Haptic Technology Handbook

Haptic Technology Handbook

**Edited by
Natalia Roberts**

WILLFORD PRESS
www.willfordpress.com

Published by Willford Press,
118-35 Queens Blvd., Suite 400,
Forest Hills, NY 11375, USA

ISBN: 978-1-64728-444-2

Cataloging-in-Publication Data

Haptic technology handbook / edited by Natalia Roberts.
    p. cm.
Includes bibliographical references and index.
ISBN 978-1-64728-444-2
1. Haptic devices. 2. User interfaces (Computer systems).
3. Computer input-output equipment. I. Roberts, Natalia.
QA76.9.H85 H373 2023
004.019--dc23

For information on all Willford Press publications
visit our website at www.willfordpress.com

Contents

Permissions

List of Contributors

Index

Preface

Haptic technology refers to a technology that uses forces, vibrations, or motions to provide the user with an experience of touch. These technologies could be utilized to construct virtual objects in a computer simulation, to control virtual objects, and improve the remote control of machines and devices. Tactile sensors which measure the forces applied by the user on the interface are used in haptic devices. Steering wheels, game controllers and joysticks are examples of simple haptic devices. Haptic technology enables researchers to better understand the workings of the human sense of touch by permitting the construction of controlled haptic virtual objects. There are a wide range of applications of haptic technology including mobile devices and personal computers. This book is a valuable compilation of topics, ranging from the basic to the most complex advancements in the field of haptic technology. It will provide comprehensive knowledge to the readers.

Various studies have approached the subject by analyzing it with a single perspective, but the present book provides diverse methodologies and techniques to address this field. This book contains theories and applications needed for understanding the subject from different perspectives. The aim is to keep the readers informed about the progresses in the field; therefore, the contributions were carefully examined to compile novel researches by specialists from across the globe.

Indeed, the job of the editor is the most crucial and challenging in compiling all chapters into a single book. In the end, I would extend my sincere thanks to the chapter authors for their profound work. I am also thankful for the support provided by my family and colleagues during the compilation of this book.

Editor

Psychophysical Studies of Interleaving Narrowband Tactile Stimuli to Achieve Broadband Perceptual Effects

Juan S. Martinez[1]*, Hong Z. Tan[1] and Roger W. Cholewiak[2]

[1]*Haptic Interface Research Laboratory, College of Engineering, School of Electrical and Computer Engineering, Purdue University, West Lafayette, IN, United States,* [2]*Cutaneous Communication Laboratory, Princeton University, Princeton, NJ, United States*

*Correspondence:
Juan S. Martinez
mart1304@purdue.edu

Despite the ubiquitous presence of tactile actuators (tactors) in mobile devices, there is a continuing need for more advanced tactors that can cover the entire frequency range of human tactile perception. Broadband tactors can increase information transmission and enrich sensory experience. The engineering challenges are multifold in that the ideal tactors should exhibit an effective bandwidth of at least 300 Hz, small form factor, robustness, power efficiency and low cost. For wearable applications, there are the additional challenges of ease of mounting and maintaining adequate skin contact during body movements. We propose an approach to interleave narrowband tactile stimuli to achieve broadband effects, taking advantage of the limited spatial resolution of the skin on the torso and limbs. Three psychophysical experiments were conducted to assess the validity of this approach. Participants performed pairwise discriminations of two broadband stimuli delivered using one or two tactors. The broadband stimuli consisted of one mid-frequency and one high-frequency component delivered through one tactor by mixing the two components, or through two tactors (one component per tactor). The first two experiments revealed extraneous cues such as localization and mutual masking of mid- and high-frequency components that were subsequently eliminated in the third experiment. Results from 12 participants confirmed that performance on pairwise comparisons was below the discrimination threshold, confirming that broadband haptic effects can be achieved through narrowband tactors placed within the skin's two-point limen.

Keywords: actuator, broadband, haptic, narrowband, psychophysics, tactile, validation, vibrotactile

1 INTRODUCTION

There has been a growing interest in wearable and array-based vibrotactile displays in academic research and commercial products in the recent years. With this interest comes a need for tactors (tactile stimulators) that can be easily attached to the skin at various body sites, and have large intensity and frequency ranges that can be independently controlled. Previous research with these type of displays include tactor arrays on hands (Hsieh et al., 2016; Park et al., 2016; Park et al., 2019), wrist (Chen et al., 2008; Lee and Starner, 2010; Matscheko et al., 2010; Liao et al., 2016), arm (Cholewiak and Collins, 2003; Brown et al., 2006; Jones et al., 2009; Culbertson et al., 2018; Reed et al., 2019), waist (Cholewiak et al., 2004; Van Erp, 2005a; Cholewiak and McGrath, 2006; Elliott et al., 2013) and torso (Ertan et al., 1998; Rupert, 2000; Jones et al., 2009; Israr and Poupyrev, 2011). Similarly, commercial products include the Optacon for persons who are visually impaired

(Telesensory Corp., Mountain View, CA), Tactaid VII for the hearing impaired (Audiological Engineering Corp., Somerville, MA) and more recent creations for virtual reality and sensory substitution (e.g., TESLASUIT by VR Electronics Ltd. in United Kingdom; SUBPAC X1 by Subpac Inc. in Palo Alto, CA; Buzz by Neosensory in San Francisco, CA; Hi5 VR Gloves by Noitom in Beijing, China; and Dot Watch by Dot Inc. in South Korea). With few exceptions, the tactors used in these examples are resonant devices that operate most efficiently within a narrow, high-frequency band (> 100 Hz). Therefore, their associated haptic sensations are limited to smooth vibrations. However, many applications would benefit from a richer set of haptic effects elicited with the addition of stimulus frequencies below 100 Hz. Such broadband tactors are capable of delivering multiple distinct effects for applications in gaming, virtual reality and sensory substitution.

In the range of sinusoidal frequencies from < 1 Hz to ≈1,000 Hz, the mechanoreceptors in the human skin can convey distinct sensations such as pressure and slow motion, flutter and roughness, and smooth vibrations (Talbot et al., 1968; Merzenich and Harrington, 1969; Mountcastle et al., 1969; Tan et al., 1999). For example, Culbertson et al. (2018) created a continuous and pleasant sensation by using slow (< 5 Hz) up-down motions in an array of tactors to simulate stroking on the forearm. Shim and Tan (2020) designed vibrotactile stimuli to represent essential features of natural phenomena in a 2-by-2 tactor array on the palm. The set of designs included slow motions at 0.8 Hz for *Breathing*, 20-Hz signals for *Bubbles* and a combination of 30-Hz signals and amplitude-modulated vibrations at 135 and 150 Hz for *Thunder*. In addition, the SUBPAC X1 and Razer Nari Ultimate (using the L5 actuator by Lofelt GmbH, Berlin, Germany) operate at frequencies as low as 35 Hz to convey bass tones in music. These tactile devices become more expressive as lower frequency components are incorporated.

Tactor arrays can also achieve high levels of information transmission by delivering multi-dimensional tactile stimuli *via* broadband actuators [see a recent review by Tan et al. (2020a)]. For instance, the OMAR device by Eberhardt et al. (1994) was used to control up to 10 channels of one-dimensional motion, or five channels of two-dimensional motion in the range from DC to 800 Hz. Studies of vibration onset asynchrony (VOA) demonstrated that participants could identify whether vibrations proceeded movement for asynchronies in the range of tens of milliseconds. This result demonstrated that VOA could be used to disambiguate lipreading of stop consonants in haptic supplements for lipreading. Another example is the Tactuator by Tan and Rabinowitz (1996). The device was composed of three independent motor assemblies used to deliver vibrotactile stimuli to the finger pads of the thumb, index and middle fingers in the range of DC to 300 Hz. Tan et al. (1999) used the device to conduct absolute identification experiments with three sets of distinct stimuli. They demonstrated a maximum information transfer rate of 12 bits/sec. More recently, Reed et al. (2019) designed a TActile Phonemic Sleeve (TAPS) for speech communication on the skin. The device consisted of a 4-by-6 broadband tactor array used to encode the 39 English phonemes

as 39 distinct multi-dimensional vibrotactile stimuli delivered to the forearm. They reported a phoneme recognition rate of 86% after one to 4 h of learning. The set of phonemic tactile codes used mid- and high-frequency signals and amplitude modulation to achieve perceptually-distinct sensations that could be easily learned and memorized. Using the same codes in the TAPS, Tan et al. (2020b) trained 51 participants on the reception of up to 500 English words. The best participants could achieve a learning rate of roughly one word per minute. Despite the success of the TAPS, the broadband tactors employed in the TAPS display are relatively large and difficult to attach to the forearm, making them suitable for lab studies but not for wearable applications.

The aforementioned research and applications make use of commercially-available tactors with different operating principles. The majority of mobile devices use either ERM (eccentric rotating mass) or LRA (linear resonant actuator) tactors, while others use solenoids or piezoelectric actuators (Jones and Sarter, 2008; Choi and Kuchenbecker, 2012). LRAs are often preferred when independent control of amplitude and frequency is required. These are high-Q actuators with a peak output over a narrow frequency range that typically centers above 100 Hz (Hayward and MacLean, 2007; Choi and Kuchenbecker, 2012), although some are designed with a lower resonant frequency. For example, the C2 tactor has a frequency range of 200–300 Hz, while the range of the C2-HDLF tactor is 50–160 Hz (Engineering Acoustics, Orlando, FL, United States). In contrast, tactors with lower Q factors have much wider bandwidths (e.g., 50–500 Hz for the Haptuator by TactileLabs in Montreal, Canada; 35–1,000 Hz for Lofelt's L5). These are commonly less power efficient, larger in form factor, heavier and more costly. A comparison of some of these commercial actuators is provided in **Table 1**.

Ideally, a tactor should be small, power efficient, low cost, easily mountable, and capable of conveying rich haptic effects over the entire frequency range of 0–1,000 Hz. However, building such a tactor is a challenging task. We hypothesize that it may not be necessary to build such a broadband actuator to achieve broadband perceptual haptic effects. In the present study, we present an alternative way to achieve rich haptic experiences using commercially-available tactors by taking advantage of the limited spectral and spatial resolution of the skin.

The frequency resolution of the human skin is very limited (Goff, 1967; Franzen and Nordmark, 1975; Verrillo and Gescheider, 1992; Israr et al., 2006; Mahns et al., 2006). Therefore, it is unnecessary for a tactor to exhibit a continuous frequency response over the entire 0–1,000 Hz range to achieve *perceptually* broadband haptic effects. In fact, previous research has shown that only three distinct sensations can be elicited from single-frequency sinusoidal stimulation over the range of 0–1,000 Hz: pressure variation/slow motion at low frequency (up to ≈6 Hz), fluttery (with low amplitude)/rough (with high amplitude) at mid frequency (≈10–70 Hz) and smooth vibration at high frequency (above 100 Hz) (Talbot et al., 1968; Merzenich and Harrington, 1969; Mountcastle et al., 1969; Tan et al., 1999). Vibrations from these ranges can be combined and remain salient perceptually (Marks, 1979; Makous et al., 1995; Tan et al., 1999). For example, a dual-frequency vibration with 30

TABLE 1 | Comparison of commercially available actuators.

Actuator	Technology	Operating frequency (Hz)	Dimensions (all in cm)				Weight (g)	Cost (USD)	Power (W)
			Height	Length	Width	Diameter			
C2	LRA	200–300	0.79	–	–	3.1	17	250	3.0 (typical)
C2-HDLF	LRA	50–160	1.30	–	–	3.0	30	250	1.1 (typical)
Haptuator	LRA	50–500	–	2.9	–	1.4	15	200	1.5 (max)
PowerHap	Piezo	50–500	0.11	0.9	0.9	–	8	21	-
L5	Voice coil	35–1,000	0.62	2.1	1.7	–	6	-	0.3 (max)
Mini Disc	ERM	183 ± 50	0.27	–	–	1.0	0.9	2	0.5 (max)

and 300-Hz components feels like a smooth vibration (due to 300 Hz) with superimposed roughness (due to 30 Hz). Research on the perception of combined frequencies from the three regions has resulted in other interesting discoveries. For example, Park and Choi (2011) studied the perceptual space of amplitude-modulated sinusoidal signals using multi-dimensional scaling (MDS). The stimuli shared a carrier frequency of 150 Hz and varied their modulating frequency from 0 (no modulation) to 80 Hz. The optimal perceptual space had two dimensions and the modulating frequencies formed a circle in the space. It was found that modulations below 10 Hz result in more discernible vibrations, i.e., it is easier to distinguish individual frequency components in the amplitude-modulated signal. Furthermore, Yoo et al. (2014) studied the degree of consonance of "vibrotactile chords," i.e., vibrotactile signals composed of superimposed frequencies that resemble musical chords. The chords were dual-frequency vibrations. In each signal, a base frequency of 40, 55, 80, or 110 Hz was paired with one of 19 semitones derived from the base frequency. The researchers demonstrated that signals sensed as high-pitch vibrations are consonant, whereas low-frequency, fluttering, pulsatory, rough and low-pitch vibrations were judged as dissonant. These studies demonstrate that a few discrete frequency values can be combined to elicit rich haptic sensations, as opposed to a continuous range of frequencies.

As far as spatial resolution is concerned, the two-point limen (threshold at which two contact points on the skin are felt as one) varies greatly across body sites. Except for the hand, the two-point limen is at least 30 mm on the body surface (Weber, 1834/1978; Weinstein, 1968). It follows that sufficiently small tactors can be placed closely on the skin and perceived as a single tactor.

With these considerations, we hypothesized that placing narrowband tactors within the two-point limen of the skin can effectively deliver broadband haptic effects indistinguishable from those delivered by one broadband tactor. Up to three narrowband tactors can be placed at each stimulation site with each tactor operating over the low-, mid- or high-frequency range, respectively. We tested our hypothesis using a paired-comparison psychophysical procedure. Participants compared a broadband stimulus delivered with one tactor and multiple narrowband stimuli simultaneously delivered with multiple tactors. We predicted that the two types of stimuli could not be distinguished provided that extraneous cues were either eliminated or matched for the two stimulus types. We

employed mid- and high-frequency vibrations in the present study.

Findings from three experiments are reported here. In the first experiment, we sought to equalize the perceived intensity of vibrotactile stimuli, but found that the participants were still able to discriminate the two types of stimuli under some conditions. In the second experiment, we refined the intensity matching procedure to take into account the mutual masking of mid- and high-frequency components and changed the stimulation site to remove localization cues. It was also found that the vibration amplitude at the lowest mid-frequency may have been limited with the tactor chosen for this study. Therefore, a higher mid-frequency was used in the third experiment. The general methods of this work and the contents of Exp. 3 were included in a previous publication by Martinez et al. (2021) This paper includes the findings and discussions from the first two experiments that informed the design of the third experiment. In the remainder of this paper, we first present the general methods that are common to the three experiments. This is followed by the design and procedures specific to each of the three experiments along with the respective results and discussion. Finally, we present guidelines for interleaving narrowband tactors to achieve broadband effects based on the findings from the present investigation.

2 GENERAL METHODS

2.1 Participants

A total of twelve participants (P01 to P12; 6F; 23–30 years old, 26.2 ± 1.9 years) took part in the present study. All had a normal sense of touch by self report. Two of the participants (P01, the first author, and P02) took part in Exp. 1 and Exp. 2. All participants were tested in Exp. 3. Each participant signed an informed consent form approved by the Purdue University IRB when they reviewed and approved the human-use protocols. They received a compensation of 10 USD per hour for their time.

In our simple discrimination test (see **Section 2.5** for details on the procedure), knowledge about the experimental design does not provide the participant with any advantage nor would it induce any additional response bias. Therefore, P01 (the first author) had to rely entirely on the perceived difference between the stimulus alternatives to perform the task, just like the other participants.

FIGURE 1 | The two tactors used in the experiment. A white 3D-printed plastic disk is attached to the underlying adhesive ring connected to the tactor diaphragm (visible as an orange border around the plastic disk).

2.2 Apparatus

Two tactors were used (**Figure 1**) in all the experiments. They were broadband audio speakers (Tectonic Elements, model TEAX13C02-8/RH) with an impedance of 8 Ω across the frequency range of 50–1,000 Hz, except for a peak impedance of 35 Ω at ≈ 600 Hz. Each tactor measures 26.3 mm in diameter (32.2 mm with soldering tab) and 9.0 mm in thickness. A circular adhesive ring on top of the diaphragm provides attachment. It is known that detection thresholds decrease with contactor area until ≈2.9 cm^2 (Verrillo, 1963). Therefore, a white 3D-printed plastic disk was attached to the adhesive ring to increase the contactor area to ≈3.8 cm^2 (see the white top in **Figure 1**; the brown rim belongs to the diaphram of the tactor underneath the plastic ring). Measurements taken with an accelerometer (Kistler 8794A500) attached to the disk verified that the tactors were able to deliver vibrations without distortion in the frequency range of 10–500 Hz. Tactors were placed side-by-side on a Velcro band

without touching (see **Figure 1**). Given their close proximity, we verified that the activation of one tactor did not induce enough electromagnetic noise in the adjacent tactor to produce a perceivable vibration. To this end, we took acceleration measurements on a resting tactor while the other tactor vibrated at 10, 30, 60, 150 and 300 Hz. Each frequency was delivered at intensities of 20 and 30 dB (relative to the maximum output of the system). We estimated the corresponding displacement of the resting tactor from the peak acceleration measured. **Table 2** shows the calculated displacements along with the detection thresholds in hairy skin reported in (Bolanowski et al., 1994). As shown, the measurements are well below the detection thresholds at each frequency.

The same tactors were used in the TAPS system for speech communication on the skin (Reed et al., 2019; Tan et al., 2020b). While the tactors work well after calibration in a laboratory setting, they are not suitable for wearable applications due to their large size, variability among individual tactors, and the difficulty of maintaining consistent contact with the skin during arm movement. For these reasons, the present study is still needed to explore the use of two or three narrowband tactors in place of one broadband tactor, when commercially-available tactors with small form factors are used in a wearable tactile display.

The tactors were connected to class D stereo amplifiers (Maxim MAX98306) that received input from a MOTU 24Ao audio interface (MOTU, Inc., Cambridge, MA, United States). The MOTU audio interface performed synchronous D/A conversion of a 2-channel MATLAB waveform played with the Playrec utility (Humphrey, 2008).

2.3 Stimulation Site

Two stimulation sites were used in the present study, as shown in **Figure 2**. In Exp. 1, the two tactors were placed on the dorsal side at the middle of the forearm (see **Figure 2A**). The upper arm was used in Exps. 2 and 3 where the tactors were placed on top of the bicep muscles (see **Figure 2B**).

2.4 Stimulus Intensity Calibration

To ensure that the stimuli were delivered to the skin at the same perceived intensity for all participants, they were

TABLE 2 | Measured displacement of the resting tactor while the other tactor is active. The detection thresholds in hairy skin from (Bolanowski et al., 1994) are shown for comparison.

Frequency (Hz)	Intensity (dB Re full output)	Peak displacement at the resting tactor (dB Re 1 μm)	Detection threshold at the same Frequency (dB Re 1 μm)
10	20	−6.94	19.75
10	30	−5.61	19.75
30	20	−24.92	17.75
30	30	−27.40	17.75
60	20	−39.23	14.625
60	30	−35.07	14.625
150	20	−55.39	3.625
150	30	−51.51	3.625
300	20	−65.76	−1.625
300	30	−63.80	−1.625

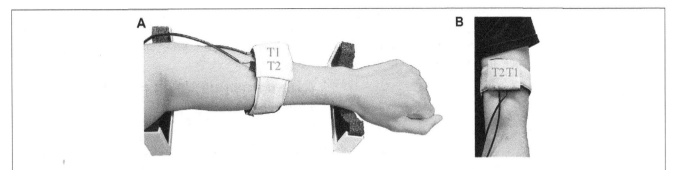

FIGURE 2 | Tactor configuration in the three experiments. The location of the two tactors underneath the Velcro band are indicated by red text. **(A)** Tactors worn at the middle of the dorsal forearm. The elbow and wrist rested on top of two foam supports. **(B)** Exps. 2 & 3: Tactors worn at the upper arm, atop the left biceps.

calibrated in two steps. First, the detection thresholds of all participants were estimated at two high frequencies (150, 300 Hz). Second, the output of the two tactors was equalized. These steps accounted for the variation in detection thresholds among the participants and possible differences between the two tactors.

2.4.1 Detection Threshold at High Frequency

Detection thresholds were measured for each participant at the beginning of the experiment using tactor T2 which was closer to the torso (see **Figure 2**). Thresholds were measured at 150 and 300 Hz using a three-interval, two-alternative, forced-choice, one-up two-down adaptive procedure with trial-by-trial response feedback. The one-up two-down rule estimates the 70.7-percentile point on the psychometric function (Levitt, 1971). The vibration amplitude was adjusted with a step size of 5 dB at the first four reversals, and 2 dB at an additional 12 reversals. On each trial, a 400-ms signal was presented in only one of the three intervals, randomly selected with equal *a priori* probabilities. Each interval was visually indicated and the gap between intervals was 500 ms. The participant indicated which interval contained the signal and received feedback for that trial. The threshold was estimated as the mean of the last twelve reversals at the smaller step size.

2.4.2 Tactor Equalization

The participants then completed a method-of-adjustment procedure to equalize the perceived intensity of the two tactors. A 400-ms long signal at 300 Hz and −10 dB (relative to the maximum output allowed by the MATLAB software) was delivered to T2, the reference tactor. The participant adjusted the amplitude of a 400-ms, 300-Hz signal on the test tactor, T1, until the two were perceived to be equally strong. The tactors were activated in the sequence reference-test-reference and the participant increased or decreased the intensity of the test tactor in steps of 1 dB. The final adjustment was recorded. On average, the adjusted values differed by 0.83 dB relative to that at the reference tactor.

The results of threshold measurement and tactor equalization were used to calculate signal amplitudes that corresponded to specific sensation levels (SLs) at high frequencies. They refer to the vibration amplitude relative to the detection threshold at the

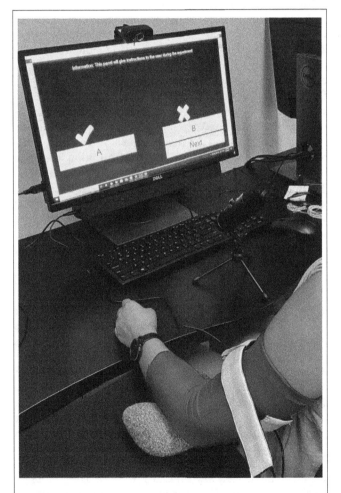

FIGURE 3 | Experimental setup in Exp. 3. The tactor band was worn on top of the left biceps. The computer screen shows the interface for pairwise discrimination.

corresponding frequency in the unit of dB SL. Verrillo et al. (1969) showed that sensation levels grow almost linearly with signal amplitudes when both are expressed in dB (see **Figures 8, 9** of (Verrillo et al., 1969) for the vibrotactile equal-sensation magnitude curves).

To account for spectral masking of mid- and high-frequency signal components, additional calibrations were performed for the mid-frequency signals. In the first two experiments, 10 and 30 Hz were used in the mid-frequency range. These changed to 30 and 60 Hz in the third experiment. The calibration procedures evolved with the experiments. They will be described later in each experiment.

2.5 Experimental Procedures

All experiments employed a one interval, two alternatives, forced choice (1I-2AFC) paired-comparison paradigm, following the design of R. Cholewiak and Collins (2000; Exp. 2) (Cholewiak and Collins, 2000) and S. Cholewiak et al. (2010; Exp. 3) (Cholewiak et al., 2010). The two stimulus alternatives included a dual-frequency vibration delivered with one tactor ("broadband") and two single-frequency vibrations delivered with the two adjacent tactors ("narrowband"). For the broadband stimulus alternative, one of the two tactors was randomly selected to be driven with the sum of two sinusoidal waveforms, one at a mid frequency (10, 30 or 60 Hz) and the other at a high frequency (150 or 300 Hz). The other tactor was not activated. For the narrowband stimulus alternative, one randomly-selected tactor was driven with a single-frequency vibration at a mid frequency, and the other tactor at a high frequency. The randomization of tactor selection was performed on each trial. The signals were 400 ms in duration and smoothed by a 5-ms Hanning window so they started and ended at zero amplitude. The specific frequency values used in an experiment varied, and will be described later in the respective experiments.

The participant wore a thin fabric sleeve on the left arm for hygiene purposes. The experimenter wrapped the tactor band around the stimulation site (forearm or upper arm) and fastened it with Velcro (see **Figure 3**). The participant sat facing the computer screen with the left arm resting comfortably on a table and the elbow supported. Audio pink noise was played through a headset throughout the experiment to mask any audible sounds from the apparatus.

After the signal-intensity calibration steps, data collection for pairwise discrimination began. At the beginning of each experimental condition, the two stimulus alternatives were presented once to the participant with their respective response labels shown as "A" or "B." This was followed by a block of 60 trials with the first 10 trials considered as training and discarded from data analysis. On each trial, one of the two stimulus alternatives was presented with an equal *a priori* probability of 0.5. The participant felt the stimulus and responded by clicking one of two buttons on the computer screen. A check mark appeared above the selection for a correct response. For an incorrect response, a cross appeared above the incorrectly selected button and a check mark was shown above the button with the correct response label. The correct-answer feedback served to ensure that the participant used the correct response labels and reduced the response bias in the two-interval discrimination task. It remained on the computer screen for 1 s and the next trial started immediately

thereafter. Participants were allowed to take a break at the end of each block of trials. They continued with the next 60-trial block by clicking on a "Next" button when ready.

2.6 Data Analysis Using Signal Detection Theory

The results of the 1I-2AFC discrimination experiment were analyzed using the decision model from Signal Detection Theory (Green and Swets, 1966; Macmillan and Creelman, 2004; Jones and Tan, 2013). Compared to many other psychophysical paradigms such as method of constant stimuli, method of adjustment and adaptive procedures, Signal Detection Theory provides a discrimination performance measure d' that is independent of response bias c. It is therefore preferred over the commonly-used percent-correct scores. A d' value of 1.0 indicates threshold performance. Therefore, if $d' \geq 1.0$ (or $d' < 1.0$), we conclude that the participants can (or cannot) distinguish the stimulus pair. Details on the theory and computation of d' and response bias c are available in **Supplementary Appendix**.

3 EXPERIMENT 1

The pairwise discrimination could be accomplished using any number of perceptual cues. The most obvious cue was that of perceived intensity of different frequency components. It was paramount that the perceived intensity of the two stimulus alternatives be equalized, not only for the high-frequency components but also for the mid-frequency components due to possible spectral masking effects. In Exp. 1, the detection thresholds at 10 and 30 Hz in the presence of 150 or 300 Hz maskers were estimated before determining the signal amplitudes at the mid frequencies. The results suggested the presence of additional perceptual cues, addressed in Exp. 2.

3.1 Experimental Conditions

There were eight conditions in Exp. 1, based on the combinations of 1) two mid frequencies (10, 30 Hz), 2) two high frequencies (150, 300 Hz), and 3) two sensation levels (20, 30 dB SL). The order of experimental conditions was randomized for each participant.

3.2 Stimulation Site

In order to eliminate any tactor localization cues, it was important to place the two tactors within the two-point limen of the body site. The tactors used in the present study needed a minimum center-to-center distance of ≈30 mm to avoid direct contact. According to Weber (1834/1978) and Weinstein (1968), this was below the 40 mm two-point limen for touch on the forearm. Using vibrations at 100 and 250 Hz, Cholewiak and Collins (2003) applied an array of vibrotactile actuators spaced by 25 mm on the volar forearm to study tactor localization. Localization was poorest at the middle of the array (≈40%). Subsequent analysis showed errors to be evenly distributed between the two tactors adjacent to the middle tactor, indicating that two tactors placed 25 mm apart could not be

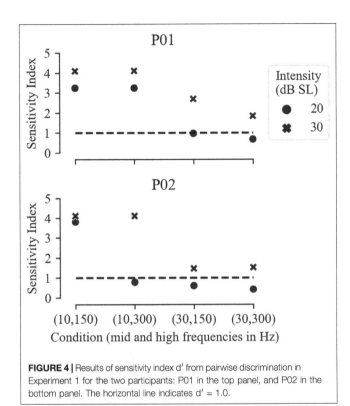

FIGURE 4 | Results of sensitivity index d' from pairwise discrimination in Experiment 1 for the two participants: P01 in the top panel, and P02 in the bottom panel. The horizontal line indicates d' = 1.0.

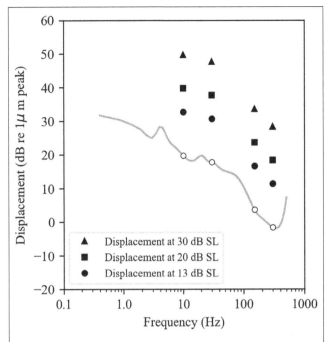

FIGURE 5 | Vibrotactile thresholds on the volar forearm. The solid gray line is re-plotted from **Figure 1** of (Bolanowski et al., 1994). The thresholds at 10, 30, 150, and 300 Hz are highlighted by four open circles. Filled circles, squares and triangles denote the displacement values at 13, 20 and 30 dB above threshold, respectively, for the four frequencies.

localized (personal communication with R. Cholewiak, 2021). Based on these findings, we chose the middle of the dorsal forearm as the stimulation site.

3.3 Calibration of Mid-Frequency Components

Gescheider et al. (1970, 1982) demonstrated that the detection threshold at the thenar eminence of a lower-frequency signal increases as a function of the intensity of a narrow-band, high-frequency masking vibration. To account for the possibility of high frequencies masking mid frequencies, we measured the detection thresholds at 10 and 30 Hz in the presence of a 150 Hz or 300 Hz masker. A total of four mid-frequency detection thresholds under masking were obtained for P01 and P02 using the same three-interval, two-alternative, forced-choice, one-up two-down adaptive procedure used to measure detection thresholds at high frequencies. However, we presented stimuli in each interval following the design in (Gescheider et al., 1982). On each trial, an 800-ms high-frequency masker at 25 dB SL was present in all three intervals. In one of the randomly-selected intervals, an additional 400-ms mid-frequency target signal was added and centered in time within the 800-ms masker.

While the signal amplitudes for the high-frequency components were computed based on the detection thresholds obtained without masking, the amplitudes for the mid-frequency components were based on the detection thresholds in the presence of high-frequency maskers.

3.4 Results

The results of d' from the discrimination procedure for each condition are shown in **Figure 4**. The sensitivity indices appeared to show two trends. First, the discriminability between the broadband and the narrowband stimulus alternatives was better (higher d') at 30 dB SL than at 20 dB SL. Second, discrimination appeared to be easier (higher d') when the mid-frequency component was at 10 Hz, except for P02's result at 20 dB SL for the (10,300) frequency combination.

3.5 Discussion

After the experiment, the participants were asked about the cues they used to perform the pairwise discrimination. They reported that 1) sometimes, one stimulus elicited a "fluttery vibration" sensation while the other felt more like a "smooth vibration"; and 2) in other times, there appeared to be a slight shift in stimulated location on the skin. These subtle cues were reported as the strategy used to solve the discrimination task on these occasions. After revisiting the experimental conditions, it was found that the "fluttery" sensation corresponded to the conditions involving the 10-Hz mid-frequency component. This was within the frequency range for fluttery vibration reported in the literature (Talbot et al., 1968; Merzenich and Harrington, 1969; Mountcastle et al., 1969; Tan et al., 1999).

To investigate the first cue, we reasoned that for the (10, 150) and (10, 300) frequency combinations at 20 and 30 dB SL, if the perceived intensity of the 10-Hz mid-frequency component was well matched to that of the high-frequency component, then the sensation should have contained both fluttery and smooth vibrations simultaneously. Whenever the fluttery or the smooth sensation dominated perception, it indicated that the mid-frequency or the high-frequency component was felt to be more intense and possibly masked its counterpart. Both cases turned out to be explainable upon further examination of the logged data.

To understand why fluttery sensation may have dominated the perception of a combined mid- and high-frequency vibration, we note that our Exp. 1 considered only the masking effects of high-frequency components on mid-frequency components, but not vice versa. Indeed most vibrotactile masking studies use high-frequency components as the maskers (Gescheider et al., 1970, 1982; Verrillo et al., 1983). However, Verrillo et al. (1983) showed evidence of a 13-Hz stimulus masking a 300-Hz stimulus at the fingertip when the amplitude of the 13-Hz stimulus exceeded the detection threshold at 300 Hz. At the relatively high intensity levels of 20 and 30 dB SL used in our Exp. 1, masking occurred in both directions of mid-to high-frequency and vice versa. This is illustrated in **Figure 5** where vibrotactile thresholds in hairy skin and various intensity levels above threshold for 10, 30, 150 and 300 Hz are plotted on the same graph. It can be seen that the amplitudes of mid-frequency components were well above the detection thresholds of the high-frequency components, demonstrating mid-frequency masking of high frequencies. The amplitudes of high-frequency components were also above the detection thresholds of the mid-frequency components when set to 20 or 30 dB SL, albeit to a lesser degree. Our calibration of the mid-frequency components focused solely on possible masking of high-frequency components on mid-frequency, thereby resulting in mid-frequency amplitudes that were perhaps too high. This could explain why the flutter sensation dominated perception in conditions that included 10 Hz as the mid-frequency.

That the smooth vibration sensation dominated perception in some conditions was due to amplitude saturation of mid-frequency components that was discovered after Exp. 1. The software used in our experiment automatically capped vibration amplitudes to levels that would not exceed the power limit of the audio amps. Due to the relatively high detection thresholds at 10 Hz as compared to those at 30, 150 and 300 Hz [the masked threshold at 10 Hz was 7 dB higher than that at 30 Hz, which is significant compared to the amplitude discrimination threshold of 1.5–2.0 dB (Craig, 1972)], the lack of rigid surround [which is known to elevate detection threshold (Gescheider et al., 1978; Van Doren, 1990)], a 3–10 dB increase observed in the thresholds under masking conditions, and the relatively high signal intensities at 20–30 dB SL, we suspected that the 10-Hz vibration amplitudes may have exceeded the maximum limit under some experimental conditions. This was later confirmed, more often at 30 dB SL than at 20 dB SL. When the amplitude of the 10-Hz vibration was clipped to the maximum allowable value, two things would occur. First, the intensity of the 10-Hz mid-frequency component was

reduced, thereby making the fluttery sensation less noticeable. Second, some harmonic distortions occurred which may have contributed to additional masking of the 10-Hz vibration. It was therefore conceivable that the smooth sensation of the 300-Hz high-frequency component dominated perception under these conditions. Since clipping occurred more often at 30 dB SL than at 20 dB SL, it was also expected that the pairwise discrimination was easier (higher d') at 30 dB SL.

To remove the extraneous cues due to mutual masking of mid- and high-frequency vibrations, and amplitude clipping, respectively, the subsequent experiments adopted an intensity matching procedure and the intensity levels for all signals were reduced to 13 dB SL. Based on (Bolanowski et al., 1994), amplitudes corresponding to 13 dB SL at 150 and 300 Hz are below the detection thresholds of non-Pacinian receptors (nPC) at 10 and 30 Hz on hairy skin (see solid circles at 150 and 300 Hz in **Figure 5**), ensuring no masking of mid-frequency components by high-frequency vibrations [see further explanation in (Gescheider et al., 1982)]. However, since the detection thresholds at 10 and 30 Hz are higher than those at 150 and 300 Hz (Bolanowski et al., 1994), it would not be possible to choose a signal amplitude at the mid frequencies that would not activate the Pacinian channel.

To investigate the second cue of a possible shift in perceived simulation site, it should be noted that most studies of two-point discrimination threshold were conducted with touch/pressure rather than vibrotactile stimuli [although see (Cholewiak and Collins, 2003)]. Among the former method, even though Weber (1834/1978) and Weinstein (1968) reported a 40-mm two-point limen on the forearm, a more recent study by Mancini et al. (2014) reported a two-point touch threshold of 22 mm which was below the center-to-center distance of the two tactors used in Exp. 1. Similarly, Lévêque et al. (2000) reported a two-point gap discrimination of 21.23 mm on the volar forearm. Craig and Johnson (2000) explained why the two-point limen is not a good measure of tactile spatial resolution, and pointed to several potential confounds that exist in its estimates. Using vibrotactile stimuli, van Erp (2005b) conducted an experiment on vibrotactile spatial acuity by activating pairs of tactors in a linear array at different locations of the torso with 28-ms sine waves at 250 Hz. The results showed a uniform acuity of 20–30 mm except for arrays oriented horizontally and placed on the body midline. Perez et al. (2000) used an array of 16 piezoelectric vibrators with a thickness of 0.5 mm spaced by 1 mm and delivered waveforms composed of bursts of rectangular pulses to the index finger. They activated pairs of vibrators simultaneously and used the method of limits to determine the two-point threshold. They found that the threshold increases from 2.1 to 5.1 mm as the pulse repetition period decreases from 1/25 to 1/500 s. This was similar to the finding by Weinstein (1968) who reported values of ≈4 mm at the index finger. It thus appears that spatial resolution improves from forearm to the fingertips. At more proximal locations such as the upper arm, the two-point limen was reported to be 44 and 67 mm by

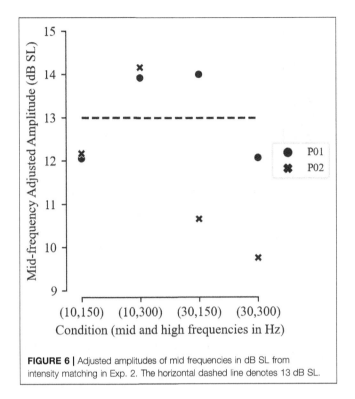

FIGURE 6 | Adjusted amplitudes of mid frequencies in dB SL from intensity matching in Exp. 2. The horizontal dashed line denotes 13 dB SL.

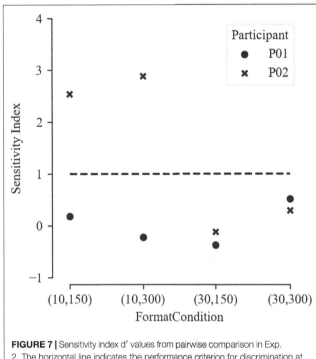

FIGURE 7 | Sensitivity index d′ values from pairwise comparison in Exp. 2. The horizontal line indicates the performance criterion for discrimination at d′ = 1.0.

Weinstein (1968) and Weber (1834/1978), respectively. Since the minimum center-to-center distance of the two tactors used in the present study needed to be ≈30 mm to avoid direct contact, it was necessary to move the stimulation site to a more proximal location with poorer spatial acuity–the upper arm. It was also important to avoid any perceptual anchors that can be easily localized [see (Cholewiak and Collins, 2003)] and to avoid bone conduction that might elicit auditory sensations (Kaufmann et al., 2012). Therefore, the fleshy surface atop the biceps on the left upper arm was chosen as the stimulation site for subsequent experiments.

4 EXPERIMENT 2

The experimental methods for Exp. 2 were similar to those for Exp. 1, except for a few modifications noted below.

4.1 Experimental Conditions
There were four conditions in Exp. 2, based on the combinations of two mid frequencies (10, 30 Hz) and two high frequencies (150, 300 Hz). Unlike Exp. 1, only one signal intensity of 13 dB SL was used.

4.2 Stimulation Site
The tactor band was fastened around the participant's left upper arm so that the tactors rested on the biceps muscle.

4.3 Calibration of Signal Intensities
Detection thresholds for the four frequencies were measured in isolation using the same three-interval, two-alternative, forced-

choice, one-up two-down adaptive procedure employed in Exp. 1. This was followed by an intensity matching procedure to calibrate the amplitudes of mid frequencies for each of the four experimental conditions. For each frequency combination, the broadband dual-frequency stimulus (the reference) used 13 dB SL (dB above detection threshold in isolation) for both the mid- and high-frequency amplitudes. For the two single-frequency stimulus alternatives (the narrowband comparison), the high-frequency amplitude was also set to 13 dB SL. The amplitude of the mid-frequency component could be changed by the participant using the method of adjustment (Jones and Tan, 2013). The participant felt a sequence of three signals in the order reference-comparison-reference, and adjusted the amplitude of the mid-frequency component until the comparison stimulus felt similar to the reference. The calibrated amplitudes were then used in the subsequent pairwise discrimination procedure.

4.4 Results and Discussion
The results of Exp. 2 are shown in two plots. First, the adjusted amplitudes of the mid-frequency components are shown in **Figure 6** after they have been converted to dB SL. The dashed line corresponds to 13 dB SL that was used with both components of the broadband stimuli and the high-frequency components of the narrowband stimuli. It can be seen that the adjusted intensity level for P01 stayed within ±1 dB around 13 dB SL, a difference that is below the 1.5–2.0 dB amplitude discrimination threshold for vibrotactile stimuli (Craig, 1972). The same was true for P02 for the two conditions where the mid-frequency was at 10 Hz. The adjusted amplitudes for the 30-Hz mid-frequency component was significantly below 13 dB SL for P02.

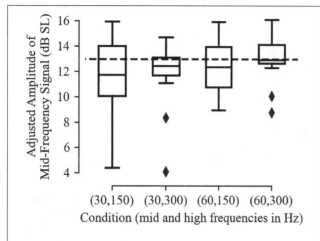

FIGURE 8 | Results of adjusted mid-frequency amplitudes from intensity matching. The horizontal dashed line corresponds to 13 dB SL.

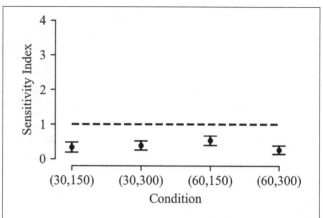

FIGURE 9 | Results of sensitivity index d′ from pairwise discrimination in Exp. 3. The dashed horizontal line indicates d′ = 1.0. Error bars denote ±1 std.err.

Second, the d′ values from pairwise comparison for each condition are shown in **Figure 7** for the two participants in separate panels. Participant P01 could not distinguish the broadband and narrowband stimuli, as demonstrated by |d′| < 1.0 in all conditions. While participant P02 showed poor discrimination for the two conditions (30,150) and (30,300), the d′ values for (10,150) and (10,300) were well above 1.0. The participant reported using the "fluttery vs. smooth" cue for pairwise comparison in the latter two conditions. Note that the d′ values for P02 when the mid-frequency was at 10 Hz were lower than those in Exp. 1 (see **Figure 4**).

An examination of logged data did not reveal a large difference in the detection thresholds between the two participants and the thresholds were more than 13 dB below the maximum allowable output (−16.7 ± 1.9 dB for P01; −15.8 ± 2.3 dB for P02; relative to maximum amplitudes). It was noticed however that the perceived intensity of the fluttery sensation due to the 10-Hz mid-frequency component changed noticeably if the tactor band was wrapped very tight around the upper arm. We reasoned that the diaphragm of the speaker could be damped by the pressure exerted by the Velcro band, especially when the displacement was high as was the case with the 10-Hz vibration. Moreover, the discriminability of signals containing 10 Hz could be related to the "borderline" characteristics of this frequency. As described by Tan et al. (1999), 10 Hz is located at the boundary between the perception of slow movement and rough/fluttery vibration. From a practical point of view, few resonance-type tactors on the market can produce discernible vibrations at 10 Hz. Therefore, we replaced the 10-Hz mid-frequency component with a 60-Hz mid-frequency component in Exp. 3 where all 12 participants were tested, including P01 and P02.

5 EXPERIMENT 3

Now that we have eliminated the extraneous cues that could contribute to the discriminability of one broadband, dual-frequency signal and two simultaneous narrowband single-frequency signals, the objective of Exp. 3 was to conduct the pairwise comparison with a large number of participants (N = 12). They included the two participants from Exp. 1 and Exp. 2 and 10 additional naive participants.

5.1 Methods

In this experiment, the two tactors were placed atop the bicep muscle on the left upper arm. There were four experimental conditions denoted by the mid- and high-frequency pairs in Hz (30,150), (30,300), (60,150) and (60,300). The procedure was the same as that in Exp. 2. Each participant was tested for detection thresholds at the four frequencies, performed intensity matching, and completed pairwise comparison of narrowband and broadband stimuli. Per additional IRB guidelines for conducting human experiments during the COVID-19 pandemic, a webcam, a microphone and TeamViewer software were installed to allow the experimenter to control programs and to monitor and communicate with participants from an adjacent room (see **Figure 3**).

5.2 Results and Discussion

The intensity matching results for all 12 participants are presented as box plots in **Figure 8**. The figure shows the distributions of the adjusted amplitudes of the single-frequency vibrations for the mid frequencies and the four experimental conditions. The adjustments are compared to the 13 dB SL amplitude level used with both components of the broadband stimuli and the high-frequency component of narrowband stimuli. As shown, there is a wide range of adjusted amplitudes with some outliers at conditions (30,300) and (60,300). However, a one-way ANOVA did not indicate a significant difference between adjustments among the four experimental conditions (F (2, 44) = 1.02, p = 0.39). In addition, individual t-tests were used to compare the intensity matching results with the 13 dB SL reference per condition. The results did not show a significant difference between the adjusted amplitudes and 13 dB SL for any condition [t (11) = −1.79, p = 0.10 for condition (30, 150); t (11) = −1.58, p = 0.14 for (30, 300); t

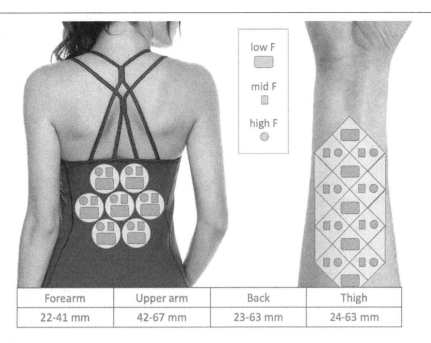

Forearm	Upper arm	Back	Thigh
22-41 mm	42-67 mm	23-63 mm	24-63 mm

FIGURE 10 | Illustration of interleaving narrowband tactors in a wearable haptic display worn on the back or volar forearm. The large circles on the back and the diamonds on the forearm indicate spatially distinct areas of stimulation. The legend shows the three types of narrowband tactors. The table at the bottom lists the two-point limens at select body sites (from (Weber, 1834/1978; Weinstein, 1968; Mancini et al., 2014)).

(11) = −0.88, p = 0.39 for (60, 150); t (11) = −0.05, p = 0.96 for (60, 300)]. The variability of the data shown in **Figure 8** suggests that intensity matching was necessary for individual participants.

The d′ values from pairwise discrimination are shown in **Figure 9**. In general, the 4 d′ values for the four experimental conditions were all between 0 and 1, indicating that the participants could not reliably distinguish between a dual-frequency vibration delivered by one tactor and two corresponding single-frequency vibrations delivered by two adjacent tactors. The d′ values were compared to the threshold value of 1.0 *via* individual t-tests per condition. The results revealed that d′ values were significantly below 1.0 across all four conditions [t (11) = −4.62 for condition (30, 150); t (11) = −4.80 for (30, 300); t (11) = −3.46 for (60, 150); t (11) = −5.88 for (60, 300); all with p < 0.01]. Furthermore, a one-way ANOVA indicated no significant differences among the 4 d′ values (F (3, 44) = 0.73, p = 0.54). The response biases, c, were relatively small, ranging from −0.16 to −0.04 for the four conditions. These results demonstrate clearly that with the removal of extraneous cues, it was feasible to achieve a broadband vibration (i.e., containing mid- and high-frequency components) with two narrowband vibrations (one mid-frequency and one high-frequency) delivered by two tactors placed in close proximity.

6 GUIDELINES FOR INTERLEAVING NARROWBAND TACTILE STIMULI FOR BROADBAND EFFECTS

Our findings that the d′ values under all experimental conditions in Experiment 3 were well below 1.0 provides psychophysical validation that broadband haptic effects can be achieved by interleaving narrowband vibrotactile stimuli, when narrowband tactors are placed within the two-point limen on the skin and signal amplitudes are properly calibrated. This result can be used to guide the design of wearable tactile displays that interleave narrowband tactors. For example, a body site can be divided into distinct stimulation areas defined by the two-point limen, as illustrated by the circular grid on the back and the diamond grid on the forearm in **Figure 10**. The exact shape of the grid element is not important, as long as 1) tactors within each area are felt as one location and 2) tactors in different areas are felt as two locations. The left panel in **Figure 10** provides an example of a haptic back display with three types of tactors in each distinct stimulation area. The right panel shows one variant where low-frequency tactors are placed along the middle of the forearm to deliver, for example, pleasant strokings using the signal patterns described in (Culbertson et al., 2018). The rest of the grid contains two parallel columns of mid- and high-frequency tactors that can be used to encode English phonemes using haptic codes similar to those in (Reed et al., 2019). Such wearable displays can differ in many ways including body site stimulated, layout of distinct stimulation areas, number and type of tactors within each stimulation area, waveforms and signal activation patterns. The distinct sensations delivered by different types of tactors can be used to encode near and far in an immersive VR game, imminent danger versus surrounding traffic to a visually-impaired pedestrian, or speed-up vs. slow-down cues in an AR workout app.

A question that naturally arises is what to do when a skin area has dense nerve innervation and hence high spatial resolution, such as the fingertip. It is unlikely to find tactors that can be squeezed into a scale on the order of millimeters (Weinstein, 1968), except for pin arrays such as the Optacon (Linvill and Bliss, 1966) and the 400-probe display (Pawluk et al., 1998). However, at very small contactor areas (below $0.08 \, cm^2$), vibrotactile detection thresholds increase significantly and flatten across the entire vibrotactile frequency range [see **Figure 7** of (Verrillo, 1963)]. As a result, perception of vibrotactile stimuli at suprathreshold levels will involve several mechanoreceptor populations. As shown by the results of experiments 2 and 3, our efforts to calibrate signal amplitudes are necessary due to the need to balance the perceived intensities associated with multiple mechanoreceptor channels. This would not be possible with very small contact areas where the detection thresholds are the same for all frequencies. Evidence of this issue is available in studies that investigate localization of low- and high-frequency vibrotactile stimuli. Rogers (1970) showed better localization of a 250-Hz stimulus compared to a 10-Hz stimulus using 1-mm-diameter probes at the finger tip, even though the Pacinian receptors (most sensitive at 250 Hz) have larger receptive fields than the non-Pacinian receptors responsible for perception at 10 Hz. It was likely that the 1-mm-diameter probes excited more mechanoreceptors than just the Pacinian corpuscles. In another study, Sherrick et al. (1990) used two 6-mm-diameter contactors in a series of four experiments to study localization. They found worse localization with 250-Hz sinusoidal stimuli than with 25-Hz stimuli in the proximal area of the metacarpus (closest to the wrist), but equal localization accuracy at the two frequencies in the distal area of the metacarpus (closest to the little finger). These findings demonstrate the difficulties that arise when trying to dissociate mechanoreceptor populations in the hand using small contactors, complicating the interpretation of experimental results. Therefore, it remains to be seen whether the approach proposed in the present study can be readily applied to the skin on the hand given the difficulty of eliciting distinct sensations such as flutter and smooth vibration. Furthermore, in most use scenarios, it would be desirable to place wearable haptic displays on the torso and limbs because the user's hand would likely be engaged in text input and menu selection tasks.

Given that the dimensions of tactors plays a key role in the selection of the stimulation site (according to the two-point limen constraint), we might wonder if vertically stacking them instead of placing them in adjacent locations is a viable way to address areas with high spatial resolution. This would seem to remove the restriction of placing tactors within the two-point limen. However, direct contact between mechanically-coupled stacked actuators would likely result in a distorted waveform. This would be owing to the difficult-to-control dynamic effects of the additional loading on each tactor. Hence, the waveforms delivered to the skin would neither be clean, independently-delivered narrowband stimuli, nor a simple broadband stimulus composed of the sum of the independent narrowband signals. This was confirmed with acceleration measurements on the two LRA tactors under several conditions. The tactors were vertically stacked and actuated with sinusoidal signals at 60, 150, and 300 Hz. We measured the acceleration at the top of the stack for all possible combinations of frequencies and configurations of the two

tactors. We observed that the response was always dominated by high frequencies, especially when delivered to the tactor closest to the accelerometer. Thus, the idea of stacking actuators to achieve broadband effects appears to be impractical.

Our work also constitutes an effort to optimize the design decisions for vibrotactile actuator manufacturing. The possibility of presenting complex haptic effects with a few narrowband signals eliminates the need for a complex and costly broadband actuator. In practice, the replacement of a single actuator with multiple interleaved narrowband actuators could represent a potential overhead in circuit complexity and mounting difficulties. Nevertheless, these complications can be resolved with better product designs. Commercially-available narrowband actuators such as LRA's are sufficiently small, cost effective and power efficient. Therefore, the advantages of interleaving narrowband actuators outweigh the trade-offs.

We hope that our approach serves as an example of how psychophysical validation and perception experiments can guide the design of new actuators. Another example of this approach is the work by Friesen et al. (2018), who asked participants to adjust the amplitude and frequency of a signal on a variable friction display to match the perception of a two-frequency reference stimulus. They demonstrated that participants matched a tactile pitch whose frequency is a function of the frequencies and amplitudes in the reference stimulus. This shows that a target texture can be achieved without a complex representation of the texture on a surface friction display.

In conclusion, we proposed, tested and validated a new way of achieving rich, broadband haptic effects by interleaving narrowband vibrotactile stimuli on the skin. We provide guidelines and examples of applying this approach in creating new wearable consumer products. Whereas the experiments in the present study used a relatively large broadband tactor, most commercially-available tactors are smaller in size (e.g., a footprint of 1 cm × 1 cm or less in mobile phones). It is therefore possible to place one mid-frequency and one high-frequency resonant tactors within the two-point limen on the skin using tactors that are on the market today. Our work also contributes to future development of tactors by providing perception-based specifications on frequency range and tactor dimensions.

AUTHOR CONTRIBUTIONS

All authors contributed to the design of all experiments, as well as writing, revising and approving the manuscript for submission. JM was responsible for conducting the three experiments, collecting and analysing the data.

ACKNOWLEDGMENTS

The content of this manuscript has been presented (in part) at the IEEE World Haptics Conference 2021, (Martinez et al., 2021).

REFERENCES

Bolanowski, S. J., Gescheider, G. A., and Verrillo, R. T. (1994). Hairy Skin: Psychophysical Channels and Their Physiological Substrates. *Somatosens. Mot. Res.* 11, 279–290. doi:10.3109/08990229409051395

Brown, L. M., Brewster, S. A., and Purchase, H. C. (2006). "Multidimensional Tactons for Non-visual Information Presentation in Mobile Devices," in Proceedings of the ACM International Conference on Human-Computer Interaction with Mobile Devices and Services (MobileHCI) (New York, NY: ACM), 231–238. doi:10.1145/1152215.1152265

Chen, H.-Y., Santos, J., Graves, M., Kim, K., and Tan, H. Z. (2008). Tactor Localization at the Wrist. *Proc. EuroHaptics 2008 LNCS* 5024, 209–218.

Choi, S., and Kuchenbecker, K. J. (2012). Vibrotactile Display: Perception, Technology, and Applications. *Proc. IEEE* 101, 2093–2104.

Cholewiak, R. W., Brill, J. C., and Schwab, A. (2004). Vibrotactile Localization on the Abdomen: Effects of Place and Space. *Percept. Psychophys.* 66, 970–987. doi:10.3758/bf03194989

Cholewiak, R. W., and Collins, A. A. (2000). The Generation of Vibrotactile Patterns on a Linear Array: Influences of Body Site, Time, and Presentation Mode. *Percept. Psychophys.* 62, 1220–1235. doi:10.3758/bf03212124

Cholewiak, R. W., and Collins, A. A. (2003). Vibrotactile Localization on the Arm: Effects of Place, Space, and Age. *Percept. Psychophys.* 65, 1058–1077. doi:10.3758/bf03194834

Cholewiak, R. W., and McGrath, C. (2006). Vibrotactile Targeting in Multimodal Systems: Accuracy and Interaction. *Proc. IEEE Haptics Symposium* 2006, 413–420.

Cholewiak, S. A., Kwangtaek Kim, K., Tan, H. Z., and Adelstein, B. D. (2010). A Frequency-Domain Analysis of Haptic Gratings. *IEEE Trans. Haptics* 3, 3–14. doi:10.1109/toh.2009.36

Craig, J. C. (1972). Difference Threshold for Intensity of Tactile Stimuli. *Percept. Psychophys.* 11, 150–152. doi:10.3758/bf03210362

Craig, J. C., and Johnson, K. O. (2000). The Two-Point Threshold. *Curr. Dir. Psychol. Sci.* 9, 29–32. doi:10.1111/1467-8721.00054

Culbertson, H., Nunez, C. M., Israr, A., Lau, F., Abnousi, F., and Okamura, A. M. (2018). A Social Haptic Device to Create Continuous Lateral Motion Using Sequential Normal Indentation. *Proc. IEEE Haptics Symposium* 2018, 32–39. doi:10.1109/haptics.2018.8357149

Eberhardt, S. P., Bernstein, L., Barac-Cikoja, D., Coulter, D., and Jordan, J. (1994). Inducing Dynamic Haptic Perception by the Hand: System Description and Some Results. *Proc. ASME Dyn. Syst. Control* 55, 345–351.

Elliott, L. R., Mortimer, B. J. P., Cholewiak, R. W., Mort, G. R., Zets, G. A., and Pittman, R. (2013). "Development of Dual Tactor Capability for a Soldier Multisensory Navigation and Communication System," in International Conference on Human Interface and the Management of Information (IEEE), 46–55. doi:10.1007/978-3-642-39215-3_6

Ertan, S., Lee, C., Willets, A., Tan, H. Z., and Pentland, A. (1998). "A Wearable Haptic Navigation Guidance System," in Digest of the Second International Symposium on Wearable Computers (Pittsburgh, PA, USA: IEEE), 164–165.

Franzén, O., and Nordmark, J. (1975). Vibrotactile Frequency Discrimination. *Percept. Psychophys.* 17, 480–484. doi:10.3758/bf03203298

Friesen, R. F., Klatzky, R. L., Peshkin, M. A., and Colgate, J. E. (2018). "Single Pitch Perception of Multi-Frequency Textures," in 2018 IEEE Haptics Symposium (HAPTICS) (IEEE), 290–295. doi:10.1109/haptics.2018.8357190

Gescheider, G. A., Capraro, A. J., Frisina, R. D., Hamer, R. D., and Verrillo, R. T. (1978). The Effects of a Surround on Vibrotactile Thresholds. *Sens. Process.* 2, 99–115.

Gescheider, G. A., Herman, D. D., and Phillips, J. N. (1970). Criterion Shifts in the Measurement of Tactile Masking. *Percept. Psychophys.* 8, 433–436. doi:10.3758/bf03207041

Gescheider, G. A., Verrillo, R. T., and Van Doren, C. L. (1982). Prediction of Vibrotactile Masking Functions. *J. Acoust. Soc. Am.* 72, 1421–1426. doi:10.1121/1.388449

Goff, G. D. (1967). Differential Discrimination of Frequency of Cutaneous Mechanical Vibration. *J. Exp. Psychol.* 74, 294–299. doi:10.1037/h0024561

Green, D. M., and Swets, J. A. (1966). *Signal Detection Theory and Psychophysics.* Wiley.

Hayward, V., and MacLean, K. (2007). Do it Yourself Haptics: Part I. *IEEE Robot. Autom. Mag.* 14, 88–104. doi:10.1109/m-ra.2007.907921

Hsieh, M. J., Liang, R. H., and Chen, B. Y. (2016). "NailTactors: Eyes-free Spatial Output Using a Nail-Mounted Tactor Array," in Proceedings of the ACM International Conference on Human-Computer Interaction with Mobile Devices and Services (MobileHCI) (IEEE), 29–34.

Humphrey, R. (2008). *Playrec.* New York, NY: Multi-channel Matlab Audio.

Israr, A., and Poupyrev, I. (2011). "Tactile Brush: Drawing on Skin with a Tactile Grid Display," in Proceedings of the SIGCHI Conference on Human Factors in Computing Systems (IEEE), 2019–2028.

Israr, A., Tan, H. Z., and Reed, C. M. (2006). Frequency and Amplitude Discrimination along the Kinesthetic-Cutaneous Continuum in the Presence of Masking Stimuli. *J. Acoust. Soc. Am.* 120, 2789–2800. doi:10.1121/1.2354022

Jones, L. A., Kunkel, J., and Piateski, E. (2009). Vibrotactile Pattern Recognition on the Arm and Back. *Perception* 38, 52–68. doi:10.1068/p5914

Jones, L. A., and Sarter, N. B. (2008). Tactile Displays: Guidance for Their Design and Application. *Hum. Factors* 50, 90–111. doi:10.1518/001872008x250638

Jones, L. A., and Tan, H. Z. (2013). Application of Psychophysical Techniques to Haptic Research. *IEEE Trans. Haptics* 6, 268–284. doi:10.1109/toh.2012.74

Kaufmann, M., Adelman, C., and Sohmer, H. (2012). Mapping Sites on Bone and Soft Tissue of the Head, Neck and Thorax at Which a Bone Vibrator Elicits Auditory Sensation. *Audiol. Neurotol. Extra* 2, 9–15. doi:10.1159/000336159

Lee, S. C., and Starner, T. (2010). "BuzzWear: Alert Perception in Wearable Tactile Displays on the Wrist," in Proceedings of CHI 2010: Computng on the Body (IEEE), 433–442.

Lévêque, J.-L., Dresler, J., Ribot-Ciscar, E., Roll, J.-P., and Poelman, C. (2000). Changes in Tactile Spatial Discrimination and Cutaneous Coding Properties by Skin Hydration in the Elderly. *J. Investigative Dermatology* 115, 454–458. doi:10.1046/j.1523-1747.2000.00055.x

Levitt, H. (1971). Transformed Up-Down Methods in Psychoacoustics. *J. Acoust. Soc. Am.* 49, 467–477. doi:10.1121/1.1912375

Liao, Y.-C., Chen, Y.-L., Lo, J.-Y., Liang, R.-H., Chan, L., and Chen, B.-Y. (2016). "EdgeVib: Effective Alphanumeric Character Output Using a Wrist-Worn Tactile Display," in Proceedings of the 29th Annual Symposium on User Interface Software and Technology (IEEE), 595–601.

Linvill, J. G., and Bliss, J. C. (1966). A Direct Translation Reading Aid for the Blind. *Proc. IEEE* 54, 40–51. doi:10.1109/proc.1966.4572

Macmillan, N. A., and Creelman, C. D. (2004). *Detection Theory: A User's Guide.* Lawrence Erlbaum Associates.

Mahns, D. A., Perkins, N. M., Sahai, V., Robinson, L., and Rowe, M. J. (2006). Vibrotactile Frequency Discrimination in Human Hairy Skin. *J. Neurophysiology* 95, 1442–1450. doi:10.1152/jn.00483.2005

Makous, J., Friedman, R., and Vierck, C. (1995). A Critical Band Filter in Touch. *J. Neurosci.* 15, 2808–2818. doi:10.1523/jneurosci.15-04-02808.1995

Mancini, F., Bauleo, A., Cole, J., Lui, F., Porro, C. A., Haggard, P., et al. (2014). Whole-body Mapping of Spatial Acuity for Pain and Touch. *Ann. Neurol.* 75, 917–924. doi:10.1002/ana.24179

Marks, L. E. (1979). Summation of Vibrotactile Intensity: An Analog to Auditory Critical Bands? *Sens. Process.* 3, 188–203.

Martinez, J. S., Tan, H. Z., and Cholewiak, R. W. (2021). "Psychophysical Validation of Interleaving Narrowband Tactile Stimuli to Achieve Broadband Effects," in 2021 IEEE World Haptics Conference (WHC) (IEEE), 709–714. doi:10.1109/WHC49131.2021.9517268

Matscheko, M., Ferscha, A., Riener, A., and Lehner, M. (2010). Tactor Placement in Wrist Worn Wearables. *Int. Symposium Wearable Comput.* 2010, 1–8. doi:10.1109/iswc.2010.5665867

Merzenich, M. M., and Harrington, T. H. (1969). The Sense of Flutter-Vibration Evoked by Stimulation of the Hairy Skin of Primates: Comparison of Human Sensory Capacity with the Responses of Mechanoreceptive Afferents Innervating the Hairy Skin of Monkeys. *Exp. Brain Res.* 9, 236–260. doi:10.1007/BF00234457

Mountcastle, V. B., Talbot, W. H., Sakata, H., and Hyvärinen, J. (1969). Cortical Neuronal Mechanisms in Flutter-Vibration Studied in Unanesthetized Monkeys. Neuronal Periodicity and Frequency Discrimination. *J. Neurophysiology* 32, 452–484. doi:10.1152/jn.1969.32.3.452

Park, G., Cha, H., and Choi, S. (2019). Haptic Enchanters: Attachable and Detachable Vibrotactile Modules and Their Advantages. *IEEE Trans. Haptics* 12, 43–55. doi:10.1109/toh.2018.2859955

Park, G., and Choi, S. (2011). "Perceptual Space of Amplitude-Modulated Vibrotactile Stimuli," in 2011 IEEE World Haptics Conference (IEEE), 59–64. doi:10.1109/whc.2011.5945462

Park, J., Kim, J., Oh, Y., and Tan, H. Z. (2016). Rendering Moving Tactile Stroke on the Palm Using a Sparse 2d Array. *Proc. EuroHaptics* 2016, 47–56. doi:10.1007/978-3-319-42321-0_5

Pawluk, D. T. V., Buskirk, C. P., Killebrew, J. H., Hsiao, S. S., and Johnson, K. O. (1998). Control and Pattern Specification for a High Density Tactile Array. *Proc. ASME Dyn. Syst. Control Div.* 64, 97–102. doi:10.1115/imece1998-0239

Perez, C. A., Holzmann, C. A., and Jaeschke, H. E. (2000). Two-point Vibrotactile Discrimination Related to Parameters of Pulse Burst Stimulus. *Med. Biol. Eng. Comput.* 38, 74–79. doi:10.1007/bf02344692

Reed, C. M., Tan, H. Z., Perez, Z. D., Wilson, E. C., Severgnini, F. M., Jung, J., et al. (2019). A Phonemic-Based Tactile Display for Speech Communication. *IEEE Trans. Haptics* 12, 2–17. doi:10.1109/TOH.2018.2861010

Rogers, C. (1970). Choice of Stimulator Frequency for Tactile Arrays. *IEEE Trans. Man. Mach. Syst.* 11, 5–11. doi:10.1109/tmms.1970.299954

Rupert, A. H. (2000). An Instrumentation Solution for Reducing Spatial Disorientation Mishaps. *IEEE Eng. Med. Biol. Mag.* 19, 71–80. doi:10.1109/51.827409

Sherrick, C. E., Cholewiak, R. W., and Collins, A. A. (1990). The Localization of Low- and High-frequency Vibrotactile Stimuli. *J. Acoust. Soc. Am.* 88, 169–179. doi:10.1121/1.399937

Shim, S.-W., and Tan, H. Z. (2020). palmScape: Calm and Pleasant Vibrotactile Signals. *Proc. HCI Int. 2020 LNCS* 12200, 1–17. doi:10.1007/978-3-030-49713-2_37

Talbot, W. H., Darian-Smith, I., Kornhuber, H. H., and Mountcastle, V. B. (1968). The Sense of Flutter-Vibration: Comparison of the Human Capacity with Response Patterns of Mechanoreceptive Afferents from the Monkey Hand. *J. Neurophysiology* 31, 301–334. doi:10.1152/jn.1968.31.2.301

Tan, H. Z., Choi, S., Lau, F. W. Y., and Abnousi, F. (2020a). Methodology for Maximizing Information Transmission of Haptic Devices: A Survey. *Proc. IEEE* 108, 945–965. doi:10.1109/jproc.2020.2992561

Tan, H. Z., Durlach, N. I., Reed, C. M., and Rabinowitz, W. M. (1999). Information Transmission with a Multifinger Tactual Display. *Percept. Psychophys.* 61, 993–1008. doi:10.3758/bf03207608

Tan, H. Z., and Rabinowitz, W. M. (1996). "A New Multi-Finger Tactual Display," in Proceedings of the ASME Dynamic Systems and Control Division (New York, NY: ASME). doi:10.1121/1.415560

Tan, H. Z., Reed, C. M., Jiao, Y., Perez, Z. D., Wilson, E. C., Jung, J., et al. (2020b). Acquisition of 500 English Words through a TActile Phonemic Sleeve (TAPS). *IEEE Trans. Haptics* 13, 745–760. doi:10.1109/TOH.2020.2973135

Van Doren, C. L. (1990). The Effects of a Surround on Vibrotactile Thresholds: Evidence for Spatial and Temporal Independence in the non-Pacinian I (NP I) Channel. *J. Acoust. Soc. Am.* 87, 2655–2661. doi:10.1121/1.399550

van Erp, J. B. F. (2005b). "Vibrotactile Spatial Acuity on the Torso: Effects of Location and Timing Parameters," in First Joint Eurohaptics Conference and Symposium on Haptic Interfaces for Virtual Environment and Teleoperator Systems (New York, NY: World Haptics Conference), 80–85.

Van Erp, J. B. (2005a). Presenting Directions with a Vibrotactile Torso Display. *Ergonomics* 48, 302–313. doi:10.1080/0014013042000327670

Verrillo, R. T. (1963). Effect of Contactor Area on the Vibrotactile Threshold. *J. Acoust. Soc. Am.* 35, 1962–1966. doi:10.1121/1.1918868

Verrillo, R. T., Fraioli, A. J., and Smith, R. L. (1969). Sensation Magnitude of Vibrotactile Stimuli. *Percept. Psychophys.* 6, 366–372. doi:10.3758/bf03212793

Verrillo, R. T., Gescheider, G. A., Calman, B. G., and Van Doren, C. L. (1983). Vibrotactile Masking: Effects of Oneand Two-Site Stimulation. *Percept. Psychophys.* 33, 379–387. doi:10.3758/bf03205886

Verrillo, R. T., and Gescheider, G. A. (1992). "Perception via the Sense of Touch," in *Tactile Aids for the Hearing Impaired* (Londong, England: Whurr Publishers), 1–36. chap. 1.

Weber, E. H. (1834/1978). *The Sense of Touch (De Subtilitate Tactus)*. London, UK: Academic Press.

Weinstein, A. (1968). The Bonanza King Myth: Western Mine Owners and the Remonetization of Silver. *Bus. Hist. Rev.* 42, 195–218. doi:10.2307/3112215

Yongjae Yoo, Y., Inwook Hwang, I., and Seungmoon Choi, S. (2014). Consonance of Vibrotactile Chords. *IEEE Trans. Haptics* 7, 3–13. doi:10.1109/TOH.2013.57

2

Haplets: Finger-Worn Wireless and Low-Encumbrance Vibrotactile Haptic Feedback for Virtual and Augmented Reality

Pornthep Preechayasomboon[1]* and Eric Rombokas[1,2]

[1]Rombolabs, Mechanical Engineering, University of Washington, Seattle, WA, United States, [2]Electrical Engineering, University of Washington, Seattle, WA, United States

*Correspondence:
Pornthep Preechayasomboon
prnthp@uw.edu

We introduce Haplets, a wearable, low-encumbrance, finger-worn, wireless haptic device that provides vibrotactile feedback for hand tracking applications in virtual and augmented reality. Haplets are small enough to fit on the back of the fingers and fingernails while leaving the fingertips free for interacting with real-world objects. Through robust physically-simulated hands and low-latency wireless communication, Haplets can render haptic feedback in the form of impacts and textures, and supplements the experience with pseudo-haptic illusions. When used in conjunction with handheld tools, such as a pen, Haplets provide haptic feedback for otherwise passive tools in virtual reality, such as for emulating friction and pressure-sensitivity. We present the design and engineering for the hardware for Haplets, as well as the software framework for haptic rendering. As an example use case, we present a user study in which Haplets are used to improve the line width accuracy of a pressure-sensitive pen in a virtual reality drawing task. We also demonstrate Haplets used during manipulation of objects and during a painting and sculpting scenario in virtual reality. Haplets, at the very least, can be used as a prototyping platform for haptic feedback in virtual reality.

Keywords: haptics, virtual reality, augmented reality, spatial computing, sensory feedback, human computer interface

1 INTRODUCTION

Hands can be considered the most dexterous tool that a human naturally possesses, making them the most obvious input modality for virtual reality (VR) and augmented reality (AR). In productivity tasks in AR and VR, natural hand tracking enables seamless context switching between the virtual and physical world i.e., not having to put down a controller first to interact with a physical keyboard. However, a major limitation is the lack of haptic feedback that leads to a poor experience in scenarios that require manual dexterity such as object manipulation, drawing, writing, and typing on a virtual keyboard (Gupta et al., 2020). Using natural hand input invokes the visuo-haptic neural representations of held objects when they are seen and felt in AR and VR (Lengyel et al., 2019). Although haptic gloves seem promising for rendering a realistic sense of touch and textures, or provide kinesthetic impedance in the virtual or augmented space, wearing a glove that covers the fingers greatly reduces the tactile information from physical objects outside the augmented space. Thus having a solution that provides believable haptic feedback with the lowest encumbrance is desirable.

Numerous research devices have shown that there is value in providing rich haptic feedback to the fingertips during manipulation (Johansson and Flanagan, 2009; Schorr and Okamura, 2017; Hinchet et al., 2018; Lee et al., 2019), texture perception (Chan et al., 2021), stiffness perception (Salazar et al., 2020), and normal and shear force perception (Kim et al., 2018; Preechayasomboon et al., 2020). Although these devices may render high fidelity haptic feedback, they often come at the cost of being tethered to another device or have bulky electronics that impede the wearability of the device and ultimately hinder immersion of the VR experience. Additionally, once devices are placed on the fingertips, any interaction with objects outside the virtual space is rendered impossible unless the device is removed or put down. Teng et al. (2021) has shown that wearable, wireless, low encumbrance haptic feedback on the fingertips is useful for AR scenarios with a prototype that leaves the fingertips free when haptic feedback is not required. Akin to the growing adoption of virtual reality, the device must be as frictionless to the user as possible—wearable haptic devices are no exception.

It has been shown that rendering haptic feedback away from the intended site does provide meaningful sensations that can be interpreted as proxies for the interactions at the hand (Pezent et al., 2019), or for mid-air text entry (Gupta et al., 2020). Ando et al. (2007) has shown that rendering vibrations on the fingernail can be used to augment passive touch-sensitive displays for creating convincing perception of edges and textures, others have extended this technique to include projector-based augmented reality (Rekimoto, 2009), and even used the fingernail as a haptic display itself (Hsieh et al., 2016). We have shown that there is a perceptual tolerance for conflicting locations of visual and tactile touch, in which the two sensory modalities are fused into a single percept despite arising from different locations (Caballero and Rombokas, 2019). Furthermore, combining multiple modalities either in the form of augmenting otherwise passive haptic sensations (Choi et al., 2020), using pseudo-haptic illusions (Achibet et al., 2017; Samad et al., 2019), or a believable simulation (Kuchenbecker et al., 2006; Chan et al., 2021), can possibly mitigate the lack of congruence between the visual and tactile sensation. We therefore extend what Ando et al. (2007) has proposed to immersive virtual reality by placing the haptic device on the fingernail and finger dorsum and compensating for the distant stimulation with believable visual and haptic rendering, which leaves the fingerpads still free to interact with real-world objects.

With the hands now free to hold and interact with physical objects, any passive object can become a tangible prop or tool. These held tools can provide passive haptic feedback while presenting familiar grounding and pose for the fingers. Gripmarks (Zhou et al., 2020) has shown that everyday objects can be used as mixed reality input by using the hand's pose as an estimate to derive the object being held. In this paper, we further this concept by introducing Haplets: small, wireless and wearable haptic actuators. Each Haplet is a self-contained unit that consists of the bare minimum required to render vibrotactile stimulus wirelessly: a linear resonant actuator (LRA), a motor driver, a wireless system-on-a-chip (SoC), and a battery. Haplets are worn on the dorsal side of the finger and fingernail, and have a footprint small enough that the hands can still be tracked using computer vision methods. Combined with a believable simulation for rendering vibrotactile feedback in VR, Haplets can be used to augment the sensation of manipulation, textures and stiffness for bare hands while still maintaining the ability to pick up and handle everyday objects outside the virtual space. With a tool held in the hand, Haplets can render haptic effects to emulate the sensations when the tool interacts with the virtual environment. We use Haplets as an exploration platform towards building low-encumbrance, wearable haptic feedback devices for virtual and augmented reality.

The rest of this paper is organized as follows: first, in **Section 2**, we describe the hardware for each Haplet and engineering choices made for each component, including our low-latency wireless communication scheme. We then briefly cover the characterization efforts for the haptic actuator (the LRA). Then, we cover our software efforts in creating a physically-believable virtual environment that drives our haptic experiences, including physics-driven virtual hands and augmented physical tools. In **Section 3**, we cover a small user study to highlight one use case of Haplets and explore the practicality of Haplets in a virtual reality scenario. In **Section 4**, we demonstrate other use cases for Haplets in virtual or augmented reality environment such as manipulation, texture discrimination, and painting with tools. Finally, in **Section 5**, we discuss our engineering efforts and the results of our user study, and provide insight for shortcomings and potential future work.

2 MATERIALS AND METHODS

Haplets can be thought of as distributed wireless wearable haptic actuators. As mentioned previously, each Haplet consists of the bare minimum required to render haptic effects: an LRA, a motor driver, a wireless SoC, and a battery (**Figure 1A**). We minimized the footprint so that Haplets, aside from our target area of the finger, can be worn on other parts of the body such as the wrist, arms, or face, or integrated into other, larger systems. Haplets is designed to be able to drive other voice-coil based actuators such as voice coil motors (VCMs), eccentric rotating mass (ERM) actuators, and small brushed DC motors, as well.

2.1 Finger-Mounted Hardware

The core electronic components of each Haplet, as shown in **Figure 1A**, are contained within one side of 13.7 mm by 16.6 mm PCB, while the other side of the PCB is a coin cell socket. We use a BC832 wireless module (Fanstel) that consists of a nRF52832 SoC (Nordic Semiconductor) and an integrated radio antenna. The motor driver for the LRA is a DRV8838 (Texas Instruments), which is chosen for its high frequency, non-audible, pulse width modulation limit (at 250 kHz) and versatile voltage input range (from 0 to 11 V). The PCB also consists of a J-Link programming and debug port, light emitting diode (LED), and two tactile buttons for resetting the device and entering device firmware upgrade (DFU) mode. The DFU mode is used for programming Haplets over a Bluetooth connection. The coin cell we use is a

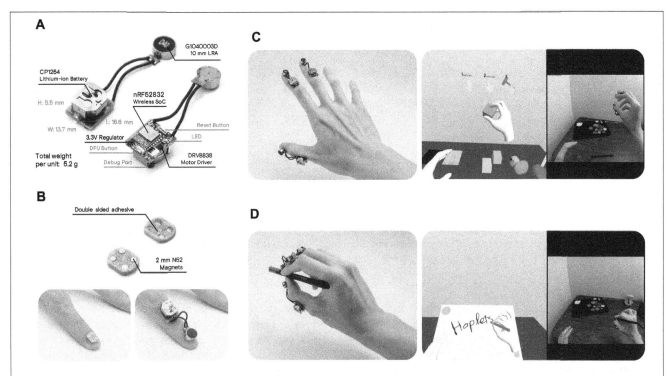

FIGURE 1 | An overview of Haplets. **(A)** Components comprising of a Haplet unit is shown, including the three key elements: the wireless SoC, the LRA, and the built-in battery. **(B)** Haplets are attached on the fingernails through fingernail-mounted magnets. The magnets are embedded in a plastic housing that is attached to the fingernail using double-sided adhesive. **(C)** The user wears Haplets on the thumb, the index finger and the middle finger. An example of a manipulation scenario as seen in VR compared to the real-world is shown. **(D)** When used with a tool (a pen, as shown), Haplets can be used to augment the virtual representation of the tool in VR by providing vibrotactile feedback in addition to the passive haptic feedback provided by the finger's grounding on the tool.

Lithium-ion CP1254 (Varta), measuring 12 mm in diameter by 5.4 mm in height, which is chosen for its high current output (120 mA) and high power density. In our tests, Haplets can be used for up to 3 h of typical usage and the batteries can be quickly replaced. The total weight of one Haplet unit, including the LRA, is 5.2 g.

We imagine Haplets as a wearable device, therefore Haplets must be able to be donned and doffed with minimal effort. To achieve this, we use 3D printed nail covers with embedded magnets, as shown in **Figure 1B**, to attach the LRA to the fingernail. The nail covers are small, lightweight, and can be attached to the fingernail using double-sided adhesive. Each cover has a concave curvature that corresponds to each fingernail. The Haplets' PCB is attached to the dorsal side of the middle phalanx using silicone-based, repositionable double-sided adhesive tape. In our user studies and demonstrations, we place the Haplets on the thumb, index finger and middle finger of the right hand, as shown in **Figure 1C**.

2.2 Low-Latency Wireless Communication

Since we target the fingers, we desire to reduce the latency from visual perception to tactile perception as much as possible, especially when considering the mechanical time constant of the LRA[1]. Although Bluetooth Low Energy (BLE) is commonplace and readily available in most systems with a wireless interface, the overall latency can vary from device to device. We therefore opted to use Enhanced ShockBurst (ESB)[2], a proprietary radio protocol developed by Nordic Semiconductor, for our devices instead. ESB enables up to eight primary transmitters[3] to communicate with a primary receiver. In our implementation, each Haplet is a primary transmitter that sends a small packet at a fixed interval to a host microcontroller, a primary receiver, which is another SoC that is connected to a VR headset, smartphone or PC (**Figure 2A**). Commands for each Haplet are sent in return along with the acknowledge (ACK) packet from the host device to the Haplets. If each Haplet transmits at an interval of 4 milliseconds, then ideally the maximum latency will be slightly over 4 milliseconds when accounting for radio transmission times for the ACK packet.

Since Haplets transmit at a high frequency (every 4 ms or 250 Hz), there is a high chance of collisions between multiple units. We mitigate this by employing a simple time-slot synchronization scheme between the Haplets and the host

---

[1]https://www.vibration-motor.com/wp-content/uploads/2019/05/G1040003D.pdf

[2]https://developer.nordicsemi.com/nRF_Connect_SDK/doc/latest/nrf/ug_esb.html

[3]It is worth noting that although this suggests that a maximum of eight Haplets can be communicating with one host microcontroller at once, there exists techniques such as radio time-slot synchronization similar to those used in Bluetooth that can increase the number of concurrent transmitters to 20.

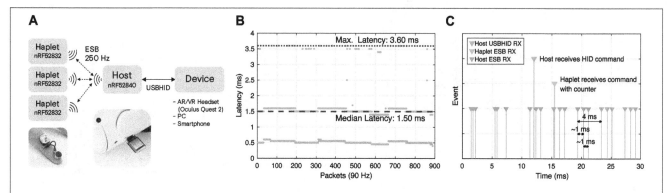

FIGURE 2 | Haplets' low-latency wireless communication architecture. **(A)** Each Haplet communicates using the Enhanced ShockBurst (ESB) protocol with a host microcontroller that receives command from a host device using USB HID. Commands are updated at the rate of 250 Hz. **(B)** Latency, as defined by the time the host microcontroller receives a command from the host device to the time a Haplet receives the command, is shown over a 10 s interval. The maximum latency and median latency is 3.60 and 1.50 milliseconds, respectively. **(C)** Events received from our logic analyzer showing our timeslot algorithm momentarily adjusting the period for sending packets over ESB to prevent radio collisions between Haplets.

microcontroller where each Haplet must transmit in its own predefined 500 microsecond timeslot. The host microcontroller keeps a 250 Hz clock and a microsecond counter that resets every tick of the 250 Hz clock. The counter value from the host is transmitted along with the command packets and each Haplet then uses the counter value to adjust its next transmitting interval to correct itself. For instance, if a Haplet receives a counter value of 750 microseconds and its timeslot is at 1,000 microseconds, it will delay its next round of transmission by 250 microseconds or 4,250 microseconds in total, after the correction, it will transmit at the usual 4,000 microsecond interval until another correction is needed.

One drawback of our implementation, as we use a proprietary radio protocol, is we cannot use the built-in Bluetooth capabilities of host devices (i.e., VR headsets or PC) to communicate with Haplets. Therefore, we use a nRF52840 SoC (Nordic Semiconductor) as a host microcontroller that communicates with the host device through a wired USB connection. In order to minimize the end-to-end latency, we use the Human Interface Device (HID) class for our USB connection. The benefits are two-fold: 1. HID has a typical latency of 1 millisecond and 2. HID is compatible out-of-the-box with most modern hardware including both Windows and Unix-based PCs, standalone VR headsets such as the Oculus Quest, and most Android-based devices (Preechayasomboon et al., 2020).

We briefly tested the communication latency of our system by running a test program that sends command packets over HID to our host microcontroller to three Haplets at 90 Hz—this frequency is chosen to simulate the typical framerate for VR applications. Two digital output pins, one from a Haplet and one from the host microcontroller, were connected to a logic analyzer. The Haplet's output pin toggles when a packet is received and the host microcontroller's output pin toggles when a HID packet is received. Therefore, latency here is defined by the interval of the time a command is received from the host device (PC) to the time the Haplet receives the command. We found that with three Haplets receiving commands simultaneously, the median latency is 1.50 ms over 10 s, with a maximum latency of 3.60 ms during

our testing window. A plot of the latency over the time period is shown in **Figure 2B** along with an excerpt of captured packet times with the timeslot correction in use in **Figure 2C**. It should be noted that the test was done in ideal conditions where no packets were lost and the Haplets are in close proximity with the host controller.

2.3 Vibration Amplitude Compensation

Haplet's LRA is an off-the-shelf G1040003D 10 mm LRA module (Jinlong Machinery and Electronics, Inc.). The module has a resonant frequency at 170 Hz and is designed to be used at that frequency, however, since the LRA is placed in such close proximity to the skin, we observed that frequencies as low as 50 Hz at high amplitudes were just as salient as those closer to the resonant frequency at lower amplitudes. Lower frequencies are important for rendering rough textures, pressure, and softness (Kuchenbecker et al., 2006; Choi et al., 2020) and a wide range of frequency is required for rendering realistic textures (Fishel and Loeb, 2012). Thus, we performed simple characterization in order to compensate for the output of the LRA at frequencies outside the resonant frequency range, from 50 to 250 Hz. **Figure 3C** shows the output response of the LRA as supplied by the manufacturer when compared to our own characterization using the characterization jig in **Figure 3A** (as suggested by the Haptics Industry Forum[4]), and when characterized on the fingertips (**Figure 3B**). The acceleration output was recorded using a micro-electromechanical-based inertial measurement unit (MEMs-based IMU) (ICM42688, TDK) on a 6.4 mm by 10.2 mm, 0.8 mm thick PCB connected to a specialized Haplet via an I^2C connection through a flat flex ribbon cable (FFC). The specialized Haplet streams readings from the IMU at 1,000 Hz to the host device for recording on a PC. We found that when using the compensation profile derived from our characterization jig (**Figure 3A**) on the fingernail, the output at higher frequencies

---

[4]High Definition Inertial Vibration Actuator Performance Specification https://github.com/HapticsIF/HDActuatorSpec

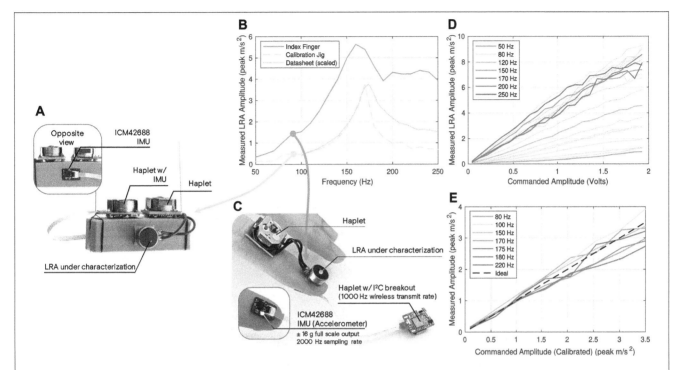

FIGURE 3 | Haplets under characterization are shown and their resulting plots. **(A)** The characterization jig used for characterizing a Haplet's LRA. The jig is hung using two threads from a solid foundation. A special Haplet with an IMU is used to record the accelerations resulting from the LRA's inputs. **(B)** The characterization results from the jig closely resembles the characterization derived from the LRA's datasheet, however, the characterization results when the LRA is placed on a fingernail is substantially different. **(C)** The same devices used in the characterization jig are placed on the fingernail and fingerpads to perform LRA characterization at the fingertips. **(D)** Results from characterization at the fingertip at various frequencies. **(E)** After compensating for reduced amplitude outputs using the model derived from characterization, commanded amplitudes, now in m/s^2, closely match the output amplitude.

were severely overcompensated for and provided uncomfortable levels of vibration. However, when characterization was performed at the target site (the fingertips), with the IMU attached on the fingerpad, the resulting output amplitudes after compensation were subjectively pleasant and more consistent to our expectations.

Characterization was performed by rendering sine wave vibrations at frequencies ranging from 50 to 250 Hz in 10 Hz increments and at amplitudes ranging from 0.04 to 1.9 V (peak-to-peak) in 0.2 V increments with a duration of 0.5 s. Acceleration data was sampled and collected at 1,000 Hz during the vibration interval. A total of five repetitions of the frequency and amplitude sweeps were performed. The resulting amplitude is the mean of the maximum measured amplitude of each repetition for each combination of frequency and amplitude, as presented in **Figure 3D**. The output compensation is then calculated first by fitting a linear model for each frequency's response, *amplitude* $= x_f V$. Then, the inverse of the model is used with the input being the desired acceleration amplitude, in m/s^2, and the output being the voltage for achieving that acceleration. Frequencies outside the characterized models are linearly interpolated. The results from our compensation on a subset of the characterized frequencies, along with frequencies outside of the characterization intervals, is shown in **Figure 3E**. We use the same compensation profile for every instance of haptic rendering throughout this paper.

2.4 Virtual Environment

Our haptic hardware is only one part of our system. Robust software that can create compelling visuals and audio as well as believable and responsive haptic effects is equally important. In this paper, we build up a software framework using the Unity game engine to create our virtual environments as described in the following sections. Our entire system is run locally on the Oculus Quest two and is completely standalone: requiring only the headset, our USB-connected host microcontroller and the Haplets themselves.

2.4.1 Haptic Rendering

Haplets are commanded to render sine wave vibrations using packets that describe the sine wave frequency, amplitude and duration. Each vibration becomes a building block for haptic effects and are designed to be either used as a single event or chained together for complex effects. For example, a small "click" that resembles a click on a trackpad can be commanded as a 10 millisecond, 170 Hz vibration with an amplitude of 0.2 m/s^2. To render textures, short pulses of varying frequencies and amplitudes are chained together in rapid succession. Due to the low-latency, haptic effects can be dynamic and responsive to the environment. Examples of interactions that highlight the responsiveness of such a low-latency system are presented in the following sections.

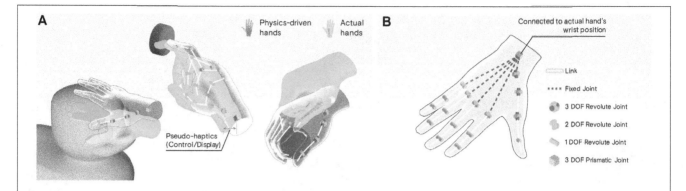

FIGURE 4 | Physics-driven hands. **(A)** Physics-driven hands shown in the following scenarios from left to right: (1) When pressing against a stationary object the physics-driven fingers conform along the object's curvature while respecting joint limits. (2) When pressing on a button with a spring-like stiffness, the fingers do not buckle under the constraints. The whole hand is also offset according to the force resisting the hand, resulting in a pseudo-haptic illusion. (3) When grasping and lifting objects, the fingers respect the geometry of the object and conform along the shape of the object. Gravity acting on the object and inertia also dictates the pseudo-haptic illusion. **(B)** A diagram showing the articulated bodies and their respective joints (The hand's base skeleton is identical to the OVRHand skeleton provided with the Oculus Integration SDK).

2.4.2 Physics-Driven Hands

The user's hands in our environment are physically simulated using NVIDIA PhysX Articulations system for robotics[5]. Articulations are abstracted as ArticulationBodies in the Unity game engine. This system enables robust hand-object manipulations and believable response towards other rigid bodies in the scene, such as pushing, prodding, and throwing. The fingers are a series of linkages connected using either 1, 2, or 3 degree of freedom revolute joints with joint limits similar to that of a human hand (Cobos et al., 2008). The wrist is connected to the tracked position of actual wrist using a 3 degree of freedom prismatic joint. As a result, pseudo-haptics (Lécuyer, 2009) is readily available as part of the system, meaning that users must extend their limbs further than what is seen in response to a larger force being applied to the virtual hands. This is also known as the pseudo-haptic weight illusion (Samad et al., 2019) or the god object model (Zilles and Salisbury, 1995). For higher fidelity, we set our simulation time step to 5 ms and use the high frequency hand tracking (60 Hz) mode on the Oculus Quest 2. A demonstration of the system is available as a video in the **Supplementary Materials** and **Figure 4**.

We take advantage of the robust physics simulation and low-latency communication to render haptic effects. A collision event that occurs between a finger and an object is rendered as a short 10 ms burst of vibration with an amplitude scaled to the amount of impulse force. Each object also has unique haptic properties: the frequency of vibration during impact with fingers and the frequency of vibration during fingers sliding across the object. For instance, a wooden surface with high friction would have a sliding frequency of 170 Hz and a rubber-like surface with lower friction would have a sliding frequency of 200 Hz. Additionally, as both our objects and fingers have friction, when a finger glides across a surface, the stick-slip phenomenon can be observed both visually and through haptic feedback (**Figures 5A,B**).

2.4.3 Tools

With the fingerpads free to grasp and hold actual objects, we augment the presence of handheld tools using visual and haptic feedback.

First, we detect the tool being held in the hand using a technique similar to template matching, as presented in GripMarks (Zhou et al., 2020). Each tool has a unique pose of the hand, such as the pose when holding a pen or the pose when holding a spray bottle (**Figure 6**), which is stored a set of joint angles for every joint of the hand. Our algorithm then compares each tool's predefined pose to the current user's pose using the Pearson correlation coefficient in a sliding 120 frame window. If 80% of frames in the window contains a pose with over a coefficient over 0.9, then it is deemed that the tool is being held in the user's hand. To "release" a tool, the user would simply open their hand fully for 1 s (**Figure 6**). Any tool can now be altered in shape and experience both visually and through haptics through the headset. For instance, the user can physically hold a pen but in a pose akin to holding a hammer, and in their VR environment, they would see and feel as if they are holding a hammer. Additionally, since our algorithm relies only on the hand's pose, an actual tool does not have to be physically held by the user's hand, we also explore this in our user study in the following sections.

When a tool is detected, the tool is visually rendered attached to the hand. In our physics simulation, the tool's rigid body is attached to the wrist's ArticulationBody and thus the tool can respond dynamically to the environment as if the tool and the hands are a single object, maintaining the same pseudo-haptic capabilities as presented in the previous sections. The physically held tools provide passive haptic feedback in the form of pressure and familiar grounding while Haplets can be used to render vibrotactile feedback to augment the presence of the held tool in response to the virtual environment. Three examples of haptic rendering schemes for tools are presented in **Figure 7**.

---

[5]https://gameworksdocs.nvidia.com/PhysX/4.0/documentation/PhysXGuide/ Manual/Articulations.html

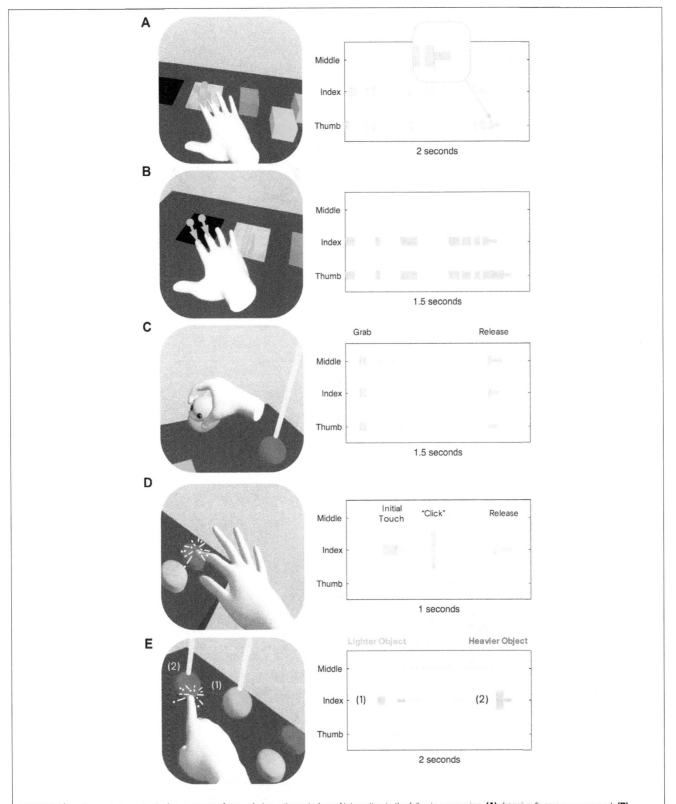

FIGURE 5 | Haptic rendering output, shown as waveforms, during a time window of interaction in the following scenarios: **(A)** dragging fingers across wood, **(B)** dragging fingers across smooth plastic, **(C)** picking up and letting go of a plastic toy, **(D)** pressing a button, and **(E)** prodding two similar spheres with different masses.

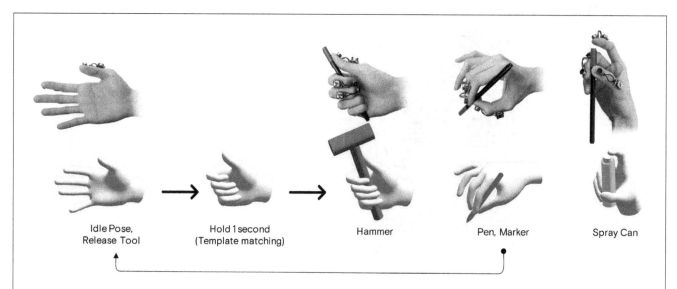

FIGURE 6 | An illustration of the tool activation system. The user starts with an open hand and holds the desired pose for each tool for 1 s. The user can also hold a physical proxy of the tool in the hand. After 1 s, a tool is visually rendered in the virtual hands and the haptic rendering system augments any interaction of the tool with environment. To release a tool, the user fully opens their hand for 1 s. Switching between tools requires the user to release the current tool first.

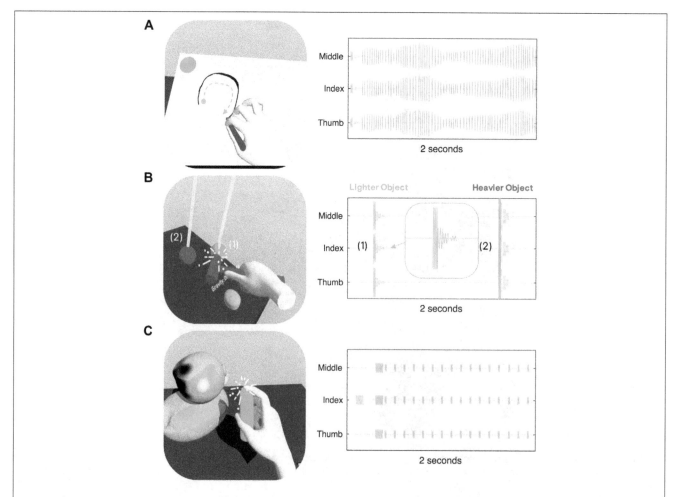

FIGURE 7 | Haptic rendering output, shown as waveforms, during a time window of tool interaction in the following scenarios: **(A)** when drawing with the pen tool, **(B)** when striking objects of different weights with the hammer tool, **(C)** when spraying paint using the spray painting tool.

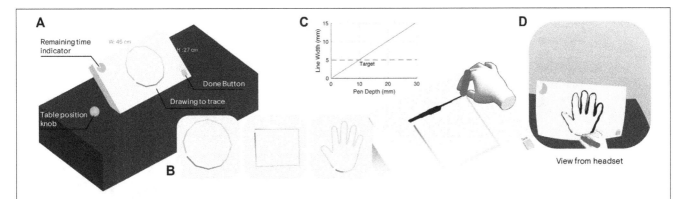

FIGURE 8 | An overview of the user study environment: **(A)** An adjustable floating desk is presented to the user along with a canvas. The canvas contains template for the user to trace with along with an indicator for the remaining time in each repetition. The canvas can also present buttons for the user to indicate that they're done with the drawing or answers to questions. **(B)** Three shapes are used in the user study: a circle, a square and an outline of a hand. Participants start tracing at the green line section and end at the red line section. **(C)** A plot of the line width that results from how deep the users actual hand is penetrating the surface of the canvas. Participants must aim for the 5 mm line width which corresponds to a 10 mm depth. Vibrotactile feedback is provided as shown in **Figure 7A**. **(D)** An example of the participant's view captured from the headset during a trial.

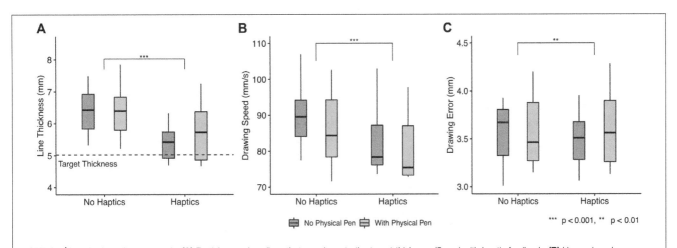

FIGURE 9 | Results from the user study: **(A)** Participants draw lines that are closer to the target thickness (5 mm) with haptic feedback. **(B)** Users slow down significantly when haptic feedback is provided. **(C)** Users produce less 2D error when drawing with haptic feedback.

3 USER STUDY

In this section, we introduce a sketching user study to evaluate the feasibility of using Haplets in a productivity scenario. We chose a sketching task because it encompasses the main concepts introduced in this paper: 1) a physical tool (a pen) is held by the user, thus allowing Haplets to augment the tool with vibrotactile haptics, 2) upon the pen contacting with a surface and while drawing, Haplets renders impacts and textures, and 3) physics-driven hands and tools respond to the sketching environment, introducing pseudo-haptic force and friction. The main task is loosely based on VRSketchPen (Elsayed et al., 2020) where the user would trace a shape shown on a flat canvas. With a simulated pressure sensitive pen, users would need to maintain a precise distance from the canvas in order to draw a line that matches the line thickness of the provided guide. We hypothesize that with Haplets providing vibrotactile

feedback, users would be able to draw lines closer to the target thickness. In addition to the sketching task, after the end of the session, the user is presented with a manipulation sandbox for them to explore the remaining modalities that Haplets has to offer such as texture discrimination, object manipulation, and pseudo-haptic weight. The details for this sandbox is described in **Section 4.1**.

3.1 Experimental Setup

We recruited eight right-handed participants (2 females, aged 22–46, mean = 32.75, SD = 7.44) to participate in the study. Proper social distancing and proactive disinfection according to local guidance was maintained at all times and the study was mostly self-guided through prompts in the VR environment. The study was approved by our institution's IRB and participants gave informed consent. Participants were first seated and started by donning three Haplets on the thumb, index and middle fingers of

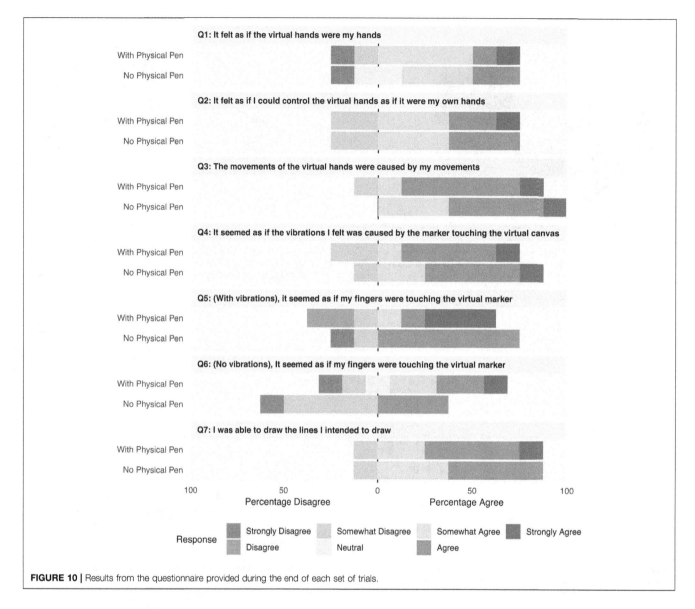

FIGURE 10 | Results from the questionnaire provided during the end of each set of trials.

their right hand. Then they donned an Oculus Quest two headset. Participants then picked up a physical pen and held it in their left hand using the headset's AR Passthrough mode, then a standalone VR Unity application was launched. All experiments were run and logged locally on the headset. All interactions in VR were done using on-device hand tracking (Han et al., 2020).

The VR environment consists of a single desktop with a large canvas, as shown in **Figure 8** The canvas is used to present instructions, questions and the actual tracing task. Participants were first instructed to hold the physical pen in their right hand, which will also create a virtual pen in their hand using the tool detection system presented in the previous section. The participant uses the pen to interact with most elements in the environment including pressing buttons and drawing.

The main task consists of participants tracing three shapes with the virtual pen: a square, a circle and a hand, as shown in **Figure 8**. The shapes are presented in a randomized order and each shape is given 15 s to complete. The virtual pen is pressure sensitive and the lines the users draw vary in thickness depending on how hard the user is pressing against the canvas—we simulate this using our physically simulated hands, which means that the further the user's real hands interpenetrates the canvas, the thicker the line will be. The target thickness for all shapes is 5 mm. Lines are rendered in VR using the Shapes real-time vector library[6].

When drawing, for every 2.5 mm the pen has traveled on the canvas, Haplets render a vibration for 10 ms at 170 Hz with an amplitude that is mapped to how much virtual force is exerted on the canvas. Since the amount of force is also proportional to the line width, the amplitude of vibration is also mapped to the line width, as shown in **Figure 8C**. In other words, the pen and Haplets emulates the sensation of drawing on a rough surface and

---

[6]Shapes by Freya Holmér https://acegikmo.com/shapes

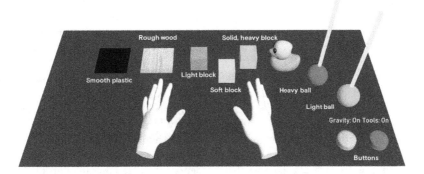

FIGURE 11 | After the user study concludes, participants are presented with a desk with various objects to interact with. From left to right: a smooth plastic square, a rough wooden square, a lightweight orange block, a soft green block, a heavy blue block, a rubber ducky (solid), a heavy tethered ball, a lightweight tethered ball. Participants can use the lower right buttons to toggle the use of tools and toggle gravity on and off. Each object responds with haptic feedback as shown in **Figures 5**, **7**.

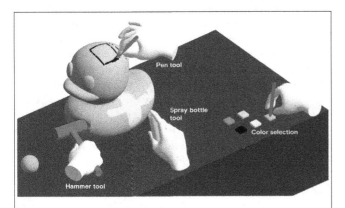

FIGURE 12 | The painting application highlights the use of haptic feedback to enhance the experience of using otherwise passive tools in the hand. Shown are four interactions overlaid from left to right: using the hammer tool to adjust the sculpture's geometry, using the pen tool to draw on the sculpture, using the spray bottle to spray paint on the sculpture, and selecting colors by tapping the tools on the swatches provided. Haptic feedback provided by the tools is visualized in **Figure 7**.

the pressure is represented as the strength of vibration. An example of the haptic rendering scheme's output is shown in **Figure 7A**.

Participants first perform 12 trials in a training phase to get familiar with the task where they would hold a physical pen but would not receive haptic feedback. Participants then performed two sets of 36 trials (12 of each shape per set) with or without holding the physical pen in their hand, totaling 72 trials. We balance the order of this throughout our participants to account for any order effects. Half of the 36 trials in each set have the Haplets turned off, presented in a randomized order. In summary, participants are given two conditions for either holding or not holding the pen and two conditions for either having or not having haptic feedback. After each set of trials, they

are presented with a short questionnaire. After all trials have concluded, the participant is given a short demo of other capabilities of Haplets, as described in the following sections.

For each trial, we collected the line thickness for every line segment, the coordinates along each line segment, and the time it took to complete the drawing. Through post-processing, we calculate the mean line thickness for each trial, the mean drawing speed and the mean 2D error from the given guide.

3.2 Results

We performed a two-way repeated measures analysis of variance (ANOVA) for each independent variable: line thickness, drawing speed and drawing error with two within-subject factors: with or without haptic feedback, and with or without a physical pen held. Our analysis, as presented in **Figure 9**, revealed main effects for haptic feedback for line thickness (F $(1,7)$ = 15.82, $p < 0.01$), drawing speed (F $(1,7)$ = 10.75, $p < 0.02$), and drawing error (F $(1,7)$ = 14.24, $p < 0.01$), but non-significance for the physical pen conditions nor the interactions between factors. Pairwise t-tests between the haptic and non-haptic conditions for each independent variable confirmed significance in line thickness ($p < 0.001$), drawing speed ($p < 0.001$), and drawing error ($p = 0.001$).

For line thickness, we can observe that participants can rely on the haptic feedback for guidance and draw lines that are closer to the guide's thickness, with an mean error across subjects of 1.58 mm with haptic feedback and 2.68 mm without haptic feedback. Having a physical pen in the hand seems to negatively impact the line thickness, we attribute this to the deteriorated tracking accuracy when the physical pen occludes parts of the tracked fingers—a limitation of our particular setup. We confirmed this by observing video recordings of the sessions, where we could correspond moments of large line width variations to temporary losses of hand tracking (indicated by malformed hand rendering or hand disappearance). We can also observe that participants slow down significantly when haptic feedback is provided. We hypothesize that participants were actively using the haptic feedback to guide their strokes. The reduced drawing error is most likely to be influenced directly by the reduced speed of drawing.

When interviewed during a debriefing session after the experiment, two participants (P3 and P5) noted that they "forgot (the Haplets) were there". Some participants (P1, P3 and P8) preferred having the physical pen in their hands, while other participants (P2 and P7) did not. One participant (P7) suggests that they were more used to using smaller styli and thus preferred not having the larger pen when using a virtual canvas. Another participant (P6) noted that they felt the presence of the physical pen even after it has been removed from their hands.

From our questionnaire (**Figure 10**), we can observe that participants had a reasonable amount of body ownership (Q1) and agency (Q2, Q3). Having a physical pen in their hands did not seem to alter the experience of drawing on a virtual canvas (Q4, Q7). However, the presence of holding a virtual pen in VR seems to be positively impacted by having active haptic rendering (from the Haplets) along with the passive haptic feedback from holding a physical pen (Q5, Q6).

4 DEMONSTRATION

We built demonstrations for highlighting two potential use-cases for Haplets: 1. manipulation in AR/VR and 2. a painting application that uses our tool system.

4.1 Manipulation Sandbox

The manipulation sandbox is a demonstration presented to participants at the end of our user study. The user is presented with a desk with several objects and widgets, as shown in **Figure 11**. A video showing the demonstration is provided with the **Supplementary Materials**.

The top-left corner of the desk consists of two squares with two different textures. The left square represents a smooth, black, plastic surface and the right square represents a grainy, wooden surface. The smooth surface has a low coefficient of friction of 0.1 while the rough surface has a high coefficient of friction of 1.0. When the user runs their fingers across each surface, the haptics system renders different frequencies for each texture, at 200 and 100 Hz, respectively. Each vibration is generated after the fingertips have traveled at least 2.5 mm, similarly to the pen's haptic rendering scheme presented in the previous section. Since the wooden texture has higher friction, the user's finger will stick and slip, rendering both visually and through haptics, the sensation of a rough surface. An example of the surfaces' haptic rendering system in use is shown in **Figures 5A,B**.

Towards the center of the desk are three cubes with varying densities. The user can either pick up or prod the cubes to figure out which cube is lighter or heavier than the others. When prodded at, visually, the lighter cube will slide while and heavier cube will topple. When picked up, the lighter cube will render a lower control-display ratio (pseudo-haptic weight illusion) than the heavier cubes. Each cube also responds to touch differently. The lighter cube will render a vibration of 100 Hz upon touch, to simulate a softer texture, while the heavier cube will render a vibration of 200 Hz to simulate contact with a dense object. Held cubes can also be tapped against the desk, and similar vibrations will be rendered upon impact. Upon release, Haplets will render a smaller amplitude vibration of the same frequency. A rubber duck is also presented nearby, with similar properties to the cubes. An example of the haptic rendering output is shown in **Figure 5C**.

Towards the right of the desk are two buttons: one for toggling gravity on and off and another for toggling the tool system on and off. The button responds to initial touch using the same system as other objects but emit a sharp click (170 Hz, 20 ms) when depressed a certain amount to signal that the button has activated. If the user turns the tool system off, tools will not be created when a pose is recognized. The buttons' haptic rendering scheme is shown in **Figure 5D**.

When the tool system is active, users can create a hammer in their hand by holding the "thumbs-up" pose (see **Figure 6**). The hammer can be used to tap and knock the items on the desk around. The hammer's haptic system is similar to the fingertips, where each object responds with different frequencies depending on pre-set properties and different amplitudes depending on how much reaction force is generated when the hammer strikes the object. All three Haplets will vibrate upon hammer strikes under the assumption that the user is holding the hammer with all three fingers. Additionally, a lower frequency reverberation is also rendered immediately after the initial impact in order to emulate stiffness. An example of the haptic rendering scheme for the hammer is shown in **Figure 7B**.

4.2 Painting

Our painting demonstration, as shown in **Figure 12**, is designed to highlight the use of our tool system. A desk with a large, gray duck sculpture is presented to the user. The sculpture can be rotated using the user's bare hands. The user can use three tools during the demonstration: a spray bottle, a pen and a hammer. Each tool is placed in the user's hand when they produce the correct pose, as shown in **Figure 6**. The lower right corner of the desk contains a palette of five colors: the user can tap the tool on the color to switch the tool to operate with that color. A video showing the demonstration is provided with the **Supplementary Materials**.

The spray bottle is used to quickly paint the duck sculpture. As the user presses down on the bottle's nozzle, a small click is rendered on the index finger Haplet. When the nozzle is engaged and the tool is producing paint, all three Haplets pulse periodically with an amplitude that corresponds to how much the nozzle is depressed. An example of the haptic rendering output is shown in **Figure 7C**. Paint is deposited onto the sculpture similar in behavior to spray painting.

The pen is used to mark fine lines on the sculpture. The haptic rendering scheme is identical to that of the pen described in the user study, where all three Haplets render vibrations with amplitudes that correspond to the depth of penetration and line width.

The hammer is used to modify the sculpture by creating indentations. The sculpture's mesh is modified in response to the reaction force caused by strikes of the hammer. Haptic feedback for the hammer is similar to that presented in the previous section (**Figure 7B**).

5 DISCUSSION

Haplets introduces a wireless, finger-mounted haptic display for AR and VR that leaves the user's fingertip free to interact with real-world objects, while providing responsive vibrotactile haptic rendering. Each Haplet is a self-contained unit with a footprint small enough to fit on the back of the fingers and fingernail. We also present an engineering solution to achieve low-latency wireless communication that adds haptic rendering to various use cases in VR such as manipulation, texture rendering, and tool usage. Our simulation system for physics-driven virtual hands complements our haptic rendering system by providing pseudo-haptics, robust manipulation, and realistic friction. With a real-world tool held in the hand, Haplets render vibrotactile feedback along with visuals from our simulation system to augment the presence of the tool. Our user study and demonstrations show that Haplets is a feasible solution for a low-encumbrance haptic device.

Although Haplets exclusively provide vibrotactile feedback, we have introduced several engineering efforts to maximize the rendering capabilities of our haptic actuator, the LRA. Our brief characterization of the LRA shows that LRAs can be used at frequencies outside the resonant frequency when properly compensated for. Furthermore, our characterization also shows that the material (or body part) on which the actuator is mounted on to can cause the output of the actuator to vary significantly and therefore needs to be characterized for the intended location of the actuator. Our low-latency wireless communication also helps minimize the total latency from visual stimuli to tactile stimuli, which is especially useful when considering the inherent mechanical time delay for LRAs.

Our user study and subjective feedback from the demonstrations have shown that Haplets and the current framework do provide adequate haptic feedback for the given tasks and experiences. However, the human hand can sense much more than simple vibrations such as the sensation of shear force, normal force, and temperature. We address this shortcoming by introducing believable visuals in the form of physics-driven hands, and make up for the lack of force rendering by introducing passive haptic feedback in the form of tools. Our low-latency solution enables impacts, touch and textures to be rendered responsively according to the simulation and visuals. Furthermore, we have yet to fully explore the voice coil-like rendering capabilities of the haptic actuator (LRA). Therefore, our immediate future improvement to our system is the ability to directly stream waveform data to the device. This will enable the ability to render arbitrary waveforms on the LRAs or VCMs which can be used to render highly realistic textures (Chan et al., 2021) or the use of audio-based tools for authoring haptic effects (Israr et al., 2019; Pezent et al., 2021).

Our implementation of passive haptic feedback for tools uses a pen for physical grounding of the fingers, which provides adequate grounding for a number of tasks. Inertial cues that provide the sense of weight to the pen are presented using pseudo-haptic weight. Shigeyama et al. (2019) have shown that VR controllers with reconfigurable shapes can provide realistic haptic cues for inertia and grounding. Therefore, a potential venue for future work is the use of Haplets in conjunction with actual tools (e.g., holding an actual hammer or an actual spray can) or reconfigurable controllers, which would not only provide realistic grips and inertia but also additional haptic feedback that the tool may provide such as depressing the nozzle of a spray bottle.

For other potential future work, our framework provides a foundation for building wearable haptic devices which are not necessarily limited to the fingers. In its current form, Haplets can be placed on other parts of the body with minimal adjustments for rapid prototyping haptic devices, such as the forearm, temple, and thighs (Cipriani et al., 2012; Sie et al., 2018; Rokhmanova and Rombokas, 2019; Peng et al., 2020). With some modifications, namely to the number of motor drivers and firmware, Haplets can also be used for rendering a larger number of vibrotactile actuators at once, which could be used to create haptic displays around the wrist or on the forearm. Furthermore, our motor drivers are not limited to driving vibrotactile actuators, skin stretch and normal force can be rendered with additional hardware and DC motors (Preechayasomboon et al., 2020).

6 CONCLUSION

We have introduced Haplets as a wearable haptic device for fingers in VR that is low encumbrance. Haplets can augment the presence of virtual hands in VR and we strengthen that further with physics-driven hands that respond to the virtual environment. We have also introduced an engineering solution for achieving low-latency wireless haptic rendering. Our user study and demonstration shows that Haplets have potential in improving hand and tool-based VR experiences. Our system as a whole provides a framework for prototyping haptic experiences in AR and VR and our immediate future work is exploring more use cases for Haplets.

AUTHOR CONTRIBUTIONS

Both authors conceptualized the device. PP designed and built the hardware, firmware and software for the devices, user study and demonstrations. Both authors conceptualized and designed the user study. PP ran the user study. PP wrote the first draft of the manuscript. Both authors contributed to manuscript revision, read, and approved the submitted version.

ACKNOWLEDGMENTS

The authors would like to thank current and former members of Rombolabs for their valuable input and insightful discussions: David Boe, Maxim Karrenbach, Abhishek Sharma, and Astrini Sie.

REFERENCES

Achibet, M., Le Gouis, B., Marchal, M., Léziart, P.-A., Argelaguet, F., Girard, A., Lecuyer, A., and Kajimoto, H. (2017). "FlexiFingers: Multi-finger Interaction in VR Combining Passive Haptics and Pseudo-haptics," in 2017 IEEE Symposium on 3D User Interfaces (3DUI), 18-19 March 2017, Los Angeles, CA, USA, 103–106. doi:10.1109/3DUI.2017.7893325

Ando, H., Kusachi, E., and Watanabe, J. (2007). "Nail-mounted Tactile Display for Boundary/texture Augmentation," in Proceedings of the international conference on Advances in computer entertainment technology, 13-15 June 2007, Salzburg, Austria (New York, NY, USA: Association for Computing Machinery), 292–293. ACE '07. doi:10.1145/1255047.1255131

Caballero, D. E., and Rombokas, E. (2019). "Sensitivity to Conflict between Visual Touch and Tactile Touch," in IEEE Transactions on Haptics 12, 78–86. doi:10.1109/TOH.2018.2859940

Chan, S., Tymms, C., and Colonnese, N. (2021). Hasti: Haptic and Audio Synthesis for Texture Interactions, 6.

Choi, I., Zhao, E., Gonzalez, E. J., and Follmer, S. (2020). "Augmenting Perceived Softness of Haptic Proxy Objects through Transient Vibration and Visuo-Haptic Illusion in Virtual Reality," in IEEE Transactions on Visualization and Computer Graphics, 1. doi:10.1109/TVCG.2020.3002245

Cipriani, C., D'Alonzo, M., and Carrozza, M. C. (2012). "A Miniature Vibrotactile Sensory Substitution Device for Multifingered Hand Prosthetics," in IEEE Transactions on Biomedical Engineering 59, 400–408. doi:10.1109/TBME.2011.2173342

Cobos, S., Ferre, M., Sanchez Uran, M., Ortego, J., and Pena, C. (2008). "Efficient Human Hand Kinematics for Manipulation Tasks," in 2008 IEEE/RSJ International Conference on Intelligent Robots and Systems, 22-26 September 2008, Nice, France, 2246–2251. doi:10.1109/IROS.2008.4651053

Elsayed, H., Barrera Machuca, M. D., Schaarschmidt, C., Marky, K., Müller, F., Riemann, J., Matviienko, A., Schmitz, M., Weigel, M., and Mühlhäuser, M. (2020). "VRSketchPen: Unconstrained Haptic Assistance for Sketching in Virtual 3D Environments," in 26th ACM Symposium on Virtual Reality Software and Technology, 1-4 November 2020, Virtual Event, Canada (New York, NY, USA: Association for Computing Machinery), 1–11. VRST '20. doi:10.1145/3385956.3418953

Fishel, J. A., and Loeb, G. E. (2012). Bayesian Exploration for Intelligent Identification of Textures. Front. Neurorobot. 6. doi:10.3389/fnbot.2012.00004

Gupta, A., Samad, M., Kin, K., Kristensson, P. O., and Benko, H. (2020). "Investigating Remote Tactile Feedback for Mid-air Text-Entry in Virtual Reality," in 2020 IEEE International Symposium on Mixed and Augmented Reality (ISMAR), 9-13 November 2020, Porto de Galinhas, Brazil, 350–360. doi:10.1109/ISMAR50242.2020.00062

Han, S., Liu, B., Cabezas, R., Twigg, C. D., Zhang, P., Petkau, J., et al. (2020). MEgaTrack. ACM Trans. Graph. 39. doi:10.1145/3386569.3392452

Hinchet, R., Vechev, V., Shea, H., and Hilliges, O. (2018). "DextrES," in Proceedings of the 31st Annual ACM Symposium on User Interface Software and Technology, 14-17 October 2018, Berlin, Germany (New York, NY, USA: Association for Computing Machinery), 901–912. UIST '18. doi:10.1145/3242587.3242657

Hsieh, M.-J., Liang, R.-H., and Chen, B.-Y. (2016). "NailTactors," in Proceedings of the 18th International Conference on Human-Computer Interaction with Mobile Devices and Services, 6-9 September 2016, Florence, Italy. (New York, NY, USA: Association for Computing Machinery), 29–34. MobileHCI '16. doi:10.1145/2935334.2935358

Israr, A., Zhao, S., Schwemler, Z., and Fritz, A. (2019). "Stereohaptics Toolkit for Dynamic Tactile Experiences," in HCI International 2019 – Late Breaking Papers. Editor C. Stephanidis (Cham: Springer International Publishing), 217–232. Lecture Notes in Computer Science. doi:10.1007/978-3-030-30033-3_17

Johansson, R. S., and Flanagan, J. R. (2009). Coding and Use of Tactile Signals from the Fingertips in Object Manipulation Tasks. Nat. Rev. Neurosci. 10, 345–359. doi:10.1038/nrn2621

Kim, H., Yi, H., Lee, H., and Lee, W. (2018). HapCube. doi:10.1145/3173574.317407513

Kuchenbecker, K. J., Fiene, J., and Niemeyer, G. (2006). "Improving Contact Realism through Event-Based Haptic Feedback," in IEEE Transactions on Visualization and Computer Graphics 12, 219–230. doi:10.1109/TVCG.2006.32

Lécuyer, A. (2009). Simulating Haptic Feedback Using Vision: A Survey of Research and Applications of Pseudo-haptic Feedback. Presence: Teleoperators and Virtual Environments 18, 39–53. doi:10.1162/pres.18.1.39

Lee, J., Sinclair, M., Gonzalez-Franco, M., Ofek, E., and Holz, C. (2019). "TORC: A Virtual Reality Controller for In-Hand High-Dexterity Finger Interaction," in Proceedings of the 2019 CHI Conference on Human Factors in Computing Systems. 6-9 May 2019, Glasgow, Scotland UK. (New York, NY, USA: Association for Computing Machinery), 1–13. doi:10.1145/3290605.3300301

Lengyel, G., Žalalytė, G., Pantelides, A., Ingram, J. N., Fiser, J., Lengyel, M., et al. (2019). Unimodal Statistical Learning Produces Multimodal Object-like Representations. eLife 8, e43942. doi:10.7554/eLife.43942

Peng, Y.-H., Yu, C., Liu, S.-H., Wang, C.-W., Taele, P., Yu, N.-H., and Chen, M. Y. (2020). "WalkingVibe: Reducing Virtual Reality Sickness and Improving Realism while Walking in VR Using Unobtrusive Head-Mounted Vibrotactile Feedback," in Proceedings of the 2020 CHI Conference on Human Factors in Computing Systems, 25-30 April 2020, Honolulu, HI, USA (New York, NY, USA: Association for Computing Machinery)), 1–12. CHI '20. doi:10.1145/3313831.3376847

Pezent, E., Cambio, B., and OrMalley, M. K. (2021). "Syntacts: Open-Source Software and Hardware for Audio-Controlled Haptics," in IEEE Transactions on Haptics, 14, 225–233. doi:10.1109/TOH.2020.3002696

Pezent, E., Israr, A., Samad, M., Robinson, S., Agarwal, P., Benko, H., and Colonnese, N. (2019). "Tasbi: Multisensory Squeeze and Vibrotactile Wrist Haptics for Augmented and Virtual Reality," in 2019 IEEE World Haptics Conference (WHC), 9-12 July 2019, Tokyo, Japan, 1–6. doi:10.1109/WHC.2019.8816098

Preechayasomboon, P., Israr, A., and Samad, M. (2020). "Chasm: A Screw Based Expressive Compact Haptic Actuator," in Proceedings of the 2020 CHI Conference on Human Factors in Computing Systems, 25-30 April 2020, Honolulu, HI, USA, (New York, NY, USA: Association for Computing Machinery), 1–13. CHI '20. doi:10.1145/3313831.3376512

Rekimoto, J. (2009). "SenseableRays," in Proceedings of the 27th international conference extended abstracts on Human factors in computing systems - CHI EA '09 (Boston, MA, USA, 4-9 April 2009, Boston, MA, USA : ACM Press), 2519. doi:10.1145/1520340.1520356

Rokhmanova, N., and Rombokas, E. (2019). "Vibrotactile Feedback Improves Foot Placement Perception on Stairs for Lower-Limb Prosthesis Users," in 2019 IEEE 16th International Conference on Rehabilitation Robotics (ICORR), 24-28 June 2019, Toronto, ON, Canada, 1215–1220. doi:10.1109/ICORR.2019.8779518

Salazar, S. V., Pacchierotti, C., de Tinguy, X., Maciel, A., and Marchal, M. (2020). "Altering the Stiffness, Friction, and Shape Perception of Tangible Objects in Virtual Reality Using Wearable Haptics," in IEEE Transactions on Haptics 13, 167–174. doi:10.1109/TOH.2020.2967389

Samad, M., Gatti, E., Hermes, A., Benko, H., and Parise, C. (2019). "Pseudo-Haptic Weight," in Proceedings of the 2019 CHI Conference on Human Factors in Computing Systems, 4-9 May 2019, Glasgow, Scotland UK. (Glasgow Scotland Uk: ACM), 1–13. doi:10.1145/3290605.3300550

Schorr, S. B., and Okamura, A. M. (2017). "Fingertip Tactile Devices for Virtual Object Manipulation and Exploration," in Proceedings of the 2017 CHI Conference on Human Factors in Computing Systems, 6-11 May 2017, Denver, CO, USA. (New York, NY, USA: Association for Computing Machinery), 3115–3119. CHI '17. doi:10.1145/3025453.3025744

Shigeyama, J., Hashimoto, T., Yoshida, S., Narumi, T., Tanikawa, T., and Hirose, M. (2019). "Transcalibur: A Weight Shifting Virtual Reality Controller for 2D Shape Rendering Based on Computational Perception Model," in Proceedings of the 2019 CHI Conference on Human Factors in Computing Systems, 4-9

Haplets: Finger-Worn Wireless and Low-Encumbrance Vibrotactile Haptic Feedback for Virtual and Augmented...

29

May 2019, Glasgow, Scotland UK. (New York, NY, USA: Association for Computing Machinery), 1–11. doi:10.1145/3290605.3300241

Sie, A., Boe, D., and Rombokas, E. (2018). "Design and Evaluation of a Wearable Haptic Feedback System for Lower Limb Prostheses during Stair Descent," in 2018 7th IEEE International Conference on Biomedical Robotics and Biomechatronics (Biorob), 26-29 August 2018, Enschede, Netherlands, 219–224. doi:10.1109/BIOROB.2018.8487652

Teng, S.-Y., Li, P., Nith, R., Fonseca, J., and Lopes, P. (2021). "Touch&Fold: A Foldable Haptic Actuator for Rendering Touch in Mixed Reality," in Proceedings of the 2021 CHI Conference on Human Factors in Computing Systems, 8-13 May 2021, Yokohama, Japan. (New York, NY, USA: Association for Computing Machinery). 1–14. doi:10.1145/3411764.3445099

Zhou, Q., Sykes, S., Fels, S., and Kin, K. (2020). "Gripmarks: Using Hand Grips to Transform In-Hand Objects into Mixed Reality Input," in Proceedings of the 2020 CHI Conference on Human Factors in Computing Systems, 25-30 April 2020, Honolulu, HI, USA, (New York, NY, USA: Association for Computing Machinery), 1–11. CHI '20. doi:10.1145/3313831.3376313

Zilles, C. B., and Salisbury, J. K. (1995). "A Constraint-Based God-Object Method for Haptic Display," in Proceedings 1995 IEEE/RSJ International Conference on Intelligent Robots and Systems. Human Robot Interaction and Cooperative Robots, 5-9 August 1995, Pittsburgh, PA, USA, 3, 146–151. doi:10.1109/IROS.1995.525876

3

Discrete Cutaneous Feedback for Reducing Dimensions of Wearable Haptic Devices

Daniele Leonardis *, Massimiliano Gabardi, Michele Barsotti and Antonio Frisoli

Percro Laboratory, Institute of Mechanical Intelligence, Scuola Superiore Sant'Anna, Pisa, Italy

*Correspondence:
Daniele Leonardis
d.leonardis@santannapisa.it

In this article, we explore alternative cutaneous haptic feedback for rendering modulation of the grasping force. The aim of the study was to reduce power requirements and in turn dimensions of the actuators, in wearable devices applied to virtual or teleoperated manipulation. This is critical in certain rehabilitation or training scenarios where haptics should not interfere with dexterity of the user. In the study, we experimented discrete, pulsed cutaneous force feedback and compared it with conventional continuous proportional feedback, in a virtual pick and place task. We made use of wearable thimbles based on voice coil actuators in order to provide high-quality, low-noise haptic feedback to the participants. The evaluation was performed on the basis of both objective measurements of task performance (measured virtual forces and correct ratio) and a questionnaire evaluating participants' preferences for the different feedback conditions. On the basis of the obtained results, in the article, we discuss the possibility of providing high-frequency, discretized cutaneous feedback only, driven by modulation of the grasping force. The opportunity is to reduce volume and mass of the actuators and also to consider alternative design solutions, due to the different requirements in terms of static and high-frequency components of the output force.

Keywords: haptic, cutaneous, feedback, touch, virtual, manipulation, discrete, wearable

INTRODUCTION

Haptic rendering of physical interaction in teleoperated or virtual manipulation tasks is a challenging and extensively explored research field; in manipulation tasks, haptic perception is a fundamental sensory pathway for task execution. On the other hand, development of haptic devices for the fingertips has to comply with strict constraints in terms of wearability, lightweight, interfinger interferences, and quality of the provided feedback. Concerning the design of wearable haptic devices for the fingertip segment, the literature includes a variety of proposed designs for rendering specific haptic cues, such as vibratory (Solazzi et al., 2010), contact orientation (Chinello et al., 2015), contact force (Leonardis et al., 2015), area of contact Fani et al. (2017), thermal (Gallo et al., 2015), or a combination of the aforementioned feedback (Wang et al., 2019; Gabardi et al., 2018). An extensive review of portable and wearable haptic devices for the fingertips can be found in Pacchierotti et al., (2017), in which also taxonomy for such devices is introduced. Recent research applications of haptic feedback include rehabilitation systems based on virtual exercises Gutiérrez et al. (2021), virtual serious games (Bortone et al., 2017), and robotic teleoperation (Klamt et al., 2020).

To replicate the correct physical interaction that occurs when the fingertip touches a virtual object is a challenging objective (Caldwell et al., 1997), and concerning fingertip haptic devices, practical requirements such as wearability and portability impose limits to the feedback the device can render or a trade-off between quality of the feedback and wearability of the device. Limitations can be, for instance, in the bandwidth and maximum output force amplitude, limits in the range of motion for shape-rendering thimbles, and heat flux intensity and dynamics for thermal devices.

About force rendering, the range of forces usually exchanged between the fingertips and a manipulated object during a natural interaction is usually too wide to be correctly reproduced by portable and wearable haptic devices. Moreover, since wearable haptic thimbles are grounded at the user fingers, such interfaces are able to provide the user with cutaneous cues only, without kinesthetic feedback. It means that in a virtual grasping task, perception of pressing forces can be delivered at the fingerpad by the actuated thimble, but the rendered force does not constrain the whole finger movement at the contact surface, as it would happen in a real physical grasping. A wearable device is only able to apply net forces between the actuated segment (i.e., the fingerpad) and segment the device is grounded at (i.e., the finger dorsum). Although it is not possible to reproduce the real contact constraints at the user's fingertips, it is still possible to provide rich and informative feedback useful to accomplish virtual (Leonardis et al., 2017), augmented (Maisto et al., 2017), or teleoperated (Pacchierotti et al., 2015) manipulation tasks. Two techniques have been proposed to use cutaneous feedback only to convey haptic information to the user: the *sensory subtraction* (Prattichizzo et al., 2012) and the *sensory substitution* (Schorr et al., 2013).

Haptic feedback related to modulation of the contact force is widely explored in teleoperation and haptic interaction research and is also relevant in fine-manipulation; modulation of the right amount of normal force is critical to overcome slippage and at the same time prevent damage to the object or to the robotic fingers. It has been shown that in manipulation tasks, such as grasping and lifting an object, healthy individuals can accurately modulate grasping forces using information obtained from mechanoreceptors in the fingertips (Westling and Johansson, 1987). In particular, in natural execution of a grasping task, fingertip forces are held just above the level of static friction required to avoid slippage (Cole and Abbs, 1988). In case of virtual environments, where the feedback modalities are limited, the safety margin in terms of forces required to grasp and lift an object is increased (Bergamasco et al., 2006). Perception of force modulation can also carry information about geometrical properties of the explored surface, such as bumps or holes (Robles-De-La-Torre and Hayward, 2001).

The simplest haptic feedback strategy to render modulated grasping force consists in a linear function between the indentation of the finger through the virtual contact surface and the output force applied by the haptic device to the user's fingerpad (Basdogan and Srinivasan, 2002). More complex models take into account also velocity and acceleration of a dynamic proxy (Niemeyer and Mitra, 2005). Furthermore, an interesting method for generating appropriate transients during virtual impacts is described in Kuchenbecker et al. (2006).

The aforementioned continuous force feedback strategies need to render a static component of the output force once the object is grasped, proportional to the grasping force required to hold the manipulated object. In terms of device design, it results, in general, in implementation of bigger actuators. Considering electromagnetic actuators (i.e., DC micromotors and voice coils), widely used in wearable haptic devices, the maximum continuous output force is limited by heat dissipation and maximum temperature reached in the windings. A bigger actuator is capable of higher output forces given the same maximum working temperature. Implementation of a mechanical reduction is another design solution that can be considered to obtain higher output forces. On the other hand, it involves several considerations and limits, especially in the wearable haptics field. Gear reduction is a conventional reduction method that can be implemented in miniaturized, lightweight servomotors, already proposed in the design of fingertip haptic devices ((Leonardis et al., 2017), (Chinello et al., 2015), (Pacchierotti et al., 2016)). However, gear reduction introduces noise and vibrations in the rendered signals, hence diminishing quality of the feedback. Also, it severely limits the output bandwidth of the rendered signals due to effects of backlash and friction. We have also proposed alternative reduction methods for fingertip haptic devices, such as screw reduction (Leonardis et al., 2020) and twist actuators (Leonardis et al., 2021), in order to limit or eliminate noise added by the reduction mechanism to the haptic rendering. The drawback remains a limited output bandwidth, friction, and non-backdrivability of the actuator, if compared with direct drive actuators (rotary motors or linear voice coils), which provide higher quality feedback at the cost of heavier and more cumbersome devices (Gabardi et al., 2016).

On the other hand, the rendering of the high-intensity, static force components might not be the most useful and informative part of the provided haptic feedback. In prosthetics, the use of discrete haptic feedback to inform the user of contact events, called DESC (Discrete Event-driven Sensory feedback Control), has been shown effective to improve control of grasp (Cipriani et al., 2014). Here, the haptic feedback is event-driven and carries information related to, i.e., object contact, liftoff, replace, and release events. The discrete nature of the feedback makes it suitable for effective implementation in prosthetics applications by means of vibrotactile motors; they can be integrated in the robotic prosthesis itself or located at a more proximal body segment, such as the arm or the forearm (Clemente et al., 2016). DESC feedback, however, does not carry information of force modulation during grasping. In Cappello et al. (2020), a study comparing DESC feedback with supplementary continuous force feedback is presented. Removal of the slow components of the continuous feedback (transient feedback) is envisaged in the study as a possibility to convey similar perceptual information to the user, diminishing required power of the haptic actuators at the same time.

In the present study, we propose the use of a discrete haptic feedback method also during the grasping loading phase, after the contact transition, in order to allow a closed-loop modulation of the grasping force, although without the use of continuous force

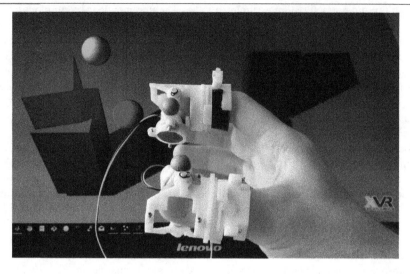

FIGURE 1 | Hand of a subject, wearing the haptic interfaces and approaching a virtual cube to accomplish the manipulation task.

components. Modulation of the grasping force is rendered here as a sequence of indentation-triggered discrete pulses.

By substituting static forces applied to the fingers with proper pulses associated to changes in the applied virtual grasping force, the user is able to keep stability of the grasping and capability of force control. By using the pulse-based force feedback strategy, the power required by the actuation system is expected to be significantly reduced. Regarding the actuator, while continuous output force components have to be limited within the nominal force value of the actuators (which in turn depends on its size and volume), isolated force peaks of much higher amplitude can be sustained without overcoming the maximum allowed temperature. Regarding perception, it has to be considered that part of the fingerpad mechanoreceptors are highly sensitive to fast dynamic signals (Bensmaia and Hollins, 2000), up to the point the tactile sensory channel mixes with the auditory channel (Yau et al., 2009). Perception of such high-frequency haptic signals becomes extremely informative during virtual exploration (Wiertlewski et al., 2011) and telemanipulation (Kuchenbecker et al., 2010). Hence, we expect cues of the pulse-based feedback can be neatly perceived by the user even if the total energy of the signal is less than the conventional continuous feedback.

Pulse-based haptic feedback have been proposed in other scenarios: in Kurihara et al. (2013), a similar feedback was proposed to provide information about the angular position of a pedal control device in a driving simulator, and in Strohmeier et al. (2018) for rendering spatial information in a hand-held device, through an inertial-mass actuator. In Stepp and Matsuoka (2011), an interesting experiment compared two different modulation methods (amplitude or rate modulation of discrete vibration bursts) to render force interaction at the fingerpad. However, the referenced works lacked an experimental comparison of discrete or vibrotactile stimuli with the conventional continuous feedback, which is the closest one to the natural perception of grasping force modulation. Also, in the

present study, we experimentally compare different feedback in a virtual pick-and-place task, allowing to better evaluate feedback effectiveness in a general and familiar manipulation task.

Summarizing, in this article, we propose and evaluate the use of discrete haptic feedback to render modulation of grasping force in virtual manipulation tasks (**Figure 1**). The aim was to reduce power requirements of the actuators and in turn dimensions while providing informative haptic feedback. The improved wearability, especially at the fingertip level, is considered critical in certain training or rehabilitation virtual task in which the addition of haptic devices should not interfere with user's dexterity. To evaluate effectiveness of the proposed feedback, a pick-and-place virtual task has been developed and experimented in different force feedback conditions. Objective metrics and a perception questionnaire were used to investigate which feedback provided better performance. The article is organized as follows: in **Section 2**, the adopted feedback strategies are described. Then, the experimental setup is presented in **Section 3.3**. Obtained results are presented in **Section 4** and discussed in **Section 5**. Finally, conclusions are reported in **Section 6**.

FORCE FEEDBACK STRATEGIES

The use of high-frequency haptic stimuli for modulating the perception of interaction with a physical, rigid surface has been proposed in Kildal (2010). In the study, the illusion of compliant surfaces was elicited by providing high-frequency vibrotactile transients at discrete thresholds of the increasing normal force. In Visell et al. (2014), authors showed the perceptual integration of vibrotactile and force–displacement cues could modulate the perceived stiffness during one finger interaction. In the study, the vibration noise was added to force–displacement feedback, and noise amplitude was modulated by the rate of increasing loading force.

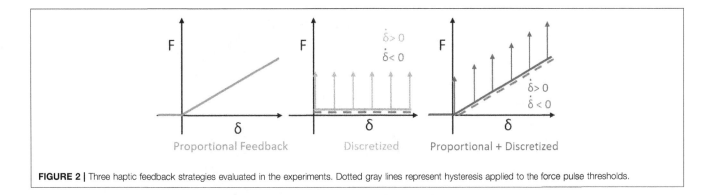

FIGURE 2 | Three haptic feedback strategies evaluated in the experiments. Dotted gray lines represent hysteresis applied to the force pulse thresholds.

In this study, we developed a conceptually similar force feedback strategy, based on discrete haptic cues triggered by the exerted virtual grasping force. The purpose was to enhance perception and control of the virtual grasping force and to eventually substitute the continuous force component. Including the conventional continuous force–displacement strategy, we developed three different feedback conditions to be experimentally evaluated and compared, depicted in **Figure 2** and analytically described as:

• Feedback 1: Proportional (P)

$$F = \begin{cases} 0 & \text{for } \delta < 0 \\ k_c\delta & \text{for } \delta \geq 0 \end{cases} \quad (1)$$

where δ is the indentation depth of the finger proxy in the virtual surface, and k_c is the constant ratio between the indentation distance and the force feedback value. k_c was set to 50 mN/mm.

• Feedback 2: Discrete (D)

$$F = \begin{cases} 0 & \text{for } \delta \leq 0 \\ k_b & \text{for } \delta \geq 0 \text{ and } \dot{\delta} \leq 0 \\ k_b + k_p III_T & \text{for } \delta \geq 0 \text{ and } \dot{\delta} \geq 0 \end{cases} \quad (2)$$

where $III_T = \sum_{k=0}^{n} \Delta(\delta - kT)$ can be described as a Dirac comb (or an impulse train) obtained as distributions of Dirac delta (Δ) functions. $T = 0.8\ mm$ is the spatial distance between successive pulses. The k_b force contribution is very low, and it is used to avoid the separation that occurs between the finger and the plate when $\delta \geq 0$. k_b was set to 50 mN, while k_p was set to 150 mN.

Each pulse lasted for 1 ms. Moreover, 0.2 mm of hysteresis has been applied to each threshold in order to avoid oscillations of the proxy position across the threshold. According to **Equation 2**, the pulses are rendered only when a quantized positive increment of the indentation depth occurs. No feedback was provided in the releasing direction, in order to make participants to unambiguously associate the feedback to a clear motor action (increment of the grasping force). In order to set a consistent value for the spacing between pulses, we conducted a brief exploratory investigation involving three subjects (male, age 29–35). The experiment involved a simplified setup (fingertip haptic devices and optical tracking system only) and proposed the subjects to precisely close the fingers between two minimum and maximum distance threshold (34: mm and 37 mm, respectively, with feedback starting below 40 mm distance). The task result was shown to the subjects after each repetition. We explored 0.4, 0.8, and 1.6 mm spacing between pulses. The averaged results in terms of variability between repetitions showed similar results for the 0.4 and 0.8 mm spacing, (respectively, 1.2 and 1.0 mm standard deviation) with a noticeably higher variability for the 1.6 mm spacing (2.5 mm standard deviation).

• Feedback 3: Proportional + Discrete

$$F = \begin{cases} 0 & \text{for } \delta \leq 0 \\ k_c\delta & \text{for } \delta \geq 0 \text{ and } \dot{\delta} \leq 0 \\ k_c\delta + k_p III_T & \text{for } \delta \geq 0 \text{ and } \dot{\delta} \geq 0 \end{cases} \quad (3)$$

Considering negligible the k_b force contribution of feedback 2, it holds the relation PD = P + D.

EXPERIMENTAL METHODS

The Virtual Task

The experiment was based on a virtual pick-and-place manipulation task. The virtual environment included a virtual desk with two fixed platforms. When a pick-and-place trial started, a cube appeared on top of the left platform. Each trial consisted in accurately moving the cube from the left platform to the right one. Each trial could end with the cube correctly placed on top of the right platform or with a failed trial; the cube could fall on the desk, due to grasping force below simulated static friction, or the cube could break when the grasping force overcame a fixed threshold.

Finally, once the cube was correctly placed on the right platform, the cube disappeared, and another trial started. Three different cube sizes were randomly presented in order to prevent subject adaptation to the cube dimensions. Each cube size was associated to a cube color. The mass of the cubes was kept constant, and the same amount of force was required to lift the cube compensating the simulated gravity

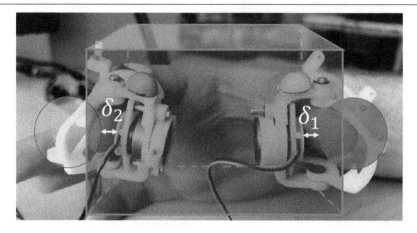

FIGURE 3 | Representation of the grasped virtual cube superimposed to the user's hand performing the grasping. δ_1 and δ_2 shown in the picture are the indentation depths of the real thimbles inside the virtual cube. They are measured as distances of the thimbles with respect to the physically constrained proxies (green and violet spheres in the picture).

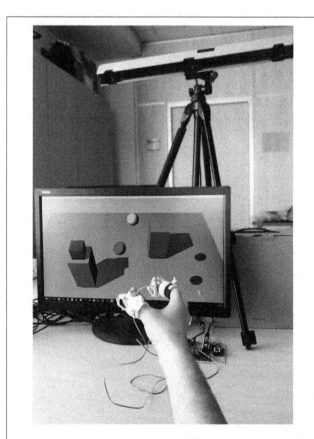

FIGURE 4 | Experimental setup including the virtual pick-and-place task presented on a screen, the wearable haptic devices, and an optical tracker.

force. No visual deformation of the cubes was implemented. Hence, once the virtual proxies were in contact with the cube, modulation of the grasping force could not be judged from visual feedback.

The subject's index and thumb fingers were represented by two spheres in the virtual scenario (proxies). Coupling between the real tracked position of subject's fingers and the position of the virtual proxies was implemented through a virtual spring. Physical simulation and virtual couplings were implemented using the NVIDIA PhysX physical engine. The frame rate was 60 fps, while physical simulation was run at 120 Hz, according to the optical tracker update frequency. With the used physical simulation parameters, the minimum indentation required to lift the cube was 1.5 mm below the contact threshold, while the virtual maximum indentation corresponded to 6 mm. The values were chosen through an exploratory experimental activity, in order to make the task challenging and enhance performance differences among the different types of feedback.

Figure 3 shows the superimposition of a grasped virtual cube to the user's hand performing the grasping. δ_1 and δ_2, shown in the figure, represent the indentation depth of the real fingers position inside the virtual cube and are measured as the distance between the tracked finger position and the virtual proxy.

An optical tracking system (Optitrack, V120 Trio) was used to track the index and thumb fingertip positions (**Figure 4**). Relative precision of the tracking system was assessed by fixing two markers on a rigid bar (4 cm distance, similar to the interfinger distance in the experimental condition). With the bar in a fixed position, the standard deviation of the tracked distance between the two markers was equal to 0.03 *mm*. We then moved the bar along a similar trajectory of the pick-and-place task proposed in the experiment. Under this condition, the standard deviation was equal to 0.11 *mm* with a maximum error equal to ± 0.2 *mm*.

The Haptic Thimble Devices

Two haptic thimble devices have been used for rendering the three different force feedback strategies described in **Section 2**. In order to obtain the most clean haptic feedback, an electromagnetic voice coil was used to actuate a moving plate in contact with the finger. The actuated core of the thimble was the same as the one preliminarily

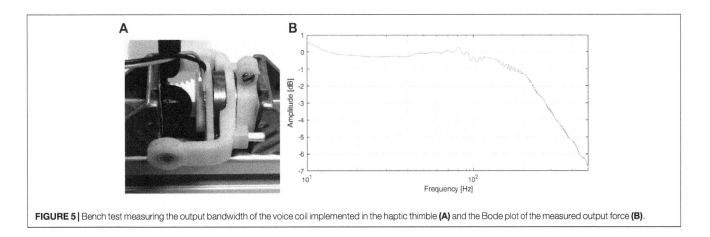

FIGURE 5 | Bench test measuring the output bandwidth of the voice coil implemented in the haptic thimble **(A)** and the Bode plot of the measured output force **(B)**.

presented in Gabardi et al., (2016). In order to enhance transparency of the device, the coil and the contact plate composed the moving part of the actuator, while the heavier ferromagnetic core and magnet were fixed to the external structure of the thimble. Design considered 1 mm clearance between the out-of-contact position and the contact threshold with the finger and 2 mm maximum normal deformation of the fingerpad during operation in the (0–0.5) N range of force. Actuator's geometry was designed in order to minimize variations in the output force characteristic depending on the position of the moving coil; the axial length of the coil was designed 2 mm higher than the internal polar expansion of the magnetic circuit. Two lateral linear guides, mounting low-friction polymer bushings, were designed to guide the linear movement of the coil.

The haptic thimbles were driven through a Texas Instruments DRV8835 compact H-bridge IC, capable of high pulse-width-modulation (PWM) frequencies (150 kHz frequency was used). The control algorithm of the two devices was run on a microcontroller board (PJRC Teensy 3.6) at a 1 kHz loop rate. The control board was connected to the host PC running the virtual environment via USB communication protocol.

The haptic thimbles were tested at the bench in order to measure the output force characteristic and the output bandwidth. The experimental setup for the bench test is shown in **Figure 5A**. The actuator was disassembled from the thimble and fixed in front of a miniaturized force sensor. The force sensor was an OptoForce OMD-10-SE-10N (three axes, range 10 N, resolution 2 mN), an optical force sensor with compact dimensions (10 mm diameter silicone rubber hemisphere). The distance between the actuator and the sensor could be adjusted in order to measure the output force characteristic at different positions of the coil. For measuring the output bandwidth of the device, the coil was actuated using a chirp voltage reference (range 10–1,000 Hz). For this specific test, reference was generated on board the controller, and the loop rate was increased to 2 kHz.

The Experimental Procedure

A total of ten subjects aged between 24–38 (mean = 31; SD = 4.3) have been involved in the study and performed the experiment. An additional subject was excluded by the experiments since in

the familiarization phase the subject was not able to accomplish the proposed task under any feedback condition. The experiment was conducted according to Declaration of Helsinki, and all the subjects provided written consent to participate in the study. The study was approved by the Ethical Board of the Scuola Superiore Sant'Anna of Pisa, Italy (approval number 15–2021). Each subject was seated on a comfortable chair, in front of a desktop and a computer monitor. The haptic thimbles were worn at the index and thumb fingers. Depending on the finger size, soft pads were used between the thimble and the finger dorsum to calibrate the distance between the plate and the fingerpad. The experimental setup is shown in **Figure 4**.

For each subject, the experiment was structured as follows: an initial phase of 5 min was presented to familiarize with the virtual task and to experience the different feedback conditions. Successively, the subject was asked to perform a session of 40 trials (pick-and-place of 40 virtual cubes) for each of the three force feedback strategies plus the only visual condition. The four different sessions were presented to the subject in a randomized order. During the visual condition, the haptic devices were worn by the subject but deactivated. After each session, the subject was asked to answer a questionnaire composed of the following questions:

- Q1: How much did you rely on the tactile feedback?
- Q2: How much did you rely on the visual feedback?
- Q3: How much was the haptic feedback realistic?
- Q4: How much were the haptic feedback and visual feedback congruent?
- Q5: How much did you manage to precisely modulate the contact force?

Concerning the only visual feedback session, only answer to Q5 has been requested. The subjects answered the questions by marking an integer value on a visual scale ranging from −3 to 3. On the same scale, it has been finally asked to the subjects to answer the following questions concerning the comparison of the four kinds of force feedback tried:

- G1: For each kind of feedback, rate your overall preference.
- G2: For each kind of feedback, rate your confidence in accomplishing the task.

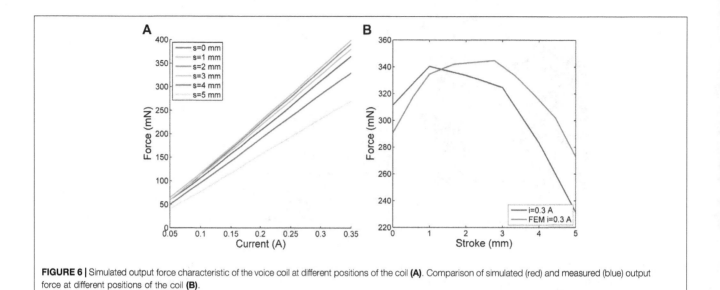

FIGURE 6 | Simulated output force characteristic of the voice coil at different positions of the coil **(A)**. Comparison of simulated (red) and measured (blue) output force at different positions of the coil **(B)**.

- G3: For each kind of feedback, rate the perceived difficulty in accomplishing the task.

Data Analysis

A total of four performance measures were extracted from the data acquired during the experiment. In particular, for each trial of each subject, only the portion of data in which the subject held the object was used for measuring the indentation of the two fingers within the virtual object, proportional to the virtual grasping force. The average, the standard deviation, and the maximum displacement have been computed in order to give a measurement of the stability of the grasp. Moreover, the correct rate was extracted for each subject by dividing the number of successful trial by the number of all trials. A one-way ANOVA test was conducted separately for each of the four performance metrics, after determining the normality of the data distribution using the Lilliefors test. *Post hoc* comparisons were corrected using the Bonferroni method. Regarding the questionnaire, the results were analyzed using the nonparametric Friedman test separately for each question. When a significant effect was found, the multiple comparisons were assessed through the Wilcoxon signed-rank test corrected with the Bonferroni method.

RESULTS

The graph in **Figure 6A** summarizes the simulated results of the current-to-force characteristic for different positions and different values of the current intensity. The slope of each line represents the force coefficient of the actuator at different positions of the moving coil. The results in **Figure 6B** show that within the designed range of motion (3 mm), the actuator output force has a variability below 0.01%. The results of the characterization at the bench of the haptic thimble are shown in **Figure 5**. The measured Bode plot of the output force shows an output bandwidth from 0 to 275 Hz.

We also conducted an estimation of the energy dissipated in the actuators' coils under the D and P conditions. Since the actuators were driven in feed-forward, the estimation had been conducted using the voltage reference signal, thus neglecting BEMF and inductance effects. The dissipated energy ratio between the D and P conditions, computed across all trials and all subjects, was below 0.005. The apparently very low value can be explained by the fact that p power dissipated under the continuous feedback condition is highly affected by duration of the grasping action. On the other hand, D feedback is active only during transients, and even there, each pulse has very limited energy consumption (proportional to the 1 ms duration of each pulse).

Figure 7 reports the correct ratio of the pick-and-place task and three metrics related to the grasping indentation measured during the experiment under the four feedback conditions. The three metrics correspond to the mean value of the indentation depth (higher value corresponds to higher virtual force exerted on the object), stability of the indentation depth (computed as the standard deviation of the indentation depth during each repetition), and peak value of the indentation depth, measured as the maximum value for each repetition. A one-way ANOVA with *post hoc* analysis was conducted over the correct ratio and the aforementioned metrics. The results related to the correct ratio show a significant main effect of the provided feedback (F (3) = 17.7, $p < 0.001$). Bonferroni post hoc tests showed that the participant's correct rate was significantly lower under the V condition (mean = 0.69; SD = 0.17) than that under all the other feedback conditions (P mean = 0.76; SD = 0.15; $p < 0.001$), (D mean = 0.58; SD = 0.23; $p < 0.05$), and (PD mean = 0.70; SD = 0.20; $p < 0.001$). The P feedback correct ratio was significantly higher than the D feedback ($p < 0.01$). The correct ratio between the PD and D feedback was not significantly different. A similar result was obtained for the grasping indentation variability metric, with all the feedback conditions reporting a significantly lower variability than the V condition (V mean = 0.96, SD = 0.13, P mean = 0.78, SD = 0.08, $p < 0.01$; D mean =

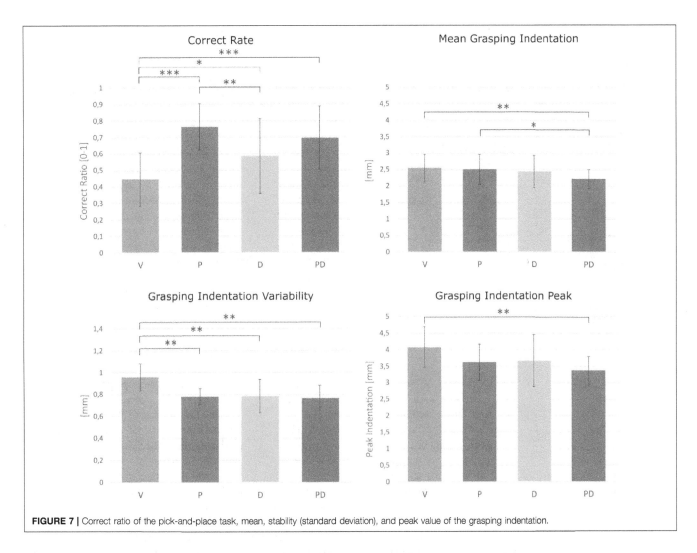

FIGURE 7 | Correct ratio of the pick-and-place task, mean, stability (standard deviation), and peak value of the grasping indentation.

0.79, SD = 0.16, $p < 0.01$; PD mean = 0.77, SD = 0.12, and $p < 0.01$). Differences were not significant between different haptic feedback conditions. Regarding the grasping indentation mean, differences were found significant only between the V and PD condition (V mean = 2.55, SD = 0.44; PD mean = 2.22, SD = 0.29, $p < 0.01$) and between the PD and P condition (P mean = 2.51, SD = 0.48, $p < 0.05$). The peak grasping indentation metric showed a significant difference only between the V and PD condition (V mean = 4.08, SD = 0.65; PD mean = 3.38, SD = 0.48, $p < 0.01$).

Figure 8 (first row) shows the averaged answers (median with 25th and 75th percentiles) of the questions related to the haptic feedback. In **Figure 8** (second row) are reported the answers to the questions regarding the overall experience. As can be noted in **Figure 8**, questions ranging from Q1 to Q4 did not include the V condition. The Friedman test provided evidence of a difference ($\chi^2 (2, 18) = 8.97$, p = 0.011) between the answers to the question Q3, "the haptic feedback was realistic." *Post hoc* analysis with Wilcoxon signed-rank tests was conducted with a Bonferroni correction applied, resulting in a significance level set at p < 0.017. There was a significant difference between the P condition [median = 7.0 (7.0 7.0)] and the D condition [median = 5 (4.0 6.0)]. A significant difference was found also

in answers to question Q5, "did you manage to precisely modulate the contact force?" ($\chi^2 (3, 27) = 21.79$, p < 0.001). The *post hoc* test, corrected with Bonferroni and resulting in a significant level set at $p < 0.008 3$, evidenced the fact that scores given to the V feedback [median = 2 (2.0 4.0)] were significantly lower than those given to the other feedback conditions for both the comparison between the P and PD feedback ($p < 0.01$) and between P and D feedback ($p < 0.01$). The similar results were found for the G1 and G2 showing a significant main effect (p < 0.001) with a lower score given to the V condition with respect to all the other feedback conditions. Regarding the perceived difficulty of the task, question G3, a significant main effect was found as well ($\chi^2 (3, 27) = 22.62$, p < 0.001). The *post hoc* comparisons, corrected with the Bonferroni method, evidenced a significant difference only between the V condition and the P condition ($p < 0.01$).

DISCUSSION

The first experimental activity aimed at characterizing the haptic actuators used in the subject study, ensuring that the

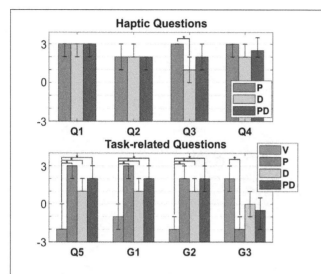

FIGURE 8 | Answers to the questionnaire. First row reports the answer to the questions related to the three implemented haptic feedback. Second row reports the answers to the questions related to the perceived performance over the task under the four different experimental conditions.

experimented feedback could be properly rendered to the subjects. An electromagnetic voice coil linear actuator was chosen as the most suitable actuator typology for a comparison experiment of different feedback signals; although heavier than alternative actuator designs, it presents, in general, a transparent response in a wide range of frequencies, including static output force, due to the absence of reduction or transformation mechanisms. The measured frequency response showed a band-pass frequency from 0 to 275 Hz, covering the range of frequencies required for cutaneous haptic feedback. Regarding the current-to-force characteristic, we designed the actuator geometry in order to keep such relationship constant in the used workspace. This was obtained by designing the length of the coil longer than the length polar expansion of the magnetic core. Measured output force at different positions of the moving plate well matched the simulated behavior of the actuator. Considering 3 mm stroke, variability of the measured output force is below 0.1%.

Regarding results of the virtual pick-and -place task, the correct rate represents the overall effectiveness of the feedback in accomplishing the proposed task. All the haptic feedback signals performed significantly better than the visual feedback alone, showing that both the P and the proposed D feedback were coherent and informative of the performed task. The grasping indentation variability reported coherent results, showing that during each manipulation task finger position and indentation with the virtual object was more stable for all the haptic feedback condition than the visual condition. Again for the correct ratio, the P feedback reported the higher performance, with a significant difference also than D feedback. It showed that the continuous feedback performed better than the proposed discrete one in terms of overall results. The possible reasons are in the continuous modulation of the feedback, achieving a higher rendering resolution of the grasping

force modulation with respect to the discrete transients of the D feedback. It also allows to discriminate the sign of variation of the grasping force, whereas discrete transients of the D feedback do not carry information about increasing or decreasing variation of the grasping force. Furthermore, the P feedback resembles the natural perception of the grasping force modulation, thus possibly becoming immediate to be effectively used by users, without adaptation or training.

On the other hand, the D feedback resulted significantly better than the V condition, suggesting that in applications where high wearability and lightweight of the haptic devices are needed, it might be profitably used. As explained in **Section 1**, by excluding the constant and slow force components by the rendering, power required by actuators is significantly lower. Furthermore, the actuator design and typology can be conceived differently, if only high frequencies have to be rendered, i.e., flexure hinges or membranes can be used to hold the moving part of voice coil actuators, in place of guides or joints, and different actuator typologies (i.e., piezo actuators) can be used, since the required stroke is considerably lower.

It is interesting to note that the superposition of the two feedback strategies under the condition PD obtained an average score for the correct ratio similar to the separated P and D feedback (with no significant differences). It suggests that the superposition of the two feedback strategies does not negatively interfere with effectiveness in the manipulation task; further investigation to improve quality of the D feedback might involve the superposition of a continuous feedback component, with reduced intensity, to the D feedback. The trade-off between effectiveness of the feedback and the required total energy of the signal should be explored. The results of the questionnaire answers of the haptic questions group showed a better performance of the P feedback with respect to the D feedback (significant for Q3). Findings are coherent with the fact that the continuous feedback is the most similar with the natural haptic perception in manipulation tasks. The results of the answers to the task-related questions group showed a better performance in terms of preferences, perceived control, and perceived difficulty of the task for all the proposed feedback with respect to the visual condition. With similar considerations to the aforementioned results, we can conclude that the proportional feedback (P) provided the overall best performance in terms of preferences and of perceived and measured effectiveness. Still, the proposed discrete feedback (D) performed significantly better than the visual condition, suggesting its possible use in applications where other advantages, in terms of reduced actuators dimensions and typology, are more relevant.

The experiment involved a discrete feedback implemented in its simplest form (a train of pulses) to obtain a first robust experimental comparison with conventional continuous feedback in a grasping task. Yet, more advanced versions can be considered and experimented. In particular, we are interested in experimenting a version of the feedback capable of conveying also the sign of the force variation. This can be envisaged in different ways, i.e., by modulating amplitude or frequency content of each discrete cue, in order to discriminate the sign of the indentation increment.

Finally, the estimation of the energy consumption ratio between the D and P feedback conditions is meaningful of the potential of the discrete feedback in terms of the smaller device design. We clarify that the noticeably high difference in energy consumption does not translate in a proportional reduction of the actuator size, and it would be difficult to generalize a scaling factor without a finalized device design. Still, heat dissipation is a critical element concurring in determining the final size of an electromagnetic actuator.

CONCLUSION

In this article, we investigated a strategy for rendering haptic feedback, informative of grasping force modulation, by means of discrete, high-frequency cues. Perception of the increasing grasping force was provided by force pulses triggered at discrete indentation thresholds. The envisaged advantage of the proposed discrete feedback was to considerably reduce the continuous output force demanded to the actuator, which in turn considerably reduces the overall dimensions of the actuator. This becomes critical in fingertip haptic devices, in which mass and size have to be limited to improve wearability and preserve dexterity, in particular for certain training and rehabilitation scenarios (i.e., Bortone et al. (2020)), in which users are children with reduced hand dimensions if compared to adult users). We experimentally evaluated effectiveness of the discrete feedback by measuring objective performance metrics in a virtual pick-and-place task of fragile objects. We compared the discrete feedback (D) with the conventional continuous proportional feedback (P), with a superposition of the two feedback strategies (PD) and with the visual only condition. The experimental setup and the implemented wearable haptic devices based on voice coil actuators were optimized for improving the quality of the feedback presented to participants.

The obtained results showed an overall better performance of the conventional continuous feedback, both in terms of users' perception and objective measurements. The correct ratio of the given pick-and-place task was significantly better for the P feedback, and answers to the feedback-related questions evidenced the P feedback was perceived significantly more natural than the D feedback. While the P feedback resembles a natural perception of the grasping force modulation, the D feedback tries to carry similar information through a different modulated signal. To this regard, an aspect to consider in future investigations is how learning might improve effectiveness of the D feedback in the objective metrics of the manipulation tasks. On the other hand, all the evaluated feedback performed significantly better than the visual condition only in terms of correct ratio, stability of the grasping pose, perceived difficulty of the task, and perceived precision in grasping modulation. This envisaged the use of the proposed D feedback in applications involving a convenient trade-off between feedback performance and physical requirements of the haptic devices, in terms of limited size and mass. The advantages of the D feedback extend also to different actuator designs that can be considered, requiring rendering of high-frequency signals only with limited stroke of the moving parts and no static components. Future investigations can be focused also on more advanced variations of the proposed discrete feedback; different discrete cues than pulses can be studied to convey additional information, such as the direction of the grasping force modulation.

AUTHOR CONTRIBUTIONS

DL and MG contributed to the development of both the haptic thimble devices and the experimental hardware/software setup. All the authors equally contributed to the design of the experiments and the data collection. Data had been analyzed by MB. The work has been revised by AF and funded by AF and DL.

REFERENCES

Basdogan, C., and Srinivasan, M. A. (2002). "Haptic Rendering in Virtual Environments," in *Handbook of virtual environments* 1.

Bensmaïa, S. J., and Hollins, M. (2000). Complex Tactile Waveform Discrimination. *The J. Acoust. Soc. Am.* 108, 1236–1245.

Bergamasco, M., Avizzano, C. A., Frisoli, A., Ruffaldi, E., and Marcheschi, S. (2006). Design and Validation of a Complete Haptic System for Manipulative Tasks. *Adv. Robotics* 20, 367–389. doi:10.1163/156855306776014367

Bortone, I., Leonardis, D., Solazzi, M., Procopio, C., Crecchi, A., Bonfiglio, L., et al. (2017). "Integration of Serious Games and Wearable Haptic Interfaces for Neuro Rehabilitation of Children with Movement Disorders: A Feasibility Study," in 2017 International Conference on Rehabilitation Robotics (ICORR), London, United Kingdom, July 17–20, 2017 (IEEE), 1094–1099. doi:10.1109/ICORR.2017.8009395

Bortone, I., Barsotti, M., Leonardis, D., Crecchi, A., Tozzini, A., Bonfiglio, L., et al. (2020). Immersive Virtual Environments and Wearable Haptic Devices in Rehabilitation of Children with Neuromotor Impairments: a Single-Blind Randomized Controlled Crossover Pilot Study. *J. Neuroeng Rehabil.* 17 (1), 1–14. doi:10.1186/s12984-020-00771-6

Caldwell, D. G., Tsagarakis, N., and Wardle, A. (1997). "Mechano Thermo and Proprioceptor Feedback for Integrated Haptic Feedback," in International Conference on Robotics and Automation, Albuquerque, ID, April 25–27, 1997, 2491–2496. Robotics and Automation.3

Cappello, L., Alghilan, W., Gabardi, M., Leonardis, D., Barsotti, M., Frisoli, A., et al. (2020). Continuous Supplementary Tactile Feedback Can Be Applied (And Then Removed) to Enhance Precision Manipulation. *J. Neuroeng Rehabil.* 17 (1), 1–13. doi:10.1186/s12984-020-00736-9

Chinello, F., Malvezzi, M., Pacchierotti, C., and Prattichizzo, D. (2015). "Design and Development of a 3rrs Wearable Fingertip Cutaneous Device," in International Conference on Advanced Intelligent Mechatronics (AIM), Busan, Korea, July 7–11, 2015, 293–298. doi:10.1109/aim.2015.7222547

Cipriani, C., Segil, J. L., Clemente, F., ff. Weir, R. F., and Edin, B. (2014). Humans Can Integrate Feedback of Discrete Events in Their Sensorimotor Control of a Robotic Hand. *Exp. Brain Res.* 232, 3421–3429. doi:10.1007/s00221-014-4024-8

Clemente, F., D'Alonzo, M., Controzzi, M., Edin, B. B., and Cipriani, C. (2016). Non-invasive, Temporally Discrete Feedback of Object Contact and Release Improves Grasp Control of Closed-Loop Myoelectric Transradial Prostheses. *IEEE Trans. Neural Syst. Rehabil. Eng.* 24, 1314–1322. doi:10.1109/tnsre.2015.2500586

Cole, K. J., and Abbs, J. H. (1988). Grip Force Adjustments Evoked by Load Force Perturbations of a Grasped Object. *J. Neurophysiol.* 60, 1513–1522. doi:10.1152/jn.1988.60.4.1513

Fani, S., Ciotti, S., Battaglia, E., Moscatelli, A., and Bianchi, M. (2017). W-fyd: A Wearable Fabric-Based Display for Haptic Multi-Cue Delivery and Tactile Augmented Reality. *IEEE Trans. Haptics* 11, 304–316. doi:10.1109/TOH.2017.2708717

Gabardi, M., Solazzi, M., Leonardis, D., and Frisoli, A. (2016). "A New Wearable Fingertip Haptic Interface for the Rendering of Virtual Shapes and Surface Features," in Haptics Symposium 2016, Philadelphia, PA, April 8–11, 2016 (IEEE), 140–146. doi:10.1109/haptics.2016.7463168

Gabardi, M., Chiaradia, D., Leonardis, D., Solazzi, M., and Frisoli, A. (2018). "A High Performance thermal Control for Simulation of Different Materials in a

Fingertip Haptic Device," in Eurohaptics 2018, Pisa, Italy, June 13–16, 2018 (Springer), 313–325. doi:10.1007/978-3-319-93399-3_28

Gallo, S., Rognini, G., Santos-Carreras, L., Vouga, T., Blanke, O., and Bleuler, H. (2015). Encoded and Crossmodal thermal Stimulation through a Fingertip-Sized Haptic Display. *Front. Robot. AI* 2, 25. doi:10.3389/frobt.2015.00025

Gutiérrez, Á., Farella, N., Gil-Agudo, Á., and de los Reyes Guzmán, A. (2021). Virtual Reality Environment with Haptic Feedback Thimble for post Spinal Cord Injury Upper-Limb Rehabilitation. *Appl. Sci.* 11, 2476. doi:10.3390/app11062476

Kildal, J. (2010). "3d-press: Haptic Illusion of Compliance when Pressing on a Rigid Surface," in International Conference on Multimodal Interfaces and the Workshop on Machine Learning for Multimodal Interaction, Beijing, China, November 8–10, 2010 (New York, NY: ACM Publications), 21.

Klamt, T., Schwarz, M., Lenz, C., Baccelliere, L., Buongiorno, D., Cichon, T., et al. (2020). Remote mobile Manipulation with the Centauro Robot: Full-body Telepresence and Autonomous Operator Assistance. *J. Field Robotics* 37, 889–919. doi:10.1002/rob.21895

Kuchenbecker, K. J., Fiene, J., and Niemeyer, G. (2006). Improving Contact Realism through Event-Based Haptic Feedback. *IEEE Trans. Vis. Comput. Graph* 12, 219–230. doi:10.1109/TVCG.2006.32

Kuchenbecker, K. J., Gewirtz, J., McMahan, W., Standish, D., Martin, P., Bohren, J., et al. (2010). "Verrotouch: High-Frequency Acceleration Feedback for Telerobotic Surgery," in IEEE Transactions on Visualization and Computer Graphics (Springer), 189–196. doi:10.1007/978-3-642-14064-8_28

Kurihara, Y., Hachisu, T., Sato, M., Fukushima, S., and Kajimoto, H. (2013). "Periodic Tactile Feedback for Accelerator Pedal Control," in Eurohaptics 2010, Amsterdam, Netherlands, July 8–10, 2010 (IEEE), 187–192. doi:10.1109/whc. 2013.6548406

Leonardis, D., Solazzi, M., Bortone, I., and Frisoli, A. (2015). "A Wearable Fingertip Haptic Device with 3 Dof Asymmetric 3-rsr Kinematics," in IEEE World Haptics Conference, Chicago, IL, June 22–26, 2015 (IEEE), 388–393. doi:10.1109/whc.2015.7177743

Leonardis, D., Solazzi, M., Bortone, I., and Frisoli, A. (2017). A 3-rsr Haptic Wearable Device for Rendering Fingertip Contact Forces. *IEEE Trans. Haptics* 10, 305–316. doi:10.1109/toh.2016.2640291

Leonardis, D., Gabardi, M., Solazzi, M., and Frisoli, A. (2020). "A Parallel Elastic Haptic Thimble for Wide Bandwidth Cutaneous Feedback," in Eurohaptics 2020, Leiden, Netherlands, September 6–9, 2020 (Springer), 389–397. doi:10.1007/978-3-030-58147-3_43

Leonardis, D., Tiseni, L., Chiaradia, D., and Frisoli, A. (2021). A Twisted String, Flexure Hinges Approach for Design of a Wearable Haptic Thimble. *Actuators* 10, 211. doi:10.3390/act10090211

Maisto, M., Pacchierotti, C., Chinello, F., Salvietti, G., De Luca, A., and Prattichizzo, D. (2017). Evaluation of Wearable Haptic Systems for the Fingers in Augmented Reality Applications. *IEEE Trans. Haptics* 10, 511–522. doi:10.1109/toh.2017.2691328

Niemeyer, G., and Mitra, P. (2005). "3 Dynamic Proxies and Haptic Constraints," in *Multi-point Interaction with Real and Virtual Objects* (Springer), 41–53.

Pacchierotti, C., Prattichizzo, D., and Kuchenbecker, K. J. (2016). Cutaneous Feedback of Fingertip Deformation and Vibration for Palpation in Robotic Surgery. *IEEE Trans. Biomed. Eng.* 63, 278–287. doi:10.1109/TBME.2015.2455932

Pacchierotti, C., Prattichizzo, D., and Kuchenbecker, K. J. (2016). Cutaneous Feedback of Fingertip Deformation and Vibration for Palpation in Robotic Surgery. *IEEE Trans. Biomed. Eng.* 63, 278–287. doi:10.1109/tbme.2015.2455932

Pacchierotti, C., Sinclair, S., Solazzi, M., Frisoli, A., Hayward, V., and Prattichizzo, D. (2017). Wearable Haptic Systems for the Fingertip and the Hand: Taxonomy, Review, and Perspectives. *IEEE Trans. Haptics* 10, 580–600. doi:10.1109/toh.2017.2689006

Prattichizzo, D., Pacchierotti, C., and Rosati, G. (2012). Cutaneous Force Feedback as a Sensory Subtraction Technique in Haptics. *IEEE Trans. Haptics* 5, 289–300. doi:10.1109/toh.2012.15

Robles-De-La-Torre, G., and Hayward, V. (2001). Force Can Overcome Object Geometry in the Perception of Shape through Active Touch. *Nature* 412, 445–448. doi:10.1038/35086588

Schorr, S. B., Quek, Z. F., Romano, R. Y., Nisky, I., Provancher, W. R., and Okamura, A. M. (2013). "Sensory Substitution via Cutaneous Skin Stretch Feedback," in Robotics and Automation (ICRA), 2013 IEEE International Conference on (IEEE), 2341–2346. doi:10.1109/icra.2013.6630894

Solazzi, M., Frisoli, A., and Bergamasco, M. (2010). "Design of a Novel finger Haptic Interface for Contact and Orientation Display," in IEEE Haptics Symposium, Waltham, MA, March 25–26, 2010 (IEEE), 129–132. doi:10.1109/haptic.2010.5444667

Stepp, C. E., and Matsuoka, Y. (2011). Vibrotactile Sensory Substitution for Object Manipulation: Amplitude versus Pulse Train Frequency Modulation. *IEEE Trans. Neural Syst. Rehabil. Eng.* 20, 31–37. doi:10.1109/TNSRE.2011.2170856

Strohmeier, P., Boring, S., and Hornbæk, K. (2018). "From Pulse Trains to" Coloring with Vibrations" Motion Mappings for Mid-air Haptic Textures," in CHI Conference on Human Factors in Computing Systems, Montreal, Canada, April 21–26, 2018, 1–13.

Visell, Y., Duraikkannan, K. A., and Hayward, V. (2014). "A Device and Method for Multimodal Haptic Rendering of Volumetric Stiffness," in Eurohaptics 2014, Versailles, France, June 24–27, 2014 (Springer), 478–486. doi:10.1007/978-3-662-44193-0_60

Wang, D., Ohnishi, K., and Xu, W. (2019). Multimodal Haptic Display for Virtual Reality: A Survey. *IEEE Trans. Ind. Electron.* 67, 610–623. doi:10.1109/TIE.2019.2920602

Westling, G., and Johansson, R. S. (1987). Responses in Glabrous Skin Mechanoreceptors during Precision Grip in Humans. *Exp. Brain Res.* 66, 128–140. doi:10.1007/BF00236209

Wiertlewski, M., Lozada, J., and Hayward, V. (2011). The Spatial Spectrum of Tangential Skin Displacement Can Encode Tactual Texture. *IEEE Trans. Robot.* 27, 461–472. doi:10.1109/tro.2011.2132830

Yau, J. M., Olenczak, J. B., Dammann, J. F., and Bensmaia, S. J. (2009). Temporal Frequency Channels Are Linked across Audition and Touch. *Curr. Biol.* 19, 561–566. doi:10.1016/j.cub.2009.02.013

4

UNREALHAPTICS: Plugins for Advanced VR Interactions in Modern Game Engines

Janis Rosskamp*, Hermann Meißenhelter*, Rene Weller*, Marc O. Rüdel,
Johannes Ganser and Gabriel Zachmann*

Computer Graphics and Virtual Reality, Faculty 03: Mathematics/Computer Science, University of Bremen, Bremen, Germany

*Correspondence:
Janis Rosskamp
j.rosskamp@cs.uni-bremen.de
Hermann Meißenhelter
hmeiss51@cs.uni-bremen.de
Rene Weller
weller@cs.uni-bremen.de
Gabriel Zachmann
zach@cs.uni-bremen.de

We present UNREALHAPTICS, a plugin-architecture that enables advanced virtual reality (VR) interactions, such as haptics or grasping in modern game engines. The core is a combination of a state-of-the-art collision detection library with support for very fast and stable force and torque computations and a general device plugin for communication with different input/output hardware devices, such as haptic devices or Cybergloves. Our modular and lightweight architecture makes it easy for other researchers to adapt our plugins to their requirements. We prove the versatility of our plugin architecture by providing two use cases implemented in the Unreal Engine 4 (UE4). In the first use case, we have tested our plugin with a haptic device in different test scenes. For the second use case, we show a virtual hand grasping an object with precise collision detection and handling multiple contacts. We have evaluated the performance in our use cases. The results show that our plugin easily meets the requirements of stable force rendering at 1 kHz for haptic rendering even in highly non-convex scenes, and it can handle the complex contact scenarios of virtual grasping.

Keywords: virtual reality, unreal engine, haptic feedback, grasping, plugin architecture, contact point, collision detection

1. INTRODUCTION

With the rise of affordable consumer devices, such as the Oculus Rift or the HTC Vive, there has been a large increase in interest and development in the area of virtual reality (VR). The new display and tracking technologies of these devices enable high fidelity graphics rendering and natural interaction with virtual environments. Modern game engines like Unreal or Unity have simplified the development of VR applications dramatically. They almost hide the technological background from the content creation process so that today, everyone can click their way to their own VR application in a few minutes. However, consumer VR devices primarily focus on outputting information to the two main human senses: seeing and hearing. Also, game engines are mainly limited to visual and audio output. Inputs processed in game engines are typically: key presses, mouse clicks, or mouse movement, controller button presses, and joystick movement. The sense of touch and a variety of untypical input devices are widely neglected.

For instance, the lack of haptic feedback can disturb the immersion in virtual environments significantly. Moreover, the concentration on visual feedback excludes a large number of people from the content created with the game engines: those who cannot see this content, i.e., blind and visually impaired people. Another important interaction technique in VR is to use our most versatile interaction tool directly, the human hand, to perform, e.g., natural grasping interactions. It can help to train (Gomes de Sá and Zachmann, 1999) and inspect (Moehring and Froehlich, 2011) objects in virtual environments more accurately and naturally. Moreover, a common way to train a robot to perform certain tasks is to apply human example grasps inside a virtual environment. Usually, modern game engines lack such fine detailed human interactions, like grasping (Lin et al., 2016).

The main reasons why such advanced input methods are widely neglected in the context of games are that haptic devices and sophisticated input devices for natural interaction methods like Cybergloves are still comparatively bulky, expensive, and do not support plug and play.

Moreover, they differ in several properties from typical input devices for games, e.g., update-rate, latency, accuracy, and resolution. The update-rate is an important property for fine interaction. It describes how many measurements are made per second and is coupled with the application and physics. Although many game engines have a built-in physics engine, they are most usually limited to simple convex shapes. They hardly deliver the complex contact information necessary to handle multiple simultaneous contacts in a stable way that typically appears during grasping. Moreover, the built-in physics engines are usually relatively slow: for the visual rendering loop it is sufficient to provide 60–120 frames per second (FPS) to guarantee smooth visual feedback. Our sense of touch is much more sensitive with respect to the temporal resolution. Here, a frequency of preferably 1,000 Hz is required to provide acceptable force feedback. It is required to decouple the physically-based simulation from the visual rendering path to reach those update rates.

In this paper, we present UNREALHAPTICS a plugin system to enable applications with specialized input devices and the demand for fast and accurate force calculations, e.g., high-fidelity haptic rendering, in a modern game engine. Following the idea of decoupling the simulation part from the core game engine, UNREALHAPTICS consists of three individual plugins:

- A plugin that we call DEVIO: It is used to implement the communication with the VR hardware devices.
- The computational bottleneck during the physically-based simulation is the collision detection. Our plugin called COLLETTE builds a bridge to an external collision detection library that is fast enough for high update rates.
- Finally, FORCECOMP computes the appropriate forces and torques from the collision information.

This modular structure of UNREALHAPTICS allows other researchers to easily replace individual parts, e.g., the force computation or the collision detection, to fit their individual needs. We have integrated UNREALHAPTICS into the Unreal Engine 4 (UE4), but the basic concept is also valid for other game engines. We use a fast, lightweight, and highly maintainable and adjustable event system to handle the communication in UNREALHAPTICS.

In this paper, we will discuss two example applications, which are using UNREALHAPTICS. While the first use case focuses on haptic rendering, our second use case shows how individual components of UNREALHAPTICS can be exchanged

for other non-haptic applications like grasping in VR. For the collision detection we use the state-of-the-art collision detection library CollDet (Zachmann, 2001) that supports complexity-independent volumetric collision detection at haptic rates. Our force calculation relies on a penalty-based approach with both 3- and 6-degree-of-freedom (DOF) force and torque computations. Our results show that UNREALHAPTICS is able to compute stable forces and torques for different 3- and 6-DOF devices in Unreal at haptic rates.

2. RELATED WORK

In section 4, we present two applications using our plugins. The first is using haptic feedback, and the second demonstrates usage for grasping. We will discuss haptic and then grasping related work here.

Game engines enable the rapid development with high-end graphics and easy extension to VR to a broad pool of developers. Hence, they are usually the first choice when designing demanding 3D virtual environments. Obviously, this is also true for haptic applications. Consequently, there exist many (research) projects that already integrated haptics into such game engines, e.g., Morris et al. (2004), Andrews et al. (2006), and de Pedro et al. (2016) to name but a few. However, they usually have spent much time developing single-use approaches that are hardly generalizable and thus, not applicable to other programs.

Only a very few approaches provide comfortable interfaces for the integration of haptics into modern game engines. Kollasch (2017) and User ZeonmkII (2016) provide plugins that serve as interfaces to the *3D Systems Touch* (formerly *SensAble PHANToM Omni*)[1] *via* the *OpenHaptics* library (3D Systems, 2018). OpenHaptics is a proprietary library that is specific to 3D Systems' devices, which means that other devices cannot be used with these plugins. Another example is a plugin for the PHANToM device presented in The Glasgow School of Art (2014), also based on the OpenHaptics library. While these plugins provide communication with some haptic devices, they do not provide a framework for a wide variety of input devices. Additionally, they are not integrated into the game engine and are missing vital elements for haptics like fast collision detection. Physics engines are often deeply integrated into game engines, and the rendering frame rate is coupled with the physics calculation. There seems to be no research on replacing the in-build physics engine in game engines like Unreal and Unity. We have only found some experimental showcases but no real project or plugin. In the case of the Unreal Engine, Steve Streeting, an independent game developer, described in his blog[2], how he has integrated bullet physics on top of PhysX. This might use unnecessary performance since PhysX is still active, and unfortunately, bullet physics does not support haptics.

Outside the context of game engines, there are a number of libraries that provide force calculations for haptic devices.

---

[1]Phantom, O. Sensable Technologies, Inc. Available online at: http://www.sensable.com (accessed November 11, 2020).
[2]Steeve Streeting. Available online at: https://www.stevestreeting.com/2020/07/26/using-bullet-for-physics-in-ue4 (accessed November 11, 2020).

A general overview is given in Kadleček and Kmoch (2011). One example is the CHAI3D library (CHAI3D, 2016b). It is an open-source library written in C++ that supports a variety of devices by different vendors. It offers a common interface for all devices that can be extended to implement custom device support. For its haptic rendering, CHAI3D accelerates the collision detection with mesh objects using an axis-aligned bounding box (AABB) hierarchy. The force rendering is based on a finger-proxy algorithm. The device position is proxied by a second virtual position that tries to track the device position. When the device position enters a mesh, the proxy will stay on the surface of the mesh. The proxy tries to minimize the distance to the device position locally by sliding along the surface. Finally, the forces are computed by exerting a spring force between the two points (CHAI3D, 2016a). Due to the simplicity of the method it only returns 3-DOF force feedback, even though the library generally allows for also passing torques and grip forces to devices. Nevertheless, we are using CHAI3D in our use case, but only for the communication with haptic devices. A comparable, slightly newer library is the H3DAPI library (H3DAPI, 2019). Same as CHAI3D, it is extensible in both the device and algorithm domain. However, by default, H3DAPI supports fewer devices and likewise does not provide 6-DOF force feedback. A general haptic toolkit with a focus on web development was presented by Ruffaldi et al. (2006). It is based on the eXtreme Virtual Reality (XVR) engine, utilizing the CHAI3D library to allow rapid application development independent from the specific haptic interface.

All approaches mentioned above are limited to 3-DOF haptic rendering and do not support 6-DOF rendering. Sagardia et al. (2014) present an extension to the *Bullet* physics engine for faster collision detection and force computation. Their algorithm is based on the Voxmap-Pointshell algorithm (McNeely et al., 1999). Objects are encoded both in a voxmap that stores distances to the closest points of the object as well as point-shells on the object surface that are clustered to generate optimally wrapped sphere trees. The penetration depth from the voxmap is then used to calculate the forces and torques. In contrast to Bullet's build-in algorithms, this approach offers full 6-DOF haptic rendering for complex scenes. However, the Voxmap-Pointshell algorithm is very memory-intensive and susceptible to noise (Weller et al., 2010).

Our second application is grasping. There are two approaches for grasping, one is based on gesture and the other is physics-based. Gesture grasps can achieve real-time computations but lack natural interaction because they are limited to two states: the grasp and release of the object. The fingers might also penetrate the object, or there is even no contact with the object while grasping it. The physics-based approaches have a trade-off between accuracy and interactivity since they are very computationally intensive. Such a physics-based approach was presented in Verschoor et al. (2018), with a library called CLAP, that was integrated into the Unreal Engine. The hand is modeled as a soft body, whereas the object is rigid. The overall simulation reached real-time, but for natural haptic feedback, this is not sufficient. A hybrid approach was presented in Liu et al. (2019), where authors introduced a caging-based system

to find a better balance between realism and performance. The hand was modeled with cylinders, and a grasp is triggered when the center of the collision contact points lies within the grasped object. Moreover, they showed a glove that has a Vive Tracker, a network of IMUs, and some vibration motors. They have integrated this system in UE4 and achieved stable grasps in real-time. The performance was evaluated only qualitatively by grasping different kinds of objects.

In the following, we will give a short overview of the structure of this paper. We will first show the UNREALHAPTICS plugin architecture by discussing the three main plugins and their communication interface in section 3. After that, we show an UE4 specific implementation. We will then present two example applications where the plugin is used. The first application (section 4.1) is haptic rendering, demonstrating a performance with haptic rates. The second use case (section 4.2) shows a grasping application with detailed collisions.

3. UNREALHAPTICS

Modern game engines support the most common devices, such as joysticks or head-mounted displays (HMDs), making them easy to set up. More specialized input, like haptic devices or elaborate hand tracking, has to be set up manually. Additionally, these applications are often in need of custom physics and high-performance collision detection. To fill that gap and provide an easy-to-use, adjustable, and generalizable framework, we have developed UNREALHAPTICS. Our software can be used in games, research, or business-related contexts, either whole or in parts. We developed our system in the Unreal Engine because of the following reasons:

- It is one of the most popular game engines with a large community, regular updates, and good documentation.
- It is free to use in most cases, especially in a research context where it is already heavily used (Mól et al., 2008; Reinschluessel et al., 2017).
- It is fully open-source, thus can be examined and adapted.
- It offers programmers access on the source code level while game designers can use a comfortable visual editor in combination with a visual scripting system called *Blueprints*. Thus, it combines the advantages of open class libraries and extensible IDEs.
- It is extendable *via* plugins.
- It is built on C++, which makes it easy to integrate external C++-libraries. This is convenient because C++ is still the first choice for high-performance libraries, e.g., haptic rendering.

Figure 1 presents the previous state before our plugins: on the one side, there are different haptic devices available with their libraries. On the other side, there is the game engine in which we want to integrate the devices. To interact with the virtual environment using input, such as haptic devices, we need (i) communication with the device, (ii) fast collision detection, and (iii) stable force computation. We solve these three major challenges by using a modular design to fulfill our goal of a flexible and adjustable system. Each module handles one of these

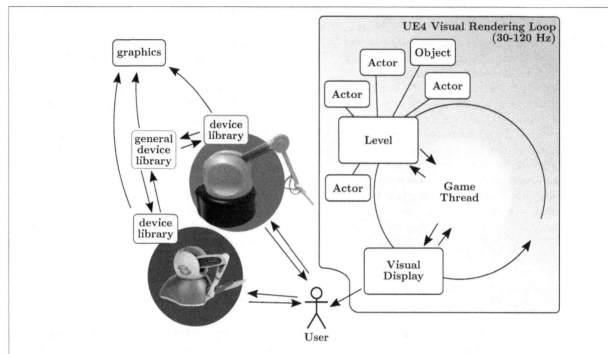

FIGURE 1 | A typical haptic integration without UNREALHAPTICS. **(Left)** Different haptic devices available with their libraries. **(Right)** Scheme of UE4, which we want to integrate the devices with.

tasks. Of course, this structure is not only valid for haptics but interaction with other input as well. Our plugins are responsible for the following tasks:

- A plugin called DEVIO that handles the communication with the input device by adding a general layer to initialize devices and to receive and send data to the device during runtime.
- A plugin called COLLETTE that communicates with an (external) collision detection library. Initially, it passes geometric objects from Unreal to the collision library (to enable it to potentially compute acceleration data structures etc.). During runtime, it updates the transformation matrices of the objects and collects collision information.
- FORCECOMP, a force rendering plugin that receives collision information and computes forces and torques. The force calculation is closely related to the collision detection method because it depends on the provided collision information. However, we decided to separate the force and torque computation from the actual collision detection into separate plugins because this allows an easy replacement, e.g., if the simulation is switched from penalty-based to impulse-based. While its main task is to compute forces, it can also be used to process collision data in general, which will be shown in section 4.2.3.

The list of plugins already suggest that communication plays an important role in the design of our plugin system. Hence, we will start with a short description on this topic before we detail the implementations of the individual plugins.

3.1. Unreal Engine Recap

Unreal Engine 4 is a game engine that comprises the engine itself as well as a 3D editor to create applications using the engine. We will start with a short recap of UE4's basic concepts.

Unreal Engine 4 follows the component-based entity system design. Every object in the scene (3D objects, lights, cameras, etc.) is at its core a data-, logic-less entity (in the case of UE4 called *actors*). The different behavior between the objects stems from *components* that can be attached to these actors. For example, a `StaticMeshActor` (which represents a 3D object) has a mesh component attached, while a light source will have different components attached. These components contain the data used by UE4's internal systems to implement the behavior of the composed objects (e.g., the rendering system will use the mesh components, the physics system will use the physics components etc.).

Unreal Engine 4 allows its users to attach new components to actors in the scene graph which allows extending objects with new behavior. Furthermore, if a new class is created using UE4's C++-dialect, variables of that class can be exposed to the editor. By doing so, users have the ability to easily change values of an instance of the class from within the editor itself, which minimizes programming effort.

Unreal Engine 4 not only provides a C++ interface but also a visual programming language called *Blueprints*. *Blueprints* abstract functions and classes from the C++ interface and present them as "building blocks" that can be connected by execution lines. It serves as straightforward way to minimize programming eßort and even allows people without programming experience to create game logic for their project.

When extending UE4 with custom classes, the general idea is noted in Epic Games (2020a): programmers extend the existing systems by exposing the changes *via* blueprints. These can be used by other users to create game behavior. Our plugin system follows this ideas.

Furthermore, UE4 allows developers to bundle their code as plugins in order to make the code more reusable and easier to distribute (Epic Games, 2020b). Plugins can be managed easily within the editor. All classes and blueprints are directly accessible for usage in the editor. We implemented our system as a set of three plugins to make the distribution eßortless and allow the users to choose which features they need for their projects.

Finally, UE4 programs can be linked against external libraries at compile time, or dynamically loaded at runtime, similar to regular C++ applications. We are using this technique to base our plugins on already existing libraries. This ensures a time-tested and actively maintained base for our plugins.

3.2. Design of the Plugin Communication

As described above, our system consists of three individual plugins that exchange data. Hence, communication between the plugins plays an important role. Following our goal of flexibility, this communication has to meet two major requirements.

- The plugins need to communicate with each other without knowledge about the others' implementation because users of our plugins should be able to use them individually or combined. They could even be replaced by the users' own implementations. Thus, the communication has to run on an independent layer.
- Users of the plugins should be able to access the data produced by the plugins for their individual needs. This means that it must be possible to pass data outside of the plugins.

To fulfill both these requirements, we implemented a messaging approach based on *delegates*. A *delegator* is an object that represents an event in the system. The delegator can define a certain function signature by specifying parameter types. *Delegates* are functions of said signature that are bound to the delegator. The delegator can issue a broadcast which will call all bound delegates. Eßectively, the delegates are functions reacting to the event represented by the delegator. A delegator can pass data to its delegates when broadcasting, completing the messaging system.

The setup of the delegates between the plugins can be handled, for example, in a custom controller class within the users' projects. We describe the implementation details for such a controller in section 3.6.

3.2.1. Our Light Delegate System

Unreal Engine 4 provides the possibility to declare different kinds of delegates out of the box. However, these delegates have a few drawbacks. Only Unreal Objects (declared with the **UOBJECT** macro etc.) can be passed with such delegates, limiting their use for more general C++ applications. They also introduce several layers of calls in the call stack since they are implemented around the reflection system of the UE4. This may influence performance when many delegates are used.

To overcome these problems we implemented our own lightweight **Delegator** class. It is a pure C++ class that can take a variable number of template arguments which represent the parameter types of its delegates. A so called *callable* can be bound with the **addDelegate(...)** function. Our solution supports all common C++-callables (free functions, member functions, lambdas, etc.). The delegates can be executed with the **broadcast()** function which will execute delegates one after another with just a single additional step in the call stack. The data are always passed around as references internally, preventing any additional copies.

3.3. Devio Plugin—Device Interface

DEVIO provides a common abstraction layer for input devices. To use a device in UNREALHAPTICS, one has to include the correct communication library and implement the abstract functions. With these functions, we gain full control of our device with either Blueprints or C++ Code. Additionally, the plugin provides bidirectional data transfer, i.e., data can be received and sent to the device.

DEVIO mainly consists of three parts: The device manager, the device thread, and the device interface. The device manager provides the user interface and is the only part used by the developer. It is represented as a UE4 actor in the scene and is used to send and receive data, e.g., positions or forces. If necessary, the execution loop of the plugin can be separated from the game thread of the UE4. This device thread allows higher framerates compared to the game thread. While this is not required for most devices, it is crucial for haptics, which can be seen in **Figure 2**. When new device data are available, a delegator-event **OnTransform** is broadcasted, which passes the data to the device manager in every tick. Users of the plugin can hook their own functions to this event, allowing them to react to the new device data. A second delegator-event **ForceOnHapticTick** is broadcasted, which allows users to hook functions like force computation into the device thread. Our own FORCECOMP plugin uses this mechanism, which is further described in section 3.6.

3.4. Collette—Collision Detection Plugin

The physics module included in UE4 has two drawbacks that makes it unsuitable for some devices:

1. It runs on the main game thread, which means it is capped at 120 FPS.
2. Objects are approximated by simple bounding volumes, which is very eßcient for game scenarios but too imprecise to compute the collision data needed for precise physics computations.

In order to circumvent these problems, we bypass the physics module of the UE4.

Our COLLETTE plugin does exactly that. We do not implement a collision detection in this plugin, but provide a flexible wrapper to bind external libraries. In our use case, we show an example how to integrate the CollDet library (see

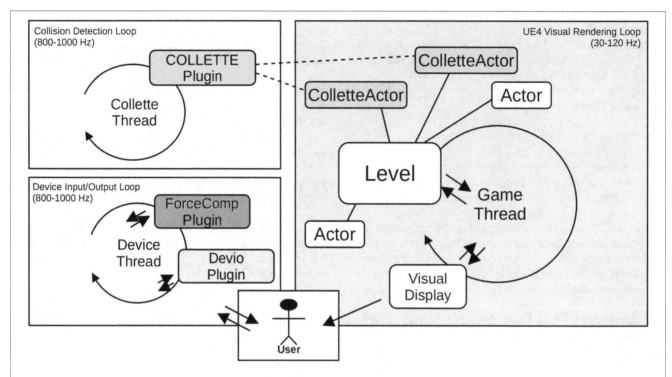

FIGURE 2 | The basic structure of our plugin system with three threads. (Right) The UE4 game thread that is responsible for the visual feedback and runs with up to 120 Hz. (Left) The haptic rendering thread and the collision detection thread. The device communication included in DEVIO and the FORCECOMP plugin run at 1,000 Hz for a stable update rate. We decided to put the collision detection in its own thread in order to not disturb the device communication, e.g., in case of deep collisions that require more computation time than 1 ms. The collidable objects in the Unreal scenegraph are represented as `ColletteStaticMeshActor`s that are derived from Unreal's built in `StaticMeshActor`s.

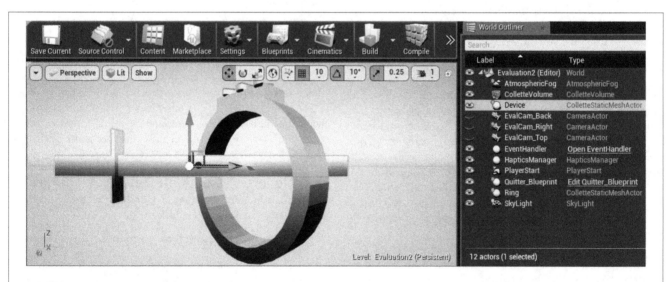

FIGURE 3 | Unreal's editor view of one of our scenes. The sword is controlled by the phantom device, whereas the ring is static. Both are `ColletteStaticMeshActor`, which is visible on the right side.

section 4.1.2). Like DEVIO, COLLETTE can run in its own thread. Thus, high framerates even for complicated scenes can be achieved. The plugin uses a `ColletteStaticMeshActor` to represent collidable objectsas shown in **Figure 3**. This is an extension to UE4's `StaticMeshActor`. It supports loading

additional pre-computed acceleration data structures to the actor's mesh component when the 3D asset is loaded. For instance, in our use case, we load a pre-generated sphere tree asset from the hard drive which is used for internal representation of the underlying algorithm.

The collision pipeline is represented by a `ColletteVolume`, which extends the UE4 `VolumeActor`. We decided to use a volume actor because it allows to restrict collision detection checks to defined areas in the level. To register collidable objects with the pipeline, they can be registered with an `AddCollisionWatcher(...)` blueprint function to the collision detection pipeline. The function takes references to the `ColletteVolume` as well as two `ColletteStaticMeshActor`s.

During runtime, the collision thread checks registered pairs with their current positions and orientations. If a collision is determined, the class `ColletteCallback` broadcasts an `OnCollision` delegator-event. Users of the plugin can easily hook their own functions to this event, allowing reactions to the collision. Blueprint events cannot be used here as they are also executed on the game thread and thus run at a low frequency. The event also transmits references to the pair of `ColletteStaticMeshActor`s involved in the collision, as well as the collision data generated by the underlying algorithm. This data can then be used, for example, to compute collision response forces.

3.5. ForceComp Plugin

The force calculation is implemented as a free standing function which accepts the data from two `ForceComponent`s that can be attached especially to `ColletteStaticMeshActor`s and depends on the current transform of the `ColletteStaticMeshActor`. The `ForceComponent` provides UE4 editor properties needed for the physical simulation of the forces: For instance, the mass of the objects, a scaling factor, or a damper (see section 4.1.3). We have separated the force data from the collision detection. This allows users to use the Collette plugin without the force computation.

3.6. Controlling Data Flow *via* Events

We already mentioned that we use a delegate-based event system to organize the data flow between the three plugins. In order to manage the events, we use an `EventHandler` actor. This guarantees a maximum of flexibility and avoids that the plugins depend on the specific implementation. Basically, the `EventHandler` has references to all involved components and game objects like actors and events. Our `EventHandler` supports drag-and-drop in the Unreal editor window, and hence, there is no coding required to establish these references. For instance, if we want to add a collidable object in the scene, we simply have to drag a `ColletteStaticMeshActor` instance on the `EventHandler` instance in the editor window.

In addition, the `EventHandler` implements various functions that it binds to the events of the plugins during initialization. For example, it provides functions for the two most important events: the `OnTransform` event sent by the device thread and for the `OnCollision` event of the `ColletteVolume` actor. The `OnTransform` event broadcasts the position and orientation data automatically to the virtual representation, e.g., a hand. This has the same effect as if the representation would be updated directly in the device

thread. Moreover, the `OnTransform` event also evokes a second delegate function from FORCECOMP that computes the collision forces based on this data. When finished, it may pass the forces back to the `DeviceManager`, which applies them to the associated device (see **Figure 4** for a simplified example).

The `OnCollision` delegator event of the `ColletteVolume` actor sends the collision data to the attached function of the `EventHandler` and finally stores it in shared variables. By doing this, the device thread will execute the delegate after it has updated the virtual tool's transform. The delegate itself reads the data from the shared variables and checks if a collision occurred. If so, the collision information is used to compute forces. The Collette thread is synchronized with the force computation. After a force is calculated the Collette thread stops waiting, reads the device data, and checks for collisions. This way the frequency of the collision thread is bounded to the device thread frequency (1,000 Hz).

With this solution, however, we keep the concrete implementations of the plugins separate from each other. **Figure 5** shows and example for the event handling between FORCECOMP and DEVIO. This modular and customizable approach guarantees a very flexible data flow between the different plugins that can be easily defined by the user within the editor. In the following sections, we want to explore UNREALHAPTICS for two concrete applications, the first being haptic rendering with a haptic device and the second grasping with a hand-tracking device.

4. APPLICATIONS

In this section, we demonstrate how UNREALHAPTICS can be used in applications. The first example focuses on haptic rendering, while the second example shows a grasping application.

4.1. Haptic Rendering

We applied UNREALHAPTICS to an application with support for haptic rendering. For haptic rendering, we use our plugin in a setup with three threads: one for the main game loop, including the visual rendering in Unreal, one for the haptic rendering that covers DEVIO and FORCECOMP and one for the collision detection. We decided to run the collision detection independently in its own thread to guarantee stable haptic rendering rates even in the case of deep interpenetrations where the collision detection could exceed the 1ms time frame. **Figure 3** shows this three-thread scenario. However, it is easy to use COLLETTE also in the haptic rendering thread—or to even use a fourth thread for FORCECOMP—by simply adjusting the configuration in the `EventHandler`. This example shows how the actual collision detection libraries, force rendering, and communication libraries can be integrated into our framework.

4.1.1. Device Communication *via* CHAI3D

We use the CHAI3D library to connect to haptic devices. As already mentioned in section 2, this library supports a wide variety of haptic devices, including the PHANToM and the *Haption Virtuose* (Haption, 2020) which we used for testing.

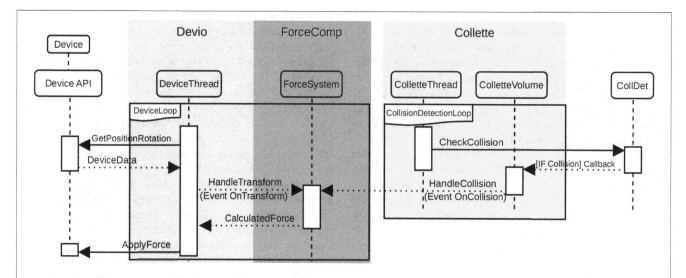

FIGURE 4 | A simplified sequence diagram of the communication of FORCECOMP, COLLETTE, and DEVIO in case of a collision: DEVIO receives the current position and orientation from the device and informs FORCECOMP *via* a `OnTransform` event. `ColletteVolume` in COLLETTE evokes an `OnCollision` event and passes the collision data to FORCECOMP. FORCECOMP computes appropriate forces and torques and passes them back to DEVIO that finally, applies them to the device. Please note, due to space constrains, we did not include transformations that are send from DEVIO to the respective `ColletteStaticMeshActor`s. Moreover, we omitted the `EventHandler` in this example.

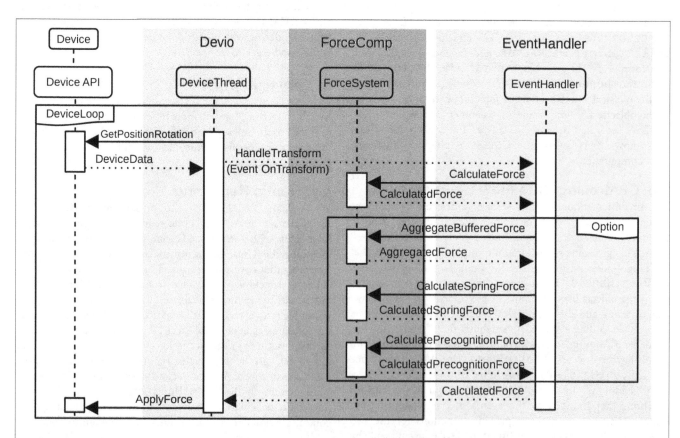

FIGURE 5 | A simplified sequence diagram of the communication of FORCECOMP, DEVIO, and our `EventHandler` that also shows the flexibility of our system. Initially, DEVIO reads the configuration from the haptic library and evokes an `OnTransform` event. This is passed to the `EventHandler` that calls the callable `HandleTransform` function that has initially registered for this event. It is easy to register more than one functions for the same event, e.g., to toggle friction or virtual coupling. The results are finally transferred back to DEVIO *via* the `EventHandler`.

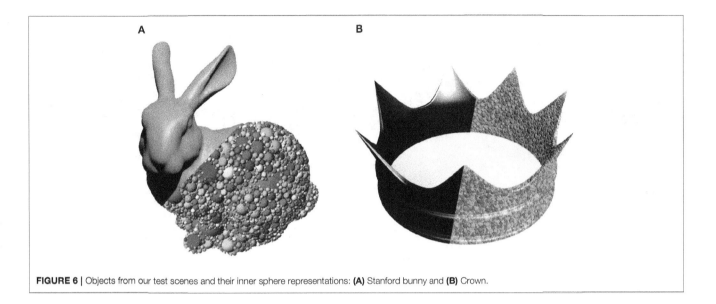

FIGURE 6 | Objects from our test scenes and their inner sphere representations: **(A)** Stanford bunny and **(B)** Crown.

DEVIO links CHAI3D as a third-party library at compile time. We primarily use CHAI3D's *Devices* module as an interface to the hardware devices, especially to set and retrieve positions and rotations. We did not use CHAI3D's force rendering algorithms as they do not support 6-DOF force calculation.

4.1.2. Collision Detection With CollDet

CollDet is a collision detection library written in C++ that implements a complete collision detection pipeline with several layers of filtering (Zachmann, 2001). This includes broad-phase collision detection algorithms like a uniform grid or convex hull pre-filtering and several narrow phase algorithms like a memory-optimized version of an AABB-tree, called Boxtree (Zachmann, 2002), and DOP-trees (Zachmann, 1998). For haptic rendering, the *Inner Sphere Trees* (ISTs) data structure fits best. Unlike other methods, ISTs define hierarchical bounding volumes of spheres *inside* the object based on a polydisperse sphere packing (see **Figure 6**). This approach is independent of the object's triangle count, and it has shown to be applicable to haptic rendering. Beyond the performance, the main advantage is the collision information provided by the ISTs: they do not simply deliver a list of overlapping triangles but give an approximation of the objects' overlap volume. This guarantees stable and continuous forces and torques (Weller et al., 2010). The source code is available under an academic-free license.

COLLETTE's `ColletteVolume` is, at its core, a wrapper around CollDet's pipeline class. Instead of adding CollDet objects to the pipeline, the plugin abstracts this process by registering the `ColletteStaticMeshActor`s with the volume. Internally, a `ColletteStaticMeshActor` is assigned a `ColID` from the CollDet pipeline through its `ColletteStaticMeshComponent`, so that each actor represents a unique object in the pipeline. When the volume moves the objects and checks for collisions in the pipeline, it passes the IDs of the respective actors to the CollDet functions

that implement the collision checking. Analog to CHAI3D, COLLETTE links to the CollDet library at compile time.

4.1.3. Force Calculation

Force and torque computations for haptics usually rely on penalty-based approaches because of their performance. The actual force computation method is closely related to the collision information that is delivered from COLLETTE. In the case of the ISTs, this is a list of overlapping inner spheres for a pair of objects. In our implementation, we apply a slightly modified volumetric collision response scheme as reported by Weller and Zachmann (2009):

For an object A colliding with an object B we compute the restitution force $\vec{F}_A$ by

$$
\begin{aligned}
\vec{F}_A &= \sum_{j \cap i \neq \varnothing} \vec{F}_{A_i} \\
&= \sum_{j \cap i \neq \varnothing} \vec{n}_{i,j} \cdot \max\left(\text{vol}_{i,j} \cdot \left(\varepsilon_c - \frac{\text{vel}_{i,j} \cdot \varepsilon_d}{\text{Vol}_{total}}\right), 0\right)
\end{aligned}
\tag{1}
$$

where (i, j) is a pair of colliding spheres, $\vec{n}_{i,j}$ is the collision normal, $\text{vol}_{i,j}$ is the overlap volume of the sphere pair, Vol_{total} is the total overlap volume of all colliding spheres, $\text{vel}_{i,j}$ is the magnitude of the relative velocity at the collision center in direction of $\vec{n}_{i,j}$. Additionally, we added an empirically determined scaling factor ε_c for the forces and applied some damping with ε_d to prevent unwanted increases of forces in the system.

Only positive forces are considered preventing an increase in the overlapping volume of the objects. The total restitution force is then computed simply by summing up the restitution forces of all colliding sphere pairs.

Torques for full 6-DOF force feedback can be computed by

$$
\vec{\tau}_A = \sum_{j \cap i \neq \varnothing} \left(C_{i,j} - A_m\right) \times \vec{F}_{A_i}
\tag{2}
$$

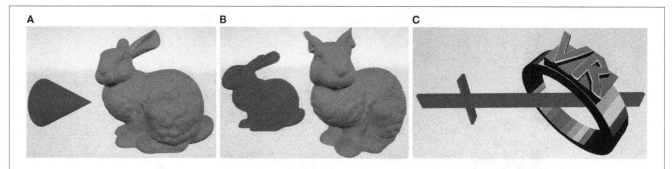

FIGURE 7 | In order to evaluate the performance of our plugins, we have used multiple complex test scenes: **(A)** Cone and bunny, **(B)** Two bunnies, and **(C)** Sword and ring. The user controls in each scene a reddish object with the phantom device to touch the other object.

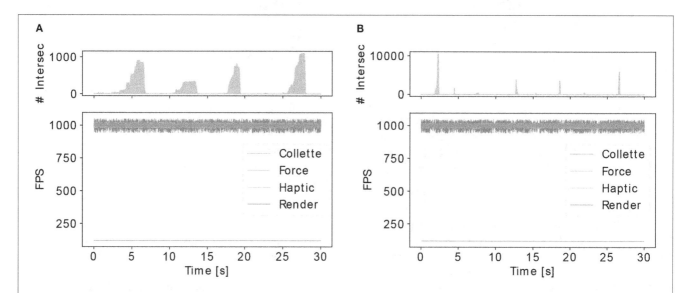

FIGURE 8 | Performance of our plugins in the cone and bunny scene. Here, we have used different sphere packing resolutions (approximation of volume) per object. Top graph shows the number of intersecting spheres. In **(A)**, we have used 10k spheres and in **(B)** we have used 100k spheres. We have achieved haptic frame rates even with large number of spheres, and also we have had a constant rendering frame rate (120 FPS).

where $C_{i,j}$ is the center of collision for sphere pair (i, j) and A_m is the center of mass of the object A. Again, the total torques of one object are computed by summing the torques of all colliding sphere pairs (Weller and Zachmann, 2009).

4.1.4. Performance

We have evaluated the performance of our implementation in UE4 on an AMD Ryzen 7 2700X (8 Cores) with 32 GB of main memory and a NVIDIA GeForce RTX 2070 running Microsoft Windows 10 Professional.

We used three different test scenes: the user explores the surface of an object (in our example, the Stanford bunny) with a Phantom device. In our test scenes, we represented the end effector with a red color (see **Figure 7**).

We achieved almost always a frequency of 850–1K Hz for the force rendering and haptic communication thread. It only dropped slightly in case of situations with a lot of intersecting pairs of spheres. The same appears for the collision detection that slightly dropped to 850 Hz in situations of heavy

interpenetrations. It is similar to the results reported in Weller et al. (2010), where a simple OpenGL test scene was used. This shows that our architecture does not add significant processing overhead (see **Figures 8, 9**).

4.2. Grasping

Due to the modular structure of UNREALHAPTICS, we can easily adapt parts of the plugin to account for different use cases. In the following, we will show how UNREALHAPTICS can be applied to a natural grasping application in VR. In this case, we change our input device to a hand tracking device, i.e., a Cyberglove, which enables natural grasping of objects in VR (**Figure 10**).

More precisely, we aim at investigating the human grasping of different object to transfer it to robots performing everyday activities. To do that, in this first step, we record sophisticated human grasping data in VR. This is done by generating heat maps during grasp experiments of the virtual objects (Tenorth et al., 2015). To record a heat map, we determine the contact points of the individual parts of the hand on object. Heat maps

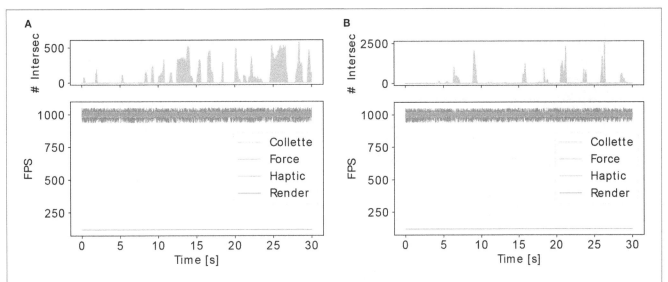

FIGURE 9 | Performance of our plugins in different scenes with 100k spheres per object. Top graph shows the number of intersecting spheres. In **(A)**, we have used two bunnies and in **(B)** a sword and ring. For these different objects in the scene, we have achieved haptic frame rates and constant 120 FPS for rendering.

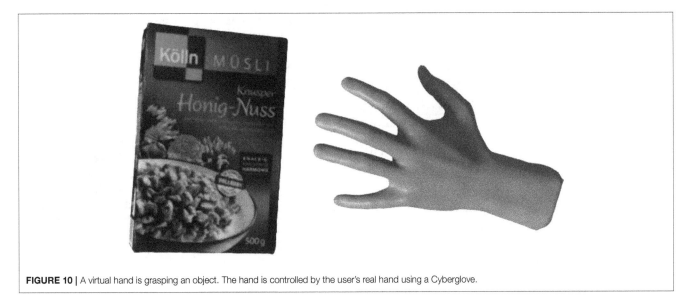

FIGURE 10 | A virtual hand is grasping an object. The hand is controlled by the user's real hand using a Cyberglove.

for a specific object show the combination of contact points from multiple grasping experiments. **Figure 11** show examples of such maps for different objects. The aggregated contact points are drawn on the texture of the object. We represent each finger with a different color, so it is easy to distinguish the grasping positions. Our generated heat maps show possible candidates for grasp points of an object. This data can be used, i.e., by robots to learn stable grasping configurations for a wide variety of objects. We will discuss the plugins in more detail in the following section.

4.2.1. Device Communication

While the CHAI3D library can be used for many different haptic devices, no such library exists for hand tracking with the many fundamentally different tracking methods, such as gloves, optical-based, or marker-based (references). For this application, we decided to use a Cyberglove, which uses bending sensors

attached to a glove to track finger motion. We have written a library that connects and retrieves signals from the glove. These signals are then transformed into joint angles by a calibration step. DEVIO links this library, and by implementing the abstract functions, we can use UNREALHAPTICS with a Cyberglove as an input device.

4.2.2. Collision Detection With CollDet

Similar to our haptic application, we use the COLLETE plugin with the CollDet library to precisely detect collisions between the hand and objects. CollDet can easily handle multiple contacts from different fingers and the palm while delivering sophisticated collision information. Each graspable object is represented by a `ColleteStaticMeshActor`. For the virtual hand, 16 `ColleteStaticMeshActors` are registered in the `ColletteVolume`, three actors for each finger and one for

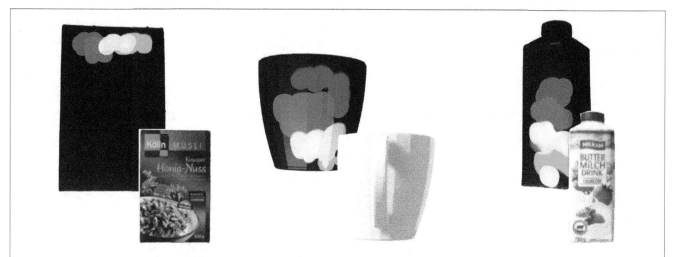

FIGURE 11 | Heatmaps for a cerial box, a cup, and a milk box. The colors denote the finger used for grasping the object: ● index finger, ● middle finger, ring finger, ● pinky finger, ● thumb.

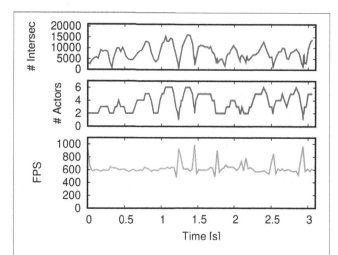

FIGURE 12 | Performance of our plugin for the grasping application with 17 interacting *ColleteStaticMeshActors*. We used multiple grasping operations and only used frames with collisions for the analysis. The top graph shows the number of intersecting spheres. The middle graph shows the number of colliding *ColleteStaticMeshActors*. In the bottom graph, the framerate is shown. The framerate never drops below 550 Hz even for complicated collisions.

the palm. This separation of actors is necessary because fingers are movable, and `ColleteStaticMeshActors` are rigid objects. At first glance, this may look complex, but in the case of collisions, we automatically know which part of the hand is in contact with the object. Moreover, we can also detect self-collisions between fingers easily. Information about the positions of the collision on the object allows both grasping and creating heat maps.

4.2.3. Force Calculation and Heat Maps

To manipulate objects in VR, knowledge of the force acting on objects from the virtual hand is essential. We can only estimate the force in our setup because our hand tracking device has no haptic feedback. Nonetheless, the force calculation introduced in section 4.1.3 using the overlapped volume can be used to approximate the force acting on objects. In this application, the main goal is the generation of heat maps. Hence, during a grasping operation, the contact points of the hand with the object are computed. We do this in the following way: If the hand is in contact with an object, the collision detection returns a list of overlapping spheres. To generate heat maps from pairs of overlapping spheres, we need to compute the corresponding points on the surface of the object. We can use Unreal's linetrace function to determine the nearest point on the surface with a raycast. Using Unreal's complex collision detection, we get a good approximation of the collisions on the surface. For the linetrace, we define as a starting point, the center of the hand's sphere and as an endpoint the center of the object's sphere.

4.2.4. Performance

We, again, tested the performance of our collision detection loop. In comparison with section 4.1.4, the number of ColldetActors increased from 2 to 17, which in principle could all collide simultaneously and increase the complexity significantly. We evaluated the performance on a machine running Windows 10 with an AMD Ryzen 9 3900X (12 cores), 16 GB of main memory, and an NVIDIA GeForce RTX 2080 SUPER. The results are shown in **Figure 12**. To focus only on the interesting case where the hand is grasping an object, we only considered frames with collisions and limited the maximal framerate to 1,000 Hz. Each of the 16 finger parts is packed with 5,000 spheres and the graspable object with 10,000 spheres. The maximum number of intersecting spheres is around 30,000, and the maximum number of colliding actors is 11, as can be seen in the upper graph. The frame rate never drops below 150 Hz, and our application is easily running in real-time.

5. CONCLUSIONS AND FUTURE WORK

We have presented a new plugin system for integrating more specialized VR input devices into modern plugin-orientated game engines. Our system consists of three individual plugins that cover the complete requirements for most devices: communication with different hardware devices, collision detection, and force rendering. Intentionally, we used an abstract design of our plugins. This abstract and modular setup makes it easy for other developers to exchange parts of our system to adjust it to their individual needs. Our results show that our plugin system is stable, and the performance is well-suited for our applications of haptic rendering and virtual grasping, even for complex non-convex objects.

With our plugin system, future projects have an easy way to include special devices in games, research, and business related applications. Even though other developers may decide to use different libraries for their work, we are confident that our experiences reported here in combination with our high-level UE4 plugin system will simplify their integration effort enormously.

However, our system and the current CollDet-based implementation also have some limitations that we want to solve in future developments. Currently, our system is restricted to rigid body interaction. Further work may entail the inclusion of deformable objects. In this case, a rework of the interfaces is necessary because the amount of data to be exchanged between the plugins will increase significantly; instead of transferring simple matrices that represent the translation and orientation of an object, we have to augment complete meshes. Direct access to UE4s mesh memory could be helpful to solve this challenge.

Also, our use cases offers interesting avenues for future works. Currently, we plan a user study with blind video game players to test their acceptance of haptic devices in 3D multiplayer environments. Moreover, we want to investigate different haptic object recognition tasks, for instance, with respect to the influence of the degrees of freedom of the haptic device or with bi-manual vs. single-handed interaction.

AUTHOR CONTRIBUTIONS

JR: evaluation of grasping and research. HM: evaluation of haptic feedback and research. RW: review and general ideas. MR: some part of implementation and technical help. JG: some part of implementation. GZ: review, general help and supervision. All authors contributed to the article and approved the submitted version.

ACKNOWLEDGMENTS

Some part of this work has previously been published at the EuroVR 2018 conference in London, United Kingdom, October, 22–23, 2018 (Rüdel et al., 2018). We extended the original plugin for haptic-based devices to other specialized input devices, e.g., Cybergloves, in this follow-up work.

REFERENCES

3D Systems (2018). *Geomagic OpenHaptics Toolkit*. Available online at: https://www.3dsystems.com/haptics-devices/openhaptics (accessed September 3, 2020).

Andrews, S., Mora, J., Lang, J., and Lee, W. S. (2006). "Hapticast: A physically-based 3D game with haptic feedback," in *Proceedings of FuturePlay 2006* (Ontario, CA).

CHAI3D (2016a). *CHAI3D Documentation–Haptic Rendering*. Available online at: http://www.chai3d.org/download/doc/html/chapter17-haptics.html (accessed March 9, 2020).

CHAI3D (2016b). Available online at: http://www.chai3d.org/ (accessed March 9, 2020).

de Pedro, J., Esteban, G., Conde, M. A., and Fernández, C. (2016). "Hcore: a game engine independent OO architecture for fast development of haptic simulators for teaching/learning," in *Proceedings of the Fourth International Conference on Technological Ecosystems for Enhancing Multiculturality* (New York, NY: ACM), 1011–1018. doi: 10.1145/3012430.3012640

Epic Games (2020a). *Introduction to C++ Programming in UE4*. Available online at: https://docs.unrealengine.com/en-US/Programming/Introduction

Epic Games (2020b). *Plugins*. Available online at: https://docs.unrealengine.com/latest/INT/Programming/Plugins/index.html (accessed March 9, 2020).

Gomes de Sá, A., and Zachmann, G. (1999). Virtual reality as a tool for verification of assembly and maintenance processes. *Comput. Graph.* 23, 389–403. doi: 10.1016/S0097-8493(99)00047-3

H3DAPI (2019). Available online at: http://h3dapi.org/ (accessed March 9, 2020).

Haption, S. A. (2020). *Virtuose 6D Desktop*. Available online at: https://www.haption.com/pdf/Datasheet_Virtuose_6DDesktop.pdf (accessed March 9, 2020).

Kadleček, P., and Kmoch, S. P. (2011). "Overview of current developments in haptic APIs," in *Proceedings of CESCG* (Vienna: Vienna University of Technology).

Kollasch, F. (2017). *Sirraherydya/Phantom-Omni-Plugin*. Available online at: https://github.com/SirrahErydya/Phantom-Omni-Plugin (accessed Septemper 3, 2020).

Lin, J., Guo, X., Shao, J., Jiang, C., Zhu, Y., and Zhu, S. C. (2016). "A virtual reality platform for dynamic human-scene interaction," in *SIGGRAPH ASIA 2016 Virtual Reality Meets Physical Reality: Modelling and Simulating Virtual Humans and Environments* (New York, NY: ACM), 1–4. doi: 10.1145/2992138.2992144

Liu, H., Zhang, Z., Xie, X., Zhu, Y., Liu, Y., Wang, Y., et al. (2019). "High-fidelity grasping in virtual reality using a glove-based system," in *2019 International Conference on Robotics and Automation (ICRA)* (Piscataway, NJ: IEEE), 5180–5186. doi: 10.1109/ICRA.2019.8794230

McNeely, W. A., Puterbaugh, K. D., and Troy, J. J. (1999). "Six degree-of-freedom haptic rendering using voxel sampling," in *Proceedings of the 26th Annual Conference on Computer Graphics and Interactive Techniques, SIGGRAPH '99* (New York, NY: ACM Press/Addison-Wesley Publishing Co.), 401–408. doi: 10.1145/311535.311600

Moehring, M., and Froehlich, B. (2011). "Effective manipulation of virtual objects within arm's reach," in *2011 IEEE Virtual Reality Conference* (Piscataway, NJ: IEEE), 131–138. doi: 10.1109/VR.2011.5759451

Mól, A. C. A., Jorge, C. A. F., and Couto, P. M. (2008). Using a game engine for VR simulations in evacuation planning. *IEEE Comput. Graph. Appl.* 28, 6–12. doi: 10.1109/MCG.2008.61

Morris, D., Joshi, N., and Salisbury, K. (2004). "Haptic battle pong: High-degree-of-freedom haptics in a multiplayer gaming environment," in *Proceedings of*

Experimental Gameplay Workshop (San Jose: Game Developers Conference). Available online at: https://www.microsoft.com/en-us/research/publication/haptic-battle-pong-high-degree-freedom-haptics-multiplayer-gaming-environment-2/

Reinschluessel, A. V., Teuber, J., Herrlich, M., Bissel, J., van Eikeren, M., Ganser, J., et al. (2017). "Virtual reality for user-centered design and evaluation of touch-free interaction techniques for navigating medical images in the operating room," in *Proceedings of the 2017 CHI Conference Extended Abstracts on Human Factors in Computing Systems, CHI EA '17* (New York, NY: ACM), 2001–2009. doi: 10.1145/3027063.30 53173

Rüdel, M. O., Ganser, J., Weller, R., and Zachmann, G. (2018). "Unrealhaptics: a plugin-system for high fidelity haptic rendering in the unreal engine," in *International Conference on Virtual Reality and Augmented Reality* (Chem: Springer International Publishing), 128–147. doi: 10.1007/978-3-030-01790-3_8

Ruffaldi, E., Frisoli, A., Bergamasco, M., Gottlieb, C., and Tecchia, F. (2006). "A haptic toolkit for the development of immersive and web-enabled games," in *Proceedings of the ACM Symposium on Virtual Reality Software and Technology* (New York, NY: ACM), 320–323. doi: 10.1145/1180495.11 80559

Sagardia, M., Stouraitis, T., and Silva, J. L. E. (2014). "A new fast and robust collision detection and force computation algorithm applied to the physics engine bullet: method, integration, and evaluation," in *EuroVR 2014–Conference and Exhibition of the European Association of Virtual and Augmented Reality*, eds J. Perret, V. Basso, F. Ferrise, K. Helin, V. Lepetit, J. Ritchie, C. Runde, et al. (The Eurographics Association).

Tenorth, M., Winkler, J., Beßler, D., and Beetz, M. (2015). Open-EASE: a cloud-based knowledge service for autonomous learning. *KÜnstl. Intell.* 29, 407–411. doi: 10.1007/s13218-015-0364-1

The Glasgow School of Art (2014). *Haptic Demo in Unity Using OpenHaptics With Phantom Omni.* Online Video. Available online at: https://www.youtube.com/watch?v=nmrviXro65g (accessed September 3, 2020).

User ZeonmkII (2016). *Zeonmkii/Omniplugin.* Available online at: https://github.com/ZeonmkII/OmniPlugin (accessed September 3, 2020).

Verschoor, M., Lobo, D., and Otaduy, M. A. (2018). "Soft hand simulation for smooth and robust natural interaction," in *2018 IEEE Conference on Virtual Reality and 3D User Interfaces (VR)* (Piscataway, NJ: IEEE), 183–190. doi: 10.1109/VR.2018.8447555

Weller, R., Sagardia, M., Mainzer, D., Hulin, T., Zachmann, G., and Preusche, C. (2010). "A benchmarking suite for 6-DOF real time collision response algorithms," in *Proceedings of the 17th ACM Symposium on Virtual Reality Software and Technology* (New York, NY: ACM), 63–70. doi: 10.1145/1889863.1889874

Weller, R., and Zachmann, G. (2009). "A unified approach for physically-based simulations and haptic rendering," in *Sandbox 2009*, ed D. Davidson (New York, NY: ACM), 151. doi: 10.1145/1581073.1581097

Zachmann, G. (1998). "Rapid collision detection by dynamically aligned DOP-trees," in *Proceedings of IEEE Virtual Reality Annual International Symposium; VRAIS '98* (Atlanta, GA), 90–97. doi: 10.1109/VRAIS.1998.658428

Zachmann, G. (2001). "Optimizing the collision detection pipeline," in *Procedings of the First International Game Technology Conference (GTEC)* (Hong Kong).

Zachmann, G. (2002). "Minimal hierarchical collision detection," in *Proceedings of ACM Symposium on Virtual Reality Software and Technology (VRST)* (Hong Kong), 121–128. doi: 10.1145/585740.585761

5

A Haptic Virtual Reality Control Station for Model-Mediated Robotic Applications

Jean Elsner [1,2]*, Gerhard Reinerth [1,2], Luis Figueredo [1], Abdeldjallil Naceri [1], Ulrich Walter [2] and Sami Haddadin [1]

[1] Munich Institute of Robotics and Machine Intelligence (MIRMI), Technical University of Munich (TUM), Munich, Germany, [2] Chair of Astronautics, TUM School of Engineering and Design, Technical University of Munich (TUM), Munich, Germany

*Correspondence:
Jean Elsner
j.elsner@tum.de

In this paper, we introduce a tele-robotic station called "*PARTI*" that leverages state-of-the-art robotics and virtual reality technology to enable immersive haptic interaction with simulated and remote environments through robotic avatars. Our hardware-in-the-loop framework integrates accurate multibody system dynamics and frictional contacts with digital twins of our robots in a virtual environment with real-time computational capabilities. This model mediated hardware-in-the-loop approach to robotic control allows a teleoperator to use the PARTI system to teach, evaluate, and control various robotic applications. In the current contribution, we focus on the general system description, integrated simulation and control framework, and a series of experiments highlighting the advantages of our approach.

Keywords: haptics, virtual reality, robotics, digital twin, simulation, model mediated, control, teleoperation

1 INTRODUCTION

As changing demographics lead to increasingly aging populations many recent research efforts focus on robotic applications to support elderly users in every-day tasks in order to increase the user's autonomy and support care providers. One such effort is the humanoid robot assistant GARMI, which was specifically designed to support elderly users at home (cf. Tröbinger et al. (2021)). Indeed, bimanual manipulation tasks and skills of caregivers are crucial for elderly care scenarios. In this work, we introduce the haptic virtual reality control station and counterpart to GARMI, called PARTI. The PARTI system was designed to closely mimic the kinematic and dynamic configuration of a caregiver and mapping it to the humanoid's two-arm system. By doing so, the system can function as a haptic input interface for bilateral teleoperation architecture, similar to an upper-body exoskeleton. Much beyond that the system integrates an advanced simulation framework and virtual reality user interfaces to facilitate immersive real-time interaction with digital twins. The digital twins in turn can be transparently coupled to their real-world counterparts. Such a system not only is beneficial for training the caregivers to use such a complex robotic system but also for sending/teaching nursing skills to GARMI.

Multimodal telepresence systems are gaining interest due to the demand for remote interaction with haptic feedback. There already exist a variety of different teleoperation-/telepresence systems such as NimbRo (Schwarz et al., 2021) and DLR's HUG (Hulin et al., 2011), just to name a few. The systems were designed for different use case scenarios, NimbRo focusses on teleoperation of a humanoid avatar, while DLR's HUG system also considers interaction with virtual environments for training purposes (Sagardia et al., 2016). Delay compensation techniques for NimbRo are neglected, since the distance between operator and teleoperator is assumed to be small. Balachandran et al. (2018) investigate HUGs feedback behaviour under delay.

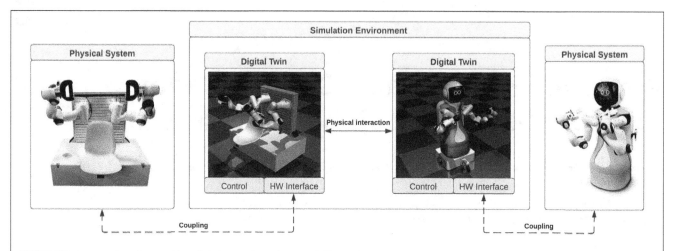

FIGURE 1 | System overview of our model-mediated approach to robot control. The simulation environment is populated with digital twins that may interact with each other and the environment. Hardware interfaces allow for transparent coupling of the digital twin to its real world counterpart to close the control loop in the physical world.

As in Sagardia et al. (2016), we also develop a simulation environment with different use cases such as training medical and technical personal. Therefore realistic simulated haptic force feedback is required that also needs to consider the hardware on the simulated remote side. We opt MuJoCo's (Todorov et al., 2012) convenient representation in generalized coordinates for kinematic chains, yielding haptic feedback in case of undesired (self-) collisions. A notable byproduct of the simulation of the systems is a digital twin, which can be used for system diagnostics. However the focus of our simulation lies on physical realism and real-time aspects for haptic force feedback. This system allows us to explore complex scenarios where various physical and virtual agents interact with each other in a simulated environment, not unlike a haptic meta-verse for robotic systems (see **Figure 1**). We refer to this approach as model-mediated robot control and present several experiments to highlight the potential of this paradigm. The main components of our system, which we explore further, are namely:

- State-of-the-art digital twins based on a multibody dynamics physical engine with real-time capability;
- Haptic real-time interface rendering constraint forces from the virtual physics engine in generalized coordinates;
- Hardware-in-the-loop interface for model-mediated closed-loop control.

Our model-mediated robot control paradigm can be linked to the model-mediated teleoperation (MMT) approach (Xu et al., 2016). To our knowledge this is the first work that considers a physics engine as model for MMT. Virtual reality (VR)-based teleoperation is widely used for MMT to provide a non-delayed force and visual feedback and thus guarantee system stability and transparency. Many studies on VR-based MMT have focused on estimating the environment geometry. Valenzuela-Urrutia et al. (2019) have built a virtual workspace that is created directly from point cloud data. Similarly in Ni et al. (2017), the remote real

world is modeled in a local virtual environment with the help of RGB information and a 3D registration method. Both virtual environments, however, do not provide sufficient physical properties. The gap between the virtual model and the real world is still large. Recently, the digital twin methodology is applied to a robot-environment interaction for enhancing task performance with the help of Unity (Li et al., 2021). A 3-D generic graphic model as well as the contact dynamics of the real entities is modeled to mirror a real interactive scene. Physical properties of the real environment are also extracted, simultaneously. This work, however, does not consider real teleoperation scenarios with communication unreliability. System control schemes to deal with various tasks and communication delays are not studied. As a contrast, in this paper, we have proposed a digital twin system with a physical engine to describe the full dynamics of the real environment. This minimizes the gap between visual-haptic rendering in virtual environment and the real-world interaction. In addition, our work considers teleoperation over real communication networks, where time delay and packet loss are inevitable. To address these issue, stability-ensuring control schemes such as the *Time Domain Passivity Approach* (TDPA, Ryu and Preusche (2007)) and MMT are investigated on our system.

2 PARTI: SYSTEM OVERVIEW

2.1 Hardware

PARTI is designed to emulate and mirror the same physical properties of humanoid avatar GARMI, whilst at the same time enabling a pleasant human-robot and haptic interaction. To this aim, the first design choice concerns the hardware layout. The robot arms were mounted horizontally, rather than vertically—with care consideration with respect to the reachability space of the human operator. This mode of operation requires a modified firmware on each of the robots master controllers for proper gravity

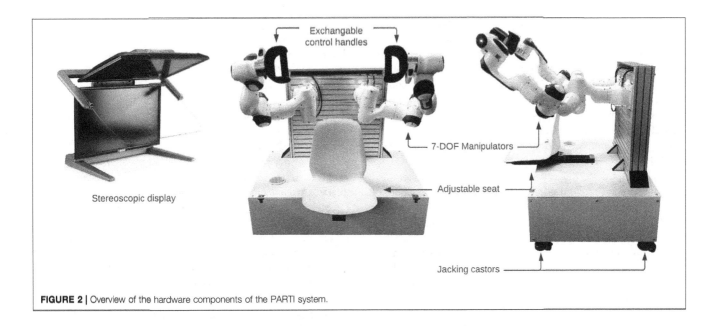

FIGURE 2 | Overview of the hardware components of the PARTI system.

FIGURE 3 | Visualization of our two primary digital twin models in MuJoCo. The model of the humanoid robot GARMI shown on the left includes fully actuated arms, head and a friction driven differential drive system with castor wheels and passive suspension. The model of PARTI to the right also features a fully actuated two-arm system. These models can run purely in a software environment or be coupled to the real hardware using the haptic or HIL interfaces.

compensation. Also precise adjustment of the main frame is mandatory, such that gravity compensation works as intended. Therefore, PARTI's baseframe is supported by four height-adjustable wheels for leveling purposes. The seat as well as robotic arms are adjustable to fit the operators demands while mirroring the properties of the humanoid avatar GARMI. A second obvious design choice was to use the Panda robot from Franka Emika, a torque-actuated 7-DoF robotic system, for each arm. The robotic arm is embedded with torque sensors on every joint, which in turn properly emulated the GARMI robot and, most importantly, provided precise (cf. Kirschner et al. (2021)) wrench estimation on task-space on different levels of the robotic kinematics, i.e., in different parts of the serial chain. Such feature enabled real-time wrench rendering in our HIL framework at the custom end-effectors is shown in **Figure 2**. For

haptic- and visual rendering, a performant computer (Intel® Core™ i7-9700F, 16 GiB RAM, NVIDIA GeForce RTX 2080 Ti) is connected to both master controllers via a switch generating torque signals for the robotic arms or reading telemetry data in a 1 kHz control loop. Since teleoperation requires depth perception, we use a 3D-PluraView monitor for stereoscopic rendering. The PARTI hardware framework, as described above, is shown in **Figure 2** with its base frame and backwall consisting of a robust construction of *item*-profiles enabling flexible prototyping.

2.2 Simulation and Control
Our framework integrates physically accurate digital twins (see **Figure 3**) directly into the real-time control loop of our hardware to provide a framework for model-mediated hardware-in-the-

loop control. The hardware-in-the-loop requirements of our framework—that integrates virtual worlds and a bimanual-robot digital-twin to our haptic framework and real-world applications—calls for most recent developments in robotics' hardware, as previously described, as well as for new control algorithms and state-of-the-art physics engines. Indeed, our proposed framework has only be made feasible due to separated developments from the past 5–10 years.[1] For the physics engine and core virtual environment, our system relies on MuJoCo[2] as it is one of the modicum engines that satisfies our requirements, that is, it is capable of running highly constrained and contact rich simulations in real-time at a control frequency of 1 kHz (cf. Todorov et al. (2012)). Compared to other popular robot simulators such as Gazebo, MuJoCo has the additional advantage of simulating in generalized coordinates (cf. Erez et al. (2015)). We use the latter to define an interface between the physical system and its digital twin for haptic interaction with the simulation environment. Given the Lagrangian describing the system dynamics of an n-degree-of-freedom digital twin as

$$M\left(q_{dt}\right)\ddot{q}_{dt} + c\left(q_{dt}, \dot{q}_{dt}\right) + g\left(q_{dt}\right) = \tau_{dt,d} + \tau_{constr} + \tau_{bias}, \quad (1)$$

where $M \in \mathbb{R}^{n \times n}$ is the total inertia, $c\left(q, \dot{q}\right), g\left(q\right) \in \mathbb{R}^n$ the Coriolis and centrifugal and gravity forces, $q, \dot{q} \in \mathbb{R}^n$ position and velocity and $\tau_{dt,d}, \tau_{constr}, \tau_{bias} \in \mathbb{R}^n$ the applied, constraint and bias forces all in generalized coordinates. We couple the digital twin's motion to the physical system using a PD control law in generalized coordinates

$$\tau_{dt,d} = K\left(q_{phys} - q_{dt}\right) - D\dot{q}_{dt} \quad (2)$$

where $K, D \in \mathbb{R}^{7 \times 7}$ are gain matrices and the subscripts $_{phys}$ and $_{dt}$ are used to refer to the physical system and digital twin respectively. Note that while we could set the position of the digital twin directly, we use a tracking controller instead. This way the dsigital twin is subject to the entire simulation pipeline, including computation of the constraint force τ_{constr} and bias force $\tau_{bias} = c\left(q, \dot{q}\right) + g\left(q\right)$. The constraint force computed by MuJoCo includes the forces produced by contacts and joint limits (cf. Todorov (2014)) and can be directly applied to the physical system as

$$\tau_{phys,d} = \lambda \tau_{constr} \quad (3)$$

where $\lambda \in \mathbb{R}^{n \times n}$ is a gain matrix that usually comes down to a single scalar to adjust for the reality gap between the digital twin and the physical system. In addition, we usually apply a slight low-pass IIR filter to τ_{constr} to make haptic interactions smoother for the user. We also implemented a hardware-in-the-loop (HIL) interface that allows us to run closed-loop controllers from within the simulator on the physical system. This is done by superseding the state of the digital twin with that of the physical system and

applying the computed control signal on the physical system, thus closing the loop. Using the HIL interface, we can run experiments developed in the simulator on real hardware without any development overhead.

3 EXPERIMENTS

We performed a series of experiments to highlight the advantages provided by our model-mediated approach to robot control and the design of our control station. The first experiment uses the real-time interface to our digital twin to haptically render generalized constraint forces on the robot. Using this methodology, we can transfer physical behavior modelled in the simulation environment to reality with minimal effort. This is demonstrated by applying a safety margin to the collision meshes of the digital twin. The real robot consequently adheres to this updated model, which serves as a form of collision avoidance—and enables the design of geometric-based virtual walls for task-specific applications. In the second experiment, we evaluate the physical fidelity of our digital twin for the Franka Emika Robot System. We compare the tracking performance as well as the estimated contact wrenches of our model for the MuJoCo simulator to those of the real system as well as a model for the Gazebo simulation environment provided by Franka Emika. Finally, we explore the use of our system as a teleoperation station controlling a humanoid robot in a contact-rich scenario. We compare different approaches such as bilateral position-force computed teleoperation as well as model mediated control.

3.1 Collision Avoidance

We use the haptic interface introduced in **Section 2.2** to connect the PARTI system to its digital twin. For this experiment, the collision model of the digital twin is extended with a safety margin in the form of two spherical meshes around the end effectors as seen in **Figure 4**. While our approach allows the use of arbitrary meshes[3], we chose spherical shapes for salient visualization and affordable computation of distances. The haptic interface will then render the generalized constraint forces as torques on the robot arms with regard to this updated model, effectively preventing any collisions between the end effectors and the rest of the system. To demonstrate the emerging collision avoidance behavior, an operator attempts to bring the end effectors into collision with each other and the main body of the PARTI system, while we record the shortest distance between the surfaces of the involved collision meshes during the motion. The compiled results in **Figure 5** confirm that our approach successfully prevented the intersection of collision geometries.

3.2 Digital Twin

The second experiment explores the physical fidelity of our digital twin. We compare our MuJoCo model of the Franka Emika Robot System as well as the Gazebo model, provided by Franka Emika, to

---

[1] Notice the Panda system, as well as, any other collaborative robot with joint-torque sensors have only be made available around 2017, the study of digital twins as dynamic proxies in model-mediated control applications is a recent development (cf. Mitra and Niemeyer (2007)), and MuJoCo was firstly made available in Todorov et al. (2012).

[2] www.mujoco.org

---

[3] MuJoCo uses the Minkowski Portal Refinement algorithm to detect collisions and as such requires convex meshes. However, non-convex geometries may be modelled by decomposing them into a union of convex geometries (Todorov et al., 2012)

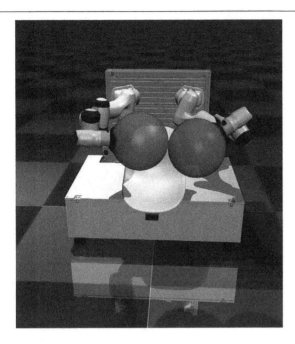

FIGURE 4 | Visualization of the digital twin of the PARTI system in MuJoCo (left) and the coupled real hardware (right) during the first experiment, where the operator actively attempts to bring the system into collision. The additional collision meshes around the end effectors to facilitate the collision avoidance behavior are seen in red.

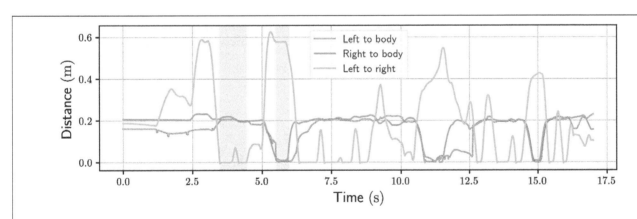

FIGURE 5 | Shortest distances between the collision surfaces of the PARTI system's left and right end effectors as well as the main body during the first experiment. The constraint forces from the simulator applied to the physical system prevent the collision meshes from intersecting, i.e. the distances remain greater or equal to 0. Note that the sections highlighted in grey mark active attempts by the operator to bring the respective bodies into collision.

the physical robot, which serves as a ground truth. For this purpose, we prepared a trajectory, which we taught kinesthetically using the PARTI system. The trajectory includes fast free motion as well as contacts with a solid plane below the base, which is perpendicular to the robot's first axis. We execute this trajectory using a task space PD control law with additional nullspace control running at a frequency of 1 kHz, which reads

$$\tau_d = J(q)^\top \left(K_d (x_d - x) - K_p \dot{x} \right) + K_{null} \left(I - J(q)^\top J(q)^{\top\dagger} \right) \left(q_{null,d} - q \right) \quad (4)$$

where $\tau_d \in \mathbb{R}^7$ is the control torque applied to the robot, $J(q) \in \mathbb{R}^{6\times7}$, $x_d \in \mathbb{R}^6$ and $\dot{x} \in \mathbb{R}^6$ are the end effector Jacobian,

pose, and twist respectively, $q \in \mathbb{R}^7$ are the joint positions, and $I \in \mathbb{R}^{7\times7}$ is the identity matrix. The trajectory is given to the controller as a list of Cartesian end effector poses $x_d \in \mathbb{R}^6$. The gain matrices $K_p, K_d \in \mathbb{R}^{6\times6}$ and $K_{null} \in \mathbb{R}^{7\times7}$ as well as the desired nullspace configuration $q_{null,d}$, which is equal to the initial joint positions[4], are identical across the experiments. We present the resulting end effector positions and external force estimates in **Figure 6** and a more detailed view of the model errors compared to the real hardware in **Figure 7**. The

_____
[4]The initial joint positions are chosen such that they have the largest distance to the joint limits

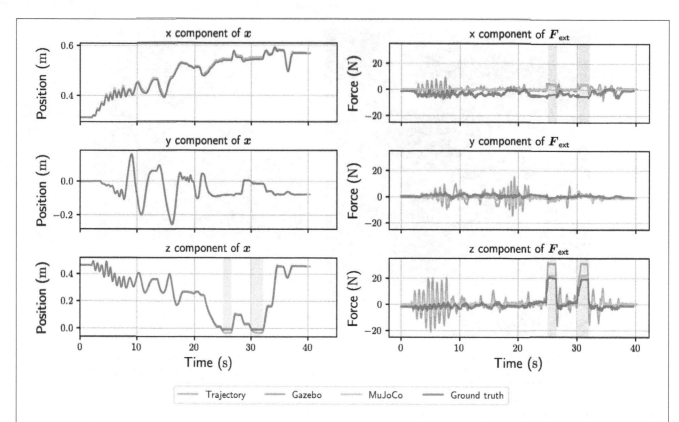

FIGURE 6 | The left column of graphs shows the resulting end effector positions as well as the tracked trajectory for the second experiment, while the right column displays the respective models' estimated external forces acting at the end effector during the same time period. All quantities are expressed relative to the robot's base frame. Periods of contact are highlighted by the grey vertical bars. Note that the robot is mounted 2 cm above the plane and contact is therefore established slightly below 0 on the z-axis while the reference trajectory reaches below the plane to facilitate solid contact wrenches given the controller's impedance.

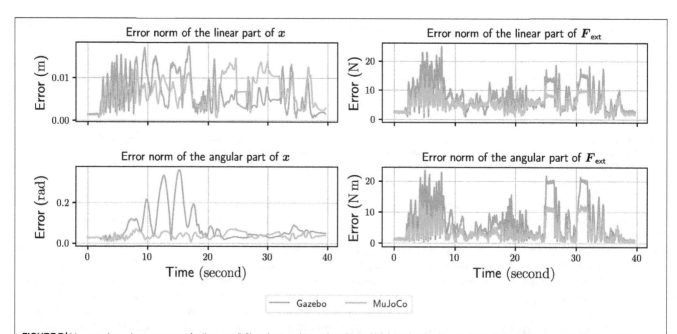

FIGURE 7 | Linear and angular error norms for the pose (left) and external wrench estimate (right) as observed in the second experiment. The model error of the Gazebo implementation is compared to the error of our own digital twin based on MuJoCo, where telemetry from the real system serves as ground truth.

robot shows some characteristics that are difficult to model due to the proprietary nature of the control and signal processing system. Especially the estimates for external wrenches show an offset and sensitivity to configuration and regions of the workspace (cf. Petrea et al. (2021)).

3.2.1 Gazebo Model

Franka Emika provides a simulation environment, which is well embedded in the ROS framework, granting the user all parameters for implementing custom control laws. Also the telemetry data for evaluation can be accessed easily. Within the ROS framework, we implement a simple ROS node, which *publishes* each point of the recorded trajectory. We then record the telemetry data with another node. Surprisingly, the Gazebo simulation behaved not as expected. The results diverged, both from the estimates provided by the MuJoCo environment and from the real system. The estimated forces showed a greater magnitude during movement and static contacts. A closer look to the code base revealed that it utilizes a type of *direct estimator* with further moving average filtering for computing external torques

$$\tau_{ext}^{(t)} = \tau_d^{(t)} - \tau_m^{(t)} + g(q^{(t)}),$$
$$\hat{\tau}_{ext}^{(t)} = \gamma \tau_{ext}^{(t)} + (1 - \gamma)\hat{\tau}_{ext}^{(t-1)} \tag{5}$$

where superscript (t) denotes the current timestep, and $\tau_{ext} \in \mathbb{R}^7$ and $\hat{\tau}_{ext} \in \mathbb{R}^7$ the estimated torque and the filtered torque estimate, respectively. $\tau_m \in \mathbb{R}^7$ represents the measured torque and $g(q) \in \mathbb{R}^7$ denotes the gravitational induced generalized forces. The filter parameter γ should be chosen such that $\gamma \in (0, 1]$. In order to get more insight to the simulation, we inquired Franka Emika. The main reason for employing the estimation, stems from the underlying ODE engine, which enforces constraints for each joint and therefore does not know the external torques in joint space.

The implemented *observer* resembling the *direct observer* (Haddadin et al., 2017) uses commanded torque signals generated by some control law, while neglecting inertia and coriolis/centrifugal terms. We assume that these approximations have an significant effect for the external torque estimates especially during free end effector motion. During the first 10 s of the traversed trajectory in **Figure 6**, the forces of the Gazebo environment are notably overestimated, most likely due to the uncompensated inertia terms.

3.2.2 MuJoCo Model

The kinematic and geometric properties of our digital twin for the MuJoCo simulation environment are based on information provided by the manufacturer, specifically the Denavit–Hartenberg parameters and the visual meshes for the robot links, respectively. For the dynamic model, i.e. the links' inertia tensors, mass and center of mass, and the friction in the joints, we use the parameters identified in Gaz et al. (2019). Mechatronic components like the motors, torque sensors, or the position encoders in the joints are modelled using MuJoCo's equivalent native components. Given these definitions, the simulator's computational engine provides us with the

necessary dynamic model quantities for robot control, such as the Jacobian matrix for all the bodies, Coriolis and gravity forces, and inertia in generalized coordinates. While we can retrieve the generalized constraint forces from MuJoCo to numerical precision, we opted to implement a momentum observer for estimating the external torque at the joints τ_{ext} to more closely model the behavior of the real robot (cf. Haddadin et al. (2017)). Given the definition of the robot's momentum p as

$$p = M(q)\dot{q}, \tag{6}$$

the external torques can be estimated as

$$\hat{\tau}_{ext} = K_O\left(p(t) - \int_0^t \tau_m - \left(g(q) + c(q, \dot{q}) - \dot{M}(q)\dot{q} + \hat{\tau}_{ext}\right)ds - p(0)\right) \tag{7}$$

where $\tau_m, c(q, \dot{q}), g(q) \in \mathbb{R}^7$ are the applied motor force, centrifugal and Coriolis forces, and gravity force, respectively, as computed by MuJoCo in the robot's generalized coordinates, and $K_O = \text{diag}\{k_{O,i}\} > 0$ is the observer's gain matrix. Additionally, we compute $\dot{q}$ numerically using the Euler method for the observer instead, as joint velocities are not directly measured by the robot. The estimated external wrench acting at the end effector is then simply computed as

$$F_{ext} = J(q)\tau_{ext}. \tag{8}$$

This estimate shares characteristics with the ground truth, such as a high frequency but low magnitude noise and sensitivity to robot movements, while the estimated wrench corresponds well with the robot's own estimates during contacts (cf. **Figure 6**).

3.3 Two-Arm Teleoperation

This experiment demonstrates our system's versatility as a teleoperation station by controlling the digital twin of the robot humanoid GARMI in a contact-rich cooperative two-arm manipulation scenario. The task consists of lifting a box out of a socket and putting it inside a shelve with only small clearance (cf. **Figure 8**). During this task, the box is only held in place by the resulting friction due to the pressure exerted by the arms. The operator controls both arms independently using the two robot arms of the PARTI system and receives haptic force feedback for both. The virtual scene is graphically rendered in stereo from the perspective of the humanoid's head camera and displayed stereoscopically on the PARTI display to provide the operator with depth perception. For this experiment, we coupled the controlled velocity of the GARMI mobile base to the arms' displacements along the humanoid's sagittal axis [5]. This way, the operator can focus on the manipulation task without the additional mental load of having to explicitly control the robot's mobile drive system. We evaluated different control schemes to perform this task. First, we directly control the humanoid, i.e. we use the haptic interface introduced in

---

[5] We mapped the net displacement along the robot's saggital axis (the x axis in the robot base frame) of the end effectors relative to the initial pose to the mobile base velocity in x direction

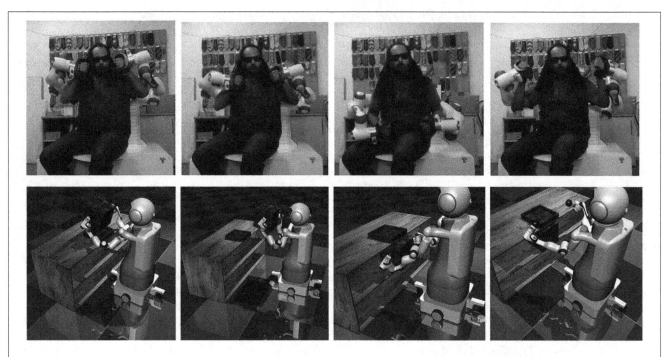

FIGURE 8 | Visualized sequence of the digital twin of GARMI (bottom row) and the coupled real PARTI system (top row) during the third experiment. The operator is tasked with lifting the box from its socket, which has a clearance of only 2 mm and putting it into the shelve below with a clearance of 2 cm.

Section 2.2 to connect the physical PARTI system to the digital twin of GARMI. This is possible as the systems were designed to have identical kinematic and dynamic configurations. We refer to this approach as model-mediated teleoperation (MMT), as the physical system interacts solely with a local representation of the remote environment and as such is not subject to communication delays (cf. Xu et al. (2016)). As an alternative approach, we implemented a more traditional bilateral position-force computed (PFC) architecture. Within this approach, the twists of the leader system's end effector are applied to the follower system, while estimated wrenches at the respective follower's end effectors are reflected as haptic force feedback. We complement this architecture with passivity controllers informed by energy observers to compensate for communication delays as introduced in Ryu and Preusche (2007). Our implementation of the latter method—commonly referred to as time domain passivity approach (TDPA)—uses a six degree of freedom two channel architecture for each arm. In total, our experiment consists of three teleoperator configurations, namely the MMT variant as well as the PFC architecture with and without TDPA and a round-trip delay of around 35 ms. For analysis, we compute the net external force of GARMI's end effectors and the relative transform between the end effectors over time as depicted in **Figure 9**.

4 DISCUSSION

The results of our experiments show the benefits of a model-mediated approach to robot control in various applications,

including scenarios with a human operator in the loop. The first experiment demonstrated how a simple change in the model can result in complex behavior, which can be transferred to the real hardware using the haptic interface. While the emerging collision avoidance behavior is useful in itself, it is worth noting that this approach allows us to focus on the physical modeling of a desired behavior without having to concern ourselves with the implementation of any controllers generating said behavior. We also showed that given identical dynamic parameters the behavior of our digital twin of the Franka Emika Robot System is closer to the real hardware than the provided Gazebo model, reinforcing our choice for MuJoCo as a simulator for model-mediated control. Finally, we demonstrated the advantage of using a model-mediated approach in teleoperation. Analysis shows that activity of the passivity controllers in TDPA results in small oscillations while the box is grasped. This can be explained by the fact that the pressure exerted by the arms on each other acts as an active disturbance, which in turn leads to dissipative action from the passivity controllers. While the arms remain stable, this small oscillation is enough to release the grasp of the box, leaving the operator unable to complete the task. In comparison, the grasp of the PFC architecture without active TDPA is more stable. However, the teleoperator quickly becomes unstable due to external disturbances such as contacts with the shelve. The MMT approach proved to be most successful for this task. Not only was the operator able to complete the task, but the system remained stable even during the challenging action of sliding the box into the shelve, which involves multiple contacts similar to the classical peg-in-hole problem of robotics.

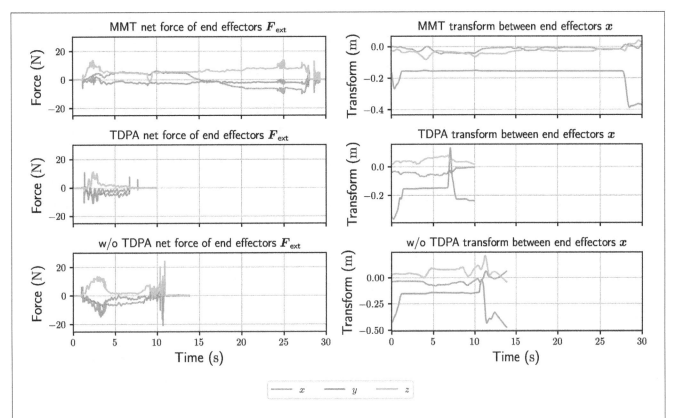

FIGURE 9 | The graphs in the left column show the net force of the estimated external wrenches acting on GARMI's end effectors during the teleoperatoin task of the third experiment. The column on the right displays graphs of the displacement between the end effectors. Note that the force and displacement induced by the grasp are primarily expressed around the y-axis of this experiment. The MMT method allowed for the successful completion of the task, while the oscillations and instability of the PFC architecuteres with and without TDPA respectively resulted in the grasp being released before the task could be completed.

5 CONCLUSION

We introduced the PARTI system, a multimodal teleoperation station, intended for teleoperation tasks under a hardware-in-the-loop framework for improved performance even in the presence of uncertainties and time delay. For the physics engine deployed in the HIL framework, experiments in virtual envrionment reveal that MuJoCo is advantageous for simulating kinematic chains during physical interaction as it enforces constraints in generalized coordinates. This in turn can be directly leveraged for self collision avoidance by designing collision meshes in simulation that enforce a certain safety margin. Furthermore, in a bimanual teleoperated manipulation task, we see that TDPA led to unstable system behaviour, emphasizing the model mediated teleoperation approach for future research. Since MuJoCo offers physical realism, we see our simulation environment as an ideal testbench for future research, including model-mediated teleoperation, system identification, and model-based/predictive control. The simulation can also serve as digital twin, providing an operator with additional information on the teleoperated system status in a human-understandable (visual) representation. For increasing the autonomy of the humanoid robot GARMI, the simulation might be potentially useful for kinesthetic teaching purposes. We also plan to incorporate VR in the near future, which will provide additional interaction options during teleoperation in tradeoff for situational awareness in the operators environment. We interpret a VR set as a minor restriction, since the operator is losing environmental awareness when wearing the head mounted display.

AUTHOR CONTRIBUTIONS

JE: Implemented the HIL and haptic interfaces, digital twins in MuJoCo, two-arm teleoperation and wrote the corresponding sections. GR: Implemented and ran the experiments for Gazebo. He wrote **Section 5**, **Section 3.2.1**, and **Section 2.1**. LF, AN, and UW: Supervised the study, provided feedback and wrote/edited the manuscript. SH: Contributed the idea and concept of PARTI and collected the funding to perform the study.

ACKNOWLEDGMENTS

We would like to thank Nicolas Zunhammer for his valuable contributions to earlier prototypes of the PARTI system and Franka Emika for their support in developing the hardware. We especially thank Xiao Xu, who provided us with valuable feedback for the manuscript. We gratefully acknowledge the funding of the Lighthouse Initiative Geriatronics by StMWi Bayern (Project X, grant no. IUK-1807-0007//IUK582/001).

REFERENCES

Balachandran, R., Kozlova, N., Ott, C., and Albu-Schäeffer, A. (2018). Non-Linear Local Force Feedback Control for Haptic Interfaces. *IFAC-PapersOnLine* 51, 486–492. doi:10.1016/j.ifacol.2018.11.587

Erez, T., Tassa, Y., and Todorov, E. (2015). "Simulation Tools for Model-Based Robotics: Comparison of Bullet, Havok, Mujoco, Ode and Physx," in 2015 IEEE international conference on robotics and automation (ICRA), Seattle, WA, USA, May 26–30, 2015 (IEEE), 4397–4404. doi:10.1109/icra.2015.7139807

Gaz, C., Cognetti, M., Oliva, A., Robuffo Giordano, P., and De Luca, A. (2019). Dynamic Identification of the Franka Emika Panda Robot with Retrieval of Feasible Parameters Using Penalty-Based Optimization. *IEEE Robot. Autom. Lett.* 4, 4147–4154. doi:10.1109/LRA.2019.2931248

Haddadin, S., De Luca, A., and Albu-Schäffer, A. (2017). Robot Collisions: A Survey on Detection, Isolation, and Identification. *IEEE Trans. Robot.* 33, 1292–1312. doi:10.1109/TRO.2017.2723903

Hulin, T., Hertkorn, K., Kremer, P., Schätzle, S., Artigas, J., Sagardia, M., et al. (2011). "The Dlr Bimanual Haptic Device with Optimized Workspace," in 2011 IEEE International Conference on Robotics and Automation, Shanghai, China, May 9–13, 2011, 3441–3442. doi:10.1109/ICRA.2011.5980066

Kirschner, R. J., Kurdas, A., Karacan, K., Junge, P., Baradaran Birjandi, S. A., Mansfeld, N., et al. (2021). "Towards a Reference Framework for Tactile Robot Performance and Safety Benchmarking," in 2021 IEEE/RSJ International Conference on Intelligent Robots and Systems (IROS), Prague, Czech Republic, September 27–October 1, 2021, 4290–4297. doi:10.1109/IROS51168.2021.9636329

Li, X., He, B., Wang, Z., Zhou, Y., Li, G., and Jiang, R. (2021). Semantic-Enhanced Digital Twin System for Robot-Environment Interaction Monitoring. *IEEE Trans. Instrum. Meas.* 70, 1–13. doi:10.1109/TIM.2021.3066542

Mitra, P., and Niemeyer, G. (2007). Haptic Simulation of Manipulator Collisions Using Dynamic Proxies. *Presence Teleoperators Virtual Environ.* 16, 367–384. doi:10.1162/pres.16.4.367

Ni, D., Song, A., Xu, X., Li, H., Zhu, C., and Zeng, H. (2017). 3d-point-cloud Registration and Real-World Dynamic Modelling-Based Virtual Environment Building Method for Teleoperation. *Robotica* 35, 1958–1974. doi:10.1017/S0263574716000631

Petrea, R. A. B., Bertoni, M., and Oboe, R. (2021). "On the Interaction Force Sensing Accuracy of Franka Emika Panda Robot," in IECON 2021 – 47th Annual Conference of the IEEE Industrial Electronics Society, Toronto, ON, Canada, October 13–16, 2021, 1–6. doi:10.1109/IECON48115.2021.9589424

Ryu, J.-H., and Preusche, C. (2007). "Stable Bilateral Control of Teleoperators under Time-Varying Communication Delay: Time Domain Passivity Approach," in Proceedings 2007 IEEE international conference on robotics and automation, Rome, Italy, April 10–14, 2007 (IEEE), 3508–3513. doi:10.1109/robot.2007.364015

Sagardia, M., Hulin, T., Hertkorn, K., Kremer, P., and Schätzle, S. (2016). "A Platform for Bimanual Virtual Assembly Training with Haptic Feedback in Large Multi-Object Environments," in Proceedings of the 22nd ACM Conference on Virtual Reality Software and Technology, Munich, November 2–4, 153–162. doi:10.1145/2993369.2993386

Schwarz, M., Lenz, C., Rochow, A., Schreiber, M., and Behnke, S. (2021). "Nimbro Avatar: Interactive Immersive Telepresence with Force-Feedback Telemanipulation," in 2021 IEEE/RSJ International Conference on Intelligent Robots and Systems (IROS), Prague, Czech Republic, September 27–October 1, 2021, 5312–5319. doi:10.1109/IROS51168.2021.9636191

Todorov, E., Erez, T., and Tassa, Y. (2012). "Mujoco: A Physics Engine for Model-Based Control," in 2012 IEEE/RSJ International Conference on Intelligent Robots and Systems, Vilamoura-Algarve, Portugal, October 7–12, 2012 (IEEE), 5026–5033. doi:10.1109/iros.2012.6386109

Todorov, E. (2014). "Convex and Analytically-Invertible Dynamics with Contacts and Constraints: Theory and Implementation in Mujoco," in 2014 IEEE International Conference on Robotics and Automation (ICRA), Hong Kong, China, May 31–June 7, 2014 (IEEE), 6054–6061. doi:10.1109/icra.2014.6907751

Tröbinger, M., Jähne, C., Qu, Z., Elsner, J., Reindl, A., Getz, S., et al. (2021). Introducing GARMI - A Service Robotics Platform to Support the Elderly at Home: Design Philosophy, System Overview and First Results. *IEEE Robot. Autom. Lett.* 6, 5857–5864. doi:10.1109/lra.2021.3082012

Valenzuela-Urrutia, D., Muñoz-Riffo, R., and Ruiz-del-Solar, J. (2019). Virtual Reality-Based Time-Delayed Haptic Teleoperation Using Point Cloud Data. *J. Intell. Robot. Syst.* 96, 387–400. doi:10.1007/s10846-019-00988-1

Xu, X., Cizmeci, B., Schuwerk, C., and Steinbach, E. (2016). Model-mediated Teleoperation: Toward Stable and Transparent Teleoperation Systems. *IEEE Access* 4, 425–449. doi:10.1109/access.2016.2517926

6

Novel Neurostimulation-Based Haptic Feedback Platform for Grasp Interactions with Virtual Objects

Aliyah K. Shell, Andres E. Pena*, James J. Abbas and Ranu Jung

Adaptive Neural Systems Laboratory, Department of Biomedical Engineering and the Institute for Integrative and Innovative Research, University of Arkansas, Fayetteville, AR, United States

*Correspondence:
Andres E. Pena
andresp@uark.edu

Haptic perception is a vital part of the human experience that enriches our engagement with the world, but the ability to provide haptic information in virtual reality (VR) environments is limited. Neurostimulation-based sensory feedback has the potential to enhance the immersive experience within VR environments by supplying relevant and intuitive haptic feedback related to interactions with virtual objects. Such feedback may contribute to an increase in the sense of presence and realism in VR and may contribute to the improvement of virtual reality simulations for future VR applications. This work developed and evaluated xTouch, a neuro-haptic platform that extends the sense of touch to virtual environments. xTouch is capable of tracking a user's grasp and manipulation interactions with virtual objects and delivering haptic feedback based on the resulting grasp forces. Seven study participants received haptic feedback delivered via multi-channel transcutaneous electrical stimulation of the median nerve at the wrist to receive the haptic feedback. xTouch delivered different percept intensity profiles designed to emulate grasp forces during manipulation of objects of different sizes and compliance. The results of a virtual object classification task showed that the participants were able to use the active haptic feedback to discriminate the size and compliance of six virtual objects with success rates significantly better than the chance of guessing it correctly ($63.9 \pm 11.5\%$, chance $= 16.7\%$, $p < 0.001$). We demonstrate that the platform can reliably convey interpretable information about the physical characteristics of virtual objects without the use of hand-mounted devices that would restrict finger mobility. Thus, by offering an immersive virtual experience, xTouch may facilitate a greater sense of belonging in virtual worlds.

Keywords: non-invasive electrical stimulation, peripheral nerve stimulation, transcutaneous electrical stimulation, haptic feedback, neuromodulation, virtual interaction, neuro-haptics

1 INTRODUCTION

The ability to navigate the tactile world we live in through haptic perception provides us with an experience that facilitates engagement with our surrounding environment. Haptic cues allow us to interpret physical properties of our surroundings and use the knowledge in unison with other senses to formulate interactive approaches with objects in our environment. We also use haptics to form a sense of connectedness with our physical environment, which includes other living organisms such as pets and plants as well as with other human beings. Social distancing conditions such as those imposed by a pandemic limit social haptics and interpersonal interactions. As we shift towards more virtual settings and remote operations (e.g., Metaverse (Dionisio et al., 2013; Mystakidis, 2022)), we risk losing the sense of connection we receive through touch. The lack of haptic feedback in the virtual reality (VR) environment prevents full interaction with the virtual environment which can have limiting effects on immersion and user connection (Price et al., 2021). Including haptic feedback in the VR environment may allow more meaningful interactions in the virtual world, which can have implications for stronger user engagement and task performance.

Typically, VR environments are limited to providing the user with an audio-visual experience. The addition of haptic feedback could enhance the sensorial experience by allowing users to navigate the virtual environment through the sense of touch (Preusche and Hirzinger, 2007). Haptic feedback has been delivered to users in a virtual environment through several types of haptic interfaces, with the most common being handheld and wearable devices. Handheld devices most commonly integrate vibrotactile actuators into handheld controllers to track and simulate hand movements. Handheld devices such the Haptic Revolver (Whitmire et al., 2018) provide users with the experience of touch, shear forces and motion in the virtual environment by using an interchangeable actuated wheel underneath the fingertip that spins and moves up and down to render various haptic sensations. Other handheld devices such as the CLAW (Choi et al., 2018) provide kinesthetic and cutaneous haptic feedback while grasping virtual objects. While functional and easy to mount, these devices occupy the hands and fail to consider the role our fingers play in our ability to dexterously manipulate and interact with objects in virtual environments.

On the other hand, wearable haptic systems (Pacchierotti et al., 2017; Yem and Kajimoto, 2017) provide feedback to the hand and fingertips through hand-mounted actuators. These technologies can take the form of exoskeletons (Hinchet et al., 2018; Wang et al., 2019) and fingertip devices (Maereg et al., 2017; Yem and Kajimoto, 2017) to provide cutaneous and/or kinesthetic feedback to the hands while allowing dexterous movement of the fingers. Wearable devices such as the Grabity (Choi et al., 2017) simulate the grasping and weight of virtual objects by providing vibrotactile feedback and weight force feedback during lifting. Maereg et al. developed a fingertip haptic device which allows users to discriminate stiffness during virtual interactions. While these devices may be cost-effective and wireless with good mounting stability, these wearable systems are often bulky, cumbersome and limit user mobility.

Consideration has also been given to the use of non-invasive sensory substitution techniques such as mechanical (Colella et al., 2019; Pezent et al., 2019) and electro-tactile (Hummel et al., 2016; Kourtesis et al., 2021; Vizcay et al., 2021) stimulation, which activate cutaneous receptors in the user's skin, to convey information about touch and grasping actions in virtual environments. But these approaches are not intuitive, can restrict finger mobility if mounted on the hands or fingers, and often require remapping and learning due to percept modality and location mismatch. A non-restrictive wearable haptic system that is capable of providing relevant and intuitive feedback to facilitate user interaction with virtual environments or remote systems may address these shortcomings.

We explored the use of ExtendedTouch (xTouch), a novel Neuro-Haptics Feedback Platform, to enable meaningful interactions with virtual environments. xTouch utilizes transcutaneous electrical nerve stimulation (TENS), a non-invasive approach that targets the sensory pathways in peripheral nerves to evoke distally-referred sensations in the areas innervated by those nerves (Jones and Johnson, 2009). TENS has previously been combined with VR as an intervention for treating neuropathic pain (Preatoni et al., 2021) and as a tool to reduce spatial disorientation in a VR-based motion task for flying (Yang et al., 2012). Outside of VR applications, TENS of the peripheral nerves is frequently used in prostheses research to convey sensations from prosthetic hands about hand grasp force (D'Anna et al., 2017) and physical object characteristics (Vargas et al., 2020). D'Anna et al. showed that prosthesis users were able to feel distally-referred sensations in their phantom hand with TENS at the residual median and ulnar nerves and that they were able to use the information to perceive stimulation profiles designed to emulate the sensations felt during manipulation of objects with varying shapes and compliances. However, with their stimulation approach localized sensations in the region of the electrode were found to increase with increasing current, which can be distracting and irritable to the user, thereby restricting the discernability of distinct object characteristics. On the contrary, xTouch implements a novel stimulation strategy that was previously developed by Pena et al. (2021), which has been shown to elicit intuitive distally-referred tactile percepts without the localized discomfort associated with conventional transcutaneous stimulation methods (Li et al., 2017; Stephens-Fripp et al., 2018). With this approach, peripheral nerves can be activated by delivering electrical stimuli from surface electrodes placed proximal to the hand (i.e., the wrist). This means that haptic feedback can be provided to the hand and fingers without restrictive finger-mounted hardware, allowing for enhanced manipulation and movement.

In this work, we aimed to investigate the capabilities of xTouch to deliver interpretable information about the physical characteristics of virtual objects. xTouch integrates contactless motion tracking of the hand with a custom software program to calculate grasp forces and deliver haptic feedback related to interactions with virtual objects. The objective of this study was to evaluate the extent to which haptic feedback provided by this platform enables users to classify virtual objects by their size and compliance. We also evaluated the capability of the xTouch to provide a wide range of intensities users could perceive as they manipulated the object. We hypothesized that participants would be able to characterize the size and compliance of virtual objects and classify them with success rates significantly better than the chance of guessing them correctly. A haptic interface that could provide such information during virtual object interactions would have the potential to improve remote work engagement, telepresence and social haptics, and object manipulation during teleoperation.

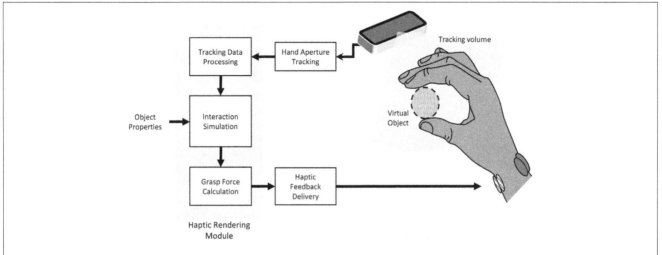

FIGURE 1 | xTouch: a neuro-haptic feedback platform for virtual object interaction. During virtual object exploration, measurements of hand aperture are used by a haptic rendering module with information from an object properties database to calculate forces resulting from user interaction. The haptic feedback profiles are mapped to determine parameters of the stimulation delivered by the neurostimulation system.

2 METHODS

2.1 Participants

Written informed consent was obtained from seven right-handed adult study participants (five males, two females, mean age ±SD: 24.6 ± 3.0) in compliance with the Institutional Review Board of Florida International University (FIU) which approved this study protocol. All prospective study participants were screened prior to the study to determine eligibility. All participants were able-bodied, with no sensory disorders or any self-reported condition listed as a contraindication for transcutaneous electrical stimulation (pregnancy, epilepsy, lymphedema, and or cardiac pacemaker) (Rennie, 2010).

2.1.1 Sample Size Justification

An a priori power analysis was conducted on preliminary data obtained in a pilot study (Pena, 2020) to determine the effective sample size for this study at $\alpha = 0.05$ and $\beta = 0.2$. The pilot study indicated that a sample size of four was sufficient to determine if subjects could identify the virtual objects at rates significantly better than chance (16.7%). To account for participant errors and potential censor data, seven participants were recruited.

2.2 xTouch: A Neuro-Haptic Feedback Platform for Interacting With Virtual Objects

The xTouch haptic feedback platform (**Figure 1**) has three functional blocks: contactless motion capture to track the hand as user's interact with a virtual environment, a haptic rendering module to generate haptic feedback profiles based on calculated forces resulting from user interaction with virtual objects, and non-invasive peripheral nerve stimulation via surface electrodes on the wrist, to deliver the haptic feedback profiles (Jung and Pena, 2021; Pena et al., 2021).

Contactless motion tracking was performed using a Leap Motion Controller (Ultraleap, Mountain View CA United States), a video-based hand-tracking unit. The hand aperture tracker was used to capture the movements of the right hand during the virtual object classification studies. The computational module consisted of a custom MATLAB® program (v2020b, MathWorks® Inc., Natick, MA) interfaced with the Leap software (Orion 3.2.1 SDK) and was used to process the tracking data and determine hand aperture distance by calculating the linear distance between the thumb pad and the average of the index, middle, and ring finger pad locations (**Figure 2C**). This distance was used to determine virtual object contact, compute the resulting interaction forces, and generate haptic feedback profiles matching the virtual interaction. The MATLAB® program was also interfaced with a custom stimulation control module, developed on the Synapse Software (version 96, Tucker-Davis Technologies (TDT), Alachua FL United States), and running on the TDT RZ5D base processor. This enabled real-time modulation of electrical stimulation parameters based on the haptic feedback profiles.

Electrical stimulation was delivered transcutaneously through four small self-adhesive hydrogel electrodes (Rhythmlink International LLC, Columbia, SC) strategically located around the participant's right wrist to activate their median nerve sensory fibers. Two small stimulating electrodes (15 × 20 mm) were placed on the ventral aspect of the wrist and two large return electrodes (20 × 25 mm) were placed on the opposite (dorsal) side. An optically isolated, multi-channel bio-stimulator (TDT IZ2-16H, Tucker-Davis Technologies, Alachua FL United States) was used to deliver charge-balanced, current-controlled biphasic rectangular pulses following the channel-hopping interleaved pulse scheduling (CHIPS) strategy (Pena et al., 2021). The interleaved current pulses delivered in CHIPS produce electric field profiles that activate underlying nerve fibers without activating those close to the surface of the skin, thus eliciting

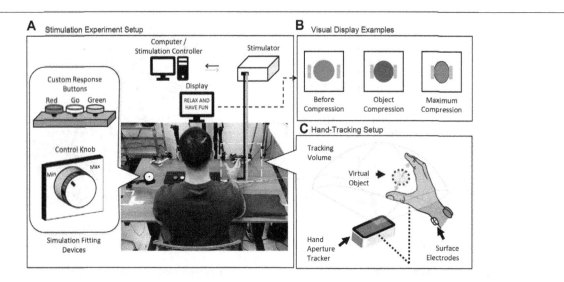

FIGURE 2 | Schematics of the experimental setup for stimulation parameter fitting and virtual object classification task. **(A)** During the stimulation parameter fitting procedure, custom response buttons and a control knob were used. **(B)** During practice trials, the visual display was used to show changes in compression of the object as hand aperture changed. **(C)** The hand aperture tracker (Leap Motion Controller) was placed on the right side of the table.

comfortable referred sensations in the hand while avoiding localized discomfort near the electrodes.

2.3 Experimental Design
2.3.1 Experimental Setup
Study participants sat in a chair with their arms resting on a table facing a computer monitor used for displaying instructions (**Figure 2**). The right forearm rested on an elevated support pad with the hand resting on the ulnar side. Electrodes were placed around the right wrist using the approach described by Pena et al. (2021) to find the electrode locations that elicited distal percepts for each channel. Participants used custom response buttons to provide percept responses, and a control knob to explore different stimulation parameters during the stimulation fitting procedure. The hand aperture tracker was placed on the right side of table. A computer monitor was placed on the table to display task instructions.

2.3.2 Experimental Procedure
2.3.2.1 Stimulation Parameter Fitting
A participant-controlled calibration routine was utilized to streamline the stimulation parameter fitting process. Strength-duration (SD) profiles were derived using the Lapicque-Weiss's theoretical model (Weiss, 1901; Lapicque, 1909). After comfortable placement of the electrodes, pulse amplitude (PA) thresholds were obtained from all participants at five different pulse width (PW) values (300–700 µs, at 100 µs intervals) in randomized order (Forst et al., 2015). Participants interacted with a custom MATLAB® interface designed to control the delivery of electrical stimuli and collect the participant's responses. The "Go" button was pressed to trigger the delivery of a pulse train with a constant 5 Hz pulse frequency (PF). To find the lowest possible current pulse amplitude that evoked a percept, perception threshold (PA_{th}), participants adjusted the PA (from 0

to 3000 µA) using the custom control knob. Throughout this study, the stimulation PA was set to 50% above the percept threshold ($1.5 \times PA_{th}$) at a PW of 500 µs This duration was selected to allow for a wide range of PW to be used at this PA, as it lays beyond the nonlinear region of the SD profile.

A similar participant-controlled calibration routine was implemented to determine the lower and upper limits for the operating ranges of PW and PF at $1.5 \times PA_{th}$ using the custom control knob. First, stimulation was delivered at a fixed PF of 100 Hz while participants explored a wide range of PW (from 100 to 800 µs) to find the lowest possible level that evoked a reliable percept, and the highest possible level that did not cause discomfort. From pilot studies, 100 Hz was determined as a frequency that lied between the fusion and saturation points for most participants, therefore it was chosen as the test PF value so that participants did not feel pulsating stimulation and focused on the PW range. Next, the stimulation PW was set to the midpoint of the recently obtained PW range, and the participants used the knob to explore a wide range of PF (from 30 to 300 Hz) to find the lowest possible frequency that was not perceived as pulsating (fusion), and the level at which the perceived stimulation intensity did not change (saturation).

The activation charge rate (ACR) model (Graczyk et al., 2016) was used to predict the perceived intensity as a combination of PF and charge per pulse (Q). The ACR model was found to be a strong predictor for graded intensity perception during extraneural neurostimulation with cuff electrodes (Graczyk et al., 2016), and during pilot studies with transcutaneous neurostimulation. PW and PF were adjusted simultaneously along their operating ranges to modulate activation charge-rate and convey a wide range of graded percept intensities. For each participant, the pulse charge at perception threshold (Q_{th}) was derived from their SD profile and was used with the ACR model ($ACR=(Q - Qth) \times PF$ where $Q = PA \times PW$) to calculate the equivalent ACR range values that would result from each PF and PW adjustment.

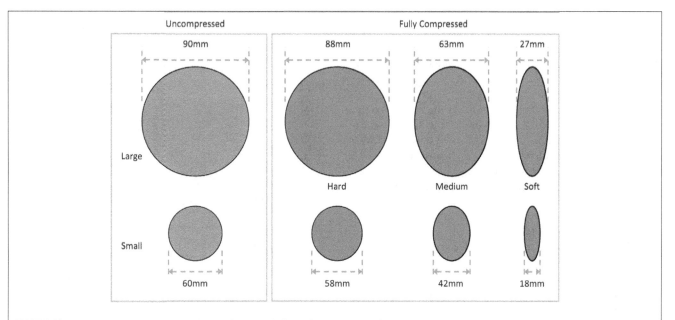

FIGURE 3 | Virtual object profiles used during the classification task. Six profiles were created from combinations of two sizes and three compliance levels. The maximum compression distance of each object, which is dependent on the compliance of the object, is presented.

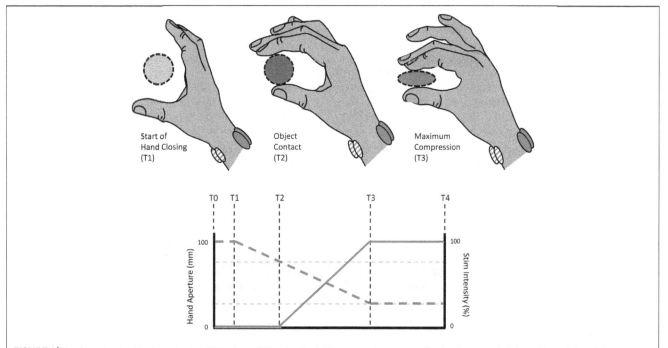

FIGURE 4 | Hand aperture tracking from the start (T0) to the end (T4) of a virtual object exploration attempt. The hand aperture (red dashed trace; left y-axis) was tracked during exploration to determine when the hand made contact with the object (T2) up to the maximum compression of the object (T3). The hand aperture data was used to estimate the resulting grasping force as the user interacted with the object (blue solid trace; right y-axis). The full compressive range of the virtual object (shaded region) was linearly mapped to the full range of stimulation intensities.

2.3.2.2 Magnitude Estimation Task

Magnitude estimation tasks were performed to assess the span of evoked percept intensities perceived within the ACR range. This task followed a protocol consistent with the one used during the extraneural neurostimulation study with the ACR model (Graczyk et al., 2016). For each magnitude estimation trial, a 1-second-long stimulation burst was delivered, and the participant was asked to state a number that represented the perceived intensity or magnitude of the evoked sensation by comparing it with the previous burst. Each burst was calculated using the ACR model, while varying the PF and PW parameters over the ranges collected in the fitting procedure. An open-ended scale was used to allow relative comparison of the perceived strength levels. For example, if one stimulus felt twice or half as intense as the previous one, it could be given a score that is half or twice as large (Stevens, 1956; Banks and Coleman, 1981). A score of 0 was used when no sensation was perceived. All participants completed 3 experimental blocks, each consisting of 10 randomized trials. Ratings were normalized by dividing the values by the grand mean rating on their respective blocks.

2.3.2.3 Virtual Object Classification

Virtual object classification tasks were performed to test the ability to distinguish different percept intensity profiles designed to emulate grasping forces during manipulation of various objects of different physical characteristics. Six unique virtual object profiles were created from all possible combinations of 2 sizes (small, large) and 3 compliance levels (soft, medium, and hard) (**Figure 3**).

Virtual object grasping trials began with the participant's right hand placed within the hand aperture tracking space as shown in **Figure 2C**, and open to an aperture greater than 100 mm. Once the hand was detected in place, participants were instructed to slowly close their hand until they began to perceive the stimulation, indicating they had contacted the virtual object (i.e., their hand aperture was equal or less than the uncompressed size of the virtual object). The participants explored the compressive range of the object by "squeezing" it and paying attention to how the resulting percept intensity changed (**Figure 4**). For instance, squeezing a hard object would ramp up the grasp force faster than a more compressible, softer object. Based on the compressive ranges shown in **Figure 3**, the rate of intensity changes for large-medium and large-soft objects were 3.7%/mm and 1.6%/mm respectively, while small-medium and small-soft objects had rates of 5.6%/mm and 2.4%/mm, respectively. For hard objects, the stimulation parameters were increased over 2 mm of compression, allowing for a rapid increase in percept intensity at a rate of 50%/mm. To indicate size, percepts were initiated at greater hand apertures for large objects relative to small objects. If the hand went beyond the object's maximum compression limit, breakage of the object was emulated by cutting off stimulation. Object exploration after breakage restarted when the hand reopened to an aperture greater than 100 mm. For all virtual grasp trials, participants were blindfolded to prevent the use of visual feedback of hand aperture. A 60 s limit was enforced for each grasp trial, with no restrictions on the number of times the hand could be opened and closed. Participants then verbally reported the perceived size and compliance of the virtual object. For example, if the perceived object was a small and hard object, they would state, "small and hard".

A practice block was presented at the onset of the experiment to introduce and allow participants to become familiar with each unique profile. Participants were instructed

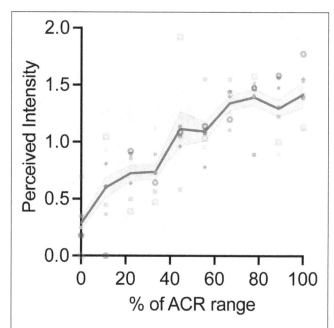

FIGURE 5 | A wide range of intensities were perceived by all participants. The individual markers represent the percept intensities reported by each participant across the chosen ACR range, normalized to the grand mean rating of their respective blocks. The solid blue line and blue shade represent the average of the normalized perceived intensities and SEM respectively, across all participants.

to pay attention to the hand aperture at which the percept began and the rate at which the intensity increased, indicating that contact was made with the object and the compliance of the object, respectively. The practice block included a 2D virtual interactive display as shown in **Figure 2B**, to provide participants with a visualization of the object during exploration. The purpose of this practice phase was to induce learning so that the participants felt confident enough to be able to identify the profiles without visual feedback. There were no time constraints for exploration or limits to the number of presentations of the objects in this phase. Participants then completed 2 experimental blocks of 18 non-repeating, randomized grasp trials each (6 repetitions per profile), resulting in a total of 36 double-blinded presentations. The virtual object profile that was presented was compared to the participant's response for each trial. The performance measure was the frequency of correct responses. Throughout the experiment, they were encouraged to stretch during breaks and frequently asked about their comfort levels or if additional breaks were needed after each task to prevent discomfort.

2.3.3 Statistical Analysis

One-sample t-tests at significance level 0.05 were performed to determine if the success rate of identifying the virtual object profile was significantly greater than chance. The chance of correctly identifying the object size or compliance alone was 50 and 33.3% respectively, while the chance of correctly identifying size and compliance together was 16.7%. The

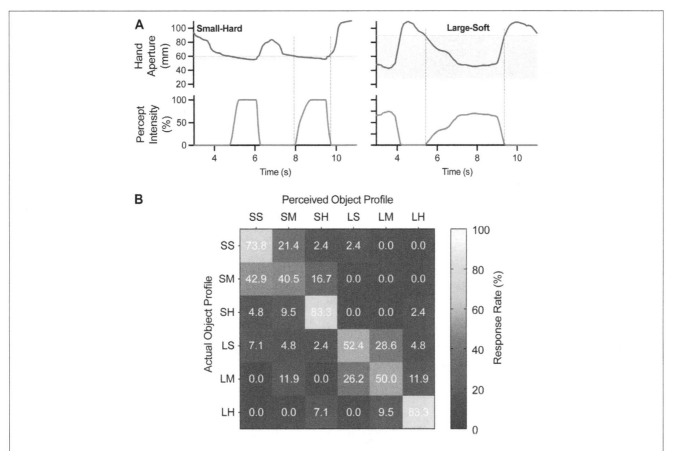

FIGURE 6 | Feedback of grasp force profiles enables identification of virtual object size and compliance. **(A)** Example of hand aperture (blue) and virtual grasp force profile (red) traces when grasping a Small-Hard object (left) and a Large-Soft object (right). The shaded regions represent the compressive range of the object. **(B)** Confusion matrix quantifying the perceived size and compliance combined (left-right), in relation with the presented profile (up-down) across 36 trials per participant. Each block represents the frequency of responses provided by all participants when they were presented with a profile (actual) and classified it (perceived). The first letter indicates the size (small/large) and the second letter indicates the compliance (soft/medium/hard). Successful identification of both size and compliance (diagonal) by chance is 16.7%.

perceived intensity as a function of charge-rate is presented for all participants. A post-hoc test was conducted to assess the statistical power achieved.

3 RESULTS

For all seven participants, comfortable distally referred sensations were evoked in the general areas of the hand innervated by the sensory fibers in the median nerve (palmar surface, index, middle, and part of the ring finger). The participant-controlled calibration routine allowed participants to select appropriate stimulation amplitude levels and operating ranges for PW and PF. No local sensations or side effects like irritation or redness of the skin were observed in any of the participants.

3.1 Participants Perceived a Wide Range of Intensities

Participants reported an operating range for PW spanning from (mean ± SD) 360 ± 70 μs to 550 ± 100 μs, while the operating

range for PF spanned from 73.9 ± 35.1 Hz (fusion) to 213.6 ± 65.1 Hz (saturation). Intensity ratings given by the participants were normalized to the grand mean of their respective blocks for comparison. **Figure 5** shows the normalized perceived intensity range as a function of the ACR range used for each participant.

3.2 Virtual Objects Were Successfully Classified by Their Size and Compliance With Haptic Feedback From xTouch

Participants were able to integrate percept intensity information delivered by xTouch as they grasped virtual objects (**Figure 6A**) to successfully determine their size and compliance, (**Figure 6B**). Most participants spent an average of 8 min exploring and learning cues for the different virtual objects during the practice block. The most one participant spent in this block was 16 min. During an experimental session, each of six virtual object profiles were presented six times, for 36 double-blinded presentations. Participants were able to differentiate between large and small objects with an average success rate (mean ± SD) of 93.7 ± 7.6%, $p < 0.001$. Participants successfully classified

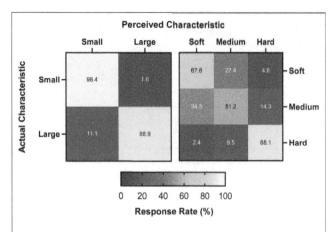

Perceived Characteristic

FIGURE 7 | Frequency of classifying objects by their size independent of compliance or compliance independent of size. All classification combinations of size and compliance were assessed, with 4 and 9 possible combinations of classification in size (left) and compliance (right), respectively. Successful identification of size or compliance by chance are 50% and 33%, respectively.

virtual objects by their compliance with success rates significantly greater than chance for large objects (70.6 ± 10.0%, $p < 0.001$) and small objects (67.5 ± 14.9%, $p < 0.001$). Participants were most successful in identifying Small-Hard and Large-Hard objects (**Figure 6B**).

On average, participants were more successful in classifying some virtual object characteristics more frequently than other characteristics. Participants were most successful in identifying hard objects (88.1 ± 13.5%) and small objects (98.4 ± 4.2%) (**Figure 7**). Overall participants identified both the size and compliance of objects together with success rates significantly better than chance (63.9 ± 11.5%, $p < 0.001$).

The response rates for identifying both size and compliance of the virtual object correctly were utilized to perform a post-hoc power analysis. Results of the analysis indicated that the effect size ($d = 4.11$) is large, giving a low Type II error ($\beta < 0.01$) and high statistical power. This suggests that the sample size of seven participants is sufficient to detect an effect.

4 DISCUSSION

This study sought to evaluate the extent to which a novel neuro-haptic feedback platform enables users to classify virtual objects by their size and compliance. Study participants received relevant and intuitive haptic feedback based on virtual grasping actions, facilitated by a novel stimulation strategy that evoked comfortable sensations in the hand, with a wide range of graded intensities. This study demonstrates that this platform can facilitate feedback with virtual objects that are interpretable by users. The integration of xTouch with the visual and auditory feedback provided through current VR systems can improve the realism of the simulation, which can enhance immersion and user experience in the simulation.

Similar to the reports in Pena et al., 2021, participants subjectively reported sensations in the hand regions innervated by the median nerve. To ensure congruency, the electrodes were adjusted as needed at the beginning of the experiment until the reported percept areas included the fingertips. After the participant-controlled calibration procedures, a magnitude estimation task was performed to identify the perceived ranges of intensity. Modulation of charge-rate was accomplished along the participant-calibrated operating ranges by adjusting pulse width and pulse frequency simultaneously. Generally, participants perceived greater intensities with increasing ACR (**Figure 5**), showing that several discriminable levels of intensities were perceivable within the ACR range. These different levels of intensity are also likely to be usable for conveying information about different object characteristics. Therefore, the full compressive range of each unique virtual object was linearly mapped to the full range of percept intensities.

The grasping action performed while exploring the object's characteristics was guided by the feedback received from xTouch. The object's full compressive range contained the full range of percept intensities, which encoded the size and compliance of different virtual objects by the intensity of the percepts during changes in the grasping action. When exploring the full compressive range of a soft or medium compliance object, participants typically reversed course and began to open the hand (**Figure 6A**), suggesting that they perceived the object as fully compressed. Participants were allowed to squeeze the virtual object as many times as needed to identify the perceived size and compliance.

Participants successfully recognized virtual objects by their size and compliance combined about 64% of the time, indicating that they were able to distinguish the virtual object profiles through the haptic feedback they received. Object compliance was recognized correctly in about 70% of the trials using the xTouch. These results are better than those obtained to correctly classify objects of three compliances (60% accuracy) using traditional TENS (D'Anna et al., 2017) or to classify objects with four compliances (60% accuracy) when using vibrotactile feedback (Witteveen et al., 2014). Our results suggest that the xTouch system can provide interpretable information on the compliance of virtual objects which users can accurately identify better than other haptic feedback methods.

To achieve the best precision with the Leap Motion Controller, routine maintenance was performed to ensure the sensor was properly calibrated and that the sensor surface was clean. The Leap software version used (Orion 3.2.1 SDK) featured improved hand reconstruction and tracking stability over previous versions. To further reduce tracking error, participants were instructed to close the hand slowly while keeping the hand at a fixed distance from the sensor. Whether hand-closing speed may have played a role in classification performance is unclear. During preliminary performance testing, we observed end-point tracking errors that were <5 mm under more dynamic conditions (worst-case) than the conditions tested in this study.

The highest percentages of misclassification were due to incorrect perception of compliance. The differences in object compliance were determined by several factors, including the compression distances and the rate at which the intensity ramped up during grasping. While each compliance profile consisted of unique characteristics, it was frequently reported that the soft and medium compliant objects were the most challenging to differentiate between. Of the soft compliant objects presented, 27.4% were misidentified as medium compliance and 34.5% of the medium compliant objects were misidentified as soft (**Figure** 7), making up the highest percentages of misidentification. This may be due to the perceived similarity in sensation intensity provided at the beginning of the stimulus. Participants often reported that hard objects were significantly easier to identify due to the high intensity felt immediately after contacting the object. However, the soft and medium compliant objects felt similar upon contact to them, and hence they required more time and exploration to provide a response. Perhaps an approach where the intensity at contact for each compliance is noticeably different would make it easier to differentiate between the two compliances. Fewer objects were misclassified by size. Of the large objects presented, 11.1% were perceived as small objects (**Figure** 7). This may be due to a sequencing order effect on perception, as these misidentifications of size for large objects mostly occurred when a large-hard or large-medium object was presented in the trial before.

Additionally, all participants performed a practice block where they were introduced to the six unique profiles and provided cues to assist in identifying the physical characteristics. It was observed during the experiment that one participant was only reporting objects of two compliances—soft and hard. After the block, the participant was reminded that there were 6 object profiles to differentiate between; here the participant reported that they were not aware that there were objects with medium compliance. This error may have contributed to the lower success rates in identifying objects of medium compliance.

4.1 Future Directions

The magnitude estimation performance could have been masked by potentially narrow pulse frequency operating ranges due to the fusion-saturation limits. Other studies have shown that participants often use individual pulse timings as supplementary cues. Because of this, frequency discrimination performance is often better with low frequency references (George et al., 2020). Since the intent of the study was to pay attention to the perceived intensity and not the frequency, participants were instructed to pick the point where individual pulses were no longer detectable (fusion) as the lower end of the operational frequency range. This may have increased the difficulty of the task by avoiding the presence of low frequency references and test bursts during the magnitude estimation trials.

In this study we focused on percept intensity only. Percept modality is also an important dimension of artificial feedback. While intensity is encoded by rate and population recruitment, modality seems to be encoded by the spatiotemporal patterning of this activity (Tan et al., 2014). Sensations delivered by conventional surface stimulation methods have often been reported as artificial or unnatural electrical tingling, or paresthesia. Synchronous activation within a population of different fibers is believed to cause these sensations (Ochoa and Torebjork, 1980; Mogyoros et al., 1996), which contrast with the more complex spatiotemporal patterns recognized during natural sensory perception (Weber et al., 2013). Future advancements to xTouch could incorporate ability to study percept modalities contribution to more intuitive and natural sensations.

When grasping objects, there is often a physical restraint on the distance our hands can close upon contact. This resistance provides haptic feedback that restrains us from going beyond the compression limits of objects, thereby preventing breakage. With virtual objects, there is no physical resistance at the fingertips and therefore, nothing preventing participants from closing their hands beyond the compressive range of each object. Taking this into account, the experience of breakage was emulated by stopping stimulation when the hand closed beyond the maximum compressive range for respective objects. In some instances, participants reported a response after breaking the object, which was most notably used when classifying hard objects, despite size. However, the participants were strongly discouraged from using this tactic. Perhaps a method incorporating physical resistance such as in augmented reality applications could be explored to prevent participants from using similar tactics.

In the interest of time, the just noticeable difference (JND) was not evaluated. Instead, we relied on results from a series of intensity discrimination tasks during a previous study (Pena, 2020) with ten participants which suggested that intensity mapping along the ACR range could potentially allow for an average of ten noticeably different intensity levels. The full compressive range of each unique virtual object was linearly mapped to the full range of percept intensities, which are achieved by simultaneously modulating PW and PF along the ACR range. Prior to performing the virtual object classification task, participants completed multiple magnitude estimation trials over ten different ACR levels equally distributed along the full ACR range. The magnitude estimation tasks showed that participants perceived a wide range of intensities within their fitted ACR range. However, whether participants could reliably discriminate between adjacent levels was not determined.

To reliably classify virtual objects with complex characteristics, xTouch must be able to convey detectable changes with a high enough intensity resolution. Assuming that we could achieve ten noticeably different intensity levels with this approach, a participant would need to change their aperture by more than 10% of the object's compressive range as depicted in **Figure 3** to experience a distinguishably different percept intensity. For instance, large-soft objects would require the most change in aperture (>6.3 mm) to produce a detectable change in intensity based on its 63 mm compressive range. The relatively coarse intensity change makes these objects less sensitive to aperture tracking errors. In contrast, a small-medium object would require the least change in aperture (>1.8 mm) making it the most sensitive to aperture tracking errors. The ability to convey multiple levels of discriminable intensities is not as critical for hard objects as it is for more compressible objects. Future work should include JND determination tasks to determine the smallest detectable increments in intensities that can be used. The effect of tracking accuracy on the JND should also be explored for different tracking approaches.

Additionally, participants had the opportunity to explore the object as many times as needed before providing a response. If the object was grasped beyond the compressive range and breakage was initiated, participants were able to restart exploration by opening the hand to a distance greater than the objects uncompressed width (>100 mm). This may not be representative of typical daily life activities, where reaching force targets with one attempt is often required. Future studies could use a single attempt method in which participants are instructed to approach the target from one direction and stop once they feel they have reached compressive bounds.

Throughout the study participants were encouraged to take breaks and stretch when needed to mitigate discomfort. However, it was not considered whether stretching could have affected the perceived intensity ranges. Ultrasound studies have shown that stretching the wrist can cause displacement of the median nerve (Nakamichi and Tachibana, 1992; Martínez-Payá et al., 2015). Previous studies with transcutaneous stimulation (Forst et al., 2015; Shin et al., 2018) at the arm suggest that some degree of position dependence exists and influences the perceived sensations, suggesting that potential displacement of the nerve does affect the perceived sensations. A potential solution to this problem is the adoption of an electrode array design [patent pending]. The haptic-feedback platform has the potential to utilize an array design which can create unique touch experiences to better match the environment. The array design may mitigate substantial changes in stimulation due to movements of the nerve, as different electrode locations within the array may activate similar populations of the nerve. Additionally, the information delivered by the feedback system could be further expanded by implementing multi-channel stimulation schemes where multiple electrode pairs target different parts of the nerve to evoke percepts in different areas of the hand. Potential combinations of electrode pairs within the array can be used to simultaneously stimulate percept locations, opening the opportunity to elicit whole hand sensations (Shin et al., 2018). These enhanced percepts could be used to replicate a variety of interactions with different types of objects, providing more realistic cues that go beyond size and compliance (Saal and Bensmaia, 2015). Development of this platform in an array form may also be used to better replicate complex interactions of event cues such as object slippage, thus enabling users to execute virtual or remote manipulation tasks with high precision.

VR is often characterized by visual dominance and previous work has shown that sense of agency in VR can be altered when the visual feedback provided is incongruent with the participant's actual movements (Salomon et al., 2016). However, more recent work challenges this visual dominance theory with haptic feedback manipulation during multisensory conflicts in VR (Boban et al., 2022). Boban et al. found that active haptic feedback paired with congruent proprioceptive and motor afferent signals and incongruent visual feedback can reduce visual perception accuracy in a changing finger movement task in VR. When subjects were provided haptic feedback inconsistent with the finger they saw moving, they were more uncertain about which finger they saw moving, thereby challenging the visual-dominance theory. This phenomenon could be examined using the xTouch

system in the future. Here, we understand how the information from the xTouch system can be utilized in isolation. Hence, the haptic feedback was provided by the xTouch system without confounding effects of visual feedback of hand aperture, which may have given away the size of the object. These data lay the groundwork for investigating the use of xTouch in more complex situations such as in the presence of other forms of feedback.

In this study, the electrical stimulation provided by the xTouch platform is driven by a benchtop stimulation system and controlled by the experiment computer. This imposes obvious mobility constraints on the user. Recent advances in portable neuromodulation technology could enable the development of a portable xTouch system for real-world VR/AR applications capable of delivering neuro-haptic feedback without restricting user mobility. The types of electronics needed to stimulate peripheral nerves have become much smaller in recent years and have demonstrated safety and reliability in widely used commercial systems. For example, commercially available TENS units are portable battery-powered devices that are slightly larger than most smartphones. These devices can deliver enough current to safely evoke muscle contractions (between 10 and 30 mA depending on the application). For comparison, the amount of current used to elicit the kinds of sensations provided by xTouch were no higher than 6 mA and therefore compatible with a portable smaller form-factor stimulator design.

A desired feature of VR experiences is interaction transparency. This is when users cannot distinguish between operating in a local (or real) environment, and a distant (or virtual) environment (Preusche and Hirzinger, 2007). While it was out of the scope of this study to evaluate immersion and realism, future studies should investigate how haptic feedback affects realism and presence in VR simulations. It has been shown that the quality of realism of virtual environments promotes a greater sense of presence in VR (Hvass et al., 2018; Newman et al., 2022). A previous study (Huffman et al., 1998) investigated how realism of a virtual environment was influenced by tactile augmentation and found that the group that received tactile feedback was likely to predict more realistic physical properties of other objects in the virtual environment. This shows that presenting stimuli that match real physical characteristics will lead users' expectations in the environment to be congruent with their expectation of reality, which in turn may induce users to interact, perform and interpret virtual interactions more like how they would in real environments. In other words, providing users with stimuli similar in quality and experience to real environments has the potential to enhance realism of VR simulations. Perhaps the addition of xTouch can also enhance the user's perception of the environment, creating a more realistic experience for the user and greater sense of presence, ultimately promoting interaction transparency.

5 CONCLUSION

This work evaluated the use of a novel neuro-haptics feedback platform that integrates contactless hand tracking and non-invasive electrical neurostimulation to provide relevant and intuitive haptic information related to user interactions with virtual objects. This approach was used to simulate object manipulation cues such as object contact, grasping forces, and breakage during a virtual object classification task, without restrictive hand-mounted hardware.

VR has been used in a variety of research applications and has been growing in interest to live up to our ideas of existing in a virtual world, such as in the Metaverse (Dionisio et al., 2013; Mystakidis, 2022). With the translatable use of virtual reality across multiple sectors (i.e. gaming, telehealth, and defense, etc.), this haptic interface has the potential for use in a variety of research and social applications. For example, the presented platform can be used to enhance immersion of simulated environments in gaming applications, facilitate stronger interactions with rehabilitative tasks in telehealth applications, advance non-invasive applications of neuroprosthetics, and allow haptic communication with other users in collaborative virtual environments. Since the hands of the user are not restrained by the wearable device, xTouch has potential uses within augmented reality applications, allowing the user to experience augmented virtual sensations while freely manipulating physical objects.

Intuitive sensory feedback is crucial to enhancing the experience of virtual reality. This study demonstrates that this platform can be used to facilitate meaningful interactions with virtual environments. While additional studies are required to investigate whether additional sensory channels can be added (e.g., delivering proprioceptive feedback to the ulnar nerve), this study demonstrated that the artificial sensory feedback delivered by xTouch may enable individuals to execute virtual or remote manipulation tasks with high precision without relying solely on visual or auditory cues. In future work, we will consider the neural mechanisms by which we interpret touch in VR and how the interactive engagement with objects in VR affects realism, immersion, haptic perception, and user performance. This may have implications for the benefits of xTouch as an addition to VR and provide insight into the mechanisms our brains use to translate haptic perception in virtual reality simulations. Identifying xTouch's capability to provide interpretable haptic information in virtual environments may potentially improve virtual reality simulations for future research and industry applications.

AUTHOR CONTRIBUTIONS

Development of xTouch, AP. Data collection and analyses, AS Writing—original draft preparation, AS. Figures, AP and AS. Writing, figure review and editing, AS, AP, JA, and RJ. Supervision, JA and RJ. All authors have read and agreed to the published version of the manuscript.

ACKNOWLEDGMENTS

We thank Heriberto A. Nieves for characterizing the hand aperture tracker and conducting pilot studies with the xTouch. In addition, we thank Sathyakumar S. Kuntaegowdanahalli for his help in conducting the experiments.

REFERENCES

Banks, W. P., and Coleman, M. J. (1981). Two Subjective Scales of Number. *Percept. Psychophys.* 29, 95–105. doi:10.3758/BF03207272

Boban, L., Pittet, D., Herbelin, B., and Boulic, R. (2022). Changing Finger Movement Perception: Influence of Active Haptics on Visual Dominance. *Front. Virtual Real.* 3. doi:10.3389/frvir.2022.860872

Choi, I., Culbertson, H., Miller, M. R., Olwal, A., and Follmer, S. (2017). "Grabity," in Proceedings of the 30th Annual ACM Symposium on User Interface Software and Technology. UIST 2017. doi:10.1145/3126594.3126599

Choi, I., Ofek, E., Benko, H., Sinclair, M., and Holz, C. (2018). "Claw," in Conference on Human Factors in Computing Systems - Proceedings. doi:10.1145/3173574.3174228

Colella, N., Bianchi, M., Grioli, G., Bicchi, A., and Catalano, M. G. (2019). A Novel Skin-Stretch Haptic Device for Intuitive Control of Robotic Prostheses and Avatars. *IEEE Robot. Autom. Lett.* 4, 1572–1579. doi:10.1109/LRA.2019.2896484

D'Anna, E., Petrini, F. M., Artoni, F., Popovic, I., Simanić, I., Raspopovic, S., et al. (2017). A Somatotopic Bidirectional Hand Prosthesis with Transcutaneous Electrical Nerve Stimulation Based Sensory Feedback. *Sci. Rep.* 7. doi:10.1038/s41598-017-11306-w

Dionisio, J. D. N., Iii, W. G. B., and Gilbert, R. (2013). 3D Virtual Worlds and the Metaverse. *ACM Comput. Surv.* 45, 1–38. doi:10.1145/2480741.2480751

Forst, J. C., Blok, D. C., Slopsema, J. P., Boss, J. M., Heyboer, L. A., Tobias, C. M., et al. (2015). Surface Electrical Stimulation to Evoke Referred Sensation. *J. Rehabil. Res. Dev.* 52. doi:10.1682/JRRD.2014.05.0128

George, J. A., Brinton, M. R., Colgan, P. C., Colvin, G. K., Bensmaia, S. J., and Clark, G. A. (2020). Intensity Discriminability of Electrocutaneous and Intraneural Stimulation Pulse Frequency in Intact Individuals and Amputees. *Annu. Int. Conf. IEEE Eng. Med. Biol. Soc.* 2020, 3893–3896. doi:10.1109/EMBC44109.2020.9176720

Graczyk, E. L., Schiefer, M. A., Saal, H. P., Delhaye, B. P., Bensmaia, S. J., and Tyler, D. J. (2016). The Neural Basis of Perceived Intensity in Natural and Artificial Touch. *Sci. Transl. Med.* 8. doi:10.1126/scitranslmed.aaf5187

Hinchet, R., Vechev, V., Shea, H., and Hilliges, O. (2018). "DextrES," in Proceedings of the 31st Annual ACM Symposium on User Interface Software and Technology. UIST 2018. doi:10.1145/3242587.3242657

Hoffman, H. G., Hollander, A., Schroder, K., Rousseau, S., and Furness, T. (1998). Physically Touching and Tasting Virtual Objects Enhances the Realism of Virtual Experiences. *Virtual Real.* 3, 226–234. doi:10.1007/bf01408703

Hummel, J., Dodiya, J., Center, G. A., Eckardt, L., Wolff, R., Gerndt, A., et al. (2016). "A Lightweight Electrotactile Feedback Device for Grasp Improvement in Immersive Virtual Environments," in Proceedings - IEEE Virtual Reality. doi:10.1109/VR.2016.7504686

Hvass, J., Larsen, O., Vendelbo, K., Nilsson, N., Nordahl, R., and Serafin, S. (2017). "Visual Realism and Presence in a Virtual Reality Game," in Proceedings of the 3DTV-Conference. doi:10.1109/3DTV.2017.8280421

Jones, I., and Johnson, M. I. (2009). Transcutaneous Electrical Nerve Stimulation. *Continuing Educ. Anaesth. Crit. Care & Pain* 9, 130–135. doi:10.1093/BJACEACCP/MKP021

Jung, R., and Pena, A. E. (2021). *Systems and Methods for Providing Haptic Feedback when Interacting with Virtual Objects.* 199903–b1. U.S. Patent 11

Kourtesis, P., Argelaguet, F., Vizcay, S., Marchal, M., and Pacchierotti, C. (2021). Electrotactile Feedback for Hand Interactions: A Systematic Review, Meta-Analysis, and Future Directions. doi:10.48550/arxiv.2105.05343

Lapicque, L. (1909). "Definition experimentale de l'excitabilite", in *Social Biology* 77.

Li, K., Fang, Y., Zhou, Y., and Liu, H. (2017). Non-Invasive Stimulation-Based Tactile Sensation for Upper-Extremity Prosthesis: A Review. *IEEE Sensors J.* 17, 2625–2635. doi:10.1109/JSEN.2017.2674965

Maereg, A. T., Nagar, A., Reid, D., and Secco, E. L. (2017). Wearable Vibrotactile Haptic Device for Stiffness Discrimination during Virtual Interactions. *Front. Robot. AI* 4. doi:10.3389/frobt.2017.00042

Martínez-Payá, J. J., Ríos-Díaz, J., del Baño-Aledo, M. E., García-Martínez, D., de Groot-Ferrando, A., and Meroño-Gallut, J. (2015). Biomechanics of the Median Nerve during Stretching as Assessed by Ultrasonography. *J. Appl. Biomechanics* 31, 439–444. doi:10.1123/jab.2015-0026

Mogyoros, I., Kiernan, M. C., and Burke, D. (1996). Strength-duration Properties of Human Peripheral Nerve. *Brain* 119, 439–447. doi:10.1093/brain/119.2.439

Mystakidis, S. (2022). Metaverse. *Encyclopedia* 2, 486–497. doi:10.3390/encyclopedia2010031

Nakamichi, K., and Tachibana, S. (1992). Transverse Sliding of the Median Nerve beneath the Flexor Retinaculum. *J. Hand Surg. Br.* 17, 213–216. doi:10.1016/0266-7681(92)90092-G

Newman, M., Gatersleben, B., Wyles, K. J., and Ratcliffe, E. (2022). The Use of Virtual Reality in Environment Experiences and the Importance of Realism. *J. Environ. Psychol.* 79, 101733. doi:10.1016/j.jenvp.2021.101733

Ochoa, J. L., and Torejök, H. E. (1980). Paræsthesiæ from Ectopic Impulse Generation in Human Sensory Nerves. *Brain* 103, 835–853. doi:10.1093/brain/103.4.835

Pacchierotti, C., Sinclair, S., Solazzi, M., Frisoli, A., Hayward, V., and Prattichizzo, D. (2017). Wearable Haptic Systems for the Fingertip and the Hand: Taxonomy, Review, and Perspectives. *IEEE Trans. Haptics* 10, 580–600. doi:10.1109/TOH.2017.2689006

Pena, A. E., Abbas, J. J., and Jung, R. (2021). Channel-hopping during Surface Electrical Neurostimulation Elicits Selective, Comfortable, Distally Referred Sensations. *J. Neural Eng.* 18, 055004. doi:10.1088/1741-2552/abf28c

Pena, A. E. (2020). *Enhanced Surface Electrical Neurostimulation (eSENS): A Non-invasive Platform for Peripheral Neuromodulation.* Dissertation. Florida International University.

Pezent, E., Israr, A., Samad, M., Robinson, S., Agarwal, P., Benko, H., et al. (2019). "Tasbi: Multisensory Squeeze and Vibrotactile Wrist Haptics for Augmented and Virtual Reality", in Proceeding of the IEEE World Haptics Conference(WHC). doi:10.1109/WHC.2019.8816098

Preatoni, G., Bracher, N. M., and Raspopovic, S. (2021). "Towards a Future VR-TENS Multimodal Platform to Treat Neuropathic Pain," in Proceeding of the International IEEE/EMBS Conference on Neural Engineering(NER). doi:10.1109/NER49283.2021.9441283

Preusche, C., and Hirzinger, G. (2007). Haptics in Telerobotics. *Vis. Comput.* 23. 273–284. doi:10.1007/s00371-007-0101-3

Price, S., Jewitt, C., Chubinidze, D., Barker, N., and Yiannoutsou, N. (2021). Taking an Extended Embodied Perspective of Touch: Connection-Disconnection in iVR. *Front. Virtual Real.* 2. doi:10.3389/frvir.2021.642782

Rennie, S. (2010). ELECTROPHYSICAL AGENTS - Contraindications and Precautions: An Evidence-Based Approach to Clinical Decision Making in Physical Therapy. *Physiother. Can.* 62, 1–80. *Physiotherapy Canada.* doi:10.3138/ptc.62.5

Saal, H. P., and Bensmaia, S. J. (2015). Biomimetic Approaches to Bionic Touch through a Peripheral Nerve Interface. *Neuropsychologia* 79, 344–353. doi:10.1016/j.neuropsychologia.2015.06.010

Salomon, R., Fernandez, N. B., van Elk, M., Vachicouras, N., Sabatier, F., Tychinskaya, A., et al. (2016). Changing Motor Perception by Sensorimotor Conflicts and Body Ownership. *Sci. Rep.* 6. doi:10.1038/srep25847

Shin, H., Watkins, Z., Huang, H., Zhu, Y., and Hu, X. (2018). Evoked Haptic Sensations in the Hand via Non-invasive Proximal Nerve Stimulation. *J. Neural Eng.* 15, 046005. doi:10.1088/1741-2552/aabd5d

Stephens-Fripp, B., Alici, G., and Mutlu, R. (2018). A Review of Non-invasive Sensory Feedback Methods for Transradial Prosthetic Hands. *IEEE Access* 6, 6878–6899. doi:10.1109/ACCESS.2018.2791583

Stevens, S. S. (1956). The Direct Estimation of Sensory Magnitudes: Loudness. *Am. J. Psychol.* 69, 1. doi:10.2307/1418112

Tan, D. W., Schiefer, M. A., Keith, M. W., Anderson, J. R., Tyler, J., and Tyler, D. J. (2014). A Neural Interface Provides Long-Term Stable Natural Touch Perception. *Sci. Transl. Med.* 6. doi:10.1126/scitranslmed.3008669

Vargas, L., Shin, H., Huang, H., Zhu, Y., and Hu, X. (2020). Object Stiffness Recognition Using Haptic Feedback Delivered Through Transcutaneous Proximal Nerve Stimulation. *J. Neural Eng.*. doi:10.1088/1741-2552/ab4d99

Vizcay, S., Kourtesis, P., Argelaguet, F., Pacchierotti, C., and Marchal, M. (2021). *Electrotactile Feedback for Enhancing Contact Information in Virtual Reality.* arXiv preprint arXiv:2102.00259.

Wang, D., Guo, Y., Liu, S., Zhang, Y., Xu, W., and Xiao, J. (2019). Haptic Display for Virtual Reality: Progress and Challenges. *Virtual Real. Intelligent Hardw.* 1, 136–162. doi:10.3724/SP.J.2096-5796.2019.0008

Weber, A. I., Saal, H. P., Lieber, J. D., Cheng, J.-W., Manfredi, L. R., Dammann, J. F., et al. (2013). Spatial and Temporal Codes Mediate the Tactile Perception of Natural Textures. *Proc. Natl. Acad. Sci. U.S.A.* 110, 17107–17112. doi:10.1073/pnas.1305509110

Weiss, G. (1901). Sur la possibilité de rendre comparable entre eux les appareils servant à l'excitation électrique. *Arch. Ital. Biol.* 35 (1), 413–445. doi:10.4449/AIB.V35I1.1355

Whitmire, E., Benko, H., Holz, C., Ofek, E., and Sinclair, M. (2018). "Haptic Revolver," in Proceeding of the Conference on Human Factors in Computing Systems - Proceedings. doi:10.1145/3173574.3173660

Witteveen, H. J. B., Luft, F., Rietman, J. S., and Veltink, P. H. (2014). Stiffness Feedback for Myoelectric Forearm Prostheses Using Vibrotactile Stimulation. *IEEE Trans. Neural Syst. Rehabil. Eng.* 22, 53–61. doi:10.1109/TNSRE.2013.2267394

Yang, S.-R., Shi-An Chen, S.-A., Shu-Fang Tsai, S-F., and Lin, C.-T. (2012). "Transcutaneous Electrical Nerve Stimulation System for Improvement of Flight Orientation in a VR-Based Motion Environment," in ISCAS 2012 - 2012 IEEE International Symposium on Circuits and Systems. doi:10.1109/ISCAS.2012.6271686

Yem, V., and Kajimoto, H. (2017). "Wearable Tactile Device Using Mechanical and Electrical Stimulation for Fingertip Interaction with Virtual World," in Proceedings - IEEE Virtual Reality. doi:10.1109/VR.2017.7892236

7

Triggermuscle: Exploring Weight Perception for Virtual Reality Through Adaptive Trigger Resistance in a Haptic VR Controller

Carolin Stellmacher[1]*, Michael Bonfert[1], Ernst Kruijff[2] and Johannes Schöning[3]

[1]Faculty of Mathematics and Computer Science, University of Bremen, Bremen, Germany, [2]Institute of Visual Computing, Bonn-Rhein-Sieg University of Applied Sciences, Sankt Augustin, Germany, [3]School of Computer Science , University of St. Gallen, St. Gallen, Switzerland

*Correspondence:
Carolin Stellmacher
cstellma@uni-bremen.de

It is challenging to provide users with a haptic weight sensation of virtual objects in VR since current consumer VR controllers and software-based approaches such as pseudo-haptics cannot render appropriate haptic stimuli. To overcome these limitations, we developed a haptic VR controller named *Triggermuscle* that adjusts its trigger resistance according to the weight of a virtual object. Therefore, users need to adapt their index finger force to grab objects of different virtual weights. Dynamic and continuous adjustment is enabled by a spring mechanism inside the casing of an HTC Vive controller. In two user studies, we explored the effect on weight perception and found large differences between participants for sensing change in trigger resistance and thus for discriminating virtual weights. The variations were easily distinguished and associated with weight by some participants while others did not notice them at all. We discuss possible limitations, confounding factors, how to overcome them in future research and the pros and cons of this novel technology.

Keywords: haptics, virtual reality, weight perception, adaptive trigger, controller design, psychophysics

1 INTRODUCTION

Grabbing objects in reality provides humans with a haptic sensation of weight (Loomis and Lederman, 1986). Muscles, tendons and skin receptors sense the gravitational pull through proprioceptive and cutaneous stimuli (McCloskey, 1974; Brodie and Ross, 1984) and enable the natural perception of weights. Users of consumer virtual reality (VR) systems, however, cannot experience the same haptic weight sensation when grabbing virtual objects. Current consumer VR controllers are unable to render appropriate haptic feedback associated with weight, leaving users with identical haptic weight perception of virtual objects. In many cases, only visual cues are ambiguous and insufficient in conveying weight information. This limits a natural and realistic experience of weight in VR and results in a discrepancy between what users are familiar with from the real world and what they experience in virtual environments (VE).

Handheld controllers are typically used in consumer VR systems. With increasing consumer attention, these lightweight and mobile VR controllers become more relevant for designing interactions in VEs. They offer various components to register user input such as buttons, a trigger, or a trackpad, which provide users with different techniques to interact with the VE. However, to provide a haptic response during the interaction (e.g., the weight of a virtual object), current state-of-the-art VR controllers such as the HTC Vive or Oculus Touch controllers only offer vibrotactile rendering. This prevents users from having an appropriate haptic experience. It also rules out haptic feedback, which is specific to user input. To nevertheless enhance weight perception with consumer VR controllers and to overcome their current hardware limitations, pseudo-haptics were explored. This software-based approach manipulates the control/display (C/D) ratio between a user's hand movements and the rendered position in the VE during a lifting motion (Rietzler et al., 2018). This sensation of weight is caused by the user's arm movements being amplified when lifting heavier virtual objects with the controller. This effect was also observed when users lifted physical props in VR (Samad et al., 2019). While this method enables conveying a sense of weight in current consumer VR, it cannot resemble an actual haptic sensation of weight since users only receive visual feedback, but no haptic weight information.

Other researchers have addressed the hardware limitations of haptic weight rendering by proposing various lightweight and mobile VR devices. For such ungrounded haptic devices, it is particularly challenging to provide proprioceptive information as they cannot generate externally grounded forces that act on users. As an alternative, cutaneous stimuli are often used as a substitute to offset the lack of force feedback. For instance, a simulation of muscular grip forces is imitated through skin deformation at the finger pads of the index finger and thumb (Minamizawa et al., 2007a; Schorr and Okamura, 2017; Suchoski et al., 2018) or through skin stretch with asymmetric vibrations (Choi et al., 2017). Other wearable technology utilises electrical muscle stimulation to resemble a proprioceptive sensation by artificially pulling the user's arm downwards (Lopes et al., 2017). Other research has explored handheld devices with liquid-based haptic feedback to simulate the weight of fluid objects (Cheng et al., 2018), shape-changing abilities to provide haptic feedback through air resistance (Zenner and Krüger, 2019) or weight-shifting abilities (Zenner and Krüger, 2017) to generate haptic sensations for weight.

While these proposed haptic interfaces have succeeded in enhancing weight perception in VR, they are either designed for specific cases, rely on complex and expensive systems or need to be manufactured for different hand sizes. This makes them currently unsuitable for mass production and the consumer market. So far, no approach has considered established input components of current consumer VR controllers to render haptic stimuli for weight perception in VR.

In this paper, we propose an approach that—in contrast to related studies—utilises a standard button available in any consumer VR controller: the trigger. By varying the resistance of the trigger, which is normally constant by default, we extend the input component through output rendering to provide users with haptic feedback during the interaction. Hence, when users pull the trigger to grab a virtual object in VR, they need to scale their index finger force accordingly to the configured resistance displaying the virtual weight: The heavier a held virtual object is, the more finger force needs to be exerted onto the trigger.

We present *Triggermuscle*, a novel haptic controller that simulates the weight of virtual objects in VR through adjustable trigger resistance. As proof of concept, our system is built into the casing of an HTC Vive controller (see **Figure 1**). The novel spring mechanism is connected internally to the original trigger and dynamically modifies the trigger resistance according to the weight of the grabbed virtual object. A demonstration video of Triggermuscle is submitted as a **Supplementary Material**. The mechanism is built with inexpensive hardware components and can be easily tailored to other form factors due to the principle of force redirection, which demonstrates the potential for haptic weight rendering in different VR controllers. Additionally, as a handheld device, Triggermuscle fits a large range of users with various hand sizes. Enriching buttons with additional haptic feedback is increasingly evident in input device development. For instance, Sony recently released the DualSense controller for PlayStation 5 with actuated triggers (Sony, 2020), while Microsoft announced a locking feature for the triggers of the Xbox Elite controller (Microsoft, 2021).

What follows explores the capacity of variable trigger resistance to display virtual weight in VR. To do so, we

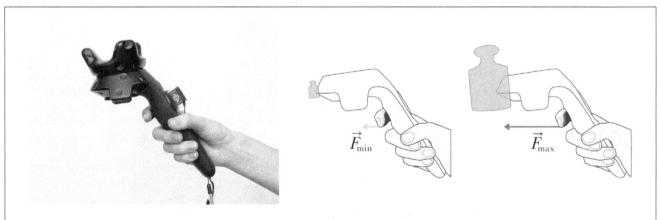

FIGURE 1 | (left) Our haptic controller Triggermuscle simulates the weight of virtual objects in VR through adapting the trigger resistance. The spring mechanism for a dynamic adjustment is built into the casing of an HTC Vive controller. An HTC Vive tracker is mounted to the top to enable spatial tracking. **(right)** Triggermuscle allows a continuous regulation of the trigger resistance according to the weight of the grabbed virtual object.

present the design and implementation of a preliminary prototype and of Triggermuscle as well as their different spring mechanisms, which we developed in an iterative and human-centred design process. In two user studies, we evaluate both controllers' hardware designs and investigate users' ability to discriminate different levels of resistance as well as the effect on weight perception in VR. Our research addresses two research questions:

RQ1: Do different trigger resistances influence the haptic perception of different virtual weights in VR?
RQ2: How can the intensity of the trigger resistance be quantified and mapped to convey distinguishable virtual weights?

We found large differences between participants for sensing change in trigger resistance and thus for discriminating different virtual weights based on the resistance. The variations were easily distinguished by some participants while others did not notice them at all. This points towards an association between trigger resistance and a sense of virtual weight in VR, but also towards confounding factors interfering with the perception of the trigger resistance. We discuss these issues to provide better insight into the problem space, to illustrate potential perceptual mechanisms that may have affected the experiment outcomes and to propose further studies and hardware designs based on our findings. We thus provide a novel hardware solution and, better understanding of the underlying (perceptual) mechanisms.

2 RELATED WORK

Extensive research in VR haptics has explored various strategies to enable experiencing physical properties of virtual objects during the interaction. This section presents an overview of grounded and handheld haptic technologies and emphasises approaches that convey a sense of weight in VR.

2.1 World- and Body-Grounded Haptic Devices

Humans feel an object's mass through the gravitational force pulling down the hand. To simulate this external pull in a force feedback display, the interface can be anchored in the environment or to the user's body. A widespread example for world-grounded interfaces is the Phantom Premium by 3D Systems (Massie and Salisbury, 1994; Systems, D., 2020), a 6 degrees-of-freedom (DoF) interface with a stylus as an effector mounted to the desk. A different approach anchors the force to the users' fingers via strings as done by the various SPIDAR interfaces (Sato, 2002) for simulating virtual weight in an early implementation (Ishii and Sato, 1994). Such wire-based force display systems were also adapted into body-grounded technologies to increase portability such as the HapticGEAR (Hirose et al., 2001) or Wireality for rendering complex shapes (Fang et al., 2020). Another wire-based variant anchors the user's hand to the respective upper arm (Tsai et al., 2019). By

stretching the arm, the wire gets tightened and the user experiences multilevel resistive force and impact. Thanks to their mobility, these body-grounded interfaces allow users to move freely within the tracking area and are suitable if a larger space is required. At the same time, they typically need cumbersome and complex equipment that is time-consuming to set up.

Haptic interfaces worn on users' hands such as exoskeletons provide force feedback (Burdea et al., 1992; Bouzit et al., 2002; Ben-Tzvi and Ma, 2015; Gu et al., 2016; HaptX, 2020) that is grounded to different parts of the hand or arm (Nisar et al., 2019) and that can actively restrict the finger movement with motors and complex mechanics. This can make such devices bulky, tethered, expensive or limit hand flexibility. In contrast, gloves (Giannopoulos et al., 2012; Martínez et al., 2016; Marquardt et al., 2018; Manus, 2020) typically do not use motors and can, therefore, overcome shortcomings related to the actuation. Gloves can also track users' fingers and provide vibrotactile feedback or other cutaneous stimuli. Researchers rendered various physical properties of virtual objects including shape (Solazzi et al., 2007), contact forces (Leonardis et al., 2015), texture (Gabardi et al., 2016), or inertia (Girard et al., 2016). Nonetheless, putting on gloves or hand-mounted equipment like exoskeletons and thimbles can be time-consuming and requires hygienic considerations. Further, they need to be adjustable or manufactured in different sizes to fit a diverse range of users.

2.2 Handheld Haptic Devices

In contrast to such wearable haptic interfaces, handheld haptic devices are ready for use when picked up. They do not physically restrict the user's movements and flexibly fit a large range of hand sizes. Most current consumer VR systems include such handheld controllers by default. In recent years, the development of handheld haptic devices that generate physical forces for haptic feedback as well as controller-based interaction techniques has received considerable attention. For instance, the CapstanCrunch allows to feel rigid and compliant objects (Sinclair et al., 2019), the TORC creates a haptic sensation for texture and compliance (Lee et al., 2019) and the controllers NormalTouch and TextureTouch render shape and texture through tilting a platform at the user's index finger pad (Benko et al., 2016). PaCaPa is a haptic display for an object's size, shape and stiffness by tilting movable wings, but cannot render resistance (Sun et al., 2019). Haptic Links generates resistance by mechanically constraining the relative movement between two controllers (Strasnick et al., 2018), while Thor's Hammer creates force feedback through airflow with propellers (Heo et al., 2018). The CLAW is a handheld device that integrates multiple haptic technologies to simulate a range of haptic sensations (Choi et al., 2018). It renders kinaesthetic forces at the index finger during grasping and touching which allows feeling the shape and stiffness of virtual objects. Additionally, a voice coil actuator produces vibrations for different surface textures. Another interface for displaying surface properties is the Haptic Revolver (Whitmire et al., 2018). Shapes and shear forces that occur when gliding along a surface are rendered at the fingertip by rotating a wheel with a direct current (DC) motor. The haptic wheels are customisable and can provide various textures and shapes, but can also comprise active electronic components such as buttons, switches and joysticks. Transcalibur enables shape perception through inertia (Shigeyama et al., 2019). Variable weight distributions along the controller are realised with shifting weights. Moving the controller through space makes the inertia noticeable for users and creates a haptic shape illusion. A similar concept was proposed with ShapeSense. Movable surface elements increase or decrease the surface area of the controller (Liu et al., 2019). While these mechanisms can render the distribution of an object's mass, they cannot render the absolute mass of objects. Furthermore, even though the proposed devices allow haptic rendering for various object properties, they do not address the weight of virtual objects.

2.3 Haptic Devices for Weight Simulation

To provide users with a weight sensation during the interaction with virtual objects in VR, previous work explored diverse approaches. For example, electrical muscle stimulation was used to induce contractions of the user's muscles while lifting virtual objects. The system actuates the user's triceps to simulate the weight of a held virtual object by inducing a downward movement of the arms (Lopes et al., 2017). Another concept of inducing a sense of weight for VR applications is skin deformation on the finger pad. This imitates the stretch of the skin from the downward pull of the object's surface. One way to do so is using small actuated belts that are strapped around users' finger pads which has been shown to generate a reliable weight sensation (Minamizawa et al., 2007b). The refined implementation of this approach induced the impression of grip force, gravity and inertia by stretching the skin on the finger pad with the attached belt, without the need for proprioceptive sensations (Minamizawa et al., 2007a). This type of approach was also explored in the context of augmented reality (AR) rendering weight and shear forces (Scheggi et al., 2010). To account for the combination of physical and virtual objects in AR, another implementation placed the finger-worn device as a ring around users' fingers leaving the finger pads free for the interaction with physical objects (Pacchierotti et al., 2016; Maisto et al., 2017). Other haptic devices use actuated plates to achieve skin stretch such as a finger-worn device that slides the contact area at the user's index finger pad to mimic weight and friction (Kurita et al., 2011). Further, scaling inertial forces rendered with a 3DoF wearable device on the finger pad showed an increase of the perceived weight of an object moved by the user (Suchoski et al., 2018). A different implementation demonstrates a handheld controller with movable plates in its handle to resemble the friction between an object and the hand during grasping (Provancher, 2014). Another finger-mounted device is Grabity, which simulates grip forces and a sensation of weight. The device is mounted on the thumb, index and middle finger and applies kinaesthetic forces for rendering shape. To render weight, asymmetric vibrations of voice coil actuators stretch the skin at the finger pad resembling the pull of gravity. The participants in the evaluation successfully distinguished the objects of different weight but felt the vibration cues even stronger than the weight cues (Choi et al., 2017).

The handheld VR controller Drag:on adjusts its surface area to generate varying haptic sensations for experiencing drag and weight. As the concept depends on air resistance, the different object properties are only noticeable when the device is moved through space. Due to the flat controller design built with fans, the effect is dependent on the orientation of the controller (Zenner and Krüger, 2019). The same authors also created Shifty, which enhances the perception of the dimensions of virtual objects by changing the controller's weight distribution. An internal weight is moved along the longitudinal axis shifting the centre of mass away from the hand. This increases the leverage and therefore feels like holding a heavier object (Zenner and Krüger, 2017). An increase in the possible rendered shift was achieved through combining the haptic device with haptic retargeting (Zenner et al., 2021). Rendering shifting weights on a 2D plane was also achieved in a handheld controller using jet propellers. Aeroplane generates force feedback with up to 14 N that can be interpreted by the user as weight while holding the device level. This was found to increase the perceived immersion and realism (Je et al., 2019). Finally, in GravityCup, the actual weight of the device changes. It is filled with water or emptied again to render inertia and weight of liquids. The user holds the interface by a handle like a cup. The interface requires a separate wearable bag with water to fill the haptic display as needed (Cheng et al., 2018). So far, these proposed devices often rely on complex hardware, might feel cumbersome to users or target specific use cases which limits their use for haptic weight rendering in commercial VR.

2.4 Software-Based Approaches for Weight Simulation

As discussed, haptic devices are limited in their application by a number of factors. Moreover, one additional constraint is the availability of the hardware. Beyond technical feasibility, a haptic display needs to be universal, flexible and affordable enough to be established as a standard interface in VR interaction. To overcome hardware limitations and deliver haptic experiences readily available to users, researchers proposed various software solutions for pseudo-haptics. This term describes haptic illusions through visual, auditory or multimodal stimuli without actual touch.

In terms of weight perception, the manipulation of the C/D ratio between users' hand movements and the rendered position in VR has proven effective. It was demonstrated in a non-VR setup that this mismatch strongly influences the perception of mass (Dominjon et al., 2005). The effect has been replicated successfully in VR. In an experiment, participants lifted two physical boxes with their hands. An increase in the offset for heavier virtual boxes resulted in an amplification of users' hand movements and a heavier perceived weight (Samad et al., 2019). This method was also applied to the interaction with a consumer VR controller and produced corresponding results (Rietzler et al., 2018).

Analogously to the modification of the translational C/D ratio, another approach changed the rotational C/D ratio depending on an object's weight, thus, the rotational motion is scaled relative to the mass of the object. A user study confirmed that this method effectively, realistically and robustly conveys different weights. At the same time, it does not compromise the perceived controllability. Furthermore, the authors proposed the manipulation of the pivot point during rotation and the scaling of rotational motion to convey the distribution of mass within an object (Yu and Bowman, 2020).

Such software-based approaches have been shown to provide users with an experience of virtual weight, but they cannot render actual force stimuli. This limits their ability to haptically convey weight in VR. Unlike previous devices or software-based approaches, Triggermuscle offers a novel hardware solution built into a commercial handheld VR controller to enhance weight perception during the interaction with a virtual object in VR. With our technology, we extend the trigger's capabilities towards generating haptic feedback and explore the effect of adaptive trigger resistance on the perception of virtual weight in VR.

3 ADAPTIVE TRIGGER

This section describes the background in haptic weight perception during grasping and how we addressed this in the concept and the first implementation of the adaptive trigger inside a prototype. The section concludes with the evaluation of the prototype in a pilot study and the findings that influenced the development of Triggermuscle.

3.1 Background in Weight Perception

Our adaptive trigger is informed by humans' perception of weight cues through the haptic sense (Loomis and Lederman, 1986). In addition, to grasp and lift an object the human brain initially incorporates visual cues (Gordon et al., 1991) and previous lifting experiences (Van Polanen and Davare, 2015) to predict an object's weight and scale finger forces accordingly. Touching and lifting the object then supplies simultaneous haptic cues obtained from cutaneous stimuli registered by receptors in the skin and proprioceptive stimuli obtained from muscles and tendons (McCloskey, 1974; Brodie and Ross, 1984). Depending on the updated weight perception, enough grip force is applied to overcome the gravitational pull, but at the same time causing no damage to the object (Westling and Johansson, 1984). The result

is a direct relationship between the physical weight and the applied grip forces: The heavier the object, the more manual force needs to be applied. This principle forms the main instigator for our hardware design. Increasing the grip force to a sufficient amount is enabled by isometric contractions in the muscles of the hand and arm (Johansson and Westling, 1988), meaning the muscle tension is adjusted accordingly to the weight, but no muscle movement takes place. When lifting the object away from the supporting surface, the contractions switch to isotonic which keeps the muscle tension static while the length of the muscle changes, e.g., to flex the elbow.

Grip forces are not only scaled according to the gravitational pull, but are also influenced by various tactile cues derived from material properties such as surface texture (surface-weight illusion) (Johansson and Westling, 1984; Flanagan et al., 1995) or material (material-weight illusion) (Ellis and Lederman, 1999) and spatial properties such as shape (shape-weight illusion) (Jenmalm and Johansson, 1997) or size (size-weight illusion) (Ellis and Lederman, 1993). These studies have shown that the illusions provoke modulated grip forces and influence the perceived weight. For instance, an increased grip force due to smoother surface texture leads to higher perceived weight (Johansson and Westling, 1984; Flanagan et al., 1995). In such cases, cutaneous receptors detect less frictional force between the skin and the object's surface leading to higher grip forces to prevent the object from slipping. Based on their findings, the researchers argued that "grip force may be a useful cue for discriminating weight" (Flanagan et al., 1995).

Such haptic illusions caused by stimuli unrelated to gravity could contribute to a successful substitution of haptic weight cues occurring during the grip. The sensory substitution implies that haptic stimuli are registered through another sense as they normally are or at a different location (Kaczmarek et al., 1991). This is necessary for most haptic interfaces to compensate for the lack of corresponding physical stimulation when virtually interacting with an object. Especially handheld VR devices displaying virtual weight rely on substitutional stimuli to compensate for the lack of gravitational force pulling down the user's hand. Simulating this force has been previously done, e.g., by deforming the user's skin at the fingertips through stretching the skin or through asymmetric vibrations (Choi et al., 2017). Moreover, as haptic stimuli unrelated to gravity such as surface texture or material have been shown to create weight illusions and

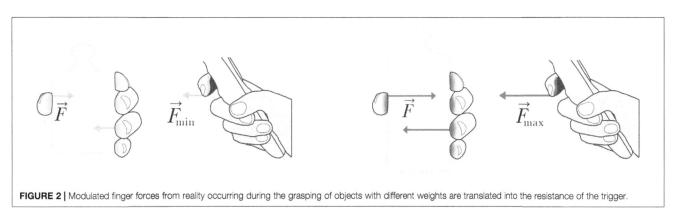

FIGURE 2 | Modulated finger forces from reality occurring during the grasping of objects with different weights are translated into the resistance of the trigger.

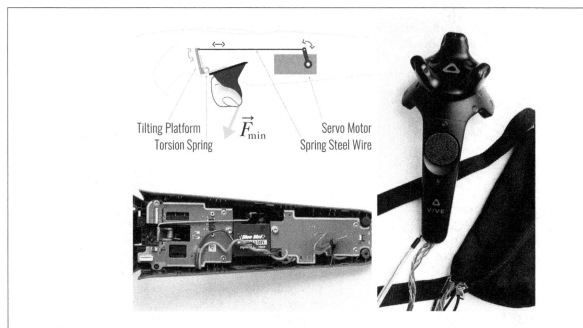

FIGURE 3 | (top left) Schematic illustration of the spring mechanism of our prototype utilising a torsion spring. **(bottom left)** Spring mechanism embedded into the casing of an HTC Vive controller. **(right)** Our prototype for adaptive trigger resistance. Electrical components are connected via cable to the prototype's bottom and carried in a small bag. An HTC Vive tracker attached on top ensures the spatial tracking of the device.

induce a modulation of grip forces, we assume that providing variable resistances as a haptic stimulus at the users' index fingers and thereby provoking a modulation of grip forces might enable a haptic weight perception in VR.

3.2 Concept

The concept of our adaptive trigger incorporates the previously described relation between grip forces and the perceived weight and transfers it to the established interaction technique of any consumer VR controller. With such devices, grabbing a virtual object typically involves pulling the trigger, which requires muscle force of users' index fingers to overcome the constant resistance. By adjusting this resisting force, substitutional stimuli (Kaczmarek et al., 1991) are displayed as weight cues and users need to adjust their index finger forces according to the weight of the grabbed virtual object. For example, the heavier the virtual object, the stronger the trigger must be pulled. An illustration of the intended effect is shown in **Figure 2**. Early evidence has demonstrated that the pull of the trigger can be interpreted as varying the grip force that the user exerts onto a virtual object enabling loose and firm grasping for controlling the object's rotation (Bonfert et al., 2019). As the grip force required for holding an object correlates with its weight, higher trigger resistance provoking higher index finger forces might consequentially be interpreted as increased weight.

While our adaptive trigger transfers the haptic recognition of weight onto a one-finger interaction, other haptic interfaces have demonstrated that rendering haptic stimuli only at users' index fingers can be sufficient to enhance haptic object perception in VR (Benko et al., 2016; Choi et al., 2018; Whitmire et al., 2018). In particular, applying resistive forces to restrict the index finger's

movement during grasping has been shown to enhance the perception of rigid and compliant objects (Sinclair et al., 2019). With Sony and Microsoft incorporating haptic feedback into their triggers for game experience, the future availability thereof is another strong argument for exploring the potential of triggers with adaptive resistance for the perception of various haptic events, in our case weight perception.

We implemented our adaptive trigger in an iterative process following a human-centred design approach. First, we built a prototype of a spring mechanism to dynamically adjust the trigger resistance which we present in **section 3.3**. We evaluated the effectiveness of the resistance range and the technical implementation in a pilot study. Based on our findings, we revised the spring mechanism and built the improved haptic controller Triggermuscle, shown in **section 4**.

3.3 Prototype

The first implementation of our adaptive trigger is based on the typical construction of standard triggers: Pulling the trigger compresses one leg of a torsion spring whereby its tension exerts a force in the opposite direction, i.e., resisting the finger's pull. To establish a change in tension force, we constructed a mechanism that rotates the spring's second leg before a pull motion, increasing or decreasing its angle. The resulting adjustment of the trigger resistance is dynamically performed by a high-voltage (7.4 V) digital micro servo (BMS-115HV) which rotates the usually fixed leg via a connected tilting platform. The entire mechanism is built into the casing of an HTC Vive controller and connected to the original trigger, as illustrated in **Figure 3**. In contrast to the later Triggermuscle controller, the prototype fully accommodates the servo inside the casing.

FIGURE 4 | Setup in the VE used for the main user study. Both boxes had to be lifted and placed onto the platform right next to it. Virtual "HEAVIER"-buttons on both target platforms allowed participants to log in their response. The same setup was used for the preliminary testing of the pilot study.

With our used spring model, the prototype renders a continuous range of resistance between 19.27 Nmm and 47.61 Nmm with a fully pulled trigger. Beyond that, users could increase the finger force further, but without moving the trigger or changing the input, identical to a conventional trigger. The chosen spring model offered the greatest possible resistance range when installed inside the mechanism and its level of resistance was closely located to the one of an original Vive controller. Informal testing in the lab with three users suggested comparability between the middle value of the prototype's range and the trigger resistance of the original HTC Vive controller. The resistance values are calculated based on the path-force ratio of the spring model (29.44 Nmm/103.89°), the respective compression angle computationally set by the servo, the additional 18° compression when the trigger is pulled and the spring's preloaded angle of 50° when installed inside the mechanism. The latter two angles were carefully measured manually using visual scales. The prototype's total resistance range achieves a maximum increase of 147%. Humans are known to perceive a difference in spring stiffness between 15 and 22%, also known as the Weber Fraction (WF) (Jones and Tan, 2013).

Apart from the modified resistance, the haptic sensation of pulling the trigger is maintained, including the final *click*. This occurs when users fully pull the trigger which then mechanically pushes the original mini button that registers the digital signal at the maximum limit. The signal is send via cable to an ESP32 microcontroller unit (MCU) which also drives the servo and communicates with Unity 2018.3 via Bluetooth. Along with a 11.1 V lithium polymer battery and a battery eliminator circuit (BEC) component, the MCU is carried in a small bag on the user's back and connected to the controller's bottom via cable. Since the original tracking components were removed, an HTC Vive tracker 1.0 is mounted to the top of the controller.

3.4 Pilot Study

Our pilot study evaluated users' ability to perceive and discriminate different resistances in VR while using the prototype. Similar to previous haptic device research (Dominjon et al., 2005; Maereg et al., 2017; Suchoski et al., 2018; Ryu et al., 2020), we conducted a psychophysical experiment to measure the just noticeable difference (JND) of adaptive trigger resistance in VR. In addition, we also carried out semi-structured interviews to qualitatively assess subjective perception. In accordance with our research goal, to explore weight perception through adaptive trigger resistance, our initial objective also included the prototype's effect on the perception of virtual weight. However, preliminary testing, in which eight participants lifted and compared the weight of two boxes in VR (see **Figure 4** for the VE), suggested that weight perception was not influenced by the varying intensity of the trigger resistance. Based on participants' reports, we assumed that the visual modality of the box-lifting task dominated the perception. To address this issue, we simplified the visual input and focused, as a first step in the pilot study, only on users' ability to discriminate different trigger resistances, without additional weight perception. The simplified pilot study is described below.

3.4.1 Experiment

We recruited nine participants (two females, seven males) aged 21–50 (M = 28, SD = 9.22), of which the majority (7) reported previous VR experience. One participant did not produce valid data and was excluded from further analysis. At the beginning of the experiment, participants gave their consent to take part in the study and were not made aware of the altered trigger resistance to ensure unbiased experience. Throughout the experiment, participants used the prototype and wore the head-mounted display (HMD) of the HTC Vive system. Noise-cancelling headphones played neutral music to block the motion noise of the servo and to avoid possible bias.

To implement an interaction task that involved pulling the trigger, participants were asked to change the colour of a grey virtual wall in VR by pressing the button. In each trial, participants consecutively activated two colours, magenta or green. For each activation, a different trigger resistance was rendered. Each colour was then deactivated, returning the wall to grey, as soon as the trigger was released. At the end of each trial, participants chose that colour that felt heavier to activate and logged their response by touching the virtual interface button in the respective colour. To assess participants' ability to discriminate different resistances, we followed the method of constant stimuli with a two-alternative forced choice (2AFC) paradigm (Jones and Tan, 2013), as this is said to produce more accurate results than alternative methods (Simpson, 1988; Guilford, 1955). Each activation was haptically rendered with different trigger resistances using the prototype described in **section 3.3**. In each trial, participants were presented with the same standard resistance (19.27 Nmm) and with one of four preselected comparison resistances (26.35, 33.44, 40.52, 47.61 Nmm). These were equally distributed along the prototype's resistance range. The comparison resistances were computed based on the compression angles set by the servo and by the path-force ratio of our used torsion spring model. Typically, the comparison values are spaced on either side of the standard value (Jones and Tan, 2013). However, we were concerned that presenting only half of the range as the maximum resistance change might be too subtle to be noticed by participants. We, therefore, chose the minimum resistance as the standard value, similar to (Maiero et al., 2019). Each comparison stimulus was tested 10 times, resulting in a total of 40 trials. The order of all trials and the appearance of the standard and comparison resistance as well as the appearance of green and magenta within one trial were randomised. Three pre-task trials allowed participants to familiarise themselves with the procedure. Upon task completion, we carried out semi-structured interviews to assess participants' self-reported experience.

3.4.2 Results

We measured the proportions of "heavier"-responses for each tested comparison resistance, plotted psychometric functions (PFs) and assessed the goodness-of-fit (Schütt et al., 2016) using the MATLAB toolbox psignifit 4 (Schütt, 2019). Based on the results, only three participants qualified for further JND computation, the point of subjective equality (PSE) and the WF. Three of the excluded data sets performed around the guess rate. The other two performed almost perfectly, not allowing an assessment of discrimination sensitivity, since the method of constant stimuli of psychophysical testing requires a decreasing range of correct responses between 100 and 50% in the case of our 2AFC task. For the remaining three participants, the average JND was 3.90 Nmm (SD = 0.79), resulting in an average WF of 14.70% (SD = 3.60). This level of sensory precision is slightly below the previously mentioned 15–22% WF in the literature of spring stiffness discrimination. However, due to the small number of considered data sets, the results should be treated with caution.

3.4.3 Discussion and Implications

At this point, the results remain inconclusive if the adaptive trigger resistance can be discriminated sufficiently in VR. Nonetheless, our findings offer the incentive to continue exploring the adaptive trigger resistance since the data sets of three participants suggest that their identification of the heavier activation was influenced by the intensity of the resistance. Further, two participants achieved an almost always perfect identification which further indicates an influence of the adaptive trigger resistance on their perception. Our findings also highlight two key limitations with the prototype's haptic feedback which we will discuss in the following.

Simplifying the visual input after the preliminary testing showed an improvement in participants' perception of the adaptive trigger resistance. We assume it enabled a shift in their attention and allowed participants to detect the provided haptic feedback by themselves, as they were kept unaware of it. This assumption is in line with other haptic VR research also observing a domination of the haptic sense by the visual sense (Ban et al., 2012; Azmandian et al., 2016; Choi et al., 2018; Degraen et al., 2019). Providing stronger haptic stimuli in future investigation might, therefore, achieve a more balanced perception of both senses. Consecutively, this might allow more users to sense the resistance as well as sense the resistance more strongly. To continue the exploration and investigate whether higher resisting forces improve the sensing of the adaptive trigger resistance and if they can influence the perception of weight in VR, we plan to establish a wider resistance range.

Furthermore, statements obtained from the interview showed that a subtle vibration occurring as a side effect during the servo's adjustment was noticed by all participants. This suggests another possible diversion of participants' haptic attention, additionally preventing them from recognising the resistance change. This could have again been amplified by the fact that participants did not know about the adaptive trigger resistance. We plan to address the vibration as a possible side effect through modifications in the hardware as well as software design. Modifying the hardware design by increasing the distance between the servo and participants' hands, adding additional damping or by using a different type of actuation might help to reduce the exposure to the servo's subtle adjustment vibrations. Implications for the software design are derived from our observations during the preliminary testing with the box-lifting task. The implemented software for that task adjusted the servo angle when participants reached for the virtual box and intersected its collider with the one from the virtual controller. To decouple the controller's adjustment from the moment of participants preparing to pull the trigger, we plan to set the servo's angle independent from the lifting motion.

4 TRIGGERMUSCLE

To overcome the drawbacks of the prototype, we built Triggermuscle, which is shown in **Figure 1**. The key change implemented in Triggermuscle is the revised spring mechanism that utilises an extension spring. This allows a larger manipulation of the exerted force in contrast to the torsion spring used for the prototype. Therefore, pulling the trigger of Triggermuscle stretches the attached extension spring and makes the exerted force noticeable to users' index fingers as the trigger resistance. Thus, changing the length of the extension spring enables the adjustment of the trigger resistance.

4.1 Implementation

The revised spring mechanism is again built into the casing of an HTC Vive controller and attached to the original trigger, as illustrated in **Figure 5**. The dynamic adjustment of the extension spring is established with a high-voltage (6.0 V)

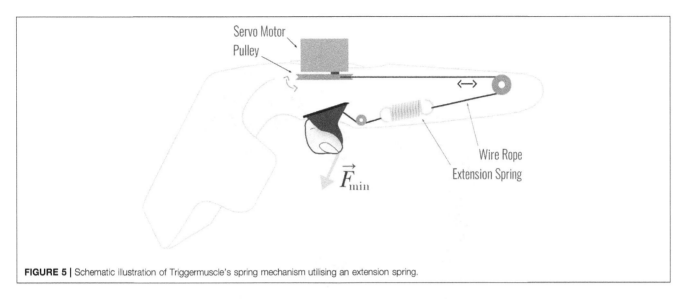

FIGURE 5 | Schematic illustration of Triggermuscle's spring mechanism utilising an extension spring.

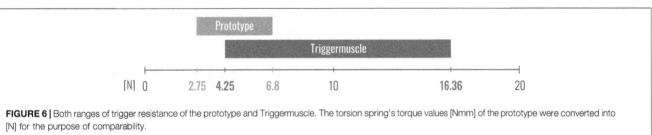

FIGURE 6 | Both ranges of trigger resistance of the prototype and Triggermuscle. The torsion spring's torque values [Nmm] of the prototype were converted into [N] for the purpose of comparability.

digital micro servo (BMS-210DMH). However, in contrast to the prototype, the servo was moved upwards and installed into the original trackpad component of the controller. The revised servo position increases the distance to the user's hand and was intended to reduce the sensed vibrations reported in the pilot study. To provide further damping, a protective silicon cover for the HTC Vive controller was wrapped around the handle. With an attached pulley on top, the servo is connected to the extension spring via a thin 1 mm wire rope. Despite its small diameter, the wire rope is strong enough to handle the forces and inelastic to ensure accurate translation. Changing the servo's angle rotates the attached pulley and winds the connected wire rope, thus pulling or releasing the spring. A second, smaller redirect pulley in the controller's bottom secures a stable guiding of the wire rope. Due to this principle of force redirect, the mechanism can be tailored to other form factors for different interaction devices.

The dimensions of the controller casing allow a spring stretch of up to 20.3 mm. For the selection of the suitable spring model, the same selection criteria were applied for Triggermuscle as for the prototype. In combination with the used extension spring model (spring rate of R = 0.592 N/mm, minimum force 1.33 N), a continuous regulation of the resistance is achieved from approximately 4.29–16.36 N with a fully pulled trigger (5 mm stretch adding 2.96 N). Increasing the finger force further beyond the set maximum limit does not move the trigger or change the input, identical to a conventional trigger. Note that we use the force unit [N] for the extension spring which differs from the unit [Nmm] for the torsion spring torque of the prototype to

emphasise the correct units of the spring types and for the readers to easily identify the prototype and Triggermuscle. The total resistance range illustrates an increase of over 281%. In contrast, the prototype allowed a smaller increase of 147%. Triggermuscle, therefore, exceeds the previously tested range of trigger resistance of the prototype by 134%. For the purpose of comparison, both ranges are illustrated in **Figure 6** in which the resistance values of the prototype were converted into [N].

Similar to the prototype, the haptic sensation of pulling the trigger is maintained, apart from the modified resistance. The MCU, the lithium polymer battery and the BEC are again carried in the bag previously used for the prototype. The final controller is shown in **Figure 7**. An HTC Vive tracker 1.0 attached to the controller's top provides spatial tracking since the original tracking components were removed from the casing. The total weight of Triggermuscle including the HTC Vive tracker 1.0 (90 g) and its mounting (10 g) is 300 g. In comparison, the original HTC Vive controller weighs 200 g. The bag carrying the battery (250 g), MCU (10 g) and BEC (22 g) weighs 350 g. Further details are described in the workshop paper (Stellmacher, 2021).

5 STUDY

Our main user study evaluated the revised technical implementation of the adaptive trigger that is built into

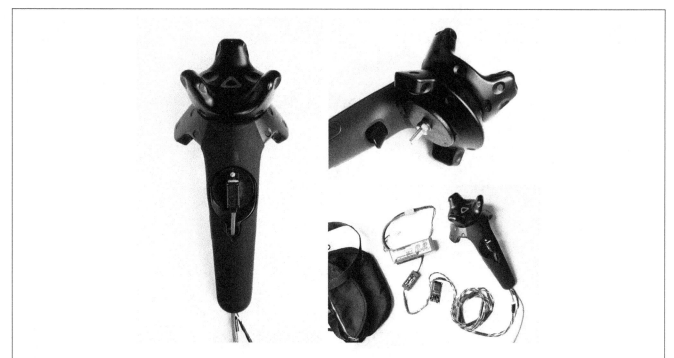

FIGURE 7 | **(left)** Our haptic VR controller Triggermuscle. **(top right)** Attachment of the HTC Vive tracker to enable spatial tracking. **(right bottom)** Electronic components (MCU, the battery and the BEC) are carried in a small bag.

Triggermuscle. Our main objective was to explore whether the increased resistance range makes more users notice the change in intensity. In addition, we investigated whether differently intense trigger resistances resemble a perception of virtual weight in VR. To do so, this study repeated the psychophysical experiment of our pilot study by using the method of constant stimuli. However, we adapted the interaction task to the main goal of the user study and repeated the box-lifting task used in the preliminary testing of the pilot study.

5.1 Participants

We recruited 21 participants (five females, 16 males) aged 19–29 (M = 22.67, SD = 2.78). Most of them (19) stated previous VR experience, more than half (16) were familiar with non-VR game controllers. No participant was previously involved in the pilot study.

5.2 Task and Stimuli

Participants lifted and compared two visually identical boxes and identified the heavier one. The setup in the VE is shown in **Figure 4**. The virtual weight of both boxes was haptically rendered with different trigger resistances. In each trial, participants were presented with the same standard resistance and with one of five preselected comparison resistances. The value of the standard resistance was 4.29 N (0% of the range). The five comparison resistances were 4.46 N (2%), 4.79 N (5%), 6.09 N (19%), 8.67 N (46%) and 13.82 N (100%), with each being repeated ten times. Therefore, a

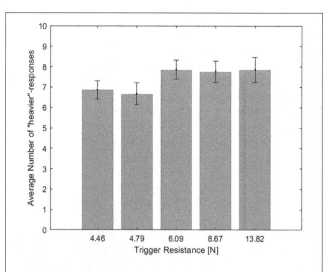

FIGURE 8 | Average number of "heavier"-responses for each tested resistance intensity from our main user study with error bars representing the standard errors. The maximum possible value is ten due to the total amount of ten trials per intensity level. A decrease was expected for the number of "heavier"-responses over the decreasing range of the resistance intensity, which, however, cannot be observed in the average responses.

total of 50 trials were conducted. The order of all trials and the appearance of the standard and comparison resistance within one trial was randomised. The possible maximum value of 16.36 N of Triggermuscle was restricted to 13.82 N for this user study to avoid wearing out the

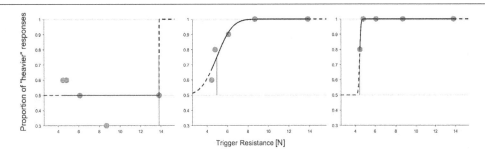

FIGURE 9 | Psychometric functions of three participants representing three commonly observed behaviours in our user study for the perception of Triggermuscle's adaptive trigger resistance. **(left)** "Heavier"-responses are located closely around and below guess rate not allowing a direct conclusion for the perception of different resistances. **(middle)** Proportion of "heavier"-responses decreases with the decrease of resistance intensity. This perception shows the full range of discrimination sensitivity of the sensory system. **(right)** High proportion of "heavier"-responses even with smaller resistances.

components. The lower half of the tested resistance range was covered by four comparison values since we considered the highest resistance to be easily recognised. We also assumed that participants would easily become aware of the change in the haptic feedback and consequently be more attentive to smaller changes. We also expected our sample to include participants who almost always successfully identify the heavier resistance as observed in two participants in the pilot study, and thus motivating the small 2% value. The crooked percentage values are due to the resolution of the servo angles.

5.3 Procedure

At the beginning of the task, participants received instructions but were kept unaware of the adaptive trigger resistance and possible vibrations as a side effect. They performed three pre-task trials in the VE to familiarise themselves with the procedure of lifting the boxes and selecting the heavier one. Three comparison resistances were rendered during those trials: 7.29 N (25% of the range), 7.72 N (29%) and 8.15 N (32%). Since we considered higher resistances of Triggermuscle to be easily recognised, the values were distributed around the lower third of the range to ensure an unbiased starting position for the psychophysical testing during the experiment task. To avoid possible influences of the servo's motion noise, participants wore noise-cancelling headphones and listened to neutral music. After completing the experiment task, we carried out semi-structured interviews to assess the self-reported experience of participants.

6 RESULTS

We assessed the influence of adaptive trigger resistance on the perception of virtual weight based on quantitative data recorded during the task and qualitative data from the interview.

6.1 Trigger Resistance Discrimination

The average number of "heavier"-responses for each tested resistance intensity are shown in **Figure 8**. We expected the

TABLE 1 | Results of four participants of our psychophysical user study.

Participant	JND [N]	WF [%]	PSE [N]
5	0.81	16.27	4.96
13	0.06	1.25	4.46
17	0.13	2.23	5.72
18	0.13	2.14	6.11
Mean	0.28	5.47	5.31
SD	0.35	7.21	0.74

number of "heavier"-responses to clearly decrease with decreasing resistance intensity. This behaviour, however, could not be observed in the average responses. For a more differentiated assessment, PFs for all 21 participants were fitted, again using the MATLAB toolbox psignifit 4 (Schütt, 2019). We also reassessed goodness-of-fit based on the calculated deviance to assess the proximity between the fitted dataset and the underlying model. It asymptotically converges to 1.0. However, the lower the mean proportion of correct responses, the higher the expected deviance is. A "typical cut off [is] around the value 2 for what is often regarded as a still" well behaved" data set" (Schütt et al., 2016).

The results demonstrate highly diverse subjective perception of trigger resistance. The observed perception can be categorised into three behavioural patterns based on their deviance values and average percentages of "heavier"-responses. Each category is represented by one of the three exemplary PFs (see **Figure 9**). Seven PFs are located at the lower end of the spectrum (represented by **Figure 9** (left)). The average percentage was of 50.3% (SD = 5.50) for the "heavier"-responses with a deviance often well above 2.00. Since these responses are located closely around the guess rate of 50% (in our 2AFC case), not enough evidence exists to support our assumption that they were influenced by the intensity of the trigger resistance. The second category includes four data sets that exhibit the expected decrease in discrimination ability with a decrease in resistance level (represented by **Figure 9** (middle)). Another seven PFs are located at the higher end (represented by **Figure 9** (right)). They show an average success rate of

94.30% (SD = 1.80). Five exhibited a deviance well above 2.00, two a value of 0.00 and 0.02, respectively. These participants almost always perfectly identified the heavier box, even with smaller resistances, and did not produce data within a resistance range where their perception changes according to the level of resistance. Three PFs showed a deviance above 2.0, indicating a high discrepancy from the underlying model. Since the method of constant stimuli of psychophysical testing requires a decreasing range of correct responses between 100 and 50% in the case of our 2AFC task, only the four data sets represented by **Figure 9** (middle) qualify for JND calculation. The remaining 17 data sets did not produce data that would allow understanding the discrimination sensitivity of the sensory system around the threshold and the resulting perception. Most of these participants are associated with both ends of the spectrum depicted in **Figure 9**. The results of the four qualified participants for JND, WF and PSE are listed in **Table 1**. Their sensory precision was determined with an average JND of 0.28 N (SD = 0.35). This resulted in an average WF of 5.47% (SD = 7.21), which is below the reported WF of 15–22% in the literature of spring stiffness discrimination. However, due to the small number of included data sets these values can only be interpreted as a first indicator of future studies. Nonetheless, the low average is caused by three out of four participants exhibiting a WF of equal or below 2.23%. Only one participant produced a WF of 16.27%, which is in line with the literature.

6.2 Interview Feedback

Statements obtained in the interview revealed that one-third of participants self-reported the adaptive trigger resistance as the cue for identifying the heavier box. Two of them additionally incorporated subtle vibrations which occur as a side effect during the servo's adjustment. The perception of virtual weight was described through "the trigger was harder to press for heavier boxes" or "depending on how much I had to press the index finger". Lifting the boxes was described as "heavier or less heavy", lifting heavier boxes was characterised as "more demanding" and one participant reported that grabbing a heavier box took "much longer" to grab than lighter ones. One participant stated he was initially unable to identify the cause of his sense of weight before noticing that the trigger "was harder to press". However, he stated that he stopped being consciously aware of the change after some time since he felt so immersed in the virtual world.

The remaining two-thirds of participants reported vibrations only, visual input or sound as the basis for their decision process, or they were unable to tell. Vibrations only were mentioned by six participants who further described different intensities, moments of appearance and different ways of how vibrations ended. One participant stated he focused on the vibration and perceived a sound when he experienced more vibrations, despite the noise-cancelling headphones with neutral music. One participant who was unable to identify the reason for his selection process still described the boxes as "much heavier" and "much lighter".

During the interview, participants were also asked if they had spontaneous associations for the content of the boxes during the task. Nine did not, but twelve did. For them, light boxes felt empty and were associated with feathers while heavy boxes felt solid and as if they were filled with sand, stones, gravel, brick or a book. One participant stated he imagined the boxes empty, but made from different materials.

7 DISCUSSION AND FUTURE WORK

The evaluation of Triggermuscle showed that the revised spring mechanism with a larger resistance range improved the perception of adaptive trigger resistance compared to the pilot study using the prototype system. However, it also showed some limitations of the current spring mechanism to simulate weight over variable resistance. In this section, we examine our results by identifying the advantages and limitations of our design from a perceptual and a hardware perspective and laying out potential directions for improvement in hardware design and follow-up studies.

7.1 RQ1—Do Different Trigger Resistances Influence the Haptic Perception of Different Virtual Weights in VR?

The interview responses of our main study revealed seven participants—one third of the sample—self-reporting the change in trigger resistance and discriminating different virtual weights according to the intensity of the resistance. These reports about the weight experience demonstrate that higher resistances were associated with heavier virtual weights, smaller resistances with lighter virtual weights. While this applies only to a limited number of our participants, it presents early indications that different trigger resistances can provide substitutional haptic weight cues at the index finger and, therefore, induce a sense of lighter and heavier virtual objects. However, at the current time, our results remain inconclusive and we cannot fully confirm our assumptions as a considerable number of users were also unable to effectively sense, interpret and associate the cues. This raises the question of why some participants experienced virtual weight using Triggermuscle while others did not.

The quantitative data of our main study highlights the users' ability to discriminate resistances for 13 data sets. This suggests that 3/5 of the participants were able to successfully differentiate between the resistance intensities rendered by Triggermuscle. The data sets consist of four participants with moderate success rates qualifying for the JND calculation, seven participants almost always identifying the heavier box and two additional participants showing an average success rate of 80 and 84%. Surprisingly, this number of data sets exceeds the number of self-reports about the change in trigger resistance by six. This discrepancy may indicate that some participants registered different resistances, but were not consciously aware of it.

7.1.1 Visual Dominance

We believe that the often reported visual dominance in human perception (Posner et al., 1976; Hecht and Reiner, 2009) might have caused the differences in the individual haptic sensing of the trigger resistance and shifted the focus for some participants away from the haptic sensation at their index finger towards the visually identical-looking boxes. Our assumption is supported by the results of our pilot study in which more participants noticed the change in trigger resistance after we simplified the visual input in response to the observations during the preliminary testing. The modification removed the visual sensation of identical-looking boxes which might have previously dominated the perception of the varying haptic feedback. In addition, the visual dominance has been previously reported in VR in the context of pseudo-haptics to overwrite haptic cues, e.g., in haptic retargeting (Azmandian et al., 2016; Zenner et al., 2021), shape rendering (Ban et al., 2012) or the perception of different surface textures in VR (Choi et al., 2018; Degraen et al., 2019). While these approaches purposely made use of this effect, it might have disrupted the haptic perception of the trigger resistance in case of Triggermuscle. We intend to follow this up in future work by exploring the ability to discriminate the trigger resistance in a non-VR setting where participants are blindfolded. This might focus participants' attention on the haptic sense and, further, remove the aspect of weight association. Since this setup would be similar to typical studies investigating the discrimination of stiffness, we would expect the results to be in line with the reported weber fractions from such studies. Nonetheless, we would also like to explore the pseudo-haptics approach through meaningfully combining the trigger resistance with virtual objects that visually indicate different weights. Comparing the weight perception based on only the adaptive resistance, only visual input and a combination of both could identify if visual input could also improve the ability to discriminate between resistances and facilitates an association with virtual weight in VR.

7.1.2 Subtle Vibrations

To better understand participants' discrimination mechanisms and to detect the causes of individual differences, we cross-referenced our qualitative and quantitative results for each participant by comparing the reported decision factors with the psychometric functions. This helped to identify the environmental vibration of the controller's handle, which occurred as an unintended side effect of the servo's adjustment, as a potential haptic confounding factor. Psychometric functions indicating an influence of the resistance on the perception system belonged to interview statements reporting either only the altered trigger resistance, or only vibration, or a combination of both. More precisely, participants who stated that their decision relied entirely on trigger resistance exhibited the expected decrease in their discrimination ability for smaller resistances. While these cases emphasise a relationship between the level of trigger resistance and the perceived weight, those participants who performed best stated both resistance change and vibration, but also vibration on its own as decisive factors. This reveals that vibrations, as an additionally perceived haptic cue, might have interfered with the ability to sense different resistances and their association with weight difference. This assumption, however, is challenged by our data. Five of our participants

also stated that they based their decisions on the sensed vibrations while producing poor success rates closely around the guess rate. Due to these two extremes, we cannot make a clear assumption about the influence of vibrations, positive or negative, on the ability to discriminate variable resistances rendered by Triggermuscle and on the association with virtual weight. While previous work has intentionally utilised vibrotactile feedback to render contact forces in addition to asymmetric skin deformation for weight sensation, it has also identified vibration amplitude as a possible confounding factor with an unknown effect on the perception of skin deformation (Choi et al., 2017).

One possible explanation for the differences in differentiating resistances could be the weber fraction of vibrotactile frequency, which ranges widely from 3 to 30% (Jones and Tan, 2013). Some participants might have been, therefore, more receptive to vibrations than others, causing different degrees of distraction away from the change in trigger resistance. This assumption is supported by participants describing vibrations to different extents: One participant reported that he did not notice any vibrations, while others described them as a side effect and yet others focused on them as the main indicator of virtual weight. Since participants were not informed about the adaptive trigger, this might have consolidated a focus on vibration. Further, this possible shift in attention to vibration could also have been promoted by servo adjustment (i.e., the occurrence of vibration). To prevent adjustment during grasping in the main study, the servo changed its angle at the beginning of each trial and before grasping the second box. However, observations during the task showed that some participants released the trigger very slowly and carefully when placing the box. In the case of the first box, the servo's adjustment for the second box was then provoked when participants were still focused on the previous box. In addition, the very first servo adjustment in the initial trial appeared even before participants pulled the trigger for the first time, hence before they experienced any resistance. Nonetheless, the occurrence of vibration does not follow a clear pattern. Vibrations occur not only as soon as the servo registers a pulling force inside the mechanism (e.g., when resistance exceeds the standard value), but also when the trigger is pulled during standard value configuration. Additionally, in this state, a reverberation sometimes occurs when the trigger is released, meaning the servo is active, i.e., causing subtle vibrations. Vibrations as a distraction in haptic devices were previously described as "one of the most noticeable disturbances in a force reflecting device" (Tan et al., 1994). To quantify participants' exposure to the reported subtle vibrations, we took measurements using the digital vibration meter no. 480 600 from VOGEL GERMANY (VOGEL GERMANY, 2021). While all servo adjustments from the main study were tested, only the switch between the minimum and maximum resistances created measurable vibrations. However, these vibrations are below the perceivable range. Importantly, this effect occurs mainly only during the brief period of servo adjustment and does not mature into a continuous vibration.

In future studies, we would like to clarify these possible limitations concerning vibrations. To approach a consistent sensing of the varying resistance, we would like to investigate the role of attention by informing users about the adaptive trigger and by additionally instructing them to ignore the current mechanism's side effect. In addition, shifting the focus away from vibration and to the trigger's intended feedback could be further facilitated by implementing a short adjustment phase. This would ensure that the servo's angle is not configured while participants are close to a virtual object.

7.1.3 Hardware

To address this matter in future hardware design and decrease users' exposure to unintended vibrations, other types of actuation technologies could be tested, such as a micro linear actuator for controlling the spring's length or exploring magnetic repulsion forces which are used in magnetic force-feedback joysticks. This could, additionally, increase the stimulus range and emphasise the trigger resistance as the weight cue. Apart from that, vibrations could also be intentionally used to enhance the experience of virtual weight. A perspective on this matter is demonstrated by previous work which explored vibratory stimulation and patterns for weight perception during the interaction with a vision-tactile-force display (Mizuno et al., 2013). As a movable weight shifts along the display's back towards one of the display's handles, the perceived weight of that handle seems heavier when strong vibrations are rendered. Vibrations were also observed to enhance other virtual object properties such as virtual stiffness in combination with visual information (Maereg et al., 2017). To better understand the possibility to enhance Triggermuscle's weight perception meaningfully with vibrations, further research is necessary.

To achieve a simple weight rendering technique that could potentially be integrated into consumer VR controllers, our approach took only into account the trigger and its level of resistance. While participants were, therefore, presented with different resistive forces at their fingertip, Triggermuscle did not render skin stretch as an additional weight cue. This stimulus is often provided in other haptic devices also focusing on rendering haptic feedback at users' fingers, such as (Minamizawa et al., 2007a; Scheggi et al., 2010; Kurita et al., 2011; Suchoski et al., 2018). While it is common for approaches of sensory substitution to not address the receptors that are addressed in reality, this limitation could have contributed to the different reactions towards the same haptic feedback of Triggermuscle. As the previous finger-worn haptic interfaces for skin stretch use belts or plates stretching and pressing the finger pad, users passively experience the skin modulation in mid-air without physical counter forces to the hand. Since, in contrast, users of the handheld Triggermuscle actively apply pressure on their skin by pulling the trigger and experiencing the counter force of the held device, an additional integration of skin stretch rendering at the trigger might enhance the weight sensation of Triggermuscle. While previous research has shown to successfully render haptic feedback only to users' index fingers for object properties (Benko et al., 2016; Choi et al., 2018; Whitmire et al., 2018; Sinclair et al., 2019), not receiving a sensation to the full hand during grasping might have further impacted the weight sensation of Triggermuscle.

7.2 RQ2—How can the Intensity of the Trigger be Quantified and Mapped to Convey Distinguishable Virtual Weights?

Our findings show that some participants easily detected smaller changes in the resistance, thus enabling them to haptically and precisely render lighter objects, while other participants did not notice any influence of the intensity level even with large differences. Sensitivity differences towards resistance might have been affected by the previously discussed limitations. Nonetheless, self-reports on absolute weight and on the respective box content associations revealed comparable statements for lower and higher resistances. While these reported impressions indicated a possible influence of the visual appearance of the virtual boxes used in the experimental task, they suggest the possibility of using visual input to map the level of resistance and the perceived absolute virtual weight. Future investigating adaptive trigger resistance as a weight metaphor could determine whether haptic feedback could be used to convey a large range of different relative virtual weights. This could be achieved by creating a visual weight context through visually rendering objects of a similar weight class in the VE and through testing the same resistances in different visual weight classes. To advance the experience of virtual weight during interaction, auditory cues could also be presented to convey weight information. For example, a hollow sound could convey an empty, light object whereas a dull sound could convey a filled, heavy object. This arrangement could also be applied to objects of different materials due to different weights.

In summary, designing triggers with adaptive resistance could be one way of equipping VR controllers with enriched haptic feedback in the future. Since the trigger is a commonly used button that can be found in other VR controllers such as Oculus Touch or game controllers, actuated triggers could be integrated into a various interaction devices, also beyond the VR domain. To achieve the intended effect, Triggermuscle's spring mechanism could be tailored to other controller shapes. Alternatively, actuation could be modified with various technical approaches including motors, springs, magnets, and gears, to flexibly fit a wide array of form factors. Particular attention should be paid to the discussed limitations in order to achieve a consistent sensing of the haptic feedback for all users. These limitations should be addressed through hardware design by minimising unintended vibrations. Our findings also indicate possible cross-modal effects, which need to be considered when designing adaptive trigger resistance for VR. One possible limitation of our study is that we asked participants about the object's weight, as this may have biased their association with the provided feedback. Although, participants were not informed of the type of haptic feedback provided, one third linked the stimulus to weight perception. Based on user reports, we further assume that some participants had a real sense of weight as they spontaneously imagined light boxes being filled with feathers, and the heavy ones with sand, stones or gravel.

In the future, we are also interested in expanding the scope of applications for adaptive trigger resistance in VR beyond weight perception by exploring visual cues for other physical properties. As studies (Johansson and Westling, 1984; Flanagan et al., 1995; Ellis and Lederman, 1999) have documented that different material properties impact the level of applied grip forces when lifting an object and its perceived weight, this effect could be potentially be used to further enhance weight rendering in VR and additionally convey different materials of the lifted object. Adapting the trigger resistance then not only to the object's weight but also to its surface roughness or smoothness could account for the naturally performed grip force modulation as reported in the studies and contribute to a more realistic weight experience. Further, we are interested in whether the trigger resistance can substitute haptic cues for virtual stiffness and if different grasp animations can further convey various surface tensions of different materials. We also imagine an integration of resistive forces beyond the trigger in other haptic devices, such as the haptic VR controller Haptic Revolver (Whitmire et al., 2018) to simulate surface stiffness. Users of this device are presented with textured wheels at their index finger to haptically experience shear forces and textures. By adding resistive forces to the textured wheel, varying surface stiffness could be rendered when the textured wheel is pressed down. Additionally, introducing an active modulation of the resistance during the pull of the trigger could render a modulation of surface tension, e.g., depending on how much a deformable material is squeezed. The resistance modulation could also convey weight shifts, e.g., as the liquid inside a cup moves around when balancing it or when an object is accelerated in order to be thrown. The brief increase or decrease of trigger resistance could furthermore be applied for haptic feedback of operating virtual UI elements.

8 CONCLUSION

We explored adaptive trigger resistance as a novel approach for weight perception in VR. The adaptive trigger inside our haptic VR controller *Triggermuscle* modifies the level of resistance according to the weight of a grabbed virtual object. Users, therefore, need to scale their index finger force to grab objects with different virtual weights. We presented the design and implementation of the prototype's initial and Triggermuscle's revised spring

mechanism, which adjusts the trigger resistance dynamically and continuously. As proof of concept, our systems are built into the casing of an HTC Vive controller. The mechanisms, however, can easily be adapted to various of form factors of different interaction devices. In two user studies, we evaluated both technical implementations and explored the positive as well as the negative effects of actuated adaptive trigger resistance on users' discrimination ability and associations with virtual object weight in VR. Our findings show large differences between participants. While Triggermuscle's adaptive trigger enabled 3 out of 5 participants to sense and discriminate different levels of resistance, only 1 out of 3 participants self-reported an association with weight. In the successful weight illusion, lower resistances were associated with lighter objects and higher resistances with heavier objects. While these findings reveal early indications for using adaptive trigger resistance to simulate virtual weight in VR, they reveal limitations regarding the sensing of variable resistance, perceptual mechanisms and hardware design. We have discussed and wish to address these limitations in future studies. Our findings provide a first important step towards using adaptive trigger resistance in VR. We hope that this work motivates further research on transforming established input elements into input-output components, so as to enhance the haptic experience of handheld VR controllers.

AUTHOR CONTRIBUTIONS

CS was the primary author and developed both systems, conducted user studies, data analysis, literature review, manuscript writing and manuscript review. MB contributed to the discussion of the research idea as well as the literature review, manuscript writing and manuscript review. EK contributed to the discussion of the research idea, provided feedback on the prototypes, and took part in manuscript writing and manuscript review. JS contributed to the discussion of the research idea, provided feedback on the prototypes, took part in the manuscript writing and manuscript review and supervised the project. All authors contributed to the article and approved the submitted version.

REFERENCES

Azmandian, M., Hancock, M., Benko, H., Ofek, E., and Wilson, A. D. (2016). "Haptic Retargeting: Dynamic Repurposing of Passive Haptics for Enhanced Virtual Reality Experiences," in *Proceedings of the 2016 CHI Conference on Human Factors in Computing Systems* (New York, NY, USA: Association for Computing Machinery), 1968–1979. CHI '16. doi:10.1145/2858036.2858226

Ban, Y., Kajinami, T., Narumi, T., Tanikawa, T., and Hirose, M. (2012). "Modifying an Identified Curved Surface Shape Using Pseudo-haptic Effect," in *Proceeding of the 2012 IEEE Haptics Symposium (HAPTICS)*, Vancouver, BC, Canada, 4-7 March 2012 (Vancouver, BC: IEEE), 211–216. doi:10.1109/HAPTIC.2012.6183793

Ben-Tzvi, P., and Ma, Z. (2015). Sensing and Force-Feedback Exoskeleton (SAFE) Robotic Glove. *IEEE Trans. Neural Syst. Rehabil. Eng.* 23, 992–1002. doi:10.1109/TNSRE.2014.2378171

Benko, H., Holz, C., Sinclair, M., and Ofek, E. (2016). "NormalTouch and TextureTouch: High-fidelity 3D Haptic Shape Rendering on Handheld Virtual Reality Controllers," in *Proceedings of the 29th Annual Symposium on User Interface Software and Technology* (New York, NY, USAUIST '16: Association for Computing Machinery), 717–728. doi:10.1145/2984511.2984526

Bonfert, M., Porzel, R., and Malaka, R. (2019). "Get a Grip! Introducing Variable Grip for Controller-Based VR Systems," in *Proceeding of the 2019 IEEE Conference on Virtual Reality and 3D User Interfaces (VR)*, Osaka, Japan, 23-27 March 2019 (IEEE), 604–612. doi:10.1109/VR.2019.8797824

Bouzit, M., Burdea, G., Popescu, G., and Boian, R. (2002). The Rutgers Master II-

New Design Force-Feedback Glove. *Ieee/asme Trans. Mechatron.* 7, 256–263. doi:10.1109/TMECH.2002.1011262

Brodie, E. E., and Ross, H. E. (1984). Sensorimotor Mechanisms in Weight Discrimination. *Perception & Psychophysics* 36, 477–481. doi:10.3758/BF03207502

Burdea, G., Zhuang, J., Roskos, E., Silver, D., and Langrana, N. (1992). A Portable Dextrous Master with Force Feedback. *Presence: Teleoperators & Virtual Environments* 1, 18–28. doi:10.1162/pres.1992.1.1.18

Cheng, C.-H., Chang, C.-C., Chen, Y.-H., Lin, Y.-L., Huang, J.-Y., Han, P.-H., et al. (2018). "GravityCup: A Liquid-Based Haptics for Simulating Dynamic Weight in Virtual Reality," in *Proceedings of the 24th ACM Symposium on Virtual Reality Software and Technology* (New York, NY, USA: Association for Computing Machinery), 1–2. VRST '18. doi:10.1145/3281505.3281569

Choi, I., Culbertson, H., Miller, M. R., Olwal, A., and Follmer, S. (2017). "Grabity: A Wearable Haptic Interface for Simulating Weight and Grasping in Virtual Reality," in *Proceedings of the 30th Annual ACM Symposium on User Interface Software and Technology* (New York, NY, USA: Association for Computing Machinery), 119–130. UIST '17. doi:10.1145/3126594.3126599

Choi, I., Ofek, E., Benko, H., Sinclair, M., and Holz, C. (2018). "CLAW: A Multifunctional Handheld Haptic Controller for Grasping, Touching, and Triggering in Virtual Reality," in *Proceedings of the 2018 CHI Conference on Human Factors in Computing Systems* (New York, NY, USA: Association for Computing Machinery). CHI '18, 1–13. doi:10.1145/3173574.3174228

Degraen, D., Zenner, A., and Krüger, A. (2019). "Enhancing Texture Perception in Virtual Reality Using 3D-Printed Hair Structures," in *Proceedings of the 2019 CHI Conference on Human Factors in Computing Systems* (New York, NY, USA: Association for Computing Machinery), 1–12. CHI '19. doi:10.1145/3290605.3300479

Dominjon, L., Lecuyer, A., Burkhardt, J., Richard, P., and Richir, S. (2005). "Influence of Control/Display Ratio on the Perception of Mass of Manipulated Objects in Virtual Environments," in Proceedings - IEEE Virtual Reality, Bonn, Germany, 12-16 March 2005 (IEEE). doi:10.1109/vr.2005.1492749

Ellis, R. R., and Lederman, S. J. (1999). The Material-Weight Illusion Revisited. *Perception & Psychophysics* 61, 1564–1576. doi:10.3758/BF03213118

Ellis, R. R., and Lederman, S. J. (1993). The Role of Haptic versus Visual Volume Cues in the Size-Weight Illusion. *Perception & Psychophysics* 53, 315–324. doi:10.3758/BF03205186

Fang, C., Zhang, Y., Dworman, M., and Harrison, C. (2020). "Wireality: Enabling Complex Tangible Geometries in Virtual Reality with Worn Multi-String Haptics," in *Proceedings of the 2020 CHI Conference on Human Factors in Computing Systems* (New York, NY, USA: Association for Computing Machinery). CHI '20, 1–10. doi:10.1145/3313831.3376470

Flanagan, J. R., Wing, A. M., Allison, S., and Spenceley, A. (1995). Effects of Surface Texture on Weight Perception when Lifting Objects with a Precision Grip. *Perception & Psychophysics* 57, 282–290. doi:10.3758/BF03213054

Gabardi, M., Solazzi, M., Leonardis, D., and Frisoli, A. (2016). "A New Wearable Fingertip Haptic Interface for the Rendering of Virtual Shapes and Surface Features," in Proceeding of the 2016 IEEE Haptics Symposium, HAPTICS, Philadelphia, PA, USA, 8-11 April 2016 (IEEE), 140–146. doi:10.1109/haptics.2016.7463168

Giannopoulos, E., Pomes, A., and Slater, M. (2012). Touching the Void: Exploring Virtual Objects through a Vibrotactile Glove. *Ijvr* 11, 19–24. doi:10.20870/IJVR.2012.11.3.2847

Girard, A., Marchal, M., Gosselin, F., Chabrier, A., Louveau, F., and Lécuyer, A. (2016). Haptip: Displaying Haptic Shear Forces at the Fingertips for Multi-finger Interaction in Virtual Environments. *Front. ICT* 3, 718. doi:10.3389/fict.2016.00006

Gordon, A. M., Forssberg, H., Johansson, R. S., and Westling, G. (1991). Visual Size Cues in the Programming of Manipulative Forces during Precision Grip. *Exp. Brain Res.* 83, 477–482. doi:10.1007/BF00229824

Gu, X., Zhang, Y., Sun, W., Bian, Y., Zhou, D., and Kristensson, P. O. (2016). "Dexmo: An Inexpensive and Lightweight Mechanical Exoskeleton for Motion Capture and Force Feedback in VR," in *Proceedings of the 2016 CHI Conference on Human Factors in Computing Systems* (New York, NY, USA: Association for Computing Machinery), 1991–1995. CHI '16. doi:10.1145/2858036.2858487

Guilford, J. P. (1955). *Psychometric Methods.* 2nd edn. New York: McGraw-Hill.

HaptX (2020). *Haptx Gloves.* Available at: https://haptx.com/ (Accessed June 15, 2020).

Hecht, D., and Reiner, M. (2009). Sensory Dominance in Combinations of Audio, Visual and Haptic Stimuli. *Exp. Brain Res.* 193, 307–314. doi:10.1007/s00221-008-1626-z

Heo, S., Chung, C., Lee, G., and Wigdor, D. (2018). "Thor's Hammer: An Ungrounded Force Feedback Device Utilizing Propeller-Induced Propulsive Force," in *Proceedings of the 2018 CHI Conference on Human Factors in Computing Systems* (New York, NY, USA: Association for Computing Machinery), 1–11.

Hirose, M., Hirota, K., Ogi, T., Yano, H., Kakehi, N., Saito, M., et al. (2001). "Hapticgear: the Development of a Wearable Force Display System for Immersive Projection Displays," in Proceedings IEEE Virtual Reality 2001, Yokohama, Japan, 13-17 March 2001 (IEEE), 123–129. doi:10.1109/VR.2001.913778

Ishii, M., and Sato, M. (1994). A 3D Spatial Interface Device Using Tensed Strings. *Presence: Teleoperators & Virtual Environments* 3, 81–86. doi:10.1162/pres.1994.3.1.81

Je, S., Kim, M. J., Lee, W., Lee, B., Yang, X.-D., Lopes, P., et al. (2019). "Aero-plane: A Handheld Force-Feedback Device that Renders Weight Motion Illusion on a Virtual 2d Plane," in *Proceedings of the 32nd Annual ACM Symposium on User Interface Software and Technology* (New York, NY, USA: Association for Computing Machinery), 763–775. UIST '19. doi:10.1145/3332165.3347926

Jenmalm, P., and Johansson, R. S. (1997). Visual and Somatosensory Information about Object Shape Control Manipulative Fingertip Forces. *J. Neurosci.* 17, 4486–4499. doi:10.1523/jneurosci.17-11-04486.1997

Johansson, R. S., and Westling, G. (1988). Coordinated Isometric Muscle Commands Adequately and Erroneously Programmed for the Weight during Lifting Task with Precision Grip. *Exp. Brain Res.* 71, 59–71. doi:10.1007/BF00247522

Johansson, R. S., and Westling, G. (1984). Roles of Glabrous Skin Receptors and Sensorimotor Memory in Automatic Control of Precision Grip when Lifting Rougher or More Slippery Objects. *Exp. Brain Res.* 56, 550–564. doi:10.1007/BF00237997

Jones, L. A., and Tan, H. Z. (2013). Application of Psychophysical Techniques to Haptic Research. *IEEE Trans. Haptics* 6, 268–284. doi:10.1109/TOH.2012.74

Kaczmarek, K. A., Webster, J. G., Bach-y-Rita, P., and Tompkins, W. J. (1991). Electrotactile and Vibrotactile Displays for Sensory Substitution Systems. *IEEE Trans. Biomed. Eng.* 38, 1–16. doi:10.1109/10.682010.1109/10.68204

Kurita, Y., Yonezawa, S., Ikeda, A., and Ogasawara, T. (2011). "Weight and Friction Display Device by Controlling the Slip Condition of a Fingertip," in Proceeding of the 2011 IEEE International Conference on Intelligent Robots and Systems, San Francisco, CA, USA, 25-30 Sept. 2011 (IEEE), 2127–2132. doi:10.1109/iros.2011.6094613

Lee, J., Sinclair, M., Gonzalez-Franco, M., Ofek, E., and Holz, C. (2019). "TORC: A Virtual Reality Controller for In-Hand High-Dexterity Finger Interaction," in *Proceedings of the 2019 CHI Conference on Human Factors in Computing Systems* (New York, NY, USA: Association for Computing Machinery), 1–13. CHI '19. doi:10.1145/3290605.3300301

Leonardis, D., Solazzi, M., Bortone, I., and Frisoli, A. (2015). "A Wearable Fingertip Haptic Device with 3 Dof Asymmetric 3-rsr Kinematics," in Proceeding of the 2015 IEEE World Haptics Conference (WHC), Evanston, IL, USA, 22-26 June 2015 (IEEE), 388–393. doi:10.1109/WHC.2015.7177743

Liu, Y., Hashimoto, T., Yoshida, S., Narumi, T., Tanikawa, T., and Hirose, M. (2019). "ShapeSense: A 2D Shape Rendering VR Device with Moving Surfaces that Controls Mass Properties and Air Resistance," in *ACM SIGGRAPH 2019 Emerging Technologies* (New York, NY, USA: Association for Computing Machinery), 1–2. SIGGRAPH '19. doi:10.1145/3305367.3327991

Loomis, J. M., and Lederman, S. J. (1986). "Tactual Perception," in *Handbook of Perception and Human Performances* (New York, NY: John Wiley & Sons), 2, 1–41.

Lopes, P., You, S., Cheng, L.-P., Marwecki, S., and Baudisch, P. (2017). "Providing Haptics to Walls & Heavy Objects in Virtual Reality by Means of Electrical Muscle Stimulation," in *Proceedings of the 2017 CHI Conference on Human Factors in Computing Systems* (New York, NY, USA: Association for Computing Machinery), 1471–1482. CHI '17. doi:10.1145/3025453.3025600

Maereg, A. T., Nagar, A., Reid, D., and Secco, E. L. (2017). Wearable Vibrotactile Haptic Device for Stiffness Discrimination during Virtual Interactions. *Front. Robot. AI* 4, 42. doi:10.3389/frobt.2017.00042

Maiero, J., Eibich, D., Kruijff, E., Hinkenjann, A., Stuerzlinger, W., Benko, H., et al. (2019). Back-of-Device Force Feedback Improves Touchscreen Interaction for Mobile Devices. *IEEE Trans. Haptics* 12, 483–496. doi:10.1109/toh.2019.2911519

Maisto, M., Pacchierotti, C., Chinello, F., Salvietti, G., De Luca, A., and Prattichizzo, D. (2017). Evaluation of Wearable Haptic Systems for the Fingers in Augmented Reality Applications. *IEEE Trans. Haptics* 10, 511–522. doi:10.1109/TOH.2017.2691328

Manus (2020). *Prime II Mocap Gloves*. Available at: https://www.manus-vr.com/mocapgloves (Accessed June 17, 2020).

Marquardt, A., Kruijff, E., Trepkowski, C., Maiero, J., Schwandt, A., Hinkenjann, A., et al. (2018). "Audio-Tactile Proximity Feedback for Enhancing 3D Manipulation," in *Proceedings of the 24th ACM Symposium on Virtual Reality Software and Technology* (New York, NY, USA: Association for Computing Machinery), 1–10. VRST '18. doi:10.1145/3281505.3281525

Martínez, J., García, A., Oliver, M., Molina, J. P., and González, P. (2016). Identifying Virtual 3d Geometric Shapes with a Vibrotactile Glove. *IEEE Computer Graphics Appl.* 36, 42–51. doi:10.1109/MCG.2014.81

Massie, T. H., and Salisbury, J. K. (1994). "The Phantom Haptic Interface: A Device for Probing Virtual Objects," in *Proceedings of the ASME Winter Annual Meeting, Symposium on Haptic Interfaces for Virtual Environment and Teleoperator Systems* (Chicago), 295–300.

McCloskey, D. I. (1974). Muscular and Cutaneous Mechanisms in the Estimation of the Weights of Grasped Objects. *Neuropsychologia* 12, 513–520. doi:10.1016/0028-3932(74)90081-5

Microsoft (2021). *Xbox Elite Wireless Controller*. Available at: https://www.xbox.com/en-US/accessories/controllers/elite-wireless-controller (Accessed June 3, 2021).

Minamizawa, K., Fukamachi, S., Kajimoto, H., Kawakami, N., and Tachi, S. (2007a). "Gravity Grabber: Wearable Haptic Display to Present Virtual Mass Sensation," in *ACM SIGGRAPH 2007 Emerging Technologies* (New York, NY, USA: Association for Computing Machinery), 3–6. SIGGRAPH '07. doi:10.1145/1278280.1278289

Minamizawa, K., Kajimoto, H., Kawakami, N., and Tachi, S. (2007b). "A Wearable Haptic Display to Present the Gravity Sensation - Preliminary Observations and Device Design," in *Proceeding of the 2013 Second Joint EuroHaptics Conference and Symposium on Haptic Interfaces for Virtual Environment and Teleoperator Systems* (WHC'07), Tsukuba, Japan, 22-24 March 2007 (IEEE), 133–138. doi:10.1109/WHC.2007.15

Mizuno, T., Maeda, J., and Kume, Y. (2013). "Weight Sensation Affected by Vibrotactile Stimulation with a Handheld Vision-Tactile-Force Display Device," in *Proceeding of the 2013 10th International Conference on Electrical Engineering/Electronics, Computer, Telecommunications and Information Technology*, Krabi, Thailand, 15-17 May 2013 (IEEE), 1–6. doi:10.1109/ECTICon.2013.6559590

Nisar, S., Martinez, M. O., Endo, T., Matsuno, F., and Okamura, A. M. (2019). Effects of Different Hand-Grounding Locations on Haptic Performance with a Wearable Kinesthetic Haptic Device. *IEEE Robot. Autom. Lett.* 4, 351–358. doi:10.1109/lra.2018.2890198

Pacchierotti, C., Salvietti, G., Hussain, I., Meli, L., and Prattichizzo, D. (2016). "The hRing: A Wearable Haptic Device to Avoid Occlusions in Hand Tracking," in *Proceeding of the 2016 IEEE Haptics Symposium (HAPTICS)*, Philadelphia, PA, USA, 8-11 April 2016 (IEEE), 134–139. doi:10.1109/haptics.2016.7463167

Posner, M. I., Nissen, M. J., and Klein, R. M. (1976). Visual Dominance: An Information-Processing Account of its Origins and Significance. *Psychol. Rev.* 83, 157–171. doi:10.1037/0033-295X.83.2.157

Provancher, W. (2014). Creating Greater VR Immersion by Emulating Force Feedback with Ungrounded Tactile Feedback. *IQT Quarterly* 6, 18–21.

Rietzler, M., Geiselhart, F., Gugenheimer, J., and Rukzio, E. (2018). "Breaking the Tracking: Enabling Weight Perception using Perceivable Tracking Offsets," in *Proceedings of the 2018 CHI Conference on Human Factors in Computing Systems* (New York, NY, USA: Association for Computing Machinery), 1–12. CHI '18. doi:10.1145/3173574.3173702

Ryu, N., Lee, W., Kim, M. J., and Bianchi, A. (2020). "ElaStick: A Handheld Variable Stiffness Display for Rendering Dynamic Haptic Response of Flexible Object," in *Proceedings of the 33rd Annual ACM Symposium on User Interface Software and Technology* (New York, NY: Association for Computing Machinery). UIST '20. doi:10.1145/3379337.3415862

Samad, M., Gatti, E., Hermes, A., Benko, H., and Parise, C. (2019). "Pseudo-Haptic Weight: Changing the Perceived Weight of Virtual Objects By Manipulating Control-Display Ratio," in *Proceedings of the 2019 CHI Conference on Human Factors in Computing Systems* (New York, NY, USA: Association for Computing Machinery). CHI '19, 1–13. doi:10.1145/3290605.3300550

Sato, M. (2002). Development of String-Based Force Display: Spidar. *8th International Conference on Virtual Systems and Multimedia*. 1034–1039. Citeseer.

Scheggi, S., Salvietti, G., and Prattichizzo, D. (2010). "Shape and Weight Rendering for Haptic Augmented Reality," in *Proceedings - IEEE International Workshop on Robot and Human Interactive Communication*, Viareggio, Italy, 13-15 Sept. 2010 (IEEE), 44–49. doi:10.1109/roman.2010.5598632

Schorr, S. B., and Okamura, A. M. (2017). "Fingertip Tactile Devices for Virtual Object Manipulation and Exploration," in *Proceedings of the 2017 CHI Conference on Human Factors in Computing Systems* (New York, NY: Association for Computing Machinery), 3115–3119. CHI '17. doi:10.1145/3025453.3025744

Schütt, H. H., Harmeling, S., Macke, J. H., and Wichmann, F. A. (2016). Painfree and Accurate Bayesian Estimation of Psychometric Functions for (Potentially) Overdispersed Data. *Vis. Res.* 122, 105–123. doi:10.1016/j.visres.2016.02.002

Schütt, H. H. (2019). *Psignifit*. Available at: https://github.com/wichmann-lab/psignifit/wiki (Accessed June 16, 2020).

Shigeyama, J., Hashimoto, T., Yoshida, S., Narumi, T., Tanikawa, T., and Hirose, M. (2019). "Transcalibur: A Weight Shifting Virtual Reality Controller for 2D Shape Rendering based on Computational Perception Model," in *Proceedings of the 2019 CHI Conference on Human Factors in Computing Systems* (New York, NY, USA: Association for Computing Machinery), 1–11. CHI '19. doi:10.1145/3290605.3300241

Simpson, W. A. (1988). The Method of Constant Stimuli Is Efficient. *Perception & Psychophysics* 44, 433–436. doi:10.3758/bf03210427

Sinclair, M., Ofek, E., Gonzalez-Franco, M., and Holz, C. (2019). "CapstanCrunch: A Haptic VR Controller with User-supplied Force Feedback," in *Proceedings of the 32nd Annual ACM Symposium on User Interface Software and Technology* (New York, NY, USA: Association for Computing Machinery), 815–829. UIST '19. doi:10.1145/3332165.3347891

Solazzi, M., Frisoli, A., Salsedo, F., and Bergamasco, M. (2007). "A Fingertip Haptic Display for Improving Local Perception of Shape Cues," in *Proceeding of the Second Joint EuroHaptics Conference and Symposium on Haptic Interfaces for Virtual Environment and Teleoperator Systems* (WHC'07), Tsukuba, Japan, 22-24 March 2007 (IEEE), 409–414. doi:10.1109/WHC.2007.3

Sony (2020). *Dualsense Wireless Controller*. Available at: https://www.playstation.com/en-gb/accessories/dualsense-wireless-controller/ (Accessed September 4, 2020).

Stellmacher, C. (2021). "Haptic-Enabled Buttons through Adaptive Trigger Resistance," in *Proceeding of the 2021 IEEE Conference on Virtual Reality and 3D User Interfaces Abstracts and Workshops (VRW)*, Lisbon, Portugal, 27 March-1 April 2021 (IEEE), 201–204. doi:10.1109/VRW52623.2021.00044

Strasnick, E., Holz, C., Ofek, E., Sinclair, M., and Benko, H. (2018). "Haptic Links: Bimanual Haptics for Virtual Reality Using Variable Stiffness Actuation," in *Proceedings of the 2018 CHI Conference on Human Factors in Computing Systems* (New York, NY, USA: Association for Computing Machinery), 1–12.

Suchoski, J. M., Martinez, S., and Okamura, A. M. (2018). "Scaling Inertial Forces to Alter Weight Perception in Virtual Reality," in *Proceeding of the 2018 IEEE International Conference on Robotics and Automation (ICRA)*, Brisbane, QLD, Australia, 21-25 May 2018 (IEEE), 484–489. doi:10.1109/icra.2018.8462874

Sun, Y., Yoshida, S., Narumi, T., and Hirose, M. (2019). "PaCaPa: A Handheld VR Device for Rendering Size, Shape, and Stiffness of Virtual Objects in Tool-based Interactions," in *Proceedings of the 2019 CHI Conference on Human Factors in*

Computing Systems (New York, NY, USA: Association for Computing Machinery), 1–12. CHI '19. doi:10.1145/3290605.3300682

3D Systems (2021). *Phantom Premium*. Available at: https://www.3dsystems.com/haptics-devices/3d-systems-phantom-premium (Accessed June 15, 2020).

Tan, H. Z., Srinivasan, M. A., Eberman, B., and Cheng, B. (1994). "Human Factors for the Design of Force-Reflecting Haptic," in *Dynamics Systems and Control* (American Society of Mechanical Engineers (ASME)), 55, 353–359.

Tsai, H.-R., Rekimoto, J., and Chen, B.-Y. (2019). "ElasticVR: Providing Multilevel Continuously-Changing Resistive Force and Instant Impact Using Elasticity for VR," in *Proceedings of the 2019 CHI Conference on Human Factors in Computing Systems* (New York, NY: Association for Computing Machinery), 1–10. CHI'19. doi:10.1145/3290605.3300450

Van Polanen, V., and Davare, M. (2015). Sensorimotor Memory Biases Weight Perception during Object Lifting. *Front. Hum. Neurosci.* 9, 1–11. doi:10.3389/fnhum.2015.00700

VOGEL GERMANY (2021). Electr. Digital Vibration Meter. Available at: https://www.vogel-germany.de/en/produkte-kataloge-prospekte-edition.html.

Westling, G., and Johansson, R. S. (1984). Factors Influencing the Force Control during Precision Grip. *Exp. Brain Res.* 53, 277–284. doi:10.1007/BF00238156

Whitmire, E., Benko, H., Holz, C., Ofek, E., and Sinclair, M. (2018). "Haptic Revolver: Touch, Shear, Texture, and Shape Rendering on a Reconfigurable Virtual Reality Controller," in *Proceedings of the 2018 CHI Conference on Human Factors in Computing Systems* (New York, NY, USA: Association for Computing Machinery), 1–12. CHI '18. doi:10.1145/3173574.3173660

Yu, R., and Bowman, D. A. (2020). Pseudo-haptic Display of Mass and Mass Distribution during Object Rotation in Virtual Reality. *IEEE Trans. Vis. Comput. Graphics* 26, 2094–2103. doi:10.1109/TVCG.2020.2973056

Zenner, A., and Krüger, A. (2019). "Drag:on: A Virtual Reality Controller Providing Haptic Feedback Based on Drag and Weight Shift," in *Proceedings of the 2019 CHI Conference on Human Factors in Computing Systems* (New York, NY, USA: Association for Computing Machinery), 1–12. CHI '19. doi:10.1145/3290605.3300441

Zenner, A., and Krüger, A. (2017). Shifty: A Weight-Shifting Dynamic Passive Haptic Proxy to Enhance Object Perception in Virtual Reality. *IEEE Trans. Vis. Comput. Graphics* 23, 1285–1294. doi:10.1109/TVCG.2017.2656978

Zenner, A., Ullmann, K., and Krüger, A. (2021). Combining Dynamic Passive Haptics and Haptic Retargeting for Enhanced Haptic Feedback in Virtual Reality. *IEEE Trans. Vis. Comput. Graphics* 27, 2627–2637. doi:10.1109/TVCG.2021.3067777

8

Exodex Adam—A Reconfigurable Dexterous Haptic User Interface for the Whole Hand

Neal Y. Lii[1]*, Aaron Pereira[1], Julian Dietl[2], Georg Stillfried[1†], Annika Schmidt[1,3], Hadi Beik-Mohammadi[1†], Thomas Baker[1], Annika Maier[1], Benedikt Pleintinger[1], Zhaopeng Chen[4], Amal Elawad[5], Lauren Mentzer[6], Austin Pineault[6], Philipp Reisich[1] and Alin Albu-Schäffer[1]

[1]Institute of Robotics and Mechatronics, German Aerospace Center (DLR), Wessling, Germany, [2]Faculty of Mechanical Engineering, Munich University of Applied Science, Munich, Germany, [3]Faculty of Informatics, Technical University of Munich, Munich, Germany, [4]Department of Informatics, Faculty of Mathematics, Informatics and Natural Science, University of Hamburg, Hamburg, Germany, [5]Department of Electrical Engineering, Chalmers University of Technology, Göteborg, Sweden, [6]Department of Computer Science and Electrical Engineering, Stanford University, Stanford, CA, United States

*Correspondence:
Neal Y. Lii
neal.lii@dlr.de

†Present address:
Georg Stillfried,
Agile Robots AG, Wessling, Germany;
Hadi Beik-Mohammadi, Bosch Center
for Artificial Intelligence, Renningen,
Germany

Applications for dexterous robot teleoperation and immersive virtual reality are growing. Haptic user input devices need to allow the user to intuitively command and seamlessly "feel" the environment they work in, whether virtual or a remote site through an avatar. We introduce the DLR Exodex Adam, a reconfigurable, dexterous, whole-hand haptic input device. The device comprises multiple modular, three degrees of freedom (3-DOF) robotic fingers, whose placement on the device can be adjusted to optimize manipulability for different user hand sizes. Additionally, the device is mounted on a 7-DOF robot arm to increase the user's workspace. Exodex Adam uses a front-facing interface, with robotic fingers coupled to two of the user's fingertips, the thumb, and two points on the palm. Including the palm, as opposed to only the fingertips as is common in existing devices, enables accurate tracking of the whole hand without additional sensors such as a data glove or motion capture. By providing "whole-hand" interaction with omnidirectional force-feedback at the attachment points, we enable the user to experience the environment with the complete hand instead of only the fingertips, thus realizing deeper immersion. Interaction using Exodex Adam can range from palpation of objects and surfaces to manipulation using both power and precision grasps, all while receiving haptic feedback. This article details the concept and design of the Exodex Adam, as well as use cases where it is deployed with different command modalities. These include mixed-media interaction in a virtual environment, gesture-based telemanipulation, and robotic hand–arm teleoperation using adaptive model-mediated teleoperation. Finally, we share the insights gained during our development process and use case deployments.

Keywords: haptic user interface, hand exoskeletons, human–machine interface (HMI), human–robot interface (HRI), teleoperation

1 INTRODUCTION

With our hands, we can communicate (read Braille, make gestures, or speak sign language), explore the world around us (feel surface impedances, textures, weights, temperature, pressure), manipulate it, and mold it. For all these functionalities, the somatosensory system of the human is essential. This includes the knowledge about the orientation and position of our body in space (proprioception) and the sense of motion in our joints (kinesthesia) as well as perception of sensory signals from the mechanoreceptors in our skin (cutaneous perception) (Hannaford and Okamura, 2016). All these senses contribute to our ability to receive haptic feedback when interacting with the environment.

In recent years, we have become increasingly used to interacting with remote or virtual environments visually and auditorily, considering voice or video calling, and virtual reality headsets or video games. Haptic interaction is still less widespread but is gaining more interest as haptic technology develops.

This article presents our novel dexterous haptic hand–arm user interface (UI) concept and the development of the Exodex Adam (referred to simply as Exodex for the remainder of the article). Using our preliminary concept for a UI as the starting point (Lii et al., 2017), we developed and integrated various features to make the Exodex a safe and functional haptic user input system for the whole hand. It takes the form of a front-facing, mirror attachment system connected to the user's fingers and palm. Thanks to its dexterous robotic fingers, each with three actuated degrees of freedom (DOF), joint torque, and angular position sensing, the Exodex is able to render omnidirectional force reflection to the fingertips and the palm triggering mechanoreceptors in the skin. The palm interaction not only allows the pose and joint configuration of the hand to be accurately determined but also allows force reflection during power grasps and whole-hand exploration. A dexterous robotic arm can be mounted on the Exodex to extend the user's workspace, as well as additional force reflection and gravity compensation. Furthermore, as human hands come in a variety of sizes and shapes, the Exodex can be adjusted through eight reconfigurable mechanisms for the desired fit.

The user is attached to the Exodex at each attachment point through a passive 3-DOF gimbal with low-friction ball bearings. Magnetic clutches ensure safe detachment in case of excessively high torques during operation. Safety is a critical part of the physical human–robot interaction (pHRI). While no pHRI can be perfectly safe, the Exodex is designed to minimize the chance of injury. The mirroring design means that the mechanical parts do not go between the human fingers, reducing the risk of pinching or clamping.

In the next section, we visit the state of the art in dexterous haptic UIs, showing how our device addresses previously unexplored challenges. We then detail the design concepts and developed system device in **Section 3** and describe the process for obtaining the best workspace through the placement of attachment positions and configuration adjustments in **Section 4**. We discuss the optimization of the device kinematics to best suit the set of positions expected of the human hand in **Section 5**. We detail the low-level control of the Exodex in **Section 6**: how friction and inertia are reduced, and how the human's position is estimated for accurate haptic rendering. **Section 7** evaluates our system's effectiveness in different teleoperation modalities through deployment in several use cases: in whole-hand perception of a virtual environment, gesture-commanded telemanipulation, and adaptive model-mediated teleoperation (MMT) of a hand–arm avatar robot. Finally, **Section 8** concludes with our closing thoughts on Exodex's design and deployment, as well as looking to the work ahead.

2 RELATED WORK

Our hands are our most capable instruments for intuitively exploring and manipulating the environment. To enable such intuitive interactions in the virtual or in remote environments, hand exoskeletons and haptic UI have been developed, which can track the finger kinematics and reflect reaction forces of the environment back to the user.

2.1 Haptic User Interface and Exoskeleton Designs for the Hand

The first commercially available hand exoskeleton, the CyberGrasp, was introduced in the 1990s. It is a tendon-driven device that applies (uni-directional) tensile forces to the human fingers and has been used in many applications and different iterations (Lii et al., 2010; Aiple and Schiele, 2013). The CyberGrasp System continues to serve as a benchmark for the development of new systems. The HaptX Glove goes a step further by adding tactile feedback to force feedback at the fingertip, to introduce cutaneous perception. This is realized by the addition of a custom-designed textile laid out with micro-fluidic channels that can be actuated to press against the user's skin at commanded locations (Goupil et al., 2019). Some use cases do not require the whole hand or all the fingers for interaction. The PERCRO dual-finger exoskeleton has 3-DOF mechanisms each for the thumb and index finger. It can provide up to 5 N of force at the fingertip. A 3-DOF force sensor is implemented to measure user feedback at each finger (Fontana et al., 2009). The Rutgers Master II (Bouzit et al., 2002) is another such hand exoskeleton attached to the thumb and three fingers of the user and is driven by pneumatic actuators to eliminate the need for tendons and pulleys, such as in the CyberGrasp system. Hall effect and infrared sensors built into the exoskeleton helps track the motion of the operator's hand. Pneumatic actuators are also implemented in the Festo ExoHand (Festo, 2012).

For coupling between the user's hand and the haptic UI at the joint level, the Maestro Hand Exoskeleton (Yun et al., 2017) uses a novel mechanism to attach individual actuators and position sensing for each phalanx of the user's finger. This has been realized into a multi-finger solution. To tackle cost constraints of such systems, the Dexmo (Gu et al., 2016) and HEXOTRAC (Sarakoglou et al., 2016) exoskeletons both aim to be inexpensive and lightweight to make exoskeletons available to a broader market. Dexmo renders haptic feedback through a shifting servo-unit. As a result, the forces can only be displayed in a binary manner. This makes it incapable of rendering more complex object properties, such as stiffness discrimination. The HEXOTRAC employs a different approach to reduce cost, by making it highly under-actuated. It is attached to three of the user's fingers (the thumb, index, and middle), each with a 6-DOF mechanism driven by a single motor (Gu et al., 2016). The system implements a novel set of kinematics, leaving a wide, natural workspace for each digit. The system is suitable for a wide variety of hand sizes without adjustments being necessary, but this makes it bulky. The force rendering resolution is limited (Sarakoglou et al., 2016).

Another way of realizing in-hand haptic UI is through a mirror attachment solution (e.g., attaching in front of the hand) (Barbagli et al., 2003; Kawasaki et al., 2003; Kawasaki and Mouri, 2007). A full five-fingered Haptic Interface Robot (HIRO) realizing this concept has been presented by Endo et al. (2009) and Endo et al. (2011). HIRO is mounted on a robotic arm making it a grounded device, in contrast to all the aforementioned systems which can be categorized as ungrounded. This is further discussed in the following section.

2.2 Grounded Haptic User Interface Devices

Most hand or hand–arm exoskeletons fall in the category of ungrounded devices, which are directly attached to the human hand and body. This makes them flexible and enlarges the workspace of the human user, but comes at the cost of adding the weight of the system to be carried by the human which can lead to fatigue over time. Additionally, with these types of devices, it is impossible to render forces acting on the whole hand, such as reaction forces from large solid/deformable surfaces or immersion in a fluid.

By contrast, grounded devices such as the HIRO (Endo et al., 2011) and the Exodex presented in this article, as well as some non–whole-hand devices such as Force Dimension's sigma.7 (Tobergte et al., 2011), and the Phantom Omni (Silva et al., 2009), can counter these problems. Since a grounded UI is mounted on a base fixed to the environment, the user need not actively support the weight of the system. This also allows alternative ways of coupling between the exoskeleton and the user's hand, such as the HIRO's mirror attachment concept (Endo et al., 2011). It places the UI in front of the user, rather than directly on their appendages.

2.3 Haptic Feedback in Teleoperation and Virtual Reality

With haptic feedback, the operator can receive calculated feedback from an environment in virtual reality (VR), whereas in teleoperation, feedback is measured from the remote environment (Stone, 2000). In augmented reality scenarios, where the environment can have an overlay of virtual cues to better assist the user, even a combination of the two is possible (Hedayati et al., 2018).

In all these cases, adding haptic feedback can help improve the user performance in comparison to tasks that were carried out with visual feedback only (Son et al., 2011; Wildenbeest et al.,

2012; Weber and Eichberger, 2015). Particularly in the medical field, the augmentation of reality and the implementation of haptic feedback has proven to greatly improve the performance of surgeons, e.g., for minimally invasive surgery situations (Gerovichev et al., 2002).

Since humans are well trained to use their hands for daily interactions, allowing the user to use and receive feedback directly via haptic UI to their hands would be, we expect, more intuitive. The user can explore the virtual or remote environment with natural exploration procedures and intuitive motions, a feature that is increasingly exploited for interactive hand rehabilitation (Missiroli et al., 2019). However, interactions with whole-hand input devices require an estimation of the human hand position and configuration to apply appropriate feedback to multiple areas on the hand. In Endo et al. (2011), the fingertips were tracked and users could manipulate a simple virtual object in precision grasp with force feedback to the fingertips. Although coupled to the user only at the fingertips, rather than the whole hand, the HaptX glove with tangible tactile sensors was shown to teleoperate a Shadow robotic hand (Goupil et al., 2019).

2.4 Moving Toward Shared Control for Haptic Hand and Hand–Arm User Interface

Pairing shared control strategies with a haptic UI enables user interaction at different levels of immersion or abstraction, which allows the operator to choose the most effective mode of teleoperation for given tasks. To date, a haptically coupled hand exoskeleton has rarely been applied in such a fashion.

However, the desire and success for shared control capability has been seen with other UI devices. This was especially observed in several space telerobotics experiments. In Kontur-2 and METERON SUPVIS Justin, both carried out from the International Space Station (ISS) to ground, DLR's dexterous humanoid robot Justin (Fuchs et al., 2009) was commanded using a 2-DOF force-reflection joystick (Artigas et al., 2016) and task-driven supervised autonomy based GUI (Schmaus et al., 2019), respectively, to perform a variety of dexterous robotic tasks. Although the ISS crew members in both experiments were able to successfully complete their given tasks, they have expressed the desire for different UI modalities to be available for more effective teleoperation (Lii et al., 2018).

In light of this, the Analog-1 experiment demonstrated the first successful UI console on board the ISS, combining a GUI, open-loop joystick, and the aforementioned Force Dimension sigma.7 haptic input device. The UI console was used to command a dual-arm rover on ground to perform driving and sample return tasks (Krueger et al., 2020). A similar approach of shared control was also applied for home elderly care using an intuitive GUI for task level command and a dual-arm haptic input device for more dexterous unplanned tasks (Vogel et al., 2020).

As previously mentioned, hand-based shared control teleoperation, particularly with haptic feedback, has been rare. Lii et al. (2012) succeeded in combining joint-level, Cartesian-level, and gesture/task-level teleoperation into a robotic hand grasping and manipulation strategy, albeit without haptic

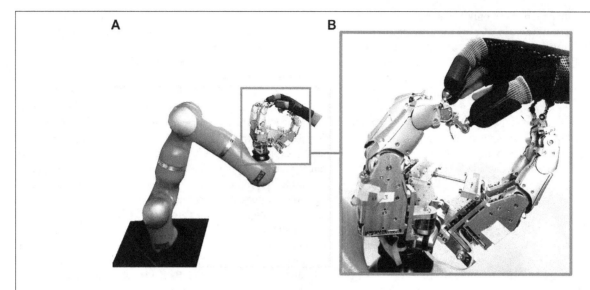

FIGURE 1 | The Exodex whole-hand haptic interface. With multiple robot fingers attached to the fingertips and palm of the user, it is capable of capturing the user's hand pose in real-time **(B)**. A DLR LWR arm **(A)** greatly increases the available workspace for the user to teleoperate robotic avatars or in virtual reality.

feedback. It nonetheless reduced user mental and physical workload, while improving task success rate.

3 DESIGN CONCEPT AND REALIZATION

The Exodex's main design aim is to create an immersive haptic user input device for the whole hand. We introduce a front-facing, mirror-attachment haptic robotic hand UI with a total of 22 active DOF, with an additional eight passive user-reconfigurable DOF to accommodate most hand sizes and shapes. This section describes our overall design concept, which enables Exodex to capture the hand pose and provide whole-hand user immersion with force reflection. Furthermore, a number of features have been developed to help achieve our design goal. These features are also detailed here, including the dexterous robotic finger, reconfigurable palm, robotic arm implementation, user attachment system, as well as safety design. A view of the overall system can be seen in **Figure 1**. An overview of the system specification is given in **Table 1**.

3.1 Overall Concept to Realize Immersive Whole-Hand Interaction

Unlike most hand exoskeleton and haptic UIs implementations that are fitted over the back of the hand (Lii et al., 2010; Endo and Kawasaki, 2014), the proposed design of Exodex employs a front-facing, mirror attachment design, with the system in front of the user's hand. Exodex aims to achieve several features that differ from existing haptic hand UI designs. To deliver a safe, immersive haptic experience, the Exodex (see **Figure 1**) combines the following features into a novel package:

- whole-hand haptic experience for the fingers and the palm surface,

- hand pose estimation capability,
- reconfigurability to accommodate most or all hand geometry and sizes,
- less interference with user movement,
- easy attachment and detachment, and
- user safety.

The Exodex differs from other front-facing fingertip UIs such as the HIRO (Endo et al., 2009; Endo et al., 2011) in its aim to serve the whole hand of the user, i.e., the fingers and the palm surface. The latter two heavily involve the human palm (Gonzalez et al., 2014; Chabrier et al., 2015). Functionality for haptic feedback to the palm is lacking in the grounded hand exoskeletons cited so far. The Exodex introduces attachment points to the user's palm with dexterous robotic fingers, as well as the fingertips, as shown in **Figure 1**. The user's hand is attached to the Exodex through a magnetic clutch and 3-DOF free-rotating gimbal mechanism. The addition of palm interaction is not merely adding more robotic fingers to the system. Rather, it changes the nature of the UI from a fingertip interface, as introduced in Barbagli et al. (2003), Kawasaki et al. (2003), Kawasaki and Mouri (2007), Endo et al. (2009), and Endo et al. (2011), to a UI for the whole-hand haptic interaction. The holistic haptic interaction enables not only precision grasps and manipulation but also power grasps and whole-hand exploration. As presented by in-hand taxonomies (Cutkosky, 1989; Bullock et al., 2013; Feix et al., 2016), we see that grasping and manipulation of objects involve not only the fingers but also the palm, in many cases. With Exodex's approach, we have the possibility to reproduce the full in-hand haptic experience.

Furthermore, the Exodex can capture the user's hand pose without additional sensors being placed directly on the user's hand. This would not be possible if the user is only attached at the fingertips to a UI device. **Figure 2** illustrates this point, where vastly different hand poses having the same fingertip positions. By

TABLE 1 | Overview of Exodex specifications.

Modular robotic fingers	
Total fingers	5
Total actuated DOF	15 (3 per finger)
Range of motion	±20° abduct/adduct (base joint)
	5°–85° flexion (base joint)
	5°–85° flexion (1:1 coupled distal/medial joint)
Max. joint velocity	180°/sec
Max. force	10 N (at TCP)
Sensing	Joint torque sensor and angular position sensor at each joint
Robotic arm	
Total actuated DOF	7
Range of motion	±170° (joints 1, 3, 5, 7)
	±120° (joints 2, 4, 6)
Max. joint velocity	112.5°/sec (except joint 5)
	180°/sec (joint 5)
Max. force	130 N (at TCP)
Sensing	Joint torque sensor and angular position sensor at each joint
Passive reconfigurable DOF (in the palm base)	
Sliding adjustment	
Total DOF for manual adjustment	4 (at the base of each attached robotic finger)
Rotational adjustment	
Total DOF for manual adjustment	3 (co-located at the base of robotic finger for the user's thumb)
Palm base cupping angle adjustment	
Total DOF for manual adjustment	1

DOF, degrees of freedom; TCP, tool center point.

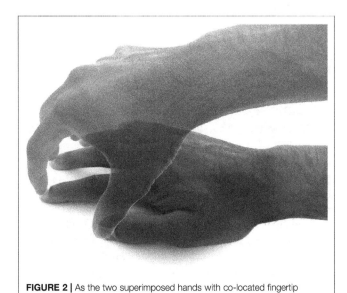

FIGURE 2 | As the two superimposed hands with co-located fingertip positions show, the position of the fingertips alone is not sufficient to determine the pose of the hand.

connecting the user's palm into the teleoperation, the palm can also become an active contributor to use command input.

Human hands vary widely in geometry and sizes, even when only considering adult users (Greiner, 1991). To serve all of these different hands, an 8-DOF reconfigurable palm base has been developed in the Exodex, which can be configured to fit the vast majority of, if not all, users, including children and adults.

With a device capable of delivering large forces at high speeds, safety against injury is paramount. The front-facing arrangement enables the possibility to implement release mechanisms for safe, fast, detachment to protect the user at any sign of danger. Since the user would be placed in front of, and away from, most of the haptic UI's mechanisms, they can simply physically pull back to be safely released from the haptic UI and away from its workspace. Finally, to give the user more usable workspace, the Exodex is integrated with a 7-DOF KUKA-DLR Light Weight Robot (LWR) arm (Bischoff et al., 2010) to provide an extension of haptically coupled workspace.

In its current configuration, the Exodex can be used to reconstruct the pose of the human hand except for the ring and little fingers, as they are not yet attached to the system. However, they can be served by adding more robotic fingers to the modular palm base in future implementations. The reconstruction of the use's hand pose is described in **Section 6**.

3.2 Modular Dexterous Robotic Fingers

The Exodex employs a modular design with self-contained robotic fingers to interact with the user's hand through angular and force/torque sensing, and force reflection.

The current version of the Exodex employs customized robotic fingers (see **Figure 3**) based on those from the DLR Five-Finger Hand (Liu et al., 2008; Chen et al., 2014). Each finger has three DOF, including two active DOF at the base for flexion and abduction/adduction, and an additional 1:1 coupled distal–medial flexion joint. The three active joints of each

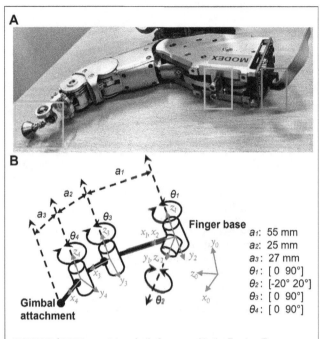

FIGURE 3 | (A) The modular robotic finger used in the Exodex. Two screws (marked by the green box), and a single data/power (marked by the red box) cable complete the physical and electrical installation. Each finger is equipped with brushless direct current motors, angular position, and joint torque sensors at each of the three active DOFs. A 3-DOF gimbal (marked in the blue box) enables free rotation at the attachment point to the user. **(B)** The kinematic definition of the robotic finger as modified from a standard DLR Five-Finger Hand. Specifically, the link length has been modified to fit the added gimbal mechanism.

finger are driven by brushless direct current (BLDC) motors. The joint angular position is measured via a hall effect sensor and potentiometer, whereas the interaction force is measured through a joint torque sensor. Motor command and sensor data are transmitted in a 200 μs cycle through a point-to-point high-speed serial communication at 25 Mbps in a time-triggered fashion.

Its self-contained actuation, sensing, and local data processing enable each finger to serve as a self-contained module. The Exodex fingers can be easily detached and reattached with two screws and a single ribbon data connector, making them easy to replace in the field. For more specifications (see **Table 1**).

3.3 Reconfigurable Modular Palm Base

The human hand come in a large variety of sizes and shapes: from 212 mm for a 95th percentile adult male to 163 mm for a fifth percentile adult female (Greiner, 1991). Therefore, it is advantageous to be able to adjust the distance between the robot fingers attached to the human fingertips and those attached to the palm. This would allow most, if not all, users' thumb, fingers, and palm surfaces to be in the manipulable workspace of the robotic finger.

To realize this, the Exodex palm base is designed with a total of eight reconfigurable DOF. These include one palm cupping angle, four translational positioning, and three rotational DOF for the

human thumb's interacting robot finger. These adjustment mechanisms for reconfiguring the palm base are shown in **Figure 4**.

Including passive DOF while increasing flexibility of the design in terms of optimal placement of the robotic fingers and hence manipulability during operation also comes with design challenges. Mechanisms take up space and also compromise the mechanical stiffness of the device—the entire device becomes less rigid. Furthermore, the passive DOF are envisioned to be automated in future designs. However, this will introduce further challenges for packaging and increased system complexity.

In the current design, four individual linear adjustments (see **Figure 4B**) are provided for four of the robotic fingers (two connected to the user's palm, one to the index finger, and one to the middle finger). They are constructed on high precision, low friction linear bearings with an unobtrusive profile. Quick release screw-type brakes keep the robotic fingers in their desired positions. The linear DOF are particularly suited to address the different hand widths, as they allow for the adjustment to suit the spacing between the user's fingers, as well as the palm width. The cupping angle (see **Figure 4C**) of the Exodex palm base can also be adjusted to accommodate different lengths of the user's hand. As the thumb is the most important member of the hand (Chalon et al., 2010), it is also given the most adjustment DOF in our design to better accommodate different users and use cases. Three rotational joints are incorporated to the base of the robotic finger (see **Figure 4A**) for pose and position adjustments.

Finally, the palm base also houses the communication gateway and power source to manage the data transition and power supply for the robotic fingers.

3.4 Gimbal Joint: Enabling Free Rotational Motion While the User is Connected to the System

To allow free movement of the user's hand while being attached to the haptic UI, free rotation at the attachment points is required. In Endo et al. (2011), a magnetic ball-in-socket joint is used to allow omnidirectional rotation. The human is attached to a magnetic ball, which fits into a hemispherical socket on the robot side.

An alternative solution is a triaxial gimbal, which has been proposed for force reflection haptic devices (Massie and Salisbury, 1997). A gimbal with ball bearings allows nearly frictionless movement, whereas a ball-in-socket joint can have higher friction at the contact surface. Furthermore, a gimbal mechanism can provide significantly more range of motion.

Our design, as shown in **Figure 5**, employs three rotational axes going through a single center of rotation, which provides the point of reference for the user's attachment to the system. The three rotational directions of our gimbal design can rotate 180 deg (see **Figure 5**, green axis), 250 deg (see **Figure 5**, red axis), and endlessly (see **Figure 5**, blue axis) in three rotational DOF. This compares favorably against commercial ball-and-socket joints typically capable of a pivot angle of about 40 deg at most (Igus, 2020).

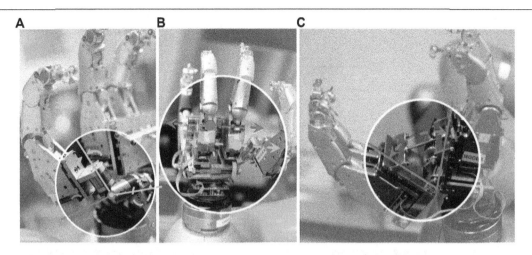

FIGURE 4 | Mechanisms of the eight passive reconfigurable DOFs in the Exodex palm base enabling adjustments to fit different hand sizes. **(A)** Three rotational DOF with friction stop mechanisms. **(B)** Sliding mechanisms for the adjustment of Exodex fingers' linear positions, which allows for accommodation of different user finger spread distance, as well as palm widths. A total of four such mechanisms are implemented, with two for the user's index and middle fingers, as well as two for the palm. **(C)** The cupping angle to adjust the palm size, which allows for accommodating different user palm lengths. These adjustment mechanisms also enable the workspace to be tailored to different tasks, such as more open-palm and power grasp of larger objects, or dexterous in-hand manipulation that utilizes the user's fingertips more.

In addition, a gimbal mechanism allows straightforward inclusion of decoupled sensors to measure position or torque in each rotational DOF. This would allow the orientation of the attachment points of the user with respect to the UI system to be measured. This is, however, not yet implemented in the current version of Exodex.

A drawback of gimbals is that they can be subject to gimbal lock. This situation is a singularity which occurs when the first and third axes of the gimbal are aligned. We therefore developed different gimbal configurations as shown in **Figure 5**. For attachments to the user's palm, the first axis of the gimbal is parallel to the long axis of the robotic finger's distal link. For the attachment to the user's fingers and thumb, the first axis of the gimbal is parallel to the last joint axis of the robot finger. With these different axis-arrangements, we could avoid the occurrence of gimbal lock within the range of motion of the human hand while being attached to the Exodex.

3.5 Connecting the User to Exodex

The user's hand is attached to the Exodex via a magnetic clutch connected to the aforementioned gimbal mounted on the robot fingers. The index and middle fingers and the thumb of the user are fitted into rigid plastic thimbles with a fixed-pose magnetic clutch at the fingertip, as shown in the left side of **Figure 6**. An elastic sleeve lined with silicone ensures a snug but comfortable fit, while eliminating slippage and reducing play. The transformation from the user's distal phalanx to the intersection of the gimbal's axes is therefore constant. The rigidity allows the rendered forces to be transmitted crisply (see **Figures 6B,D**). We have carried out tests with three different sizes of thimbles, which so far could accommodate all finger sizes that we have encountered.

Magnetic clutches are also placed on the palm on two form-fitting plastic plates on an open-finger glove worn by the user, as shown in **Figures 6C,D**. These provide the rigidity necessary to transmit forces crisply to the user's palm surface. This also allows the rendering of a more intuitive force reflection to an area of the palm, rather than feeling like being poked.

To ensure safety, the magnetic clutches detach automatically should a dangerously high force be exerted. The user can simply pull back and away from the haptic UI to safety at anytime. The magnet positions are adjustable to regulate the coupling force according to user and target application requirements. An additional dead man's switch to automatically bring the system into a safe mode (e.g., compliant mode or full shut down) is being considered to provide additional safety.

An additional benefit of a magnetic clutch is the improvement in the ease of usage for the user to clutch into the Exodex. As the magnets on the user's hand attract the clutch holders on robotic fingers, they conveniently snap into position when the hand is close by, which makes clutching quite easy for the user.

3.6 Extending Exodex Workspace With a Dexterous Robot Arm

The Exodex can function as a stand-alone UI for the hand, particularly in locations with limited space such as inside a spacecraft or research submarine. It is already capable of complex in-hand gesture and manipulation commands, as discussed in **Section 7**. However, it also limits the workspace of the system for the user. The use of a robotic arm as a haptic UI has been introduced in a recent work on the applications in user arm manipulation (Hulin et al., 2011) and reconfigurable vehicle UI console (Lii and Neves, 2021). We extend upon this approach by integrating the arm as a component of the haptic UI to form a hand–arm UI system.

Figure 1 (at the beginning of **Section 3**) shows the Exodex with the integrated 7-DOF robotic arm. Specifically, we integrated a DLR-

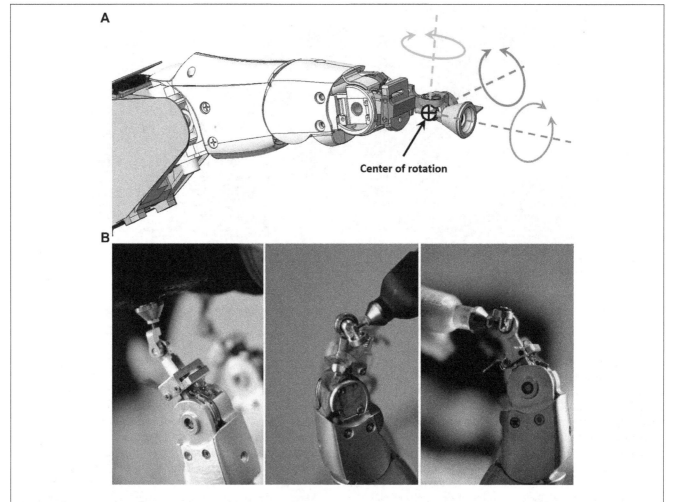

FIGURE 5 | Gimbal rotational DOF and different gimbal arrangements as implemented on the Exodex. The three rotational directions of our gimbal design can rotate 180 deg (green axis), 250 deg (red axis), and endlessly (blue axis). Thanks to low friction bearings, the friction is negligible. **(A)** Three rotational DOF go through a single center point. **(B)** Different mechanisms are needed to avoid gimbal lock on the robotic fingers connected to the palm (left) and those connected to the fingers and thumb (centre, right).

KUKA LWR arm into the Exodex. With seven BLDC motor–driven DOF and joint torque sensing at each joint, as well as a possible additional 6-DOF force–torque sensor at the tool center point (TCP), the robotic arm can truly extend the user's workspace. With such an extension, the user can employ their arm to explore the environment. It also allows a larger range of motion for the user. The integration of the dexterous arm provides gravity compensation to relieve the user of carrying the weight of the system. It also allows for force reflection to be transmitted to the user's arm, thus completing an immersive hand–arm haptic UI experience.

4 USER ATTACHMENT POINT PLACEMENTS FOR FITTING EXODEX'S WORKSPACE

To make the best use of the robotic fingers' workspace and match the desired movement of the human hand, the robotic fingers must be placed such that they allow maximum manipulability in the applications for which Exodex was envisioned. To help enable an effective whole-hand haptic experience, this section examines some of the key workspace considerations to finding suitable attachment configurations, including the positioning of the 3-DOF gimbal, pose and positioning of the robotic finger to the user's thumb, and effective attachment points on the user's palm.

4.1 Gimbal Placement Considerations for User Workspace

To ascertain a desirable point for attachment for the user's index and middle fingers to the robotic fingers, we examined the available workspace for three planar locations: plain distal, distal-palmar, and distal-dorsal. **Figure 7** gives an illustration of these attachment positions. Their respective workspaces are visualized in **Figure 8**, with the robotic finger and a user's hand superimposed for reference.

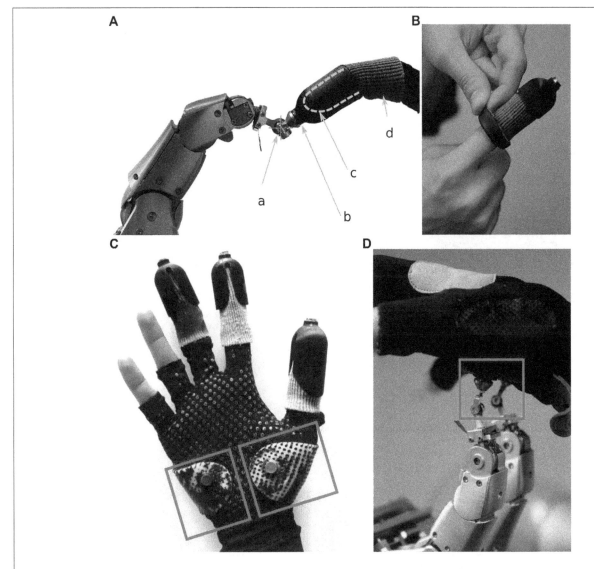

FIGURE 6 | User attachments to the Exodex. **(A)** The 3-DOF gimbal (a) is integrated at the tip of the robotic finger. The magnetic clutch (b) is attached to the gimbal for a rigid connection from the distal phalanx of the user. (c) The positions of the gimbals' centers are found from forward kinematics of the Exodex. The elastic sleeve is shown in (d). **(B)** Close up of the elastic cloth–silicone attachment: the elastic cloth sleeve is flipped back to show the black silicone lining. **(C)** Open-finger glove with palm attachment points. The attachments are marked in the red boxes. **(C)** The glove as worn by a user. A magnet is integrated into each attachment point on a supporting plate, which allows the forces to be distributed over an area on the palm. **(D)** The user's hand with the glove attached to the Exodex.

The workspace of the plain distal attachment provides the largest available planar workspace at 755.24 mm². The workspace using the distal-palmar attachment measured 392.50 mm² (51.97% of the plain distal workspace). Finally, the distal-dorsal attachment configuration only allowed a very thin, crescent-shaped workspace measuring 20.82 mm² (2.76% of the plain distal workspace). The significantly larger workspace achieved by the plain distal attachment configuration is therefore implemented in the Exodex.

4.2 Examining the User's Thumb Workspace
The thumb and its omnidirectional range of motion is essential for dexterous (in-hand) tasks. Consequently, we implemented the most reconfigurability for its corresponding attachment with

three adjustable joints. To examine the suitable workspace that these pose adjustments can provide for the user, we explored different attachment configurations of the user's thumb by examining the possible workspace with the user's thumb attached to the robotic finger in different base configurations. This is made possible utilizing various hand poses taken from magnetic resonance imaging (MRI) measurements (Stillfried et al., 2014). Examples of their workspace with a variety of base positions and orientations of the robot finger are visualized in **Figure 9**. The center position of the gimbal joint with the thumb connected to the robotic finger is calculated for each pose, as denoted by the blue dots. Furthermore, the workspace of the center of the gimbal joint on the TCP of the robotic finger is plotted as a thin line mesh. The base of the robot

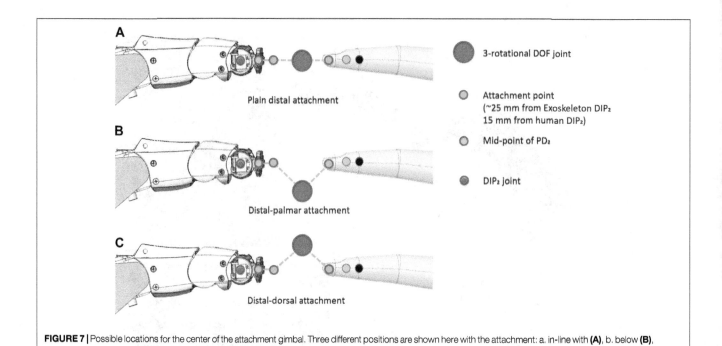

FIGURE 7 | Possible locations for the center of the attachment gimbal. Three different positions are shown here with the attachment: a. in-line with **(A)**, b. below **(B)**, and c. above **(C)** the distal links of the robotic fingers.

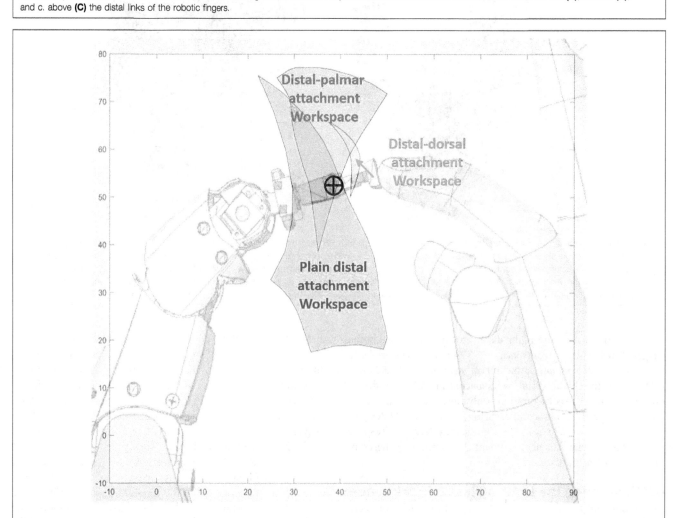

FIGURE 8 | Workspace boundaries of the gimbal center in three different attachment configurations. An overlay of the Exodex finger attached to the user's index finger is included for clarity. Blue: plain distal attachment. Red: distal-palmar attachment. Green: distal-dorsal attachment.

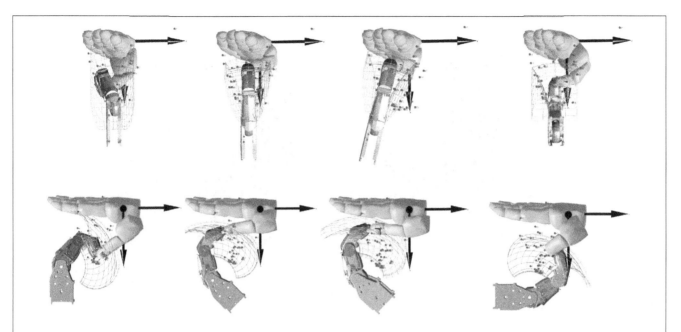

FIGURE 9 | Different options of placing the robot finger base with respect to the palm that allow good workspace of the thumb for in-hand manipulation. Top: views from the fingertip side (dorsal views). Bottom: views from the thumb side (radial views).

finger is moved until there is a good congruence between the gimbal center positions from the MRI measurements and the gimbal range of motion from the robot finger.

We observe in **Figure 9** that the workspace of the robotic finger becomes long and thin as the finger becomes extended. However, full extension is a singularity, and near full extension, manipulability is low. As such, this part of the workspace is limited in usefulness. To avoid bringing the robotic fingers into full extension, the palm of the Exodex is designed in such a way that the distance between the opposing robotic fingers can be adjusted using the adjustable cupping angle. This way, depending on the size of the operator's hand, the cupping can be adjusted so that the robotic finger is always in at least a slightly flexed posture.

As expected, the entire range of motion of the human thumb cannot be covered with the robotic finger's available workspace. A further observation is that all different poses achieve similar workspace volumes. This is particularly noticeable from the dorsal view in **Figure 9**. This is a result of the human thumb's vastly larger reachable workspace as compared to the robotic finger. Conversely, we can conclude that the human thumb can exploit the full workspace of the robotic finger. Nevertheless, the achieved workspace would already allow good performance by matching the palm base configuration to the desired tasks, such as gesture command, or in-hand dexterous manipulation. This is further confirmed in several use cases, which are detailed in **Section 7**. This also confirms our design strategy of implementing a reconfigurable base to compensate for the limitation of the robotic fingers available.

An interesting, albeit failed, attempt was made to increase the workspace for the user's thumb by increasing the length of

the distal link of the robotic finger connected to the thumb tip. However, this led to instability in the form of vibration during testing. This appeared to be caused by the flexibility in the mechanism for actuating the distal phalanx of the robotic finger. Specifically, this may stem from the cable-driven coupling between the distal and medial links, combined with the flexibility from the aluminum extension to the distal phalanx. Setting the finger feed-forward gains (see **Section 6.4**) lower in turn resulted in a large perceived inertia, which made it difficult for the user to move the thumb when attached to the Exodex.

4.3 Providing Whole-Hand Immersion Through Palm Attachment

As already discussed earlier, the incorporation of palm interaction enables the Exodex to provide a whole-hand interaction, as well as to estimate the pose and gesture. Two attachment points have been implemented on the user's palm, as shown in **Figure 10**. With sparser touch receptors in the palm than at the fingertips, we expect that one attachment on each side of the palm would provide sufficient haptic feedback to the user. The support plates allow the reflected forces to be distributed more evenly over the palm surface.

For pose estimation, the placement of the attachment points on the thenar bulge (thumb side) and hypothenar (little finger side) also enables the two robotic fingers to capture the pose of the palm, as well as the circumduction folding angle, which in turn helps estimate the whole-hand gesture. Furthermore, as the thenar bulge is directly connected to thumb metacarpal link, it is also helpful in estimating the thumb's pose relative to the whole hand. The effectiveness of this setup is particularly evident

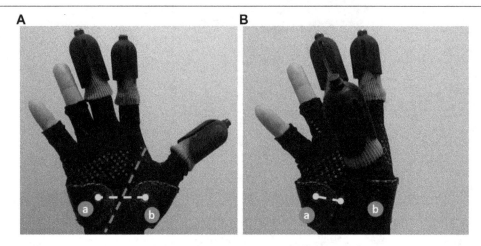

FIGURE 10 | Demonstration of the palm motion that can be captured by the Exodex. The attachments on the support plates covering the thenar bulge (a) and the hypothenar bulge (b) transmit the forces and motion between the user and the Exodex. The red dashed line notes the axis of the circumduction/folding motion of the palm. By placing the two attachments points on either side of this line, this motion can be captured by the Exodex. The difference in the green dashed line between the **(A,B)** figures gives an impression of the movement possible by the user's palm.

in the gesture recognition experiments as discussed later in **Section 7.2**.

5 OPTIMIZATION OF DEVICE KINEMATICS

Given the inherent workspace and collision limitations of a front-facing haptic UI or hand exoskeleton, it is impossible to achieve the entire range of movement of a healthy human hand while connected to the Exodex, since 1) the attachment points are at the fingertips, meaning it is impossible to, e.g., ball the hand into a tight fist without detaching the fingers, and 2) due to the limited range of motion of the robot fingers compared to that of the human fingers and the need to avoid collisions between robot fingers (e.g., one cannot cross one's fingers while connected to the Exodex).

Nevertheless, some key hand configurations required to explore or manipulate a real or virtual environment should be achievable, and manipulability of the system should be maximized for a hand configuration (or configurations) relevant to manipulation. As shown in **Figure 4**, the Exodex has eight passive DOF to accommodate users with various hand sizes and shapes.

In this section, we show how we set the positions of the eight passive DOFs shown in **Figure 4** and described in **Section 3.3** to optimize the workspace for different users. The optimization is high-dimensional, since there are not only the eight passive DOF y of the palm base, which can be optimized for any given hand pose, but also the transformation q_{pose} between the human hand's base coordinate system and the base coordinate system of the Exodex is not fixed.

We use a two-step, iterative approach to tackle this problem. Starting with an initial guess of the positions y of the passive DOF, the first step (lines 6–9 of **Algorithm 1**) is to determine whether there exists a pose of the hand's base coordinate system for which the joint angles of the robotic fingers are within limits, for each

key hand configuration. The second step (lines 16–19) is to modify the positions y to increase manipulability of the robotic fingers for the configurations relevant for manipulation. These two steps are iterated until convergence or until a maximum number of iterations. In case, in the first step, there are some configurations for which no pose of the hand base brings the joint angles within limits, we go back to the last feasible y, and perform the second optimization step, i.e., maximizing the manipulability, for these failing configurations instead of the configurations relevant for manipulation. This is shown in lines 10–14.

5.1 Manipulability Measure

Central to the optimization algorithm is a manipulability measure, defined per robotic finger, of the contact point with respect to the base of the finger i with joint values $\boldsymbol{\theta}_i = [\theta_1, \theta_2, \theta_3]^\top$, shown in **Eq. 3**. If the contact point is within the workspace of the robotic finger, the manipulability measure is Yoshikawa's manipulability measure (Yoshikawa, 1985) combined with a penalization function $P(\boldsymbol{\theta}_i)$ for joint limits as described in Tsai (1986, Eq. 84). The parameter k regulates the slope near the boundary of the workspace, and θ_j, $\theta_{\min,j}$, and $\theta_{\max,j}$ are the values of the jth joint and its lower and upper limits, respectively. Note that if J is a square matrix, as it is in our case, then $\sqrt{\det(JJ^\top)} = \det(J)$. If the contact point is outside the robotic finger workspace, then the measure is $ad(x)^2 + 2bd(x)$, where d is the distance to the closest point on the finger workspace and $a > 0$ is the gradient at the workspace boundary. We set $k = 100$, $a = 1$, and $b = .2$.

$$[\boldsymbol{\theta}_i, inBounds] = \texttt{inverse\_kinematics\_finger}(\boldsymbol{x}_i) \tag{1}$$

$$P(\boldsymbol{\theta}_i) = 1 - \exp\left(-k\prod_{j=1}^{3} \frac{\left(\theta_j - \theta_{\min,j}\right)\left(\theta_{\max,j} - \theta_j\right)}{\left(\theta_{\max,j} - \theta_{\min,j}\right)^2}\right) \tag{2}$$

$$m(\boldsymbol{x}) = \begin{cases} \det(J_F(\boldsymbol{\theta}_i))P(\boldsymbol{\theta}_i), & \text{if } inBounds \\ ad(\boldsymbol{x})^2 + 2bd(\boldsymbol{x}), & \text{otherwise} \end{cases} \quad (3)$$

Algorithm 1. Update hand state.

Require: set of key configurations $C = \{C_1, C_2, ...C_k\}$, subset of key manipulable configurations $C_m \subseteq C$, weights α, hand scale $scale$, maximum iterations max_iter
Ensure: optimal y
1: update_human_hand_model($scale$)
2: $y \leftarrow y_{init}$
3: $iter \leftarrow 0$
4: **while** $\neg converged \wedge iter < max\_iter$ **do**
5:   $C_{unsatisfied} \leftarrow \emptyset$
6:   **for** $i \in \{1, ...k\}$ **do**
7:     $q_{pose,i} \leftarrow$ find_viable_pose(C_i, y)
8:     **if** $\neg$is_valid_pose($q_{pose,i}$) **then**
9:       append_to_list($C_{unsatisfied}, C_i$)
10: **if** $C_{unsatisfied} = \emptyset$ **then**
11:    $C_{relevant} \leftarrow C_m$
12: **else**
13:    $C_{relevant} \leftarrow C_{unsatisfied}$
14:    restore_previous_values($y, \{q_{pose,1}, ..., q_{pose,k}\}$)
15: save_previous_values($y, \{q_{pose,1}, ..., q_{pose,k}\}$)
16: **for** $C_i \in C_{relevant}$ **do**
17:    $dy \leftarrow$ compute_correction($C_i, q_{pose,i}, y$)
18:    $y \leftarrow \alpha_i dy$
19:    $y \leftarrow$ saturate_at_joint_limits(y, y_{max}, y_{min})
20: $iter ++$
21: check_for_convergence(y)

5.2 Determining a Valid User Hand Pose

To find a valid pose, we use **Algorithm 2**: find_viable_pose. This first tries gradient descent, and if this fails, tries Particle Swarm Optimization (PSO). PSO (Clerc, 2006) is a sampling-based method that works in the non-convex and non-smooth domains and may find a viable q_{pose} where gradient descent fails.

Our implementation of gradient descent finds, at each step, the gradient of the manipulability index (**Eq. 3**) at each contact point. It then sums these gradients and multiplies by a gain to yield the change in translation of q_{pose} and sums their cross products with the distances from the hand's base coordinate system to each contact point, multiplied by another gain, to yield the change in orientation of q_{pose}.

Algorithm 2. find_viable_pose

Require: configuration C, passive DOF positions y, previous pose $q_{pose, old}$
Ensure: pose of hand q_{pose}
1: **if** $\neg$is_valid_pose($q_{pose, old}$) **then**
2:   $q_{pose, old} \leftarrow$ identity_transformation
3: $iter \leftarrow 0$
4: $q_{pose} \leftarrow q_{pose, old}$
5: **while** $iter < max\_iter\_gradient\_descent$ **do**
6:   $\{c_1, ...c_5\} \leftarrow$ get_contact_points_in_human_hand_frame(C)
7:   **for** $j \in \{1, ..., 5\}$ **do**
8:     $x_j \leftarrow \frac{\partial m}{\partial x}|_{c_j}$ // this direction leads to better manipulability for the robot finger
9:     $x_j \leftarrow$ transform_to_human_hand_frame(x_j, y, q_{pose}, C)
10:    $\Delta z \leftarrow k_{pos}\sum_{i=1}^{i=5} x_i$ // translational correction with gain
11:    $\Delta \psi \leftarrow k_{rot}\sum_{i=1}^{i=5} c_i \times x_i$ // rotational correction with gain
12:    $q_{pose} \leftarrow$ apply_translational_and_rotational_corrections($q_{pose}, \Delta z, \Delta \psi$)
13:    $iter ++$
14: **if** is_valid_pose(q_{pose}) **then return** q_{pose}
15: $iter \leftarrow 0$
16: **while** $iter < max\_iter\_PSO$ **do**
17:   $state\_space =$ initialize_state_space()
18:   $q_{pose} \leftarrow$ particle_swarm_optimization($state\_space$)
19:   **if** is_valid_pose(q_{pose}) **then return** q_{pose}
20:   enlarge($state\_space$) // more iterations, larger state space
21: $q_{pose} \leftarrow NaN$

5.3 Optimization of Passive Degree of Freedom Using Nullspace Projection

The calculation of the iterative correction dy in line 17 of **Algorithm 1** is described in **Algorithm 3**. It is found by

calculating, for each contact point, the gradient of the manipulability index (**Eq. 3**) with respect to the joint angles of the robotic finger. These are then multiplied by a gain, and projected into the nullspace of the entire Exodex, i.e., the finger joints and the passive DOF. The nullspace projector projects any vector of forces on the Exodex's DOF into a subspace: the nullspace. Any force in the nullspace will not produce a resultant force at the contact points.

Letting $x_i \in \mathbb{R}^3$ be the Cartesian position of the ith attachment point, then $x = [x_1^\top, x_2^\top, x_3^\top, x_4^\top, x_5^\top]^\top$ is the vector of attachment points. Letting $\boldsymbol{\theta}_i \in \mathbb{R}^3$ be the joint positions of the ith robotic finger, $\boldsymbol{\theta} = [\boldsymbol{\theta}_1^\top, \boldsymbol{\theta}_2^\top, \boldsymbol{\theta}_3^\top, \boldsymbol{\theta}_4^\top, \boldsymbol{\theta}_5^\top]^\top$ is similarly the vector of the Exodex's active joint positions (just like y is the passive DOF positions). Then let J_θ be the Jacobian of x with respect to θ, J_y be the Jacobian with respect to y, and $J_{y,\theta} = [J_y, J_\theta]$.

The static nullspace projector N was calculated as in Dietrich et al. (2015):

$$N = I - J^\top (J^{W+})^\top, \quad (4)$$

$$J^{W+} = W^{-1}J^\top (JW^{-1}J^\top)^{-1}, \quad (5)$$

where J^{W+} is the weighted pseudoinverse of the Jacobian using diagonal weighting matrix W (we omit the dependency on q for brevity). Depending on W, we can increase or decrease the contribution of various DOF. Since we are interested in the contribution of the passive DOF of the Exodex, we adjust the weighting accordingly, setting the values of W on the diagonal which correspond to the passive DOF low, and the others, which correspond to pose, high.

Algorithm 3. compute_correction

Require: configuration C, pose of hand q_{pose}, passive DOF positions y, robot finger joint positions $\theta \in \mathbb{R}^{15}$
Ensure: correction dy
1: $\{c_1, ...c_5\} \leftarrow$ contact_points_in_robot_finger_frame(C, y, q_{pose}) // the Cartesian positions of the 5 contact points in the base frame of each robotic finger, for this configuration
2: **for** $i \in \{1, ..., 5\}$ **do**
3:   $\Delta \theta_i = \beta \frac{\partial m}{\partial \theta}|_{c_i}$ // this is the change in θ that would lead to better manipulability for the robot finger
4:   $J^{W+} \leftarrow$ weighted_pseudoinverse($J_{y,\theta}(y, \theta)$)
5:   $N = I - J^\top J^{W+\top}$
6:   $dy = N[0_{8\times1}, \Delta\theta_1^\top, \Delta\theta_2^\top, \Delta\theta_3^\top, \Delta\theta_4^\top, \Delta\theta_5^\top]^\top$
---

6 USER STATE ESTIMATION AND CONTROL

For accurate contact rendering and force-feedback from a virtual or remote environment, it is required to know the position and orientation of the hand (hand pose), and the positions of the joint angles in the fingers and the palm (hand configuration).

There are a number of ways to measure these. The configuration could be acquired from strain gauges on a sensorized glove, e.g., Cyberglove. The pose could be found from IMUs placed on the human hand, as long as the device is used in microgravity. These methods require electronics to be attached on the user's hand. Another possible method is through vision or motion-capture systems to capture pose and finger angles. However, this can be susceptible to occlusion and mislabeling.

In Pereira et al. (2019), we show how to reconstruct the hand pose and configuration only from the positions of the attachment points of the Exodex to the human hand. These can be determined from the angular position sensors on the robot finger joints, and the known kinematics of the system. Inverse kinematics can then be performed on a joint model of the human hand to determine the pose and configuration. The user does not need to wear any sensors.

6.1 Hand Model

The human hand model for the pose estimation is derived from MRI data and is based on Stillfried et al. (2014). The original model has 22 DOF: five in the thumb, four in each finger, and the intermetacarpal joint in the palm. However, neglecting the human's last two fingers and setting the distal interphalangeal joint (DIP) and proximal interphalangeal joint (PIP) to be proportional (constant k is the ratio DIP:PIP), the number of DOF reduces to 12. Added to this the six DOF in the hand pose (i.e., position and orientation of the hand's base coordinate system) and there are 18 DOF to be determined from 15 constraints [three-dimensional (3D) positions of each attachment points]. The kinematic model is shown in **Figure 11** overlaid on an image of the glove and attachment points.

In Pereira et al. (2019), constant k is found to give the most accurate tracking at $k = \frac{1}{2}$ and $k = \frac{2}{3}$. This corresponds with the value from the empirical measurements in Rijpkema and Girard (1991) and the value of $\frac{1}{2}$ suggested for power grasps in Cobos et al. (2008). We used a value of $k = \frac{2}{3}$ in our trials in **Section 7**.

6.2 Iterative Hand State Update

The well-known iterative method for the inverse kinematics which minimizes the joint error using the transpose of the Jacobian (Balestrino et al., 1984; Wolovich and Elliott, 1984) is used. As there are more DOF than constraints, a nullspace of dimension 18 − 15 = 3 exists. In the nullspace, we optimize away from the joint limits in the hand to achieve a more natural posture. The full algorithm is recapitulated in **Algorithm 4**.

Algorithm 4. Update hand state.

Require: observed attachment point positions x, previous hand state q'
Ensure: updated hand state q
1: $x_{\mathrm{calc}} \leftarrow \mathtt{forwardKinematics}(q')$ // *calculate positions of attachment points on hand given previous state*
2: $\delta x \leftarrow x - x_{\mathrm{calc}}$ // *deviation measured to calculated*
3: $q_{\mathrm{pose}} \leftarrow q'_{\mathrm{pose}} + A_{\mathrm{pose}} J_{\mathrm{pose}}(q')^{\top} \delta x$
4: $\hat{q} \leftarrow [q_{\mathrm{pose}}^{\top}, q_{\mathrm{conf}}'^{\top}]^{\top}$
5: $\hat{x}_{\mathrm{calc}} \leftarrow \mathtt{forwardKinematics}(\hat{q})$ // *calculate positions of attachment points on hand given intermediate state*
6: $\delta \hat{x} \leftarrow x - \hat{x}_{\mathrm{calc}}$ // *deviation measured to calculated*
7: $q_{\mathrm{conf}} \leftarrow q'_{\mathrm{conf}} + A_{\mathrm{conf}} J_{\mathrm{conf}}(\hat{q})^{\top} \delta \hat{x}$
8: $\delta q_{\mathrm{cor,N}} \leftarrow \mathtt{nullspaceCorrection}(J(\hat{q}), \hat{q}, q_{\mathrm{max}}, q_{\mathrm{min}})$
9: $q_{\mathrm{unsat}} \leftarrow [q_{\mathrm{pose}}^{\top}, q_{\mathrm{conf}}^{\top}]^{\top} + \delta q_{\mathrm{cor,N}}$
10: $q \leftarrow \mathtt{saturateAtJointLimits}(q_{\mathrm{unsat}}, q_{\mathrm{max}}, q_{\mathrm{min}})$

In the algorithm, $q \in \mathbb{R}^3 \times SO(3) \times \mathbb{R}^{12}$ is the 18-dimensional vector of joints of the hand. This consists of $q_{\mathrm{pose}} \in \mathbb{R}^3 \times SO(3)$ as the pose of the hand (orientation given in roll-pitch-yaw) and $q_{\mathrm{conf}} \in \mathbb{R}^{12}$ as the configuration of all the independent DOF in the hand as described in the previous section. The hand state at the previous time step is q', the vector of attachment point positions

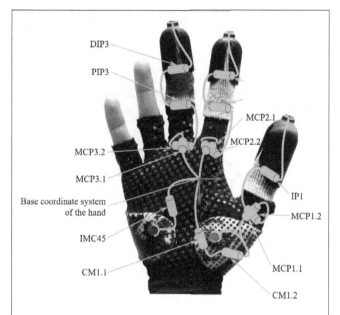

FIGURE 11 | Diagram of hand kinematic model overlaid on human hand wearing glove and finger socks. Cylinders represent revolute joints; green lines represent links. Not shown: three prismatic and revolute joints linking world coordinate system with the hand's base coordinate system (this shown here in red).

at the current time step is x, and the partial derivatives matrices of x with respect to q_{pose} and q_{conf} are J_{pose} and J_{conf}, respectively. A_{pose} and A_{conf} are gain matrices.

A two-step approach is applied where first the pose is updated in line 3, the estimated contact points are recalculated, and then the configuration is updated in line 7. This was found during development to allow higher gains A_{pose} and A_{conf} without becoming unstable, and therefore a faster convergence, than if all state elements were updated at once.

The joint ranges are enforced in line 10; the values are taken from González Camarero et al. (2015), with the exception of PIP2 and PIP3, which are limited in extension to .03 rad. The reason for disallowing full extension and hyperextension was that the restoring values when moving back into flexion, $A_{\mathrm{conf}} J_{\mathrm{conf}}(\hat{q}) \delta x$ in line 7 would be zero at full extension (since this is a singularity). In hyperextension, these would instead try to pull the joints further into extension.

6.3 Nullspace Projection

To move joints away from their limits where possible, which also results in a more natural-looking reconstruction, a correction in the nullspace was defined. This is shown in lines 8 and 9. The nullspace projector was calculated with the intermediate values $\hat{q}$, to avoid recalculating J_{conf}, since this is computationally expensive.

For each DOF, a correction was calculated so:

$$\delta q_{i,\mathrm{cor}} = \alpha_i \frac{q_{i,\max} + q_{i,\min} - 2q_i}{q_{i,\max} - q_{i,\min}}, \tag{6}$$

where for the ith DOF, α_i is a gain; q_i, $q_{i,\max}$, $q_{i,\min}$, and $\delta q_{i,\mathrm{cor}}$ are the ith elements of the vectors q, the joint limits $q_{\max}$ and $q_{\min}$, and δq_{cor}, respectively. We then project this into the nullspace: $\delta q_{\text{cor, N}} = N\delta q_{\text{cor}}$, and add it to the hand state in line 9.

The nullspace projector is calculated as in **Eq. 4**. We omit the dependency on q for brevity. Since the unweighted pseudoinverse (i.e., with $W = I$) can be calculated using singular value decomposition (SVD) (Golub and van Loan, 2013) in polynomial time, we rearrange the Jacobian, defining:

$$W^{-1} = \Omega\Omega^{\top}, \quad H = J\Omega, \tag{7}$$

Hence **Eq. 5** becomes:

$$J^{W+} = \Omega H^{\top}\left(HH^{\top}\right)^{-1} = \Omega H^{I+}, \tag{8}$$

which can be solved using SVD. Our weighting matrix was a diagonal matrix with low weights for the elements of the pose and the intermetacarpal joint, and high weights for most other joints, as in Pereira et al. (2019). The nullspace projector was calculated in parallel with the robot control at 1 kHz, since the computation was too intensive to be done in serial in a single control cycle.

6.4 Control of the Hand–Arm System

When used in combination with the Exodex, the LWR is controlled in torque mode, compensating only for its weight and compliant to external torques. Attaching the Exodex to the end effector and compensating for its weight means that the Exodex behaves as a floating object in zero-gravity, except that the inertia of the system and a small amount of friction is felt by the user (Schmidt et al., 2020). Forces exerted by the robotic fingers of the Exodex on the human hand leads to a movement of the base of the Exodex if not also counteracted by the LWR (see **Figure 12**). For this reason, forces from the virtual or remote environment are also applied on the base of the robot similar to that in Endo et al. (2011).

Each of the five robotic fingers are also compliant to external forces and torques, and are gravity-compensated. However, the non-backdrivability of the robotic fingers, as well as their high friction and inertia, mean that feed-forward control and friction compensation are necessary to bring the user closer to an impression of moving in free space. Measured torques on each of the three joints of each finger $\tau_{\text{msr, exo}} \in \mathbb{R}^{15}$ are fed forward with a feed-forward diagonal gain matrix K_{FF}, which lowers the perceived inertia in the mechanism. Gravity compensation $\tau_{\text{g, exo}} \in \mathbb{R}^{15}$ is added. The forces from the virtual environment on each finger $f_{\text{env, exo}} = [f_{\text{env,1}}^{\top}, f_{\text{env,5}}^{\top}]^{\top}$, where $f_{\text{env},i}$ is the force from the environment on the ith robotic finger, are transformed into the joint space using the transpose of the Jacobian $J_{\text{exo}}^{\top}$, which relates the Cartesian velocity of the contact points in the Exodex base frame to the velocity of each joint. Friction compensation as in Le Tien et al. (2008) is performed on the resulting commanded torque.

$$\tau_{\text{des, exo}} = K_{\text{FF}}\tau_{\text{msr, exo}} + \tau_{\text{g, exo}} + K_{\text{FF}}J_{\text{exo}}^{\top}f_{\text{env, exo}} \tag{9}$$

$$\tau_{\text{cmd, exo}} = \tau_{\text{des, exo}} + \tau_{\text{fric, exo}}\left(\tau_{\text{des, exo}}, \tau_{\text{msr, exo}}, \dot{q}\right) \tag{10}$$

where $f_{\text{env},i}$ is the desired force-feedback from the virtual environment. The Exodex base frame is coincident with the end effector frame of the LWR. The control of the LWR is therefore:

$$w_{\text{env}} = \sum_{i\in\{1,\ldots,5\}}\begin{bmatrix} f_{\text{env},i} \\ r_i \times f_{\text{env},i} \end{bmatrix} \tag{11}$$

$$\tau_{\text{LWR,cmd}} = \tau_{\text{LWR,g}} + J_{LWR}^{ET}w_{\text{env}} + (\tau_{\text{ff}}) \tag{12}$$

The term τ_{ff} is optional feed-forward term for reducing inertia in free space and is detailed in the next section. Note, as it is only used in free space, the wrench from the environmental forces on the Exodex w_{env} will be zero, and this term does not need to be scaled with the feed-forward gains.

6.5 Inertia Reduction in Free Space

Since forces on the LWR and the Exodex are not measured at the end effectors but only in the joints, the movement in free space is not without some perceivable resistance (see **Section 7.4**). To attempt to remove this resistance, when working in free space, an extra feed-forward wrench on the end effector of the LWR can be introduced. However, using the torques measured at the LWR joints themselves can be inaccurate. As there is a chain of mechanisms between the human hand and the LWR joints (e.g., magnetic clutch attachments, gimbals, Exodex fingers, modular palm, etc.), each component in this mechanism chain can introduce some element of elasticity and play. Therefore, in order to capture the forces that the human exerts as accurately as possible, we measure them as close as possible to the point where they are exerted on the Exodex's fingers. More accurate would be to measure the forces directly exerted by the human hand on the Exodex. To do this, the forces exerted at the attachment points to the robotic fingers, $f_{\text{ext},i}$, are calculated from the torques on the robotic finger joints and are used to determine the total force and torque that the user exerts on the Exodex.

The world frame of the human hand is the same as that of the LWR. The transformation T_0^H is the transformation from the world to the human hand coordinate system (i.e., applied to coordinates of a point in the hand frame, yielding the coordinates in the world frame) obtained from the first six elements of the hand state q_{pose}. T_0^E is the transformation from the world to the end effector. $T_H^E = (T_0^H)^{-1}T_0^E$ is therefore the transformation from human hand to end effector.

The torque around the hand's base coordinate system is also found, as shown in **Figure 12**. This is the wrench exerted on the robot measured at the base coordinate system of the human hand,

$$w_{\text{ext, H}} = \sum_{i\in\{1,\ldots,5\}}\begin{bmatrix} f_{\text{ext},i} \\ (T_H^E r_i) \times f_{\text{ext},i} \end{bmatrix}, \tag{13}$$

where r_i is the finger contact in the frame of the LWR end effector as in **Eq. 11** and shown in **Figure 12**. Hence, **Eq. 13** gives the wrench around the human hand coordinate system in the hand frame. This is translated to the desired LWR joint torques using the transpose of the Jacobian J_{LWR}^H of the forward kinematics of the human hand's base coordinate system. This is calculated from the Jacobian at the end effector J_{LWR}^E and the adjunct of the transformation from the end effector to hand base. The gain $K_{\text{FF,free}}$ is a diagonal matrix regulating the strength of the feed-forward.

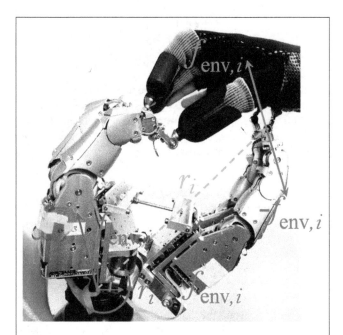

FIGURE 12 | The wrench at the Exodex base (attachment to tool center point of the Light Weight Robot) from an external force at the attachment point to the human. The freely rotating gimbals at the attachment points mean that torques from the human are not transmitted, only forces.

$$J_{LWR}^H = \mathrm{adj}\left(T_H^E\right)J_{LWR}^E \qquad (14)$$

$$\boldsymbol{\tau}_{\mathrm{ff}} = K_{FF,free}J_{LWR}^{H\top}\boldsymbol{w}_{\mathrm{ext,h}} \qquad (15)$$

7 EXODEX DEPLOYMENT AND EVALUATION

To examine Exodex's ability to effectively serve as a hand haptic UI in a variety of use cases and command modalities, we deployed it in three different scenarios. We first discuss its use in a virtual environment for interacting with mixed media of both solid objects of different shapes and liquids of different viscosities. The second use case realizes hand gesture recognition and telecommand of an avatar robot, for a variety of hand sizes. Thirdly, we present hand–arm teleoperation utilizing adaptive MMT.

7.1 Whole-Hand Perception of Liquid and Solid in a Virtual Environment

A virtual environment was created with a cylinder, sphere, and flat surface. The surface object could be switched between the solid mode, as a virtual wall, or liquid mode, which changes the perceivable viscosity when going below the surface level.

To render solids, a god-object method implementing a simple spring-damper impedance was used. Spring stiffness of up to 1000 N/m could be achieved without leading to significant instability. Adding force sensors at the attachment points (see **Section 8.1**) should further improve this.

For the liquid media, only viscosity forces were rendered, which mainly stimulate proprioceptive and kinesthetic senses, while other fluid cues require cutaneous and temperature sensing. The viscosity forces were calculated based on a simplified drag equation (Schmidt et al., 2020). With this trade-off in accuracy, high enough frequencies could be achieved for the viscosity rendering to run simultaneously with the solid interaction loop. Despite the physical hardware limitations restricting the rendering of very low viscosity such as that of water, users were able to perceive media as fluid in the virtual environment and could clearly distinguish these from solids. In a user study (Schmidt et al., 2020), the viscosities between 1 and 30 Pa s were achieved stably on the Exodex. Especially in the higher viscosity range, the participants were able to distinguish different rendered fluid viscosities as in real-life experiments, with a Weber fraction of .3. Using Exodex as an UI, it was observed that virtual viscosity is mainly perceived through larger arm motions, e.g., as people do when checking the water in a bathtub, whereas more dexterous interactions with solid objects occur at the in-hand level. This suggests that the viscosity rendering could be mainly implemented in the robotic arm, while the robotic fingers are free to render crisp solid body interactions. Thus, exploration of more complex virtual environments is enabled, where both solids and fluids can be simultaneously rendered and explored as can be seen in **Figure 13** and in the **Supplementary Video**.

7.2 Gesture-Commanded Telemanipulation

Earlier work has shown the gesture-driven approach to telecommand robotic end effectors using a data glove to be particularly effective for high dexterity tasks such as in-hand manipulation, while reducing the teleoperator's workload (Lii et al., 2012). For the Exodex, a neural network–based gesture command concept has been implemented.

A two-layer neural network was trained on six hand gestures, with

P_1: outstretched fingers,
P_2: index finger pointing,
P_3: diver's "OK,"
P_4: power-grasp, small object (e.g., size of an apricot),
P_5: power-grasp, larger object (e.g., size of a grapefruit), and
P_6: (attempt to) touch bottom of the little finger with thumb tip.

The gesture recognition was tested as an input method to a graphical UI which controls the robot, as well as for telemanipulating another robot, as shown in **Figure 14B**. The gesture command in operation can be seen in the **Supplementary Video**.

To examine the ability to accommodate different hand sizes, we tested the gesture recognition on three adult females and two adult males, from a 15th percentile adult female hand span of 168 mm to an 86th percentile adult male at 205 mm (Greiner, 1991, p. 157). The device kinematics was optimized for each hand size as in **Section 5**. The gestures from **Section 7.2** were used as the set C of required hand configurations, and we used gesture P5

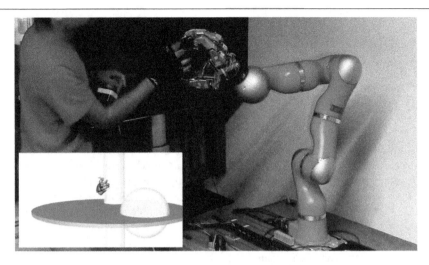

FIGURE 13 | User interaction in a virtual environment with liquid and solid objects. The operator of the Exodex can be seen using a virtual hand in the virtual environment on screen (shown bottom left). The surface of a virtual fluid is represented by a purple disk. Solid bodies are rendered in the shape of a cylinder (in cyan) and a sphere (in pink). For a better view of the user interaction in the virtual reality environment, please refer to the **Supplementary Video**.

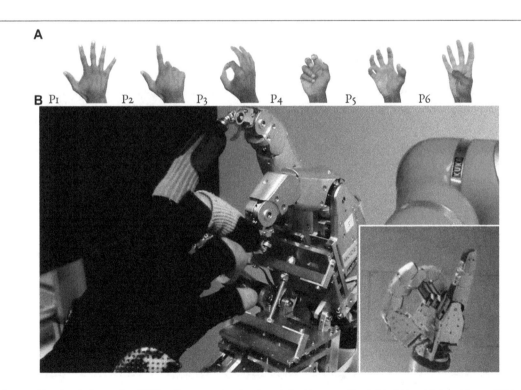

FIGURE 14 | Gesture-driven hand teleoperation. **(A)** The different user hand gestures trained for recognition: left to right: outstretched fingers (P1), index finger pointing (P2), diver's "OK" (P3), power-grasp, small object (P4), power-grasp, larger object (P5), touch bottom of little finger with thumb tip (P6). **(B)** An example of telecommanded gesture being executed by a DLR Five-Finger Hand (bottom right). More examples can be seen in the Supplementary Video.

as $\mathcal{C}_m$ the (set of) gestures around which to maximize manipulability. In addition, we tried two children's hand sizes with spans of 138 and 158 mm. Kinematics were optimized manually for the experiments with the child subjects, due to time constraints on running the optimization and the availability of the children.

Subjects had photographs in front of them showing the six positions in **Figure 14A** with their corresponding number. The trial progressed as follows:

(1) The subject practiced the six positions to get adjusted to the haptic UI.

(2) The number of each position was shown on screen for 16 s, during which time the subject had to form the corresponding position with their hand. All six positions were cycled through in order, twice.

(3) The second step was repeated, but the subject had visual feedback on screen of both the number of the recognized gesture, and a simulation of a teleoperated (robot) hand making the gesture.

Results are presented in **Table 2**. For each subject, we show which gestures were not achieved (on either attempt) either with or without visual feedback. We show whether this was within 8 s (the reaction time of subjects was sometimes several seconds, so a gesture being recognized within 8 s corresponds to a problem-free formation and recognition of the gesture) or within 16 s. The recognized gesture was counted only if it was constant for 2 s. Gesture P_6 is difficult to form when connected to the exoskeleton. This is discussed in the following section. Gesture P_5 is difficult for the neural network to tell apart from P_4, as they are both power grasps.

Interestingly, the child of hand size 158 mm was unable to achieve gesture P_6 at all after the first attempt at manually optimizing the Exodex kinematics. When the kinematics were readjusted, the child could achieve all gestures. However, this suggests that 1) rather than a one-size-fits-all design, passive DOF allow the design to be optimized and function well for a range of hand sizes, and 2) manual optimization does not always yield a valid solution, further motivating the automated optimization in **Section 5**.

7.3 Teleoperation of a Dexterous Hand–Arm System

The Exodex can also be used as an input device to teleoperate a real or virtual avatar robot (see **Figure 15**) with haptic and/or visual feedback. We used the Exodex to command a anthropomorphic hand–arm setup (see **Figure 15**) composed of a custom configured KUKA DLR-LWR 4+ (with joints reconfigured to match human arm kinematics) and a DLR Five-Finger hand with a two-channel teleoperation setup (Frisoli et al., 2004). The visual feedback from the remote

environment plus additional task-specific information are provided through a Microsoft Hololens.

Both direct teleoperation and an MMT (Passenberg et al., 2010; Xu et al., 2016) approach were tested. In direct teleoperation, an impedance controller on the avatar tracks the input device in the task space. The haptic feedback displayed on the Exodex to the teleoperator's hand is calculated based on environmental forces measured on the avatar. In our MMT approach, both the different kinematics of Exodex and avatar as well as possible communication delays are accounted for by a virtual model at the local site. The user interacts haptically directly with this intermediate model. Differences between the virtual model and the real avatar's environment are reconciled using Dynamic Motion Primitives and Reinforcement Learning. More detailed description and evaluation are found in Beik-Mohammadi et al. (2020).

7.4 Summary and Discussion

Looking at the overall success of the different use cases deployed, we believe that the Exodex has fulfilled the functions of a haptic interface that we set out for. In a mixed media virtual environment, the users can interact with and distinguish different stiffness (e.g., like a drum-skin, dough, or air-balloon), shapes (i.e., plane, sphere, cylinder), and curvature. They were also able to differentiate between different media, such as solids and fluids of different viscosities. The users could also grasp and manipulate objects in a virtual world using intuitive exploration procedures. This set of capabilities shows great potential for applications such as underwater exploration.

Looking at a more abstract level of teleoperation through gestures, the Exodex was able to facilitate the recognition of the set of different gestures in the experiment, and in turn command the avatar robotic hand. This also helped validate our hand state and pose estimation approach presented in **Sections 5, 6**.

The successful teleoperation of a hand–arm robotic avatar through adaptive MMT demonstrates the Exodex's ability to command a high complexity robot in performing different hand--arm motion skills such as object handling.

TABLE 2 | Gestures not recognized within 8 and 16 s, with and without visual feedback.

Subject	Gender[a]	Hand size	Gestures not achieved, no feedback[b]		Gestures not achieved, with feedback[b]	
		(mm)	(<8 s)	(<16 s)	(<8 s)	(<16 s)
Adult 1	F	168				
Adult 2	F	174	P5, P6	P5, P6	P6	
Adult 3	F	182	P6	P6	P6	
Adult 4	M	186				
Adult 5	M	205				
Child 1[c]	M	138	P5, P6	P5	P3, P6	
Child 2[c]	F	158				

[a]F, female; M, male.
[b]Only the gestures not achieved are listed in the interest of legibility.
[c]Exodex Adam configuration was manually optimized.

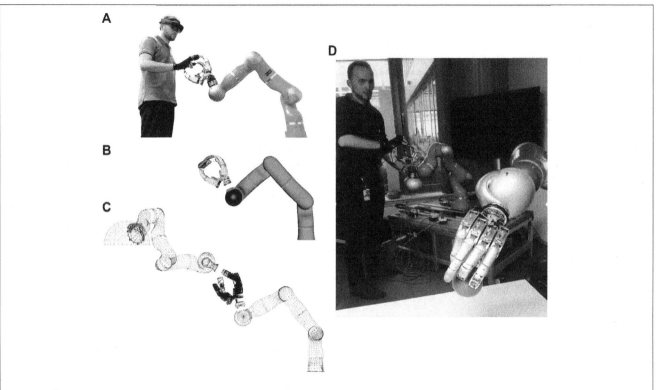

FIGURE 15 | Exodex employed as a haptic UI to teleoperate a hand–arm system. **(A)** The operator's hand is attached to Exodex. **(B)** The contact points of the hand and interface are calculated using the forward kinematics. The contact points are then used to estimate the human hand posture using the inverse kinematics in **Section 6**. **(C)** A joint-to-joint approximation of avatar robot hand is calculated to match the operator's hand. **(D)** Exodex being used to teleoperate a hand–arm system to pick up an object.

Furthermore, it shows the feasibility to delegate some autonomy (more of the lower level robotic tasks) to the avatar.

However, our first attempt at a whole-hand haptic UI still has shortcomings that can be addressed. Firstly, there was no tactile perception, as the fingers were inside silicone sleeves. This gives the user a somewhat insulated feel, even with force reflection. The experience can be likened to exploring the physical world with gloves on. Furthermore, although the finger sleeves are usually comfortable to wear, with a limited number of sizes, the fit is not always perfect. This can sometimes cause unwanted pressure on the distal links of the user's finger. If the rigid thimble part of the finger sleeve was too tight, this could be uncomfortable over longer periods of time. An adjustable finger sleeve, or more gradations in the size can address the discomfort.

Secondly, the operator of the Exodex should be able to move their hand and arm in space freely, feeling as little of the mechanism's inertia and friction as possible. To reduce the inertia, feed-forward control was implemented (see **Section 6.5**) and to reduce the friction in the fingers, a friction observer was implemented (see **Section 6.4**). Friction in the LWR is barely perceptible, and so was not compensated. Despite these measures, inertia and friction effects can still be felt. Since excessively high feed-forward gains lead to instability in the fingers, it is not possible to completely remove the feeling of inertia by increasing feed-forward gain. Sometimes, users had to use their other hand to move the LWR or readjust the Exodex. Reducing the weight (the current version weighs approximately 2.5 kg) and moment of inertia of the Exodex can help. Additional force/torque sensors at the attachment points can also help improve the control performance to reduce unwanted perceivable dynamics.

Thirdly, the workspace of the robotic fingers of the Exodex is limited, and this led to a compromise, as detailed in **Section 4**, of ensuring that the most useful human hand positions for grasping and manipulation were within the workspace. However, other hand positions were difficult, e.g., P_6 in **Section 7.2**, or impossible. Since the workspace of the human's thumb is so large, some thumb positions (e.g., full flexion), lie outside the workspace of the robotic finger. We observed that subjects would sometimes contort their hands to achieve the gesture despite the constraints of the system's mechanics.

The reason gesture P_6 (see **Section 7.2**) was problematic was its difficulty to be detected, even when achievable. In this position, some of the human hand joints were near their joint limits. Since the null space optimization of the human hand kinematics estimation (see **Section 6.3**) optimizes away from joint angles, it could be that this makes P_6 more difficult for the algorithm to reconstruct the angles of the human hand joints accurately.

Another drawback, related to the limited workspace, was that joint limits of the LWR and of the Exodex's robotic fingers are often reached. To protect the joints from damage, we implemented a virtual impedance (spring-damper system) at the joint limits which prevents the user from reaching the physical limits. However, this may be perceived as a virtual object by the user, or may simply be confusing.

To address this, a variety of solutions are possible. On the control side, virtual forces pulling away from joint limits could be projected into the null space with a suitable dynamic null space projector (Dietrich et al., 2015), reorienting the device away from the joint limits without exerting forces at the attachment points. Another solution is to limit the workspace in which the human operates, and instead use metaphor 3D interaction techniques such as go-go (Poupyrev et al., 1996) or ray-casting (Mine et al., 1997) as proposed in Bowman and Hodges (1997) and Ouramdane et al. (2006), to allow the user to reach objects beyond their physical workspace. Concretely, the users are lead to believe—via visual cues—that their hand has reached a position, which is in reality unattainable while attached to the haptic UI.

In the Exodex, the forces exerted at the center of the gimbal are the same as those exerted on the human. However, there is often a small torque induced since the distance from the attachment point to the human is often not parallel to the force acting at the gimbal. In our design, we kept these torques to a minimum by keeping the attachment point as close to the gimbal as was mechanically possible. Nevertheless, this inherent issue of the human–Exodex attachment should be examined with new attachment concepts. This, along with other drawbacks that we discovered during this work can be addressed in our continuing development on the Exodex.

One key feature omitted in this first version of Exodex is the dedicated haptic interaction for the ring and little fingers, which we plan to add in the follow-up version. Nevertheless, users were able to perform the necessary precision and power grasps without feedback to the ring and little fingers. They would generally hold these fingers in full flexion when power-grasping and extend them when precision grasping. Feix et al. (2016) have shown that some power grasps can be performed with the thumb, index, and middle fingers and the palm. However, adding two more robotic fingers to Exodex would finally enable a full(er) variety of grasps and in-hand manipulations.

By comparison, a fingertip-only system, such as the HIRO, gives the user more possibilities to move the UI through its workspace. A somewhat apt analogy is our operation of a steering wheel, where the user can take the hand off the wheel, then place it back on to regain range of motion on the user side, and continue manipulating the input device. With Exodex, this whole-hand attachment scheme takes away this possibility. What it gains, in turn, is the whole-hand immersive interaction. One can say that although the HIRO is more of an input style suitable to manipulating the input device, the Exodex's strength lies in its close coupling of the whole user's hand. As a first version of integrated system from our ground whole-hand haptic UI system, the Exodex succeeded in providing a safe and comfortable operation, immersive user experience, user hand pose capturing, and enabling several command modalities. This gave us the confidence to continue forward with it as a capable device for a wide array of applications.

8 CONCLUSION

We present a novel whole-hand haptic input device, the Exodex Adam, a front-facing, mirror attachment haptic UI for the hand. Attached to the user at the fingers and the palm, it not only allows tracking of the human hand pose but also offers an immersive haptic experience. This enables the rendering of forces from power grasps, precision grasp, in-hand manipulation, as well as whole-hand exploration of a remote or virtual environment.

Through the deployment of the Exodex in different use cases, we validated our haptic UI concept's viability for a wide array of applications. Its combination of force reflection and whole-hand interaction enables the user to intricately interact with complex environments. We also showcased its effectiveness in different command modalities, making it a viable system for shared control strategies and scalable autonomy based telerobotics. The reconfigurable design has been shown to safely accommodate users of different hand sizes and shapes.

We believe with the current Exodex, and its further development, such a haptic UI system shall serve a growing array of fields and applications from space and underwater exploration, physical therapy, or rehabilitation, VR activities, to an assortment of telerobotic applications.

8.1 Future Work

As already discussed in **Section 7.4**, the most immediate improvement to the Exodex is the addition of dedicated haptic interaction for the ring and little fingers, by adding two more robotic fingers to the system. Furthermore, by automating the palm base's adjustable DOF with actuation and sensorization, the robotic fingers' base pose and position can be automatically generated, thus streamlining the hand pose estimation. It may also be possible to further incorporate the actuated palm base DOF into the motion of the Exodex to increase the active workspace during operation.

Currently, the Exodex only stimulates proprioceptive and kinesthetic perception (i.e., by rendering forces), which are only two components of haptic feedback. In future development, miniaturized vibrotactile actuators in the finger sleeves may be able to provide additional cutaneous feedback (Bolanowski Jr et al., 1988; Biswas, 2015). Adding tactile or cutaneous feedback (i.e., feeling warmth, texture, etc. on the skin) as part of future work would further enrich user experience.

Better estimation of the human hand pose would allow us to apply more accurate rendering algorithms taking into account the different frictional and mechanical properties of the human hand. An area of future work that should be continued is the implementing and testing of these rendering algorithms.

Although Exodex's current implementation already allows good hand pose estimation, its accuracy can be improved by adding angular sensors on each of the DOF on the gimbal. Furthermore, by introducing force sensors at the attachment points, we could acquire more detailed measurements of the applied force from the user, which can in turn improve feed-forward control performance.

Finally, this work demonstrates the broad usability of the Exodex with different command modalities. Another urgent next step is to identify more specifically relevant applications in need of such a capable hand-arm haptic UI, so that development can focus on their specific requirements.

AUTHOR CONTRIBUTIONS

NYL led the project, including conceptualization, development, and realization of the Exodex Adam. APe carried out work on pose estimation, control implementation and gesture command, together with APi and LM. JD carried out ideation on mechanical design and realization of the Exodex Adam palm base. GS and AE carried out work on workspace and finger placement strategy. AS carried out work on mixed media VR teleoperation. HB-M and PR carried out work on MMT hand-arm teleoperation. TB carried out work on system model development, as well as user attachment mechanisms. AM carried out work on gimbal mechanical design and realization. BP took part in early ideation of Exodex Adam, and provided mechatronics support throughout. ZC participated in early ideation, and supported in low level controller design. AA-S provided research guidance throughout the concept, validation and deployment. NYL, APe, AS, GS, and HB-M jointly wrote the manuscript.

ACKNOWLEDGMENTS

The authors would like to express their deep gratitude to several of our current and former DLR colleagues for their kind assistance toward the development of this work: Vanessa Hofbauer (now with Aitme GmbH) and Andreas Meissner (now with the German Central Office for Information Technology in the Security Sector) on Exodex Adam reconfigurable palm development, Thomas Hulin and Philipp Kremer (now with BMW AG) for the setup and debugging of the LWR, Florian Schmidt for middleware support, Robert Burger for firmware support, and Miguel Neves for CAD design.

REFERENCES

Aiple, M., and Schiele, A. (2013). "Pushing the Limits of the Cybergrasp™ for Haptic Rendering," in IEEE International Conference on Robotics and Automation (ICRA), 3541–3546.

Artigas, J., Balachandran, R., Riecke, C., Stelzer, M., Weber, B., Ryu, J.-H., et al. (2016). "Kontur-2: Force-Feedback Teleoperation from the International Space Station," in 2016 IEEE International Conference on Robotics and Automation (ICRA), 1166–1173. doi:10.1109/ICRA.2016.7487246

Balestrino, A., De Maria, G., and Sciavicco, L. (1984). Robust Control of Robotic Manipulators. IFAC Proc. Volumes 17, 2435–2440. doi:10.1016/s1474-6670(17)61347-8

Barbagli, F., Salisbry, K., and Devengenzo, R. (2003). "Enabling multi-finger, Multi-Hand Virtualized Grasping," in 2003 IEEE International Conference on Robotics and Automation (Cat. No. 03CH37422) (Taipei, Taiwan: IEEE), 809–815. Vol. 1.

Beik-Mohammadi, H., Kerzel, M., Pleintinger, B., Hulin, T., Reisich, P., Schmidt, A., et al. (2020). "Model Mediated Teleoperation with a Hand-Arm Exoskeleton in Long Time Delays Using Reinforcement Learning," in IEEE International Conference on Robot and Human Interactive Communication (Ro-Man). doi:10.1109/ro-man47096.2020.9223477

Bischoff, R., Kurth, J., Schreiber, G., Koeppe, R., Albu-Schaeffer, A., Beyer, A., et al. (2010). "The Kuka-Dlr Lightweight Robot Arm - a New Reference Platform for Robotics Research and Manufacturing," in ISR 2010 (41st International Symposium on Robotics) and ROBOTIK 2010 (6th German Conference on Robotics), 1–8.

Biswas, A. (2015). Characterization and Modeling of Vibrotactile Sensitivity Threshold of Human Finger Pad and the Pacinian Corpuscle. Ph.D. thesis. doi:10.13140/RG.2.2.18103.11687

Bolanowski, S. J., Jr, Gescheider, G. A., Verrillo, R. T., and Checkosky, C. M. (1988). Four Channels Mediate the Mechanical Aspects of Touch. The J. Acoust. Soc. America 84, 1680–1694. doi:10.1121/1.397184

Bouzit, M., Burdea, G., Popescu, G., and Boian, R. (2002). The Rutgers Master Ii-New Design Force-Feedback Glove. Ieee/asme Trans. Mechatron. 7, 256–263. doi:10.1109/tmech.2002.1011262

Bowman, D. A., and Hodges, L. F. (1997). An Evaluation of Techniques for Grabbing and Manipulating Remote Objects in Immersive Virtual Environments, 35–38.

Bullock, I. M., Zheng, J. Z., De La Rosa, S., Guertler, C., and Dollar, A. M. (2013). Grasp Frequency and Usage in Daily Household and Machine Shop Tasks. IEEE Trans. Haptics 6, 296–308. doi:10.1109/TOH.2013.6

Chabrier, A., Gonzalez, F., Gosselin, F., and Bachta, W. (2015). Analysis of the Directions in Which Forces Are Applied on the Hand during Manual Manipulation and Exploration. Proc. IEEE World Haptics Conf. 2015, 280–285. doi:10.1109/whc.2015.7177726

Chalon, M., Grebenstein, M., Wimboeck, T., and Hirzinger, G. (2010). "The Thumb: Guidelines for a Robotic Design," in IEEE/RSJ International Conference on Intelligent Robots and Systems (IROS). doi:10.1109/iros.2010.5650454

Chen, Z., Lii, N. Y., Wimböck, T., Fan, S., Liu, H., and Albu-Schäffer, A. (2014). Experimental Analysis on Spatial and Cartesian Impedance Control for the Dexterous DLR/HIT II Hand. Internation J. Robotics Automation 29, 1. doi:10.2316/Journal.206.2014.1.206-3669

Clerc, M. (2006). Particle Swarm Optimization. Washington, DC, USA: ISTE.

Cobos, S., Ferre, M., Uran, M. A. S., Ortego, J., and Pena, C. (2008). "Efficient Human Hand Kinematics for Manipulation Tasks," in Proc. IEEE/RSJ International Conference on Intelligent Robots and Systems, 2246–2251. doi:10.1109/iros.2008.4651053

Cutkosky, M. R. (1989). On Grasp Choice, Grasp Models, and the Design of Hands for Manufacturing Tasks. IEEE Trans. Robot. Automat. 5, 269–279. doi:10.1109/70.34763

Dietrich, A., Ott, C., and Albu-Schäffer, A. (2015). An Overview of Null Space Projections for Redundant, Torque-Controlled Robots. Int. J. Robotics Res. 34, 1385–1400. doi:10.1177/0278364914566516

Endo, T., and Kawasaki, H. (2014). Collision Avoidance and its Experimental Investigation for a Side-faced-type Multi-Fingered Haptic Interface. IEEE Int. Conf. Systems, Man. Cybernetics 2014, 3984–3989. doi:10.1109/smc.2014.6974554

Endo, T., Kawasaki, H., Mouri, T., Doi, Y., Yoshida, T., Ishigure, Y., et al. (2009). "Five-fingered Haptic Interface Robot: Hiro Iii," in World Haptics 2009-Third Joint EuroHaptics conference and Symposium on Haptic Interfaces for Virtual Environment and Teleoperator Systems (Salt Lake City, UT, USA: IEEE), 458–463. doi:10.1109/whc.2009.4810812

Endo, T., Kawasaki, H., Mouri, T., Ishigure, Y., Shimomura, H., Matsumura, M., et al. (2011). Five-fingered Haptic Interface Robot: HIRO III. *IEEE Trans. Haptics* 4, 14–27. doi:10.1109/toh.2010.62

Feix, T., Romero, J., Schmiedmayer, H.-B., Dollar, A. M., and Kragic, D. (2016). The Grasp Taxonomy of Human Grasp Types. *IEEE Trans. Human-mach. Syst.* 46, 66–77. doi:10.1109/THMS.2015.2470657

Festo (2012). *Festo ExoHand*. Esslingen, Germany: Festo AG & Co. KG, 54791.

Fontana, M., Dettori, A., Salsedo, F., and Bergamasco, M. (2009). "Mechanical Design of a Novel Hand Exoskeleton for Accurate Force Displaying," in IEEE International Conference on Robotics and Automation (ICRA), 1704–1709. doi:10.1109/robot.2009.5152591

Frisoli, A., Sotgiu, E., Checcacci, D., Simoncini, F., Marcheschi, S., Avizzano, C. A., et al. (2004). "Theoretical and Experimental Evaluation of a 2-channel Bilateral Force Reflection Teleoperation System," in International Conference on Integrated Modeling and Analysis in Applied Control and Automation (IMAACA).

Fuchs, M., Borst, C., Giordano, P. R., Baumann, A., Kraemer, E., Langwald, J., et al. (2009). "Rollin' Justin - Design Considerations and Realization of a mobile Platform for a Humanoid Upper Body," in 2009 IEEE International Conference on Robotics and Automation, 4131–4137. doi:10.1109/ROBOT.2009.5152464

Gerovichev, O., Marayong, P., and Okamura, A. M. (2002). "The Effect of Visual and Haptic Feedback on Manual and Teleoperated Needle Insertion," in International Conference on Medical Image Computing and Computer-Assisted Intervention (Berlin, Germany: Springer), 147–154. doi:10.1007/3-540-45786-0_19

Golub, G. H., and van Loan, C. F. (2013), *Matrix Computations*. 4 edn. Baltimore, Maryland, USA: Johns Hopkins Univ. Press.

González Camarero, R., Hulin, T., and Vodermayer, B. (2015). "The Stamas Simulator: A Kinematics and Dynamics Simulator for an Astronaut's Leg and Hand Exoskeleton," in STAMAS Workshop - Smart technology for artificial muscle applications in space.

Gonzalez, F., Gosselin, F., and Bachta, W. (2014). Analysis of Hand Contact Areas and Interaction Capabilities during Manipulation and Exploration. *IEEE Trans. Haptics* 7, 415–429. doi:10.1109/toh.2014.2321395

Goupil, M. Y., Rojanachaichanin, B. L., Sjoberg, K. C., Piller, P., Nicholas, J., Bonafede, J., et al. (2019). *Haptic Feedback Glove US Patent Pending*.

Greiner, T. M. (1991). *Hand Anthropometry of US Army Personnel*.

Gu, X., Zhang, Y., Sun, W., Bian, Y., Zhou, D., and Kristensson, P. O. (2016). "Dexmo: An Inexpensive and Lightweight Mechanical Exoskeleton for Motion Capture and Force Feedback in Vr," in Proceedings of the 2016 CHI Conference on Human Factors in Computing Systems (ACM), 1991–1995.

Hannaford, B., and Okamura, A. M. (2016). *Haptics*. Berlin, Germany: Springer, 1063–1084. doi:10.1007/978-3-319-32552-1_42

Hedayati, H., Walker, M., and Szafir, D. (2018). "Improving Collocated Robot Teleoperation with Augmented Reality," in Proceedings of the 2018 ACM/IEEE International Conference on Human-Robot Interaction, 78–86. doi:10.1145/3171221.3171251

Hulin, T., Hertkorn, K., Kremer, P., Schätzle, S., Artigas, J., Sagardia, M., et al. (2011). "Mechanical Design of a Novel Hand Exoskeleton for Accurate Force Displaying," in IEEE International Conference on Robotics and Automation (ICRA).

[Dataset] Igus (2020). *Igubal Plastic Spherical Bearings*. Cologne, Germany: Igus.

Kawasaki, H., and Mouri, T. (2007). Design and Control of Five-Fingered Haptic Interface Opposite to Human Hand. *IEEE Trans. Robot.* 23, 909–918. doi:10.1109/tro.2007.906258

Kawasaki, H., Takai, J., Tanaka, Y., Mrad, C., and Mouri, T. (2003). "Control of Multi-Fingered Haptic Interface Opposite to Human Hand," in Proceedings 2003 IEEE/RSJ International Conference on Intelligent Robots and Systems (IROS 2003)(Cat. No. 03CH37453) (Las Vegas, NV, USA: IEEE), 2707–2712. Vol. 3.

Krueger, T., Ferreira, E., Gherghescu, A., Hann, L., den Extera, E., van der Hulst, F., et al. (2020). "Designing and Testing a Robotic Avatar for Space-To-Ground Teleoperation: the Developers' Insights," in 71th International Astronautical Congress (IAC).

Le Tien, L., Albu-Schäffer, A., Luca, A. D., and Hirzinger, G. (2008). "Friction Observer and Compensation for Control of Robots with Joint Torque Measurement," in Proc. IEEE/RSJ Int. Conf. Intell. Robots and Systems, 3789–3795. doi:10.1109/iros.2008.4651049

Lii, N. Y., Chen, Z., Pleintinger, B., Borst, C. H., Hirzinger, G., and Schiele, A. (2010). "Toward Understanding the Effects of Visual- and Force-Feedback on Robotic Hand Grasping Performance for Space Teleoperation," in IEEE/RSJ International Conference on Intelligent Robots and Systems (IROS), 3745–3752. doi:10.1109/iros.2010.5650186

Lii, N. Y., Chen, Z., Roa, M. A., Maier, A., Pleintinger, B., and Borst, C. (2012). "Toward a Task Space Framework for Gesture Commanded Telemanipulation," in IEEE RO-MAN: The 21st IEEE International Symposium on Robot and Human Interactive Communication, 925–932. doi:10.1109/roman.2012.6343869

Lii, N. Y., and Neves, M. (2021). *Eingabesystem*. German patent DE 10 2017 220 990.

Lii, N. Y., Riecke, C., Leidner, D., Schätzle, S., Schmaus, P., Weber, B., et al. (2018). "The Robot as an Avatar or Co-worker? an Investigation of the Different Teleoperation Modalities through the Kontur-2 and Meteron Supvis justin Space Telerobotic Missions," in 69th International Astronautical Congress (IAC).

Lii, N. Y., Stillfried, G., Chen, Z., Chalon, M., Pleintinger, B., and Maier, A. (2017). *Handexoskelett sowie Roboterarm mit solchem Handexoskelett*. German patent DE102017220996.8, pending.

Liu, H., Wu, K., Meusel, P., Seitz, N., Hirzinger, G., Jin, M. H., et al. (2008). "Multisensory Five-finger Dexterous Hand: The DLR/HIT Hand II," in Proc. IEEE/RSJ Int. Conf. Intell. Robots and Systems, 3692–3697. doi:10.1109/iros.2008.4650624

Massie, T. H., and Salisbury, J. K. J. (1997). *Force Reflecting Haptic Interface US Patent 5,625,576*.

Mine, M., Brooks, F., and Sequin, C. (1997). "Moving Objects in Space: Exploiting Proprioception in Virtual Environment Interaction," in International Conference on Computer Graphics and Interactive Techniques (SIGGRAPH), 19–26.

Missiroli, F., Barsotti, M., Leonardis, D., Gabardi, M., Rosati, G., and Frisoli, A. (2019). Haptic Stimulation for Improving Training of a Motor Imagery Bci Developed for a Hand-Exoskeleton in Rehabilitation. *IEEE Int. Conf. Rehabil. Robot* 2019, 1127–1132. doi:10.1109/ICORR.2019.8779370

Ouramdane, N., Davesne, F., Otmane, S., and Mallem, M. (2006). "3d Interaction Technique to Enhance Telemanipulation Tasks Using Virtual Environment," in IEEE/RSJ International Conference on Intelligent Robots and Systems, 5201–5207. doi:10.1109/iros.2006.281658

Passenberg, C., Peer, A., and Buss, M. (2010). "Model-mediated Teleoperation for Multi-Operator Multi-Robot Systems," in IEEE/RSJ International Conference on Intelligent Robots and Systems, 4263–4268. doi:10.1109/IROS.2010.5653012

Pereira, A., Stillfried, G., Baker, T., Schmidt, A., Maier, A., Pleintinger, B., et al. (2019). "Reconstructing Human Hand Pose and Configuration Using a Fixed-Base Exoskeleton," in Proc. IEEE/RAS Int. Conf. Robotics and Automation, 3514–3520. doi:10.1109/icra.2019.8794059

Poupyrev, I., Billinghurst, M., Weghorst, S., and Ichikawa, T. (1996). "The Go-Go Interaction Technique: Non-linear Mapping for Direct Manipulation in Vr," in ACM Symposium on User Interface Software and Technology (UIST), 79–80.

Rijpkema, H., and Girard, M. (1991). Computer Animation of Knowledge-Based Human Grasping. *SIGGRAPH Comput. Graph.* 25, 339–348. doi:10.1145/127719.122754

Sarakoglou, I., Brygo, A., Mazzanti, D., Hernandez, N. G., Caldwell, D. G., and Tsagarakis, N. G. (2016). "Hexotrac: A Highly Under-actuated Hand Exoskeleton for finger Tracking and Force Feedback," in Proc. IEEE/RSJ Int. Conf. Intell. Robots and Systems (Daejeon, South Korea: IEEE), 1033–1040. doi:10.1109/iros.2016.7759176

Schmaus, P., Leidner, D., Bayer, R., Pleintinger, B., Krüger, T., and Lii, N. Y. (2019). "Continued Advances in Supervised Autonomy User Interface Design for Meteron Supvis justin," in 2019 IEEE Aerospace Conference, 1–11. doi:10.1109/aero.2019.8741885

Schmidt, A., Pereira, A., Baker, T., Pleintinger, B., Hulin, T., Chen, Z., et al. (2020). "Enabling Interaction with Virtual Fluids and Mixed media Using a High Dexterity Hand Exoskeleton," in IEEE International Conference on System, Man and Cybernetics (SMC). doi:10.1109/smc42975.2020.9283274

Silva, A. J., Ramirez, O. A. D., Vega, V. P., and Oliver, J. P. O. (2009). "Phantom

Omni Haptic Device: Kinematic and Manipulability," in 2009 Electronics, Robotics and Automotive Mechanics Conference (CERMA), 193–198. doi:10.1109/cerma.2009.55

Son, H. I., Chuang, L. L., Kim, J., and Bülthoff, H. H. (2011). "Haptic Feedback Cues Can Improve Human Perceptual Awareness in Multi-Robots Teleoperation," in 2011 11th International Conference on Control, Automation and Systems (Gyeonggi-do, South Korea: IEEE), 1323–1328.

Stillfried, G., Hillenbrand, U., Settles, M., and van der Smagt, P. (2014). "Mri-based Skeletal Hand Movement Model," in *The Human Hand as an Inspiration for Robot Hand Development*. Editors R. Balasubramanian and V. J. Santos (Berlin, Germany: Springer), 49–75. doi:10.1007/978-3-319-03017-3_3

Stone, R. J. (2000). "Haptic Feedback: A Brief History from Telepresence to Virtual Reality," in *International Workshop on Haptic Human-Computer Interaction* (Berlin, Germany: Springer), 1–16.

Tobergte, A., Helmer, P., Hagn, U., Rouiller, P., Thielmann, S., Grange, S., et al. (2011). "The sigma.7 Haptic Interface for Mirosurge: A New Bi-manual Surgical Console," in 2011 IEEE/RSJ International Conference on Intelligent Robots and Systems, 3023–3030. doi:10.1109/IROS.2011.6094433

Tsai, M.-J. (1986). *Workspace Geometric Characterization and Manipulability of Industrial Robots*. Ph.D. thesis (Columbus, OH, USA: The Ohio State University).

Vogel, J., Leidner, D., Hagengruber, A., Panzirsch, M., Bauml, B., Denninger, M., et al. (2021). An Ecosystem for Heterogeneous Robotic Assistants in Caregiving: Core Functionalities and Use Cases. *IEEE Robot. Automat. Mag.* 28, 12–28. doi:10.1109/MRA.2020.3032142

Weber, B., and Eichberger, C. (2015). "The Benefits of Haptic Feedback in Telesurgery and Other Teleoperation Systems: a Meta-Analysis," in International Conference on Universal Access in Human-Computer Interaction (Berlin, Germany: Springer), 394–405. doi:10.1007/978-3-319-20684-4_39

Wildenbeest, J. G., Abbink, D. A., Heemskerk, C. J., Van Der Helm, F. C., and Boessenkool, H. (2012). The Impact of Haptic Feedback Quality on the Performance of Teleoperated Assembly Tasks. *IEEE Trans. Haptics* 6, 242–252. doi:10.1109/TOH.2012.19

Wolovich, W. A., and Elliott, H. (1984). "A Computational Technique for Inverse Kinematics," in IEEE Conf. Decision and Control, 1359–1363. doi:10.1109/cdc.1984.272258

Xu, X., Cizmeci, B., Schuwerk, C., and Steinbach, E. (2016). Model-mediated Teleoperation: Toward Stable and Transparent Teleoperation Systems. *IEEE Access* 4, 425–449. doi:10.1109/access.2016.2517926

Yoshikawa, T. (1985). Manipulability of Robotic Mechanisms. *Int. J. Robotics Res.* 4, 3–9. doi:10.1177/027836498500400201

Yun, Y., Dancausse, S., Esmatloo, P., Serrato, A., Merring, C. A., Agarwal, P., et al. (2017). "Maestro: An Emg-Driven Assistive Hand Exoskeleton for Spinal Cord Injury Patients," in IEEE International Conference on Robotics and Automation (ICRA), 2904–2910. doi:10.1109/icra.2017.7989337

9

Perception by Palpation: Development and Testing of a Haptic Ferrogranular Jamming Surface

Sigurd Bjarne Rørvik, Marius Auflem *, Henrikke Dybvik and Martin Steinert

TrollLABS, Department of Mechanical and Industrial Engineering, Faculty of Engineering, Norwegian University of Science and Technology (NTNU), Trondheim, Norway

*Correspondence:
Marius Auflem
mariuauf@stud.ntnu.no

Tactile hands-only training is particularly important for medical palpation. Generally, equipment for palpation training is expensive, static, or provides too few study cases to practice on. We have therefore developed a novel haptic surface concept for palpation training, using ferrogranular jamming. The concept's design consists of a tactile field spanning 260 x 160 mm, and uses ferromagnetic granules to alter shape, position, and hardness of palpable irregularities. Granules are enclosed in a compliant vacuum-sealed chamber connected to a pneumatic system. A variety of geometric shapes (output) can be obtained by manipulating and arranging granules with permanent magnets. The tactile hardness of the palpable output can be controlled by adjusting the chamber's vacuum level. A psychophysical experiment (N = 28) investigated how people interact with the palpable surface and evaluated the proposed concept. Untrained participants characterized irregularities with different position, form, and hardness through palpation, and their performance was evaluated. A baseline (no irregularity) was compared to three irregularity conditions: two circular shapes with different hardness (Hard Lump and Soft Lump), and an Annulus shape. 100% of participants correctly identified an irregularity in the three irregularity conditions, whereas 78.6% correctly identified baseline. Overall agreement between participants was high (κ= 0.723). The Intersection over Union (IoU) for participants sketched outline over the actual shape was IoU *Mdn* = 79.3% for Soft Lump, IoU *Mdn* = 68.8% for Annulus, and IoU *Mdn* = 76.7% for Hard Lump. The distance from actual to drawn center was *Mdn* = 6.4 mm (Soft Lump), *Mdn* = 5.3 mm (Annulus), and Mdn = 7.4 mm (Hard Lump), which are small distances compared to the size of the field. The participants subjectively evaluated Soft Lump to be significantly softer than Hard Lump and Annulus. Moreover, 71% of participants thought they improved their palpation skills throughout the experiment. Together, these results show that the concept can render irregularities with different position, form, and hardness, and that users are able to locate and characterize these through palpation. Participants experienced an improvement in palpation skills throughout the experiment, which indicates the concepts feasibility as a palpation training device.

Keywords: haptic interface, tactile surface, simulation, palpation, granular jamming, tactile perception, ferromagnetic granules

1 INTRODUCTION

In simulated training environments (i.e., augmented, virtual, and mixed reality), realistic rendering of tactile interactions with the physical world is challenging, yet meaningful. This is because haptic interfaces enabling such tactile interactions must complement (and reflect) the vivid audiovisual feedback provided by the simulation (Woodrum et al., 2006). This combination could yield deeper immersion and thus facilitate the transfer of tactile experiences when transitioning to real-world scenarios. Furthermore, by realistically bridging the physical and digital world, users can develop, improve, and maintain critical psychomotor skills (Lathan et al., 2002; Zhou et al., 2012; Zhao et al., 2020). Hence, haptic interfaces in simulation can enable safe, repetitive, and available training alternatives for various professions that require dexterous hands-on experience (Carruth, 2017; Lelevé et al., 2020).

In a medical context, simulation can help narrow the gap of required clinical experience and mitigate the risk of harming or providing unsatisfactory patient treatment. However, various medical procedures require not only hands-on, but hands-only training. One of these procedures is palpation, which is used to examine a patient through touch. By palpation, diagnosis is based on tactile findings such as irregularities (lumps, fluids, tenderness) and locating pain-points. Unfortunately, common equipment such as wearable tactile devices and kinesthetic devices are less suited in this use-case given their current resolution, Degrees of Freedom (DOF), and tactile limitations (Licona et al., 2020). Consequently, simulated palpation exercises are mainly performed using static case-specific models (phantoms) or mannequins (patient simulators). While these can provide safe and repetitive training conditions, their fixed number of study cases, task-specific functionalities, and limited tactile realism are collectively obstacles for current healthcare training and education.

Haptic interfaces designed for palpation training should enable users to practice locating and describing tactile irregularities, as they would when palpating a real patient. Hence, multiple tactile displays are promising in this context by utilizing technology ranging from pin arrays (Wagner et al., 2002), to shape memory alloy actuators (Taylor et al., 1998) and airborne ultrasound (Iwamoto et al., 2008). However, such solutions are generally expensive, complex in operation and non-continuously available, thus limiting their use and widespread in research and education. Moreover, as these solutions rely on using a matrix of actuators or tactile outputs, it restricts the obtainable resolution, scalability and robustness of such interfaces. Furthermore, compliance and flexibility are often compromised by using rigid mechanisms to achieve haptic feedback. Therefore, attention has been brought to using soft robotics principles for haptic applications, as these can approximate soft body animations and organic behaviors suitable to medical training, among others (Manti et al., 2016).

An interesting area of soft robotics for medical training applications is the use of granular jamming mechanisms for haptic feedback. Granular jamming enables interfaces to alter stiffness and thus simulate compliant objects with variable hardness. This technology has been explored in medical training devices as embedded tactile modules (He et al., 2021), multi-fingered palpation interfaces (Li et al., 2014), and as actuation to enable objects and surfaces to alter shape and hardness for palpation (Stanley et al., 2016; Koehler et al., 2020). While this technology looks promising, current solutions often require complex pneumatic systems, since a matrix of actuated cells or objects is needed. Thus, this could limit the tactile resolution and geometrical freedom of rendered objects. Based on this existing work on granular jamming interfaces, we have developed a simple and low-cost technology utilizing ferromagnetic granulate. Our technology enables the granules to be remotely manipulated in an unjammed state and thus create customized tactile objects. Furthermore, when jammed, the hardness of these objects can be altered by the applied vacuum, i.e., how firmly the granules are packed together in a sealed chamber. In a haptic interface prototype described in **Figure 1**, the ferrogranular jamming principle is used to render palpable irregularities between two compliant layers. The prototype was developed to examine the feasibility and usability of this technology in a tactile display application. Moreover, this technology could be used to challenge the complexity, accessibility and cost of current haptic interfaces.

This work relates to the existing literature on tactile interactions, and more precisely, users' tactile perception of hardness and geometrical shapes. Hence, studies investigating the psychophysical perception of hardness and shapes have been of interest (Tan et al., 1992; Srinivasan and LaMotte, 1995; Bergmann Tiest and Kappers, 2009; Frisoli et al., 2011). However, the use-case of palpable interfaces that requires a perceptual exploration and manipulation is a less explored area with fewer examples (Lederman and Klatzky, 1993; Genecov et al., 2014). As this encourages more research on users' interaction and performance using haptic interfaces, our conceptual prototype has been piloted in a palpation experiment. This experiment investigates whether untrained users can locate and determine the form and hardness of rendered irregularities by palpation. Information of hardness, speed (time used to find irregularity) and accuracy of form and position has been collected, together with users' subjective experience throughout the experiment.

This paper examines using soft-robotics principles to alter the characteristics of a haptic interface for medical diagnostics training. This investigation has resulted in the concept shown in **Figure 1**, which uses granular jamming and ferromagnetic granulate manipulation to achieve various palpable outputs. The concept is used to assess untrained users' ability to locate and characterize the shape and hardness of different irregularities using palpation. Considering this concept for a novel haptic interface and the context of medical palpation training, we try to answer the following research questions in this paper:

i. Can the novel ferrogranular jamming concept be used as a haptic interface for palpation exercises?
ii. How well can untrained users determine the position, form and hardness of irregularities rendered by the haptic interface using palpation techniques?

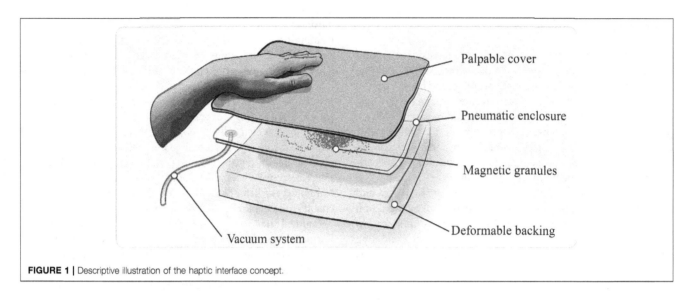

FIGURE 1 | Descriptive illustration of the haptic interface concept.

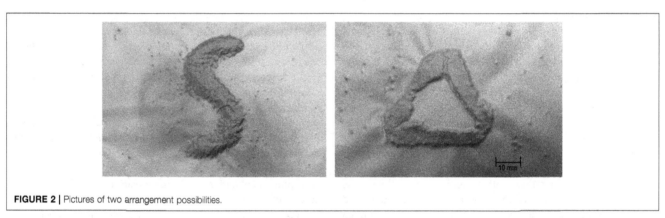

FIGURE 2 | Pictures of two arrangement possibilities.

iii. Did participants think their palpation skills improved during the experiment?

2 MATERIALS: DESIGN OF THE FERROGRANULAR JAMMING INTERFACE

This chapter starts with a short introduction to the ferrogranular jammer. Secondly, the theory of granular jamming and magnetic manipulation is presented. Lastly, the manufacturing of the magnetic granules and chamber is presented before the pneumatic setup.

The prototype was developed to examine the feasibility and usability of a ferrogranular jamming interface in a tactile display for palpation. The novelty of the proposed concept is the introduction of magnetic manipulation of granules in a jamming application. This innovation provides the opportunity to manipulate the granular media inside a compliant vacuum chamber, thus managing the position, form and hardness of the palpable outputs. Some examples are shown in **Figure 2**, where the jammed granulate shapes are visible within the translucent chamber. To act as a deformable and palpable

structure the vacuum chamber is sandwiched between a deformable polyurethane (PU) foam backing (60 mm) and a flexible polyethylene (PE) fabric cover (4 mm) (as seen in **Figure 5B**).

2.1 Granular Jamming and Magnetic Manipulation

Granular jamming works by transitioning granular matter from a low-density compliant packing to a high-density rigid packing. This change is done by removing the fluid/medium surrounding the granulate, which produces an external hydrostatic pressure. From this, the granules can behave both like a fluid and a solid. When the granules are in a low-density packing, the intergranular friction is low, resulting in a fluid-like state. Vice versa, when the vacuum level increases, higher intergranular friction results in a jammed and solid-like state. In the jammed state, the granules distributes applied force through the grains so that the group of particles functions as a stiff and compliant material (Cates et al., 1998).

Particle jamming has been a big research topic for engineers and material scientists for the last few decades. The principle of reversibly transitioning the granular media from a fluid-like state to a more rigid state has been seen to be applicable to various domains, such as industrial grippers (Harada et al., 2016; D'Avella et al., 2020), minimally invasive surgery (Jiang et al., 2012) and robotic locomotion (Steltz et al., 2009). Granular jamming is a prevalent type of actuation within soft robotics applications because of two main reasons: 1) considerable stiffness variation with little volume change, and 2) possibility to adjust the stiffness variability area so it can be easily adapted to different soft robotics applications (Fitzgerald et al., 2020).

There has been research on optimizing granules for granular jamming with different aspects; size, shape and volume fraction (Jiang et al., 2012), chamber material (Jiang et al., 2012) and using soft granules (Putzu, Konstantinova, and Althoefer 2019). However, a common feature for these studies is the stasis of the granulate. To the best of our knowledge, there has been no research focusing on the movability of granules in a jamming context. For example, Follmer et al. (2012) reviewed jamming in a user-interface context, where none of the technologies utilized movement of the granules.

Using magnetic fields is an effective way to transport and position magnetic particles in a medium. The most prominent concept of ferromagnetic particles in a fluid is ferrofluid. This colloidal liquid consists of surfactant-coated magnetic particles with a size order of 10 nm suspended in a liquid medium. When the fluid is subjected to a magnetic field, it forms a shape like the magnetic field and acts more like a solid. Generally, ferromagnetic particles are induced by two types of interaction energy: the one between the particles and the magnetic field E^H, and between particles E^M (Cao et al., 2014). Using a magnetic field to manipulate magnetic particles has been used in microfluidic systems, such as magnetorheological fluid in user interfaces (Hook et al., 2009; Jansen et al., 2010) and biological analysis and catalysis (Gijs et al., 2010).

The advantages of using ferromagnetic granules include: 1) Controllability—Ferro-granulate can be arranged numerous ways by designing magnetic fields. 2) Noncontact—Magnetic particles can be remotely manipulated. 3) Precision—Ferromagnetic granules can be placed at a target region with high precision by precisely designing a magnetic field with local maximum field strength at preferred areas (Cao et al., 2014).

2.2 Manufacturing of Magnetic Granulate

Based on the previous research done on granular jamming, manufacturing of ferromagnetic granules to be used in a haptic interface were investigated. A central factor for the granulate in this research is how high interparticle friction yields higher viscosity in the un-jammed state but yields higher hardness when jammed and vice versa. Since moving the granules in the unjammed state is essential, we investigated the granule material and manufacturing methods that produce granules with lower interparticle friction in the unjammed state but still yielding sufficient hardness in the jammed state.

Ground coffee, which Putzu, Konstantinova, and Althoefer (2019) refer to as the gold standard within the field of granular jamming, was evaluated as the most viable option for our case.

Ground coffee has been proven to be a successful granulate for jammers that need a large stiffness range (Brown et al., 2010; Cheng et al., 2012). The magnetic coffee ground was produced by mixing fine coffee ground and magnetic paint with a 1:1 volumetric ratio as seen in **Figure 3** (Magnetic undercoat, Lefranc and Bourgeois Déco). After the mixture dried, it was ground to a size of approximately 2 mm using a mortar. Using a crushing technique, instead of grinding, produced less size dispersion of the granulate. Granules with a 1–2.4 mm size were filtered out with a perforated filter with circular holes (see **Figures 3D,E**). It is advantageous to use homogeneous monodisperse granules to make the output more repeatable (Genecov et al., 2014).

The manipulation of the ferromagnetic granulate using a permanent magnet is presented in **Figure 4**. The same type of spikes can be observed in both ferrofluids and iron shavings when in the presence of a magnetic field.

2.3 Chamber Design

Since the concept of this technology is different from traditional granular jamming, the choice of chamber material was evaluated on having surface friction that enabled the granules to be remotely manipulated inside the sealed chamber. Further, the material needed to be flexible to jam the particles together when a vacuum was applied. Different heat-sealing plastic types were evaluated, and a corrugated polyvinylchloride (PVC) film (0.2 mm for vacuum sealing applications) was deemed the most viable due to its flexibility and least warping lines. With the corrugated pattern, we avoided self-sealing as this was a problem with other materials.

2.4 Pneumatic Setup

The pneumatic setup for the ferrogranular jamming concept is shown in **Figure 5**. The chamber is connected to the rest of the pneumatic system through a filter (**Figure 5D**). The 12 V vacuum pump (D2028B, SparkFun Electronics) delivers a vacuum level down to −0.54 bar. Next, a manometer is connected to measure the vacuum level. The vacuum pump is controlled using a speed controller. The chamber was made using an Impulse Heat Sealer (Audion Elektro Sealboy 235). A 3D-printed nozzle connects the chamber to the rest of the system, as seen in **Figure 5E**. Together with butyl vacuum sealant tape, it ensures minimal leakage at the inlet. A ball valve connects the system to atmospheric pressure when open.

3 METHOD: EXPERIMENT

A psychophysical experiment was designed to evaluate the functional abilities of the proposed concept by evaluating the user's performance in locating and characterizing rendered irregularities. The experiment encompassed a palpation task, where qualitative and quantitative data were gathered on both participant performance and prototype reliability.

3.1 Experimental Test Setup

The pneumatic system presented in 2.4 was integrated into the test cabinet shown in **Figure 6A**. A camera is fixed above the

FIGURE 3 | Manufacturing of magnetic granulate **(A)** 1:1 mixing ratio of coffee ground and magnetic paint **(B)** Consistency of the mixture **(C)** Grounding using mortar **(D)** and **(E)** Filtering **(F)** Finished result.

FIGURE 4 | Manipulation of the magnetic coffee ground using a permanent magnet.

haptic interface. The cabinet walls ensure no bias from visual perception during the transition between conditions and provides a consistent working environment. In addition, an overhead LED panel eases picture processing by ensuring consistent lighting. The two different geometrical shapes were created with two arrangements of permanent neodymium magnets, as seen in **Figure 6B**. These magnets were held above the vacuum chamber, arranging the granules in the desired shape, before applying the vacuum. When vacuum was applied, the magnets could be removed and the granulate remained jammed in place. To alter the shape, or remove it, the vacuum was released, before the granules were manually dispersed, rearranged, or moved out of the palpable field. The structural parts of the test rig are laser-cut MDF. The palpable field (260 × 160 mm) is seen as the pink

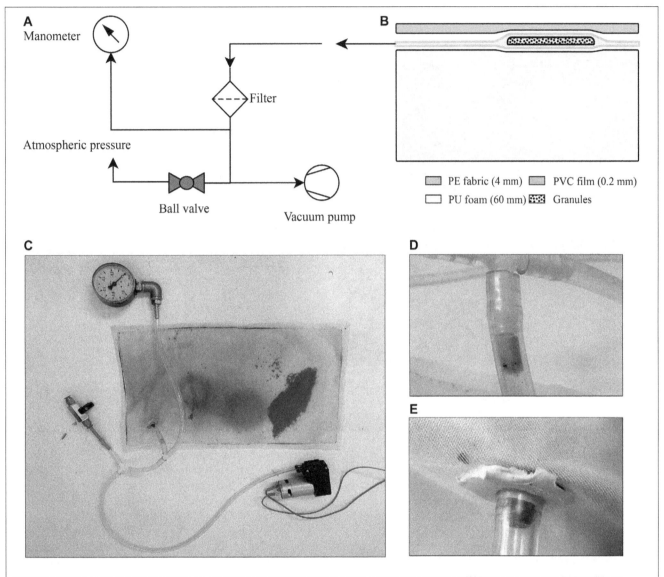

FIGURE 5 | (A) Schematic presentation of the pneumatic setup **(B)** Palpation interface with layer material and thickness **(C)** The pneumatic setup **(D)** Filter **(E)** Inlet seal for vacuum chamber.

area in **Figure 6A**. We used 12 g of filtered ferromagnetic granulate in the chamber.

3.2 Experiment Design

All participants repeated the palpation task four times, under four different conditions. The irregularity could differ in hardness, position and form. The four conditions were as follows:

- C1: Baseline. No irregularity in the palpation field.
- C2: Annulus. Annular-shaped irregularity rendered with the magnet configuration seen in **Figure 6B**. Vacuum level: −0.4 to −0.6 bar, whereas −1 bar is a complete vacuum. Located in the lower left part of the field. Approximately 82 mm outer diameter and 29 mm inner diameter with area $M = 4{,}915$ mm^2 $SD = 371$ mm^2 $SE = 70$ mm^2.

- C3: Hard Lump. A circular-shaped irregularity rendered with the magnet configuration seen in **Figure 5B**. Vacuum level: 0.4 to −0.6 bar. Located in the top right part of the field. Approximately 100 mm diameter with area $M = 7{,}912$ mm^2 $SD = 474$ mm^2 $SE = 89$ mm^2.
- C4: Soft Lump. A circular-shaped irregularity rendered with the magnet configuration seen in **Figure 5C**. Vacuum level: 0.1 bar. Located in the top right part of the field. Approximately 100 mm diameter with area $M = 8{,}094$ mm^2 $SD = 641$ mm^2 $SE = 121$ mm^2.

The sequence of the testing conditions was randomized to avoid potential learning or order effects. The order of conditions was also balanced, i.e., they appear the same number of times in each procedure step.

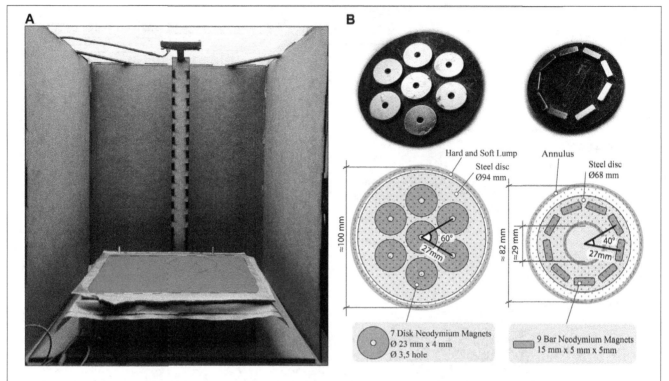

FIGURE 6 | (A) Test rig with camera and cabinet setup (pink area is the palpable field) **(B)** Magnet arrangement with angular and radial distance shown. Approximated outlines for the generated outputs are also illustrated with measurements. (Left) Circular shape for Hard and Soft Lump (Right) Annulus shape with the hollow center.

3.2.1 Participants

N = 28 healthy engineering students were recruited to participate (21 male (75%) and 7 female (25%)). Twenty-seven participants were in the 21–29 years range and one participant in the 18–20 years range. None of the participants were trained in the test or had any relevant knowledge about the technology before participation. Participation was voluntary, and all gave informed consent to be part of the study.

3.2.2 Experimental Procedure and Data Collection

The experimental procedure can be seen in **Figure 7**. After signing a consent form, the participants filled out a demographic questionnaire. Durometer and manometer readings and pictures of the granulate were sampled before the participant was seated in front of the test setup. The hardness of the irregularities was measured with a commercially available Shore durometer (Shenzhen Gairan Tech Co., X.F Type 00), following the requirements described in ISO 48-4:2018. A minimum of three measurements at different positions on the flat parts of the irregularity was performed. After objective data was collected, participants were instructed regarding the proceedings of the experiment. First, participants were told to palpate for a potential irregularity and say stop when they had control of the position and form. The participants did not get any instructions regarding technique to be used, other than using their hands to explore and feel for any irregularities in the field. We measured the time

the participant used to find position and form of the irregularity. After completing each palpation, participants were asked to draw the contours of a possible irregularity on a sheet placed above the palpation field. More specifically, they were told to draw the outside and possible inside contours and put an x inside the area enclosing the proposed identified irregularity (see **Figure 8B**). Pilot experiments showed that this instruction facilitated the participants who found an inside contour to also draw it, instead of drawing the outer contour only. Drawing data were captured using the camera.

To evaluate the hardness of the irregularity, a sampled selection of objects of varying hardness was used. These samples were numbered from 1 to 5 and had a Shore hardness of 00–20, 00–35, 00–55, 00–65, and 00–90, from soft to harder. The objects were presented similarly to the test setup using the same deformable backing and palpable cover as the palpation field. Thus, the participant could palpate the irregularity when doing the hardness test.

After each condition, participants reported their degree of agreement to a series of statements using a Likert Scale from 1 (Totally disagree) to 5 (Totally agree). The statements were: 1) It was hard to find the irregularity. 2) I am confident that I found the position and shape of the irregularity. 3) The irregularity had a constant/homogeneous hardness. To get a measure of a potential learning effect occurring during the experiments, participants also evaluated the statement: 4) I became better at finding the irregularity during the experiment., after completing the experiment.

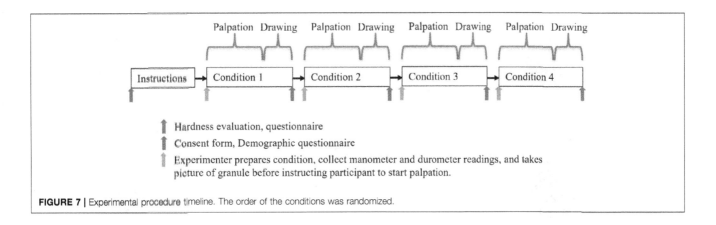

FIGURE 7 | Experimental procedure timeline. The order of the conditions was randomized.

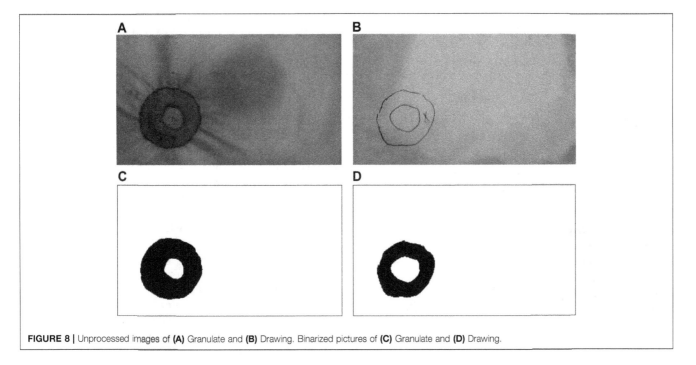

FIGURE 8 | Unprocessed images of **(A)** Granulate and **(B)** Drawing. Binarized pictures of **(C)** Granulate and **(D)** Drawing.

3.3 Data Analysis

The data was collected throughout the experiment to answer the study's research questions. Thus, experiment pictures were processed into binarized matrices that yielded objective data points describing irregularities' and drawings' respective positions and geometrical form. These data, together with the questionnaire and objective measurements, were statistically analyzed for reliability and differences between variables with SPSS Statistics (IBM SPSS Statistics 27, 2020).

3.3.1 Picture Processing

Data about position and form was collected through images. The images of the granulate and drawings were then processed and analyzed using package OpenCV 4.5.1 in Python 3.0. The capturing code also took photos of the manometer during each test. The images were blurred before grayscaling and binarizing to remove noise. An adaptive Gaussian threshold was used on the pictures of

the drawings to improve accuracy. The binarized results are shown in **Figures 8C,D**.

3.3.1.1 Distance From Center to Center

The center point distance between granulate and drawings were calculated by finding the center of mass for both the granulate and the drawings using cv2.moments in Python. Then, the Euclidean distance (ΔD) was calculated between the two coordinates, using **Eq. 1**. x_1 and y_1 representing the coordinates for the granulate, while x_2 and y_2 representing the drawing.

$$\Delta D = \sqrt{(x_1 - x_2)^2 + (y_1 - y_2)^2} \tag{1}$$

3.3.1.2 Intersection Over Union

Intersection over Union (IoU) was used to evaluate the form. First, matrices of the intersection and union of the two binarized pictures were calculated using Python. Then, the number of black

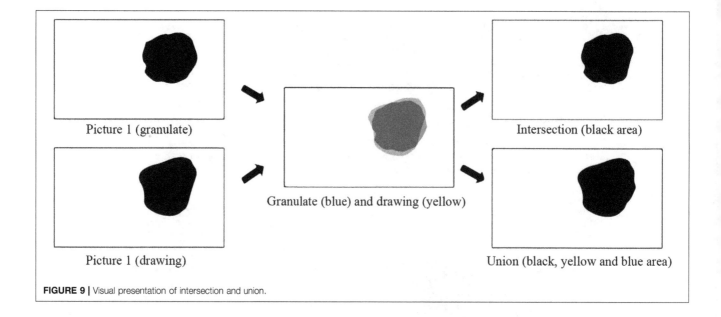

FIGURE 9 | Visual presentation of intersection and union.

pixels (pixels with value 0) in the intersection was divided by the number of black pixels in the union, using **Eq. 2**. A visual representation of intersection and union is shown in **Figure 9**.

$$IoU = \frac{Area\ of\ Intersection}{Area\ of\ Union} \qquad (2)$$

3.4 Statistical Tests

To assess reliability, Fleiss' kappa was ran to determine if there was an agreement between participants' judgment of whether there was an irregularity or not (Lump or No Lump) in the four conditions. Fleiss' kappa does not assume that the raters are identical for each condition (which is the case here), but this is the only test we know of that assesses the case when there are multiple raters. Therefore, we report this test along with the frequency. One-way repeated measures ANOVAs were used to investigate differences between conditions for continuous variables. Those were: IoU, hardness (durometer reading) and vacuum level (manometer reading). Assumptions regarding no outliers, normality, and sphericity were inspected with boxplots, histograms and Normal Q-Q Plots, and Mauchly's Test of Sphericity. Violations of the outlier assumption were not removed since it only applied to Durometer and Manometer readings, which were used to corroborate that the conditions Hard Lump and Soft Lump differed in terms of hardness. In addition, a Friedman test was also conducted to ensure similar differences. A Greenhouse-Geisser correction was applied in the case of violating sphericity (Wickens and Keppel, 2004; Field, 2018). A Friedman test was used to investigate differences between conditions for discontinuous variables (the remaining variables), and in the case of more severe violations to ANOVA's assumptions. Pairwise comparisons were performed with a Bonferroni correction for multiple comparisons for both ANOVA and Friedman. Some

variables produced a statistically significant Friedman test, but without any significant pairwise comparisons. One reason might be the conservative nature of the multiple comparisons correction. An additional approach, multiple Wilcoxon signed-rank tests, was therefore used to follow up the Friedman tests. We deemed it acceptable to be less conservative since it is the first investigation of an early-stage prototype, and it was important to gain an understanding of where potential differences were. The Wilcoxon signed-rank tests was also used to obtain a z-score, used to estimate effect size (r) (Rosenthal, 1986; Field, 2018). For the ANOVAs, the sample effect size partial eta squared (η^2), and population effect size partial omega squared (ω^2) (Rosenthal, 1986) are reported. The significance level $p < 0.05$ was chosen for highly significant differences. p–values ≤ 0.10 were considered as interesting effects, again due to the experiment involving human participants evaluating an early-stage prototype. We believe a 10% probability for Type 1 error is acceptable in this case.

4 RESULTS

Both objective and subjective data points were gathered throughout all four conditions described in 3.2.2. Each condition focused on localizing and characterizing a potential irregularity based on position, form and hardness. Additional descriptive statistics can be found in **Supplementary Material**.

4.1 Lump or No Lump: How Many Found an Irregularity?

In all three conditions with an irregularity (Annulus, Hard Lump and Soft Lump), all participants found an irregularity (100%

agreement). In Baseline condition six participants (21.4%) found an irregularity, despite there not being one. The remaining 22 participants (78.6%) failed to find an irregularity. Fleiss' kappa determined if there was an agreement between participants' judgment of whether there was an irregularity or not (Lump or No Lump) in the four conditions. The agreement between participants' judgements was statistically significant with κ= 0.723, 95% CI [0.722, 0.725], p < 0.001. The individual kappa's for Lump and No Lump categories were also κ= 0.723, 95% CI [0.722, 0.725], p < 0.001. This statistic is the proportion of agreement over and above chance agreement, with 0 being no agreement and 1 being perfect agreement. An agreement of 0.723 can be classified as a good agreement (Landis and Koch, 1977).

As stated, six out of 28 participants found an irregularity in the baseline condition. Of these six, three participants drew contours with areas of 22, 64 and 147 mm², which are small compared to the actual size of the irregularities. They are similar to granular remnants, which means they could be discarded as an error in the setup. Other participants commented on particle-sized irregularities in the Baseline condition but decided that they were not of sufficient size to be an actual irregularity. Removing these three participants results in three participants (12.0%) finding an irregularity in the Baseline condition, whereas 22 participants (88%) did not find an irregularity. Fleiss' kappa was ran again with these three participants removed to investigate the magnitude of the potential error from the setup. The agreement between the remaining 25 participants was statistically significant with κ= 0.840, 95% CI [0.783, 0.896], p < 0.001. The individual kappa's for Lump and No Lump categories were also κ= 0.840, 95% CI [0.783, 0.896], p < 0.001.

22 of 28 (78.57%) of the participants found the inner circle. In the two irregularity conditions 50 of 56 (89.29%) drawings were filled circles without any inner contour.

In summary, all participants agreed that there was an irregularity present in all irregularity conditions. Despite a few participants finding an irregularity where there was none, the overall agreement between participants was high.

4.2 Time

The users were not instructed to be as fast as possible but rather spend enough time to be sure of position and form of the irregularity. Therefore, the time represents the procedure time needed to find position and form of the irregularity to the best of the participant's ability.

Time was statistically significantly different in the four conditions, $\chi^2(3)$ = 29.460, p < 0.001 as shown in **Figure 10**. Post hoc analysis revealed significant differences in Time from Baseline (Mdn = 37.0 s), 95% CI [25.0, 61.0] to Annulus (Mdn = 13.50 s), 95% CI [7.0, 21.0] (p < 0.001) and Soft Lump (Mdn = 16.00), 95% CI [11.0, 40.0] (p = 0.001) condition. It took longer to determine that there was no irregularity in Baseline condition, compared to finding it in Annulus and Soft Lump condition. The contrast comparing Annulus to Hard Lump (Mdn = 17.50), achieved a significance level p = 0.050 and effect size r = −0.50, and Hard Lump to Baseline had a significance level of p = 0.067 and effect size r = 0.48. We interpret this to be a notable difference. There

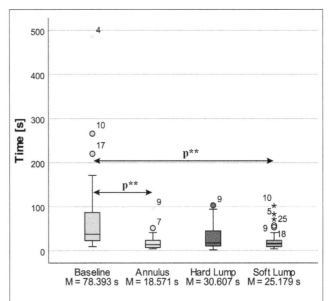

FIGURE 10 | Descriptive statistics of procedure time to find the position and form of the irregularities. Statistically significant differences at p < 0.05 are indicated by p**.

was no significant difference between Annulus and Soft Lump (p = 0.80, r = −0.28) and Soft Lump and Hard Lump (p = 1.00, r = 0.22).

4.3 Position: Distance From Center to Center

The distance between the center of the irregularity to the center of the participants' drawing was statistically significantly different in the three irregularity conditions, $\chi^2(2)$ = 16.357, p < 0.001. Post hoc analysis revealed statistically significant differences in center distance from Annulus (Mdn = 5.2920 mm), 95% CI [2.978, 7.097], to Hard Lump (Mdn = 7.4366 mm), 95% CI [6.331, 12.217] (p < 0.001), and from Soft Lump (Mdn = 6.3908 mm), 95% CI [3.836, 9.654], to Hard Lump condition (Mdn = 7.4366 mm) (p = 0.01). There was no significant difference in center distance between Annulus and Soft Lump (p = 1). We also observe that there was a greater spread in the Hard Lump condition. These results are plotted in **Figure 11A**.

4.4 Form: IoU

IoU was statistically significantly different in the three conditions, $\chi^2(2)$ = 12.071, p = 0.002. Post hoc pairwise comparisons with a Bonferroni correction for multiple comparisons yielded one significant difference between Soft Lump (Mdn = 0.793), 95% CI [0.728, 0.825], and Annulus (Mdn = 0.688), 95% CI [0.579, 0.735], p = 0.002, and a corrected p = 0.247 for both the Soft Lump vs Hard Lump (Mdn = 0.767), 95% CI [0.568, 0.754] comparison, and Hard Lump vs Annulus comparison (uncorrected p-value was p = 0.082). Post hoc Wilcoxon tests revealed a statistically significant difference between Annulus (Mdn = 0.688) and Soft Lump (Mdn = 0.793), T = 316.00, p = 0.010, r = 0.49, and a significant difference between Hard Lump (Mdn = 0.767), 95%

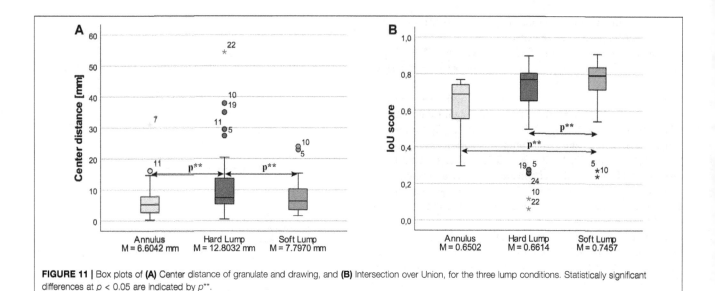

FIGURE 11 | Box plots of **(A)** Center distance of granulate and drawing, and **(B)** Intersection over Union, for the three lump conditions. Statistically significant differences at $p < 0.05$ are indicated by p^{**}.

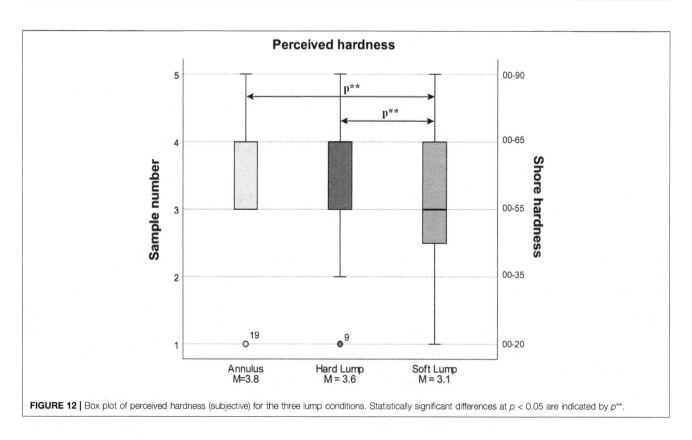

FIGURE 12 | Box plot of perceived hardness (subjective) for the three lump conditions. Statistically significant differences at $p < 0.05$ are indicated by p^{**}.

CI [0.703, 0.0794], and Soft Lump (Mdn = 0.793), $T = 304.00$, $p = 0.021$, $r = 0.43$. There was no difference between Annulus and Hard Lump, $T = 263.00$, $p = 0.021$, $r = 0.26$ as plotted in **Figure 11B**.

4.5 Hardness

We compared perceived hardness, objective hardness measurements, and vacuum levels of the irregularity conditions.

4.5.1 Perceived Hardness

Perceived hardness was statistically significantly different in the three conditions, χ^2 (2) = 9.129, $p = 0.010$. Post hoc pairwise comparisons with a Bonferroni correction for multiple comparisons yielded one significant difference between Soft Lump (Mdn = 3) and Annulus (Mdn = 4), $p = 0.033$, and a corrected $p = 0.184$ for the Soft Lump and Hard Lump comparison (uncorrected p-value was $p = 0.061$). Post hoc Wilcoxon tests revealed a statistically significant difference

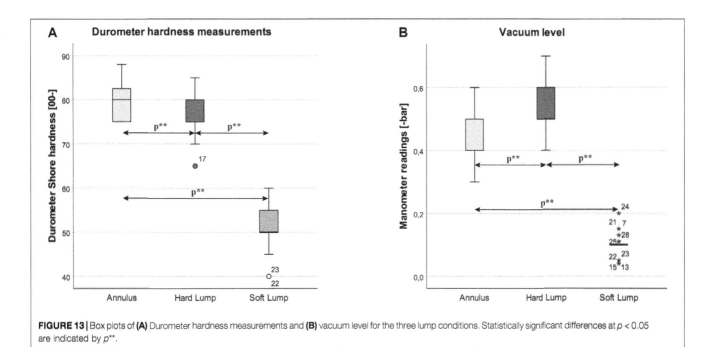

FIGURE 13 | Box plots of **(A)** Durometer hardness measurements and **(B)** vacuum level for the three lump conditions. Statistically significant differences at $p < 0.05$ are indicated by p^{**}.

between Soft Lump (Mdn = 3) and Hard Lump (Mdn = 4), $T = 132.00$, $p = 0.032$, $r = -0.41$, and a significant difference between Annulus (Mdn = 4) and Soft Lump (Mdn = 3), $T = 55.00$, $p = 0.015$, r = -0.46. There was no difference between Annulus and Hard Lump, $T = 87.00$, $p = 0.474$, $r = -0.14$. These results are as expected. Participants perceived the hardness of Soft Lump to be less than that of both Hard Lump and Annulus which is shown in **Figure 12**.

4.5.2 Durometric Measurements

There were 3 outliers as assessed by boxplot in **Figure 13A**. By visual inspection, the data was approximately normally distributed. The assumption of sphericity was violated, as assessed by Mauchly's test of sphericity, $\chi^2(2) = 6.825$, $p = 0.033$. Therefore, a Greenhouse-Geisser correction was applied ($\varepsilon = 0.812$). Results was statistically significant different in the three conditions F $(1.625, 43.872) = 278.699$, $p < 0.001$, $\eta^2 = 0.912$, $\omega^2 = 0.869$. Durometric readings were: Annulus ($M = 79.96$), Hard Lump ($M = 76.79$), Soft Lump ($M = 51.25$). Post hoc analysis with a Bonferroni correction yielded statistically significantly difference between Annulus and Hard Lump (M = 3.179, 95% CI [0.63, 5.72], $p = 0.011$), between Annulus and Soft Lump (M = 0.28.714, 95% CI [24.71, 32.72], $p < 0.001$), and between Hard Lump and Soft Lump (M = 25.536, 95% CI [22.04, 0.29.03], $p < 0.001$).

4.5.3 Manometer

There were several outliers as assessed by boxplot in **Figure 13B**. The data was approximately normally distributed by visual inspection. The assumption of sphericity was violated, as assessed by Mauchly's test of sphericity, $\chi^2(2) = 13.713$, $p = 0.001$. Therefore, a Greenhouse-Geisser correction was applied ($\varepsilon = 0.709$). Manometer was statistically significant different in the three conditions F $(1.419, 38.301) = 228.636$, $p < 0.001$, $\eta^2 = 0.894$,

$\omega^2 = 0.844$. Manometer readings were: Annulus ($M = 0.431$), Hard Lump ($M = 0.536$), Soft Lump ($M = 0.101$). Post hoc analysis with a Bonferroni adjustment was statistically significantly different between Annulus and Hard Lump (M = -0.105, 95% CI [-0.17, -0.04], $p = 0.002$), between Annulus and Soft Lump (M = 0.330, 95% CI [0.29, 0.368], $p < 0.001$), and between Hard Lump and Soft Lump (M = 0.435, 95% CI [0.38, 0.49], $p < 0.001$).

4.6 Questionnaire

Participants completed the questionnaire in the three irregularity conditions.

4.6.1 How Hard Was It to Find the Position?

Participants' evaluation of how hard it was to find the irregularity was statistically significantly different in the three conditions, $\chi^2(2) = 7.423$, $p = 0.024$. Post hoc pairwise comparisons with a Bonferroni correction for multiple comparisons yielded no significant differences. Post hoc Wilcoxon tests revealed a statistically significant difference between Soft Lump (Mdn = 1) and Hard Lump (Mdn = 1), $T = 63.00$, $p = 0.006$, $r = -0.52$. There were no significant differences between Annulus (Mdn = 1) and Soft Lump (Mdn = 1), $T = 27.00$, $p = 0.957$, r = -0.01, or between Annulus and Hard Lump, $T = 89.00$, $p = 0.096$, $r = -0.32$. Participants found it hardest to locate the irregularity in the Hard Lump (see **Figure 14A**).

4.6.2 Confidence in Finding Position and Shape of the Irregularity

Participants' confidence in finding position and shape of the irregularity was statistically significantly different in the three irregularity conditions, $\chi^2(2) = 8.926$, $p = 0.012$. Post hoc pairwise comparisons with a Bonferroni correction for multiple

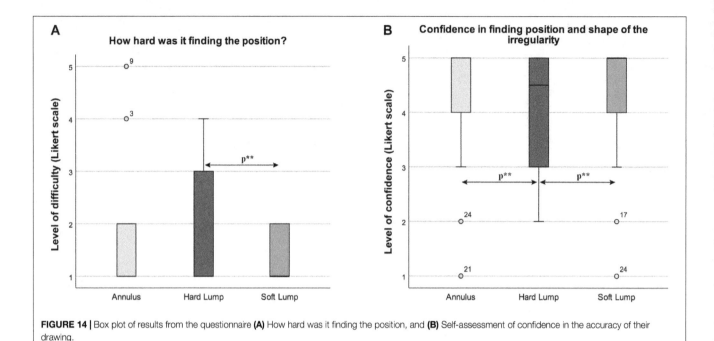

FIGURE 14 | Box plot of results from the questionnaire **(A)** How hard was it finding the position, and **(B)** Self-assessment of confidence in the accuracy of their drawing.

comparisons yielded no significant differences. Post hoc Wilcoxon tests revealed a statistically significant decrease in confidence from Annulus (Mdn = 5) to Hard Lump (Mdn = 4.5), $T = 12.00$, $p = 0.032$, r = −0.40, and a significant decrease in confidence from Soft Lump (Mdn = 5) to Hard Lump (Mdn = 4.5), $T = 13.50$, $p = 0.038$, r = −0.39. There was no significant difference between Annulus and Soft Lump, $T = 31.00$, $p = 0.276$, $r = −0.21$. Participants were most confident in finding the position and shape of the irregularity in the Annulus and Soft Lump condition and less confident in finding the irregularity's position and shape in the Hard Lump condition (see **Figure 14B**).

4.6.3 Homogeneous Hardness
Participants' evaluation of whether the irregularity had a constant/homogeneous hardness was not significantly different in the three irregularity conditions, χ^2 (2) = 3.410, $p = 0.182$.

4.6.4 Self-Assessed Improvement in Palpation
After completing the experiment, participants evaluated whether they thought they improved their palpation skills throughout the experiment. 20 participants (71.4%) thought they improved, 3 disagreed (10.7%), and 5 were neutral (17.9%).

5 DISCUSSION

Introducing ferromagnetic granules in a jamming haptic interface has the quality to be a promising solution to produce larger tactile displays cheaply with high accuracy. Palpation trainers need to be robust, safe and have a high level of repeatability. Using adaptable palpation trainers increases the number of study cases and task-specific functionalities the trainer can accomplish. Thus, we think

our concept can be taken further for use in a medical training equipment environment. Before that, however, there is a need for further development of the technology and contextual testing.

When comparing our data with relevant research (as mentioned in the Introduction), we have good results for people's perception of both hardness and position. Bergmann Tiest and Kappers (2009) states that users are pretty good at determining hardness. Frisoli et al. (2011) states that cutaneous sensor modality is not affected by size, but kinesthetic performance is reduced with smaller-sized objects. To our knowledge, there is a lack of research on people's perceptual exploration and characterization. Thus, this study could add to the body of knowledge concerning this aspect of both machine interaction and human tactile perception. The following section discusses the objective and subjective results gathered and how they answer our research questions. Further, an evaluation of the participant sampling is presented before we discuss the limitations and outlook of the study.

5.1 Interpreting Results
We defined that our haptic interface should be able to change the position, form and hardness of an irregularity recognizable by palpation. We chose a circle and an annulus as our two shapes to evaluate if people could locate and characterize them. A major part of the participants could differentiate between the circular lumps and the Annulus (78.57% recognized the inner circle of the Annulus, and 89.29% drew the circular lumps with no inner circle). Furthermore, all the participants found an irregularity in all conditions that had an irregularity. For the Baseline condition, six participants found a false positive. When determining the participants' ability to describe the form, we used Intersection over Union (IoU). The median was promising for all three

irregularity conditions, with the highest score for Soft Lump (0.793). From these three observations, we could conclude that the overall agreement between participants was great for form. Thus, our concept can manipulate the granules into different shapes that laypersons can distinguish by palpation.

However, an interesting result is that the IoU was significantly lower for Annulus than for Hard Lump and Soft Lump, while Annulus scored best at center point distance. A more logical assumption would be that IoU and center point distance is inversely proportional. There could be at least two reasons why we get a lower IoU score for Annulus. Initially, we observed from the participants contouring the Annulus that they struggled to get the size and position of the inner circle right. Due to how we calculated IoU, a wrong positioned hole yielded a more considerable difference in IoU than a similar error in outer contour. Also, the same error in the center point difference for Lump and Annulus gives a more significant change in IoU for Annulus because of the inner circle.

The results show a statistical difference for both objectively measured and perceived hardness between Soft lump and Hard Lump. Furthermore, when performing Wilcoxon tests on perceived hardness, there was a significantly lower value of the Soft Lump than the Hard Lump and Annulus condition. Thus, we have shown that participants can distinguish between hard and soft objects that the prototype produces, which is essential for palpation tasks, whereas characterizing the physical attributes such as form and hardness of identified irregularities is essential.

Considering how participants conducted the palpation tasks, time spent is of interest. The five most extended procedure times were on baseline condition, and three of them had baseline as the first condition. For example, participant No. 4 stated that there was no irregularity after 90 s before spending six more minutes to palpate before finding a false positive. No. 21 expressed hesitancy after 1 minute, and then spent two more minutes palpating before concluding with a true negative. No. 17 expressed insecurity before spending 2–3 more minutes searching, ending with a true negative. From the respective participant's confidence data, the participant with the false positive (no. 4) answer a four on the Likert scale, i.e., partially agreeing that they were sure they found the correct position and form of the irregularity. Also, all three participants had good results in all irregularity conditions. This connection could mean that some people struggle to trust their sense of touch. The baseline condition presents ambiguity as there is nothing to palpate, and we believe having it as the first condition increased ambiguity and thus uncertainty in participants who probably expected an irregularity.

Another aspect is the repeatability of our testing equipment. We tried to develop a haptic interface that can alter and maintain hardness, position and form of palpable outputs with high repeatability. However, while prototyping the granular jammer, it became apparent that repeatedly creating geometries with identical shape and hardness was challenging. While the outline for the shapes varied for each sample as a result of the manual setup and granule dispersion, the gathered images showed only a small deviation of rendered area for each irregularity condition. The durometric

measurements did, however, show a wide hardness range within a prepared condition. This inhomogeneous hardness from granular jamming is similar to the findings of Genecov, Stanley, and Okamura (2014). We thought of two reasons for this, firstly, how the hardness is highly dependent on how the granules interlock or position themselves across the irregularity. Secondly, because the arrangement of granules was made manually, there was an unavoidable variation in the produced output geometries and thus granulate concentration across the area.

Considering the pressure readings for the setup, Soft Lump had more outliers as a result of the vacuum level being manually set (and adjusted). Compared to Hard Lump and Annulus which had a hard stop, governed by the maximum vacuum the setup could provide. Given these being different geometries thus yielding different volumes to drain the air from, this could cause the difference in obtained vacuum level. However, our results from the perceived hardness showed no significant difference between Annulus and Hard Lump. As this being a first prototype, challenges concerning repeatability is expected and the overall results show great promise for this concept to be improved further to address these limitations.

When looking at the questionnaire data, confidence was highest in finding the position and shape of the Annulus and Soft Lump condition. We expected that the Hard Lump would be the easiest to find due to a sharper edge and thus greater difference between the Hard Lump and the palpable area. However, this was not the case. In retrospect we suspect this was due to the increased vacuum level instantly jamming the granules not allowing them to evenly distribute and conform to a smooth shape. This could cause the edges of the Hard Lump to be more jagged/rivet than the edge of the Soft Lump, which had a more circular shape in comparison. We therefore believe this might have made participants more uncertain of where the edge was. Moreover, since the edge of the Hard Lump varied more compared to a circle, this may have contributed to that it was more difficult to find the center of it.

Participants reported they got better at finding the irregularity throughout the experiment, meaning it could be used as a training device for palpation exercises. However, a reported high level of confidence and low level of difficulty for each condition could mean the task being too easy to perform, not leaving much room for progression and learning. Given the ability to find and characterize the irregularities sufficiently, and having a high confidence in doing so, further steps should be made to tailor level of difficulty to specific scenarios and investigating the use of the device in a medical context. The concept has been experimentally, shown to facilitate users' palpation skills by speed, location, shape, and hardness differentiation of palpable findings. Other learning objectives could involve motoric technique and following procedural algorithms, which should be explored in further development of the concept.

5.2 Participant Sampling

In this experiment, the 28 participants were all engineering students who did not have any previous experience with palpation as a medical examination technique. The participants did not get any technical or strategic instructions, meaning their palpation approach would be different to a medical professional. Therefore, we have shown that our concept works for presenting generic geometric shapes for laypersons, which is a promising result considering this a training device. Moreover, having participants with prior medical experience, would thus require a higher level of difficulty. A sample size of 28 was adequate compared to similar studies (Gerling et al., 2003; Asgar-Deen et al., 2020). Also, as we got statistically significant differences between relevant data points, such as the hardness of Soft Lump and Hard Lump, more participants would most likely not produce other results. However, a higher sample size would reduce the possibility of an accepted hypothesis being incorrect.

5.3 Limitations and Further Work

In this research, sensing, automation or participant feedback has not been addressed nor implemented in the palpation concept. The prototype and subsequently the experiments with the prototype are not tied to a medical context. Instead, it explores some of the capabilities and extreme conditions the haptic device can output. Hence, it has not been within the scope of this research to model, synthesize, or simulate physiological attributes for palpation. Nevertheless, we lack to prove that our haptic interface is helpful in medical training because of a simplified experiment focusing on planar perceptual exploration. Therefore, in further development, more levels of difficulty, complex geometries, hardness profiles, locations, and dynamic abilities should be explored. As palpation tasks seldom concerns irregularities in one plane, investigating multiple jamming layers, or simulating depth of palpation by dynamic stiffness control should be investigated. A positive backpressure in combination with ferrogranular jamming could yield 3D-shapes with high tactile resolution and geometrical freedom (Koehler et al., 2020; He et al., 2021). In further work, we seek to test the concept with users who can provide feedback and evaluation on a medical basis. This could reveal hitherto unexplored concept potentials and critical functions to pursue.

6 CONCLUSION

This work has described the development and testing of a novel haptic interface concept that uses ferrogranular jamming. This concept was developed as a compliant simulation interface for medical palpation training, with the ability to simulate geometrical objects of various shapes and tactile properties. The concept was tested by having 28 untrained participants perform a set of structured palpation tasks in an experiment. The experiment consisted of four conditions, one baseline and three containing a palpable irregularity. These conditions were chosen to evaluate if the interface could produce various shapes and hardness levels, while also investigating participants palpation skills. Given the results of the experiment, we conclude that the concept can create palpable objects with variable hardness by adjusting the jamming vacuum. Laypersons can distinguish these objects by palpation, both by the hardness, location, and shape of objects with good accuracy. Thus, this study also provides insights on peoples' perceptual abilities in explorative palpation. It shows the ability to locate and characterize palpable objects of varying shape and hardness in a satisfactory manner. Further, the results show that, the task was not considered very challenging. This combined with participants reported high level of confidence in performance, indicates that increased difficulty might be required to ensure room for improvement and learning. However, as participants also reported improvements in their palpation skills during the experiment, the technology looks promising to be further developed for medical training applications.

Considering this being an early conceptual prototype, this study revealed opportunities and challenges yet to be addressed. In further work, we want to explore whether the interface can be used as a palpation tool in medical simulation by qualitative testing with expert users. This will require palpable objects where both hardness, shape, and difficulty are tailored to the medical scenarios we want to simulate. Other technical aspects of the ferrogranular jamming concept we want to explore are sensing and feedback, automation, and dynamic and responsive tactile abilities. Collectively, this could improve the experience of using this technology in simulation-based medical training.

AUTHOR CONTRIBUTIONS

All authors contributed ideas and concepts throughout the development of the device. SR did the technical work and execution of the experiment. MS provided laboratory and testing facility. All authors contributed and agreed to the final wording of the submission. HD conducted the statistical analysis. MA contributed to the development of the concept and design of the experiment.

ACKNOWLEDGMENTS

Thanks to Sindre Wold Eikevåg for the experiment procedure timeline figure and thanks to Håvard Vestad for creative ideas concerning the ferrogranular jamming concept.

REFERENCES

Asgar-Deen, D., Carriere, J., Wiebe, E., Peiris, L., Duha, A., and Tavakoli, M. (2020). Augmented Reality Guided Needle Biopsy of Soft Tissue: A Pilot Study. *Front. Robot. AI* 7, 72. doi:10.3389/frobt.2020.00072

Bergmann Tiest, W. M., and Kappers, A. (2009). Cues for Haptic Perception of Compliance. *IEEE Trans. Haptics* 2, 189–199. doi:10.1109/TOH.2009.16

Brown, E., Rodenberg, N., Amend, J., Mozeika, A., Steltz, E., Zakin, M. R., et al. (2010). Universal Robotic Gripper Based on the Jamming of Granular Material. *Proc. Natl. Acad. Sci.* 107, 18809–18814. doi:10.1073/pnas.1003250107

Cao, Q., Han, X., and Li, L. (2014). Configurations and Control of Magnetic fields for Manipulating Magnetic Particles in Microfluidic Applications: Magnet Systems and Manipulation Mechanisms. *Lab. Chip* 14, 2762–2777. doi:10.1039/c4lc00367e

Carruth, D. W. (2017). "Virtual Reality for Education and Workforce Training," in 2017 15th International Conference on Emerging eLearning Technologies and Applications (ICETA) (IEEE), 1–6. doi:10.1109/ICETA.2017.8102472

Cates, M. E., Wittmer, J. P., Bouchaud, J.-P., and Claudin, P. (1998). Jamming, Force Chains, and Fragile Matter. *Phys. Rev. Lett.* 81, 1841–1844. doi:10.1103/PhysRevLett.81.1841

Cheng, N. G., Lobovsky, M. B., Keating, S. J., Setapen, A. M., Gero, K. I., Hosoi, A. E., et al. (2012). "Design and Analysis of a Robust, Low-Cost, Highly Articulated Manipulator Enabled by Jamming of Granular media," in 2012 IEEE International Conference On Robotics And Automation (IEEE), 4328–4333. doi:10.1109/ICRA.2012.6225373

D'Avella, S., Tripicchio, P., and Avizzano, C. A. (2020). A Study on Picking Objects in Cluttered Environments: Exploiting Depth Features for a Custom Low-Cost Universal Jamming Gripper. *Robotics and Computer-Integrated Manufacturing* 63, 101888. doi:10.1016/j.rcim.2019.101888

Field, A. (2018). *Discovering Statistics Using IBM SPSS Statistics*. Los Angeles: SAGE.

Fitzgerald, S. G., Delaney, G. W., and Howard, D. (2020). A Review of Jamming Actuation in Soft Robotics. *Actuators* 9, 104. doi:10.3390/act9040104

Follmer, S., Leithinger, D., Olwal, A., Cheng, N., and Ishii, H. (2012). "Jamming User Interfaces," in Proceedings of the 25th Annual ACM Symposium on User Interface Software and Technology UIST '12 (New York, NY, USA: Association for Computing Machinery), 519–528. doi:10.1145/2380116.2380181

Frisoli, A., Solazzi, M., Reiner, M., and Bergamasco, M. (2011). The Contribution of Cutaneous and Kinesthetic Sensory Modalities in Haptic Perception of Orientation. *Brain Res. Bull.* 85, 260–266. doi:10.1016/j.brainresbull.2010.11.011

Genecov, A. M., Stanley, A. A., and Okamura, A. M. (2014). "Perception of a Haptic Jamming Display: Just Noticeable Differences in Stiffness and Geometry," in 2014 IEEE Haptics Symposium (HAPTICS) (IEEE), 333–338. doi:10.1109/HAPTICS.2014.6775477

Gerling, G. J., Weissman, A. M., Thomas, G. W., and Dove, E. L. (2003). Effectiveness of a Dynamic Breast Examination Training Model to Improve Clinical Breast Examination (CBE) Skills. *Cancer Detect. Prev.* 27, 451–456. doi:10.1016/j.cdp.2003.09.008

Gijs, M. A. M., Lacharme, F., and Lehmann, U. (2010). Microfluidic Applications of Magnetic Particles for Biological Analysis and Catalysis. *Chem. Rev.* 110, 1518–1563. doi:10.1021/cr9001929

Harada, K., Nagata, K., Rojas, J., Ramirez-Alpizar, I. G., Wan, W., Onda, H., et al. (2016). Proposal of a Shape Adaptive Gripper for Robotic Assembly Tasks. *Adv. Robotics* 30, 1186–1198. doi:10.1080/01691864.2016.1209431

He, L., Herzig, N., Lusignan, S. d., Scimeca, L., Maiolino, P., Iida, F., et al. (2021). An Abdominal Phantom with Tunable Stiffness Nodules and Force Sensing Capability for Palpation Training. *IEEE Trans. Robot.* 37, 1051–1064. doi:10.1109/TRO.2020.3043717

Hook, J., Taylor, S., Butler, A., Villar, N., and Izadi, S. (2009). "A Reconfigurable Ferromagnetic Input Device," in Proceedings of the 22nd Annual ACM Symposium on User Interface Software and Technology UIST '09 (New York, NY, USA: Association for Computing Machinery), 51–54. doi:10.1145/1622176.1622186

IBM SPSS Statistics 27 (2020). *Downloading IBM SPSS Statistics 27*. NY: IBM Corp..

Iwamoto, T., Tatezono, M., and Shinoda, H. (2008). "Non-contact Method for Producing Tactile Sensation Using Airborne Ultrasound," in *Haptics: Perception, Devices and Scenarios Lecture Notes in Computer Science*. Editor M. Ferre (Berlin, Heidelberg: Springer), 504–513. doi:10.1007/978-3-540-69057-3_64

Jansen, Y., Karrer, T., and Borchers, J. (2010). "MudPad," in ACM International Conference on Interactive Tabletops and Surfaces ITS '10 (New York, NY, USA: Association for Computing Machinery), 11–14. doi:10.1145/1936652.1936655

Jiang, A., Xynogalas, G., Dasgupta, P., Althoefer, K., and Nanayakkara, T. (2012). "Design of a Variable Stiffness Flexible Manipulator with Composite Granular Jamming and Membrane Coupling," in 2012 IEEE/RSJ International Conference on Intelligent Robots and Systems (IEEE), 2922–2927. doi:10.1109/iros.2012.6385696

Koehler, M., Usevitch, N. S., and Okamura, A. M. (2020). Model-Based Design of a Soft 3-D Haptic Shape Display. *IEEE Trans. Robot.* 36, 613–628. doi:10.1109/TRO.2020.2980114

Landis, J. R., and Koch, G. G. (1977). The Measurement of Observer Agreement for Categorical Data. *Biometrics* 33, 159–174. doi:10.2307/2529310

Lathan, C. E., Tracey, M. R., Sebrechts, M. M., Clawson, D. M., and Higgins, G. A. (2002). "Using Virtual Environments as Training Simulators: Measuring Transfer," in *Handbook of Virtual Environments* (Boca Raton, FL: CRC Press).

Lederman, S. J., and Klatzky, R. L. (1993). Extracting Object Properties through Haptic Exploration. *Acta Psychologica* 84, 29–40. doi:10.1016/0001-6918(93)90070-8

Lelevé, A., McDaniel, T., and Rossa, C. (2020). Haptic Training Simulation. *Front. Virtual Real.* 1, 2. doi:10.3389/frvir.2020.00003

Li, M., Ranzani, T., Sareh, S., Seneviratne, L. D., Dasgupta, P., Wurdemann, H. A., et al. (2014). Multi-fingered Haptic Palpation Utilizing Granular Jamming Stiffness Feedback Actuators. *Smart Mater. Struct.* 23, 095007. doi:10.1088/0964-1726/23/9/095007

Licona, A. R., Liu, F., Pinzon, D., Torabi, A., Boulanger, P., Lelevé, A., et al. (2020). "Applications of Haptics in Medicine," in *Haptic Interfaces for Accessibility, Health, and Enhanced Quality of Life*. Editors T. McDaniel and S. Panchanathan (Cham: Springer International Publishing), 183–214. doi:10.1007/978-3-030-34230-2_7

Manti, M., Cacucciolo, V., and Cianchetti, M. (2016). Stiffening in Soft Robotics: A Review of the State of the Art. *IEEE Robot. Automat. Mag.* 23, 93–106. doi:10.1109/MRA.2016.2582718

Putzu, F., Konstantinova, J., and Althoefer, K. (2019). "Soft Particles for Granular Jamming," in Annual Conference towards Autonomous Robotic Systems (Springer), 65–74. doi:10.1007/978-3-030-25332-5_6

Rosenthal, R. (1986). "Meta-Analytic Procedures for Social Science Research," in *Educational Researcher* (Beverly Hills: Sage Publications), 14818–14820. doi:10.3102/0013189x015008018

Srinivasan, M. A., and LaMotte, R. H. (1995). Tactual Discrimination of Softness. *J. Neurophysiol.* 73, 88–101. doi:10.1152/jn.1995.73.1.88

Stanley, A. A., Hata, K., and Okamura, A. M. (2016). "Closed-loop Shape Control of a Haptic Jamming Deformable Surface," in 2016 IEEE International Conference on Robotics and Automation (ICRA) (IEEE), 2718–2724. doi:10.1109/icra.2016.7487433

Steltz, E., Mozeika, A., Rodenberg, N., Brown, E., and Jaeger, H. M. (2009). "JSEL: Jamming Skin Enabled Locomotion," in 2009 IEEE/RSJ International Conference on Intelligent Robots and Systems (IEEE), 5672–5677. doi:10.1109/IROS.2009.5354790

Tan, H. Z., Pang, X. D., and Durlach, N. I. (1992). Manual Resolution of Length, Force, and Compliance. *Adv. Robotics* 42, 13–18. doi:10.5802/aif.1307

Taylor, P. M., Moser, A., and Creed, A. (1998). A Sixty-Four Element Tactile Display Using Shape Memory alloy Wires. *Displays* 18, 163–168. doi:10.1016/S0141-9382(98)00017-1

Wagner, C. R., Lederman, S. J., and Howe, R. D. (2002). "A Tactile Shape Display Using RC Servomotors," in Proceedings 10th Symposium on Haptic Interfaces for Virtual Environment and Tele Operator Systems. HAPTICS 2002 (IEEE), 354–355.

Wickens, T. D., and Keppel, G. (2004). *Design and Analysis: A Researcher's Handbook*. Upper Saddle River, NJ: Pearson Prentice-Hall.

Woodrum, D. T., Andreatta, P. B., Yellamanchilli, R. K., Feryus, L., Gauger, P. G., and Minter, R. M. (2006). Construct Validity of the LapSim Laparoscopic Surgical Simulator. *Am. J. Surg.* 191, 28–32. doi:10.1016/j.amjsurg.2005.10.018

Zhao, X., Zhu, Z., Cong, Y., Zhao, Y., Zhang, Y., and Wang, D. (2020). Haptic Rendering of Diverse Tool-Tissue Contact Constraints during Dental Implantation Procedures. *Front. Robot. AI* 7, 1. doi:10.3389/frobt.2020.00035

10

Model-Augmented Haptic Telemanipulation: Concept, Retrospective Overview and Current use Cases

Thomas Hulin*, Michael Panzirsch, Harsimran Singh, Andre Coelho, Ribin Balachandran, Aaron Pereira, Bernhard M. Weber, Nicolai Bechtel, Cornelia Riecke, Bernhard Brunner, Neal Y. Lii, Julian Klodmann, Anja Hellings, Katharina Hagmann, Gabriel Quere, Adrian S. Bauer, Marek Sierotowicz, Roberto Lampariello, Jörn Vogel, Alexander Dietrich, Daniel Leidner, Christian Ott, Gerd Hirzinger and Alin Albu-Schäffer

Institute of Robotics and Mechatronics, German Aerospace Center (DLR), Wessling, Germany

*Correspondence:
Thomas Hulin
thomas.hulin@dlr.de

Certain telerobotic applications, including telerobotics in space, pose particularly demanding challenges to both technology and humans. Traditional bilateral telemanipulation approaches often cannot be used in such applications due to technical and physical limitations such as long and varying delays, packet loss, and limited bandwidth, as well as high reliability, precision, and task duration requirements. In order to close this gap, we research model-augmented haptic telemanipulation (MATM) that uses two kinds of models: a remote model that enables shared autonomous functionality of the teleoperated robot, and a local model that aims to generate assistive augmented haptic feedback for the human operator. Several technological methods that form the backbone of the MATM approach have already been successfully demonstrated in accomplished telerobotic space missions. On this basis, we have applied our approach in more recent research to applications in the fields of orbital robotics, telesurgery, caregiving, and telenavigation. In the course of this work, we have advanced specific aspects of the approach that were of particular importance for each respective application, especially shared autonomy, and haptic augmentation. This overview paper discusses the MATM approach in detail, presents the latest research results of the various technologies encompassed within this approach, provides a retrospective of DLR's telerobotic space missions, demonstrates the broad application potential of MATM based on the aforementioned use cases, and outlines lessons learned and open challenges.

Keywords: telerobotics, model-augmented telemanipulation, shared control, shared autonomy, haptic constraints

1. INTRODUCTION

Telerobotics is a powerful tool to combine the benefits of robotic manipulation with human mental abilities and manipulation strategies. Modern bilateral teleoperation systems provide haptic feedback that enables a human operator to perceive interaction forces and—more importantly—to intuitively control the forces applied by a teleoperated robot on its environment. This kind of feedback is crucial for delicate applications and tasks that comprise handling of fragile, dangerous, or expensive parts, or require high precision as it enables the operator to feel guiding structures or sliding on surfaces with limited forces. Such situations typically occur for applications in space, biochemical laboratories, or radiation environments. The latter was also the motivation for the development of many of the early telemanipulation systems that handled highly radioactive materials starting in the 1940s (cyberneticzoo.com, 2014). While these early systems were purely mechanically coupled, a revolution in telemanipulation occurred with the introduction of information technology (IT), which made it possible to electronically couple the haptic interaction device to the remote system. The major advantages of this innovation were (i) the ability to cover greater distances, (ii) a greater flexibility in control, (iii) a clearer presentation of forces, but above all (iv) a drastic reduction of apparent inertia. In addition to numerous incremental improvements in hardware and control approaches, there were a few other relatively new developments that significantly advanced the applicability and ease of use of telerobotics.

First, software-generated constraints that can limit the position or force of the haptic device or remote robot were introduced as so-called virtual fixtures (VFs; Rosenberg, 1993b). They guide the robot through a predefined desired path or restrict it from getting into a forbidden region of the workspace. Thus, VFs reduce the control freedom given to the operator while enhancing task accuracy and task completion time (Kang et al., 2004). They are also ideal for tasks requiring speed and precision while being repetitive in nature (Payandeh and Stanisic, 2002). Therefore, VFs are a great candidate for applications such as laparoscopic surgery, where they add an additional layer of safety and increase the surgeon's dexterity (Turro and Khatib, 2001). However, they have also proven to be highly beneficial for telemanipulation tasks with very long time delays (Xia et al., 2012).

Second, diverse forms of cooperation between operator and robot emerged, such as *supervisory control* (Ferrell and Sheridan, 1967; Sheridan, 1992) or *shared control* (Anderson, 1994). These approaches, subsumed under the term *shared autonomy*, aim at overcoming limitations of the operator that are due to the complexity of the robot or time delay between operator and robot by transferring some workload to the robot. Embedded into this concept, shared control refers to a continuous blend of human and robot control, ranging from safeguarding techniques (Fong et al., 2001), where the robot validates the operator's input, to adaptive virtual fixtures (Aarno et al., 2005), that support the operator in achieving predicted goals. Supervisory control, on the other hand, refers to an intermittent programming of the robot while the robot engages in a closed-loop interaction with its environment.

Third, model-mediated telemanipulation (MMT) was introduced where the user interacts with a local haptically rendered model estimate of the remote environment that is constantly updated, instead of being directly coupled to a teleoperated robot (Hannaford, 1989; Mitra and Niemeyer, 2008). The closed loop controller gets split into two control loops

on either side of the communication channel, i.e., the haptic device and the remote robot side. Such an architecture reduces the conservatism while maintaining stability for arbitrary time delays. MMT has also been extended to multi-operator multi-robot systems to enhance performance compared to the classical bilateral approach (Passenberg et al., 2010). Despite its advantages, MMT has a few unresolved challenges. One of which is the unstable haptic rendering on the operator side during drastic changes in the updated local model. Another, and perhaps more significant, hurdle is the environment modeling. A model mismatch can result in transmitting dangerous position information for the robot to follow, which can end up with the robot exerting high forces and thereby damaging itself and the remote environment (Xu et al., 2016). To this end, reinforcement learning has recently been integrated into the concept of MMT in order to adapt to new environmental conditions and to cope with high uncertainties (Beik-Mohammadi et al., 2020).

While stability is not an issue in an ideal system without delays and with unlimited communication bandwidth, real-world scenarios, especially those with communication over long distances, pose additional challenges in terms of control. To this end, bilateral control approaches have been continuously evolved in parallel to the aforementioned developments, and today enable haptic telemanipulation via communication including time delays of several seconds (Panzirsch et al., 2020a). Although such approaches can guarantee stable operation, telemanipulation with such significant delay still remains demanding for the operator, and a more powerful approach facilitating the task would be useful.

One of the main research interests at DLR is to enable robots to operate in orbit and on the surface of celestial bodies and to perform exploration or construction tasks there. **Figure 1** illustrates this vision and shows a spectrum of robotic systems to realize this goal. However, since robots are currently not able to operate fully autonomously, telerobotics is key to achieve this goal. The robots on the surface can be operated either from Earth or from a spacecraft, depending on the distance and the availability of a spacecraft.

This overview paper presents the model-augmented haptic telemanipulation (MATM) approach as a promising solution for such a telerobotic scenario. This approach uses two kinds of models, a remote model to enable shared autonomous functionality of the teleoperated robot and a local model to generate assistive augmented haptic feedback for the human operator. The forces that are displayed to the operator are a combination of augmented forces from the local model and forces resulting from interaction between the robot and the distant environment. The remote model is an environmental model of the remote environment to enable shared autonomy functionality to the teleoperated robot. The MATM approach can be considered as generalization of MMT, where the user interacts with a local model that acts as medium between the haptic device and the teleoperated robot. Yet, MATM has two major differences, i.e., the feedback to the human is a combination of real and augmented virtual feedback, and a remote model is introduced to enable shared autonomy of the remote robot.

MATM can be regarded as an intermediate step toward supervised and fully autonomous manipulation. **Figure 2** illustrates how this approach differentiates from classical bilateral telemanipulation, telenavigation of mobile robots, and supervised autonomy in terms of time delay and visual feedback quality. With increasing levels of support and autonomy, higher delays can be dealt with and visual quality demands decrease. The figure also shows the delays that occurred in some of the missions and use cases described in this paper.

The paper first presents MATM in detail and provides a state-of-the-art research overview in the underlying technologies used (section 2). Second, it gives a historical overview of the robotic space missions that were the main driving force behind this technology and highlights which aspects of MATM were advanced in each mission (section 3). Third, it discusses the potential and limitations of MATM based on use cases in different applications (section 4). In addition, the paper is also intended to serve as a reference work and therefore contains references to key

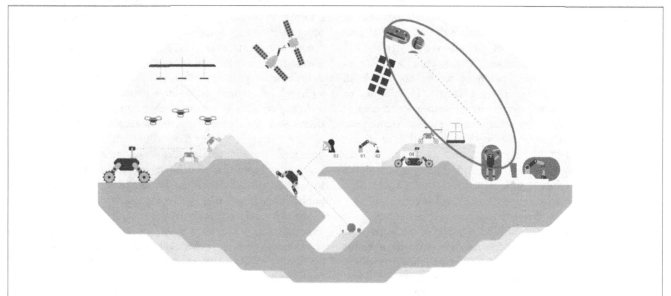

FIGURE 1 | Illustration of DLR's space robot vision. Teleoperation is a key topic of DLR's long-term research endeavors for robot applications on celestial bodies and is illustrated by the example of telemanipulation of a humanoid robot from a spacecraft. While the number of tasks that robots can perform autonomously is steadily increasing, teleoperation will still be required over the next few years or decades for situations where autonomy fails.

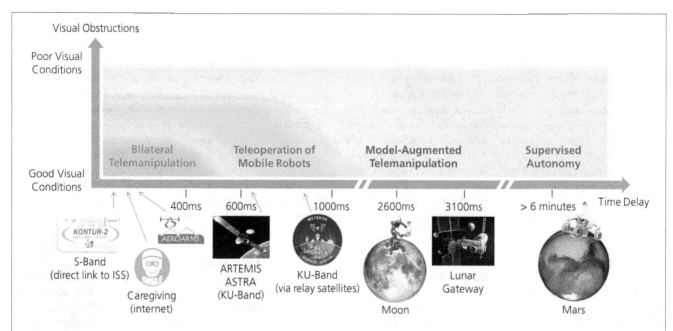

FIGURE 2 | Schematic diagram that illustrates up to which time delay and under which visual conditions different telerobotic concepts can be applied. It also shows the delays that occurred for selected missions from section 3 and use cases from section 4 (credit for photos of the Moon, the Mars, and the gateway: NASA).

publications that provide further details on specific aspects of the respective technology, mission, or use case.

2. MODEL-AUGMENTED TELEMANIPULATION

While in classical telemanipulation the operator is coupled to a remote robot via a haptic device, we aim to reach improved performance, efficiency, and ease of use during demanding telemanipulation tasks by means of two models that generate augmented feedback to the human operator and support the movements of the remote robot. **Figure 3** schematically depicts this MATM approach and illustrates the elements that play a key role in it. The haptic interaction device acts as an input and output interface for the human operator and provides haptic force feedback. The remote robot is telemanipulated by the human operator and is intended to execute the desired commands in a remote environment. The communication channel connecting the two systems can cause a significant delay due to long transmission distances or limitations in the communication infrastructure. On each side of the channel, a model supports the movements or augments feedback, respectively. The following subsections describe the most important challenges in detail and outline our proposed solution. The applications of the methods described in this section along with its project or use case description will be presented in sections 3 and 4.

2.1. Telemanipulation Under Time Delay

Traditional bilateral control approaches, such as Lawrence's well-known 4-channel architecture (Lawrence, 1993), enable telemanipulation with force feedback. For space applications, other factors need to be considered, such as motion (Onal and Sitti, 2009) and force scaling (Goldfarb, 1998), which address the differences in precision requirements and is used for training purposes, or indexing (Johnsen and Corliss, 1971) which is a displacement technique to avoid reaching the workspace limits of the haptic device (Hagn et al., 2010). Most importantly, control approaches require considering the time delay in the communication channel that originate due to the huge distances

between the operator and remote robot, which can have severe destabilizing consequences.

Extensive research has been carried out toward addressing the issue of stability for delayed bilateral teleoperation system, of which passivity-based methods are widely accepted and recognized due to their robustness and ease of applicability to any linear or nonlinear system independent of their model parameters. The Time Domain Passivity Approach (TDPA; Ryu et al., 2010) has garnered attention for being robust to variable delay and for being the least conservative of the passivity-based approaches. A novel 4-channel architecture using TDPA was implemented and tested in a real space experiment where the cosmonauts aboard the International Space Station (ISS) stably teleoperated a manipulator arm with two degrees of freedom (DoF) on Earth despite the inherent time delay (Artigas et al., 2016b). Nevertheless, TDPA too suffers from delay-dependent position drift and high frequency force oscillations. Therefore, some enhanced methods were proposed recently to remove this position mismatch between the haptic interaction device and remote robot while improving force transparency and enhancing the task performance (Coelho et al., 2018; Singh et al., 2018, 2019a; Panzirsch et al., 2020b).

Although position drift is an undesired phenomenon in telemanipulation, the authors of Panzirsch et al. (2020a) use it to their advantage to achieve a safe robot–environment interaction by using measured force feedback for the TDPA energy observations. Experimental validation for tasks such as slide & plug-in and pick & place were carried out safely and with a force feedback of sufficient quality, even with time delay of up to 3 s. This control algorithm was also extended for delayed telenavigation, where fictitious forces were generated by a set of "predictive" polygons, implemented in the driving direction of a mobile robot, overlapping with the objects in a depth data map (Sierotowicz et al., 2020).

Almost all of the state-of-the-art bilateral teleoperation controllers are implemented on both sides of the communication channel, i.e., on the local and the remote side. It would be advantageous if the stabilizing controller is implemented on either side of the communication channel, i.e., on the local side or on the remote side, as this would reduce the

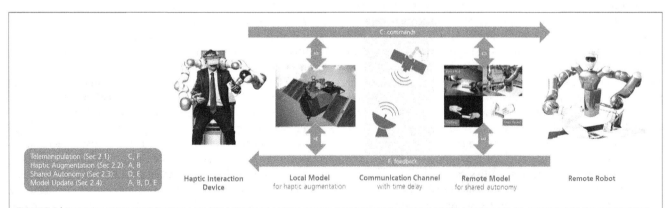

FIGURE 3 | Illustration of the control scheme of MATM. The local and the remote model can both read and modify (or augment) the commands to the remote robot and the feedback to the operator. Certain methods and situations demand such full signal access, as explained in the respective subsections.

reliability on communication bandwidth and therefore diminish the effects of packet delay, loss, and jitter. This was recently achieved by the proxy-based controller (Singh et al., 2020) that is only implemented on the local side. Experimental results showed enhanced position synchronization and realistic impedance matching for a communication suffering from unknown time-varying delays of up to 2 s, and interacting with an active environment.

The above methods form the backbone of stable bilateral control even for communication that includes a delay of several seconds. On this basis, haptic augmentation and shared autonomy can enrich the telemanipulation framework as explained in the subsequent sections.

2.2. Haptic Augmentation

Haptic augmentation is the blending of the feedback from a remote robot with the feedback from a model. This haptic feedback is augmented to the haptic device so that it can be perceived by the operator and provide support during telemanipulation. While for many telemanipulation systems with negligible communication delay a distinction between local and remote model does not play a role, the situation is different for space applications in which communication delay affects the telemanipulation. Normally this feedback is implemented on the local model in order to obtain haptic support without delay. In some applications, such augmentation is also fed to the remote robot to achieve a more direct reaction and higher precision in manipulations tasks (this signal path is represented by the bi-directional arrow B in **Figure 3**).

A standard tool in haptics for generating such feedback are *haptic constraints*—also denoted as *virtual fixtures*. The concept of virtual fixtures was introduced by Rosenberg (1992) to support the operator during a telemanipulation task and was also evaluated for time-delayed systems (Rosenberg, 1993a). Virtual fixtures are control algorithms which regulate manipulator motion, surveyed in Bowyer et al. (2013). They are typically employed to support or guide the operator for high precision tasks, avoid critical regions in which the remote robot could cause some damage, and avoid running into robotic constraints such as workspace limits or singularities.

To enable more general geometries for virtual fixtures, haptic algorithms can be used instead of geometric primitives. A prominent example of such an algorithm is the *Voxmap PointShell Algorithm* that uses volumetric data structures and is able to compute collision forces at haptic rates (1 kHz) even for extremely complex geometries in multi-object simulations (McNeely et al., 2006; Sagardia, 2019). Such an algorithm can also be combined with a physics-engine to include physical phenomena in the simulation (Sagardia et al., 2014). This capability is very useful for telemanipulation to predict object movements and poses and thus counteract the effects of time delays.

The concept of augmented haptics can also be applied for bimanual telemanipulation tasks or multilateral teleoperation in which more than one haptic device or remote robot is used. For instance, if a high precision in orientation is demanded, two haptic devices can be coupled with a virtual rigid link

to create an additional virtual grasping point that helps the operator to precisely set orientations (Panzirsch et al., 2018a). In cooperative tasks, where two operators jointly manipulate an object, knowing the intention of the respective other operator would be useful. Providing haptic information about the collaborating operator's intention is faster (force = acceleration) than on the visual/audio channel (velocity information). This concept was already evaluated in a delicate experiment with flexible objects involving the ISS (Panzirsch et al., 2017). In this experiment, the intention was measured by force sensors at the two haptic devices.

A challenge in this task is to differentiate between the feedback from intention and from the remote robot. In general, the operator should be able to distinguish between real and extended haptic feedback. One approach to achieve this is to apply a drastically higher stiffness for the amplified haptic feedback than for the one from the remote environment, which is feasible because the signals of the local path are not affected by the time delay of the communication channel (Hulin et al., 2013; Singh et al., 2019b). Another open question is how to best parameterize and distribute haptic augmentation between the local and the remote model. Future theoretical investigations and user studies should address this topic.

Feedback similar to haptic augmentation may also be implemented directly on the remote side and thus support the remote robot's movements without having to send commands over the communication channel first, making it faster and more precise compared to using a local model. This kind of model-based support of the remote robot belongs to the field of shared autonomy, which is discussed in the subsequent section.

2.3. Shared Autonomy

Commanding robots is a highly demanding, tedious task for humans. This is partially because of the sheer number of degrees of freedom that need to be orchestrated, partially because of time delays that cause adoption of the move-and-wait strategy (Ferrell, 1965). *Shared autonomy* (also known as *mixed initiative interaction*) is an umbrella term subsuming multiple techniques that aim at reducing the workload of the operator by delegating some of the control to the robot (Goodrich et al., 2013). Examples of shared autonomy are *supervised control*, where the operator commands the robot intermittently with high-level tasks while the robot engages in a closed-loop interaction with the environment, and *shared control*, where continuous input from the user is processed by the robot in order to validate, augment, or map it to higher dimensions.

In the MATM approach, we use these techniques to support the operator while performing a telemanipulation task. In shared control, the robot may relieve the operator by taking over certain subtasks of the robot. An easy-to-understand example is to constrain the orientation of a manipulated object (Quere et al., 2020). To achieve such support, the methods of the previous section on haptic augmentation can be used and applied on the remote robot. The advantage compared over applying haptic augmentation to the haptic device is higher precision and faster reaction (without the delay of the communication channel). In addition, the shared control algorithm can take control of non-telemanipulated robot parts or joints. An example is automatic positioning of robot hand fingers to establish stable grasp (Hertkorn, 2016).

In a mixed initiative shared control approach, the weighted sum of the commands (positions/forces/torques etc.) from both agents, namely the human operator and the autonomous system, is given to the remote robot as the final command signal (Musić and Hirche, 2017). The weights for the individual commands are called task or authority allocation factors (Parasuraman and Riley, 1997). These factors can be fixed (Panzirsch et al., 2018a), or time varying to account for certain situation changes (Inagaki, 2003). In a recent publication, we developed a novel time varying approach, where the authority is shifted from the autonomous system to the human operator based on real measurement noise (Balachandran et al., 2020a) using Bayesian filters. This means that in case the autonomous system is not able to complete the task at hand due to bad measurements, the human operator is asked for intervention and to implement corrective measures to complete the task. If and when the sensor measurement quality improves, the control authority is smoothly given back to the autonomous system. This reduces the physical and mental efforts demanded from the operator as he has to intervene if and only when the autonomous system has low confidence in its own task completion ability.

Although more robust, fixed authority allocation-based shared control limits possibilities of human intervention in case of failure of autonomy. On the other hand, adaptive allocation factors are more robust against autonomy failures but are sensitive to the probabilistic filters' convergence. Further improvements can be made to optimize the mixed-initiative approach by combining confidence factors from both autonomy and the human operator, availing possibilities offered by artificial intelligence and machine learning.

While shared control depends on continual input from the user, supervised control can deal with intermittent input and is thus suitable for commanding multiple robots. We apply supervised control in a two-step approach. First, the user specifies a goal in an intuitive user interface (UI) (Birkenkampf et al., 2014), which is then translated into *Planning Domain Definition Language* (Ghallab et al., 1998). Second, the robot uses its local autonomy to reach the goal without any further need of user intervention. The local autonomy is based on *action templates*, which store the symbolic and geometric descriptions for manipulation instructions. The robot creates a plan to reach the specified goal based on the symbolic description in the action template headers. Robot-specific geometric reasoning modules then evaluate the geometrical descriptions of the respective action templates. In case of an error, the planner first assesses possible alternative geometric solutions before initiating backtracking to explore different solutions by re-evaluating previous actions. The procedure is described in detail in Leidner (2019) and the approach has been validated in multiple experimental sessions with astronauts on board the ISS (Schmaus et al., 2019). We also extended this approach to probabilistic domains where actions can fail (Bauer et al., 2020). This allows operators to choose between plans that reach the goal with different likelihood. Sometimes, operators might be willing to trade success probability for completion time, number of steps of the plan, or possible side effects.

Ongoing work focuses on how to switch from teleoperation to supervised control, which requires to update the world model according to the changes induced by the teleoperated robot. The challenges that arise during model updates and their respective solutions are the subject of the following section.

2.4. Model Update

The model update represents the updating of the data of the local and the remote model as well as the synchronization between these two models. Two challenges arise directly from this task. First, how can the models be synchronized even though the data of the models may be in a different structure or representation? Second, how can stability be established despite the fact that the updating process is highly nonlinear, especially in case of time delay, jitter, and packet loss?

In the case of supervised control, model update translates to keeping the local model (that is shared between robot and operator) in synchronization with the environment the robot is acting in. This includes detection and localization of objects, but also inference of the symbolic state. Both geometric and symbolic information are needed by the user interface for providing the user with possible actions and by the robot in order to execute those actions. A viable and pragmatic solution for this is a shared knowledge base that stores the object information and provides it to both modules in order to create a knowledge common ground. Part of this knowledge base can be geometric models, available action templates, symbolic state, and pose of the objects. In our implementation, object detection and localization are performed according to Sundermeyer et al. (2018). The symbolic state of the environment is evaluated based on a digital twin of the robot and the environment in simulation as described in Bauer et al. (2018).

In order to tackle the second challenge, i.e., the stability of the overall system, we research a novel control framework. The challenges of the proposed framework in terms of closed-loop stability are the fusion of different force feedback channels with computed, measured, or fictitious forces and the design of the reference position for the devices. Those challenges also include the model update, which represents a highly nonlinear functionality especially in the presence of time delay, jitter, and packet loss, making it a potential source of instability.

The energy-based passivity principle represents a highly modular method to assure absolute stability of complex closed-loop systems since the passivity of submodules can assure the passivity of the overall system. Thus, different modules as the force feedback channel or the haptic augmentation and shared autonomy functionalities (compare **Figure 3**) can be designed and activated or deactivated, respectively, in a highly adaptive and modular manner. The fusion of different force commands to the haptic input device and remote robot can be passively designed with the help of power control units as earlier presented for multilateral telemanipulation (Panzirsch et al., 2013), telenavigation (Panzirsch et al., 2018b), and haptic augmentation (Panzirsch et al., 2017, 2018a). Exemplary, the haptic augmentation and shared autonomy modules based on local and remote models can be modeled as 1-port subsystems,

FIGURE 4 | The astronaut Hans Schlegel inside the Space Shuttle Columbia (**left**, credit: NASA) controls the robotic gripper of the ROTEX experiment (**middle**). The chaser satellite of the ETS-VII mission was equipped with a robot arm (**right**, credit: NASA).

which can be designed to be intrinsically passive (Weber Martins et al., 2018) or, alternatively, passivity controllers can assure the passivity of the modules including model updates as proposed in Xu et al. (2015) and Panzirsch et al. (2018b).

The modularity of the passivity concept simplifies combining independently developed passive modules, since no complex stability analyses of the overall control loops are required. The remaining challenge is the passive design of prospective haptic augmentation and shared autonomy features. It should be noted, though, that passivity is in general not more conservative than the popular Lyapunov stability criterion, especially since passivity does not necessarily have to be ensured in the frequency domain, but can be guaranteed in a highly adaptive manner in the time domain.

3. PAST TELEROBOTIC SPACE MISSIONS—PRIOR MILESTONES ON THE WAY TOWARD MODEL-AUGMENTED TELEOPERATION

The starting signal for DLR's telerobotic space missions was given in 1993 with ROTEX (**Figure 4**). Since then, DLR has contributed to several telerobotic space missions in cooperation with various space agencies, in particular ESA, ROSCOSMOS, and JAXA. The most significant missions for the MATM approach are briefly described in this section. In contrast to a purely historical overview on our telerobotic missions (Artigas and Hirzinger, 2016), this section is intended to relate to the MATM approach and to highlight the specific impact of our past missions, to synthesize the lessons learned, and to point out the challenges ahead.

3.1. Model Predictive Teleoperation—ROTEX and ETS-VII

The first space robotics experiment performed by DLR was the ROTEX experiment (Hirzinger et al., 1993) during the D2 mission in 1993 on board the Space Shuttle Columbia. A

multisensory robot inside the spacecraft successfully worked in four operational modes, i.e.,

- automatic (preprogramming on ground, reprogramming from ground),
- teleoperation on board (astronauts using stereo-TV-monitor),
- teleoperation from ground (using predictive computer graphics) via human operators and machine intelligence as well,
- tele-sensor-programming (learning by showing in a completely simulated world on ground including sensory perception with sensor-based execution later on board).

The main control concept behind all these modes was a shared autonomy approach, which includes shared control as well as shared intelligence, based on local autonomy loops on board. **Figure 5** shows the overall loop structures for the sensor-based telerobotic concept.

Due to the large time delays of up to 7 s that were involved during operation from ground, there was no haptic feedback in the ROTEX experiment. Instead, the human operator was enclosed in the feedback loop via stereovision and 3-D graphics on a very high level but with low bandwidth, while the low-level sensory loops were closed directly at the robot on board with high bandwidth.

To handle the large time delay, ROTEX used a predictive computer graphics approach, which seems to be the only way to overcome this problem. A human operator at the remote workstation gave robot commands by looking at a *predicted* graphics model of the robot. The control commands issued to this instantaneously reacting robot simulator are sent to the remote robot as well using the time-delayed transmission links.

Complex tasks were split up into elemental moves, represented by a certain configuration, which allows the simulated (as well as the real) robot to refine the gross commands autonomously. We introduced the term *tele-sensor-programming* that means the robot is graphically guided through the task (off-line on ground), storing not only the relevant Cartesian poses of the gripper but also the corresponding nominal sensory patterns

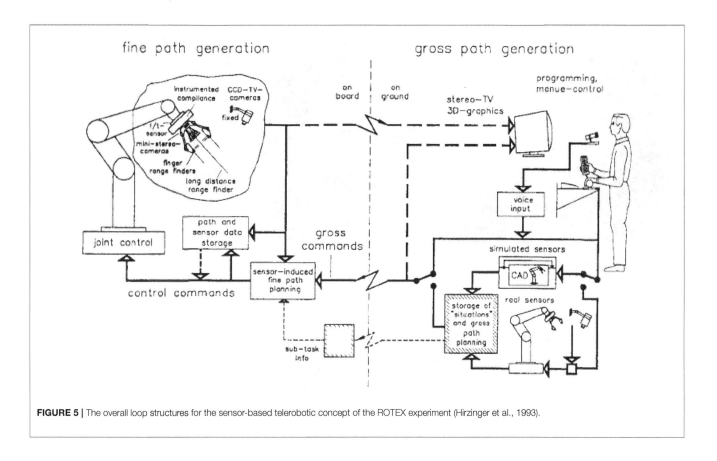

FIGURE 5 | The overall loop structures for the sensor-based telerobotic concept of the ROTEX experiment (Hirzinger et al., 1993).

(graphically simulated) for later reference in the on-board execution phase.

In summary, this mode of tele-sensor-programming is a form of off-line-programming, which tries to overcome the well-known problems of conventional approaches, especially the fact that the simulated and the real world are not identical. But instead of calibrating the robot, tele-sensor-programming provides the real robot with simulated sensory data that refer to relative positions between the end-effector and the environment, thus compensating for any kind of inaccuracies in the absolute positions of the robot and the real world. Using the simulated sensor values during the programming phase can be seen as the first model-based teleoperation approach in space robotics.

A few years later in 1999, DLR got the chance to contribute with an own experiment (German ETS-VII Technology Experiment [GETEX]) to the Japanese ETS-VII mission, which was the first space robotics mission with a focus on on-orbit-servicing tasks. For DLR the participation was the first step to a big challenge in space robotics, i.e., the capturing and repair of a failed satellite, completely controlled remotely from ground. In that context, we performed two main tasks, first a series of dynamic experiments to verify our models of free-floating space robots and the identification of the dynamic model parameters; second—and this is the more interesting one in the field of telerobotics—a peg-in-hole experiment, using VR methods and a *vision-and-force* control scheme, by closing sensor control loops directly on board (force) and via ground communication (vision). Like in ROTEX we used the tele-sensor-programming

approach to set the reference values for the visual servoing task, using some dedicated markers as image features, in a virtual environment for later usage in space. For that we developed an approach, which did not need any calibration, because it was only based on the sensor–actor relation: the desired Cartesian goal frame of the robot's tool center point was expressed only by the respective visual sensory pattern (Brunner et al., 1999).

3.2. Force-Feedback—ROKVISS and Kontur-2

Launched in 2005 and operated for nearly 5 years in space, the Robotics Component Verification Experiment on the ISS (ROKVISS) was a big success for two reasons: the first aim was the in-flight verification of highly integrated modular robotic joints (**Figure 6**, left), the second one the demonstration of different control modes, reaching from high system autonomy to force feedback teleoperation (telepresence mode). After ROTEX and GETEX, which did not cover any haptics, ROKVISS was designed to test and verify real telepresence operation using haptic and visual feedback at high data rates. For that the telepresence system of ROKVISS was equipped with

- a highly dynamic teleoperated robot including sensors and local intelligence,
- a high-bandwidth real time communication channel,
- an immersive multimodal human–machine interface.

All these components had to be connected by an advanced control concept, which combined shared autonomy and bilateral

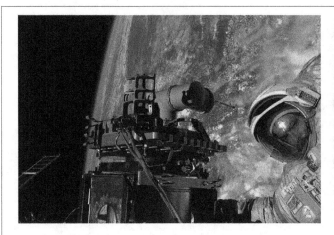 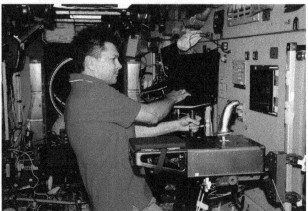

FIGURE 6 | The ROKVISS system mounted on a platform on the outside of the ISS (**left**, credit: NASA). Cosmonaut Oleg Kononenko with the Kontur-2 joystick on board the ISS (**right**, credit: ROSCOSMOS/O. Kononenko).

control of the teleoperated robot and guaranteed a synchronicity between the visual and haptic information. The human–machine interface played a major role for immersive telepresence. The operator should feel like being at the remote location. Therefore, DLR developed a new 2-DoF force-feedback joystick corresponding to the two joints of the manipulator in space. Providing the human operator with haptic feedback means to include the human into the control loop, i.e., the human arm was energetically coupled with the manipulator arm at the ISS. The stabilization of this coupled telemanipulation system was complicated due to the presence of time delay in the system (Hannaford and Ryu, 2002). An advantage of ROKVISS was that the communication delay was relatively small (10–30 ms) and predictable. This allowed to simulate additional time delays to test different control schemes and communication systems within a real space experiment (Preusche et al., 2006).

Space agencies are planning and working toward crewed lunar and planetary exploration missions to be realized within the next few decades. Sending astronauts directly to the surface of the celestial bodies is extremely dangerous and costly. Therefore, in an initial, cautious step, robots can be teleoperated from an orbital spacecraft to explore the surface, acquire samples, and construct habitats. To this end, DLR and the Russian space agency ROSCOSMOS collaborated on the Kontur-2 mission during the period 2012–2016.

The main goal of the Kontur-2 space mission was to test the feasibility of using force feedback teleoperation from a spacecraft in micro-gravity conditions and to telemanipulate robots on distant planets (Riecke et al., 2016). For this, the ISS was used as the spacecraft and the Earth as planet with a robot on its surface. It was therefore an inverted scenario compared to ROKVISS. To provide high fidelity force feedback to the cosmonauts, DLR developed a space qualified force feedback joystick, which was taken on board the ISS (**Figure 6**, right). A direct link over S band was used for communication between the ISS and Earth with short latency and ISS experiment windows. In spite of the short latency

(10–30 ms round-trip delay), it was observed that the bilateral controller was unstable due to the closed control loop with force feedback.

To reduce the performance deterioration that comes as the trade-off while ensuring stability, a novel 4-channel architecture bilateral controller was developed with passivity observers and passivity controllers as explained in section 2.1. This 4-channel bilateral controller provided a stable and highly transparent teleoperation system in spite of the communication delays and data losses and was tested in both terrestrial set-up (for cosmonaut training) and for the real space mission (Artigas et al., 2016b). In addition to the single-operator single-robot teleoperation, further tests were conducted for cooperative grasping of objects by two users.

In the scenario, a cosmonaut on board the ISS and a second operator from ground (located at our project partner in Russia) teleoperated a dual arm robot at DLR to cooperatively handle a flexible sphere. In order to handle the sphere safely (without dropping it or pressing it with too high forces), the haptic intention augmentation approach explained in section 2.2 was tested and verified during the Kontur-2 mission (Panzirsch et al., 2017). It was learned that force feedback provided the cosmonaut with a more intuitive feeling of the robot-environment interaction with which he could modulate the interaction forces more accurately as desired.

A series of human factors experiments was conducted within the Kontur-2 space mission, investigating the benefits of force feedback under conditions of weightlessness. Cosmonauts teleoperated the ROKVISS robot from the ISS with DLR's force feedback joystick. Findings indicated that force feedback is indispensable for teleoperation tasks, although the terrestrial performance level could not be reached in weightlessness. Moreover, haptic support at the joystick (e.g., motion damping) has to be adjusted to be beneficial in weightlessness conditions and higher resistive forces should be avoided (Weber et al., 2019, 2020; Riecke et al., 2020).

3.3. Supervised Autonomy—METERON SUPVIS Justin

Space telerobotics based on haptic telepresence provides close, immersive coupling between the user and the robotic asset. However, it presents two drawbacks: short effective operation time due to user fatigue, and difficulty to scale up (Lii et al., 2018). METERON SUPVIS Justin was a mission to tackle these issues with a different approach to teleoperation with supervised autonomy, or shared autonomy. Rather than using the robot as a haptically coupled avatar for the user, the robots are utilized as intelligent robotic assets, or coworkers to be commanded at the task level.

Between 2017 and 2018, three ISS-Earth telerobotic experiment sessions were carried out with five NASA and ESA astronauts. For METERON SUPVIS Justin, an analog scenario of a Martian surface environment was implemented at DLR in Germany to be serviced by DLR's humanoid robot Rollin' Justin (Borst et al., 2007, 2009). ISS in turn takes on the role of the orbiting spacecraft, from where the astronaut commands the robots on simulated Martian surface.

To test the robot's ability to carry out an increasing catalog of tasks that could be expected in a space habitat or colony, the SOLar farm EXperimental (SOLEX) environment was developed and constructed at DLR in Oberpfaffenhofen, Germany. The SOLEX environment is equipped with a wide array of systems and devices including solar panels, smart payload units, and a lander, which allowed for the design of different mission scenarios to be carried out by the human–robot team (Bayer et al., 2019).

Using action templates (Leidner, 2019) as described in section 2.3, Rollin' Justin carried out the task level commands provided by the astronaut by utilizing its local intelligence to process and execute lower level tasks. The knowledge-driven approach was also applied to the user interface design in the form of an intuitive touch screen tablet application (Schmaus et al., 2019). Implemented on a commercial off-the-shelf (COTS) tablet PC, the application provides the crew with vital information on the mission at hand, view from Justin's camera, and a dynamically updated list of relevant commands. This provides an uncluttered and intuitive user interface to command a highly complex robotic asset. **Figure 7** shows the user interface on the tablet PC being commanded by the ISS crew.

Through three sessions, increasingly complex tasks were carried out: from service and inspection, to manual device adjustment and maintenance, concluding with a full set of component retrieval and assembly tasks. **Figure 8** shows ESA astronaut Alexander Gerst performing component retrieval and assembly with Rollin' Justin. Thanks to the supervised autonomy approach, all participating ISS crew members not only were able to successfully complete all assigned tasks, their feedback

FIGURE 7 | An example layout of the knowledge-driven intuitive tablet user interface on board the ISS (Lii et al., 2018).

FIGURE 8 | ESA astronaut Alexander Gerst on board the ISS (**left**, credit: ESA) commanding DLR's Rollin' Justin in the SOLEX environment to perform component retrieval and assembly tasks (**right**).

also indicated that they would be able to handle working with larger robotic teams to perform more complex tasks with this approach.

3.4. Telenavigation—Analog-1

The Analog-1 mission (November 2019) tested geological sampling from orbit. It was intended to give insight into the feasibility of operating a robot on the surface of the moon by an astronaut aboard the Lunar Gateway, where communication latencies would be comparable to, or less than, those from ISS to ground (these were $\approx$850 ms in the K_u band link via relay satellites). In contrast to the SUPVIS-Justin experiment of the previous section, the unstructured environment and loosely defined tasks made supervised autonomy impractical. Hence, for the first time, full-DoF direct teleoperation with force feedback was tested from space to ground. The robot controlled from space was a mobile platform with two robotic manipulators and two cameras, shown in the right photo in **Figure 9**. The astronaut on the ISS drove the mobile platform to three geological sampling sites (mocked-up in a hangar in the Netherlands), investigated them and collected rock samples, all while in communication with geologists.

The astronaut's work station consisted of a laptop to display and interact with the user interface; a Sigma.7 haptic interface device from Force Dimension (modified by the company to be used in microgravity) to command position of the tool on the manipulator and receive force feedback; and an integrated joystick with keypad to drive the platform, move the cameras, and also interact with the user interface (see **Figure 9**, left). For the control, we used TDPA to deal with latency (described in section 2.1). Full details of the control are outside the scope of this paper.

The astronaut was able to command the robot stably, effectively, and intuitively. Despite the unstructured environment, it was clear from pre-trials with astronauts and astronaut trainers that certain maneuvers could also be automated, for example, the stowing of the rock. This begs the question of how to scale up and down levels of autonomy for different environments or tasks, with the same interface. Furthermore, possible uses of augmented reality were identified: to aid communication with scientists (during the experiment the astronaut benefited from a grid projected over the image), to aid driving under time delay (e.g., to show the projected path of the platform under the current steering angle) or in semi-autonomous driving, and to specify via points for the robot path on the camera image itself.

4. CASE STUDIES

While space missions were our original motivation for research on the MATM approach, it is evident that numerous other applications can also benefit from this approach. In this section, six exemplary use cases are presented to illustrate the wide variety of potential applications that reach from orbital applications over terrestrial telemanipulation in caregiving and telesurgery to applications that involve driving and flying robotic systems. In each use case description, special emphasis is given to the specific challenges, technical solutions, and experience gained. In none of these use cases, we have exploited the full spectrum of MATM so far, but rather emphasized certain aspects that appeared to be of particular interest for the respective use case. These foci are indicated in parentheses in the section headings.

4.1. In-orbit Telemanipulation (Haptic Augmentation and Shared Control)

To reduce the cost and payload volume of satellites launches, the assembly of satellites may be realized in in-orbit factories

FIGURE 9 | (Left) Astronaut Luca Parmitano used a haptic device and a joystick to control the robot arms and the mobile platform (credit: ESA). **(Right)** The Analog-1 mobile platform at a mocked-up geological sampling site (credit: ESA).

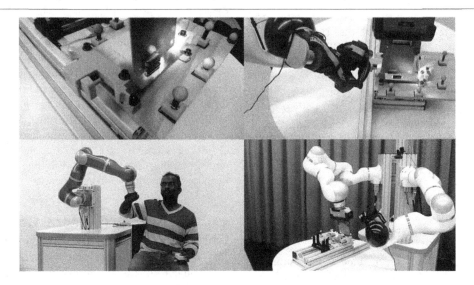

FIGURE 10 | Demonstration of a telerobotic high-precision assembly task of an electrical connector of CubeSats (Weber Martins et al., 2018).

(Spaceflight, 2020). Although manufacturing in the ISS has been recently tested with 3D printing (Napoli and Kugler, 2017), robotic assembly of satellites has not been done yet. To this end, an on-ground feasibility study was conducted within the framework of the Space Factory 4.0 project (Weber Martins et al., 2018) for the robotic assembly of CubeSats (**Figure 10**). *Space Factory 4.0* aimed at developing a bilateral controller, which allows for teleoperation of the assembly robot by a human operator using an HMI device, providing force feedback with the support of virtual fixtures, which in the control scheme of **Figure 3**, are elements of the remote model. The virtual fixtures are dynamic and are placed on the desired point by a vision-based tracking system. The final control architecture was based on a mixed-initiative approach (see section 2.3), where the final control commands to the remote robot was a weighted sum of control commands

from the teleoperator and the vision-based autonomy (virtual fixtures) with fixed authority allocation factors (Panzirsch et al., 2018a).

In order to reduce the physical effort demanded from the operator while telemanipulating the remote robot using the robot-based haptic device with its high inertia, a local explicit force controller was used to match the forces measured at the human–haptic device interface to the force measured at the remote robot's end effector (Balachandran et al., 2020b). This reduced the perceived inertia of the haptic device by the operator, during free motion of the robot, and also increased the transparency during robot–environment interaction. In addition to the feedback of the measured forces from the robot's end-effector, additional feedback was provided to the operator via the forces generated by the virtual fixtures. This supported the operator in gaining a better impression of the relative motion of the robot with respect to the workpiece and the target position and orientation. In a pilot study, it was found that such supportive feedback reduced the required completion time for an assembly task of CubeSat parts that required a high degree of precision (Weber Martins et al., 2018).

In spite of these benefits introduced by this mixed-initiative-based shared control architecture, it was observed that if the virtual fixtures were wrongly placed during certain scenarios then the tracking system produced noisy measurements. Due to the fixed authority allocation factors that were tuned beforehand, the operator had to produce more physical effort to intervene and force the robot against the virtual fixtures. Future works include applying the adaptive shared control approach (as in Balachandran et al., 2020a) with possibilities for human intervention with more ease along with optimal placement of the virtual fixtures using artificial intelligence and machine learning.

4.2. Caregiving (Shared Autonomy and Seamless Autonomy Activation)

The demographic change in most industrial countries will pose major challenges to national health-care systems and the society to be faced within the next decades. While the number of people requiring assistance and caregiving is continuously growing, the number of caregivers is not keeping up with that demand. Robotic systems can potentially contribute to bridge this gap between demand and supply (Riek, 2017). Only recently, various robotic systems were brought to market for this purpose (Ackerman, 2018; Gupta et al., 2019; Mišeikis et al., 2020). Such robots should be able to take over logistical tasks or assist in care or daily life. Besides technical aspects, also the simplicity and empathy in interactions are highly relevant for these assistance tasks (Pepito et al., 2020).

To mitigate the demographic challenges, the prototypical SMiLE[1] ecosystem has been developed as a holistic concept for robotic assistance in caregiving (Vogel et al., 2020). This ecosystem offers a variety of control modes and autonomy levels to meet the actual application at hand. However, a 100 % reliability of the autonomous capabilities is practically unrealistic and the requirements in terms of safety are enormous since the robots are operated in direct vicinity of humans. Therefore, telepresence technologies are applied to cover several aspects (see **Figure 11**). For example, in case of emergency a teleoperator can instantly gain control of the remote robot and take immediate actions before an ambulance arrives on site. Alternatively, the person in need of care can activate teleoperated human assistance, if desired, or the robot requests human support itself if the autonomous capabilities of the system do not suffice to solve a required task.

The SMiLE ecosystem foresees haptic input devices to control a large variety of heterogeneous robotic agents in order to increase their reliability and efficiency. Therefore, a uniform control structure has been developed in which the robotic agents act at the users' requests, while seamlessly switching to remote

haptic teleoperation can be performed at any time. Besides the teleoperation coupling, the methods of supervised and shared autonomy are also designed in a robot agnostic way. Within the SMiLE ecosystem, these operation modes are fused with the delayed teleoperation control structure to augment the human operator with the model-based capabilities of the robot-side intelligence. Similar to autonomous functions, advanced control methods such as hierarchical whole-body control (Dietrich and Ott, 2020), which are parameterized with the knowledge of the remote model, can help to increase the usability of the robotic system.

It was shown that seamless switching to teleoperation can be achieved through the application of one common Cartesian controller for teleoperation and autonomous operation modes on the remote robot side. Furthermore, in order to sequentially couple one haptic device to a variety of robotic systems and to augment the human operator with the shared-autonomy functionalities, the coupling has to be designed in the Cartesian space as well. The results of SMiLE further confirm that the shared-autonomy functionalities can be stably combined with the time-delayed telemanipulation framework if the generation of the respective fictitious force feedback is designed with passive characteristics, as was outlined in section 2.4.

A challenge apparent in domestic use cases is the large variety of different objects and tasks the system has to handle. Here, the human teleoperator can not only serve as a fallback solution for tasks unknown to the system but the data generated in these task executions can help to increase the functionality of the autonomous agent. To this end, we investigate task representations that enable the definition of new tasks through learning by demonstration approaches.

4.3. Telesurgery (Bilateral Control Concepts and Haptic Augmentation)

The demographic change and the accompanied continuous development of medical technology to enable high quality of life is an important driving factor for surgical robotics technology. Goals of robotically assisted surgical systems (RASS) are manifold, ranging within the enhancement of surgical treatments in terms of safety for patients and clinicians, patient outcome, and short convalescence. Already in the 1970s first concepts of RASS were considered based on telemanipulation (Alexander, 1973). Nowadays more than 7 million procedures have been performed assisted by RASS, many of them by the da Vinci Surgical System (Intuitive Surgical Inc.), which embodies a telemanipulation system, similar to the envisioned system of the 1970s (Klodmann et al., 2020).

Since the 1990s DLR contributes to this field, e.g., one of the most mature research platforms for telemanipulation in robotic surgery, the DLR MiroSurge System, was developed (**Figure 12**) (Hagn et al., 2010; Seibold et al., 2018). The modular patient-side manipulator consists of one to multiple bed-mounted 7-DoF DLR MIRO robot arms. One arm is equipped with a stereo endoscope and the others carry various types of articulated, wristed instruments (DLR MICA). The surgeon console incorporates a stereo display to visualize the situs of

---

[1] The acronym SMiLE stands for service robotics for people in restricted living situations (in German "Servicerobotik für Menschen in Lebenssituationen mit Einschränkungen").

the patient in 3-D and two *sigma.7 (force dimension)* haptic devices are used as input devices (Tobergte et al., 2011). The system is the institute's core platform to research surgical robotics in interdisciplinary collaborations with industry, clinics, and complementary research institutions (MIRO Innovation Lab, 2017). Besides a seamless integration of RASS into a digitalized hospital infrastructure, the focus areas of research range from the acquisition and natural presentation of information from the situs to the surgeon, over enhancing the surgeon's dexterity inside the patient, while keeping the trauma low and providing natural controls, which assist with individualized and task-dependent assistance functions, e.g., utilizing virtual fixtures, shared control, or semi-autonomous functions, to further decrease the physician's cognitive workload (**Figure 12** and sections 2.2 and 2.3).

The basic control architecture maps the user inputs to joint positions of the patient-side manipulators by an inverse kinematics algorithm accounting for workspace constraints, singularities, and redundancy. This basic control architecture is continuously enhanced by different MATM-based approaches, as described in the following paragraphs.

Different passivity-based force feedback control approaches to increase the system's transparency, e.g., by downscaling the felt inertia and friction and dealing with other disturbances, were developed (Tobergte et al., 2011; Tobergte and Albu-Schäffer, 2012; Tobergte and Helmer, 2013). Even though many studies show that force/torque feedback might increase also surgical performance (Weber and Schneider, 2014), cost effective, sterilizable sensors integrable directly at the instrument tips are still not commercially available.

Haptically augmented workspace limits (e.g., of the haptic device, the remote manipulators or task-dependent constraints, such as the incision point constraint), limit-indexing or velocity scaling approaches support the safe and efficient control of the system. To appropriately configure and parameterize these features, user-studies based on best practices and standards of human factors are conducted and are generally recommendable (Nitsch et al., 2012; Weber et al., 2013).

A rich set of geometric primitives is implemented to provide task-related and haptically augmented virtual fixtures that are intended to finally enhance the surgeon's

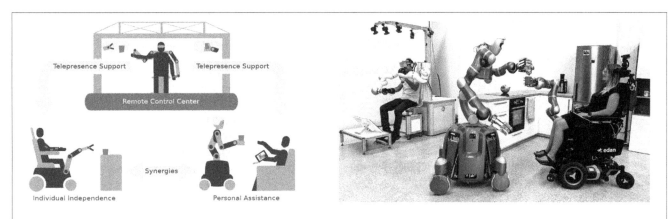

FIGURE 11 | (Left) Concept of the caregiving ecosystem *SMiLE*. **(Right)** Exemplary implementation (Vogel et al., 2020).

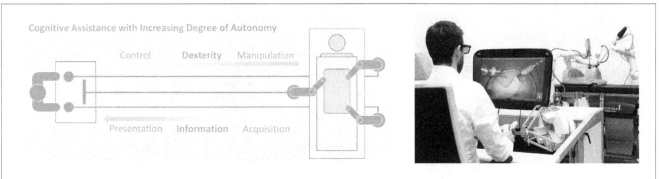

FIGURE 12 | (Left) Focus areas of surgical robotics research. (translated by permission from Springer Nature Customer Service Centre GmbH: Springer Nature, (Klodmann et al., 2020).

capabilities, e.g., by guiding toward or along target tissues or preventing unintentionally injuring critical anatomical structures. Perceiving the patient's situs accurately and reactively update the robot's knowledge or rather representation of patient and procedure (section 2.4) to appropriately configure and parameterize these features embody some still open research questions to finally integrate the concept of task-dependent assistance functions into realistic scenarios in robot-assisted laparoscopic surgery.

4.4. Telenavigation (Haptic Augmentation and Model-Mediated Telemanipulation)

The ambitious future of planetary exploration has the potential to push the boundaries of technological advancements. However, nondeterministic remote environment at communication delay might render full autonomy and supervised control as an unfeasible feat with laborious task execution times. Instead adding human to the loop, to telenavigate the robot, can bypass many of the task requirements especially in the fields of perception and cognition, and ensure safety. Unlike telemanipulation, telenavigation benefits from velocity as the command signal, instead of position. Nonetheless, it too presents us with the trade-off between performance and stability.

To examine the effect of such a trade-off, a recent study (Sierotowicz et al., 2020) was conducted to telenavigate a Light Weight Rover (LRU; Wedler et al., 2015) with and without delay, via a 2-DoF DLR force feedback joystick (Riecke et al., 2016) by using a predictive polygon-based approach with a car-like interface (Panzirsch et al., 2018b) (**Figure 13**). TDPA was extended and used as a tool to passivate the active communication channel, which injects energy to the system due to delay. The human operator commanded longitudinal velocity and lateral curvature to the LRU, by pressing the dead-man switch on the joystick, and in return received a fictitious force feedback computed by the overlapping of polygons with the obstacles in a danger map. The danger

map of the remote terrain is generated by classifying the traversability based on the depth data acquired by the LRU's pan/tilt stereo camera system (Brand et al., 2014), and is the local model that was used to generate haptic feedback (see section 2.2). A passive model update was achieved by Panzirsch et al. (2018b) (see section 2.4), which makes this a favorable approach in terms of applicability to a large variety of feedback generation types.

The main findings of the user study is that force feedback significantly improves navigation performance in the proximity of obstacles, although navigation is slower. The positive effect of the force feedback was evident in conditions without and with a communication delay of 800 ms. Altogether, these results show that a fictitious force feedback approach based on a TPDA controller is beneficial in difficult terrain and in the presence of substantial communication delay.

Apart from collision avoidance, the predictive polygon method could also help maintain a certain "safe" distance for the LRU from its environment. Since the width of the predictive polygons is a tunable factor, it can be adjusted to increase or decrease the safety factor or to allow/restrict the LRU's movement through narrow canyon-like environment. Despite of rate control, the TDPA could effectively stabilize and provide valuable force feedback with minimized position drift to the human operator. Thus, the haptic augmentation was beneficial with regard to navigation accuracy for demanding telenavigation tasks.

The 2-D danger map considers any object above a certain height as an obstacle. Thus, this would be impossible to tune when the LRU is traversing an unstructured environment. Therefore, a 2.5-D danger map with annotations would give more freedom to the operator and allow driving over small pebbles, grass, uneven roads, etc. Although a 2-DoF joystick could be used to maneuver the LRU with a car like interface, a 3-DoF haptic joystick could be used to fully explore LRU's potential of rear steering capabilities for crab-like and sideway motions.

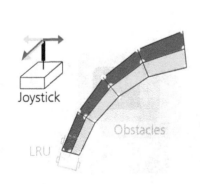 

FIGURE 13 | (Left) Schematic showing the generation of fictitious forces by polygons overlapping with obstacle in the danger map. **(Top Right)** Screenshot of the user interface. **(Bottom Right)** LRU with augmented polygons in the experimental environment.

4.5. Aerial Manipulation (Hierarchical Bilateral Teleoperation and Haptic Augmentation)

The use of aerial manipulators, i.e., unmanned aerial vehicles (UAVs) with attached robotic arms, allows for significant improvements in the reachability and versatility of manipulation tasks. Among other functionalities, such systems are able to perform inspection and maintenance tasks in high or inaccessible scenarios (e.g., oil refineries; Ollero et al., 2018). In order to exploit such systems while taking advantage of human capabilities in terms of perception and cognition, bilateral aerial teleoperation arises as a reasonable solution. In that scope, providing the user with camera images and/or virtual reality has been shown an essential feature for the successful fulfillment of the teleoperation task (Coelho et al., 2020; Lee et al., 2020).

Within the class of aerial manipulators, those presenting kinematic redundancy like the DLR Suspended Aerial Manipulator (SAM; Sarkisov et al., 2019; see **Figure 14**) are able to allow the user to not only control the robotic arm, but also steer the UAV (also called flying base) to achieve a desired camera view of the task being performed. Nevertheless, two main issues arise in that application. First, suitable control strategies have to be applied in order to ensure a strict hierarchy between the manipulation and the vision task, i.e., such that the flying base can move without disturbing the manipulation task. Additionally, as the traditional TDPA method is not capable of dealing with such a hierarchy in the presence of time delays, an extension thereof has to be applied.

An initial approach to cope with the aforementioned issues was introduced in Coelho et al. (2020) and a complete solution was subsequently presented in Coelho et al. (2021). A conceptual view of the presented approach is shown in **Figure 14** together with an overview of an experimental scenario. Using the proposed approach, the user was able to choose to command either vision or manipulation task while the other task was autonomously controlled to keep the last commanded pose in a shared-control fashion. As the vision task was restricted to the motion subset where the end-effector is not disturbed, a haptic concept called *Null-Space Wall* was created to inform the

user when the limits of that subset were reached. Moreover, the extended TDPA ensured the system passivity in simulations with up to 300 ms round-trip delay as well as in a real scenario, where command and feedback signals were exchanged through a wireless network with time delay, package loss, and jitter. The user was able to successfully perform pick-and-place tasks while keeping the manipulator and the object in the field of view. In addition, it was found that moving the flying base to align the camera image with the command directions of the input device can significantly decrease the task-completion time as well as the mental effort.

A current limitation of the proposed approach is that it does not take into account the constraints imposed by the cable system on the SAM. Therefore, it is only guaranteed to work when the oscillations of the base are negligible. An extension of the approach to deal with such constraints is planned for the near future. In addition, the visual-inertial odometry-based approach presented in Lee et al. (2020) to create a 3-D virtual-reality environment will be extended with haptic rendering capabilities. Moreover, the multilateral haptic augmentation method based on virtual grasping points (see section 2.2) could be especially meaningful in the described setup for the cases when the flying robot needs to keep some distance from obstacles. In that case, the robot grasping point on the manipulated object can be distant from the environment interaction point of the object, which can be chosen as the virtual grasping point.

4.6. On-Orbit Servicing (Shared Control)

Mitigation of space debris and servicing of dysfunctional satellites have driven space agencies and companies toward the concept of robotic on-orbit servicing (Miller et al., 1982). The term On-Orbit Servicing (OOS) refers to the maintenance in orbit, including assembly, refueling, and repair of defective satellites to extend their lifetime and to actively remove the space debris with a controlled re-entry into the Earth's atmosphere. To this end, space robotic projects consider the employment of a manipulator arm attached to a new satellite to implement the multiple phases of an OOS mission, namely, approaching a target satellite, followed by grasping, stabilization, docking, and finally servicing. In order to test and validate the low-level and

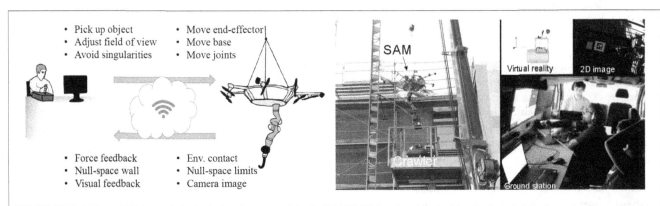

FIGURE 14 | (Left) Concept of the whole-body teleoperation approach for the SAM. **(Right)** Experimental setup, showing the robot, the ground station and the view provided to the user

high-level control strategies (aimed to be used in micro-gravity conditions) prior to the real mission, an on-ground facility to simulated the free-floating nature of the satellites. To achieve this, the OOS Simulator (OOS-Sim) hardware facility (**Figure 15**) has been developed at DLR, which comprises of two large industrial robots that simulate micro-gravity environment using model-based dynamic simulation for the satellite mock-ups attached to their end-effectors. The servicer satellite is equipped with a robot arm to service the target satellite mock-up (Artigas et al., 2015).

The manipulator arm attached to the satellite mock-up can be controlled using vision-based semi-autonomous control with the stereo camera set-up at the end-effector of the robotic arm. This semi-autonomous approach relies highly on perception of the target satellite, which is affected by internal and external factors such as camera noise, close range vision degradation, illumination changes, and reflections among many other (Schmidt et al., 2016). These factors might lead to a failure in the task execution by the autonomous system, and a human in the loop supervision is always preferred due to the critical nature of the orbital robotic missions.

To enable human intervention in the event of autonomy failure, the OOS-Sim also features teleoperation modality using a haptic device with which an operator can control the manipulator on the servicer satellite. To validate orbital teleoperation tasks in Low Earth Orbits (LEO) satellites with long operation windows using the OOS-Sim facility, experiments were conducted with the ASTRA GEO satellite acting as a relay system for the signals from the operator and the OOS-Sim manipulator, where the round-trip delay was 270 ms with standard deviation of 3 ms and a mean data loss of 24%. It was presented in Artigas et al. (2016a) that grasping and stabilization of the free-floating OOS-Sim target using the servicer manipulator with teleoperation is feasible even under large time delays and data losses.

5. CONCLUSION

Traditional bilateral teleoperation proved to be feasible up to time delays of several seconds round-trip (see section 2.1). However, task execution then becomes extremely difficult and slow. Particularly in scenarios with such long delays, a support of the operator by suitable technologies can be of great value. This paper introduced the MATM approach, which aims to enable effcient operator-assisting telemanipulation. The concept encompasses and generalizes previous approaches for enhanced telemanipulation, in particular model-mediated telemanipulation, shared autonomy, and augmented haptics. The approach employs two kinds of models to achieve this goal and to augment both the feedback to the operator and the commands for the teleoperated remote robot. In particular, a remote model enables a shared autonomous functionality of the teleoperated robot, while a local model aims at generating an assistive augmented haptic feedback to the human operator. This scope makes the MATM approach one of the

most comprehensive and powerful, but also one of the most technologically sophisticated and challenging telemanipulation approaches.

In a historical retrospective of our past telerobotic space missions, the way to this technology was described and the challenges we encountered during these missions were highlighted. The biggest challenge of the first missions we participated in, ROTEX and EST VII, was to overcome the hurdles that were imposed by the low computing power at that time that led to long time delays. Since these delays made closed-loop telemanipulation with force feedback impossible, our research concentrated on shared control and model prediction. Later, in ROKVISS and Kontur-2, the development of a control approach that allows stable and transparent bilateral telemanipulation despite delay, loss, and jitter of communication packets became the main focus of our research activities on telemanipulation. During the latter mission, basic research on the design of optimal haptic feedback was also conducted. In the more recent METERON mission, supervised autonomous operation was evaluated using a humanoid robot as an exemplary execution platform. It turned out during this mission that such an autonomous functionality can provide a great relieve for operating a robot and even allows for parallel operation of several robots. However, it also showed the limitation of autonomous operation especially in unstructured environments. Without human perception and cognition, a robot system will in the near future not be able to operate autonomously during a whole mission, although autonomy can already perform some specific robotic tasks today. These results suggest to combine autonomy and telemanipulation in an advantageous way, which is realized in particular with the remote model of MATM. In the recent Analog-1 mission, the telemanipulation technologies for the telenavigation of a rover through an unstructured environment and for the teleoperation of a robot arm mounted on this rover were evaluated. It could be shown for the first time that full-DoF direct teleoperation with force feedback can be robustly established for such a system and underlines the benefit of haptic feedback over open-loop teleoperation.

While these space missions were the main driver for our research on telemanipulation, the technology also has enormous potential for other applications, which was highlighted on the basis of six use cases. These use cases unveiled the potential and limitations of the MATM approach in the applications that reach from orbital applications over terrestrial telemanipulation in caregiving and telesurgery to applications that involve driving and flying robotic systems. In none of these use cases have we exploited the full spectrum of MATM so far, but rather emphasized certain aspects of it. The following lines give an overview of the most important results.

Haptic augmentation methods, in particular task- and system-related virtual fixtures demonstrated their usefulness in telesurgery, caregiving, and orbital robotics. In telenavigation, a predictive polygon method helped to maintain a certain "safe" distance for DLR's rover LRU from its environment and therefore to avoid collisions. We identified an enormous potential in

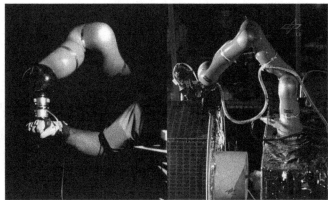

FIGURE 15 | (Left) The On-Orbit Servicing facility at DLR. **(Right)** The haptic device and the remote robot are of the same type of collaborative robot.

making haptic augmentation methods more flexible, which could be achieved by parameterizing them manually using human intervention or automatically by machine learning methods.

While in the presented use case of aerial manipulation, the autonomous functionality took control of a subtask and was thus used to support the operator, the shared control for on-orbit servicing showed that even proactive autonomous trajectory generation is comprehensible and clearly supportive for the operator. The mixed-initiative-based shared control present certain limitations, particularly if object recognition is affected by camera noise, close range vision degradation, illumination changes, and reflections. More adaptive approaches need to be developed in future enabling easier human intervention or automatic adaption of authority. With regard to the caregiving use case, it is apparent that the shared control approach is currently only able to handle objects that are previously known to the algorithm. To overcome this limitation, in the future new objects could be self-learned by learning-by-demonstration approaches.

With regard to stability, we could confirm in the caregiving use case that the combination of shared-autonomy functionalities and a time-delayed telemanipulation framework becomes stable if the respective fictitious force feedback is designed with passive features. All our available MATM modules for delayed teleoperation, bilateral, or multilateral haptic augmentation methods and model updates were implemented on the basis of passive modules, which can be almost arbitrarily combined without further stability considerations. Furthermore, seamless switching from autonomy to telemanipulation or between different teleoperated robots was enabled by a coupling control structure that can be readily transferred to comparable telerobotic systems as well.

Beyond these lessons learned and the challenges identified, a number of other important questions remain for future work, in particular to enable the MATM approach to be realized as a whole, incorporating all of its technologies. A robust and powerful solution for updating the symbolic models for supervised autonomy especially during the teleoperation phase is still an active topic of research. In relation to this task, the synchronization between the local and the remote model also needs to be developed. The passivity principle, which we applied to achieve stability, needs to be validated as a suitable tool for a general control framework to allow easy extension of the MATM approach for new applications and robots. Furthermore, a new transparency metric would be useful for comparing MATM with direct teleoperation methods and model-mediated teleoperation. Finally, as a big challenge remains the design of a user interface involving graphical, audio, and haptic channels that provides the operator access to all model-augmentation functionalities and control modalities reaching from direct teleoperation to supervised autonomy. While MATM has not been implemented as a whole, it has already proven its usefulness in numerous applications and plays an important role as intermediate step toward supervised and fully autonomous robots.

AUTHOR CONTRIBUTIONS

TH: contributed to all sections. AA-S: wrote section 1. GH: wrote section 3.1. CO: wrote section 2.1. DL: wrote sections 2.3 and 2.4. AD, JV, KH, AH, and JK: wrote section 4.3. RL: wrote section 4.6. MS: wrote section 4.4. AB: wrote sections 1, 2.3, and 2.4. GQ: wrote sections 2.2, 2.3, and 2.4. NL: wrote section 3.3. BB: wrote sections 3.1 and 3.2. CR: wrote section 3.2. NB: wrote section 2.1. BW: wrote sections 3.2, 4.3, and 4.4. AP: wrote section 3.4. AC: wrote section 4.5. RB: wrote sections 3.2, 4.1, 4.4, and 4.6. HS: wrote sections 1, 2.1, 4.4, and 5. MP: wrote sections 2.1 and 5. All authors contributed to the article and approved the submitted version.

FUNDING

This research work was funded by several funding sources. The work mention in section 2.1 was partially funded by the German

Research Foundation (DFG, Deutsche Forschungsgemeinschaft) as part of Germany's Excellence Strategy–EXC 2050/1–Project ID 390696704–Cluster of Excellence Centre for Tactile Internet with Human-in-the-Loop (CeTI) of Technische Universität Dresden. Section 4.1 contains results achieved in the project Space Factory 4.0 funded by German Aerospace Center (DLR) and the Federal Ministry for Economic Affairs and Energy (BMWi). The work of section 4.2 was partially funded by the Bavarian Ministry of Economic Affairs, Regional Development and Energy, within the projects SMiLE (LABAY97) and SMiLE2gether (LABAY102).

ACKNOWLEDGMENTS

The authors would like to thank Jordi Artigas, Katharina Hertkorn, Philipp Kremer, Carsten Preusche, Mikel Sagardia, and Simon Schätzle for the discussions and ideas about the MATM concept, and also thank Tilo Wüsthoff and Markus Grebenstein for their illustration of DLR's robotic vision in **Figure 1**. The authors would also like to express our deep appreciation for the close collaboration in METERON SUPVIS Justin and Analog-1, with our partners at the ESA Human Robot Interaction Laboratory headed by Thomas Krueger. Greatest appreciation also applies to our other partners at ESA, JAXA, and ROSCOSMOS for the productive cooperation.

REFERENCES

cyberneticzoo.com (2014). *1948-GE Master-Slave Manipulator-John Payne*. Available online at: http://cyberneticzoo.com/teleoperators/1948-ge-master-slave-manipulator-john-payne-american (accessed August 5, 2020).

Aarno, D., Ekvall, S., and Kragic, D. (2005). "Adaptive virtual fixtures for machine-assisted teleoperation tasks," in *IEEE International Conference on Robotics and Automation (ICRA)* (Barcelona), 1139–1144.

Ackerman, E. (2018). *Moxi Prototype From Diligent Robotics Starts Helping Out in Hospitals*. IEEE Spectrum. Available online at: https://spectrum.ieee.org/automaton/robotics/industrial-robots/moxi-prototype-fromdiligent-robotics-starts-helping-out-in-hospitals

Alexander, A. D. (1973). *On Theory and Practice of Robots and Manipulators*. Springer, 121–136.

Anderson, R. J. (1994). "Teleoperation with virtual force feedback," in *Experimental Robotics III*, eds T. Yoshikawa and F. Miyazaki (Berlin; Heidelberg: Springer Berlin Heidelberg), 366–375. doi: 10.1007/BFb0027608

Artigas, J., Balachandran, R., De Stefano, M., Panzirsch, M., Lampariello, R., Albu-Schaeffer, A., et al. (2016a). "Teleoperation for on-orbit servicing missions through the astra geostationary satellite," in *IEEE Aerospace Conference* (Big Sky), 1–12. doi: 10.1109/AERO.2016.7500785

Artigas, J., Balachandran, R., Riecke, C., Stelzer, M., Weber, B., Ryu, J.-H., et al. (2016b). "Kontur-2: force-feedback teleoperation from the international space station," in *IEEE International Conference on Robotics and Automation (ICRA)* (Stockholm), 1166–1173. doi: 10.1109/ICRA.2016.7487246

Artigas, J., De Stefano, M., Rackl, W., Lampariello, R., Brunner, B., Bertleff, W., et al. (2015). "The oos-sim: an on-ground simulation facility for on-orbit servicing robotic operations," in *IEEE International Conference on Robotics and Automation (ICRA)* (Seattle, WA: IEEE), 2854–2860. doi: 10.1109/ICRA.2015.7139588

Artigas, J., and Hirzinger, G. (2016). A brief history of DLR's space telerobotics and force feedback teleoperation. *Acta Polytech. Hungar.* 13, 239–249. doi: 10.12700/APH.13.1.2016.1.16

Balachandran, R., Mishra, H., Cappelli, M., Weber, B., Secchi, C., Ott, C., et al. (2020a). "Adaptive authority allocation in shared control of robots using Bayesian filters," in *IEEE International Conference on Robotics and Automation (ICRA)* (Paris). doi: 10.1109/ICRA40945.2020.9196941

Balachandran, R., Ryu, J.-H., Jorda, M., Ott, C., and Albu-Schaeffer, A. (2020b). "Closing the force loop to enhance transparency in time-delayed teleoperation," in *IEEE International Conference on Robotics and Automation (ICRA)* (Paris). doi: 10.1109/ICRA40945.2020.9197420

Bauer, A. S., Schmaus, P., Albu-Schäffer, A., and Leidner, D. (2018). "Inferring semantic state transitions during telerobotic manipulation," in *IEEE/RSJ International Conference on Intelligent Robots and Systems (IROS)* (Madrid), 5517–5524. doi: 10.1109/IROS.2018.8594458

Bauer, A. S., Schmaus, P., Stulp, F., and Leidner, D. (2020). "Probabilistic effect prediction through semantic augmentation and physical simulation," in *IEEE International Conference on Robotics and Automation (ICRA)* (Paris). doi: 10.1109/ICRA40945.2020.9197477

Bayer, R., Schmaus, P., Pfau, M., Pleintinger, B., Leidner, D., Wappler, F., et al. (2019). "Deployment of the solex environment for analog space telerobotics validation," in *Int. Astronautical Congress (IAC)* (Washington, DC: IAF).

Beik-Mohammadi, H., Kerzel, M., Pleintinger, B., Hulin, T., Reisich, P., Schmidt, A., et al. (2020). "Model mediated teleoperation with a hand-arm exoskeleton in long time delays using reinforcement learning," in *IEEE International Symposium in Robot and Human Interactive Communication (Ro-Man)* (Naples, FL). doi: 10.1109/RO-MAN47096.2020.9223477

Birkenkampf, P., Leidner, D., and Borst, C. (2014). "A knowledge-driven shared autonomy human-robot interface for tablet computers," in *2014 IEEE-RAS International Conference on Humanoid Robots* (Madrid), 152–159. doi: 10.1109/HUMANOIDS.2014.7041352

Borst, C., Ott, C., Wimböck, T., Brunner, B., Zacharias, F., Bäuml, B., et al. (2007). "A humanoid upper body system for two-handed manipulation," in *IEEE International Conference on Robotics and Automation (ICRA)* (Roma), Vol. 2, 2766–2767. doi: 10.1109/ROBOT.2007.363886

Borst, C., Wimböck, T., Schmidt, F., Fuchs, M., Brunner, B., Zacharias, F., et al. (2009). "Rollin' justin - mobile platform with variable base," in *IEEE International Conference on Robotics and Automation (ICRA)* (Kobe), 1597–1598. doi: 10.1109/ROBOT.2009.5152586

Bowyer, S. A., Davies, B. L., and y Baena, F. R. (2013). Active constraints/virtual fixtures: a survey. *IEEE Trans. Robot.* 30, 138–157. doi: 10.1109/TRO.2013.2283410

Brand, C., Schuster, M. J., Hirschmüller, H., and Suppa, M. (2014). "Stereo-vision based obstacle mapping for indoor/outdoor slam," in *IEEE/RSJ International Conference on Intelligent Robots and Systems (IROS)* (Chicago, IL), 1846–1853. doi: 10.1109/IROS.2014.6942805

Brunner, B., Landzettel, K., Schreiber, G., Steinmetz, B. M., and Hirzinger, G. (1999). "A universal task level ground control and programming system for space robot applications - the MARCO concept and it's application to the ETS VII project," in *International Symposium on Artifical Intelligence, Robotics, and Automation in Space (i-SAIRAS)* (Noordwijk), 507–514.

Coelho, A., Sarkisov, Y., Wu, X., Mishra, H., Singh, H., Dietrich, A., et al. (2021). Whole-body teleoperation and shared control of redundant robots with applications to aerial manipulation. *J. Intell. Robot. Syst.* 102, 1–22. doi: 10.1007/s10846-021-01365-7

Coelho, A., Singh, H., Kondak, K., and Ott, C. (2020). "Whole-body bilateral teleoperation of a redundant aerial manipulator," in *IEEE International Conference on Robotics and Automation (ICRA)* (Paris), 9150–9156. doi: 10.1109/ICRA40945.2020.9197028

Coelho, A., Singh, H., Muskardin, T., Balachandran, R., and Kondak, K. (2018). "Smoother position-drift compensation for time domain passivity approach based teleoperation," in *IEEE/RSJ International Conference on Intelligent Robots and Systems (IROS)* (Madrid: IEEE), 5525–5532. doi: 10.1109/IROS.2018.8594125

Dietrich, A., and Ott, C. (2020). Hierarchical impedance-based tracking control of kinematically redundant robots. *IEEE Trans. Robot.* 36, 204–221. doi: 10.1109/TRO.2019.2945876

Ferrell, W. R. (1965). Remote manipulation with transmission delay. *IEEE Trans. Hum. Fact. Electron.* HFE-6, 24–32. doi: 10.1109/THFE.1965.6591253

Ferrell, W. R., and Sheridan, T. B. (1967). Supervisory control of remote manipulation. *IEEE Spectr.* 4, 81–88. doi: 10.1109/MSPEC.1967.5217126

Fong, T., Thorpe, C., and Baur, C. (2001). "A safeguarded teleoperation controller," in *IEEE International Conference on Advanced Robotics (ICAR)* (Budapest), 351–356.

Ghallab, M., Howe, A., Christianson, D., McDermott, D., Ram, A., Veloso, M., et al. (1998). PDDL - The planning domain definition language. *AIPS98 Plann. Commit.* 78, 1–27.

Goldfarb, M. (1998). "Dimensional analysis and selective distortion in scaled bilateral telemanipulation," in *IEEE International Conference on Robotics and Automation (ICRA)*, Vol. 2, (Leuven), 1609–1614. doi: 10.1109/ROBOT.1998.677379

Goodrich, M. A., Crandall, J. W., and Barakova, E. (2013). Teleoperation and beyond for assistive humanoid robots. *Rev. Hum. Fact. Ergon.* 9, 175–226. doi: 10.1177/1557234X13502463

Gupta, N., Smith, J., Shrewsbury, B., and Börnich, B. (2019). "2D push recovery and balancing of the eve R3-a humanoid robot with wheel-base, using model predictive control and gain scheduling," in *2019 IEEE-RAS 19th International Conference on Humanoid Robots (Humanoids)* (Toronto, ON), 365–372. doi: 10.1109/Humanoids43949.2019.9035044

Hagn, U., Konietschke, R., Tobergte, A., Nickl, M., Jörg, S., Kübler, B., et al. (2010). DLR MiroSurge: a versatile system for research in endoscopic telesurgery. *Int. J. Comput. Assist. Radiol. Surg.* 5, 183–193. doi: 10.1007/s11548-009-0372-4

Hannaford, B. (1989). A design framework for teleoperators with kinesthetic feedback. *IEEE Trans. Robot. Autom.* 5, 426–434. doi: 10.1109/70.88057

Hannaford, B., and Ryu, J.-H. (2002). Time-domain passivity control of haptic interfaces. *IEEE Trans. Robot. Autom.* 18, 1–10. doi: 10.1109/70.988969

Hertkorn, K. (2016). *Shared grasping: a combination of telepresence and grasp planning* (Ph.D. thesis). Karlsruher Institut für Technologie (KIT), Karlsruhe, Germany.

Hirzinger, G., Brunner, B., Dietrich, J., and Heindl, J. (1993). Sensor-based space robotics - rotex and its telerobotic features. *IEEE Trans. Robot. Autom.* 9, 649–663. doi: 10.1109/70.258056

Hulin, T., González Camarero, R., and Albu-Schäffer, A. (2013). "Optimal control for haptic rendering: Fast energy dissipation and minimum overshoot," in *IEEE/RSJ International Conference on Intelligent Robots and Systems (IROS)* (Tokyo), 4505–4511. doi: 10.1109/IROS.2013.6697004

Inagaki, T. (2003). "Adaptive automation: Sharing and trading of control," in *Handbook of Cognitive Task Design*, Vol. 8, eds, Hollnagel, Erik (Mahawa, NJ: Lawrence Erlbaum Associates, Inc.), 147–169. doi: 10.1201/9781410607775.ch8

Johnsen, E. G., and Corliss, W. R. (1971). *Human Factors Applications in Teleoperator Design and Operation*. New York, NY: Wiley-Interscience.

Kang, H., Park, Y. S., Ewing, T. F., Faulring, E., and Colgate, J. E. (2004). "Visually and haptically augmented teleoperation in D&D tasks using virtual fixtures," in *International Conference on Robotics and Remote Systems for Hazardous Environments* (Gainesville, FL), 466–471.

Klodmann, J., Schlenk, C., Borsdorf, S., Unterhinninghofen, R., Albu-Schäffer, A., and Hirzinger, G. (2020). Robotische assistenzsysteme für die chirurgie. *Der Chirurg* 91, 533–543.. doi: 10.1007/s00104-020-01205-8

Lawrence, D. A. (1993). Stability and transparency in bilateral teleoperation. *IEEE Trans. Robot. Autom.* 9, 624–637. doi: 10.1109/70.258054

Lee, J., Balachandran, R., Sarkisov, Y., De Stefano, M., Coelho, A., Shinde, K., et al. (2020). "Visual-inertial telepresence for aerial manipulation," in *IEEE International Conference on Robotics and Automation (ICRA)* (Paris), 1222–1229. doi: 10.1109/ICRA40945.2020.9197394

Leidner, D. S. (2019). *Cognitive Reasoning for Compliant Robot Manipulation*. Springer. doi: 10.1007/978-3-030-04858-7

Lii, N. Y., Riecke, C., Leidner, D., Schätzle, S., Schmaus, P., Weber, B., et al. (2018). "The robot as an avatar or co-worker? An investigation of the different teleoperation modalities through the KONTUR-2 and meteron supvis justin space telerobotic missions," in *Int. Astronautical Congress (IAC)* (Bremen).

McNeely, W. A., Puterbaugh, K. D., and Troy, J. J. (2006). Voxel-based 6-DOF haptic rendering improvements. *Haptics-e* 3:50. doi: 10.1145/1198555.1198606

Miller, R., Minsky, M. L., and Smith, D. B. (1982). *Space Applications of Automation, Robotics and Machine Intelligence Systems (ARAMIS), Vol. 1: Executive Summary*. NASA.

MIRO Innovation Lab (2017). *MIRO Innovation Lab*. Available online at: https://miroinnovationlab.de/en/home-en/index.html (accessed September 22, 2020).

Mišeikis, J., Caroni, P., Duchamp, P., Gasser, A., Marko, R., Mišeikienė, N., et al. (2020). Lio-a personal robot assistant for human-robot interaction and care applications. *IEEE Robot. Autom. Lett.* 5, 5339–5346. doi: 10.1109/LRA.2020.3007462

Mitra, P., and Niemeyer, G. (2008). Model-mediated telemanipulation. *Int. J. Robot. Res.* 27, 253–262. doi: 10.1177/0278364907084590

Musić, S., and Hirche, S. (2017). Control sharing in human-robot team interaction. *Annu. Rev. Control* 44, 342–354. doi: 10.1016/j.arcontrol.2017.09.017

Napoli, J., and Kugler, M. S. (2017). "The additive manufacturing facility: one year on the iss national lab," in *Proceedings of the ISS Research and Development Conference*. Washington, DC.

Nitsch, V., Färber, B., Hellings, A., Jörg, S., Tobergte, A., and Konietschke, R. (2012). "Bi-modal assistance functions and their effect on user perception and movement coordination with telesurgery systems," in *2012 IEEE International Workshop on Haptic Audio Visual Environments and Games (HAVE 2012) Proceedings* (Munich), 32–37. doi: 10.1109/HAVE.2012.6374427

Ollero, A., Heredia, G., Franchi, A., Antonelli, G., Kondak, K., Sanfeliu, A., et al. (2018). The Aeroarms project: aerial robots with advanced manipulation capabilities for inspection and maintenance. *IEEE Robot. Autom. Mag.* 25, 12–23. doi: 10.1109/MRA.2018.2852789

Onal, C. D., and Sitti, M. (2009). A scaled bilateral control system for experimental one-dimensional teleoperated nanomanipulation. *Int. J. Robot. Res.* 28, 484–497. doi: 10.1177/0278364908097773

Panzirsch, M., Artigas, J., Ryu, J.-H., and Ferre, M. (2013). "Multilateral control for delayed teleoperation," in *2013 16th International Conference on Advanced Robotics (ICAR)* (Montevideo), 1–6. doi: 10.1109/ICAR.2013.6766476

Panzirsch, M., Balachandran, R., Artigas, J., Riecke, C., Ferre, M., and Albu-Schaeffer, A. (2017). "Haptic intention augmentation for cooperative teleoperation," in *IEEE International Conference on Robotics and Automation (ICRA)* (Singapore), 5335–5341. doi: 10.1109/ICRA.2017.7989627

Panzirsch, M., Balachandran, R., Weber, B., Ferre, M., and Artigas, J. (2018a). Haptic augmentation for teleoperation through virtual grasping points. *IEEE Trans. Hapt*, Big Sky. 11, 400–416. doi: 10.1109/TOH.2018.2809746

Panzirsch, M., Singh, H., Kruger, T., Ott, C., and Albu-Schaffer, A. (2020a). "Safe interactions and kinesthetic feedback in high performance earth-to-moon teleoperation," in *IEEE Aerospace Conference* (Big Sky). doi: 10.1109/AERO47225.2020.9172665

Panzirsch, M., Singh, H., and Ott, C. (2020b). The 6-dof implementation of the energy-reflection based time domain passivity approach with preservation of physical coupling behavior. *IEEE Robot. Autom. Lett.* 5, 6756–6763. doi: 10.1109/LRA.2020.3010727

Panzirsch, M., Singh, H., Stelzer, M., Schuster, M. J., Ott, C., and Ferre, M. (2018b). "Extended predictive model-mediated teleoperation of mobile robots through multilateral control," in *IEEE Intelligent Vehicles Symposium (IV)* (Changshu), 1723–1730. doi: 10.1109/IVS.2018.8500578

Parasuraman, R., and Riley, V. (1997). Humans and automation: use, misuse, disuse, abuse. *Hum. Fact.* 39, 230–253. doi: 10.1518/001872097778543886

Passenberg, C., Peer, A., and Buss, M. (2010). "Model-mediated teleoperation for multi-operator multi-robot systems," in *IEEE/RSJ International Conference on Intelligent Robots and Systems (IROS)* (Taipei), 4263–4268. doi: 10.1109/IROS.2010.5653012

Payandeh, S., and Stanisic, Z. (2002). "On application of virtual fixtures as an aid for telemanipulation and training," in *IEEE Haptics Symposium* (Orlando, FL), 18–23. doi: 10.1109/HAPTIC.2002.998936

Pepito, J. A., Ito, H., Betriana, F., Tanioka, T., and Locsin, R. C. (2020). Intelligent humanoid robots expressing artificial humanlike empathy in nursing situations. *Nursing Philos.* 21:e12318. doi: 10.1111/nup.12318

Preusche, C., Reintsema, D., Landzettel, K., and Hirzinger, G. (2006). "Robotics component verification on iss rokviss - preliminary results for telepresence," in *IEEE/RSJ International Conference on Intelligent Robots and Systems (IROS)* (Beijing), 4595–4601. doi: 10.1109/IROS.2006.282165

Quere, G., Hagengruber, A., Iskandar, M., Bustamante, S., Leidner, D., Stulp, F., et al. (2020). "Shared control templates for assistive robotics," in *IEEE International Conference on Robotics and Automation (ICRA)* (Paris), 1956–1962. doi: 10.1109/ICRA40945.2020.9197041

Riecke, C., Artigas, J., Balachandran, R., Bayer, R., Beyer, A., Brunner, B., et al. (2016). "Kontur-2 mission: the DLR force feedback joystick for space telemanipulation from the ISS," in *International Symposium on Artifical Intelligence, Robotics, and Automation in Space (i-SAIRAS)* (Beijing).

Riecke, C., Weber, B., Maier, M., Stelzer, M., Balachandran, R., Kondratiev, A., et al. (2020). "Kontur-3: Human machine interfaces for telenavigation and manipulation of robots from ISS," in *IEEE Aerospace Conference* (Big Sky), 1–10. doi: 10.1109/AERO47225.2020.9172347

Riek, L. D. (2017). Healthcare robotics. *Commun. ACM* 60, 68–78. doi: 10.1145/3127874

Rosenberg, L. B. (1992). *The Use of Virtual Fixtures as Perceptual Overlays to Enhance Operator Performance in Remote Environments*. Technical report, Wright-Patterson AFB OH: USAF Armstrong Laboratory.

Rosenberg, L. B. (1993a). "The use of virtual fixtures to enhance telemanipulation with time delay," in *Proceedings of the ASME Winter Annual Meeting on Advances in Robotics, Mechatronics, and Haptic Interfaces*, Vol. 49, (New Orleans, LA), 29–36.

Rosenberg, L. B. (1993b). "Virtual fixtures: perceptual tools for telerobotic manipulation," in *Proceedings of IEEE Virtual Reality Annual International Symposium* (Seattle, WA), 76–82. doi: 10.1109/VRAIS.1993.380795

Ryu, J.-H., Artigas, J., and Preusche, C. (2010). A passive bilateral control scheme for a teleoperator with time-varying communication delay. *Mechatronics* 20, 812–823. doi: 10.1016/j.mechatronics.2010.07.006

Sagardia, M. (2019). *Virtual manipulations with force feedback in complex interaction scenarios* (Ph.D. thesis). Technische Universität München, Munich, Germany.

Sagardia, M., Stouraitis, T., and e Silva, J. L. (2014). "A new fast and robust collision detection and force computation algorithm applied to the physics engine bullet: method, integration, and evaluation," in *EuroVR* (Bremen), 65–76.

Sarkisov, Y. S., Kim, M. J., Bicego, D., Tsetserukou, D., Ott, C., Franchi, A., et al. (2019). "Development of SAM: cable-suspended aerial manipulator," in *IEEE International Conference on Robotics and Automation (ICRA)*, 5323–5329. doi: 10.1109/ICRA.2019.8793592

Schmaus, P., Leidner, D., Krüger, T., Bayer, R., Pleintinger, B., Schiele, A., et al. (2019). Knowledge driven orbit-to-ground teleoperation of a robot coworker. *IEEE Robot. Autom. Lett*, IEEE. 5, 143–150. doi: 10.1109/LRA.2019.2948128

Schmidt, P., Balachandran, R., and Artigas Esclusa, J. (2016). "Shared control for robotic on-orbit servicing," in *The Robotics: Science and Systems*. Available online at: https://elib.dlr.de/113169

Seibold, U., Kübler, B., Bahls, T., Haslinger, R., and Steidle, F. (2018). The DLR MiroSurge surgical robotic demonstrator. *Encyclop. Med. Robot.* 1, 111–142. doi: 10.1142/9789813232266_0005

Sheridan, T. B. (1992). *Telerobotics, Automation, and Human Supervisory Control*. Cambridge, MA: MIT Press.

Sierotowicz, M., Weber, B., Belder, R., Bussmann, K., Singh, H., and Panzirsch, M. (2020). "Investigating the influence of haptic feedback in rover navigation with communication delay," in *EuroHaptics* (Paris), 1723–1730. doi: 10.1007/978-3-030-58147-3_58

Singh, H., Jafari, A., Peer, A., and Ryu, J.-H. (2018). "Enhancing the command-following bandwidth for transparent bilateral teleoperation," in *IEEE/RSJ International Conference on Intelligent Robots and Systems (IROS)* (Madrid), 4972–4979. doi: 10.1109/IROS.2018.8593866

Singh, H., Jafari, A., and Ryu, J.-H. (2019a). "Enhancing the force transparency of time domain passivity approach: observer-based gradient controller," in *IEEE International Conference on Robotics and Automation (ICRA)* (Montreal, QC), 1583–1589. doi: 10.1109/ICRA.2019.8793902

Singh, H., Janetzko, D., Jafari, A., Weber, B., Lee, C.-I., and Ryu, J.-H. (2019b). Enhancing the rate-hardness of haptic interaction: successive force augmentation approach. *IEEE Trans. Indus. Electron.* 67, 809–819. doi: 10.1109/TIE.2019.2918500

Singh, H., Panzirsch, M., Coelho, A., and Ott, C. (2020). Proxy-based approach for position synchronization of delayed robot coupling

without sacrificing performance. *IEEE Robot. Autom. Lett.* 5, 6599–6606. doi: 10.1109/LRA.2020.3013860

Spaceflight (2020). *Pricing Information*. Available online at: http://spaceflight.com/schedulepricing/pricing (accessed August 26, 2020).

Sundermeyer, M., Marton, Z.-C., Durner, M., Brucker, M., and Triebel, R. (2018). "Implicit 3d orientation learning for 6d object detection from RGB images," in *Proceedings of the European Conference on Computer Vision (ECCV)* (Munich). doi: 10.1007/978-3-030-01231-1_43

Tobergte, A., and Albu-Schäffer, A. (2012). "Direct force reflecting teleoperation with a flexible joint robot," in *IEEE International Conference on Robotics and Automation (ICRA)* (Saint Paul, MN), 4280–4287. doi: 10.1109/ICRA.2012.6224617

Tobergte, A., and Helmer, P. (2013). "A disturbance observer for the sigma. 7 haptic device," in *2013 IEEE/RSJ International Conference on Intelligent Robots and Systems* (Tokyo), 4964–4969. doi: 10.1109/IROS.2013.6697073

Tobergte, A., Helmer, P., Hagn, U., Rouiller, P., Thielmann, S., Grange, S., et al. (2011). "The sigma. 7 haptic interface for mirosurge: a new bi-manual surgical console," in *2011 IEEE/RSJ International Conference on Intelligent Robots and Systems* (San Francisco, CA), 3023–3030. doi: 10.1109/IROS.2011.6048043

Turro, N., and Khatib, O. (2001). "Haptically augmented teleoperation," in *IEEE International Conference on Robotics and Automation (ICRA)* (Seoul; Springer), 386–392.

Vogel, J., Leidner, D., Hagengruber, A., Panzirsch, M., Bäuml, B., Denninger, M., et al. (2020). An ecosystem for heterogeneous robotic assistants in caregiving. *IEEE Robot. Autom. Mag.* doi: 10.1109/MRA.2020.3032142

Weber Martins, T., Pereira, A., Hulin, T., Ruf, O., Kugler, S., Giordano, A., et al. (2018). "Space factory 4.0-new processes for the robotic assembly of modular satellites on an in-orbit platform based on industrie 4.0 approach," in *Proceedings of the International Astronautical Congress (IAC)* (Bremen: IAC).

Weber, B., Balachandran, R., Riecke, C., Stulp, F., and Stelzer, M. (2019). "Teleoperating robots from the international space station: microgravity effects on performance with force feedback," in *IEEE/RSJ International Conference on Intelligent Robots and Systems (IROS)* (Macau), 8138–8144. doi: 10.1109/IROS40897.2019.8968030

Weber, B., Hellings, A., Tobergte, A., and Lohmann, M. (2013). "Human performance and workload evaluation of input modalities for telesurgery," in *Chancen durch Produkt- und Systemgestaltung - Zukunftsfähigkeit für Produktions- und Dienstleistungsunternehmen*, ed German Society of Ergonomics (GfA) (Dortmund: GfA-Press), 409–412.

Weber, B., Panzirsch, M., Stulp, F., and Schneider, S. (2020). Sensorimotor performance and haptic support in simulated weightlessness. *Exp. Brain Res.* 238, 2373–2384. doi: 10.1007/s00221-020-05898-5

Weber, B., and Schneider, S. (2014). "The effects of force feedback on surgical task performance: a meta-analytical integration," in *International Conference on Human Haptic Sensing and Touch Enabled Computer Applications* (Versailles: Springer), 150–157. doi: 10.1007/978-3-662-44196-1_19

Wedler, A., Rebele, B., Reill, J., Suppa, M., Hirschmüller, H., Brand, C., et al. (2015). "LRU-lightweight rover unit," in *Proceedings of the 13th Symposium on Advanced Space Technologies in Robotics and Automation (ASTRA)* (Noordwijk).

Xia, T., Léonard, S., Deguet, A., Whitcomb, L., and Kazanzides, P. (2012). "Augmented reality environment with virtual fixtures for robotic telemanipulation in space," in *IEEE/RSJ Int. Conf. on Intelligent Robots and Systems (IROS)* (Vilamoura), 5059–5064. doi: 10.1109/IROS.2012.6386169

Xu, X., Cizmeci, B., Schuwerk, C., and Steinbach, E. (2016). Model-mediated teleoperation: toward stable and transparent teleoperation systems. *IEEE Access* 4, 425–449. doi: 10.1109/ACCESS.2016.2517926

Xu, X., Schuwerk, C., and Steinbach, E. (2015). "Passivity-based model updating for model-mediated teleoperation," in *2015 IEEE International Conference on Multimedia & Expo Workshops (ICMEW)* (Torino), 1–6. doi: 10.1109/ICMEW.2015.7169831

11

Visual Haptic Feedback for Training of Robotic Suturing

François Jourdes[1], Brice Valentin[1], Jérémie Allard[1], Christian Duriez[2] and
Barbara Seeliger[3,4,5,6]*

[1]InSimo SAS, Strasbourg, France, [2]DEFROST Team, UMR 9189 CRIStAL, CNRS, Centrale Lille, Inria, University of Lille, Lille,
France, [3]IHU-Strasbourg, Institute of Image-Guided Surgery, Strasbourg, France, [4]Department of General, Digestive, and
Endocrine Surgery, University Hospitals of Strasbourg, Strasbourg, France, [5]ICube, UMR 7357 CNRS, University of Strasbourg,
Strasbourg, France, [6]IRCAD, Research Institute Against Digestive Cancer, Strasbourg, France

*Correspondence:
Barbara Seeliger
barbara.seeliger@ihu-strasbourg.eu

Current surgical robotic systems are teleoperated and do not have force feedback. Considerable practice is required to learn how to use visual input such as tissue deformation upon contact as a substitute for tactile sense. Thus, unnecessarily high forces are observed in novices, prior to specific robotic training, and visual force feedback studies demonstrated reduction of applied forces. Simulation exercises with realistic suturing tasks can provide training outside the operating room. This paper presents contributions to realistic interactive suture simulation for training of suturing and knot-tying tasks commonly used in robotically-assisted surgery. To improve the realism of the simulation, we developed a global coordinate wire model with a new constraint development for the elongation. We demonstrated that a continuous modeling of the contacts avoids instabilities during knot tightening. Visual cues are additionally provided, based on the computation of mechanical forces or constraints, to support learning how to dose the forces. The results are integrated into a powerful system-agnostic simulator, and the comparison with equivalent tasks performed with the da Vinci Xi system confirms its realism.

Keywords: surgical simulation, haptics, knot-tying, collision detection, virtual reality, robotic surgery training, minimally invasive surgery

1 INTRODUCTION

Traditionally, in open surgery, surgeons' fingertips sensed tension on tissue and suture threads. In minimally invasive surgery, sensory perception is reduced as the interaction is mediated by an instrument. In robot-assisted surgery, tele-manipulation implies that there is no more direct physical interaction between surgeon and patient. Force sensing and feedback could transmit a sense of touch, but they are not typically available in current platforms Amirabdollahian et al. (2018); Miller et al. (2021). Consequently, surgeons rely on visual cues such as tissue distensibility and deformation, in order to get a "feel" for it. Perception of visual input as a tactile sense is an acquired skill and needs considerable practice.

Suturing and knot tying are basic surgical skills required for various procedures amongst all surgical specialties. In minimally invasive surgery, sutures are performed with long and rigid instruments in angles determined by the trocar positions. These constraints have to be overcome by optimal needle and instrument positioning and by a sometimes challenging surgical technique. Robotic surgical systems provide an enhanced interface with articulating instruments reproducing surgeons' wrist movements and angulation. However, robotic control interfaces typically do not provide force or tactile feedback. Thus, the application of excessive force is a common phenomenon when robotic novices familiarize with a system. During suturing tasks, such shearing and tearing forces lead to needle deformation or breaking as well as suture breakage. Training on the robotic system is needed to adapt the suturing technique in order to apply the correct amount of tension for tightening a suture or knot without too much strain. In the recent systematic review of Golahmadi et al. (2021), assessing instrument-tissue interaction forces exerted during surgery across different specialities, the comparison of mean average forces between groups showed that novices exerted 22.7% more force than experts, and that the presence of a feedback mechanism reduced exerted forces by 47.9%. Thus, trainees particularly benefit from force feedback.

Suture breakage is significantly more common in surgeons inexperienced in robotics when compared to trained robotic surgeons. Reiley et al. (2008) demonstrated that visual force feedback (VFF) is particularly advantageous for novice surgeons, with significantly reduced suture breakage rates, as well as peak and standard deviations of applied forces during knot-tying with a da Vinci robotic system equipped with force-sensing instrument tips. In contrast, the presence or absence of VFF did not change measured performance parameters among experienced robotic surgeons. It was suggested that VFF is better than physical force feedback in terms of knot quality. Interestingly, visual haptics also significantly reduced information flow as determined by brain wave sensing, suggesting a lower cognitive burden with superimposed visual cues during robot manipulation in a VR environment, while increasing task performance as presented by Haruna et al. (2020).

Virtual Reality (VR) simulators provide a unique training environment with an unlimited number of repetitions possible for suturing and knot tying tasks and practice. Additional visual cues can be integrated to enable VFF. A suture training model for robotic surgery requires the integration of a realistic suture thread performance in the virtual simulator environment. The present work proposes a new simulation approach for suture training, based on precise mechanics of suture behavior and its interactions with tissues. It integrates a realistic thread simulation for suturing and knot-tying, as well as a real-time computation of the stress fields, especially on the thread. A colour-coded force feedback based on the stress fields can be activated to alert surgeons when excessive force is applied during VR robotic suturing, in order to avoid excessive shearing forces. These haptic cues illustrating the influence of trainees' gestures on the mechanical balance can enhance training to adapt to the absence of tactile feedback in the non-virtual robotic surgery environment.

To build such a simulator, the best possible trade-off between physics realism and latency has to be found. Latency to compute physics has to be compatible with visual rendering (minimum 30 Hz) and haptic rendering (500 Hz to 1 kHz). At the same time, latency has to be minimized since it decreases surgical performance, as shown in robotic long-distance telesurgery studies like Marescaux et al. (2001) and Doarn et al. (2009). If fast (latency-less) simulation comes at the price of model inaccuracy in reproducing knot-tying or sutures, learning of the entire sequence is impaired. Therefore, a number of technical challenges have been answered in this study with new methods that are presented in this paper. Our approach is based on the work of Guébert et al. (2009) to which we bring the following contributions:

- The mechanical model of the suture thread, based on the theory of beams in global coordinates is constrained in length. The formulation is compatible with the calculation of mechanical stress on the thread and allows for adding visual cues and simulation (detection) of breakage,
- A smooth collision and contact response formulation based on curves allows for more consistent behavior than with serial segments,
- The real-time simulation of knot tying in a stable and physical way is simulated up to the end of the tightening,
- A realistic suture training simulator is demonstrated on basic exercises, where they can be compared to videos of training actually performed with a surgical robot.

2 RELATED WORK

2.1 Virtual Reality Robotic Surgery Simulators

2.1.1 Commercial Products

There are two different types of robotic surgery VR simulators: the specific "backpack" ones for each of the commercial platforms (e.g., *SimNow*, Intuitive Surgical, United states) and three stand-alone systems (*dV-Trainer*, Mimic Technologies, United states; *RobotiX Mentor*, 3D Systems/Simbionix, United states; *Robotic Surgery Simulator*, Simulated Surgical Systems, United states), of which both Simbionix and Mimic Technologies are now part of Surgical Science Sweden AB.

Due to the challenges to realistically model suture threads and their behavior in simulation environments, several "cheats" are commonly used throughout these systems to provide speed and stability in the simulation modules. As an example, suture threads not respecting the property of inextensibility, or tools blocking when a certain tension is applied, prevent the trainee to learn how much a thread can be stretched before breakage. Moreover, damped suture movements and unrealistic gravity forces lead to unnatural effects during knot-tying. Furthermore, automatic tightening of the knot when traction is applied on both ends of the thread impedes an adjustment of the knot position. Such adjustments are usually performed by adapting the traction in order to slide the knot towards one region of the thread to optimize the knot position and the length of both ends of the thread. The reason why such unrealistic behaviors are implemented is that they facilitate a fast and robust simulation. At the cost of missing technical details, users can thereby complete a given task while avoiding instabilities.

In contrast, we chose to model the suture with precise mechanical properties for a realistic training experience including suturing errors such as suture breakage, air knots and tissue tearing. However, a system of visual cues is implemented to alert the trainee of improper technique prior to reaching a "game over".

2.1.2 Haptic Rendering

Haptic rendering on surgical simulations has been the subject of numerous studies like Basdogan et al. (2004) and Marshall et al. (2006). There are many difficulties to achieve a quality haptic rendering (see the study of Hamza-Lup et al. (2019) for more information): A first challenge is to have a realistic modeling of surgical tools, of the mechanical behavior of the organs, as well as of the interaction between tools and organs. A second difficulty is based on the performance required for a realistic haptic rendering. In general, it is estimated that to simulate a haptic rendering of contact, the control must be performed at 1 kHz. Combining these two challenges already means that we need a very fast and very realistic simulation engine at the same time. But a third difficulty comes from the coupling between this simulation engine and the haptic rendering. Indeed, the robotic interface requires a control law that guarantees stability. But this control law will often disturb the quality of the haptic rendering (called its transparency).

In the end, these difficulties mean that the haptic rendering is often disappointing on surgical training simulators, and does not necessarily provide educational value, as reported by Rangarajan et al. (2020). In our study we therefore choose to only provide visual cues translating this force feedback, even if our approach theoretically allows for haptics. It should be noted that most surgical robots (notably the Da Vinci) do not offer force feedback, so it is logical that the corresponding simulator does not provide any either.

2.2 Deformation Model for the Suture Thread

We identified two main properties which need to be captured to faithfully represent the deformation of a suture thread. The first one is the ability to form loops and knots, which stems from the mechanical coupling between bending and torsional motion. The second one is the conservation of the length, which adds visual realism, and allows to perform accurate tying motions. Different families of methods exist for modeling the deformation of one-dimensional structures, also denoted as rods, ranging from purely geometric models (Brown et al., 2004; Müller et al., 2012), to more elaborate ones which derive from either Euler Bernoulli, Timoschenko, Kirchhoff or Cosserat theory. Essentially, the more complex the theory, the richer is the deformation of the model. This section introduces previous work on deformation models used to model elastic rods, categorized into two families: reduced coordinate methods, and maximal coordinate methods.

2.2.1 Reduced Coordinate Methods

With reduced coordinate methods, the number of parameters to describe the motion exactly matches the degrees of freedom of the model. As a consequence, the inextensibility property is captured natively by the model. In this setting the Cartesian coordinates of the rod centerline are an implicit function of the degrees of freedom. A tempting approach is to consider the suture thread as a particular case of a chain of articulated rigid segments, where the angles between two adjacent segments are the degrees of freedom. Using the method described by Featherstone (1983), this type of model can be solved in linear time. Rigid articulated chains perfectly preserve length, but have the major drawback of not capturing torsional motion, which plays a critical role for the formation of knots.

Bertails et al. (2006) derived a model using Kirchhoff theory, where the curvature is used as the degree of freedom of the rod. Very complex deformations can be obtained even with a coarse discretization, and both torsional and bending motions are captured by the model. A recursive solving strategy, similar in spirit as the one introduced by Roy Featherstone for articulated rigid chains, can be applied to recover the rod Cartesian coordinates from the curvature degrees of freedom in linear time (Bertails, 2009).

However, even though reduced coordinates offer an attractive formulation to solve the suture thread deformation, they require additional implementation work in order to be integrated efficiently in a simulation environment which contains other types of deformable solids. To scale well, reduced coordinates need a dedicated linear solver to alleviate for the need explicit assembly of the system matrix. Indeed the system dynamic matrix is always dense, and therefore the complexity of a direct solve is cubic with the number of degrees of freedom. Also, due to the implicit nature of the formulation, the expression of the rod centerline position and velocity can only be recovered with the application of an additional geometric function.

2.2.2 Maximal Coordinate Methods

With maximal coordinate methods, the number of parameters used to describe the model is greater than the degrees of freedom, so additional constraints are needed, e.g., to preserve the length of the model. On the numerical side, the system matrix is very sparse, so the application of its inverse can be computed efficiently using linear algebra routines like the conjugate gradient method (Shewchuk, 1994) or the direct sparse Cholesky factorization (Davis, 2006).

Mass-spring models are probably the simpler conceptual implementation for elastic rods, but they lack mechanical soundness. The rod centerline is discretized with a succession of segments, connected by linear springs. Choe et al. (2005) also added torsion to this type of model by tracking the difference in orientation between two successive segments. Spline based models by Lenoir et al. (2004) and Theetten et al. (2006) offer a continuous representation of the rod centerline, and torsion is obtained by tracking the change in orientation of the rod cross section.

Work by Spillmann and Teschner (2007) introduced the simulation of elastic rods to the computer graphics community by discretizing the Cosserat rod theory. In this setting the degrees of freedom are described by a spatially continuous material frame, called the Frenet frame, which is computed by taking the parametric derivatives of the rod centerline curve, and allows to measure both bending and torsion on top of stretching. This work was later extended by Bergou et al. (2008) who proposed a different framing for the material basis, called the Bishop framing. Contrary to Frenet framing, Bishop framing is always defined even in regions where the curvature of the centerline is zero. In Bergou et al. (2010), they provided the second derivative of the energy function of this model which makes it suitable for implicit time integration with large time steps (Baraff and Witkin, 1998).

Guébert et al. (2009) proposed to model a suture thread by resorting to the Timoschenko beam theory (Przemieniecki, 1985), which is traditionally used for the analysis of structures, and equipped it with a corotational filter to account for large displacements.

Among the family of maximal coordinates method, a popular alternative to implicit time integration is to use the Position Based Dynamics (PBD) framework (Müller et al., 2007; Macklin et al., 2016). Using just the first derivative of the energy function and a non-linear Gauss-Seidel solver, this method approximates implicit Euler integration. Position-based solving method is very robust, but requires a lot of iterations to converge to a stiff behavior. Work by Umetani et al. (2015) has shown how Cosserat rod theory can be expressed in the PBD framework using ghost particles to model orientations. Later this was work was extended by Kugelstadt and Schömer (2016) to treat orientation constraints directly in the PBD framework. However as demonstrated by Deul et al. (2018), and Xu and Liu (2018) in the more particular context of suture thread simulation, a large number of iterations are required to achieve stiff behaviors with Position-based methods, and propose to use a direct solver to obtain inextensible rods.

Still, since they allow stretching to occur, all the maximal coordinate formulations need an additional Lagrangian hard constraint in order to project the rod kinematics to a subspace where stretching motion is cancelled.

3 MECHANICAL MODELING

We present a novel simulation model of suture threads which employs:

- Corotational Timoshenko beam elements. This model accurately captures the motions of the thread and can be used to represent a large variety of suture threads ranging from very stiff to very soft.
- A discrete continuous geometrical model for the centerline based on cubic Bézier curves whose control points can be inferred from the beam configuration.
- A stable length-preserving second order Lagrange multiplier constraint based on the derivatives of the cubic Bézier curve length with respect to the beam generalized coordinates.
- A spatially continuous contact geometry which relies on the cubic Bézier curve geometry of the thread. It allows to produce an accurate and smooth contact detection which is particularly helpful during knot formation where the model becomes more and more tangled.

This section presents the parts of the overall simulation model that are specific to the suture thread. It will be illustrated with results presented in **Section 4** within a full simulation including other rigid and soft bodies, linear solvers and constraints resolution schemes from the SOFA open-source software Faure et al. (2012), with additional methods and proprietary implementation from InSimo that improve the achieved performances, stability, and precision of the tissues modeling. However, the presented suture thread model is generic and standalone and could be used within other engines.

3.1 Equations of Motion

Using Newton's second law, the acceleration of the objects can be related with the applied forces

$$
\begin{aligned}
\mathbf{M}\ddot{q} &= \mathbf{f}_{ext} - \mathbf{f}_{int} + \mathbf{H}^\top \lambda \\
\Phi(q) &= 0
\end{aligned}
\tag{1}
$$

Where $\mathbf{M} \in \mathbb{R}^{n \times n}$ is the mass matrix of the system, $q \in \mathbb{R}^n$ are the generalized coordinates, $\mathbf{f}_{ext}$ and $\mathbf{f}_{int}$ are the external and internal forces, respectively. $\mathbf{H}^\top \lambda$ are the constraint forces, where $\mathbf{H} \in \mathbb{R}^{m \times n}$ is the Jacobian matrix gives the constraint force directions of the m algebraic constraint equations Φ, and $\lambda \in \mathbb{R}^{m \times 1} \in$ is the vector of unknown Lagrange multipliers encoding constraint force intensities.

This equation is integrated using the backward Euler scheme to accommodate for large time steps, which was popularized by Baraff and Witkin (1998) in computer graphics. The system can be written in matrix form

$$
\begin{pmatrix} \mathbf{M} - h^2\mathbf{K} & -\mathbf{H}^\top \\ \mathbf{H} & \frac{1}{h^2}\mathbf{C} \end{pmatrix} \begin{pmatrix} \dot{q}_+ \\ h\lambda_+ \end{pmatrix} = \begin{pmatrix} \mathbf{M}\dot{q} + h(\mathbf{f}_{ext} - \mathbf{f}_{int}) \\ -\frac{1}{h}\Phi(q) \end{pmatrix}
\tag{2}
$$

With $\mathbf{K}$ the stiffness matrix coming from the linearization of the internal forces, $\mathbf{C}$ the optional compliance of the constraints, and h the time step. The subscript $+$ denotes an end of time step quantity. This integration scheme allows to obtain an equation of the dynamics in velocity, with impulses in the right term. It is a low order scheme but well adapted to a "time stepping" processing of the contacts.

The reduced system can be formed by taking the Schur complement of the upper left block of the system matrix. Using $\mathbf{A} = \mathbf{M} - h^2\mathbf{K}$ we obtain

$$
\left(\mathbf{H}\mathbf{A}^{-1}\mathbf{H}^\top + \frac{1}{h^2}\mathbf{C}\right)h\lambda_+ = -\frac{1}{h}\Phi - \mathbf{H}\mathbf{A}^{-1}\left(\mathbf{M}\dot{q} + h(\mathbf{f}_{ext} - \mathbf{f}_{int})\right)
\tag{3}
$$

The symmetric semi positive definite matrix $\mathbf{W} = \mathbf{H}\mathbf{A}^{-1}\mathbf{H}^\top$ is the Delassus operator (Delassus 1917), or compliance matrix projected in the constraint space. It encodes the mechanical coupling between each of the constraint equations of the system.

To solve the system 2) we first compute the free velocity, which is the velocity obtained by removing the influence of the constraint forces

$$
\dot{q}_* = \mathbf{A}^{-1}\left(\mathbf{M}\dot{q} + h(\mathbf{f}_{ext} - \mathbf{f}_{int})\right)
\tag{4}
$$

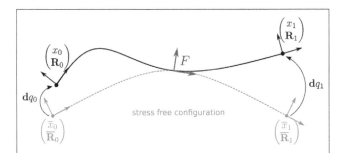

FIGURE 1 | The computation of the deformation is done in the local reference frame *F* of the beam element (in red). Using this frame, the 6D local displacements of the nodes are computed between the current configuration and their rest configuration (in orange).

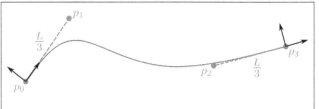

FIGURE 2 | Construction of the spline control points from the beam end nodes.

Then we compute the intensities of the constraint forces λ_+ using the reduced system. This system usually models a mixed non linear complementary problem. It is called "mixed" since it combines both equalities and inequalities constraint equations, and constraint equations may be also be non linear, like with frictional contact constraints.

Finally once the intensities λ_+ are obtained we can compute the end of time step velocity and position

$$\begin{aligned} \dot{q}_+ &= \dot{q}_* + \mathbf{A}^{-1}\mathbf{H}^\top\lambda_+ \\ q_+ &= q + h\dot{q}_+ \end{aligned} \tag{5}$$

3.2 Deformation Model of the Suture Thread

To model the suture thread deformation we extend the Timoschenko linear beam finite element method presented in Przemieniecki (1985) to account for large displacements by using a corotational formulation.

3.2.1 Corotational Beam Elements

We will provide a succinct introduction to the corotational method in this section, and we refer the reader to Felippa and Haugen (2005) for extensive details.

The generalized coordinates q of a beam node which captures the deformation of its cross section are defined by a positional vector $x \in \mathbb{R}^3$ and a rotation matrix $\mathbf{R} \in SO(3)$. Its general velocities $\dot{q}$ are defined using a linear velocity vector $v \in \mathbb{R}^3$ and an angular velocity vector $\omega \in \mathbb{R}^3$. We use the following update rule to integrate the new positions and orientations of the beam cross section from the end of time step linear and angular displacements:

$$\begin{aligned} x_+ &= x + hv_+ \\ \mathbf{R}_+ &= \exp\left(h\left[\omega_+\right]_\times\right)\mathbf{R} \end{aligned} \tag{6}$$

With $[\cdot]_\times$ the operator which converts a vector into a skew symmetric matrix

$$[a]_\times = \begin{pmatrix} 0 & -a_3 & -a_2 \\ a_3 & 0 & -a_1 \\ a_2 & a_1 & 0 \end{pmatrix}$$

And exp the matrix exponential function whose closed form in the case of skew symmetric matrices is given by the Euler Rodrigues formula.

Using the corotational method, we decompose the motion of a flexible beam in two parts, a rigid body motion and a deformation motion. We add, to each flexible beam, a reference frame $F = [x_F, \mathbf{R}_F]$ at the center of the element and we use it as a local coordinate system where the deformation is measured (see **Figure 1**). To define the orientation of this local frame F, we first construct a cubic spline using the position and orientation of the beam end nodes. The position of the control points at both end of the cubic spline is given by the position of the corresponding beam nodes. The second and third control points are constructed using the orientation of the $\mathbf{u}_x$ axis of each node and the rest length L of the beam (see **Figure 2**).

$$\mathbf{p}_0 = x_0 \qquad \mathbf{p}_1 = x_0 + \frac{L}{3}\mathbf{R}_0\begin{pmatrix} 1 \\ 0 \\ 0 \end{pmatrix}$$

$$\mathbf{p}_2 = x_1 - \frac{L}{3}\mathbf{R}_1\begin{pmatrix} 1 \\ 0 \\ 0 \end{pmatrix} \qquad \mathbf{p}_3 = x_1 \tag{7}$$

From the control points we can define the position x_F of corotational frame F at the mid point of the beam element, by evaluating the interpolation function of the cubic spline at the parameter value 0.5.

$$\mathbf{p}(u) = (1-u)^3\mathbf{p}_0 + 3u(1-u)^2\mathbf{p}_1 + 3u^2(1-u)\mathbf{p}_2 + u^3\mathbf{p}_3 \tag{8}$$

The steps used to construct the orientation $\mathbf{R}_F$ of corotational frame F are illustrated in **Figure 3**.

First, we evaluate the mid point tangent $\vec{t}$ by taking the normalized gradient of the cubic spline interpolation function.

$$\nabla\mathbf{p}(u) = (1-u)^2 3(\mathbf{p}_1 - \mathbf{p}_0) + 2(1-u)^2 3(\mathbf{p}_2 - \mathbf{p}_1) + u^2 3(\mathbf{p}_3 - \mathbf{p}_2) \tag{9}$$

$$\vec{t} = \frac{\nabla\mathbf{p}(0.5)}{\|\nabla\mathbf{p}(0.5)\|}$$

Then, for each beam end node we find the rotation $\mathbf{R'}_i$ which aligns the node u_{x_i} axis with the mid point tangent $\vec{t}$ (see **Figure 4**). From there, the orientation of F is derived with spherical linear interpolation.

We then construct $\mathbf{R}_F$ using:

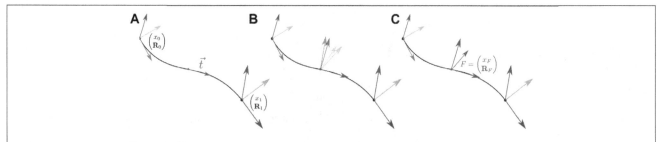

FIGURE 3 | To construct $\mathbf{R}_F$ we first evaluate the tangent at the cubic Bézier curve mid point **(A)** We then transform each beam end point orientation to align its first axis with the mid point tangent **(B)** We finally compute the orientation of F by taking the average of these two rotations **(C)**.

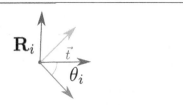

FIGURE 4 | Alignment of u_{x_i} with the mid point tangent.

$$R'_i = R_{\theta_i} R_i$$
$$\mathbf{R}_F = R'_0 \exp\left(0.5 \cdot \log\left(R'^{\top}_1 R'_0\right)\right)$$

3.2.2 Elastic Force and Stiffness

The assumption of the corotational method is that in the reference frame, the deformation remains small at the level of each element, and we can compute in the local frame the element force $\mathbf{f_e}$ with the linear relation:

$$\mathbf{f_e} = \mathbf{K_e}(\mathbf{u} - \bar{\mathbf{u}}) \tag{10}$$

With.

- $\mathbf{u} = F^{\top}\begin{bmatrix} q_0 \\ q_1 \end{bmatrix}$ the column vector containing the coordinates of the beam nodes in the deformed configuration expressed in its local frame F.

- $\bar{\mathbf{u}} = \bar{F}^{\top}\begin{bmatrix} \bar{q}_0 \\ \bar{q}_1 \end{bmatrix}$ the column vector containing the coordinates of the beam nodes in the stress free configuration expressed in its local frame $\bar{F}$.

- $\mathbf{K_e}$ the 12 × 12 elementary stiffness matrix given by Przemieniecki (1985).

The elementary stiffness matrix $\mathbf{K_e}$ relates the positional and rotational motion of each of the beam nodes to forces and torques applied to them.

With $G = \frac{E}{2*(1+\nu)}$ where E is the Young modulus and ν Poisson ratio; A is the cross-sectional area of the beam, l is its length; I_y and I_z are the cross-section moments of inertia; Φ_y and Φ_z are deformation parameters related to the shearing of the cross section and are given by the following relation: $\Phi_y = \frac{12EI_z}{GA_{sy}l^2}$ and $\Phi_z = \frac{12EI_y}{GA_{sz}l^2}$ with A_{sy} and A_{sz} the shearing area in the y and z.

We use the orientation of corotational frame $\mathbf{F}$ to transform the force $\mathbf{f} = \mathbf{R}_F\mathbf{f_e}$ and the stiffness matrix $\mathbf{K} = \mathbf{R}_F\mathbf{K_e}\mathbf{R}_F^{\top}$ from the local to the global coordinate system.

3.3 Length-Preserving Lagrangian Constraint

To model a suture thread, we need to equip the beam model with an additional length-preserving constraint. Indeed, during suturing, the traction loads applied to the thread are very high, and a simple increase of the beam rigidity in the stretching direction cannot enforce the inextensibility property.

For a Bézier curve, we can compute its length L with the arc length function

$$L = \int_0^1 \|\nabla\mathbf{p}(u)\|\,du \tag{11}$$

In the case of cubic Bézier curves this function has no closed form solution, and we use Gauss quadrature to approximate the integral. We sample the integral using the following Gauss points (with $A = 2\sqrt{6/5}$)

$$u_0 = \frac{-\sqrt{(3-A)/7}+1}{2} \quad u_1 = \frac{\sqrt{(3-A)/7}+1}{2}$$
$$u_2 = \frac{-\sqrt{(3+A)/7}+1}{2} \quad u_3 = \frac{\sqrt{(3+A)/7}+1}{2}$$

Which using the quadrature rule gives

$$L \approx \frac{18+\sqrt{30}}{72}\left(\|\nabla\mathbf{p}(u_0)\| + \|\nabla\mathbf{p}(u_1)\|\right) + \frac{18-\sqrt{30}}{72}\left(\|\nabla\mathbf{p}(u_2)\| + \|\nabla\mathbf{p}(u_3)\|\right)$$

$$\tag{12}$$

For each beam segment, we can then formulate the length-preserving constraint equation as a composition of two functions of the beam generalized degrees of freedom

$$\Phi(q) = \Phi_2 \circ \Phi_1(q) - \bar{L} \tag{13}$$

Where.

- Φ_1 is the function which gives the position of the control points $\mathbf{p}$ in terms of the beam end nodes $q = \begin{pmatrix} q_1 \\ q_2 \end{pmatrix}$. See **Eq. 7**
- Φ_2 the function which gives the length of the cubic Bézier curve L in terms of its four control points $\mathbf{p}_0 \cdots \mathbf{p}_3$. See **Eq. 11**
- $\bar{L}$ is the length of the beam segment in its stress free configuration, $\bar{L} = \Phi_2 \circ \Phi_1 (\bar{q})$

Linearizing Φ with respect to the generalized coordinates of the beam gives the constraint Jacobian $\mathbf{H}$, which in this case is a 1×12 matrix

$$\frac{\partial \Phi}{\partial q} = \mathbf{H} = \frac{\partial \Phi_2}{\partial \mathbf{p}} \cdot \frac{\partial \Phi_1}{\partial q}$$

$$\frac{\partial \Phi_1}{\partial q} = \mathbf{H}_1 = \begin{pmatrix} \mathbf{I}_3 & 0 & 0 & 0 \\ \mathbf{I}_3 & -[\mathbf{p}_1 - \mathbf{p}_0]_\times & 0 & 0 \\ 0 & 0 & \mathbf{I}_3 & -[\mathbf{p}_2 - \mathbf{p}_3]_\times \\ 0 & 0 & \mathbf{I}_3 & 0 \end{pmatrix}$$

$$\frac{\partial \Phi_2}{\partial \mathbf{p}} = \mathbf{H}_2 = \left(\int_0^1 \frac{\partial \|\nabla \mathbf{p}(u)\|}{\partial \mathbf{p}_0} du \int_0^1 \frac{\partial \|\nabla \mathbf{p}(u)\|}{\partial \mathbf{p}_1} du \int_0^1 \frac{\partial \|\nabla \mathbf{p}(u)\|}{\partial \mathbf{p}_2} du \int_0^1 \frac{\partial \|\nabla \mathbf{p}(u)\|}{\partial \mathbf{p}_3} du \right)$$

Again, since no close form for the integrals which compose the components of $\frac{\partial \Phi_2}{\partial \mathbf{p}}$ exists, we also resort to Gauss quadrature to evaluate the terms numerically.

Note that Φ is highly non-linear, so depending on the chosen time integration and numerical resolution solver, it may be necessary to apply an adequate stabilization strategy.

3.4 Contact and Collision Model of the Suture Thread

To be able to perform knots we need to robustly capture thread-thread interactions. In our simulation we model contact using the Signorini's contact law (Duriez et al., 2006) which gives a complementary condition between the contact force λ and the proximity distance (or gap) function $\mathbf{g}(q)$

$$0 \le \lambda \perp \mathrm{g}(q) \ge 0 \tag{14}$$

We use collision detection to discretize the distance function $\mathbf{g}$ for the suture thread by computing at each time step its closest vertex-edge and edge-edge features. We use bounding volume hierarchies (BVH) to prune distant features to focus the computations on features that are close by (see Bergen (1997) for instance).

It is common in simulators to model the geometry of the suture thread with piecewise continuous geometry like line segments (Wang et al., 2017), (Qi et al., 2017), or cylinders with fixed radius (Hüsken et al., 2013). Because each geometry primitive is only locally continuous and not smooth, discretization artifacts will always occur. In our work, we instead rely on the cubic Bézier geometry associated with each beam segment to get an accurate and spatially continuous contact definition.

3.4.1 Vertex-Edge Distance Function

The closest point on a cubic Bézier curve from another curve vertex $\mathbf{q} \in \mathbb{R}^3$ can be obtained by minimizing the following square distance function

$$\mathbf{d}(u) = \frac{1}{2} (\mathbf{p}(u) - \mathbf{q}) \cdot (\mathbf{p}(u) - \mathbf{q})$$

A minimum u_{min} of the $\mathbf{d}$ function is reached when its gradient is zero

$$\nabla \mathbf{d}(u) = \nabla \mathbf{p}(u) \cdot (\mathbf{p}(u) - \mathbf{q})$$

Since no closed form exists to express the minimum of the $\nabla \mathbf{d}$ function we use a Newton Raphson iterative scheme to converge toward a local minimum of the function. This requires at each iteration the evaluation of the Hessian $H(\mathbf{d})$ of the square distance function which is given by

$$H(\mathbf{d})(u) = H(\mathbf{p})(u) \cdot (\mathbf{p}(u) - \mathbf{q}) + \nabla \mathbf{p}(u) \cdot \nabla \mathbf{p}(u)$$

3.4.2 Edge-Edge Distance Function

The closest points between two cubic Bézier curves $\mathbf{p}$ and $\mathbf{q}$ with parameters u and v can be obtained by minimizing the square distance function

$$\mathbf{d}(u, v) = \frac{1}{2} (\mathbf{p}(u) - \mathbf{q}(v)) \cdot (\mathbf{p}(u) - \mathbf{q}(v))$$

Again, to find a local minimum (u_{min}, v_{min}) of this function, we look for a root of its the gradient

$$\nabla \mathbf{d}(u, v) = \begin{pmatrix} \nabla \mathbf{p}(u) \cdot (\mathbf{p}(u) - \mathbf{q}(v)) \\ -\nabla \mathbf{q}(v) \cdot (\mathbf{p}(u) - \mathbf{q}(v)) \end{pmatrix}$$

The Hessian used during each Newton Raphson iteration being

$$H(\mathbf{d})(u,v) = \begin{pmatrix} H(\mathbf{p})(u) \cdot (\mathbf{p}(u) - \mathbf{q}(v)) + \nabla \mathbf{p}(u) \cdot \nabla \mathbf{p}(u) & -\nabla \mathbf{p}(u) \cdot \nabla \mathbf{q}(v) \\ -\nabla \mathbf{p}(u) \cdot \nabla \mathbf{q}(v) & H(\mathbf{q})(v) \cdot (\mathbf{q}(v) - \mathbf{p}(u)) + \nabla \mathbf{q}(v) \cdot \nabla \mathbf{q}(v) \end{pmatrix}$$

3.4.3 Collision Detection

To produce the contact geometry, we run collision detection at every time step of the simulation. Collision detection typically uses two stages to produce the contact information. The first stage, called the broad phase algorithm, uses bounding volume hierarchies—a hierarchy of axis aligned bounding boxes in our simulation—to prune distant features. The only cubic Bézier lines that are tested for proximity are the one which are enclosed by intersecting bounding boxes. The second stage, called the narrow phase, uses the potential colliding pair of primitives provided by the broad phase to test for potential contact by computing the Vertex-Edge and Edge-Edge distance. The result of the narrow phase gives us the contact geometry, from which we can generate non-penetration constraints.

3.4.4 Unilateral Contact Constraint

Sampling the distance function using closest point features gives us a list of pairs of contact points together with their parametric location on the cubic Bézier curve and their contact normal. For each pair $(\mathbf{p}(u), \mathbf{q}(v))$ of contact points the non-penetration contact constraint can be written as

$$\mathbf{n}^\top (\mathbf{p}(u) - \mathbf{q}(v)) - 2r - \epsilon \geq 0 \tag{15}$$

With.

- $\mathbf{n} = \frac{\mathbf{p}(u) - \mathbf{q}(v)}{\|\mathbf{p}(u) - \mathbf{q}(v)\|}$ the contact normal
- r the radius of the suture thread
- ϵ is a user-defined safety tolerance

To enforce the non-penetration constraint at the end of the time step we linearize the gap function with respect to the degrees of freedom q

$$\mathbf{g}(q^+) \approx \mathbf{g}(q) + \frac{\partial \mathbf{g}}{\partial q}(q^+ - q) \tag{16}$$

The constraint Jacobian $\mathbf{H_n} = \frac{\partial \mathbf{g}}{\partial q}$ at a contact location $\mathbf{p}(u)$ with normal $\mathbf{n}$ being

$$\mathbf{H_n} = \mathbf{n} \cdot \left(\frac{\partial \mathbf{p}(u)}{\partial \mathbf{p}_i} \right) \cdot \left(\frac{\partial \mathbf{p}_i}{\partial q_j} \right)$$
$$\mathbf{H_n} = \mathbf{n} \left((1-u)^3 \quad u(1-u)^2 \quad u^2(1-u) \quad u^3 \right)$$
$$\begin{pmatrix} \mathbf{I}_3 & 0 & 0 & 0 \\ \mathbf{I}_3 & -[\mathbf{p}_1 - \mathbf{p}_0]_\times & 0 & 0 \\ 0 & 0 & \mathbf{I}_3 & -[\mathbf{p}_2 - \mathbf{p}_3]_\times \\ 0 & 0 & 0 & \mathbf{I}_3 \end{pmatrix}$$

We can then express the contact constraint inequality at the velocity level as.

$$\mathbf{A}\Delta\dot{q} = \mathbf{H_n}^\top \lambda_+ \tag{17}$$
$$\Delta\dot{q} = \dot{q}_+ - \dot{q}_* \tag{18}$$
$$0 \leq \lambda_+ \perp \mathbf{H_n}\Delta\dot{q} \geq -\frac{1}{h}\mathbf{g}(q) - \mathbf{H_n}\dot{q}_* \tag{19}$$

3.4.5 Coulomb Frictional Contact

Friction plays an important role during the formation of knots, where the suture thread motion alternates between sticking and sliding. For each contact, we construct an orthonormal frame $\mathbf{n}$, $\mathbf{t}_1$, $\mathbf{t}_2$ to measure the tangential gap together with the normal gap.

Noting μ the friction coefficient, the Coulomb's law can be then written as.

$$\mathbf{A}\Delta\dot{q} = \mathbf{H_n}^\top \lambda_{\mathbf{n}_+} + \mathbf{H_t}^\top \lambda_{\mathbf{t}_+} \tag{20}$$
$$0 \leq \lambda_{\mathbf{n}_+} \perp \mathbf{H_n}\Delta\dot{q} \geq -\frac{1}{h}\mathbf{g}(q) - \mathbf{H_n}\dot{q}_* \tag{21}$$
$$\|\lambda_{\mathbf{t}_+}\| \leq \mu\lambda_{\mathbf{n}_+} \perp \mathbf{H_t}\Delta\dot{q} \geq -\mathbf{H_t}\dot{q}_* \tag{22}$$

3.5 Suture Thread Tension

At each time step of the simulation the solution of the reduced system gives us the intensity λ_{l_+} of the forces that need to be applied to preserve the length of each of the beam segments that compose the suture thread deformable model. These intensities directly reflect the degree of tension on the suture thread, and we use them to construct the colour code to provide visual haptic cues. For each type of suture thread we specified a rupture threshold λ_{yield} above which breakage occurs, and defined a colour code accordingly to notify the user.

The mechanical work $\|h\lambda_{l_+} (-\frac{1}{h}\Phi_l(q) - \mathbf{H}_l^\top \dot{q}^*)\|$ is the energy that needs to be injected in the system to respect the length-preserving constraint during the time step, and directly depends on the mechanical parameters of the suture thread.

Based on this energy, we render a gradient of signal colours (from yellow to red) on the stretched areas of the suture thread (see **Figures 5, 13**). When the thread is subject to excessive force, it turns red until reaching the breakage point, after which it switches back to its normal colour without any tension (**Figure 5**).

3.6 Summary

We use a continuous representation of the suture thread based on cubic Bézier curves to address the stability challenges that arise during the formation of knots in the simulation. From this continuous setting, we obtain an accurate definition of the suture thread length from which a length-preserving constraint function can be derived. Additionally, as the support geometry is continuous and smooth, we generate spatially continuous contact geometry which can capture precisely the moment at which a knot is formed in the simulation. The intensity of the length-preserving constraint can be mapped to a colour code reflecting the proficiency of the user manipulation.

4 RESULTS

Standard robotic knot-tying and suturing tasks were performed on a current robotic surgical system (da Vinci Xi, Intuitive Surgical) in order to assess comparability with the proposed simulation model. Both the robotic and the simulated knot-tying and suturing tasks were recorded on video for visual comparison of suture thread behavior during manipulation. The Fundamentals of Robotic Surgery (FRS) dome was chosen as a benchmark model for robotic surgical skills training Satava et al. (2019). Measures were taken of the FRS dome and of commonly used suture threads for an accurate representation in the robotic simulation module.

The simulations were computed in real time at over 50 frames per second on a computer with an AMD Ryzen 9 5900X CPU, a NVIDIA GeForce RTX 3070 GPU, and 64 GB of RAM. As the simulation scenarios are sufficiently simple, there was no need for specific efforts to reach this 50 frames per second target. For integration of more complex simulations, we envision several ways to enhance the computational performances of our simulation if needed, such as work by Otaduy et al. (2009) and Hecht et al. (2012).

The results presented are subdivided into the following categories:

- A series of behavior tests to illustrate the soundness of our model (**Section 4.1**)
- The suture thread model properties and its applications to knot-tying and suturing (**Section 4.2**)

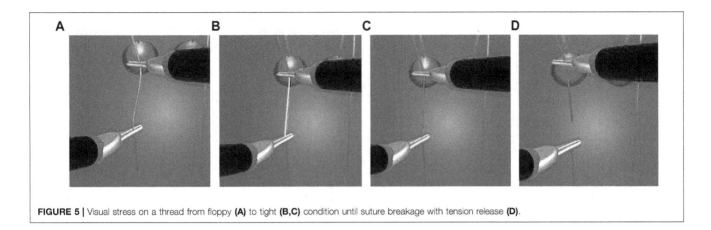

FIGURE 5 | Visual stress on a thread from floppy **(A)** to tight **(B,C)** condition until suture breakage with tension release **(D)**.

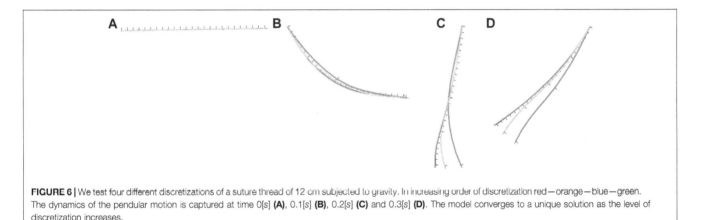

FIGURE 6 | We test four different discretizations of a suture thread of 12 cm subjected to gravity. In increasing order of discretization red−orange−blue−green. The dynamics of the pendular motion is captured at time 0[s] **(A)**, 0.1[s] **(B)**, 0.2[s] **(C)** and 0.3[s] **(D)**. The model converges to a unique solution as the level of discretization increases.

- The visual haptic feedback (**Section 4.3**)
- The comparison of the knot-tying exercise between the simulation and the reality on a da Vinci Xi system (**Section 4.4**)

4.1 Thread Behavior Tests

In order to test the behavior of our model we reproduced several of the experiments proposed in Xu and Liu (2018). These interactive experiments helped to confirm that our deformation model converges to a unique solution as the mesh discretization increases (**Figure 6**), its ability to reproduce the well known phenomena of plectonemes (**Figure 7**), its ability to remain inextensible even in scenarios where the suture thread is highly constrained (**Figure 8**), and finally its ability to form a knot (**Figure 9**).

4.2 Suture Thread Model
4.2.1 Mechanical Properties

We developed the deformation model of the suture thread proposed in **Section 3.2**. The model reproduces a realistic thread behaviour during manipulation, which was demonstrated in comparison with several types of surgical suture threads. **Figure 7** illustrates the coupling between torsion and bending when applying a torsional load at both ends of the thread. In order to preserve movement dynamics for a realistic gesture, the model is damped at a low level (the minimum needed for the purpose of numerical stability). In contrast to models encountered in common robotic VR simulations, our model overcomes the challenge of thread inextensibility (see **Section 3.3**). The strategy is sufficiently robust to offer an immersive thread manipulation to the user.

4.2.2 Collision

The developed method (see **Section 3.4**) to handle thread contact is robust enough to support various manipulations including thread wrapping around instruments, thread-thread interaction, as well as contact between the thread and other elements. During the knot-tying task, the thread touches the rings (linear collision model) and the dome (triangular collision model). It is in contact with the instruments when being grasped, and when being wrapped around an instrument tip for single or multiple loops. When the knot is formed, but not yet pulled tight, the thread is mainly in self-collision. We introduce an offset between the contacts to prevent the suture thread from tunneling (typically a small fraction of the thread's radius, see ϵ parameter in **Eq. 15**). Maintaining a minimal distance between adjacent threads enables precise recognition of the created pattern. If the pattern does not correspond to the desired one, it can thus be identified and corrected.

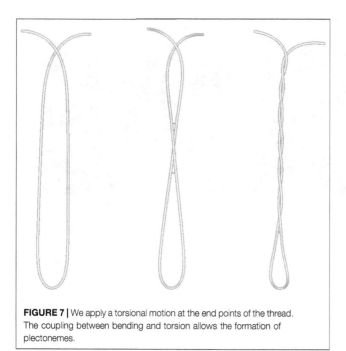

FIGURE 7 | We apply a torsional motion at the end points of the thread. The coupling between bending and torsion allows the formation of plectonemes.

4.2.3 Knot Tying

The present method enables the user to tie various knots in different scenarios and correct them if needed. As an example, the

first step of the blocking sequence of a surgeon's knot is a double overhand knot. It is a half knot with an extra turn, illustrated in **Figure 10**. The double loop provides additional friction to impede loosening of the first while the subsequent throws are performed. Before tightening, the knot position can be adjusted by means of traction on one end of the thread while holding the other end loosely. This way, the knot moves over to the desired position and the remaining length of each end can be optimized for subsequent knots (**Figure 10C,D**). The surgeon's knot is then completed by adding a half knot wrapped in the opposite sense, and additional knots can be added (sequence in **Figure 15**).

In contrast to other existing simulators, our approach does not presuppose the knot pattern by use of an analysis of the tool gesture. In the present approach, the precise mechanics and collision lead to the exact patterns that correspond to the performed manipulation. Consequently, our simulation approach complies with errors due to incorrect loop formation or knot tightening. This results in an accurate representation of the faulty pattern, just like with a real thread (see **Figure 11**). These precise thread characteristics are key to allow to substitute a robotic knot-tying and suturing training on the real console system with a simulation module.

4.2.4 Suturing

Based on the proposed approach, we developed interrupted suturing and continuous suturing tasks (see **Figure 12**). In these modules, the thread is attached to a needle. The collision

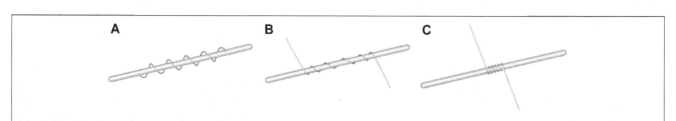

FIGURE 8 | A suture thread is wrapped around a fixed rigid cylinder by pulling at its ends. The wrapping motion is sampled at time 0 [s]**(A)**, 0.5 [s]**(B)**, and 1 [s]**(C)**. The model remains inextensible during this simulation, which is why the loops around the rigid cylinder get closer and closer.

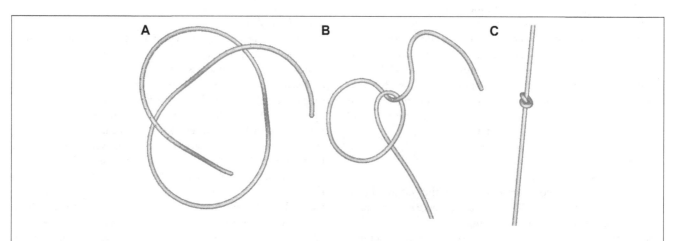

FIGURE 9 | Gradual tightening of a simple knot. The motion is sampled at time 0 [s]**(A)**, 1 [s]**(B)**, and 2 [s]**(C)**. The accurate contact model allows to form the knot and to tighten it.

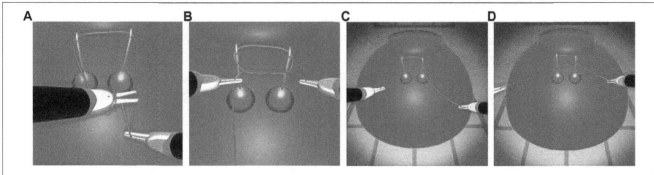

FIGURE 10 | First step of a surgeon's knot. The double overhand knot is created by wrapping the thread around an instrument tip **(A)**, grasping the other end, and pulling it through the double loop, resulting in a pattern with two twists **(B)**. The knot position can be adjusted by exerting traction on one end, thus moving the knot over to the other end **(C,D)**. The collision is sufficiently robust to support thread interactions with itself and with the other elements.

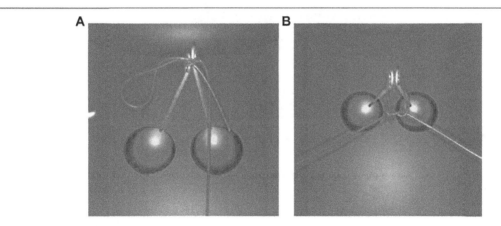

FIGURE 11 | Simulation accurately reproducing knot-tying errors. An accidental loop is created when one end of the thread is not completely pulled through the loop before tightening the knot on the rings **(A)**. An air knot is created when the knot is not properly guided down onto the rings before tightening it with traction on both ends of the thread **(B)**.

strategy of the rigid needle is the same as the one described for the thread. The interrupted suturing task involves placing the stitch and surgical knot-tying as outlined above. For the continuous suturing task, one end of the thread is anchored at the edge of the incision. The suture can be gradually tightened during each step of the task, and can be corrected at the end in order to ensure that the gap is well closed. Finally, a pair of scissors (third instrument) allows to cut the thread at the end of each task.

4.3 Visual Haptic Feedback

In order to reproduce the conditions of the majority of current robotic surgical systems, our simulation does not provide haptic feedback. Instead, we augment the graphics rendering of the simulation with visual cues. Visual force feedback has been demonstrated to enhance knot quality and reduce applied forces as well as suture breakage rates in robotic suturing Reiley et al. (2008). By mapping the intensity of the length-preserving constraints in a colour-code, our model indicates the degree of closeness to the rupture threshold of a suture thread or to damage from shear forces on tissues.

Such visual cues alert users that errors are about to occur when continuing to work with excessive force. In order to demonstrate the consequences of inappropriate handling, our simulation still progresses at this point and includes suture breakage or tissue tearing conditions (see **Figure 5**). This section presents the different types of visual cues we propose in our simulator.

4.3.1 Stress on Tissue

Our simulator represents stress on tissue with the same colour code. The signal colours appear on the stressed area, such as when puncturing with a needle or when applying counter-pressure with the needle driver (**Figure 13B**). Moreover, when excessive traction is applied, tissue tearing can occur, as represented with a red mark on the tissue where the thread has torn through (**Figure 13 C, D**).

4.3.2 Stress on Rigid Objects

When rigid objects are subject to excessive force, a change in color alerts the user of a collision (see **Figure 14**). If the collision is resolved, these objects return to their original colour. In contrast,

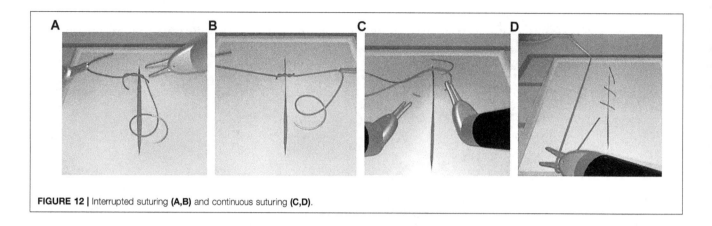

FIGURE 12 | Interrupted suturing **(A,B)** and continuous suturing **(C,D)**.

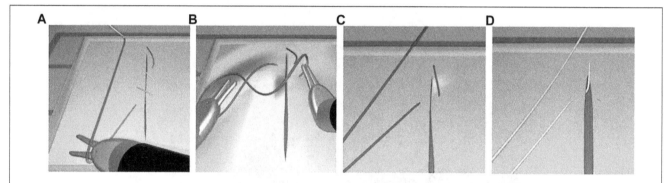

FIGURE 13 | Visual stress gradients on a thread when tightening a continuous suture **(A)**, and on tissue when driving a needle through tissue (right instrument) while applying a counter-pressure (left instrument) **(B)**. Combined visual cues on thread and tissue when applying excessive force **(C)** leading to a tear in the tissue and subsequently reduced tension on the thread **(D)**.

without a trajectory correction the simulation can become unstable and a game-over state is reached.

4.4 Preliminary Evaluation by Surgeons

At the IRCAD Strasbourg training platform, a trained robotic surgeon (BS) performed and recorded various knot-tying and suturing steps using the da Vinci Xi surgical system (Intuitive Surgical). The same tasks were then performed on the simulator by several of the authors. The gestures performed were slow on purpose, in order to ensure visibility of the thread behaviour and knot pattern in the video recordings. According to the measures taken on the real FRS dome, a stylized FRS dome version was

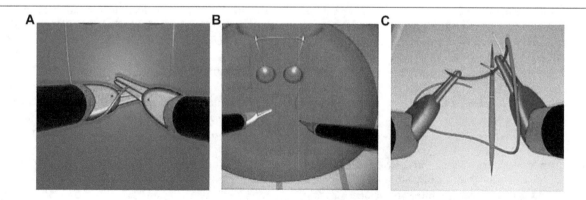

FIGURE 14 | Visual cues for excessive forces during collisions: Visual cues for excessive forces during collisions. Instrument tips turning from silver to orange during collision when forming a loop with a thread for knot-tying **(A)**, right instrument tip turning orange during collision with the dome, which turns from blue to pink **(B)**, double grasping with shearing forces during needle manipulation with both instrument tips turning orange, and the needle approximating the breakage point as represented by its color change to red **(C)**. Animated scenes are shown in the **Supplementary Video S1**.

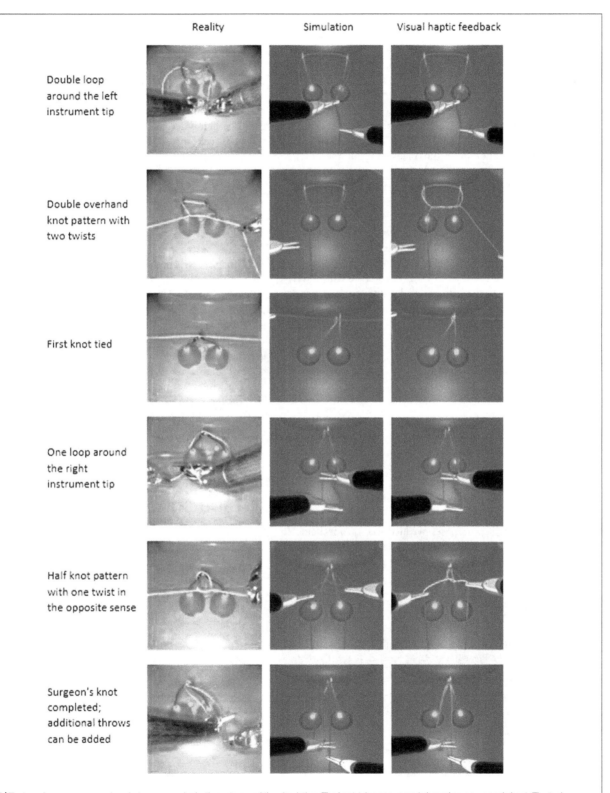

FIGURE 15 | Task performance comparison between a real robotic system and the simulation. The knot-tying sequence is based on a surgeon's knot. The task with the da Vinci Xi system is shown on the left, and the simulated task is shown without (middle) and with visual haptic cues (right).

implemented into the simulation module for the task of knot-tying around rings known from the FRS curriculum (see https:// frsurgery.org/). During development of the simulation approach, instrument articulation and range were adjusted to represent the typical degrees of freedom and thread movements observed in the real scenario. The FLS curriculum (required for US board certification in general surgery) includes suturing with intracorporeal knot-tying as one of the five laparoscopic tasks. After placing a stitch, it comprises a sequence of knots: a double overhand knot followed by two half knots (Qi et al., 2017). Consequently, this step sequence was chosen to illustrate the degree of realism in **Figure 15**. The suturing and knot-tying simulation exercises were then demonstrated to various surgeons. During the French national surgical conference 2021 (Association Française de Chirurgie, AFC), feedback was collected from 20 surgeons. They all underlined the plausibility of the thread simulation. The main positive feedback aspects were the overall realism of the suture, its fluidity, and the precise control of the knot tightening. The visual cues, and in particular the visual stress on suture threads, were perceived as a valuable tool to prevent beginners from breaking the suture. As a current limitation, our thread simulation lacks performance metrics (position, instrument path, duration, etc.). These will further be implemented in order to perform a study quantitatively assessing trainee performance with and without visual haptic cues, and evaluate training progress in comparison with commercial simulation systems.

Parameters	Reality	Simulation
Young Modulus	7 GPa	3 GPa
Poisson ratio	0.35	0.35
Diameter	0.25 mm	1.5 mm/0.4 mm (*)
Mass density	1,530 g.cm-3	1,530 g.cm-3
Length	165 mm	165 mm

(*) 1.5 mm for mechanics and 0.4 mm for collision.

For a braided absorbable suture (Vicryl 3–0, Ethicon) the characteristics compared to the simulated one are as follows:

For numerical stability purposes, we increased the mechanical diameter of our model, and then reduced the Young Modulus to compensate.

REFERENCES

Amirabdollahian, F., Livatino, S., Vahedi, B., Gudipati, R., Sheen, P., Gawrie-Mohan, S., et al. (2018). Prevalence of Haptic Feedback in Robot-Mediated Surgery: a Systematic Review of Literature. *J. Robotic Surg.* 12, 11–25. doi:10.1007/s11701-017-0763-4

Baraff, D., and Witkin, A. (1998). "Large Steps in Cloth Simulation," in SIGGRAPH 98 Conference Proceedings, 43–54. doi:10.1145/280814.280821

Basdogan, C., De Rensselaer, S., Jung Kim, J., Muniyandi, M., Hyun Kim, H., and Srinivasan, M. A. (2004). Haptic Rendering - beyond Visual Computing - Haptics in Minimally Invasive Surgical Simulation and Training. *IEEE Comput. Grap. Appl.* 24, 56–64. doi:10.1109/mcg.2004.1274062

Bergen, G. v. d. (1997). Efficient Collision Detection of Complex Deformable Models Using Aabb Trees. *J. graphics tools* 2, 1–13. doi:10.1080/10867651.1997.10487480

Bergou, M., Audoly, B., Vouga, E., Wardetzky, M., and Grinspun, E. (2010). "Discrete Viscous Threads," in *ACM SIGGRAPH 2010 PapersSIGGRAPH '10* (New York, NY, USA: Association for Computing Machinery). doi:10.1145/1833349.1778853

Bergou, M., Wardetzky, M., Robinson, S., Audoly, B., and Grinspun, E. (2008). "Discrete Elastic Rods," in *ACM SIGGRAPH 2008 Papers*, 1–12. doi:10.1145/1399504.1360662

Bertails, F., Audoly, B., Cani, M.-P., Querleux, B., Leroy, F., and Lévêque, J.-L. (2006). Super-helices for Predicting the Dynamics of Natural Hair. *ACM Trans. Graph.* 25, 1180–1187. doi:10.1145/1141911.1142012

Bertails, F. (2009). Linear Time Super-helices. *Comp. graphics Forum* 28, 417–426. Wiley Online Library. doi:10.1111/j.1467-8659.2009.01381.x

Brown, J., Latombe, J.-C., and Montgomery, K. (2004). Real-time Knot-Tying Simulation. *Vis. Comp.* 20, 165–179. doi:10.1007/s00371-003-0226-y

Choe, B., Choi, M. G., and Ko, H.-S. (2005). "Simulating Complex Hair with Robust Collision Handling," in Proceedings of the 2005 ACM SIGGRAPH/Eurographics symposium on Computer animation, 153–160. doi:10.1145/1073368.1073389

Davis, T. A. (2006). *Direct Methods for Sparse Linear Systems (Fundamentals of Algorithms 2).* USA: Society for Industrial and Applied Mathematics.

5 CONCLUSION

We present novel contributions on the wire model with constraints on elongation and on the continuous modeling of the contacts. The robust collision detection and suture thread modeling enable suturing and knot-tying in an interactive and real-time simulation environment running on a standard personal computer. Based on these advancements, virtually all types of thread manipulation can be performed in the simulation, just as in real life, and the knot can be tightened relatively far without compromising stability. Our simulation integrating visual haptic cues has the potential to facilitate learning of suturing and knot-tying tasks, since visual haptic feedback was already shown to be advantageous for novice surgeons to reduce applied forces and avoid suture breakage. Moreover, numerous interactive tests are provided to assess the quality of the results. Additionally, we compare the simulation results with a suture task performed with a da Vinci robotic system. Future work will include a model of the wire plasticity. Additionally, assessment metrics such as task completion time, accomplishment of the required knot-tying sequence and knot tightness will be integrated. Based on physical forces/stresses calculated in the simulation, exerted forces during a task can be extracted and used as performance metrics. Comparison of learning curves with and without visual haptic cues will then quantify the economy of motion and presumed learning advantage for training with visual haptic feedback. Performance evaluation scores with quantitative data will enable objective training assessment and inter-user comparability.

AUTHOR CONTRIBUTIONS

All authors listed have made a substantial, direct, and intellectual contribution to the work and approved it for publication.

Delassus, É. (1917). Mémoire sur la théorie des liaisons finies unilatérales. *Ann. Sci. École Norm. Sup.* 34, 95–179. doi:10.24033/asens.701

Deul, C., Kugelstadt, T., Weiler, M., and Bender, J. (2018). Direct Position-Based Solver for Stiff Rods. *Comp. Graphics Forum* 37, 313–324. doi:10.1111/cgf.13326

Doarn, C. R., Anvari, M., Low, T., and Broderick, T. J. (2009). Evaluation of Teleoperated Surgical Robots in an Enclosed Undersea Environment. *Telemed. e-Health* 15, 325–335. doi:10.1089/tmj.2008.0123

Duriez, C., Dubois, F., Kheddar, A., and Andriot, C. (2006). Realistic Haptic Rendering of Interacting Deformable Objects in Virtual Environments. *IEEE Trans. Vis. Comput. Graphics* 12, 36–47. doi:10.1109/TVCG.2006.13

Faure, F., Duriez, C., Delingette, H., Allard, J., Gilles, B., Marchesseau, S., et al. (2012). "SOFA: A Multi-Model Framework for Interactive Physical Simulation," in *Soft Tissue Biomechanical Modeling for Computer Assisted Surgeryof Studies in Mechanobiology, Tissue Engineering and Biomaterials*. Editor Y. Payan (Springer), 11, 283–321. doi:10.1007/8415_2012_125

Featherstone, R. (1983). The Calculation of Robot Dynamics Using Articulated-Body Inertias. *Int. J. Robotics Res.* 2, 13–30. doi:10.1177/027836498300200102

Felippa, C. A., and Haugen, B. (2005). A Unified Formulation of Small-Strain Corotational Finite Elements: I. Theory. *Comp. Methods Appl. Mech. Eng.* 194, 2285–2335. Computational Methods for Shells. doi:10.1016/j.cma.2004.07.035

Golahmadi, A. K., Khan, D. Z., Mylonas, G. P., and Marcus, H. J. (2021). Tool-tissue Forces in Surgery: A Systematic Review. *Ann. Med. Surg.* 65, 102268. doi:10.1016/j.amsu.2021.102268

Guébert, C., Duriez, C., Cotin, S., Allard, J., and Grisoni, L. (2009). "Suturing Simulation Based on Complementarity Constraints," in *Symposium on Computer Animation*, 2009.

Hamza-Lup, F. G., Bogdan, C. M., Popovici, D. M., and Costea, O. D. (2019). *A Survey of Visuo-Haptic Simulation in Surgical Training*. arXiv preprint arXiv:1903.03272.

Haruna, M., Ogino, M., and Koike-Akino, T. (2020). Proposal and Evaluation of Visual Haptics for Manipulation of Remote Machine System. *Front. Robot AI* 7, 529040. doi:10.3389/frobt.2020.529040

Hecht, F., Lee, Y. J., Shewchuk, J. R., and O'Brien, J. F. (2012). Updated Sparse Cholesky Factors for Corotational Elastodynamics. *ACM Trans. Graph.* 31, 1–13. doi:10.1145/2231816.2231821

Hüsken, N., Schuppe, O., Sismanidis, E., and Beier, F. (2013). Microsim - a Microsurgical Training Simulator. *Stud. Health Technol. Inform.* 184, 205–209. doi:10.3233/978-1-61499-209-7-205

Kugelstadt, T., and Schömer, E. (2016). "Position and Orientation Based Cosserat Rods," in *Proceedings of the ACM SIGGRAPH/Eurographics Symposium on Computer Animation* (Goslar, DEU: Eurographics Association (SCA), 16. 169–178.

Lenoir, J., Grisoni, L., Meseure, P., Rémion, Y., and Chaillou, C. (2004). "Smooth Constraints for Spline Variational Modeling," in *ACM International Conference on Computer Graphics and Interactive Techniques in Australasia and South East Asia (Graphite)* (Singapour, France), 58–64. doi:10.1145/988834.988844

Macklin, M., Müller, M., and Chentanez, N. (2016). "Xpbd," in *Proceedings of the 9th International Conference on Motion in Games*, New York, NY, USA (Association for Computing Machinery)MIG), 16. 49–54. doi:10.1145/2994258.2994272

Marescaux, J., Leroy, J., Gagner, M., Rubino, F., Mutter, D., Vix, M., et al. (2001). Transatlantic Robot-Assisted Telesurgery. *Nature* 413, 379–380. doi:10.1038/35096636

Marshall, P., Payandeh, S., and Dill, J. (2006). "A Study on Haptic Rendering in a Simulated Surgical Training Environment," in *2006 14th Symposium on Haptic Interfaces for Virtual Environment and Teleoperator Systems (IEEE)*, 241–247.

Miller, J., Braun, M., Bilz, J., Matich, S., Neupert, C., Kunert, W., et al. (2021). Impact of Haptic Feedback on Applied Intracorporeal Forces Using a Novel Surgical Robotic System-A Randomized Cross-Over Study with Novices in an Experimental Setup. *Surg. Endosc.* 35, 3554–3563. doi:10.1007/s00464-020-07818-8

Müller, M., Heidelberger, B., Hennix, M., and Ratcliff, J. (2007). Position Based Dynamics. *J. Vis. Commun. Image Representation* 18, 109–118. doi:10.1016/j.jvcir.2007.01.005

Müller, M., Kim, T.-Y., and Chentanez, N. (2012). Fast Simulation of Inextensible Hair and Fur. *VRIPHYS* 12, 39–44.

Otaduy, M. A., Tamstorf, R., Steinemann, D., and Gross, M. (2009). Implicit Contact Handling for Deformable Objects. *Computer Graphics Forum (Proc. Eurographics)* 28. doi:10.1111/j.1467-8659.2009.01396.x

Przemieniecki, J. S. (1985). *Theory of Matrix Structural Analysis*. Courier Corporation.

Qi, D., Panneerselvam, K., Ahn, W., Arikatla, V., Enquobahrie, A., and De, S. (2017). Virtual Interactive Suturing for the Fundamentals of Laparoscopic Surgery (Fls). *J. Biomed. Inform.* 75, 48–62. doi:10.1016/j.jbi.2017.09.010

Rangarajan, K., Davis, H., and Pucher, P. H. (2020). Systematic Review of Virtual Haptics in Surgical Simulation: a Valid Educational Tool. *J. Surg. Educ.* 77, 337–347. doi:10.1016/j.jsurg.2019.09.006

Reiley, C. E., Akinbiyi, T., Burschka, D., Chang, D. C., Okamura, A. M., and Yuh, D. D. (2008). Effects of Visual Force Feedback on Robot-Assisted Surgical Task Performance. *J. Thorac. Cardiovasc. Surg.* 135, 196–202. doi:10.1016/j.jtcvs.2007.08.043

Satava, R. M., Stefanidis, D., Levy, J. S., Smith, R., Martin, J. R., Monfared, S., et al. (2019). Proving the Effectiveness of the Fundamentals of Robotic Surgery (FRS) Skills Curriculum. *Ann. Surg. Publish Ahead Print* 272, 384–392. doi:10.1097/SLA.0000000000003220

Shewchuk, J. R. (1994). *An Introduction to the Conjugate Gradient Method without the Agonizing Pain*. USA: Tech. rep.

Spillmann, J., and Teschner, M. (2007). "Corde: Cosserat Rod Elements for the Dynamic Simulation of One-Dimensional Elastic Objects," in *Proceedings of the 2007 ACM SIGGRAPH/Eurographics symposium on Computer animation*, 63–72.

Theetten, A., Grisoni, L., Andriot, C., and Barsky, B. (2006). Geometrically Exact Dynamic Splines. *Research Report*.

Umetani, N., Schmidt, R., and Stam, J. (2015). "Position-based Elastic Rods," in *Proceedings of the ACM SIGGRAPH/Eurographics Symposium on Computer Animation* (Goslar, DEU: Eurographics Association) (SCA), 14, 21–30.

Wang, Z., Fratarcangeli, M., Ruimi, A., and Srinivasa, A. R. (2017). Real Time Simulation of Inextensible Surgical Thread Using a Kirchhoff Rod Model with Force Output for Haptic Feedback Applications. *Int. J. Sol. Structures* 113-114, 192–208. doi:10.1016/j.ijsolstr.2017.02.017

Xu, L., and Liu, Q. (2018). Real-time Inextensible Surgical Thread Simulation. *Int. J. CARS* 13, 1019–1035. doi:10.1007/s11548-018-1739-1

Watch out for the Robot! Designing Visual Feedback Safety Techniques When Interacting with Encountered-Type Haptic Displays

Victor Rodrigo Mercado[1]*, Ferran Argelaguet[1], Gery Casiez[2] and Anatole Lécuyer[1]

[1]*Inria Rennes—Bretagne Atlantique, Rennes, France,* [2]*Univ. Lille, Inria, CNRS, Centrale Lille, UMR 9189 CRIStAL, Lille, France*

*Correspondence:
Victor Rodrigo Mercado
vrmercado@outlook.com

Encountered-Type Haptic Displays (ETHDs) enable users to touch virtual surfaces by using robotic actuators capable of co-locating real and virtual surfaces without encumbering users with actuators. One of the main challenges of ETHDs is to ensure that the robotic actuators do not interfere with the VR experience by avoiding unexpected collisions with users. This paper presents a design space for safety techniques using visual feedback to make users aware of the robot's state and thus reduce unintended potential collisions. The blocks that compose this design space focus on what and when the feedback is displayed and how it protects the user. Using this design space, a set of 18 techniques was developed exploring variations of the three dimensions. An evaluation questionnaire focusing on immersion and perceived safety was designed and evaluated by a group of experts, which was used to provide a first assessment of the proposed techniques.

Keywords: virtual reality, encountered-type haptic display, immersion, perceived safety, human robot interaction, visual feedback

1 INTRODUCTION

Human-robot interaction (HRI) in virtual reality (VR) promises to enhance immersive applications by adding a new level of interaction between users and machines. This paper focuses on Encountered-Type Haptic Displays (ETHDs), which represent a case of HRI in which robots are used as a means to render haptic feedback in VR. ETHDs possess a surface display, which is displaced by actuators through the real environment to render surfaces that can be touched by users in a virtual environment (VE). ETHDs depend on technologies such as head-mounted displays (HMDs) to "hide" their actuators and to show a VE that contextualizes the haptic feedback rendered by their surface displays. The combination of these technologies allows users to touch surfaces in a VE without disclosing the fact that these surfaces are being brought and placed by a robotic actuator in the real environment (Mercado et al., 2021).

Researchers have considered collisions between users and elements of the real environment fundamental when planning the use of a space for interacting in VR (Kanamori et al., 2018). Commercial VR systems such as SteamVR request users to establish a zone where they could be "safe" from any unexpected collision with elements they cannot see when wearing an HMD (Yang et al., 2018; Steam, 2021). Interacting with an ETHD when wearing an HMD adds a degree of complexity: users are interacting with a moving machine they cannot see. Thus, one of the main challenges of ETHDs is to ensure that the robotic actuators do not interfere with the VR experience.

ETHD systems use path planning algorithms for conceiving a trajectory that optimizes the placement of their end-effector and for avoiding collisions with users at the same time (Yokokohji et al., 2001). This premise has been present in ETHD literature ever since its earliest days (Hirata et al., 1996; Yokokohji et al., 1996). ETHDs need to take into account several factors to position their end-effector in an encountered position: 1) the actuators' configuration, 2) the actuators' movement speed, 3) users' position, 4) users' movement, and 5) users' speed (Yokokohji et al., 2005). These factors have been considered in previous path planning research for ETHDs and yet researchers still consider that there is work to be done to properly optimize this feature for ETHDs (Yokokohji et al., 2005; Araujo et al., 2016; Vonach et al., 2017; Kim et al., 2018). The displacements and movements of a user are often hard to predict and increase the chance of collisions. Additionally, the complexity of calculating an optimal trajectory escalates when the precision of the tracking systems is taken into account. Therefore, this paper explores the use of visual feedback for representing the robotic actuators which are normally hidden from the user's view within VR.

Related research works have proposed solutions integrating visual feedback for avoiding collisions with other users and objects that could be located in the same physical room where the interaction in VR occurs (Lacoche et al., 2017; Scavarelli and Teather, 2017; Kang and Han, 2020). Additionally, commercial VR systems such as SteamVR Steam (2021) and Oculus SDK Oculus (2021) use visual feedback that displays the workspace limits. In the case of human-robot collaboration, literature suggests giving users visual feedback about the robotic system's behavior as a way to increase users' perceived safety when interacting with a robot in virtual reality (Guhl et al., 2018; Kästner and Lambrecht, 2019; Oyekan et al., 2019). However, in the case of ETHDs, disclosing too much information about the robotic actuator's behavior might break users' immersion in a VR application. Recent research works for ETHDs have considered the use of visual feedback integrated into interaction techniques that are designed to optimize the use of an ETHD and also to inform the user about possible collisions (Abtahi et al., 2019; Mercado et al., 2020a). Nevertheless, to the best of our knowledge, related works in the ETHD field have not considered clear design guidelines that address the user's perceived safety when interacting with an ETHD without compromising their immersion in a VE. Many different visual feedback types can be considered, but some may be more efficient than others to inform the user about possible collisions. Safety techniques that disclose more information about the ETHD hidden in the VE might be more effective than other techniques providing more subtle feedback when a collision may occur. However, if the user's perceived safety is increased with techniques displaying the robotic actuator all the time, this might degrade immersion. Thus, signaling a potential trade-off between immersion and perceived safety. The challenge is to find visual techniques that provide at the same time a high sense of perceived safety while degrading the immersion as little as possible.

After discussing the related work, we present our first contribution, 1) a design space for safety techniques for ETHDs that intends to serve as a guide for researchers who desire to provide feedback for avoiding collisions between users and ETHDs. Then, we introduce our second contribution: 2) 18 techniques designed to explore the generative power of our design space. Later we present our third contribution which is 3) the definition of criteria for evaluating safety techniques for ETHDs.

And finally 4), we present a preliminary evaluation with expert users to investigate the trade-off performance of the safety techniques in terms of immersion and perceived safety.

2 RELATED WORK

Collisions with elements that are hidden from the users' view when interacting in VR can not only break the immersion provided by the system but also compromise users' safety (Cirio et al., 2012). Integrating visual feedback that represents objects that are occluded in VEs has been explored by previous research as a means to increase usability in VR scenarios (McGill et al., 2015; Yang et al., 2018). The presented related works can be classified into visual feedback made for avoiding collisions with robots and feedback for avoiding elements present in the real environment such as walls and/or people. We describe these efforts hereby.

2.1 Visual Feedback for Avoiding Collisions With Robots

Avoiding collisions between users and robots within VEs has been explored primarily in the context of user training for robot teleoperation (Kuts et al., 2017; Guhl et al., 2018; Oyekan et al., 2019; Chen et al., 2020). The work of Oyekan et al. (2019) reported that users' stress concerning the robot's presence in a shared workspace increased under three conditions: when the robot's speed increased 1), when the user and robot were close 2), and when the user did not know what the robot was going to do next 3). The importance of knowing about the robot's actions was also highlighted in the work of Guhl et al. (2018). Their research reported that in order to increase users' perceived safety when interacting with a robot in a VE, users should be aware of the intentions of the robot, particularly concerning the knowledge of the robot's trajectory. Thus, these researchers conceived an AR system that displayed the robot's path planning for avoiding potential risks of collisions with users. Other approaches come from visualizing robot navigation data in mixed reality as in Kästner and Lambrecht (2019) system, and Shepherd et al. (2019) system that displays the co-located robot's trajectory.

In the field of ETHDs, safety techniques revolve around visual feedback to indicate where users can and cannot touch. Abtahi et al. (2019) interaction technique considers the display of a panel in the VE when users are at risk of collision with their ungrounded drone-based ETHD.

The works of Mercado et al. (2020b,a) and Posselt et al. (2017) displayed the contact area when their grounded ETHDs displace from one position to another as a means to indicate to the user when to enter in contact with the surface.

2.2 Visual Feedback for Avoiding Collisions With Elements in Real Environments

Large environments where users can navigate can often be crowded with elements that could break users' immersion when a collision occurs. Kanamori et al. (2018) explored methods for displaying elements of a real environment in VR, consisting of superimposing a virtual point cloud to represent objects in the real environment. The results of their user study suggested that VR objects did not reduce immersion as much as compared the point cloud and commercial chaperone methods such as SteamVR's Steam (2021). In the former method, real objects are represented in the VE as a point cloud presented using the same shapes as the real object. In the latter method, a circle is projected on the floor of the VE indicating the boundaries of the interaction zone.

In addition, the work of Hartmann et al. (2019) proposed an approach for displaying in VR the real environment elements that are close to colliding with users. Their approach was compared to the SteamVR chaperone in a user study where participants played VR games in a room with obstacles. After the experiment, participants were asked to answer a subjective questionnaire to evaluate users' reflections about the approaches in matters of safety, physical manipulations, communication, their transition between virtual and real environments, and immersion. Results yielded a higher perceived immersion and safety coming from approaches that integrated real-life elements in the VE. Recent research work from Kang and Han (2020) proposed a series of visual feedback to represent real objects that users could encounter when navigating in VR based on point clouds that appeared in the VE. A user study was conducted to evaluate users' experience with the visual feedback techniques. The user study considered the following conditions for displaying the point cloud: once per trial; gradually as the users got closer to the object; and permanently during the entire trial. Participants were asked to walk in an area with obstacles in the real environment that were not depicted in the VE. After the experimental trials, participants were asked to answer a subjective experience questionnaire that asked them about their experience in terms of awareness of the surrounding environment, task attention, perceived safety, and their preferences for all the techniques. Participants reported that they preferred the feedback display using the gradual approach. This approach also yielded the highest scores in task attention and perceived safety.

Safety techniques in VR also consider the possibility of colliding with walls or boundaries of the workspace where interaction takes place in the real environment. Cirio et al. (2012) proposed several visual metaphors to indicate to users the presence of a screen in an immersive projection system. Researchers conducted a user study where they assessed the performance of the visual metaphors for helping users to avoid collisions with the CAVE walls when walking in VEs. Results from the analysis of the participants' walking indicated that using a virtual companion was efficient for keeping participants in a "safe zone" relatively far from the CAVE walls.

Lacoche et al. (2017) proposed different visual feedback approaches to help users to acknowledge the presence of collaborators sharing the same physical workspace when interacting in VR. A subjective questionnaire about users' global satisfaction was used to measure users' experience quality, aestheticism, and efficiency for each visual feedback condition. Results suggested that users appreciated more sharing a virtual space with a ghost avatar of the user's when sharing a workspace in VR.

Another example of user collision avoidance methods is considered by the work of Medeiros et al. (2021). In their work, they explored visual feedback for users in VR for disclosing the position of other people present in the real environment. They implemented several techniques based on UI overlays and virtual elements. Researchers conducted a user study where participants played a game in a VE in which recorded motions of people were used as obstacles. After the experimental trials, researchers assessed participants' perceived presence in the VE, focus on the task, their alert preference, and the alert's efficiency. Participants stressed that even if visual feedback was useful for indicating the presence of other people in the real environment, receiving alerts of possible collisions compromised their immersion in the system.

2.3 Summary

Related research works suggest the use of visual feedback to indicate the presence of objects in the real environment that could collide with users when executing a task in the VE.

This feedback considers integrating elements of the real environment into the virtual one or displaying a warning to indicate to users that a possible collision could take place.

However, displaying information and/or warnings about the real environment's configuration could compromise users' immersion (Medeiros et al., 2021).

To the best of our knowledge, and more especially when it comes to ETHDs, there are no design guidelines that suggest how to balance the trade-off between providing visual feedback to increase users perceived safety without compromising their immersion in the VE.

3 DESIGN SPACE

The first contribution of this paper is a design space meant to classify the previous work from the literature and help researchers to generate new safety techniques for ETHDs. As such, our design space allows to generate different possibilities of visual feedback meant to represent the ETHD system's status when rendering haptic feedback. The design space considers several blocks with features that describe the way the safety techniques could be implemented.

3.1 Design Space Organization

The design space is organized in three blocks that describe the feedback given to the user by answering three questions: *what?*, *when?*, and *how?*

- The **what?** block answers to the question: *what information is the user receiving from the feedback delivered by the safety technique?*
- The **when?** block answers to the question: *when is the feedback is delivered by the safety technique?*
- The **how?** block answers to the question: *how is the feedback is displayed by the safety technique?*

TABLE 1 | Design Space with related research works and the 18 techniques we designed. This table represents the three blocks of the design space along with their respective features. The conceived techniques along with related literature research works represent different combinations of the design space's features.

Blocks	Block What?		Block When?						Block How?			
Category	Feedback Information		Feedback Persistence			Protection Strategy			Visual Integration		Representation	
Technique/Feature	W	SS	S	G	P	BE	VB	ID	UI	VE	R	M
Revealers												
Full Reveal		○	○		○			○		○	○	
Partial Reveal		○	○					○		○	○	
Gradient Reveal		○		○				○	○	○		
Magic Light Reveal		○	○					○	○	○		
X-Ray		○	○					○		○		
Hartmann et al. (2019) Full		○	○					○		○	○	
Lacoche et al. (2017) Ghost Avatar	○	○	○					○		○		○
Kang and Han (2020) SafetyXR (VR-OP)	○	○	○					○		○		○
Kang and Han (2020) SafetyXR (VR-GP)	○	○		○				○		○		○
Kang and Han (2020) SafetyXR (VR-CP)	○	○			○			○		○		○
Trajectory Beams												
Trajectory Beam		○			○				○	○		
Guhl et al. (2018)		○			○			○	○			
Loading Trajectory Beam		○								○		
Bounds												
Hiding Box		○	○		○					○		○
Trajectory Bounds		○	○				○			○		
Hartmann et al. (2019) Grid		○	○				○			○		
Lacoche et al. (2017) Extended Grid		○	○				○		○	○		
Kanamori et al. (2018)		○	○						○	○		
Vosniakos et al. (2019)		○		○			○					
Device Bounds	○	○		○	○		○			○		○
Radar		○	○						○			
Blockers												
Guardian Angel	○		○			○				○		
Cirio et al. (2012) Virtual Companion	○		○			○				○		
Shield	○		○			○			○			
Signals	○		○						○			
Warning												
Arrow			○			○			○			○
Cirio et al. (2012) Signs	○		○			○			○			○
Cirio et al. (2012) Magic Barrier	○					○	○			○		
Medeiros et al. (2021) 3DArrow		○			○			○	○			
Medeiros et al. (2021) Color Glow	○		○		○			○		○		
Abtahi et al. (2019)	○		○					○	○			
Screen Overlay		○						○	○	○	○	
Lacoche et al. (2017) Safe Navigation Space		○	○									
Projector		○	○						○			
Timer					○			○	○			○

The features' names are abbreviated: W, warning; SS, system's state; S, sudden; G, gradual; P, permanent; BE, blocking element; VB, virtual bounds; ID, information display; UI, user interface; VE, virtual element; R, realistic; M, metaphorical.

These blocks are further described hereby:

3.1.1 Block What

3.1.1.1 Feedback Information

This design space category refers to the information the user is going to receive as feedback. The two features considered are *warning* and *system state*. *Warning* consists of displaying a warning about a possible collision with a real element in the environment. *System State* consists of providing information about the system state when the user gets close to the ETHD.

Examples of *warning* are the works of Abtahi et al. (2019) and Cirio et al. (2012) that display an abstract warning for indicating users not to get close to the robot. Some techniques use visual feedback for describing the *system state* in matters of position, configuration, and trajectory. An example of the state of the art is the robot integration in the VE proposed by Vosniakos et al. (2019) where users can also acknowledge the robot's actions in the VE (**Table 1**).

3.1.2 Block When

This block comprises the *feedback persistence* category which is described hereby:

3.1.2.1 Feedback Persistence

This category refers to the time and the way feedback appears in the VE. The feedback can be displayed only for a moment (sudden), gradually (gradual), or permanently (permanent). The *gradual* feature consists of gradually making the feedback appear based on a parameter such as the distance between the user and the element being represented. The work of Kang and Han presented a set of visual feedback techniques using a point cloud representing an object that could come in collision with the users. Their work considers a point cloud that could appear suddenly (once), gradually as the users come closer to the object, or permanently (Kang and Han, 2020).

3.1.3 Block How

This block comprises the *protection strategy*, *visual integration*, and *representation*. The categories comprised in this block aim at describing how the safety technique protects the user (*protection strategy*) and integrates itself in the VE (*visual integration* and *representation*). These categories are described hereby:

3.1.3.1 Protection Strategy

This category refers to how the feedback protects users. Three different features are considered for this category: *blocking elements*, *virtual bounds*, and *information display*. The *Blocking Element* feature consists in having a virtual element that interposes itself between the user's hand and the haptic display. This allows having a blocking element that could avoid undesired contact with the haptic device. The *Virtual Bounds* feature consists in having bounds surrounding elements of the VE for avoiding any possible collisions between the user and a part of the VE that is still to be rendered or that is occluding the haptic display's virtual position. The *information display* feature consists in displaying information about the real elements that are occluded in the VE. The displayed information could allow the users to acknowledge the position of real elements for avoiding any undesired collisions with those elements. In the context of ETHD interaction, *information display* can comprise the robot's position, trajectory, and actuator configuration.

An example of a blocking element in the literature comes from the work of Cirio et al. (2012). Their work presents a virtual companion that interposes itself between users and an element that could collide with the users in the real environment. In the case of the *virtual bounds*, the extended grid technique proposed by Lacoche et al. (2017) uses bounding for an object/person that could collide with users when interacting in a VE. In the case of *information display* the Area technique proposed by Lacoche et al. presents information about the position of the other person who could collide with the user (**Table 1**).

3.1.3.2 Visual Integration

This category refers to the way the information is going to be displayed to the user concerning the visual elements. The two branches considered are information displayed on the *user interface* or as a *virtual element* integrated into the environment. The *user interface* feature consists in displaying an element as if it was part of the system's user interface. The virtual element feature consists in using or integrating an element into the VE that could serve as visual support or metaphor for displaying information.

The work of Medeiros et al. (2021) illustrates an example of the *user interface* feature. This work used visual feedback overlaid on the system's UI in the case of their Color Glow and 3DArrow techniques. The *virtual element* feature is represented in the works of Cirio et al. for the magic barrier tape and the virtual companion (**Table 1**).

3.1.3.3 Representation

This category refers to the way the techniques can be represented in the VE. Two different features are considered: *realistic* and *metaphorical*. In the *realistic* feature category, the safety elements are represented as realistic as they can be in the VE as in the work of Hartmann et al. (2019) where elements of the real environment are inserted as they are captured from images of the real environment. On the other hand, the *metaphorical* feature category refers to feedback representations based on metaphors and/or analogies. For this feature, safety elements are adapted into metaphors to provide more congruence between the task and/or the VE's context such as the virtual companion proposed by Cirio et al. (2012).

Table 1 presents all safety techniques identified in the literature according to the different features of our design space. **Figure 1** depicts the design space's features and how they are illustrated through some of the safety techniques.

3.2 Safety Techniques

The second contribution of this paper is the development of a set of 18 safety techniques that illustrate the generative power of the previously presented design space. These techniques were largely inspired by

Watch out for the Robot! Designing Visual Feedback Safety Techniques When Interacting...

175

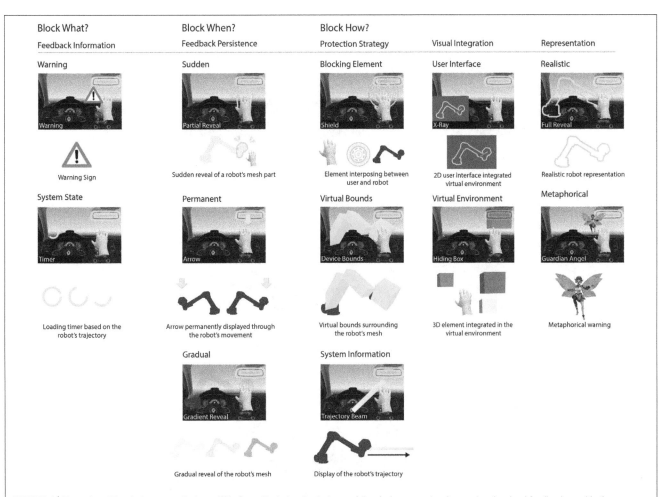

FIGURE 1 | Examples of the design space features. This figure illustrates the features of the design space by showcasing the visual feedback used in the implemented in some of the safety techniques.

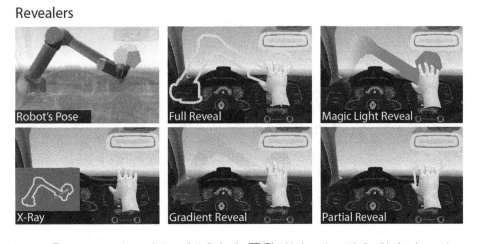

FIGURE 2 | The revealers group. This group comprises techniques that display the ETHD's virtual counterpart in the virtual environment.

previous techniques proposed in the literature and adapted to the context of interaction with an ETHD. All the conceived techniques were implemented in a simulation made in Unity where a virtual model of a grounded ETHD based on the Universal Robot's UR5 cobot was used to render different elements of a virtual automobile cockpit. **Figures 2–6** depict the implementation of all the techniques

Beams

Robot's Pose | Trajectory Beam | Loading Trajectory Beam

FIGURE 3 | The trajectory beams group. This group comprises techniques that display the ETHD's trajectory when moving to one point to another.

Blockers

Robot's Pose | Guardian Angel | Shield

FIGURE 4 | The blockers group. This group comprises techniques that interpose a virtual object between user and ETHD to block/avoid a possible unexpected collision.

Signals

Robot's Pose | Timer | Warning

Arrow | Projector | Screen Overlay

FIGURE 5 | The signals group. This group comprises techniques that use basic signaling metaphors for displaying information about the position of the ETHD's end-effector.

in this VE. More details about the techniques are available in the accompanying video. The techniques were grouped into five groups that represent the techniques' main features. The conceived groups are presented hereby:

3.2.1 Revealers

This group comprises several techniques dedicated to displaying and rendering the haptic device in the VE. The revealers group integrates techniques inspired by the works of Lacoche et al. (2017), Kang and Han (2020), and Kanamori et al. (2018) that represent a part of the environment or an element close to colliding with the users. This information display is made for users to acknowledge the presence of near elements and thus helping users to avoid collisions with the elements.

Several visual feedback strategies are comprised in this group such as revealing the haptic display entirely, gradually or partially. In the *Full Reveal* technique, the haptic display mesh is rendered entirely through the whole simulation. This technique is inspired by the constant point cloud display proposed by Kang and Han (2020) and the contour display presented by Kanamori et al. (2018). The difference from the previous research work relies on the fact that our technique displays the device's contour rather than a point cloud (**Figure 1**, top-right). We conceived a technique to gradually display the ETHD (*Gradient Reveal*) in which the robot's virtual mesh transparency is modified according to the distance between the robot and the users' hands. Beyond a certain threshold, the robot's mesh becomes more opaque as the hand gets closer to it (**Figure 1**, bottom-left).

FIGURE 6 | The bounds group. This group comprises techniques that bound the ETHD device for protecting the user from getting closer to the ETHD.

The implementation of this technique is inspired by the gradient point technique proposed by Kang and Han (2020). We considered the option of only displaying the parts of the robot that were the closest to the user for the *Partial Reveal* technique. When the user approaches the ETHD, the mesh of the closest part activates and gets displayed in the VE. This indicates the user of the presence and proximity of the robot without disclosing the entire device and compromising the users' immersion. This technique requires dividing the ETHD's mesh into several parts (**Figure 1**, second column from the left, top). In our case, we divided the ETHD's based on the joints that compose the robot. The implementation of this technique is inspired by the partial rendering of the user virtual representation by Lacoche et al. (2017). Their technique consisted in representing a ghost avatar of another user's HMD as a means to represent the users' positions in a collaborative VE. We also considered the opportunity of revealing the robot under other approaches based on real-life methods for revealing hidden objects such as the *Magic Light Reveal* and *X-Ray* techniques. This first technique consists of a "black light" that emanates from the user's virtual hand model that shows the haptic display's mesh within the light range. When the users come close to the robot, the part of the robot's mesh that enters the light range is displayed, as if it was revealed the same way that invisible ink is revealed under a black light. The *X-Ray* technique consists of a viewport screen located in the VE that displays the users' hand and the haptic display. The metaphor was inspired by the use of x-rays in medicine to see through the skin of patients. This technique is conceived to inform the users about the proximity of their hands to the haptic display without displaying a co-located mesh in the VE (**Figure 1**, second column from the right, top). **Figure 2** showcases the techniques that are part of this group.

3.2.2 Trajectory Beams

This group comprises the safety techniques that visually represent the haptic device trajectory when the movement is discrete and the trajectory is planned with anticipation. This principle is inspired by the technique proposed by Guhl et al.

(2018) that consists in displaying the robot's trajectory when in motion.

The *Trajectory Beam* technique consists in displaying the predefined trajectory of the haptic device's end-effector in the VE (**Figure 1**, bottom-right). This allows users to better acknowledge the space where the haptic interface will travel. The *Loading Trajectory Beam* technique has a similar behavior compared to the previous one. The main difference is that the rendered trajectory shrinks as the haptic display arrives from the starting position to the final one. **Figure 3** displays the two techniques that are part of this group.

3.2.3 Blockers

This group comprises safety techniques that use a blocking virtual element between the user and the haptic device. These techniques use visual feedback that interposes itself between the user and the device to catch the user's attention and "block" any possible movement that would yield a direct collision with the haptic device (**Figure 1**, middle column, top).

The *Guardian Angel* technique uses a virtual guardian that places itself between the user's hand and the haptic device (**Figure 1**, right column, middle). When the user's hand is far from the robot, the guardian enters an "idle" state. In this state the guardian wanders around the users, out of their vision field. Once the user's hand becomes closer to the device, the guardian "reacts" and appears immediately between the users' hand and a part of the device where contact could have taken place. We conceived a similar technique using more abstract visual feedback called *Shield*. This technique, as its name suggests, consists of a virtual shield that appears between the user's hand and the device. This "shield" permits users to acknowledge they might enter in collision with the haptic device at the moment users enter in proximity with it. Both techniques require detecting the distance from the users' hand to the closest point of the haptic display virtual representation into the VE. Once a proximity threshold has been detected, the blocker element (in these cases: the guardian angel and the shield) will appear in the midpoint between the users' hand and the closest point between the hand and the haptic display mesh. The main difference between these techniques is that the guardian angel uses an animated character that can be integrated in the VE, while the shield appears as a 2D UI for blocking any contact between users and robot. These safety techniques were conceived under the inspiration of the work of Cirio et al. (2012) who proposed a virtual companion for helping users to avoid collisions with the walls in a CAVE system. **Figure 4** showcases the techniques that comprise this group.

3.2.4 Signals

This group comprises safety techniques that consist of metaphorical signaling methods. This group considers the use of basic signs such as arrows or the conventional warning signs used in work environments. The *Arrow* technique consists of an arrow placed at the top of the haptic display's end-effector. This arrow is always visible throughout the whole simulation and it allows the user to acknowledge the device's end-effector position (**Figure 1**, second column from the left, middle). This technique is somehow inspired by the 3D Arrow metaphor presented in the work of Medeiros et al. (2021). The *Warning* technique consists of a virtual warning signal that appears right next to the user's hand when the latter is close to the haptic display (**Figure 1**, top-left). This technique is inspired by the work of Abtahi et al. (2019) which displays a warning panel when users get close to the ungrounded UAV-based ETHD. We also considered retrieving a warning technique used frequently in gaming contexts such as *Screen Overlay*. This technique consists of a screen overlay that colors the contour of the users' field of view in red whenever their hand gets close to the haptic display. A similar work in the literature is the Color Glow technique presented by Medeiros et al. (2021).

We considered another approach for "signaling" the robot's position through a more abstract metaphor. The *Projection* technique consists in projecting in the VE a floor representing a walking user sharing the interaction workspace in the real environment. Projections are made to display the position and area that an element has in the VE so users can avoid collisions with the aforementioned element. This technique is inspired by the safe navigation space technique presented by Lacoche et al. (2017) that projects on the floor of the VE the position of another user sharing the same physical workspace in a VR application. The techniques proposed in this group can also indicate other properties of the robot's movement beyond its position. For instance, the *Timer* technique consists of a timer displayed when the robot is moving in a predefined trajectory. The timer indicates the amount of completion of the predefined trajectory thus indicating when the user can interact with a rendered surface by the haptic display (**Figure 1**, left column, middle). **Figure 5** illustrates the techniques that comprise this group.

3.2.5 Bounds

This group comprises safety techniques that use barriers and/ or bounds that surround the elements that the user could collide with. These bounds can surround the device, the device trajectory path, or the target contact area. The bounds techniques are inspired by the work proposed by Lacoche et al. (2017) and in the SteamVR Chaperone Steam (2021).

This group comprises techniques that bound the workspace and/or the haptic device as a means to indicate the user that the interaction space is limited or constrained. Examples of this group are: *Hiding Box*, *Trajectory Bounds*, and *Device Bounds*, and *Radar* (**Figure 6**).

In order to add bounds around the device's mesh, we conceived the *Device Bounds* technique. This technique consists of mesh boxes surrounding the haptic display's virtual model (**Figure 1** middle column, middle row). When the user gets close to these bounds, the mesh will appear to disclose the device configuration as well as its position. We also considered bounding the final position of the ETHD's trajectory. To do so, we designed the *Hiding Box* technique which consists of a box mesh placed at a desired end-effector's final position. As the haptic display arrives at this desired position, the box's mesh starts to fade and reveals the zone that can be explored and touched once the ETHD has reached its target. The possibility of surrounding the device's trajectory was also considered with the *Trajectory Bounds* technique. When users cross a given proximity threshold to any point of the trajectory, the mesh surrounding the entire trajectory will appear to indicate that the haptic rendering process is not finished and that the haptic display is displacing its end-effector from one position to another. We conceived a technique that acts as an "inverse" bound called *Radar*. This technique consists of a spinning arrow attached to the users' virtual hand models that acts as a compass and radar, indicating the haptic display's position and proximity. The arrow changes color from green to red as the users' hand gets closer to the haptic device. The technique's behavior as an inverse bound is justified in the sense that the information displayed by this technique is expected to "bound" the users' hand from any involuntary contact with the ETHD's hidden mesh. The technique is based on radars for detecting objects mainly in military contexts.

3.3 Example

Our design space can be used as a tool for creating safety techniques for ETHDs. **Table 1** depicts how the 18 safety techniques presented in this research address the blocks and features of our design space. Hereby an example is provided on how the "guardian angel" safety technique was created using our design space. The first block that was considered was the block **what?** In this case, the guardian angel technique delivers *warning* feedback information. Then the block **when?** was addressed by selecting a *sudden* appearance of the guardian angel when the users come close to colliding with the ETHD. The block **how?** was addressed as follows: a protection strategy consisting of a *blocking element* was used since it is the guardian angel that interposes itself between the users' hand and the robot; a visual integration consisting of a virtual element (the guardian angel) integrated in the VE; and a metaphorical representation since the blocking element is represented as a "guardian" that interposes itself between the user and the robot to keep the former safe. The rest of the techniques presented in this paper followed the same approach when they were created, with the only difference being that other branches in the blocks' categories were explored.

4 EVALUATION WITH ENCOUNTERED-TYPE HAPTIC DISPLAYS EXPERTS

An evaluation was conducted with a group of ETHD experts for assessing the performance of the safety techniques mainly in the dimensions of users' immersion and perceived safety. This led to the third contribution of this paper: the definition of a set of evaluation criteria from the literature and an interview with experts. These criteria were designed to be used for assessing qualitatively safety techniques for ETHDs.

4.1 Evaluation Criteria

The proposed criteria were retrieved from insights of the literature on evaluation methods for assessing the performance of their safety techniques and also discussed with four experts in the ETHD and haptic research fields. Two primary criteria were identified: immersion and perceived safety. In this paper, we consider *immersion* as the capability that the system (the ETHD and visual display technologies) has for ensuring users' immersion in the VE by properly rendering sensory feedback without disclosing the presence of real elements behind the scene rendering. Research works such as the works of Kanamori et al. (2018) and Hartmann et al. (2019) considered immersion as a criterion to evaluate their techniques.

In the context of interacting with an ETHD in VR, we considered *perceived safety* as the users' sensation of being safe during their interaction with the haptic display in VR. This criterion has been considered in the literature for assessing if the users feel comfortable when interacting with elements that could come in physical contact with them such as robots (Bartneck et al., 2017; Oyekan et al., 2019), walls (Hartmann et al., 2019), and other objects present in the workspace (Kang and Han, 2020).

Our literature review and discussion with the experts identified a set of complementary criteria, which could also be linked with immersion and perceived safety. We first considered other criteria that can be related to properties directly associated with the visual feedback used by safety techniques such as *visual clutter* and *ecological adaptability*. For example, Lacoche et al. (2017) assessed the efficiency of the visual feedback proposed by their safety techniques. We considered measuring the visual efficiency of our techniques through cluttering (visual clutter) and aesthetics (ecological adaptability). Visual clutter refers to the degree to which the additional visual feedback occludes the virtual environment, and is linked with the additional virtual elements added to the environment. If the visual feedback used within a safety technique clutters the VE, then users' immersion could be compromised since there could exist a larger number of distractors when users are performing a task in the VE. Ecological adaptability addresses an aspect of visual feedback more oriented towards aesthetics and pertinence to the context of the VE. We defined ecological adaptability as the visual feedback's adaptability level for being represented in different tasks and contexts in VE. In this context, a safety technique with high ecological adaptability should be able to be implemented using different visual metaphors for a large diversity of contexts and use-case scenarios. On the other hand, a technique with low ecological adaptability might be inefficient under different scenarios and thus it might break users' immersion in the task carried out within a VE.

The safety techniques should also be evaluated in matters of their capability of accurately representing information about the presence of the ETHD. We considered the use of *co-location* as an important factor that might help users to acknowledge the presence of the ETHD when they are using an HMD. In the context of visual feedback for safety techniques for ETHDs, co-location refers to the correspondence of the visual feedback with respect to the ETHD's position in the real environment. In the literature, co-location has been considered to display visual feedback about the robot's behavior (Shepherd et al., 2019) in an HMD. We considered that safety techniques should also make users aware that they are interacting with a robot in real-life. Therefore, we included the feature *device awareness*. This feature refers to how much users are aware of the ETHD's position and state in the VE. Being aware of the actuator's presence is useful for users' perceived safety since they acknowledge the presence of something that can collide with them as signaled in previous research works (Hartmann et al., 2019; Oyekan et al., 2019; Kang and Han, 2020).

We further considered two additional criteria referred as *users' trust* and *mental workload*. In the context of safety techniques, we defined mental workload as the demand imposed on users in the process of understanding the safety techniques. This notion of mental workload is derived from that of Moray (2013). A Low mental workload should be favorable for user safety since users could be easily focused on simple tasks and therefore it could be easier for them to avoid any involuntary collision with the system. Mental workload could also be linked to immersion, as low mental workload could also be linked with less noticeable safety techniques. We considered mental workload based on the study of Kang and Han (2020) and Medeiros et al. (2021) who assessed users' subjective perception of the attention they invested in doing tasks in VR while avoiding at the same time collisions with elements present in the real environment. Finally, we defined user trust as the level of trust users can have towards the system based on the understanding of the ETHD behavior within the VE. The higher the level of trust in the system, the higher the sense of perceived safety for potential users could be. In the literature, the work of Oyekan et al. (2019) evaluated user trust for their studies.

The eight different criteria were assembled in a unique questionnaire with eight items scored with a 7-Likert scale. For each criterion, the definition was provided to ensure that participants well understood the different concepts. Except for visual clutter and mental workload, higher values mean better. For the sake of clarity, the analysis of the results will consider inverse scores (8 − 1) for visual clutter and mental workload to ensure that for all criteria higher values means better.

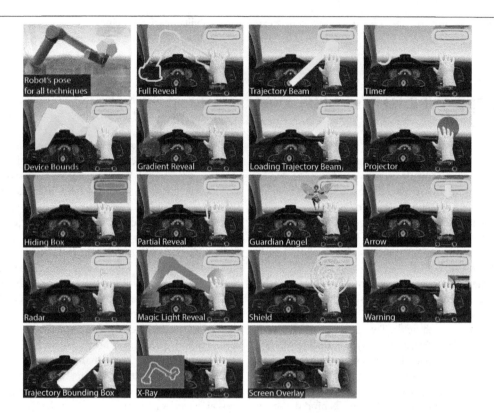

FIGURE 7 | Illustration of the conceived 18 safety techniques designed. The safety techniques are represented in a virtual environment representing an automobile interior. All the technique screenshots represent a status with a robot pose as similar as possible to the robot pose shown on the top left.

The fourth contribution of this paper consists in an preliminary evaluation carried out by a set of experts. Further details about the preliminary evaluation procedure and results are presented hereby.

4.2 Participants

Ten participants (2 female, 24–57, M = 34) took part in the experiment. They were all international experts with an average of 2.8 years spent in the fields of haptics and VR in both academia and industry. The four participants of the preliminary evaluation participated in this experiment. Each member of this set of experts has at least one scientific publication in the field of ETHDs and has been involved in a project with ETHDs for more than two years. We used experts instead of non-experts given the form of the experiment. As an important note, none of the authors participated in the two evaluations carried out in this paper.

4.3 Experimental Procedure

Due to the COVID-19 sanitary situation, the experiment was conducted through an online questionnaire sent to the participants so they could answer it individually. This questionnaire required participants to visualize videos of each safety technique and then provide the score for each evaluation criteria. Although it would have been ideal to let participants test the actual ETHD system, we assumed the experts would be able to imagine the technique in an immersive setting when watching the videos, compared to non-experts. Each technique was presented as a ~25s video showing the ETHD rendering several interest points of an automobile interior, highlighted in blue as presented in **Figure 7**. The **Supplementary Video S1** displayed two views: 1) a view of the robot moving through the automobile model and 2) the user's view. This allowed participants to see the users' view and, at the same time, the actual movement of the ETHD, to better assess the safety issues by comparing the actual robot configuration in the real workspace to the visual feedback provided by the techniques in the VE. Participants could play the video as many times as they wanted before answering the questions. They were instructed to imagine being in a VR setting with the video showing the technique presented in the VR headset. The participants were then prompted to evaluate on a 7-point Likert scale each one of the criteria discussed in the previous section. Descriptions from the criteria were included for each question to remind the participants about the meaning of each criterion.

4.4 Results

During an initial analysis, we explored the role of the principal criteria, immersion and perceived safety (**Figure 8**). The visual inspection of the data showed one big cluster, with techniques with mean immersion scores between 3.5 and 5.5 and mean perceived safety scores between 3.5 and 4.5. *Full Reveal* and *Gradient reveal* techniques stood out in the perceived safety score. Although the Friedman ANOVA

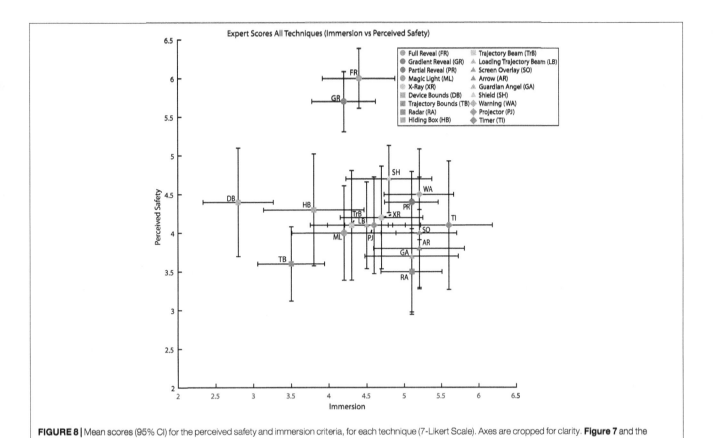

FIGURE 8 | Mean scores (95% CI) for the perceived safety and immersion criteria, for each technique (7-Likert Scale). Axes are cropped for clarity. **Figure 7** and the accompanying video for watching the illustrations of the techniques.

TABLE 2 | The principal component analysis from the questionnaire data. The first part details the correlations for each criterion. The second part presents the eigenvalues and the percent of the variance explained by the principal component. Finally, the third part shows the correlation between principal components.

Criteria	PC1	PC2
Device Awareness	**0.86**	−0.22
Co-Location	**0.85**	0.00
Perceived Safety	**0.81**	0.17
User Trust	**0.80**	0.12
Immersion	0.06	**0.84**
Visual Clutter	−0.19	**0.80**
Ecological Adaptability	0.18	**0.65**
Mental Workload	0.10	**0.60**
Eigenvalues	2.86	2.22
Percent of variance	36%	28%
Correlation with PC1	100%	6%
Correlation with PC2	6%	100%

The bold values were highlighted to show their pertinence to PC1 and PC2. The first four highlighted values (top to bottom) correspond to PC1 which integrates the Device Awareness, Co-Location, Perceived Safety, and User trust criteria. The rest of the highlighted values correspond to PC2, which integrates Immersion, Visual Clutter, Ecological Adaptability, and Mental Workload.

found significant differences for the perceived safety ($\chi^2(17) = 38.8$, $p < 0.001$) and immersion scores ($\chi^2(17) = 54.18$, $p < 0.001$), post-hoc tests (Wilcoxon pairwise with Bonferroni correction) were not significant (all $p > 0.05$). The non-significance of the results can mainly be attributed to the high number of conditions and the correction for multiple pairwise tests.

In a second step, we explored the potential relationships between the primary (immersion and perceived safety) and the secondary criteria (device awareness, co-location, user trust, visual clutter, ecological adaptability, and, mental workload). For this purpose, instead of using cross-correlations, we decided to conduct a principal component analysis (**Table 2**) to extract meaningful relationships among all criteria.

Before conducting the PCA analysis, we checked for the sampling adequacy using the Kaiser-Meyer-Olkin (KMO) measure. The overall KMO was 0.7, which can be considered as moderate sampling adequacy. In addition, we used the Bartlet's test of sphericity to observe if the correlations between the criteria were enough for running a PCA ($\chi^2(28) = 160.107$; $p < 0.001$). Considering the limited sample size, we considered that this was sufficient for a preliminary assessment.

TABLE 3 | Average response scores for all the techniques and all the evaluation criteria. The three highest values are highlighted in blue while the three lowest values are highlighted in orange.

Evaluation Criteria/Safety Techniques	Immersion	Visual Clutter	Ecological Adaptability	Mental Workload	Immersion Subscale	Perceived Safety	Co-Location	Device Awareness	User Trust	Safety Subscale
Revealers										
Full Reveal	4.4	4.2	5.4	5.1	4.8	6	5.6	6.1	5.4	5.8
Gradient Reveal	4.2	3.6	5.3	4.1	4.3	5.7	5.7	6.1	5.4	5.7
Partial Reveal	5.1	5	4.8	4	4.7	4.4	4.5	4.5	4	4.4
Magic Light	4.2	4.3	4.1	3.1	3.9	4	4.5	4.2	4	4.2
X-Ray	4.7	3.5	5.6	3.6	4.4	4.2	3.9	4.1	4.5	4.2
Trajectory Beams										
Trajectory Beam	4.3	3.7	5.2	4.2	4.4	4.1	4.5	3.9	3.8	4.1
Loading Trajectory Beam	4.5	3.9	5.2	4.3	4.5	4.1	4.3	4	4	4.1
Bounds										
Device Bounds	2.8	1.8	4.7	3.6	3.2	4.4	5.1	5.3	3.9	4.7
Hiding Box	3.8	3.2	4.6	5.1	4.2	4.3	3	2.8	3.2	3.3
Trajectory Bounds	3.5	2.8	4.4	3.4	3.5	3.6	3.7	3.5	3.3	3.5
Radar	5.1	5.1	5.1	3.5	4.7	3.5	3.8	3.6	3.6	3.6
Blockers										
Guardian Angel	5.1	4.6	5.6	5	5.1	3.7	3.6	2.5	3.1	3.2
Shield	4.8	3.5	5.4	4.6	4.6	4.7	4.8	3.9	4.2	4.4
Signals										
Projector	4.6	4.2	4.7	3.8	4.3	4.1	4.2	3.6	4.1	4.0
Screen Overlay	5.2	6.1	6.5	4.5	5.6	4	2.3	2.5	3.8	3.2
Warning	5.2	4.8	5.6	4.6	5.1	4.5	4.1	3.8	4.1	4.1
Arrow	5.2	5.9	5.4	5	5.4	3.8	4.2	2.7	4.2	3.7
Timer	5.6	5.9	6.6	4.8	5.7	4.1	3.2	3	4.1	3.6

When considering only two components, the PCA analysis showed that they could explain the 64% of the observed variance and provided a fit of 0.92.

The PCA analysis, see correlation coefficients in **Table 2**, revealed a clear dichotomy of the criteria enabling to split them into two major clusters. The first one considering device awareness, co-location, perceived safety, and user trust. The second one considering immersion, visual clutter, ecological adaptability, and mental workload. The separation between the two clusters was clear, as the correlation between the unused criteria is weak (smaller or equal than |0.22|). Furthermore, the correlations between principal components were low (≈ 0.06). The first cluster aggregates criteria related to the subjective perception and awareness of the robot, while the second cluster focuses more on the impact and adequation of the visual components in the VE. As our main criteria were safety and immersion, and considering that each one was in a different cluster, we decided to name the clusters as "Safety Subscale" and "Immersion Subscale".

We also explored the addition of a third factor, which increased the variance explained to 11% and increased the fit by 0.03. With three factors configuration, the main difference was

that the mental workload was strongly correlated with the third component and not the second one. The remaining correlation remained similar. We did not consider the third component for simplicity and the good fit for two first components.

Table 3 presents the average score for each safety technique for each evaluation criterion and the aggregated scores for both subscales. The aggregation was computed by averaging the criteria scores for each cluster.

Moreover, **Figure 8** displays the mean and confidence intervals for each technique concerning the immersion and safety subscales.

The Friedman ANOVA analysis showed a similar result as the one conducted on the immersion and perceived safety criteria, thus we present the results considering the rank among each subscale to provide qualitative results.

Regarding the technique clusters, overall, revealer techniques obtained higher scores in the safety-related subscale while presenting average scores in the immersion-related subscale.

The trajectory beam techniques obtained average scores in both subscales, while bound techniques tended to obtain the lowest scores in both subscales.

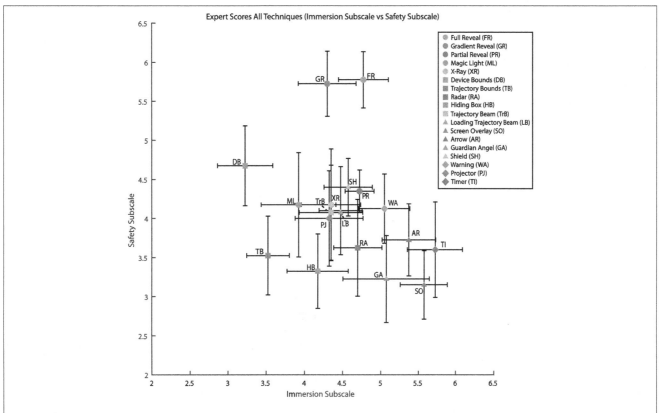

FIGURE 9 | Overall average scores for the Safety and (PC1) and Immersion (PC2) subscales, for each technique. Axes are cropped in order to display values and 95% confidence intervals as clearly as possible. **Figure 7** and the accompanying video for seeing the illustrations of the techniques.

For blockers, both techniques obtained average scores, although the guardian angel technique obtained one of the worst scores in the safety subscale.

Finally, signal techniques obtained in overall the highest scores for the immersion-related subscale, while presenting lower scores for the safety-related subscale.

Technique-wise, the *Full reveal* obtained the highest scores for both subscales, while *Partial reveal*, *Shield* and *Warning* and *Gradient reveal* techniques presented a good trade-off between subscales.

5 DISCUSSION

This paper presented a design space for safety techniques for ETHDs based on visual feedback. This contribution intends to serve as a tool for researchers to create safety techniques for ETHDs within multiple-use contexts. This design space is based on previous research works from both VR and HRI research fields. This combination allows exploring possible solutions from two disciplines that we consider to be fundamental within the ETHD field. The generative power of our design space is seen in the diversity of techniques presented in this paper. The factor that makes the techniques specialized in ETHDs consists in providing

information of an element outside the VE that users should be aware of, that ideally should not be seen, and that has to be touched by users at some point during interaction. The 18 techniques presented in this paper explore factors related to feedback information, permanence, and representation so as to provide as much information as possible to the user without breaking the illusion of touching elements that are in the VE but rendered through an ETHD. Another difference between these techniques and other approaches for avoiding collisions in VR is that these techniques are triggered whenever the users' hands get close to the ETHD specifically when the robotic device has not yet placed the surface display in a position where users can actually engage contact. We considered primarily hand collisions with the ETHD since the user's hand is the extremity that is commonly in contact with the robot, mainly for surface exploration and object manipulation Mercado et al. (2021).

In order to evaluate the safety techniques, we proposed a set of criteria to characterize the techniques in their immersion and perceived safety (primary criteria), and six additional criteria corresponding to visual clutter, co-location, ecological adaptability, device awareness, mental workload, and user trust (secondary criteria). While there are indeed questionnaires to assess in depth each one of these factors, we decided to keep the evaluation focused on the factors that the

ETHD experts suggested that could be useful for evaluating our techniques.

The use of the design space could help researchers to optimize the performance of a safety technique on the criteria previously mentioned. Since the results of this preliminary evaluation suggest that different technique clusters have different performance on the different evaluation criteria, we decided to provide design guidelines so researchers and designers might find or create the most suitable technique for their needs. In the following, we discuss the scores obtained for each presented technique, design recommendations for safety techniques, the limitations of our study, and future work.

5.1 Results Discussion

The statistical analysis of the preliminary results suggests that there were relationships among the different criteria considered. Two independent clusters of criteria were formed, one aggregating criteria strongly correlated with immersion (Immersion subscale) and another one strongly correlated with perceived safety (Safety subscale).

First, although we hypothesized that there would be a trade-off between Immersion and Perceived Safety, none of the subscales had a significant correlation (≈ 0.06).

From **Figure 9**, we can observe that the majority of the techniques obtained average scores for both subscales. If we observe the techniques obtaining higher scores in the immersion and safety subscale, we can find techniques with higher safety scores but lower immersion scores (e.g., *Device Bounds*) and vice versa (e.g., *Screen Overlay*). Two outliers can also be found, *Full Reveal* and *Gradient Reveal*, which resulted in the techniques with the highest safety scores.

The balance between immersion and perceived safety for *Full Reveal* and *Gradient Reveal* might be because the whole device is being represented and therefore it indicates the device's configuration and position. However, the fact that the device is being fully shown but in a subtle way had only a moderate impact on immersion according to the experts.

We further discuss the results for each subscale.

5.1.1 Safety Subscale

The safety subscale, in addition to the perceived safety criteria, also included co-location, device awareness, and user trust.

We can hypothesize that co-location and device awareness increased the knowledge about the robot state, which can be linked with perceived safety. User trust was also positively correlated with perceived safety.

The highest scores were obtained with the techniques that displayed the entire robotic actuator, *Full Reveal*, *Gradient reveal*.

Both techniques use visual feedback to represent the haptic display as accurately as possible and accordingly to the actuator's configuration and position in the real environment, thus achieving the highest scores in co-location and device awareness. In addition, these two techniques also reported the highest scores for device awareness and user trust. These results are in agreement with results in HRI stating that it is important to

disclose the robot's position and configuration when it is integrated into a VE (Guhl et al., 2018).

The *Device Bounds* technique also obtained a high score in the safety subscale, yet, the fact that the representation of the robot was more "clumsy" could have generated a lower perceived safety and user trust.

In contrast, the lowest scores were obtained with the techniques that did not display the robot actuator such as the *Screen Overlay*, the *Guardian Angel* or the *Hiding Box*.

The only technique that achieved a moderate safety score without displaying the robot actuator was the *Shield* technique, which provided a moderate perceived safety and co-location, but was penalized by a lower device awareness and user trust.

5.1.2 Immersion Subscale

The immersion subscale, in addition to the immersion criterion, also included visual clutter, ecological adaptability, and mental workload.

We can hypothesize that subtle techniques (low visual clutter), and techniques that can be seamlessly integrated with the VE (high ecological adaptability) have a smaller negative impact on user immersion. Finally, we expect that mental workload would be more correlated with safety, yet this was not the case. This suggests that techniques that were easier to interpret had a lower impact on immersion.

The techniques achieving the highest scores were mainly techniques in the Signals cluster, in particular *Timer*, *Arrow*, and *Screen Overlay*. These three techniques subtly displayed information regarding the robot, thus obtaining the highest scores in immersion and visual clutter. In addition, as the feedback was subtle, they also obtained high scores in ecological adaptability.

In contrast, the techniques that were ranked lower on immersion were those that used bounds around the device (*Device Bounds*), its trajectory (*Trajectory Bounds*), and its final position (*Hiding Box*). The evaluation results suggest that these techniques also ranked high on visual clutter as can be seen in **Figure 7**. These techniques, when active, display large and colorful mesh boxes that highly contrast with the VE used as a use-case scenario.

Concerning mental workload, the *Magic Light Reveal* technique reported the lowest score. This might be because users needed to place their hand in a position close to the robot but also in an angle that permitted to "reveal" the robot's mesh. Paying attention to those factors while "avoiding" a collision with something that cannot be directly seen in the VE could be highly demanding for users' mental workload. At the opposite, the *Full Reveal* technique yielded one of the highest scores for the aforementioned feature since the information of the haptic display is always shown in the VE and thus it is easier to understand what is going on in the real environment.

5.2 Design Recommendations

From the results on the immersion and safety subscales, several design recommendations could be provided regarding the potential application requirements.

For applications focusing on safety, safety techniques that display the entirety of the ETHD's, such as *Full Reveal* and *Gradient Reveal* seem the best choices. Moreover, both techniques had a moderate impact on the user's immersion. The use of *Device Bounds* although having a high perceived safety score is discouraged as its impact in immersion is too high. However, it is important to consider that the bounds' mesh could be adapted to be less strident and visually cluttering.

In contrast, for applications having its focus on immersion techniques such as *Timer*, *Arrow* and *Screen Overlay* seem the best choices. However, these three techniques obtained relatively low scores on safety. Thus, potentially being only usable in an expected context in which users are well aware of the ETHD behavior. With this same rationale, the *Radar* technique could also be considered, but it had a strong negative impact on mental workload, which could be overcome with training.

Other methods also presented some good trade-offs between safety and immersion, although they did not excel in any of them. These techniques were the *Shield*, *Partial Reveal* and *Warning*. We believe that these three methods are worth being considered in further analysis.

Furthermore, for particular applications requiring displaying the trajectory of the robot, could also consider both *Trajectory Beam* and *Loading Trajectory Beam*. Although not achieving high scores, they obtained average scores.

Finally, the graphical representation can be considered a key factor in designing the visual feedback. In this work, we considered the use of colors that are highly contrasted with the VE since we wanted to design visual elements that could be easily perceived.

However, in a real application, the visual feedback's aesthetics should be adapted to the context of the VE.

Adapting the visual feedback as much as possible to the context of use could enhance safety and increase immersion. However, designers should be aware that users should perceive the visual feedback, and therefore, visual contrast should be considered for alerting users of possible collisions.

For example, the *Guardian Angel* low performance in the evaluation might be related to the graphic representation of the blocking element, which contrasted notably with the automobile scenario. A notably similar technique, *Shield* yielded a better perceived safety score. This could be due to the simpler visual representation and metaphor presented in the technique's visual feedback.

Balancing the trade-off between immersion and perceived safety is a challenge that could not be ultimately solved by the implementation of a safety technique. The best that researchers and designers could do is to select and/or design the most appropriate technique for a given context. Providing feedback about the real environment behavior is crucial when interacting within an immersive VE. Previous research works in VR and HRI have already signaled the problems that come up when feedback is not provided to the users. Even when having an ideal ETHD capable of dodging and adapting to every user's movement, the variables of human error and trust will still be present. Thus, we consider that as long as users are informed about

a robotic device "hidden" in a VE, then the risk of collision could be lower.

5.3 Limitations and Future Work

One of the main objectives of this paper was to design and evaluate a wide range of safety techniques for ETHDs. In order to increase the number of techniques evaluated, we decided to run an online evaluation based on video examples for all the techniques. We assumed the experts could imagine being in a real VR environment with an ETHD, which remains different from actually experiencing each technique in a real VR setup. Remotely testing a VR setup using an ETHD brings up challenges in matters of having the same setup (PCVR, HMD, and ETHD) for controlling variability in visual and haptic feedback.

However, some of the criteria might have been harder to evaluate than others. For example, being immersed in a virtual environment would have increased the depth perception of the users and they would not have to imagine themselves performing actions in the VE. One of such criteria might have been the mental workload, as users were passive and not active. Furthermore, an increased exposure time would have been beneficial for a better assessment.

Nevertheless, the initial evaluation has provided a wide range of relevant results, first providing a validation of the different criteria proposed and highlighting a set of safety techniques that stood out from the rest. These preliminary results could serve as a base for future research as it is detailed in the following paragraphs.

Another aspect that could be further explored is the creation of additional safety techniques. In this paper, we proposed a set of distinct techniques which explored the proposed design space. However, although finding techniques, which a good balance of immersion and safety, none of the proposed techniques was able to achieve high scores in both subscales. Considering that the principal component analysis showed that there was no correlation between the immersion and the safety subscales, techniques for achieving high scores in both subscales seem still possible.

The relevance of our design space and the findings of this paper rely on highlighting the importance of the aspects that compose a safety technique for ETHDs, and how design decisions could have an impact on user experience. Factors such as the application context, users' previous experience and background, interactions, and tasks performed in the VE could influence on the performance of the techniques for informing users about the risk of collision with the ETHD. These factors could be explored in future research.

The presented virtual car-cockpit scenario is dedicated entirely to surface exploration. However, the use of ETHDs can also consider object manipulation in a part assessment scenario for the industry, for instance. The technique's feedback information (Block What?) could be adapted to the industrial scenario and the warnings that are emitted to users in that context. The permanence of the visual feedback (Block When?) should be adapted to the length of the object manipulation task. A safety technique designed for industrial part assessment could consider a protection strategy (Block How?) based on virtual bounds since the user is going to manipulate a volume. The aesthetics of the visual feedback case could be adapted to represent the seriousness of the use context. Future work could dive deeper into the use and integration of the design space and the techniques in different use contexts.

Future works should consider the evaluation of safety techniques in the actual VR system. The techniques, which obtained better scores in the different subscales, should be further evaluated to ensure that the same scores could be replicated.

Future work could dive even further into the techniques aesthetics and the use of other types of feedback for signaling the possibility of collision. One possibility could be the creation of a meta-technique that selects the most suitable safety technique according to the users' proximity to the ETHD. In the case of multimodal feedback, the visual feedback displayed by the techniques could also be complemented with additional auditory and haptic cues for warning users about a possible collision.

An orthogonal approach could be the combination of several safety techniques, yet, there is a high risk of complexifying their interpretation and adding too many visual elements to the virtual environment.

The evaluation was carried out with a limited number of ETHD experts, who were expected to well apprehend the pros and cons of every safety technique. The statistical analysis displayed interesting tendencies. However, these are still preliminary results. Future work could explore the insights of a larger user population considering both experienced and novice profiles. The favored techniques might vary for different user groups based on their experience with HRI in VR.

The safety techniques for ETHDs proposed in this paper intend to serve as visual feedback for making users aware that they are interacting with a robot. Visual feedback has already been used in VR research as a means to prevent and warn users about the presence of objects that could collide with them in the interaction environment (Cirio et al., 2012; McGill et al., 2015; Yang et al., 2018; Kang and Han, 2020). This measure is complementary to the path planning strategies used in ETHD research to "help" the robotic device for avoiding the user (Araujo et al., 2016; Yokokohji et al., 2005, 2001). Since human behavior is often unpredictable, we consider that the design space we propose in this paper could help ETHD researchers and designers to find strategies to disclose the presence of a robotic actuator without sacrificing immersion nor users' perceived safety.

6 CONCLUSION

This paper presented a design space for safety techniques based on visual feedback for avoiding collisions when using an ETHD in a VE. Ensuring user safety when interacting with an ETHD within an immersive VE represents a challenge for designers and researchers, as two key factors need to be balanced to ensure optimal interaction with the system. On one hand, users' immersion needs to be favored to not disrupt the task and the "realism" the ETHD is providing when rendering haptic feedback. On the other hand, users' perceived safety needs to be ensured by providing appropriate information about the system's behavior.

This trade-off between immersion and perceived safety needs to be addressed with the design of safety techniques for avoiding involuntary collisions with an ETHD. For this purpose, inspired by previous works, we designed a total of 18 different safety techniques and a set of eight evaluation criteria. In order to assess the proposed techniques with the proposed evaluation criteria, we recruited a group of experts in ETHDs. Preliminary results from this evaluation pave the way to design guidelines for visual feedback for avoiding collisions that balance immersion and perceived safety. Taken together, the contributions of this paper could help designers and researchers to explore different possibilities to augment users' perceived safety and immersion by using visual feedback when integrating an ETHD for rendering haptic feedback in a VE.

AUTHOR CONTRIBUTIONS

VRM contributed with the manuscript writing, the literature review, the conduction of the user evaluations, and the design and implementation of the safety techniques. FA contributed with the scientific design of this paper and the statistical analysis. GC contributed with the scientific design and vision of this paper. AL contributed with envisioning and guiding the research conducted in this paper.

ACKNOWLEDGMENTS

The authors would like to thank the French National Research Agency (ANR) for the funding of the LobbyBot project.

REFERENCES

Abtahi, P., Landry, B., Yang, J., Pavone, M., Follmer, S., and Landay, J. A. (2019). Beyond the Force. *Proc ACM CHI* 1. 589. doi:10.1145/3290605.3300589

Araujo, B., Jota, R., Perumal, V., Yao, J. X., Singh, K., and Wigdor, D. (2016). Snake Charmer. *Proc. ACM TEI*, 218–226. doi:10.1145/2839462.2839484

Bartneck, C., Kulic, D., and Croft, E. (2017). *Measuring the Anthropomorphism, Animacy, Likeability, Perceived Intelligence, and Perceived Safety of Robots*. Amsterdam, Netherlands: Artwork Size: 311700 Bytes Publisher: figshare.

Chen, C., Pan, Y., Li, D., Zhang, S., Zhao, Z., and Hong, J. (2020). A Virtual-Physical Collision Detection Interface for AR-based Interactive Teaching of Robot. *Robotics Computer-Integrated Manuf.* 64, 101948. doi:10.1016/j.rcim.2020.101948

Cirio, G., Vangorp, P., Chapoulie, E., Marchal, M., Lecuyer, A., and Drettakis, G. (2012). Walking in a Cube: Novel Metaphors for Safely Navigating Large Virtual Environments in Restricted Real Workspaces. *IEEE Trans. Vis. Comput. Graph.* 18, 546–554. doi:10.1109/TVCG.2012.60

Guhl, J., Hügle, J., and Krüger, J. (2018). Enabling Human-Robot-Interaction via Virtual and Augmented Reality in Distributed Control Systems. *Procedia CIRP* 76, 167–170. doi:10.1016/j.procir.2018.01.029

Hartmann, J., Holz, C., Ofek, E., and Wilson, A. D. (2019). "RealityCheck," in Proceedings of the 2019 CHI Conference on Human Factors in Computing Systems (ACM), 1. doi:10.1145/3290605.3300577

Hirata, R., Hoshino, H., Maeda, T., and Tachi, S. (1996). A Force and Shape Display for Virtual Reality System. *Trans. Virtual Real. Soc. Jpn.* 1, 32

Kanamori, K., Sakata, N., Tominaga, T., Hijikata, Y., Harada, K., and Kiyokawa, K. (2018). "Obstacle Avoidance Method in Real Space for Virtual Reality Immersion," in 2018 IEEE International Symposium on Mixed and Augmented Reality (ISMAR), Munich, Germany, October 16–20, 2018 (IEEE), 80. doi:10.1109/ISMAR.2018.00033

Kang, H., and Han, J. (2020). SafeXR: Alerting Walking Persons to Obstacles in Mobile XR Environments. *Vis. Comput.* 36, 2065–2077. doi:10.1007/s00371-020-01907-4

Kästner, L., and Lambrecht, J. (2019). *Augmented-Reality-Based Visualization of Navigation Data of Mobile Robots on the Microsoft Hololens – Possibilities and Limitations* Bangkok, Thailand: IEEE. *arXiv:1912.12109 [cs, eess]* ArXiv: 1912.12109.

Kim, Y., Kim, H. J., and Kim, Y. J. (2018). Encountered-type Haptic Display for Large VR Environment Using Per-Plane Reachability Maps. *Comput. Anim. Virtual Worlds* 29, e1814. doi:10.1002/cav.1814

Kuts, V., Modoni, G. E., Terkaj, W., Tähemaa, T., Sacco, M., and Otto, T. (2017). "Exploiting Factory Telemetry to Support Virtual Reality Simulation in Robotics Cell," in *Augmented Reality, Virtual Reality, and Computer Graphics Series Title: Lecture Notes in Computer Science.* Editors L. T. De Paolis, P. Bourdot, and A. Mongelli (Ugento, Italy: Springer International Publishing), 10324, 212–221. doi:10.1007/978-3-319-60922-5_16

Lacoche, J., Pallamin, N., Boggini, T., and Royan, J. (2017). "Collaborators Awareness for User Cohabitation in Co-located Collaborative Virtual Environments," in Proceedings of the 23rd ACM Symposium on Virtual Reality Software and Technology (ACM), 1. doi:10.1145/3139131.3139142

McGill, M., Boland, D., Murray-Smith, R., and Brewster, S. (2015). A Dose of Reality: Overcoming Usability Challenges in VR Head-Mounted Displays. *Proc. ACM CHI (ACM)*, 2143–2152. doi:10.1145/2702123.2702382

Medeiros, D., Anjos, R. d., Pantidi, N., Huang, K., Sousa, M., Anslow, C., et al. (2021). "Promoting Reality Awareness in Virtual Reality through Proxemics," in 2021 IEEE Virtual Reality and 3D User Interfaces (VR), Lisboa, Portugal, March 27–April 1, 2021 (IEEE), 21–30. doi:10.1109/VR50410.2021.00022

Mercado, V., Marchal, M., and Lecuyer, A. (2021b). ENTROPiA: Towards Infinite Surface Haptic Displays in Virtual Reality Using Encountered-type Rotating Props. *IEEE Trans. Vis. Comput. Graph.* 27, 2237–2243. doi:10.1109/TVCG.2019.2963190

Mercado, V. R., Marchal, M., and Lecuyer, A. (2021). "Haptics On-Demand": A Survey on Encountered-type Haptic Displays. *IEEE Trans. Haptics* 14, 449–464. doi:10.1109/TOH.2021.3061150

Mercado, V. R., Marchal, M., and Lecuyer, A. (2020a). "Design and Evaluation of Interaction Techniques Dedicated to Integrate Encountered-type Haptic Displays in Virtual Environments," in *IEEE VR* Atlanta, GA, United States: IEEE. doi:10.1109/vr46266.2020.00042

Moray, N. (2013). *Mental Workload: Its Theory and Measurement*, 8. Boston, MA, United States: Springer Science & Business Media.

Oculus (2021). *Oculus Guardian System.* Meta Platforms, Inc.

Oyekan, J. O., Hutabarat, W., Tiwari, A., Grech, R., Aung, M. H., Mariani, M. P., et al. (2019). The Effectiveness of Virtual Environments in Developing Collaborative Strategies between Industrial Robots and Humans. *Robotics Computer-Integrated Manuf.* 55, 41–54. doi:10.1016/j.rcim.2018.07.006

Posselt, J., Dominjon, L., Bouchet, A., and Kemeny, A. (2017). "Toward Virtual Touch: Investigating Encounter -type Haptics for Perceived Quality Assessment in the Automotive Industry," in *Industrial Track.* EuroVR: Inustrial Track Laval, France.

Scavarelli, A., and Teather, R. J. (2017). "VR Collide! Comparing Collision-Avoidance Methods between Co-located Virtual Reality Users," in Proceedings of the 2017 CHI Conference Extended Abstracts on Human Factors in Computing Systems (ACM), Denver, Colorado, United States, May 6–11, 2017. 2915. doi:10.1145/3027063.3053180

Shepherd, D. C., Kraft, N. A., and Francis, P. (2019). "Visualizing the "Hidden" Variables in Robot Programs," in 2019, Visualizing the "Hidden" Variables in Robot Programs IEEE/ACM 2nd International Workshop on Robotics Software Engineering (RoSE) (IEEE), Montreal, QC, Canada, May 27, 2019. 13. doi:10.1109/RoSE.2019.00007

Steam (2021). *Steamvr Chaperone Faq.* Valve Corporation.

Vonach, E., Gatterer, C., and Kaufmann, H. (2017). "VRRobot: Robot Actuated Props in an Infinite Virtual Environment," in *Proc of IEEE VR* Los Angeles, CA, United States, 74–83. doi:10.1109/vr.2017.7892233

Vosniakos, G.-C., Ouillon, L., and Matsas, E. (2019). Exploration of Two Safety Strategies in Human-Robot Collaborative Manufacturing Using Virtual Reality. *Procedia Manuf.* 38, 524–531. doi:10.1016/j.promfg.2020.01.066

Yang, K.-T., Wang, C.-H., and Chan, L. (2018). "ShareSpace," in *Proc. UIST (ACM)* Berlin, Germany, 499. doi:10.1145/3242587.3242630

Yokokohji, Y., Hollis, R. L., and Kanade, T. (1996). "What You Can See Is what You Can Feel-Development of a Visual/haptic Interface to Virtual Environment," in *Proc. IEEE VRAIS* Santa Clara, CA, United States, 46–53. doi:10.1109/VRAIS.1996.490509

Yokokohji, Y., Kinoshita, J., and Yoshikawa, T. (2001). "Path Planning for Encountered-type Haptic Devices that Render Multiple Objects in 3d Space," in *Proc of IEEE VR* Yokohama, Japan, 271. doi:10.1109/VR.2001.913796

Yokokohji, Y., Muramori, N., Sato, Y., and Yoshikawa, T. (2005). Designing an Encountered-type Haptic Display for Multiple Fingertip Contacts Based on the Observation of Human Grasping Behaviors. *Int. J. Robotics Res.* 24, 717–729. doi:10.1177/0278364905057123

Design of a Wearable Haptic Device for Hand Palm Cutaneous Feedback

Mihai Dragusanu[1], Alberto Villani[1], Domenico Prattichizzo[1,2] and Monica Malvezzi[1]*

[1]Department of Information Engineering and Mathematics, University of Siena, Siena, Italy, [2]Department of Advanced Robotics, Istituto Italiano di Tecnologia, Genova, Italy

*Correspondence:
Monica Malvezzi
monica.malvezzi@unisi.it

This study describes the main design and prototyping steps of a novel haptic device for cutaneous stimulus of a hand palm. This part of the hand is fundamental in several grasping and manipulation tasks, but is still less exploited in haptics applications than other parts of the hand, as for instance the fingertips. The proposed device has a parallel tendon-based mechanical structure and is actuated by three motors positioned on the hand's back. The device is able to apply both normal and tangential forces and to render the contact with surfaces with different slopes. The end-effector can be easily changed to simulate the contact with different surface curvatures. The design is inspired by a smaller device previously developed for the fingertips; however, in the device presented in this study, there are significant differences due to the wider size, the different form-factor, and the structure of hand palm. The hand palm represents the support for the fingers and is connected to the arm through the wrist. The device has to be developed taking into account fingers' and wrist's motions, and this requirement constrains the number of actuators and the features of the transmission system. The larger size of the palm and the higher forces challenge the device from a structural point of view. Since tendons can apply only tensile forces, a spring-based support has been developed to keep the end-effector separated from the palm when the device is not actuated or when the force to be rendered is null. The study presents the main design guidelines and the main features of the proposed device. A prototype has been realized for the preliminary tests, and an application scenario with a VR environment is introduced.

Keywords: cutaneous stimuli, force feedback, device design, hand palm, wearable haptic device

1 INTRODUCTION

Nowadays technology is increasingly present in our everyday lives, and among the emerging technologies those oriented to the reproduction of tactile, kinesthetic, and skin sensations are getting interest in several application fields. These technologies allow enriching the sensory experience of humans, for instance in virtual environments, in augmented or mixed-reality applications, and/or during teleoperation tasks. Recent studies available in literature confirm that the use of tactile technologies not only increases the involvement of users in teleoperation tasks but also increases their accuracy and performance (Abbott et al., 2007; Battaglia et al., 2011). Interesting applications of haptic technologies are also present in telemedicine and in tele-rehabilitation, these applications have become particularly significant since the beginning of the past year, when the pandemic situation required solutions for guaranteeing social distance and human/human physical contacts.

The hand is one of the primary interfaces connecting humans and the surrounding environment, and it is also one of the main targets of haptics technology development. Most of the haptic devices for tactile stimuli are located on the fingers or on the wrist, while fewer are developed specifically for the palm (Pacchierotti et al., 2017); although Klatzky and Lederman's studies demonstrated that the hand-closing task depends on haptic information in the palm (Lederman and Klatzky, 1987). Haptic devices developed for the hand palm can be broadly divided in two types: the grounded ones, having a base external to the user's body and connected to a fixed base; and the wearable ones. Concerning grounded devices, for instance, in Iwata et al. (2001), the authors presented a device that can change the shape of the surface in contact with the hand using vertical motions of some pistons, while in Borst and Cavanaugh (2004) an array of actuators returns vibrotactile stimuli on users' palm. In Martinez et al. (2018), a grounded planar device returns haptic stimuli and several sensations on users' palms, and the ultrasound technology allows us to provide stimuli on hand that is detached from the surface of the device, so that the hand is free to move in a wider workspace.

The research in this topic is increasingly oriented towards wearable devices to completely free the users and their workspace. To date, wearability is a fundamental requirement for haptic devices, and in this context the trade-off between the extension of the area of the palm that can be stimulated and the number of actuators used is almost inevitable (Pacchierotti et al., 2017).

In this study we present a haptic wearable device for rendering forces in the palm that attempts to find a trade-off between the aforementioned requirements. The state-of-the-art devices are mostly based on localized and fixed contact points on the palm. Among these, there are two main typologies of devices: devices based on vibrotactile actuations, and devices using mechanical actuation. The last ones usually employ tightening bands reproducing only a normal pressure on the palm, as presented in Minamizawa et al. (2008a). However, this kind of technology allows the user to feel a limited and predetermined type of sensations. Similarly Minamizawa et al. (2008b) presented a band with a mobile contact surface on the palm, while Achibet et al. (2015) showed a passive device composed by an elastic band to return distance hand/body by haptic feedback.

In Son and Park (2018a) and Son and Park (2018b) two haptics gloves with several mechanical active points are designed and developed: the first uses small rigid links, while the second is tendon actuated. The limit of these devices is the high number of actuators needed to reproduce haptic stimuli in an extended area as the human palm, for this reason the authors of Gollner et al. (2012); Martínez et al. (2014); Borja et al. (2018) chose vibrotactile matrices in contact with the palm to reduce the clutter of mechanical actuators, reducing, however, the similarity between the desired stimulus and the transmitted one. A combination of mechanical stimuli and vibrotactile stimuli was shown by Kovacs et al. (2020) where a mobile mass comes in touch with a palm in case of collision between a hand avatar and the surrounding environment in virtual reality; while pneumatic solutions were presented by Kajimoto (2012) and Zubrycki and Granosik (2017). The authors in de Tinguy et al. (2020) presented a wearable haptic interface for natural manipulation of tangible objects in virtual reality that render contact force using a sensorized mobile mass grounded on wrist.

Haptic devices with mobile and an orientable contact area such as those presented by Trinitatova et al. (2019) and Trinitatova and Tsetserukou (2019) are closer to what we propose in this study for what concerns the design; however, in this study we want to investigate the possibility of reducing the footprint in the palm and the overall mechanical load on the hand through the use of cables for the transmission of forces.

In order to summarize and clarify the solutions available in the literature, **Table 1** shows the details of the implementation and electronics of the devices mentioned above and of the device presented in this study.

The device presented in this study is able to stimulate a large area of the palm with a limited number of actuators (three), therefore assuring a good wearability. In order to achieve these objectives a parallel mechanism has been designed in which the mobile platform (end-effector) has interchangeable contact interfaces. The various contact interfaces, having different shapes, can be easily connected and disconnected to/from the device to reproduce a tactile sensation more similar to the desired stimulus in different tasks.

Inspired from a family of wearable devices that we developed for fingertip stimulation (Chinello et al., 2018; Chinello et al., 2020), the mobile platform has a "Y" shape, and it is actuated by three servomotors positioned on the back of the hand by means of tendons, allowing the transmission motion. Notwithstanding the kinematic structure of the device presents some similarities with the devices previously presented for the fingertips; the solicitation of hand palm presents several different challenges, due to the different size, the kinematic structure, the form factor, and the force level. In order to provide to the user the possibility to easily wear the device and avoid the continuous contact with the palm, we added an elastic element at the base of the platform. The tendons and the springs allow us to reproduce the cutaneous stimulus both in static and dynamic conditions. The use of three actuators, furthermore, allows reproducing both normal and tangential components of the contact force (necessary for simulating shear forces) and the contact with virtual/remote surfaces with different orientations (that can be used for instance for reproducing the contact with variable curvature surfaces).

The wearable haptic device for hand palm stimulation is shown in **Figure 1**. In particular, in this study, we will: 1) describes the haptic device for hand palm stimulation based on tendons, designed taking into account the physical/anatomical features of the palm; 2) presents the design of interchangeable modules for simulations of different types of contact; 3) details the mechanical, mechatronics, and manufacturing aspects of the device, including the finite element method (FEM) analysis, hardware, and control description; and 4) presents a working prototype of the device with some preliminary applications.

2 BIOMECHANICS AND PERCEPTIVE RECEPTOR OF THE PALM

The design of the wearable haptic device started from the analysis of the hand palm: its biomechanical structure and the features of

TABLE 1 | Comparison between the proposed haptic device (indicated as HaptiPalm, last row) and other solutions available in the literature.

Name	Type of actuation	Contact area	Form factor of electronics
Ghostglove (Minamizawa et al., 2008a; Minamizawa et al., 2008b)	Squeezing band	Fixed and extended	On board
Achibet et al. (Achibet et al., 2015)	Passive elastic band	Fixed and point-like	–
Son et al. (Son and Park, 2018a)	Four pressure points	Fixed and point-like	On arm
Son et al. (Son and Park, 2018b)	10 pressure points tendon drive	Fixed and point-like	Delocalized
Gollner et al. (Gollner et al., 2012)	35 vibrating motors	Fixed and point-like	On arm
Martinez et al. (Martínez et al., 2014)	Six vibrating motors	Fixed and point-like	Delocalized
Borja et al. (Borja et al., 2018)	Five vibrating motors	Fixed and point-like	On arm
Haptic pivot (Kovacs et al., 2020)	Mobile vibrating mass	Fixed and extended	on arm
Zubrycki et al. (Zubrycki and Granosik, 2017)	10 pneumatic pad	Fixed and extended	Delocalized
Weatavix (de Tinguy et al., 2020)	Mobile mass	Fixed and extended	On arm
Deltatouch (Trinitatova et al., 2019; Trinitatova and Tsetserukou, 2019)	3D Mobile platform	Mobile and point-like	Delocalized
HapticPalm	3D Mobile platform tendon drive	Mobile and interchangeable	On board

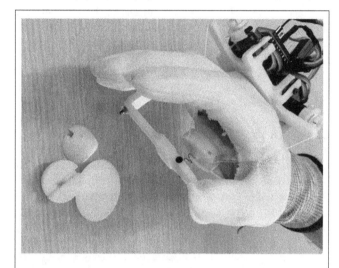

FIGURE 1 | Prototype of the wearable haptic device for hand palm stimulation worn by a user.

the stimuli to be rendered define the requirements and the constraints. From an anatomical point of view, the palm of the hand is the ventral (or anterior) region of the hand, the one to which the fingers converge when punching. The back of the hand, on the other side, is the posterior region of the hand, located from the opposite side of the palm. The bones of the palm can be divided into carp bones and metacarpal bones. The metacarpus is the set of five long bones that connect the carpus to the phalanges, and they are numbered from 1 to 5 starting from the thumb to the little finger. The carpus consists of eight short bones spread over two rows, the proximal and the distal row, and connects the radio with the metacarpus.

The proximal row is composed by scaphoid, lunate, triquetrum, and pisiform bones, while the distal row is defined by trapezium, trapezoid capitate, and hamate bones. The biomechanical structure of palm bones, muscles, and ligaments allows the radial abduction, the ulnar adduction, the palmar flexion/dorsiflexion, and combined movement, all depicted in **Figure 2**. According to Swartz (2002), the palmar flexion is the flexion of the wrist towards the palm and ventral side of forearm,

while the dorsiflexion is the hyperextension of the wrist joint, towards the dorsal side of forearm; radial abduction is a motion that pulls a structure or part away from the midline of wrist and ulnar adduction is a motion that pulls the hand structure toward the midline of wrist. Other two principal motions are provided by the biomechanical structure of the palm: the opposition and apposition of thumb. In apposition, the side part of thumb is in touch with other fingers, while the pulp side of thumb distal is in contact with fingertips of other digits during opposition (Van Nierop et al., 2008).

The contact surface of the developed haptic device has been dimensioned and placed according with biomechanics of palm, avoiding cluttering of palm and the reduction of carpus mobility. The mobile platform should not constrain and limit any motion described above; it should be placed under metacarpal bone *in situ* and extended from upper bound of first row of carpal bone to transverse metacarpal ligament.

The articulation of the bones of the carpus constitutes, on the handheld side, a cavity called the carpal tunnel. The carpal tunnel develops a flywheel on the wrist and is crossed by the superficial and deep flexor muscles of the fingers and the long flexor of the thumb. The median nerve also runs through the carpal tunnel, and its palmar branches, called digital cutaneous branches or cutaneous digital nerves, are distributed to the palmar skin up to the first three fingers (thumb, index finger, and middle). The palm, like the fingertips, is one of the densest regions of the human body of mechanoreceptors. Then channel of haptic stimulus transmission is the same for fingertips and palm. However, biomechanics of palm is more complex than finger one, as the geometry, anatomic constrains, and mechanical compliance (Kubo et al., 2018) are different, and the increased extension of the device is the cause of greater structural fragility, while the forces to render on palm are higher and, consequently, the structural stress on the device is greater too.

3 HAPTIC STIMULUS OF THE HAND PALM: DESIGN PRINCIPLES AND MODELING

The proposed device is able to both push the end-effector towards the palm and differentiate the applied force direction, contact

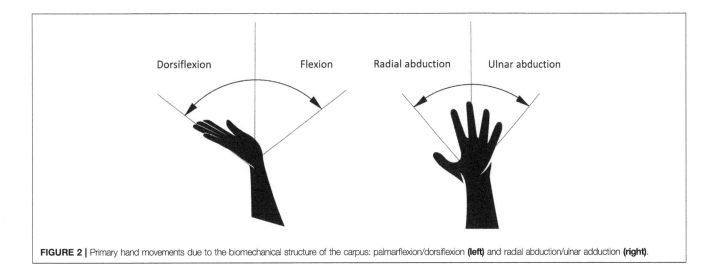

FIGURE 2 | Primary hand movements due to the biomechanical structure of the carpus: palmarflexion/dorsiflexion **(left)** and radial abduction/ulnar adduction **(right)**.

location, and the orientation, ensuring robustness, ergonomics, and low weight. To achieve these requirements, the end-effector is passively supported by a spring connected to a C-shape structure fixed on one side on the hand's back. The end-effector is then moved by three tendons actuated by three motors positioned on the hand's back. Both the part fixed on the hand's back and the active end-effector has a Y-shape, whose vertices are connected by three tendons actuated by three motors. This structure allows to apply a wide set of movements to the end-effector and to interact with most of the palm surface. In the following we will introduce a simplified mathematical model that relates with the force applied to the hand palm to the forces applied by the motors to the tendons.

The problem of cable driven parallel mechanisms is an interesting topic studied by several researchers in robotics context. Using cables and tendons to transmit movements allows designers and engineers to obtain compact and small-size devices, reducing the weight and inertial effects of mechanical components. The solution of the direct geometric-static problem of three cable-driven parallel robots by interval analysis is presented in Berti et al. (2013), while the case of direct geometric-static analysis of an underconstrained 4-cables parallel robot is presented in Carricato and Abbasnejad (2013). In Miermeister et al. (2013) the differential kinematics is studied for calibration, system investigation, and force-based forward kinematics. Moreover, the dynamic modeling of cable-driven parallel robots for a fully constrained planner case is investigated in Khosravi and Taghirad (2013) and for an underconstrained spatial case is presented in Yao et al. (2013).

Solving the forward kinematics problem means finding the relationship between lengths of the cables and posture of the moving platform; this information is important for the device control, but it is not easy to be solved in parallel mechanisms. On the other hand, the inverse kinematics problem evaluates the lengths of the cables corresponding to a given platform posture. Static analysis defines the relationship between cable tensions and wrench exchanged with the palm.

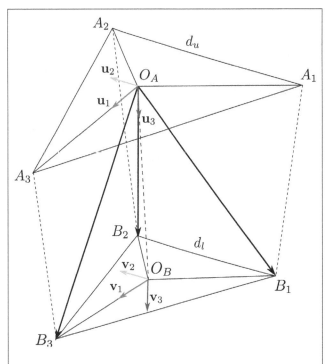

FIGURE 3 | Main points and coordinate frames for the analysis of the wearable haptic device.

To describe the device as a cable-driven parallel robot, two coordinate frames are defined. The first one $\mathscr{A} = \{O_A, \mathbf{u}_1, \mathbf{u}_2, \mathbf{u}_3\}$ is fixed on the device body on the hand back, while the second one $\mathscr{B} = \{O_B, \mathbf{v}_1, \mathbf{v}_2, \mathbf{v}_3\}$ is fixed on the mobile platform in contact with hand palm, as shown in **Figure 3**. In the following, to simplify the notation, if quantities are expressed in $\mathscr{A}$ frame, the superscript $\mathscr{A}$ is omitted.

On the device body we define three connection points A_1, A_2, A_3, representing the points where the tendons pass through in the device-fixed part; assuming they define an equilateral triangle, their coordinates are:

$$\mathbf{a}_1 = \left[\frac{\sqrt{3}\,d_u}{-6}, \frac{d_u}{-2}, 0\right]^{\mathrm{T}} \mathbf{a}_2 = \left[\frac{\sqrt{3}\,d_u}{-6}, \frac{d_u}{2}, 0\right]^{\mathrm{T}} \mathbf{a}_3 = \left[\frac{\sqrt{3}\,d_u}{3}, 0, 0\right]^{\mathrm{T}} \tag{1}$$

where d_u is the upper triangle side length. The wires are connected to the mobile platform in three points B_1, B_2, B_3, defining an equilateral triangle with center O_B, their coordinates in $\mathscr{B}$ frame are:

$$\mathbf{b}_1^{\mathscr{B}} = \left[\frac{\sqrt{3}\,d_l}{-6}, \frac{d_l}{-2}, 0\right]^{\mathrm{T}} \mathbf{b}_2^{\mathscr{B}} = \left[\frac{\sqrt{3}\,d_l}{-6}, \frac{d_l}{2}, 0\right]^{\mathrm{T}} \mathbf{b}_3^{\mathscr{B}} = \left[\frac{\sqrt{3}\,d_l}{3}, 0, 0\right]^{\mathrm{T}} \tag{2}$$

where, d_l is the length side of lower triangular plate, while their coordinates in $\mathscr{A}$ reference frame are indicated as:

$$\mathbf{b}_1 = [x_1, y_1, z_1]^{\mathrm{T}}, \mathbf{b}_2 = [x_2, y_2, z_2]^{\mathrm{T}}, \mathbf{b}_3 = [x_3, y_3, z_3]^{\mathrm{T}},$$

and vary according to the platform motion. The coordinates of O_B point, expressed in $\mathscr{A}$ frame, are defined by the vector $\mathbf{o}_B = [x, y, z]^{\mathrm{T}}$.

Let us define a rotation matrix $\mathbf{R}(\eta) = \mathbf{R}_z(\phi)\mathbf{R}_y(\theta)\mathbf{R}_x(\psi)$ representing the orientation of $\mathscr{B}$ frame w.r.t. $\mathscr{A}$ frame. We indicate with $\eta = [\psi, \theta, \phi]^{\mathrm{T}}$ a vector containing roll, pitch, and yaw angles, respectively.

3.1 Inverse Kinematics

The inverse kinematic problem consists in finding the values of cable lengths l_i for a given position $\mathbf{o}_B$ and orientation $\mathbf{R}$. The geometric constraints of the parallel structure relate to the length of the cables to the norm of the geometric vectors connecting B_i to A_i, that is,

$$\|\mathbf{b}_i - \mathbf{a}_i\| = l_i \quad i = 1, 2, 3 \tag{3}$$

where l_i is the length of cable i that can be controlled by the motors. The coordinates of the mobile platform connection points can be evaluated as:

$$\mathbf{b}_i = \mathbf{o}_B + \mathbf{R}\mathbf{b}_i^{\mathscr{B}} \quad i = 1, 2, 3 \tag{4}$$

By substituting (**Eq. 4**) in the cable constraint relationship (**Eq. 3**), we can easily evaluate l_i as a function of $\mathbf{o}_B$ and $\mathbf{R}$.

3.2 Statics

In stationary conditions, the sum of the forces and torques (wrench) applied to the platform through the wires is balanced by the forces and torques (wrench) due to the physical contact with the finger pad as follows:

$$\sum_{i=1}^{3} \mathbf{f}_i + \mathbf{f}_{\mathbf{o}_B} + \mathbf{f}_s = 0 \tag{5a}$$

$$\sum_{i=1}^{3} \boldsymbol{\tau}_i + \boldsymbol{\tau}_{\mathbf{o}_B} + \boldsymbol{\tau}_s = 0 \tag{5b}$$

We indicate with $\mathbf{f}_i \in \mathbb{R}^3$ the forces applied by the cables, with $\boldsymbol{\tau}_i \in \mathbb{R}^3$ the corresponding momentum, with $\mathbf{f}_{\mathbf{O}_B} \in \mathbb{R}^3$ the reaction force applied by the hand palm to the platform, with $\mathbf{f}_s \in \mathbb{R}^3$ the force due to spring deformation, with $\boldsymbol{\tau}_{\mathbf{O}_B} \in \mathbb{R}^3$ the reaction torque, and with $\boldsymbol{\tau}_s \in \mathbb{R}^3$ the torque due to spring

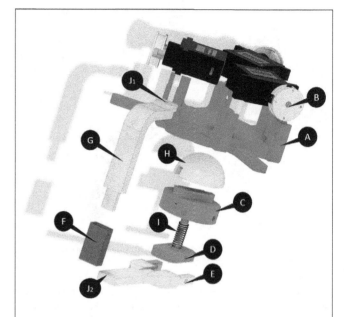

FIGURE 4 | Exploded CAD view of the device. The end-effector of the device is composed of the components indicated with (**C,I,D**). (**H**) indicates the end-effector's module while the "Y-shaped" platform is indicated with (**A**) and the pulleys are indicated with (**B**). (**E–G**) are the elements that realize the link between the two platforms. (**J₁**) and (**J₂**) are the two joints that allowed to rotate the end-effector.

deformation, both expressed w.r.t. the O_B point. Expanding the equilibrium equations (**Eq. 5**) we get:

$$\sum_{i=1}^{3} \rho_i \mathbf{u}_{\mathbf{f}_i} + \mathbf{f}_{\mathbf{o}_B} + \mathbf{f}_s = 0 \tag{6a}$$

$$\sum_{i=1}^{3} \rho_i \mathbf{b}_i \times \mathbf{u}_{\mathbf{f}_i} + \boldsymbol{\tau}_{\mathbf{o}_B} + \boldsymbol{\tau}_s = 0 \tag{6b}$$

where ρ_i is the tension cable i, and $\mathbf{u}_{\mathbf{f}_i}$ is the unit vector representing the cable direction, and can be evaluated as:

$$\mathbf{u}_{\mathbf{f}_i} = \frac{\mathbf{b}_i - \mathbf{a}_i}{l_i} \tag{7}$$

From (**Eq. 6**), and (**Eq. 7**), we can express (**Eq. 5**) in the matrix form:

$$\begin{bmatrix} \mathbf{u}_{\mathbf{f}_1} & \mathbf{u}_{\mathbf{f}_2} & \mathbf{u}_{\mathbf{f}_3} \\ \mathbf{b}_1 \times \mathbf{u}_{\mathbf{f}_1} & \mathbf{b}_2 \times \mathbf{u}_{\mathbf{f}_2} & \mathbf{b}_3 \times \mathbf{u}_{\mathbf{f}_3} \end{bmatrix} \begin{bmatrix} \rho_1 \\ \rho_2 \\ \rho_3 \end{bmatrix} + \begin{bmatrix} \mathbf{f}_{\mathbf{o}_B} + \mathbf{f}_s \\ \boldsymbol{\tau}_{\mathbf{o}_B} + \boldsymbol{\tau}_s \end{bmatrix} = 0 \tag{8}$$

which is well-known as geometric-statics equation of cable driven parallel robots (Berti et al., 2013).

4 DESIGN AND ANALYSIS

The device presented in this study is the result of a trade-off between wearability, weight, and resistance to mechanical stress. The symmetrical geometry of the supports on the back of the hand and under the palm allows a homogeneous distribution of the forces applied by the motors and transmitted through tendons. One of the drawbacks of tendon-actuated devices is that the end-effector has to be always in contact with the hand and the tendons have to be stretched. To overcome this issue and allow the device to activate and deactivate the contact with the palm, the end-effector is connected to a C-shaped fixed element by means of an elastic element.

In the following, we describe with more details the device from the design point of view, the interchangeable end-effector's modules that are in contact with the palm, and some results of a structural mechanical analysis.

4.1 HapticPalm

The device has a parallel structure and consists of two main parts: one on the back of the hand and the other below the palm, defined as the end-effector of the device.

The part on the hand's back consists of a mechanical support for the force actuation/transmission system, the microcontroller, and the power supply (indicated with A in **Figure 4**). Three tendons are routed in three paths extruded from the support, arranged at 120°deg from each other in order to achieve an equilateral "Y-shape". The tendons transmit the forces applied by the motors, through the pulleys, from the back of the hand to the device's end-effector (B), and therefore to the palm. This type of actuation has an easy wearability and avoids the problems present in parallel mechanisms based on rigid links, that have higher weight, lower flexibility/adaptability, and requires suitable procedures to be adapted to different users and needs (Malvezzi et al., 2021).

The end-effector is composed of two platforms (D) and (C). The first is connected to the actuation system through the tendons, and the second is connected directly to the part on the back by means of a "C-shaped" rigid link (E). The two platforms are connected by an elastic element (a spring, I) that allows the tip-palm disconnection when no contacts and forces have to be applied. The connection points between tendons and the platform have a "Y-shaped" structure similar to the support on the back of the hand. A magnetic "T-shaped" interlocking system is designed on the first platform, allowing to easily interchange the different end-effectors' modules (H) realized to reproduce different types of cutaneous stimuli.

The rigid link connecting the two main parts (G, F, E) has an adjustable telescopic height to adapt the device dimension to the needs of users with different anthropometric dimension of the hand, and can be rotated through two revolute joints (J1, J2), with the aim to ensure the ergonomics for several users and allow them to temporary move away the end-effector from the palm without remove the device.

4.2 Modules

As mentioned before the end-effector modules of the device are manually interchangeable. They are fixed to the device by means of a "T-shaped" interlocking system. The modules can be connected/disconnected easily to the end-effector platform thanks to the "T-shaped" path and are fixed by a magnet inserted in each module. The magnets allow the modules to position themselves exactly in the center of the "Y-shaped" platform and to keep them fixed during the force rendering. In order to transmit the sensation of touching objects and surfaces that are interesting in haptics applications, four different end-effector modules have been created. The basic idea is to let the user feel common shapes such as spheres, corners, edges, and a flat surface. In this study, we have created two spherical modules with different radii of curvature with the aim to reproduce the curved surfaces (H1, H4 in **Figure 5**), a rectangular-shaped module and a plane-shaped module in order to reproduce the contact with edges and flat shapes, respectively (H2, H3).

4.3 FEM Analysis

Even if the basic structure of the device is similar to the one developed for the fingertip, for instance in Chinello et al. (2018), the larger dimensions and the magnitude of the applied forces are more challenging from the mechanical point of view. A structural stationary FEM analysis was carried out for evaluating the overall stress/deformation of the device in four different loading cases representing typical operative conditions. Three of them analyze the behavior of the device when a set of forces defined according to the model described in **Section 3.2** are applied, while the fourth investigate the response of the device when the skin elasticity is saturated, that is, when the end-effector is fixed. The analysis was performed with 3D-CAD/CAE software, Fusion360 (Autodesk Inc., United States). The materials of the components used in these cases are ABS for all the components of the device except for the spring, realized in steel.

The behavior of the device was analyzed when the forces indicated with blue arrows in **Figure 6** are applied on the three vertices of both platforms. A fixed constraint was set on the bottom part of the back hand's platform to simulate the contact with the hand. Six forces are applied to the fixed and mobile "Y" vertices, the directions of the forces are selected to simulate tendons' actions. Their magnitudes are chosen according to the overall interaction force direction to be simulated.

Figure 6 shows the results of FEM analysis for the three-axis directions. All the subfigures on the top side report the results in terms of displacements while the subfigures on the bottom side show the results in terms of deformations. In **Figures 6A, D**, the results of the analysis corresponding to an overall force acting along the z direction are reported. In this case, the forces' magnitudes are the same for all the simulated tendons and equal to 1 N. Concerning the corresponding displacement, **Figure 6D** shows that, as expected, it occurs mainly along the "z" axis.

Figures 6B, E show the results of the simulation of an overall force with components along the z and the y direction. For this simulation, we have symmetrically modified four forces, by reducing their module to 0.5 N.

In **Figures 6C, F**, we finally reported the results when an equivalent force with components along x and z directions is applied. As in the previous case, the forces have been modified symmetrically.

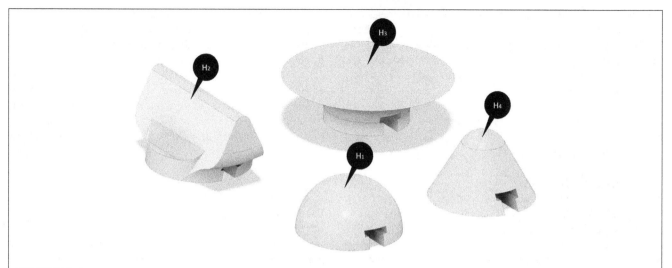

FIGURE 5 | CAD models of the end-effector' modules. (H₁) and (H₄) indicate the spherical modules with different radii of curvature while (H₂) and (H₃) are, respectively, the rectangular-shaped module and the plane-shaped module.

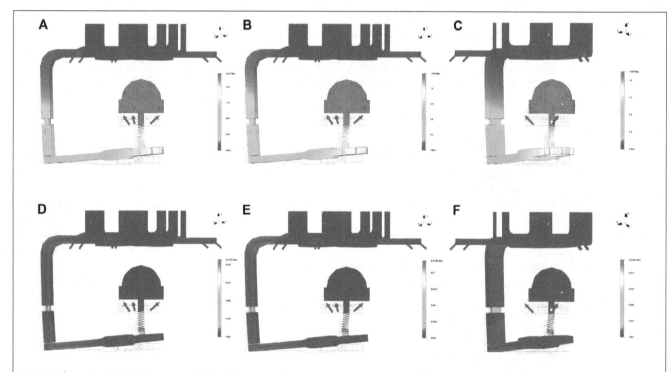

FIGURE 6 | Results of the FEM structural analysis. The blue arrows indicate the forces applied in the simulations, the wireframe transparent CAD model represents the undeformed model, while a 1X deformation of the device is represented in the colored surfaces. **(A)** The displacements when a force with only a z-component is applied, **(B,C)** show, respectively, the results of the displacements when a force with a z-component and an x-component or a y-component is applied; subfigures **(D–F)** on the right side report the results of the deformation for the same loading cases.

Finally, we verified the response of the device when the skin elasticity is saturated, to check the resistance of the platform on the back of the hand. The forces applied in this case are all with the same direction and intensity, that is, 5 N while the fixed constrains are two: one on the end-effector's module and the other on the bottom part of the back hand's platform (**Figure 7**).

In general, results from the FEM analysis shows that the mechanical structure of the device can resist to the forces that are applied in haptics applications. The results of FEM analysis also show that, as expected, the main critical points of the structure are represented by the rigid link and the base of the spring. Moreover, the choice of the spring is very another critical

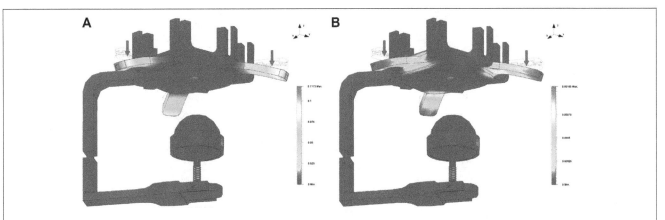

FIGURE 7 | Results of the FEM analysis for the platform of the back of the hand under the action of an overall 15 N force (5 N for each side of the "Y-shape"). Blue arrows indicate the forces applied while the transparent wireframe, the CAD model, is the reference undeformed model, while the colored surface corresponds to a 1X deformation of the haptic palm device. Subfigure **(A)** shows the displacement of the platform and the subfigure **(B)** reports the deformation of the platform.

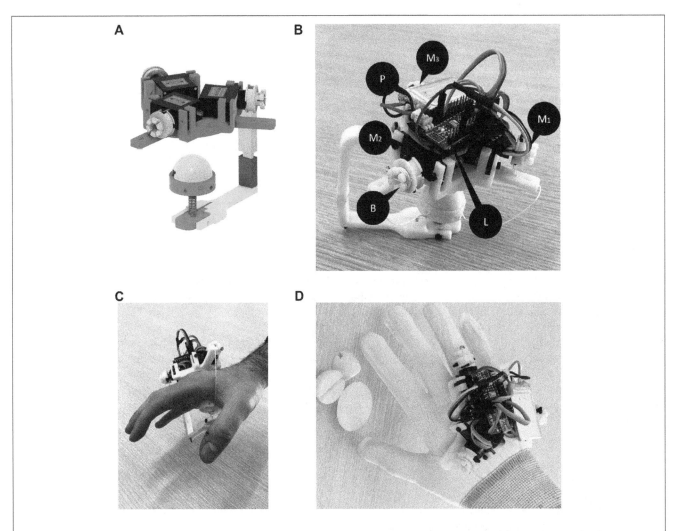

FIGURE 8 | Prototype of the device presented in this study. Subfigure **(A)** shows the final CAD model of prototype, while **(B)** shows the device hardware components. Subfigure **(C)** report the "naked" device worn by a user. Subfigure **(D)** shows the final prototype worn by the user together with the different modules.

aspect to be considered to guarantee a suitable level of robustness and functionality of the device.

5 PROTOTYPE, HARDWARE AND COMPONENTS, CONTROL, AND APPLICATION

Figure 8 shows the first prototype of the developed device for hand palm haptics stimulation. All the structural components are manufactured using an FDM (fused deposition modeling) process with ABS material, except for the elastic element that is a standard off-shelf steel spring.

For the transmission of forces, three MG-90S microserves were used (M_i in **Figure 8B**), powered by a 5V battery (P). Each of them has a stall torque of 20 Ncm. For the control and data processing part, we used the Elegoo Nano V3+ microcontroller (ELEGOO Inc., CHN) (L), while the transmission with the virtual environment was carried out using serial communication. As previously introduced, the rendering of the force on the hand palm uses a tendon-based transmission. The tendons are anchored on one side to the pulleys of the motors fixed on the "Y-shaped" platform (A) of the back of the hand, on the other side to the "Y-arranged" connectors of the end-effector. The minimum size of each tendon is defined by the length of the thread needed, when it is under tension, to connect the platform of the end-effector to the "Y-shaped" platform on the back of the hand. In order to adjust this length, the pulleys have been designed with an external part that allows to wrap the excess amount of tendon. A first version of the pulleys is shown in the CAD model (B in **Figure 4**), while an updated version is shown in the prototype in **Figure 8B**.

Figure 8C shows the first prototype worn by a user. From the first users' feedback, we realized that the "naked" device was not easy and intuitive to wear it due to the uncertainties on the orientation caused by the symmetrical shape of the device. Then with the aim to avoid this ambiguity in the orientation and to help/guide the user's hand between the tendons when wearing the device, the device was embedded in a glove with a properly shaped hole in the center of the palm allowing the contact with the end-effector (**Figure 8D**).

As mentioned before, an elastic element was used in order to passively support the end-effector when it is not in contact with the palm. On one side the spring should be enough stiff to keep the end-effector in an upright position even when the tendons are not actuated. On the other side, the spring should be enough soft to avoid an overload to the motor, that should spend a part of their torque to apply the required haptic force and a part to deform the spring, as highlighted in **Section 3.2**. To meet this trade-off, we adopted a spring with a stiffness coefficient equal to 6.7 N/mm. Moreover, we decided to use a short spring, with a length of 7 mm, to keep the end-effector's size as compact as possible and with this choice, in the prototype, we observed a symmetric behavior of the spring both along the axial and radial directions.

Table 2 summarizes the main characteristics of the developed prototype. The maximum and minimum theoretical forces that

TABLE 2 | Haptic palm device prototype; main hardware/software details and technical specifications. The dimensions of device are measured without the glove, and the value of Δh is equal to the capability to extend and shorten the rigid link F with respect to the G link.

	Technical specifics
Weight	89.92g
Dimensions $L \times l \times (h \pm \Delta h)$	$104 \times 81 \times (97 \pm 0.7)mm$
Degrees of freedom	3
Microprocessor	ATmega328
Clock speed of microcontroller	16 MHz
Computer interface	Serial COM
Input voltage	5.0V
Battery life	$\approx 5h$
Maximum speed	9.5$\frac{rad}{s}$
Maximum resisting force	60.0N
Maximum theoretical force on palm	29.5N
Minimum theoretical force on palm	0.81N
Maximum recall force	30.5N
Maximum contact surface	$\approx 7.06\ cm^2$
Cost	$\approx$ \$50

can be applied on palm are evaluated according to the model presented in **Section 3.2**.

5.1 An Example of VR Application

We have created a virtual reality scenario to demonstrate the functionality of the device in the case of different extended contacts. The scenario was developed in CoppeliaSim (Coppelia Robotics AG., CHE) and it is a replica of a common office station. In the simulated environment, it is possible to interact with a series of objects on a desk and with the desk itself, in detail, each object is designed to test a specific haptic device end-effector.

The module H2 is suitable for the exploration of laptop frames (**Figure 9B**), and circular module H1 is intended for the interaction with the paperweight (**Figure 9A**), while the modules H3 and H4 are suitable for interacting with the desk plane and stacked books (**Figures 9C,D**). Interaction with these objects is possible through a hand avatar sensorized in the palm and controllable by LeapMotion controller (Ultraleap.inc., United States), a camera hand tracker system. As a further development of this study, an IMU-based tracking system will be integrated with the haptic device (Baldi et al., 2017). The forces, estimated by the triaxial virtual sensor, are the result of collisions with the dynamic model of the hand and objects, the collision forces are processed through a Bullet 2.78 physical engine. The contact forces are then transmitted to the device during navigation, and it is also possible to generate an on-demand signal from a recorded force profile from a previous exploration. The device and the virtual environment communicate *via* the serial port.[1]

---

[1]A video demonstration is available at the following link: https://drive.google.com/file/d/15YgSfVR1ygYl6Do9mY12Ms9qyvuKcaSI/view?usp=sharing.

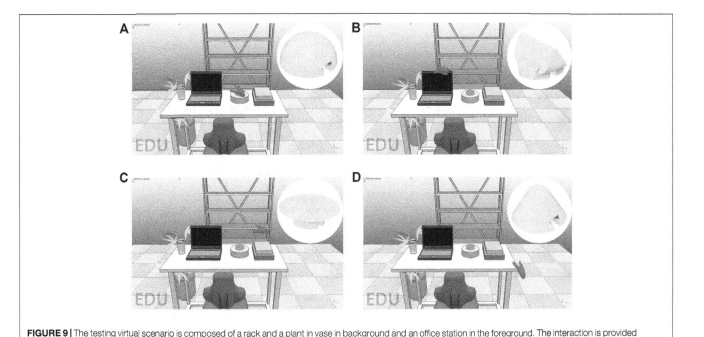

FIGURE 9 | The testing virtual scenario is composed of a rack and a plant in vase in background and an office station in the foreground. The interaction is provided by the red hand avatar of and the objects in foreground are chosen to use all modules: paperweight for H1 module **(A)**; laptop frames for H2 module **(B)**; cover of book and the surface of desk for H3 module **(C)**; and desk, laptop, and book peaks for H4 module **(D)**.

6 CONCLUSION

This study introduces a wearable haptic device for a hand palm cutaneous stimulation, suitable to render the forces generated from palm/environment interactions in a virtual reality environment. As discussed in the initial part of the study, due to the biomechanical structure, constraints of the palm, and the need of wearability, the design of this device prototype is the result of different requirements, including limited dimensions, weight, capability to reproduce contact interactions, and force components in a large surface as the palm. Ideally, the device should be very light, should not over constrain the hand, should not encumber palm, and should apply forces suitable for accurately reproducing desired haptic simulations. The study proposes a tendon driven solution with a passive element that allows disconnecting the end-effector from the palm in absence of force to render.

The starting idea is a parallel tendon-driven mechanism actuated by three motors on the hand back. In the first part of the study, the mechanism has been studied from the theoretical point of view by means of a simplified mathematical model. Then the idea has been detailed and a CAD model of the device has been realized, and a FEM analysis has been conducted to simulate the behavior of device in case of skin elasticity saturation. A first prototype of the device has been realized and some preliminary functional tests have been conducted. Three servomotors actuate the tendons and transmit symmetrical force from a "Y-shaped" platform to an end-effector platform with a "Y-arrangement" of

the connection points. Several modules have been designed and 3D-printed to extend set of the reproducible surface sensations. The design of modules allows the easy connection and disconnection by means of a "T-shape" socket and a magnetic clip. According to the first experiences of the users in a virtual environment and their opinions, the device was positioned and fixed on a shaped glove to guide the hand when wearing the device without covering the palm.

Future developments of this study will include the validation of forces provided by device, the change of serial communication on wire with a Bluetooth communication channel, an optimization of the design of some critical structural components, and the development of active interchangeable modules with sensors and/or multisensory actuators (e.g., thermal and vibrations) to increase capability of device in terms of precision and stimuli rendering, including cutaneous stimuli. In addition, we will conduct human studies on device usability and wearability for virtual reality applications.

AUTHOR CONTRIBUTIONS

MD: principal investigator, device design, prototype development, and paper writing. AV: device design, prototyping, and paper writing. DP: project coordination and paper review. MM: project coordination, analysis, and paper review.

REFERENCES

Abbott, J. J., Marayong, P., and Okamura, A. M. (2007). "Haptic Virtual Fixtures for Robot-Assisted Manipulation," in *Robotics Research* (Berlin, Heidelberg: Springer), 49–64.

Achibet, M., Girard, A., Talvas, A., Marchal, M., and Lécuyer, A. (2015). "Elastic-arm: Human-Scale Passive Haptic Feedback for Augmenting Interaction and Perception in Virtual Environments," in 2015 IEEE Virtual Reality (VR), Arles, France, 23-27 March 2015 (IEEE), 63–68. doi:10.1109/VR.2015.7223325

Baldi, T. L., Scheggi, S., Meli, L., Mohammadi, M., and Prattichizzo, D. (2017). GESTO: A Glove for Enhanced Sensing and Touching Based on Inertial and Magnetic Sensors for Hand Tracking and Cutaneous Feedback. *IEEE Trans. Human-mach. Syst.* 47, 1066–1076. doi:10.1109/thms.2017.2720667

Battaglia, P. W., Kersten, D., and Schrater, P. R. (2011). How Haptic Size Sensations Improve Distance Perception. *Plos Comput. Biol.* 7 (6), e1002080. doi:10.1371/journal.pcbi.1002080

Berti, A., Merlet, J.-P., and Carricato, M. (2013). "Solving the Direct Geometrico-Static Problem of 3-3 Cable-Driven Parallel Robots by Interval Analysis: Preliminary Results," in *Cable-driven Parallel Robots* (Berlin, Heidelberg: Springer), 251–268. doi:10.1007/978-3-642-31988-4_16

Borja, E. F., Lara, D. A., Quevedo, W. X., and Andaluz, V. H. (2018). "Haptic Stimulation Glove for Fine Motor Rehabilitation in Virtual Reality Environments," in International Conference on Augmented Reality, Virtual Reality and Computer Graphics, Otranto, Italy, June 24–27, 2018 (Springer), 211–229. doi:10.1007/978-3-319-95282-6_16

Carricato, M., and Abbasnejad, G. (2013). "Direct Geometrico-Static Analysis of Underconstrained Cable-Driven Parallel Robots with 4 Cables," in *Cable-driven Parallel Robots* (Berlin, Heidelberg: Springer), 269–285. doi:10.1007/978-3-642-31988-4_17

Chinello, F., Malvezzi, M., Prattichizzo, D., and Pacchierotti, C. (2020). A Modular Wearable Finger Interface for Cutaneous and Kinesthetic Interaction: Control and Evaluation. *IEEE Trans. Ind. Electron.* 67, 706–716. doi:10.1109/tie.2019.2899551

Chinello, F., Pacchierotti, C., Malvezzi, M., and Prattichizzo, D. (2018). A Three Revolute-Revolute-Spherical Wearable Fingertip Cutaneous Device for Stiffness Rendering. *IEEE Trans. Haptics* 11, 39–50. doi:10.1109/toh.2017.2755015

Borst, C. W., and Cavanaugh, C. D.(2004). "Haptic Controller Design and palm-sized Vibrotactile Array," technical report.

de Tinguy, X., Howard, T., Pacchierotti, C., Marchal, M., and Lécuyer, A. (2020). "WeATaViX: WEarable Actuated TAngibles for VIrtual Reality eXperiences," in *Haptics: Science, Technology, Applications*. Editors I. Nisky, J. Hartcher-O'Brien, M. Wiertlewski, and J. Smeets (Cham: Springer International Publishing), 262–270. doi:10.1007/978-3-030-58147-3_29

Gollner, U., Bieling, T., and Joost, G. (2012). "Mobile Lorm Glove: Introducing a Communication Device for Deaf-Blind People," in Proceedings of the sixth international conference on tangible, embedded and embodied interaction, Kingston Ontario Canada, February 19 - 22, 2012 (ACM), 127–130. doi:10.1145/2148131.2148159

Iwata, H., Yano, H., Nakaizumi, F., and Kawamura, R. (2001). "Project Feelex: Adding Haptic Surface to Graphics," in Proceedings of the 28th annual conference on Computer graphics and interactive techniques, New York, 01 August 2001 (Association for Computing Machinery), 469–476. doi:10.1145/383259.383314

Kajimoto, H. (2012). "Design of Cylindrical Whole-Hand Haptic Interface Using Electrocutaneous Display," in International Conference on Human Haptic Sensing and Touch Enabled Computer Applications, Tampere, Finland, June 13-15, 2012 (Springer), 67–72. doi:10.1007/978-3-642-31404-9_12

Khosravi, M. A., and Taghirad, H. D. (2013). "Experimental Performance of Robust PID Controller on a Planar Cable Robot," in *Cable-driven Parallel Robots* (Berlin, Heidelberg: Springer), 337–352. doi:10.1007/978-3-642-31988-4_21

Kovacs, R., Ofek, E., Gonzalez Franco, M., Siu, A. F., Marwecki, S., Holz, C., and Sinclair, M. (2020). "Haptic Pivot: On-Demand Handhelds in Vr," in Proceedings of the 33rd

Annual ACM Symposium on User Interface Software and Technology, Virtual Event USA, October 20 - 23, 2020 (ACM), 1046–1059. doi:10.1145/3379337.3415854

Kubo, K., Cheng, Y.-S., Zhou, B., An, K.-N., Moran, S. L., Amadio, P. C., et al. (2018). The Quantitative Evaluation of the Relationship between the Forces Applied to the palm and Carpal Tunnel Pressure. *J. Biomech.* 66, 170–174. doi:10.1016/j.jbiomech.2017.10.039

Lederman, S. J., and Klatzky, R. L. (1987). Hand Movements: A Window into Haptic Object Recognition. *Cogn. Psychol.* 19, 342–368. doi:10.1016/0010-0285(87)90008-9

Malvezzi, M., Chinello, F., Prattichizzo, D., and Pacchierotti, C. (2021). Design of Personalized Wearable Haptic Interfaces to Account for Fingertip Size and Shape. *IEEE Trans. Haptics* 14, 1. doi:10.1109/TOH.2021.3076106

Martínez, J., García, A., Oliver, M., Molina, J. P., and González, P. (2014). Identifying Virtual 3D Geometric Shapes with a Vibrotactile Glove. *IEEE Comput. Graph Appl.* 36, 42–51. doi:10.1109/MCG.2014.81

Martinez, J., Griffiths, D., Biscione, V., Georgiou, O., and Carter, T. (2018). "Touchless Haptic Feedback for Supernatural Vr Experiences," in 2018 IEEE Conference on Virtual Reality and 3D User Interfaces (VR), Tuebingen/Reutlingen, Germany, 18-22 March 2018 (IEEE), 629–630.

Miermeister, P., Kraus, W., and Pott, A. (2013). "Differential Kinematics for Calibration, System Investigation, and Force Based Forward Kinematics of Cable-Driven Parallel Robots," in *Cable-driven Parallel Robots* (Berlin, Heidelberg: Springer), 319–333. doi:10.1007/978-3-642-31988-4_20

Minamizawa, K., Kamuro, S., Fukamachi, S., Kawakami, N., and Tachi, S. (2008). "Ghostglove: Haptic Existence of the Virtual World," in ACM SIGGRAPH 2008 new tech demos, Los Angeles California, August 11 - 15, 2008 (ACM), 1.

Minamizawa, K., Kamuro, S., Kawakami, N., and Tachi, S. (2008). "A palm-worn Haptic Display for Bimanual Operations in Virtual Environments," in International Conference on Human Haptic Sensing and Touch Enabled Computer Applications, Madrid, Spain, June 10-13, 2008 (Springer), 458–463. doi:10.1007/978-3-540-69057-3_59

Pacchierotti, C., Sinclair, S., Solazzi, M., Frisoli, A., Hayward, V., and Prattichizzo, D. (2017). Wearable Haptic Systems for the Fingertip and the Hand: Taxonomy, Review, and Perspectives. *IEEE Trans. Haptics* 10, 580–600. doi:10.1109/toh.2017.2689006

Son, B., and Park, J. (2018). "Haptic Feedback to the palm and Fingers for Improved Tactile Perception of Large Objects," in Proceedings of the 31st Annual ACM Symposium on User Interface Software and Technology, Berlin Germany, 14 October 2018 (ACM), 757–763. doi:10.1145/3242587.3242656

Son, B., and Park, J. (2018). "Tactile Sensitivity to Distributed Patterns in a palm," in Proceedings of the 20th ACM International Conference on Multimodal Interaction, Boulder CO USA, October 16 - 20, 2018 (ACM), 486–491. doi:10.1145/3242969.3243030

Swartz, M. H. (2002). *Physical Diagnosis: History and Examination*. WB Saunders.

Trinitatova, D., and Tsetserukou, D. (2019). "Deltatouch: a 3d Haptic Display for Delivering Multimodal Tactile Stimuli at the palm," in 2019 IEEE World Haptics Conference (WHC), Tokyo, Japan, 9-12 July 2019 (IEEE), 73–78. doi:10.1109/WHC.2019.8816136

Trinitatova, D., Tsetserukou, D., and Fedoseev, A. (2019). "Touchvr: a Wearable Haptic Interface for Vr Aimed at Delivering Multi-Modal Stimuli at the User's palm," in SIGGRAPH Asia 2019 XR, Brisbane QLD Australia, November 17 - 20, 2019 (ACM), 42–43. doi:10.1145/3355355.3361896

Van Nierop, O. A., van der Helm, A., Overbeeke, K. J., and Djajadiningrat, T. J. (2008). A Natural Human Hand Model. *Vis. Comp.* 24, 31–44. doi:10.1007/s00371-007-0176-x

Yao, R., Li, H., and Zhang, X. (2013). "A Modeling Method of the Cable Driven Parallel Manipulator for FAST," in *Cable-driven Parallel Robots* (Berlin, Heidelberg: Springer), 423–436. doi:10.1007/978-3-642-31988-4_26

Zubrycki, I., and Granosik, G. (2017). Novel Haptic Device Using Jamming Principle for Providing Kinaesthetic Feedback in Glove-Based Control Interface. *J. Intell. Robotic Syst.* 85 (3-4), 413–429. doi:10.1007/s10846-016-0392-6

Haptic Feedback for Microrobotics Applications

Claudio Pacchierotti[1]*, Stefano Scheggi[2], Domenico Prattichizzo[1,3] and Sarthak Misra[2,4]

[1] Department of Advanced Robotics, Istituto Italiano di Tecnologia, Genova, Italy, [2] Surgical Robotics Laboratory, Department of Biomechanical Engineering, MIRA – Institute for Biomedical Technology and Technical Medicine, University of Twente, Enschede, Netherlands, [3] Department of Information Engineering and Mathematics, University of Siena, Siena, Italy, [4] Department of Biomedical Engineering, University of Groningen and University Medical Center Groningen, Groningen, Netherlands

*Correspondence:
Claudio Pacchierotti
claudio.pacchierotti@iit.it

Microrobotics systems are showing promising results in several applications and scenarios, such as targeted drug delivery and screening, biopsy, environmental control, surgery, and assembly. While most of the systems presented in the literature consider autonomous techniques, there is a growing interest in human-in-the-loop approaches. For reasons of responsibility, safety, and public acceptance, it is in fact beneficial to provide a human with intuitive and effective means for directly controlling these microrobotic systems. In this respect, haptic feedback is widely believed to be a valuable tool in human-in-the-loop teleoperation systems. This article presents a review of the literature on haptic feedback systems for microrobotics, categorizing it according to the type of haptic technology employed. In particular, we considered both tethered and untethered systems, including applications of micropositioning, microassembly, minimally invasive surgery, delivery of objects, micromanipulation, and injection of cells. One of the main challenges for an effective implementation is stability control. In fact, the high scaling factors introduced to match variables in the macro and the micro worlds may introduce instabilities. Another challenge lies in the measurement of position and force signals in the remote environment. The integration of microsized sensors may significantly increase the complexity and cost of tools fabrication. To overcome the lack of force-sensing, vision seems a promising solution. Finally, although the literature on haptic feedback for untethered microrobotics is still quite small, we foreseen a great development of this field of research, thanks to its flexible applications in biomedical engineering scenarios.

Keywords: haptics, microrobotics, robotics, teleoperation, micromanipulation, micropositioning, microsurgery

1. INTRODUCTION

The field of microrobotics has been progressing fast since the last decade, and its applications have shown promising results in several robotic tasks at the microscale, such as controlled positioning (Solovev et al., 2009; Woods and Constandinou, 2011; Khalil et al., 2014a,b), pick up and delivery of objects, cells, and molecules (Solovev et al., 2010; Balasubramanian et al., 2011; Sanchez et al., 2011; Zhang et al., 2012), biopsy (Gultepe et al., 2013), and drilling into soft tissue (Matteucci et al., 2008; Solovev et al., 2012; Soler et al., 2013; Xi et al., 2013).

For reasons of responsibility, safety, and public acceptance, it is beneficial to provide a *human* operator with intuitive and effective means for directly controlling these microrobots (Troccaz and Delnondedieu, 1996; Jakopec et al., 2003; Bolopion and Régnier, 2013). In this condition, the operator should receive enough information about the controlled microrobot and the remote environment. Haptic feedback is one piece of this information flow. Its benefits typically include increased manipulation accuracy and decreased completion time, peak and mean force applied to the remote environment (Massimino and Sheridan, 1994; Wagner et al., 2002; Okamura, 2004; Pacchierotti, 2015; Pacchierotti et al., 2015b,c, 2016).

2. LITERATURE REVIEW

This article reviews the literature on haptic feedback systems for microrobotics, categorizing it according to the type of haptic sensing technique employed. **Table 1** summarizes the features of the considered microrobotic systems.

2.1. Atomic Force Microscopy

Atomic force microscopy (AFM) is a high-resolution type of scanning probe microscopy with a resolution of fractions of a nanometer. An AFM probe has usually a sharp tip on the free-swinging end of a cantilever that is protruding from a holder.

TABLE 1 | Haptic feedback for microrobotics applications.

System	Force sensing	Force actuation	Information rendered with haptics		Application	Untethered	Notes
			Physical properties	Active constraint			
Sitti et al. (1999)	AFM	1-DoF (custom)	✓		Micromanipulation		Force scaling: 2×10^6 Position scaling: 4×10^3
Ferreira et al. (2001)	AFM	2-DoF (custom)	✓		Micromanipulation		
Fahlbusch et al. (2002)	AFM-based	7-DoF (Freedom)	✓		Microassembly		
Bolopion et al. (2011)	AFM, SEM	3-DoF (Omega.3)	✓		Micropositioning		Force scaling: 10^6 Position scaling: 4.8×10^3
Bolopion et al. (2012)	AFM	3-DoF (omega.3)	✓	✓	Microassembly		Force scaling: 2.5×10^6
Vogl et al. (2006)	AFM	6-DoF (phantom premium)	✓		Micromanipulation		Simulated scenario
Iwata et al. (2013)	AFM		✓		Micromanipulation		
Bhatti et al. (2015)	AFM	3-DoF (Phantom Omni)	✓		Micromanipulation		
Venture et al. (2005)	AFM	1-DoF (custom)	✓		Micromanipulation		Force scaling: 8.8×10^{-5} Position scaling: 5800
Kim and Sitti (2006)	AFM	3-DoF (omega.3)	✓		Micromanipulation		
Mohand Ousaid et al. (2015)	AFM	1-DoF (custom)	✓		Micromanipulation		Force scaling: 0.5×10^5
Ni et al. (2012)	Optical sensors	3-DoF (omega.3)	✓	✓	Micromanipulation		
Ammi and Ferreira (2005)	Optical sensor	3-DoF (phantom)	✓	✓	Micromanipulation, cell injection		
Ni et al. (2013)	Optical sensors	3-DoF (omega.3)	✓		Micromanipulation	✓	Force scaling: 4×10^{-4} Position scaling: 2×10^{11}
Kim et al. (2008)	Optical sensors	3-DoF (phantom omni)	✓		Micromanipulation, cell injection		
Shirinov and Fatikow (2003)	6-axis force/torque sensor	6-DoF (custom)	✓		Micromanipulation		Force scaling: 100 Position scaling: up to 10^6
Boukhnifer and Ferreira (2013)	Semiconductor strain gages	1-DoF (custom)	✓		Micromanipulation		
Vijayasai et al. (2010)	Capacitive sensors	3-DoF (Novint Falcon)	✓		Micromanipulation		
Menciassi et al. (2003)	Semiconductor strain gages	3-DoF (Phantom Premium)	✓		Microsurgery		
Pillarisetti et al. (2005)	PVDF	3-DoF (Phantom)	✓		Micromanipulation, cell injection		
Mehrtash et al. (2015)	Hall-effect and laser sensors	3-DoF (phantom omni)	✓		Micromanipulation	✓	
Pacchierotti et al. (2015a)	Visual estimation	6-DoF (Omega.6)	✓	✓	Micropositioning	✓	

Features of selected microrobotic systems.

The cantilever deflection due to the interaction between the tip and the surface gives information about the mechanical properties of the environment (Binnig et al., 1986). One of the first examples of haptic-enabled microrobotic system employed a scanning tunneling microscope coupled with a 6-degrees-of-freedom (6-DoF) haptic interface (Hollis et al., 1990; Bolopion and Régnier, 2013). The vertical movement of the haptic device end-effector replicates one of the microscope tip, so that users can feel the topology of the environment. Few years later, Sitti et al. (1999) presented a teleoperated microscale haptic system composed of a 1-DoF haptic device and an AFM cantilever tip. They addressed the problem of modeling the contact forces at the microscale and designed a scaled bilateral teleoperation controller for reliable contact force feedback. Using a Phantom Premium haptic device, the same group extended these results to 2-D and 3-D tele-micromanipulation scenarios (Sitti et al., 2003). In the same years, Ferreira et al. (2001) presented a teleoperated micromanipulator considering both a piezoelectric microgripper and an AFM operating under an optical microscope. The registered forces are provided to the human operator through a two-finger planar haptic device. Fahlbusch et al. (2002) focused more on the study of suitable force sensing techniques for nanohandling robotics. They used an AFM wheatstone bridge-based sensor for the measurement of gripping forces, and a haptic interface to allow the operator to feel and control these forces. Later on, Bolopion et al. (2011) described a haptic-enabled system for the remote handling of microscale objects. The micromanipulation setup is composed of an AFM manipulator integrated in a scanning electron microscope (SEM). The master teleoperation system is composed of an Omega.3 haptic interface and a virtual reality room (Grange et al., 2001). The system was validated in an approach-retract teleoperation experiment between Paris, France, and Oldenburg, Germany. The same group presented a teleoperated system with haptic feedback for 3-D AFM-based manipulation (Bolopion et al., 2012; see **Figure 1A**). It uses two independent AFM probes to collaboratively grasp and position microscale objects with known shape equations. Haptic feedback is based on dynamic-mode AFM data. It is used to provide information on the measured interaction forces and assist the user in improving dexterity and avoiding collisions. An AFM, together with a haptic interface and an augmented reality system has been also used by Vogl et al. (2006) for applications of micropositioning and sensing. Later on, also Iwata et al. (2013) described an AFM-based manipulator. It can be coupled with a SEM and provides haptic feedback through a Phantom Desktop interface, which is also in charge of controlling the cantilever-based probe of the micromanipulator. More recently, Bhatti et al. (2015) developed a custom haptic interface able to provide force feedback about the interaction forces sensed by an AFM. Interaction forces are characterized by estimating the forces sensed by the cantilever tip using geometric deformation principles.

Microscale teleoperation with haptic feedback requires scaling gains in the order of 10^4–10^7, depending on the application. These high gains impose a trade-off between stability and transparency. Venture et al. (2005) were one of the first groups to consider stability issues in remote micromanipulation systems with force feedback. They implemented a passivity-based position–position coupling scheme that ensures unconditional stability. Stability issues have been also addressed by Kim and Sitti (2006), who introduced a scaled virtual coupling concept and derived the relationship between performance, stability, and scaling factors of velocity (or position) and force.

2.2. Visual Sensing

Kim et al. (2001) developed a 3-D visuo-haptic teleoperated micromanipulation system. A 6-DoF Phantom Premium haptic interface provides the necessary force feedback and controls the positioning of the micromanipulator in the remote environment. The micromanipulator is equipped with a 2-DoF gripper, and multiple CCD cameras are used for position sensing. Similarly, Ni et al. (2012) presented a vision-based microrobotic system combining an asynchronous Address Event Representation silicon retina and a frame-based camera. The temporal precision of the asynchronous silicon retina is used to provide haptic feedback using an Omega.3 haptic device, while the camera is used to retrieve the position of the object to be manipulated. The same group also presented a haptic feedback teleoperation system for optical tweezers (OT) that attains high frequency (Ni et al., 2013). It is composed of laser OT and an Omega.3 haptic interface. The force is estimated using a trap stiffness model that

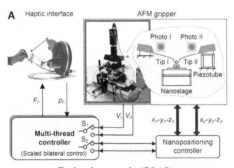
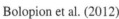

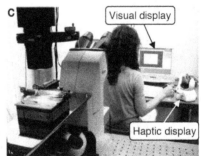

Bolopion et al. (2012)   Ammi and Ferreira (2005)   Basdogan et al. (2007)

FIGURE 1 | Three teleoperation systems for the telemanipulation of microsized objects with haptic feedback. (A) AFM gripper-based teleoperation system. **(B)** 3-D reconstructed cell deformations based on visual tracking data. **(C)** Optical tweezers. All pictures are adapted with permission.

measures the relative position of the object with respect to the laser spot. The human operator controls the OT using the master haptic interface, and the pico-newton forces detected by a vision system are provided to the operator through the same haptic device. Ni et al. (2014) recently extended this approach to multi-trap OT. Mehrtash et al. (2012) developed a haptic-enabled virtual reality interface for a magnetic-haptic micromanipulation platform. It is composed of a magnetic untethered microrobotic station and a Phantom Omni haptic interface. The difference between the actual and commanded position of the microrobot is used to provide force feedback to the human operator. Later on, the same authors also addressed the problem of estimating forces in real environments using a combination of Hall-effect and laser sensors (Mehrtash and Khamesee, 2013; Mehrtash et al., 2015). It uses the produced magnetic flux information and the real position of the microrobot to estimate the forces applied by the robot to the environment. More recently, Pacchierotti et al. (2015a) presented a haptic teleoperation system that enables a human operator to control the positioning of self-propelled catalytic microrobots. A particle-filter-based tracking algorithm tracks, at runtime, the position of the microsized agents in the remote environment. A 6-DoF Omega haptic interface then provides the human operator with haptic feedback about the interaction between the controlled microrobot and the environment, as well as enabling the operator to control the target position of the microrobot. Finally, a wireless magnetic control system regulates the orientation of the microrobot to reach the target point.

2.3. Strain Gages/Piezoresistive Sensors

Shirinov and Fatikow (2003) developed a 4-DoF haptic interface for the remote control of microrobotic cells, which are realized on the basis of a SEM. Two microrobots equipped with piezoelectric actuators operate in the cell, and a 6-axis force/torque sensor is in charge of registering the forces to be filtered, amplified, and finally provided to the human user through the haptic interface. Probst et al. (2009) presented a 6-DoF system for the assembly of 3-D bio-microrobotic devices out of individual 2.5-D microelectro-mechanical systems (MEMS) components. A gripper exchange mechanism allows reaching for parts, and a microfabricated platform provides a structured working area. The human operator controls the microgripper through a Phantom Omni haptic interface, which is also able to provide force feedback about the interaction of the microgripper with the remote environment. More recently, Boukhnifer and Ferreira (2013) used a passivity-based approach for the bilateral control and robust fault tolerant control of a two-fingered microgripper system with haptic feedback. The considered haptic interface is a custom 1-DoF haptic feedback system driven by a DC motor.

Vlachos et al. (2007) presented a haptic telemanipulation system composed of a 2-DoF slave robot driven by two centripetal force vibration micromotors and a custom 5-DoF haptic interface. Since the sensed forces have the form of impulses, the system first filters the forces, it magnifies them, and then provides them to the human operator through the custom haptic interface. The same group recently devised a shared-control steering approach for this manipulation system that uses visual servoing techniques to help the operator in completing various micromanipulation tasks (Vlachos and Papadopoulos, 2014). Sieber et al. (2008) developed a haptic platform for bilateral micromanipulation of cells with 3-D force feedback. It is composed of a MEMS-based silicon triaxial force sensor, customized to act as a sensing probe. The sensor is mounted on a nanomanipulator with 3-DoF, and a Phantom Premium device is in charge of providing the sensed force to the operator. Horan et al. (2009) proposed another system to provide the human operator with intuitive means for controlling a micromanipulator during intracellular injection. A Phantom Omni haptic device controls the position of a micropipette in the remote environment. The authors also investigated the importance of proper position and force scaling. More recently, Seifabadi et al. (2013) presented a 1-DoF macro–micro teleoperation system with haptic feedback. A micromotion piezo actuator is used as the slave robot, and a servo DC motor actuates the master handle. Force sensors are placed at both ends for haptic feedback, and a microscope system is used for real-time visual feedback. A sliding mode-based impedance controller ensures position tracking, while an impedance force controller is used at the master side to ascertain force tracking.

Salcudean et al. (1995) started to investigate the role of haptic feedback for minimally invasive surgery applications at the microscale by developing a macro–micro manipulator with a micro-motion wrist identical to the haptic-enabled master. By using a combination of position and rate control, the system requires small operator hand motions to provide low mechanical impedance, high motion resolution, and force feedback over a substantial volume. Later on, Menciassi et al. (2003) presented a set of robotic haptic-enabled microinstruments for minimally invasive surgery. At the operating table, a microgripper, instrumented with semiconductor strain gages as force sensors, is in charge of manipulating tissue samples. A fiber optic microscope monitor allows the operator to visualize the sample and the microgripper position. Finally, a Phantom haptic interface enables the human operator to control the position of the microgripper and feels the pulse in the considered microvessels. The same group leaded the collaborative project "ARAKNES"[1] on the advancement of technologies for the surgical treatment of morbid obesity and gastroesophageal reflux. Within the same project, Santos-Carreras et al. (2010) developed a bimanual haptic-enabled workstation to teleoperate surgical microrobots in the abdominal cavity of the patient. More recently, Payne et al. (2012) presented a hand-held device capable of amplifying micromanipulation forces during minimal invasive surgical tasks. The device uses a three-phase linear motor capable of generating forces that allow amplification factors up to 15 times.

---

[1]http://www.araknes.org/home.html

2.4. Capacitive Sensors

Vijayasai et al. (2010) uses a MEMS microgripper as an end-effector and a force sense circuit to measure the gripping force. Force feedback is then provided to the operator using a Novint Falcon, which is also employed to control the position of the microgripper. The same system has been also employed in a chess piece pick-and-place game at the microscale (Vijayasai et al., 2012).

2.5. Electrostatic Active Sensors

Mohand Ousaid et al. (2014) proposed a modular micro teleoperation system using custom passive components. The stability of the teleoperation loop is guaranteed as the serial connection of passive systems yield a passive system. The slave probe is equipped with a force sensor, which uses electrostatic energy. The sensed force is scaled up and provided to the human operator through a custom 1-DoF haptic interface (Mohand Ousaid et al., 2012). The authors tested the proposed system in microscale force sensing scenarios, such as feeling capillary forces while penetrating a water droplet (Mohand Ousaid et al., 2015). The same group participates in the collaborative project "REMIQUA,"[2] which aims at developing modular and versatile systems for microassembly and quality inspection.

2.6. Piezoelectric Sensors

Ammi and Ferreira (2005) presented a bio-inspired cell micromanipulation system. Stereoscopic visual information is provided to the operator through a 3-D reconstruction method using vision-based tracking of the environment deformations (see **Figure 1B**). A Phantom haptic device provides haptic feedback. Results show that the stability of the cell punction is improved when adding haptic feedback about cellular forces and the viscosity of the medium. Similarly, Pillarisetti et al. (2005) developed a haptic system capable of measuring cell injection forces and providing a suitable feedback to the user through a Phantom Premium device. All subjects were able to correctly detect the puncturing of the membrane through the haptic interface.

2.7. Physical Models

Kim et al. (2008) presented a haptic rendering technique in which interaction forces between the slave instrument, driven by a Phantom Omni haptic device, and a deformable cell are estimated in real time based on a physical model of the object. The system was evaluated in micromanipulation experiments using zebrafish embryos. Asgari et al. (2011) used a 3-D particle-based model to simulate the deformation of a cell membrane and cellular forces during microrobotic cell injection. The model is based on the kinematic and dynamic of spring–damper multi-particle joints taking into account viscoelastic fluidic properties. It simulates indentation haptic feedback as well as cell visual deformation. The model was validated using experimental data of zebrafish

embryo microinjections. A simulator for cell injection has been also presented by Ladjal et al. (2011, 2013). It is composed of a computer-generated mesh of the cell, a needle, a collision detection algorithm, a physical-based model of deformable cell modeling, and a haptic interaction controller. The authors devised two models based either on an explicit linear finite element model or on a non-linear finite element Saint Venant–Kirchhoff material. The operator is able to see the 3-D shape of the cell and interact with it using a Phantom Desktop haptic device.

2.8. Active Constraints

Haptic feedback is not only useful to render the mechanical properties of the remote environment, but it can also be used to provide the human operator with navigation information. Ghanbari et al. (2010) investigated the use of haptic active constraints for cell injection. The active constraints assist the human operator when performing intracellular injection by limiting the micropipette tip's motion to a conical volume as well as recommending the desired path for optimal injection. The same group recently extended this approach to volumetric active constraints (Ghanbari et al., 2014) and to multi-point interaction (Ang et al., 2015). Similarly, Faroque et al. (2015) used haptic constraints to assist an operator performing real-time cell injection. As the operator commands the micropipette to approach the cell, a conical potential field encourages her/him to follow an optimized trajectory toward the penetration point on the cell membrane. To prevent the operator from overshooting the deposition location, a planar active constraint is also used. Kim et al. (2012) described a shared-control framework for microinjection, in which a micromanipulator is controlled by the shared-motion commands of both the human operator and an autonomous controller. While the controller retains cells and glass pipettes within a desired path or space, the operator can concentrate on the injection task. A Phantom desktop haptic interface controls the motion of the pipette and provides the operator with haptic guidance.

Regarding untethered microrobotics, Basdogan et al. (2007) demonstrated the manipulation of polymer microspheres floating in water using OT (see **Figure 1C**). Trapped microspheres are steered using the end-effector of a haptic device that is virtually coupled to an XYZ piezo-scanner controlling the movements of the fluid bed. To ease the manipulation, the system computes a collision-free path for the particle and then provides the user with guidance through the haptic interface to keep him/her on this path.

AUTHOR CONTRIBUTIONS

CP and SS searched in the literature for relevant works and wrote the paper. SM and DP wrote the paper.

---

[2]http://www.remiqua.eu/

REFERENCES

Ammi, M., and Ferreira, A. (2005). "Realistic visual and haptic rendering for biological-cell injection," in *Proc. IEEE International Conference on Robotics and Automation* (Barcelona), 918–923.

Ang, Q.-Z., Horan, B., Abdi, H., and Nahavandi, S. (2015). Multipoint haptic guidance for micrograsping systems. *IEEE Syst. J.* 9, 1388–1395. doi:10.1109/JSYST.2014.2314737

Asgari, M., Ghanbari, A., and Nahavandi, S. (2011). "3d particle-based cell modelling for haptic microrobotic cell injection," in *Proc. International Conference on Mechatronics Technology: Precision Mechatronics for Advanced Manufacturing, Service, and Medical Sectors* (Melbourne), 1–6.

Balasubramanian, S., Kagan, D., Hu, C. M., Campuzano, S., Lobo-Castañon, M. J., Lim, N., et al. (2011). Micromachine-enabled capture and isolation of cancer cells in complex media. *Angew. Chem. Int. Ed.* 50, 4161–4164. doi:10.1002/anie.201102193

Basdogan, C., Kiraz, A., Bukusoglu, I., Varol, A., and Doganay, S. (2007). Haptic guidance for improved task performance in steering microparticles with optical tweezers. *Opt. Express* 15, 11616–11621. doi:10.1364/OE.15.011616

Bhatti, A., Khan, B., Nahavandi, S., Hanoun, S., and Gao, D. (2015). "Intuitive haptics interface with accurate force estimation and reflection at nanoscale," in *Advances in Global Optimization* (Springer International Publishing), 507–514.

Binnig, G., Quate, C. F., and Gerber, C. (1986). Atomic force microscope. *Phys. Rev. Lett.* 56, 930. doi:10.1103/PhysRevLett.56.930

Bolopion, A., and Régnier, S. (2013). A review of haptic feedback teleoperation systems for micromanipulation and microassembly. *IEEE Trans. Autom. Sci. Eng.* 10, 496–502. doi:10.1109/TASE.2013.2245122

Bolopion, A., Stolle, C., Tunnell, R., Haliyo, S., Régnier, S., and Fatikow, S. (2011). "Remote microscale teleoperation through virtual reality and haptic feedback," in *Proc. IEEE/RSJ International Conference on Intelligent Robots and Systems* (San Francisco), 894–900.

Bolopion, A., Xie, H., Haliyo, D. S., and Régnier, S. (2012). Haptic teleoperation for 3-d microassembly of spherical objects. *IEEE/ASME Trans. Mechatron.* 17, 116–127. doi:10.1109/TMECH.2010.2090892

Boukhnifer, M., and Ferreira, A. (2013). Fault tolerant control of a teleoperated piezoelectric microgripper. *Asian J. Control* 15, 888–900. doi:10.1002/asjc.593

Fahlbusch, S., Shirinov, A., and Fatikow, S. (2002). "Afm-based micro force sensor and haptic interface for a nanohandling robot," in *Proc. IEEE/RSJ International Conference on Intelligent Robots and Systems*, Vol. 2. (Lausanne), 1772–1777.

Faroque, S., Horan, B., Adam, H., Pangestu, M., and Thomas, S. (2015). "Haptic virtual reality training environment for micro-robotic cell injection," in *Haptic Interaction*, Vol. 277. (Springer), 245–249.

Ferreira, A., Cassier, C., Haddab, Y., Rougeot, P., and Chaillet, N. (2001). "Development of a teleoperated micromanipulation system with visual and haptic feedback," in *Intelligent Systems and Advanced Manufacturing*, 112–123.

Ghanbari, A., Abdi, H., Horan, B., Nahavandi, S., Chen, X., and Wang, W. (2010). "Haptic guidance for microrobotic intracellular injection," in *Proc. IEEE RAS and EMBS International Conference on Biomedical Robotics and Biomechatronics* (Tokyo), 162–167.

Ghanbari, A., Horan, B., Nahavandi, S., Chen, X., and Wang, W. (2014). Haptic microrobotic cell injection system. *IEEE Syst. J.* 8, 371–383. doi:10.1109/JSYST.2012.2206440

Grange, S., Conti, F., Helmer, P., Rouiller, P., and Baur, C. (2001). "Delta haptic device as a nanomanipulator," in *Intelligent Systems and Advanced Manufacturing*, 100–111.

Gultepe, E., Randhawa, J. S., Kadam, S., Yamanaka, S., Selaru, F. M., Shin, E. J., et al. (2013). Biopsy with thermally-responsive untethered microtools. *Adv. Mater. Weinheim* 25, 514–519. doi:10.1002/adma.201203348

Hollis, R., Salcudean, S., and Abraham, D. (1990). "Toward a tele-nanorobotic manipulation system with atomic scale force feedback and motion resolution," in *Proc. IEEE Micro Electro Mechanical Systems* (Napa Valley), 115–119.

Horan, B., Ghanbari, A., Nahavandi, S., Chen, X., and Wang, W. (2009). "Towards haptic microrobotic intracellular injection," in *Proc. ASME 2009 International Design Engineering Technical Conferences and Computers and Information in Engineering Conference* (San Diego), 135–142.

Iwata, F., Mizuguchi, Y., Ko, H., and Ushiki, T. (2013). A compact nano manipulator based on an atomic force microscope coupling with a scanning electron microscope or an inverted optical microscope. *J. MicroBio Rob.* 8, 25–32. doi:10.1007/s12213-013-0063-7

Jakopec, M., Rodriguez Baena, F., Harris, S. J., Gomes, P., Cobb, J., and Davies, B. L. (2003). The hands-on orthopaedic robot acrobot: early clinical trials of total knee replacement surgery. *IEEE Trans. Rob. Autom.* 19, 902–911. doi:10.1109/TRA.2003.817510

Khalil, I. S. M., Magdanz, V., Sanchez, S., Schmidt, O. G., and Misra, S. (2014a). The control of self-propelled microjets inside a microchannel with time-varying flow rates. *IEEE Trans. Robot.* 30, 49–58. doi:10.1109/TRO.2013.2281557

Khalil, I. S. M., Magdanz, V., Sanchez, S., Schmidt, O. G., and Misra, S. (2014b). Wireless magnetic-based closed-loop control of self-propelled microjets. *PLoS ONE* 9:e83053. doi:10.1371/journal.pone.0083053

Kim, D.-N., Kim, K., Kim, K.-Y., and Cha, S.-M. (2001). "Dexterous teleoperation for micro parts handling based on haptic/visual interface," in *Proc. IEEE Micromechatronics and Human Science* (Kawasaki), 211–217.

Kim, J., Ladjal, H., Folio, D., Ferreira, A., and Kim, J. (2012). Evaluation of telerobotic shared control strategy for efficient single-cell manipulation. *IEEE Trans. Autom. Sci. Eng.* 9, 402–406. doi:10.1109/TASE.2011.2174357

Kim, J., Sharifi, F. J., and Kim, J. (2008). "A physically-based haptic rendering for telemanipulation with visual information: macro and micro applications," in *Proc. IEEE/RSJ International Conference on Intelligent Robots and Systems* (Nice), 3489–3494.

Kim, S.-G., and Sitti, M. (2006). Task-based and stable telenanomanipulation in a nanoscale virtual environment. *IEEE Trans. Autom. Sci. Eng.* 3, 240–247. doi:10.1109/TASE.2006.876909

Ladjal, H., Hanus, J.-L., and Ferreira, A. (2011). "Microrobotic simulator for assisted biological cell injection," in *Proc. IEEE/RSJ International Conference on Intelligent Robots and Systems* (San Francisco), 1315–1320.

Ladjal, H., Hanus, J.-L., and Ferreira, A. (2013). Micro-to-nano biomechanical modeling for assisted biological cell injection. *IEEE Trans. Biomed. Eng.* 60, 2461–2471. doi:10.1109/TBME.2013.2258155

Massimino, M. J., and Sheridan, T. B. (1994). Teleoperator performance with varying force and visual feedback. *Hum. Factors* 36, 145–157.

Matteucci, M., Casella, M., Bedoni, M., Donetti, E., Fanetti, M., De Angelis, F., et al. (2008). A compact and disposable transdermal drug delivery system. *Microelectron. Eng.* 85, 1066–1073. doi:10.1016/j.mee.2007.12.067

Mehrtash, M., and Khamesee, M. B. (2013). Micro-domain force estimation using hall-effect sensors for a magnetic microrobotic station. *J. Adv. Mech. Des. Syst. Manuf.* 7, 2–14. doi:10.1299/jamdsm.7.2

Mehrtash, M., Khamesee, M. B., Tarao, S., Tsuda, N., and Chang, J.-Y. (2012). Human-assisted virtual reality for a magnetic-haptic micromanipulation platform. *Microsyst. Technol.* 18, 1407–1415. doi:10.1007/s00542-012-1560-7

Mehrtash, M., Zhang, X., and Khamesee, M. (2015). Bilateral magnetic micromanipulation using off-board force sensor. *IEEE/ASME Trans. Mechatron.* 20, 3223–3231. doi:10.1109/TMECH.2015.2417116

Menciassi, A., Eisinberg, A., Carrozza, M. C., and Dario, P. (2003). Force sensing microinstrument for measuring tissue properties and pulse in microsurgery. *IEEE/ASME Trans. Mechatron.* 8, 10–17. doi:10.1109/TMECH.2003.809153

Mohand Ousaid, A., Bolopion, A., Haliyo, S., Régnier, S., Hayward, V. (2014). "Stability and transparency analysis of a teleoperation chain for microscale interaction," in *Proc. IEEE International Conference on Robotics and Automation (ICRA)* (Hong Kong: IEEE), 5946–5951.

Mohand Ousaid, A., Haliyo, D., Regnier, S., and Hayward, V. (2015). A stable and transparent microscale force feedback teleoperation system. *IEEE/ASME Trans. Mechatron.* 20, 2593–2603. doi:10.1109/TMECH.2015.2423092

Mohand Ousaid, A., Millet, G., Régnier, S., Haliyo, S., and Hayward, V. (2012). Haptic interface transparency achieved through viscous coupling. *Int. J. Rob. Res.* 31, 319–329. doi:10.1177/0278364911430421

Ni, Z., Bolopion, A., Agnus, J., Benosman, R., and Régnier, S. (2012). Asynchronous event-based visual shape tracking for stable haptic feedback in microrobotics. *IEEE Trans. Robot.* 28, 1081–1089. doi:10.1109/TRO.2012.2198930

Ni, Z., Pacoret, C., Benosman, R., and Régnier, S. (2013). "2d high speed force feedback teleoperation of optical tweezers," in *Proc. IEEE International Conference on Robotics and Automation* (Karlsruhe), 1700–1705.

Ni, Z., Yin, M., Pacoret, C., Benosman, R., and Régnier, S. (2014). "First high speed simultaneous force feedback for multi-trap optical tweezers," in *Advanced Intelligent Mechatronics (AIM), 2014 IEEE/ASME International Conference on* (Besançon), 7–12.

Okamura, A. M. (2004). Methods for haptic feedback in teleoperated robot-assisted surgery. *Ind. Rob.* 31, 499–508. doi:10.1108/01439910410566362

Pacchierotti, C. (2015). "Cutaneous haptic feedback in robotic teleoperation," in *Springer Series on Touch and Haptic Systems* (Springer International Publishing).

Pacchierotti, C., Magdanz, V., Medina-Sanchez, M., Schmidt, O. G., Prattichizzo, D., and Misra, S. (2015a). Intuitive control of self-propelled microjets with haptic feedback. *J. MicroBio Rob.* 10, 37–53. doi:10.1007/s12213-015-0082-7

Pacchierotti, C., Meli, L., Chinello, F., Malvezzi, M., and Prattichizzo, D. (2015b). Cutaneous haptic feedback to ensure the stability of robotic teleoperation systems. *Int. J. Rob. Res.* 34, 1773–1787. doi:10.1177/0278364915603135

Pacchierotti, C., Tirmizi, A., Bianchini, G., and Prattichizzo, D. (2015c). Enhancing the performance of passive teleoperation systems via cutaneous feedback. *IEEE Trans. Haptics* 8, 397–409. doi:10.1109/TOH.2015.2457927

Pacchierotti, C., Prattichizzo, D., and Kuchenbecker, K. J. (2016). Cutaneous feedback of fingertip deformation and vibration for palpation in robotic surgery. *IEEE Trans. Biomed. Eng.* 63, 278–287. doi:10.1109/TBME.2015.2455932

Payne, C. J., Latt, W. T., and Yang, G.-Z. (2012). "A new hand-held force-amplifying device for micromanipulation," in *Proc. IEEE International Conference on Robotics and Automation* (St. Paul), 1583–1588.

Pillarisetti, A., Anjum, W., Desai, J. P., Friedman, G., and Brooks, A. D. (2005). "Force feedback interface for cell injection," in *Proc. World Haptics* (Pisa), 391–400.

Probst, M., Hürzeler, C., Borer, R., and Nelson, B. J. (2009). A microassembly system for the flexible assembly of hybrid robotic mems devices. *Int. J. Optomechatronics* 3, 69–90. doi:10.1080/15599610902894592

Salcudean, S. E., Wong, N., and Hollis, R. L. (1995). Design and control of a force-reflecting teleoperation system with magnetically levitated master and wrist. *IEEE Trans. Rob. Autom.* 11, 844–858. doi:10.1109/70.478431

Sanchez, S., Solovev, A. A., Schulze, S., and Schmidt, O. G. (2011). Controlled manipulation of multiple cells using catalytic microbots. *Chem. Commun.* 47, 698–700. doi:10.1039/c0cc04126b

Santos-Carreras, L., Leuenberger, K., Beira, R., and Bleuler, H. (2010). "Araknes haptic interface: user-centered design approach," in *pHealth* (Berlin), 2010.

Seifabadi, R., Rezaei, S. M., Ghidary, S. S., and Zareinejad, M. (2013). A teleoperation system for micro positioning with haptic feedback. *Int. J. Control Autom. Syst.* 11, 768–775. doi:10.1007/s12555-012-0139-5

Shirinov, A., and Fatikow, S. (2003). "Haptic interface for a microrobot cell," in *Proc. EuroHaptics* (Dublin), 6–9.

Sieber, A., Valdastri, P., Houston, K., Eder, C., Tonet, O., Menciassi, A., et al. (2008). A novel haptic platform for real time bilateral biomanipulation with a mems sensor for triaxial force feedback. *Sens. Actuators A Phys.* 142, 19–27. doi:10.1016/j.sna.2007.03.018

Sitti, M., Aruk, B., Shintani, H., and Hashimoto, H. (2003). Scaled teleoperation system for nano-scale interaction and manipulation. *Adv. Robot.* 17, 275–291. doi:10.1163/156855303764018503

Sitti, M., Horiguchi, S., and Hashimoto, H. (1999). "Tele-touch feedback of surfaces at the micro/nano scale: modeling and experiments," in *Proc. IEEE/RSJ International Conference on Intelligent Robots and Systems*, Vol. 2 (Kyongju), 882–888.

Soler, L., Magdanz, V., Fomin, V. M., Sanchez, S. O., and Schmidt, O. G. (2013). Self-propelled micromotors for cleaning polluted water. *ACS Nano* 7, 9611–9620. doi:10.1021/nn405075d

Solovev, A. A., Mei, Y., Urena, E. B., Huang, G., and Schmidt, O. G. (2009). Catalytic microtubular jet engines self-propelled by accumulated gas bubbles. *Small* 5, 1688–1692. doi:10.1002/smll.200900021

Solovev, A. A., Sanchez, S., Pumera, M., Mei, Y. F., and Schmidt, O. G. (2010). Magnetic control of tubular catalytic microbots for the transport, assembly, and delivery of micro-objects. *Adv. Funct. Mater.* 20, 2430–2435. doi:10.1002/adfm.201090064

Solovev, A. A., Xi, W., Gracias, D. H., Harazim, S. M., Deneke, S. M., Sanchez, S., et al. (2012). Self-propelled nanotools. *ACS Nano* 6, 1751–1756. doi:10.1021/nn204762w

Troccaz, J., and Delnondedieu, Y. (1996). Semi-active guiding systems in surgery. a two-dof prototype of the passive arm with dynamic constraints (PADyC). *Mechatronics* 6, 399–421. doi:10.1016/0957-4158(96)00003-7

Venture, G., Haliyo, D. S., Régnier, S., and Micaelli, A. (2005). "Force-feedback micromanipulation with unconditionally stable coupling," in *Proc. International Conference on IEEE/RSJ Intelligent Robots and Systems* (Edmonton), 1923–1928.

Vijayasai, A. P., Sivakumar, G., Mulsow, M., Lacouture, S., Holness, A., and Dallas, T. E. (2010). Haptic controlled three-axis mems gripper system. *Rev. Sci. Instrum.* 81, 105114. doi:10.1063/1.3499243

Vijayasai, A. P., Sivakumar, G., Mulsow, M., Lacouture, S., Holness, A., Dallas, T. E., et al. (2012). Haptic controlled three degree-of-freedom microgripper system for assembly of detachable surface-micromachined mems. *Sens. Actuators A Phys.* 179, 328–336. doi:10.1016/j.sna.2012.03.035

Vlachos, K., and Papadopoulos, E. (2014). "Design and experimental validation of a hybrid micro tele-manipulation system," in *8th Hellenic Conference on Artificial Intelligence* (Ioannina: Springer International Publishing), 164–177.

Vlachos, K., Vartholomeos, P., and Papadopoulos, E. (2007). "A haptic tele-manipulation environment for a vibration-driven micromechatronic device," in *Proc. IEEE/ASME International Conference on Advanced Intelligent Mechatronics* (Zurich), 1–6.

Vogl, W., Ma, B. K.-L., and Sitti, M. (2006). Augmented reality user interface for an atomic force microscope-based nanorobotic system. *IEEE Trans. Nanotechnol.* 5, 397–406. doi:10.1109/TNANO.2006.877421

Wagner, C. R., Howe, R. D., and Stylopoulos, N. (2002). "The role of force feedback in surgery: analysis of blunt dissection," in *Proc. International Symposium on Haptic Interfaces for Virtual Environment and Teleoperator Systems* (Orlando), 354–355.

Woods, S. P., and Constandinou, T. G. (2011). "Towards a micropositioning system for targeted drug delivery in wireless capsule endoscopy," in *Proc. International Conference of the IEEE Engineering in Medicine and Biology Society* (Boston), 7372–7375.

Xi, W., Solovev, A. A., Ananth, A. N., Gracias, D. H., Sanchez, S., and Schmidt, O. G. (2013). Rolled-up magnetic microdrillers: towards remotely controlled minimally invasive surgery. *Nanoscale* 5, 1294–1297. doi:10.1039/c2nr32798h

Zhang, L., Petit, T., Peyer, K. E., and Nelson, B. J. (2012). Targeted cargo delivery using a rotating nickel nanowire. *Nanomedicine* 8, 1074–1080. doi:10.1016/j.nano.2012.03.002

15

A Robust Approach for Reproducing the Haptic Sensation of Sandpaper with Different Roughness During Bare Fingertip Interaction

Jianyao Zhang* and Hiroyuki Kajimoto

Department of Informatics, The University of Electro-Communications, Chofu, Japan

*Correspondence:
Jianyao Zhang
zhang@kaji-lab.jp*

When reproducing realistic virtual textures for bare finger interaction, an accelerometer attached to a fingernail is commonly used. This measurement depends on the dynamic conditions during the exploration action, and slight differences in roughness are difficult to acquire accurately because of masking by shivering, low-pass filtering by the finger tissue, and sensor accuracy. We propose a simpler yet robust approach based on the 3D measurement of the surface and compare it with the conventional approach. The 3D surface images of sandpaper with different degrees of roughness were captured using a 3D microscope, and the line roughness curve was transformed into an acceleration curve by quadratic differential transformation. The real-time acceleration and frictional force were measured by an accelerometer and force sensor for comparison. A haptic device replaying acceleration-based vibrations by two audio speakers and producing tangential force by a motor-controlled liner slide was developed for reproduction. We conducted experiments with participants to evaluate the reproduction approach. Experimental results showed that the conventional approach obtained sufficient discriminability with the assistance of force, whereas the proposed approach achieved higher reproducibility and discriminability by sole vibration. Thus, our approach provides a new reference for studies of bare finger interaction with rough surfaces.

Keywords: bare finger interaction, haptic device, roughness, surface measurement, texture rendering

1 INTRODUCTION

With the rapid development of computer graphics technologies, it has become possible to construct 3D models in which virtual objects have texture details that are visually almost indistinguishable from those of real objects. This allows computers to build a virtual environment that can achieve a high degree of similarity with the real environment. However, in the field of virtual reality, interaction with virtual objects with haptic feedback is considered an integral part of immersion (Martel and Muldner, 2017). Although graphic rendering can achieve high precision for surface textures, the haptic sensation has not yet been reproduced to a degree close to the precision of visual reproduction. To achieve such high-quality haptic reproduction, a robust approach is needed to accurately capture the slight differences in the texture of a specific material and reproduce them as distinguishable.

The purpose of this research is to measure the roughness of the material surface precisely and reproduce the slightly different textures of a specific material. The reproduction objects are sandpapers with seven slightly different levels of roughness. To reproduce the haptic sensation when a finger directly contacts and explores them, we introduce a haptic rendering approach that measures the 3D surface height information under no-contact conditions. The acceleration-based vibration signal is obtained by quadratic differential transformation of the line roughness curve in the image and is then processed by an audio processing software to reproduce the textures of different sandpapers. To evaluate the proposed approach, the acceleration and frictional forces under dynamic conditions were also measured directly. Experiments were conducted to compare the reproducibility and discriminability under the combined vibration and force conditions. The device used in the experiment presents vibrations from audio speakers installed on the left and right sides. The knob of a linear slide at the top can be moved by a motor to present force to the fingers. Experimental results revealed that the conventional approach obtains sufficient discriminability with the assistance of force, whereas the proposed approach achieves higher reproducibility and discriminability by vibration only.

Our proposed approach is able to measure the roughness of the material surface more precisely and reproduce the fine differences between sandpapers. In addition, the measurement approach is easy to set up and the measurement results are stable, so it can be considered as a candidate approach to reproduce the haptic sensation of bare fingers on a flat plate. For example, showing different weave densities of the clothes in a shopping application, or showing the fine texture of an object in a game application using touch.

The remainder of this paper is organized as follows. We introduce the related work in *Related Work* Section, describe the details of the proposed reproduction approach, an overview of the conventional approach, and the setup of the haptic reproduction system in *Materials and Methods* Section. User experiments and results that reveal the reproducibility and discriminability of each approach are presented in *User Study* and *Results* Sections. The discussion of the experimental results, limitations, and future work are presented in *Discussion* Section.

2 RELATED WORK

2.1 Use of Vibration in Haptic Reproduction

A series of extant studies have demonstrated excellent performance in reproducing different types of materials, such as wood, clothes, and sandpaper (Kuchenbecker et al., 2011; Ito et al., 2017; Strese and Steinbach, 2018). Mechanical vibration is a common method for haptic reproduction. Lee et al. (2019) built TORC, a rigid haptic controller that renders virtual textures and compliance by applying a trackpad on the region where users hold and squeeze using their thumb and two other fingers. Vibrotactile motors embedded in trackpads produce sensations on each finger that represent the haptic feel of squeezing, shearing, or turning an object. Ujitoko et al. (2020) created a transparent vibrator system that absorbs the difference in the frequency characteristics of the vibrator environments. Because vibrotactile signals with various frequency patterns can arouse

different haptic sensations, processing the spectral feature of vibration to match the real one is an important process in haptic rendering. Preechayasomboon et al. (2020)'s "Chasm" reproduced rough and smooth textures using 25–40 Hz vibrations rendered from a broadband screw-based linear actuator; Hasegawa et al. (2020) attempted to reproduce the haptic sensation of 19 materials by the phase difference between normal and shear forces and obtained reproducibility with great accuracy. However, these studies all focused on reproducing the textures of completely different materials.

2.2 Augmented Reality of the Texture

In contrast to reproducing different materials, we focused on rendering and reproducing the roughness with a slight difference in a specific material, using sandpapers with different roughness as an example. This requires the reproduced virtual texture to reflect the components with changed texture in a way that is maximally and discriminatingly effective, without changing the basic haptic sensation of the material. Studies that attempted to prepare a "real object" and modulate its changed texture have been conducted; this can be regarded as augmented reality of the texture (Jeon et al., 2011). Asano et al. (2015) proposed a method to modulate the roughness of a material with characteristic textures by applying vibrations in the depth direction. Maeda et al. (2016) reported that vibrating a voice coil actuator attached to a fingertip changes the haptic perception of objects touched by the fingertip. For haptic modulation of flat surfaces, Poupyrev and Maruyama (2003) produced a click-like texture by vibrating a small touch panel. The texture of the real object itself does not change, but in terms of the haptic phenomenon that occurs, an augmented reality situation is established because the sensation of the texture of the real object has changed. This concept is considered useful for reproducing slightly different textures of specific materials (Takasaki et al., 2005; Bau et al., 2010).

2.3 Limitations and Countermeasures for Acceleration Measurement

Considering the sensory mechanoreceptors in the skin that are responsible for haptic perception, especially the Pacinian corpuscles that function in micro-textures and respond only to the accelerative vibration of skin deformation (Biswas et al., 2015), it is reasonable to replay acceleration as a vibration signal to reproduce textures with slight differences. To obtain different degrees of roughness data for modulation, it is common to use an accelerometer to measure the acceleration as the probe explores a surface. Culbertson et al. (2014) measured six types of surfaces, including rough plastic, canvas, floor tile, silk, vinyl, and wood, using a metal probe with an internally mounted accelerometer. Culbertson and Kuchenbecker (2017) restructured the recorded data for realistic rendering of textures on a SensAble Phantom Omni haptic interface augmented with a Tactile Labs Haptuator for vibration output. While these works achieved great reproducibility, there is a lack of discussion on the different textures of the same material based on bare fingers contact in these existing studies. In the case of contact with a bare finger,

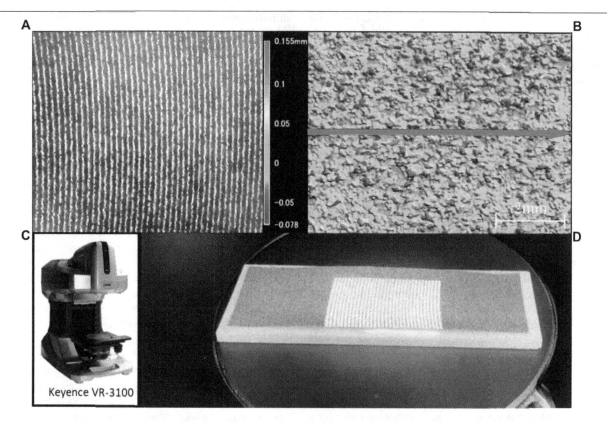

FIGURE 1 | 3D measurement of sandpaper. **(A)** The deformation of the stripe pattern. **(B)** Height image measured by **(C)** 3D microscope. The red arrow indicates where the line roughness is acquired. **(D)** Microscope projects the light of the stripe pattern onto the surface.

the fingertip needs to contact the material directly when measuring acceleration, so the accelerometer is usually attached to the fingernail. However, the accuracy of the measurement is easily affected by dynamic measurement conditions. It is difficult to accurately control the speed of finger movement and pressing force, and the finger tissue from the contact point to the sensor has a filtering effect on the transmission of vibration. These dynamic conditions may mask the slight differences in vibration due to changes in the roughness of the same material, even if the masking effect is smaller for macro differences in the haptic sensation of completely different materials. To extract more details of the material itself and improve the measurement accuracy, a more robust and condition-independent approach for haptic reproduction is required. Our study will focus on solving this problem.

3 MATERIALS AND METHODS

The studies involving human participants were reviewed and approved by the ethics committee of the University of Electro-Communications (No. 19037). The patients/participants provided their written informed consent to participate in this study. Written informed consent was obtained from the individual(s) for the publication of any potentially identifiable images or data included in this article.

3.1 Surface Measurement

Seven pieces of sandpaper were used as samples for the texture reproduction. Their granularities were #100, #120, #150, #180, #240, #320, and #400. These numbers represent the approximate number of abrasive particles per unit area according to the ISO 6344 (2013) standard. The smaller the number, the higher the roughness. For example, the average particle size of #100 sandpaper was 162 μm, and that of #400 was 35 μm. We captured the surface images of the seven sandpaper samples with an area of 43 mm^2 (with a length of 7.59 mm) using a 3D measurement microscope (VR-3100, Keyence) that uses laser scanning to obtain a 3D image of a certain area of the sample surface (**Figure 1C**). The principle of the measurement is to project the light of the stripe pattern onto the surface (**Figure 1D**) and observe the deformation of the stripe pattern (**Figure 1A**). The shape of the surface was obtained from the distortion of the stripe pattern using triangulation ranging. **Figure 1B** shows the measured surface image of sandpaper #100 as an example. The captured images were analyzed and processed using an accompanying software environment (VR-3000 G2 APPLICATION). The line roughness was obtained on the horizontal centerline, denoted by the red arrow in **Figure 1B**.

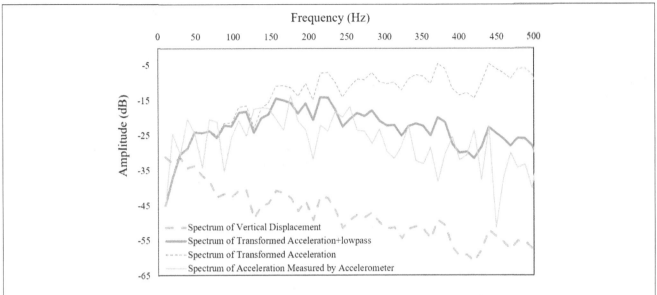

FIGURE 2 | The spectrums obtained when processing the vibration of sandpaper #100. Blue: Spectrum of the 3D measured displacement curve; Grey: Spectrum of the transformed acceleration curve; Orange: Spectrum of the acceleration curve after low-pass filtering; Yellow: Spectrum of the acceleration measured directly by accelerometer.

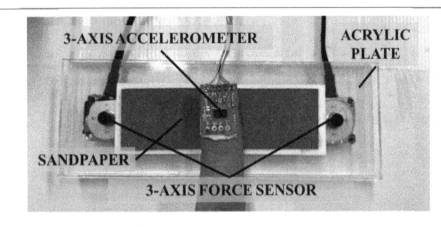

FIGURE 3 | System for direct measurement of acceleration and frictional force.

These line roughness curves indicate the height at each position on the cross section based on this centerline.

3.2 Transformation From Displacement Curve to Acceleration Curve

Because the vibration for reproduction is based on acceleration, it is necessary to transform the obtained line roughness curves into acceleration curves. The line roughness curve indicates the height of the surface at each position on the selected line. If this curve is placed on the time axis with a length of approximately 0.2 s, it can be regarded as a vertical displacement curve when the point-like probe is scanned horizontally over a distance of 7.59 mm in 0.2 s. Here we present **Figure 2** that shows the spectrums obtained from sandpaper #100 to introduce the process of vibration transformation. The blue curve in **Figure 2** is the spectrum of the displacement curve obtained with the audio software Audacity v2.3.0 (https://www.audacityteam.org/), which shows the amplitude characteristics at each frequency.

Based on the Fourier transform, this displacement curve can be decomposed into i sine waves $D(t)_i$ with i different frequencies f_i and can be expressed by **Eq 1**. Because this equation is the displacement formula, a quadratic differential calculation of this formula yields the formula of acceleration $a(t)_i$ (**Eq 2**). Thus, we only add the ω^2 quadratic factor to **Eq 1**; that is, the amplitude at every frequency is increased by a factor of ω^2. **Eq 3** is the transformation formula obtained after rewriting the amplitude A_i to the form in decibel units as $A\_unit\_dB_i$. Because the amplitude units in the spectrum are in decibels, the new amplitude $(A\_unit\_dB\_new_i)$ of the acceleration at every frequency can be calculated using **Eq 3**. An equalizer with

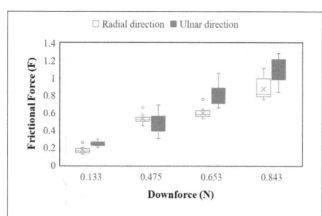

FIGURE 4 | Relationship between downforce and frictional force obtained by the results of force measurement in the case of sandpaper #100. The frictional force displayed direction-dependent difference.

logarithmic curve $(2 \times \log 2 \pi f \times 20)$ features was developed using the equalizer tool in Audacity.

$$D(t)_i = A_i \sin \omega_i t \quad \omega_i = 2\pi f_i \quad (1)$$

$$a(t)_i = (A_i \sin \omega_i t)'' = -\omega_i^2 A_i \sin \omega_i t = \omega_i^2 A_i \sin (\omega_i t + \theta) \quad (2)$$

$$A\_unit\_dB\_new_i = \log \omega_i^2 A_i = A\_unit\_dB_i + 2 \times \log 2\pi f_i \times 20 \quad (3)$$

After applying this equalizer to the displacement curve, the acceleration curve was obtained, the spectrum of which is shown as the grey curve in **Figure 2**.

3.3 Direct Measurement of Acceleration and Force

The acceleration and friction measurement system consist of a 3-axis accelerometer (MMA7361, Cixi Borui Technology) and two

3-axis force sensors, as shown in **Figure 3**. The accelerometer was attached to the nail, and the fingertip was used to touch the sample to be measured on the acrylic plate. The acceleration, lateral friction, and downforce generated during exploration were measured simultaneously. For each piece of sandpaper, 10 testers (who were also participants in the experiment) were recruited to perform the test in seven pressure ranges: 0–0.25 N, 0.25–0.5 N, 0.5–0.75 N, 0.75–1 N, 1–1.25 N, 1.25–1.5 N, and 1.5–1.75 N. The testers were required to follow a metronome rhythm of 60 bpm to trace the sandpaper from left to right (or right to left) at a speed of approximately 80 mm/s. For rougher sandpaper, when the down pressure exceeds 0.75 N, the stick-slip phenomenon is likely to occur and the finger will have difficulty sliding steadily, so we chose the acceleration measured at a relatively stable down pressure of 0.25–0.5 N for reproduction. The spectrum of acceleration measured when tracing sandpaper #100 is shown as the yellow curve in **Figure 2**. For the same reason, we reproduced only the frictional force during stable sliding. The discarded data were used to simulate the stick-slip phenomenon (see Section 2.5.3). An example of frictional force measured when ten testers traced sandpaper #100 is shown as a box-and-whisker plot in **Figure 4**. The horizontal axis is the mean value of the downforce when it was controlled in the range of 0–0.25 N, 0.25–0.5 N, 0.5–0.75 N, and 0.75–1 N. When the downforce is strong, the frictional force in the ulnar direction is stronger than that in the radial direction. The same direction-dependent phenomenon occurred with the other sandpapers.

3.4 System Description
3.4.1 Configuration of Haptic Device

The haptic device used for reproduction was designed as an encounter-type haptic display to allow the user to freely experience the reproduced haptic sensation using a bare finger. An overview of this device is presented in **Figure 5**. Two audio speakers [NSW 12058 A (2), Aurasound] were fixed on the side of the main unit to present the tangential vibrations *via* audio

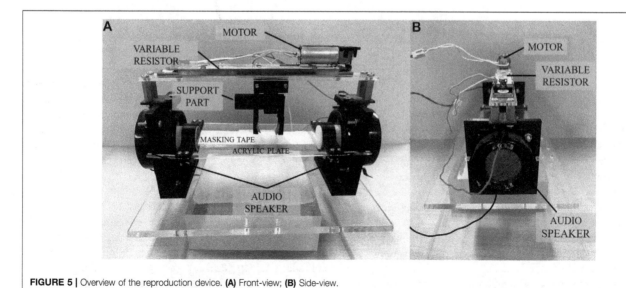

FIGURE 5 | Overview of the reproduction device. **(A)** Front-view; **(B)** Side-view.

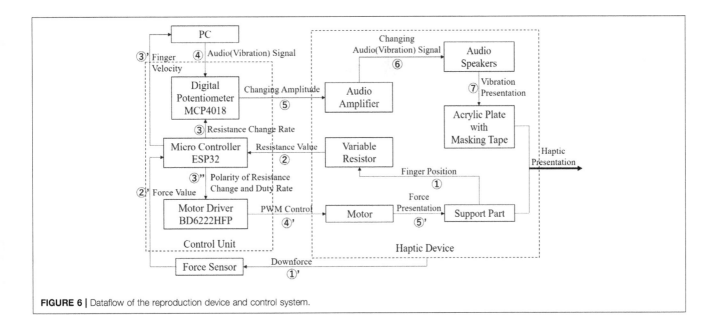

FIGURE 6 | Dataflow of the reproduction device and control system.

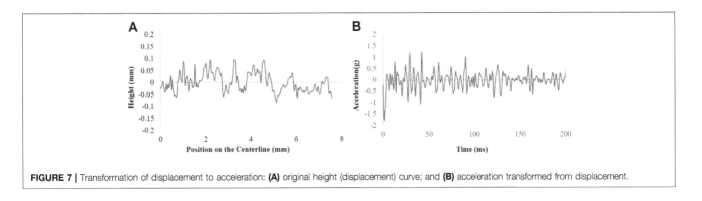

FIGURE 7 | Transformation of displacement to acceleration: **(A)** original height (displacement) curve; and **(B)** acceleration transformed from displacement.

signals and connected in series to an audio amplifier (M50, Muse). An acrylic plate with a thickness of 1 mm was connected to the speakers from the left and right so that the plate was suspended in air. A masking tape with a similar material feeling (Macroscopic perception of the material, including roughness, shape, hardness, and wetness, etc.) as the sandpaper was then pasted onto the acrylic plate. The length of the explored area was approximately 76 mm. A variable resistor with a DC motor (RSA0N11M9A0K, Alps Alpine) was set on top of the main unit, and its resistance value refers to the position of the knob on the liner slide. A support part was attached to the knob. When the user inserts the finger into the support part and moves it horizontally, the position of the finger is mapped to the resistance value. By controlling the motor, the handle can be actuated to move left or right with a settable velocity through pulse-width modulation (PWM) control. Different intensities of the resistance and propulsion forces (depending on the direction of rotation) can be provided. The downforce during the exploration can be monitored in real time

by placing the device on the measuring device (described in *Limitations and Countermeasures for Acceleration Measurement* Section). Based on these data, the frictional force can be reproduced for different downforce conditions.

3.4.2 System Control Flow

The control unit consisted of a digital potentiometer (MCP4018, Microchip Technology), motor driver (BD6222HFP, Rohm), and microcontroller (ESP32, Espressif). The data flow of the entire system is shown in **Figure 6**. The vibration signal at a fixed amplitude was input to a digital potentiometer from a personal computer. The user places the index finger into the support part and moves it to the left and right. The position of the finger is mapped from the value of the variable resistor (1). The microcontroller reads the changing resistance value (2) and calculates the finger velocity according to the changing rate. The finger velocity data are sent to a digital potentiometer (3) and personal computer (3'). Based on the finger velocity, the personal computer adjusts the playback speed (4), and the digital

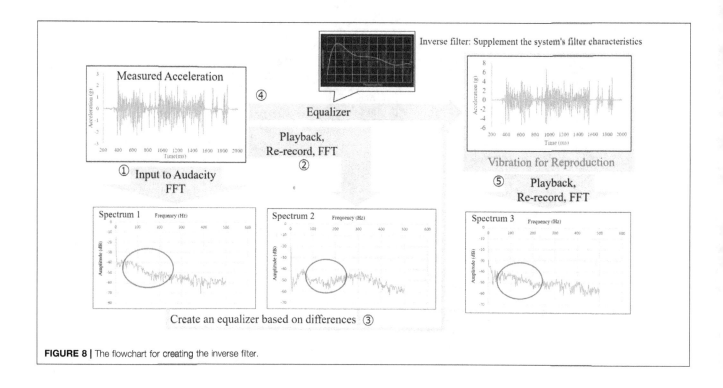

FIGURE 8 | The flowchart for creating the inverse filter.

potentiometer linearly adjusts the vibration amplitude to present a natural virtual texture to audio amplifier (5). As described later in Section 2.5.2. This adjusts the output signal amplitude with low latency, and the vibrations are only presented when the finger moves. The vibration signal is finally output to audio speakers to vibrate the acrylic plate for texture reproduction (6 7). For force presentation, the downforce data are obtained by the force sensor (1') and sent to the microcontroller (2'). Then the polarity of resistance that determines the direction of rotation, and the duty ratio of the PWM control that correspondence to downforce is output to the motor driver (3'). Finally, the motor is driven by the motor driver and present force to user's finger (4' 5').

3.5 Processing of the Reproduction Signal
3.5.1 Vibration Filters
The high frequency vibration of the transformed acceleration needs to be attenuated. In a contact action, the finger pad and sandpaper surface are in contact through a contact area rather than a point. The contact area of the finger allows the perceived roughness to be averaged by integrating multiple-line roughness. This means that the contact area acts as a low-pass filter. To confirm the effect of the low-pass filter on the contact surface, we referred to the spectrum of the directly measured acceleration. Taking the acceleration of #100 as an example, the frequency spectrum is represented by the yellow curve in **Figure 2**. The major difference compared to the grey curve is the decrease in amplitude above 150 Hz. To achieve the filtering effect of the contact area, we used the low-pass filter function of Audacity to reduce the amplitude of the vibration above 150 Hz by −12 dB, and finally obtained the

spectrum indicated by the orange curve. It can be seen that the spectral characteristics of the orange curve are close to those of the yellow curve. The acceleration that transformed from line roughness (**Figure 7A**) is shown in **Figure 7B**. We applied the same filter to all vibration curves transformed from the seven displacement curves, and these processed vibrations were used as a result of the haptic rendering for the haptic reproduction.

An inverse filter to supplement the difference between the input and output of the vibration is required. Owing to the filter feature within the entire system, such as the amplifier and audio speaker, and the skin tissue of the participant's finger, the output and input vibration signals are different in some frequency ranges. To compensate for this discrepancy, we used an equalizer to create inverse filters. The flowchart for creating the inverse filter is shown in **Figure 8**. We measured the acceleration when exploring the sandpaper and obtained its spectrum 1 (1). Then, we playback this vibration on our device and measured the acceleration with the spectrum 2 (2). Based on the difference between these two the spectrums, we created an equalization curve using Audacity (3). By applying this equalization curve to the vibration signal (i.e., reproduced texture data), we obtained the vibration for reproduction with the spectrum 3 (4). Compare spectrum 3 to spectrum 1, they are almost the same, which means we approximatively neutralized the influence of the system (5). This equalization curve plays the role of an inverse filter. For each participant, we performed the same measurement to customize the inverse filter to supplement the filter effect of their finger pad individually, and it was applied to each reproduced texture data during the haptic reproduction

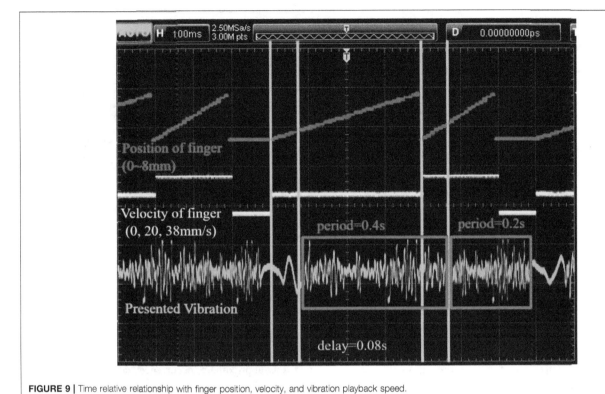

FIGURE 9 | Time relative relationship with finger position, velocity, and vibration playback speed.

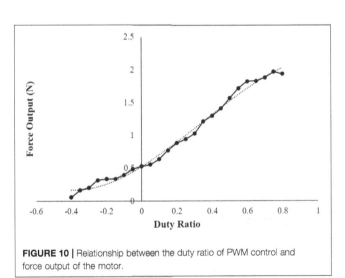

FIGURE 10 | Relationship between the duty ratio of PWM control and force output of the motor.

process and experiments. This equalization process was conducted for both the transformed and directly measured acceleration data (*Limitations and Countermeasures for Acceleration Measurement* Section).

3.5.2 Playback Cycle Corresponding to Finger Velocity

The correspondence between the playback cycle of vibration and finger velocity is important for the realism of reproduction. When using the transformed acceleration, vibration signals of 0.2 s duration were looped during the texture reproduction using

the reproduction device. In the process of transforming, we assumed that the user explores the sandpaper at a velocity of 38 mm/s and considered the line roughness curve as the vertical displacement curve of the skin deformation of the fingertip when the user tangentially explores the sandpaper of a length of 7.6 mm in 0.2 s. In fact, it is difficult for the user to always explore the sandpaper at the same velocity, and 38 mm/s is slow for the actual exploring action. It is considered that when the exploration velocity exceeds 38 mm/s, the playback speed of vibration should also be increased accordingly.

We used MAX7, a graphical integrated development environment for music and multimedia to obtain a simple correspondence between the playback speed of vibration and finger velocity. When the exploration velocity was lower than 15 mm/s, wherein the skin was primarily deformed by elasticity caused by the static friction between the fingers and the sandpaper, no significant vibration was felt. Therefore, the vibration was cycled slowly over a period of approximately 1 s. When the exploration velocity was between 15 and 35 mm/s, the period is cycled approximately 0.4 s for a stable low-frequency vibration. When it exceeds 35 mm/s, the period decreases proportionally to the exploration velocity starting from 0.2 s. The change at 35 mm/s was not perceived by the participants.

Similarly, the directly measured acceleration and duration of the vibration signal was 1 s during which the finger traced the sandpaper at a speed of 80 mm/s. When the exploring speed was lower than 20 mm/s, the playback cycle was 5 s. When the exploration velocity was between 20 and 80 mm/s, the period was cycled for approximately 2 s. When it exceeded 80 mm/s, the

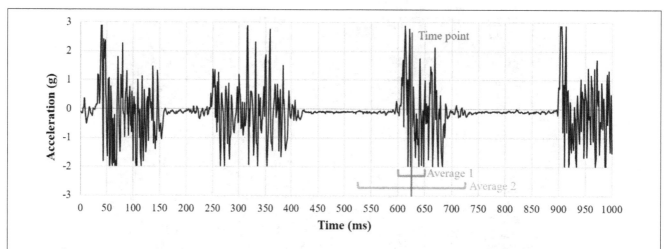

FIGURE 11 | Acceleration profile where the stick-slip phenomenon occurs. At a certain time point, if the average amplitude within 50 ms (Average 1) is greater than twice the average amplitude within 200 ms (Average 2), it is considered that stick-slip phenomenon occurred.

playback cycle decreased proportionally to the exploration velocity starting from 1 s.

To confirm the actual effect of this processing, we used a microcontroller to input dummy finger position and velocity data to MAX7, and the temporal relationship between the finger velocity and vibration playback speed is shown in **Figure 9**. The dummy data for the test were set to repeatedly output the position information of 0–8 mm at speeds of 0 mm/s, 20 mm/s, and 38 mm/s. There is a delay of approximately 80 ms between the timing of the change in the vibration playback speed and that in the exploration velocity. This delay does not appear to have a significant effect on texture perception at this time.

3.5.3 Frictional Force and Stick-Slip Simulation

We used a variable resistor in which the knob could be driven by the motor for force presentation. As shown in **Figure 10**, we tested the force intensity at −0.4 to 0.8, with a duty ratio of 0.05 increments and obtained the output *vs.* duty ratio curve. The symbol indicates the direction of the force. In the default condition (duty ratio is 0), there is a frictional force of about 0.5 N between the knob and the slide. Presenting the propulsive force in the same direction as the finger movement can eliminate intrinsic friction. In this case, the resistance force is counteracted to about 0 N when the duty ratio is 0.4 (−0.4 in **Figure 10**). Using this curve, the duty ratio required for reproducing the frictional force can be obtained. During reproduction, the downforce is constantly monitored. When the downforce increased, the resistance force increased in steps.

As shown in **Figure 11**, in the acceleration profile where the stick-slip phenomenon occurs, the amplitude suddenly increases at several periods. We calculated the duration for which a large amplitude occurred. At a certain time point, if the average amplitude within 50 ms before and after this time point is greater than twice the average amplitude within 200 ms before and after this time point, this 50 ms period is considered to be

larger than the amplitude during the surrounding period. By performing this operation during a 1 s vibration signal, we obtained the approximate occurrence rate of the stick-slip phenomenon. The maximum resistance force was output according to this occurrence rate to simulate the stick-slip phenomenon.

4 USER STUDY

The user study included two experiments to evaluate the reproducibility and discernibility of the rendered virtual texture. The participants were ten laboratory members (all males) of 25 ± 2 years of age, nine of which were right-handed. None of the participants had functional problems with haptic perception. Before the experiment, the experimenter adjusted the height of the chair so that each participant's finger could move easily on the device.

4.1 Experiment 1

Our objective was to reproduce the texture of sandpaper while focusing on reproducing the slight differences in roughness among different types of sandpapers. Thus, the first experiment was focused on whether the differences between the reproduced textures of each roughness could be correctly perceived under the three reproduction approaches.

4.1.1 Practice

The participants were asked to keep their eyes closed and put on a headset playing pink noise to mask auditory cues. Before the experiment, a practice process was conducted to familiarize the participants with the use of the haptic device and the perception of the reproduced textures. The experimenter first played one of the reproduced textures and allowed the participant to put their fingers into the support part to explore horizontally at any velocity for 10 s. Then, the experimenter switched to another

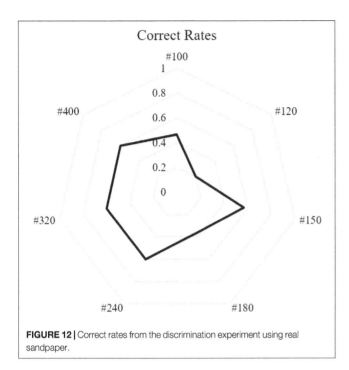

FIGURE 12 | Correct rates from the discrimination experiment using real sandpaper.

reproduced texture and repeated the same practice process until all the produced textures were presented. The basic procedure of the main experiment was as follows.

4.1.2 Procedure
Initially, the participants were provided with one of the seven real sandpapers and asked to explore the sandpaper freely for no more than 5 s. Thereafter, the experimenter randomly replayed one of the reproduced textures, and the participants explored the reproduced texture on the haptic device using the same exploration condition for no more than 10 s. The participants were allowed to go back to explore the sandpaper no more than twice during one trial. After the exploration, the degree of roughness of the real sandpaper was defined as benchmark 0. The relative degree of roughness was answered with a number from −1 to −5 in the case when the reproduced texture was smoother than real sandpaper, and with a number from 1 to 5 in the case when the reproduced texture was rougher than real sandpaper; a response of 0 was permitted. Therefore, if the replay "perfectly" matched, we expected an answer close to 0. Therefore, we expected an answer close to 0 when the real and reproduced samples were the same. Under the same benchmark, the response scores should show an increasing trend when the reproduced texture became rough, and a decreasing trend when the reproduced texture became smoother. This indicates that the change in each reproduced texture can be correctly perceived using the same benchmark. In addition, when changing the real sandpaper, the score of the same reproduced texture should show a decreasing trend when the sandpaper becomes rougher, and an increasing trend when the sandpaper becomes smoother. This indicates that the perception of the roughness of the same reproduced texture does not change despite the change in the benchmark. We evaluated the distinguishability and stability of

the three approaches with these two pieces of evidence. The experiments were conducted in 3 days for each of the three reproduction approaches: acceleration transformed from 3D measurement (VD), directly measured acceleration (VA), and frictional force (F). There was no difference in texture reproduced using the transformed acceleration among all participants. The texture reproduced using the directly measured acceleration and frictional force were based on the data obtained from individual measurement of each participant (*Limitations and Countermeasures for Acceleration Measurement* Section), and the downward pressure was limited to 0.25–0.5 N. Under one reproduction approach, there were seven reproduced textures and seven real textures, yielding 49 combinations. Each combination was randomly presented three times, with 147 trials in total.

4.2 Experiment 2
Experiment 2 evaluated the reproducibility of the reproduced textures. The following reproduction approaches were tested: acceleration transformed from 3D measurements (VD), directly measured acceleration (VA), and frictional force (F). We also added a combination of acceleration that transformed from 3D measurement and frictional force (VD + F), and a combination of directly measured acceleration and frictional force (VA + F) as new approaches to confirm the auxiliary effect of frictional force on vibration.

4.2.1 Preparatory Experiment
Because the roughness of the seven types of sandpaper was similar, it was predicted that it was not easy to distinguish among the physical objects. First, we conducted a preparatory experiment with physical objects only. During one trial, the participants were required to explore one of the sandpapers randomly with eyes closed, while the auditory cue was masked by pink noise. The participant then freely explored the seven sandpapers. After finishing this trial, participants were required to answer which of the seven pieces of sandpaper was the first explored sandpaper. Each sandpaper was randomly presented five times, with 35 trials in total. The correct rates are shown in **Figure 12**. The two lowest correct rates were obtained for sandpaper with granularities of #120 and #180, which indicates that these two sandpapers are very easily confused with similar sandpapers and would affect the reproducibility experiment afterwards; therefore, these two sandpapers were excluded from the subsequent experiment.

4.2.2 Main Experiment
In the main experiment, we used a haptic device (introduced in *Limitations and Countermeasures for Acceleration Measurement* Section) to present the virtual texture reproduced by five approaches (VD, VA, F, VD + F, VA + F). During one trial, a reproduced texture was randomly presented. Then, the participants were allowed to explore the texture alternately with each sandpaper for 5–30 s at any speed and downforce. There was no limit to the number of times they could explore the virtual texture or sandpaper. After this trial, participants were

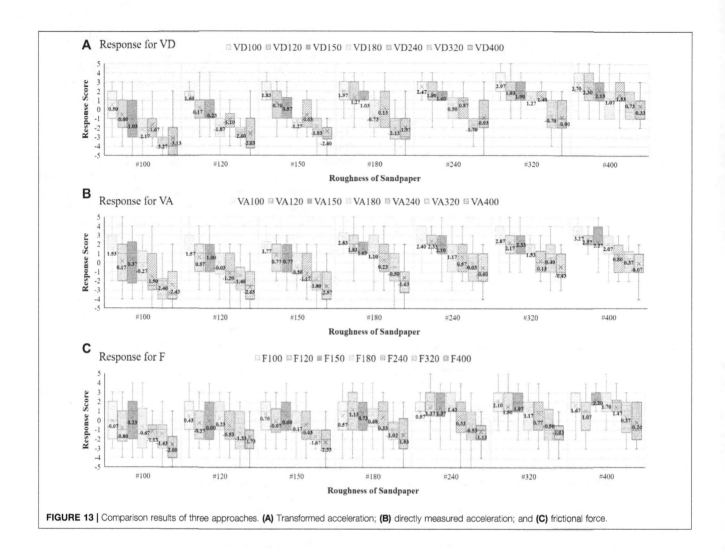

FIGURE 13 | Comparison results of three approaches. **(A)** Transformed acceleration; **(B)** directly measured acceleration; and **(C)** frictional force.

required to identify the physical sandpaper that the device was reproducing. Participants were asked to keep their eyes closed, and their hearing was masked by pink noise. Five textures reproduced by five approaches were randomly presented three times, yielding 75 trials in total.

5 RESULTS

5.1 Comparison of the Discriminability

Results of Experiment 1 is shown in **Figure 13** which illustrates the distribution of responses. The data labels indicate the mean values. The Kruskal–Wallis test with independent samples was used to identify the differences among all responses. The significance level was set at 0.05 and the degree of freedom was 6. The adjusted probability of significance for multiple tests by Bonferroni correction showed that significant differences were found among several reproduced texture under the same benchmark sandpaper.

Figure 13A shows the results obtained when using the transformed acceleration. The horizontal axis shows the roughness of each sandpaper as a benchmark. Under the same benchmark sandpaper, the response scores showed a decreasing trend when the reproduced texture became smoother, which indicates that the differences in each reproduced texture were correctly perceived. When the sandpaper became smoother, the score of the same reproduced texture showed an increasing trend, which indicates that the perception of the roughness of the same reproduced texture did not change despite the change in the benchmark. Furthermore, under all benchmarks, the score of the reproduced texture corresponding to the benchmark sandpaper was close to 0. For example, reproduced texture #100 had similar subjective roughness as sandpaper #100 and #120, and the above reproduced textures were finer than sandpaper #100. Therefore, we consider that the approach using the acceleration transformed from 3D measurement has good discriminability and stability.

Figure 13B shows the results obtained when using the directly measured acceleration. In contrast to the

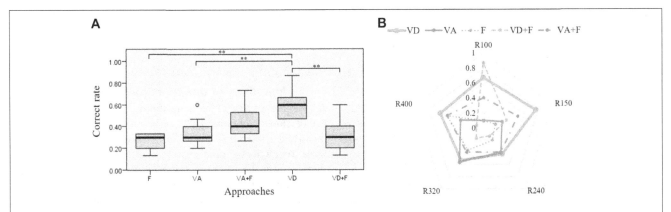

FIGURE 14 | Correct rates of five approaches. **(A)** Average of correct rates for all sandpapers among each participant, **: $p < 0.05$; and **(B)** correct rates of each of the five approaches when reproducing each sandpaper.

TABLE 1 | Confusion matrices.

	Number of responses for VD						Number of responses for VA						Number of responses for F				
	#100	#150	#240	#320	#400		#100	#150	#240	#320	#400		#100	#150	#240	#320	#400
R100	20	10	0	0	0	R100	3	16	8	3	0	R100	3	5	8	6	8
R150	4	23	3	0	0	R150	0	8	13	9	0	R150	2	5	8	6	9
R240	3	10	13	4	0	R240	0	7	12	7	4	R240	0	6	6	8	10
R320	0	4	9	16	1	R320	0	1	2	17	10	R320	0	1	10	11	8
R400	0	1	1	9	19	R400	0	1	6	13	10	R400	0	0	1	13	16

	Number of responses for VD + F						Number of responses for VA + F						—	—	—	—	—	—
	#100	#150	#240	#320	#400		#100	#150	#240	#320	#400		—	—	—	—	—	—
R100	26	4	0	0	0	R100	12	15	2	1	0	—	—	—	—	—	—
R150	20	10	0	0	0	R150	8	15	7	0	0	—	—	—	—	—	—
R240	6	20	4	0	0	R240	2	14	12	2	0	—	—	—	—	—	—
R320	0	9	16	5	0	R320	0	5	12	12	1	—	—	—	—	—	—
R400	0	2	14	11	3	R400	1	0	9	4	16	—	—	—	—	—	—

transformed acceleration, the scores of each reproduced texture were high under rougher sandpaper. For example, the score of reproduced texture VA100 was obviously higher than 0 and felt rougher than the benchmark sandpaper #100. There was no significant change in the score of VA100 among sandpapers #100, #120, and #150. This indicates that using directly measured acceleration can reproduce the different roughness of sandpaper, but the results are shifted to the rough side.

In summary, using acceleration transformed from displacement can reproduce the texture of different sandpaper as well as or better than using directly measured acceleration. When we tried using force cue alone, the results showed that the different sandpaper can be reproduced to some extent. We hypothesize that the reproduction effect may improve if the frictional force cue is combined with both transformed acceleration and directly measured acceleration. This hypothesis was verified in Experiment 2. In addition, whereas Experiment 1 focused on the differences of sandpapers, we focused on the realistic quality of the reproduced texture to

compare the reproducibility of various approaches more clearly and specifically in Experiment 2.

5.2 Evaluation of the Reproducibility

Figure 14A shows the correct rates of the five approaches. VD achieved the highest correct rate. The Kruskal–Wallis test with independent samples was used to analyze the obtained data. The significance level was set at 0.05 and the degree of freedom was 4. The adjusted probability of significance for multiple tests by Bonferroni correction showed that significant differences were found in terms of reproduction approaches. The correct rate of VD was significantly better than that of VA, F, and VD + F. VA + F obtained a reproducibility comparable to that of VD, which indicated that the reproducibility of direct acceleration was improved by the assistance of frictional force simulation. While this analysis disregarded the variable of sandpaper roughness and used the average of correct rates for all sandpapers among each participant, **Figure 14B** shows a radar chart of the correct rates of each of the five approaches when reproducing each sandpaper. When using only VA or F approaches, the overall correct rate of each sandpaper was low and varied widely by roughness, with very poor correct rates for the rougher sandpaper. The reproduction of the texture using the VD approach had a higher correct rate, and the difference between the correct rates for the roughness was smaller, indicating a better balance. This result is consistent with that of Experiment 1: using transformed acceleration can make the differences of each reproduced texture be correctly perceived. When using the VA + F approach, the correct rate for each roughness is similar to that of the VD approach, but the overall correct rate is lower.

It is worth noting that when VD + F was used, the force presentation seems to have greatly degraded the reproducibility. Whereas the correct rate for #100 was close to 1, the correct rates for the other roughness values were very low. **Table 1** shows the confusion matrix of the responses. The distribution of responses for VD + F tended to be on the rougher side, which means that although the reproduction of #100 for VD + F was not good, the participants could only choose #100 because the reproduced texture was the roughest.

6 DISCUSSION

6.1 Discussion and Limitations Based on Experimental Results

Throughout Experiments 1 and 2, we found that our proposed algorithm using 3D height measurement provided good reproducibility of roughness, compared with the acceleration- and force-based methods. Although we cannot conclude that the height-based method is better (as there are several limitations as discussed below), the height-based method is easier and more stable to setup, and we believe it is a candidate approach for bare finger texture reproduction.

6.1.1 Discussion of Reproduction Approaches

Experiment 1 revealed that rougher surfaces were more difficult to reproduce when reproducing with directly measured acceleration. Even though we used data measured in a relatively stable sliding condition, it remained difficult to avoid the occasional stick-slip phenomenon that occurred when the sandpaper was rough. When this phenomenon occurred, the measured acceleration profile contained small portions of strong amplitudes, and they were perceived as rougher when used as vibration cues. This may be the reason the performance was worse when reproducing rougher sandpaper. In contrast, when using frictional force, rougher surfaces tended to be perceived as smoother. As the masking tape on the device was very smooth, it was difficult to reproduce the feeling of unevenness on the sandpaper without vibration, and the lack of unevenness made the reproduced texture feel too smooth overall, which may be the reason the texture reproduced by the frictional force was evaluated as smoother.

This may partly explain the results of Experiment 2. In Experiment 2, VA + F yielded relatively better results than VA or F alone. As discussed above, the VA condition tends to make the rough surface rougher, and the F condition tends to make the rough surface smoother. The combination of these conditions might have compensated for the bias in each condition. In contrast, although the VD condition yielded the best scores, the addition of force cue (VD + F) degraded the results because the force cue made the virtual texture rougher.

6.1.2 Limitations of the Experimental Setup

A possible causes of reproducibility differences may be the exploration conditions. In Experiment 1, when using directly measured acceleration (VA) and frictional force (F), participants were required to monitor the real-time downforce values displayed on the screen to standardize the downforce and stay within a certain range. This type of visual information has been shown to affect the perception of macro roughness (Burns et al., 2021). As the texture of the rough sandpaper was close to macro roughness, it is possible that the interference of this visual information was one of the reasons for the worse results when reproducing rough sandpaper. In contrast, participants kept their eyes closed and were allowed to explore the reproduced texture freely in Experiment 2 to confirm the reproduction effect in the natural state. The unstandardized downforce and exploring speed may increase the variance of the response and decrease the correct rate. In addition, the pain generated by the concavity of the sandpaper caused the participants to unconsciously reduce the downforce when exploring, whereas the force was relatively stronger when using the smooth device. This may make the response for the reproduced texture be on the rough side when comparing the physical and reproduced haptic sensations, especially for the comparison of friction.

In measurement and both experiments, our participants were all from research laboratory that lacked female members, which led us to overlook possible changes in the evaluation by female participants. We will include female participants in future studies and investigate the effect of female's soft skin on the reproducibility.

Our haptic device can provide haptic cues in the horizontal direction, but not in the vertical direction. This design is based on several state-of-the-art surface haptics devices that utilize tangential vibration to present realistic textures (Basdogan et al., 2020). In contrast, our 3D measurement and transformation are based on surface "height" data. Although it is not the scope of this study to determine how the height information is converted to finger normal/tangential vibration, the mechanism should be clarified and modeled in the future.

6.1.3 Limitations of the Proposed Approach

Our newly developed algorithm transforming 3D height information to vibration yielded good reproducibility in terms of surface roughness, but it has certain limitations. In the rendering process, we applied a low-pass filter to the acceleration curve, which required acceleration measurements. In fact, the high-frequency amplitude of VD is still higher and the low-frequency amplitude is lower than that of VA (**Figure 2**). Even if the same F was added, the discrepancy in the spectra may be the reason VA + F performed better, but VD + F performed worse than VD. If the spectra were a perfect match, VA + F and VD + F may be equally good. Therefore, instead of approximating the spectrum roughly, an ideal approach should be to study the filtering effect of the contact surface to obtain an accurate model, and thus eliminate the need to directly measure acceleration.

We cycled the audio signal during the vibration cue, but this cycling could be expected to be noticeable. Although the experimental results do not appear to be unduly affected, excessive vibration from cycling need to be considered as flaws that could potentially affect the reproduction effect. In our reproduction algorithm, the amplitude of the vibration and the loop cycle of the audio signal correspond to the exploring speed of the finger, but not to the variation of the downforce.

In addition, the frictional force corresponded only to the downforce but not to the velocity variation, which is consistent with a previous study on pen-holding type replay of textures (Culbertson, 2015). This study observed that the vibration generated during exploration was minimally affected by the downforce, while the frictional force was minimally affected by the exploring speed. However, the experiments used a Phantom Omni with a hard probe, and the variation in vibration due to downforce deserves to be investigated in bare finger contact. According to Hertzian contact theory (Hertz, 1882), in the contact between a hard and a soft object, the contact area varies with the conduct load (Fischer-Cripps, 1999), which means that the filtering effect on the contact surface varies, and the resulting vibration feature also changes.

6.1.4 Future Work

In this study, we only used relatively hard sandpaper as the reproduction object. For texture reproduction only, our proposed approach is considered to be applicable to a variety of materials such as cloth and human skin. In the future, we will use soft human skin as the next objective to verify the versatility of the discussed approaches. The skin has a similar softness to the finger, so the Hertzian contact model will be difficult to apply, and a new model for the contact between soft objects is required.

By the way, during the measurement of friction, we determined the dependence of the friction force on the direction of exploration. When exploring a rough surface with finger pad, the overall friction force is stronger and the stick-slip phenomenon is more likely to occur in ulnar direction than radial direction This direction dependence has been explored by several studies (Delhaye et al., 2014; Delhaye et al., 2016), and we will also need to study the mechanism for this phenomenon.

6.2 Conclusion

In this study, we proposed an approach for measuring surface height curves using a 3D microscope and transforming them into acceleration curves to reproduce the haptic sensation of sandpaper with slight differences in roughness when being explored by bare fingers. This approach has the advantage of not being affected by the accuracy of the sensor, skin properties, or dynamic state during acceleration measurement. This approach achieved comparable reproducibility and discriminability when compared with the usual approach that directly measures acceleration. After applying the simultaneous frictional force cueing, the reproducibility of the directly measured acceleration increased, but the transformed acceleration was reproduced with a bias toward roughness. We believe that the former is due to the complementary effect of directly measured acceleration and frictional force, whereas in the latter situation, the force cue made the surface too rough. In the future, we will investigate the variation of the filtering effect on the contact surface when the finger is in contact with the surface of different materials, while reproducing different objects such as human skin. We will also investigate the reasons for the directional dependence of frictional force. These researches result provide a reference for studies that also reproduce haptic sensations on a flat plate using a bare finger, and the technique for haptic rendering are expected to be applied to new controllers for virtual reality contents and haptic reproduction devices that can reproduce high quality haptic sensation.

AUTHOR CONTRIBUTIONS

JZ developed the software/hardware setup, implemented the experiments, and analyzed the results. HK provided guidance on various aspects, such as the study design and development of the measurement system. All authors have made substantial direct and intellectual contributions to the article and have approved the submitted version.

ACKNOWLEDGMENTS

We would like to thank all the participants who participated in the study for their time and comments that provided a way to improve our work.

REFERENCES

Asano, S., Okamoto, S., and Yamada, Y. (2015). Vibrotactile Stimulation to Increase and Decrease Texture Roughness. *IEEE Trans. Human Mach. Syst.* 45 (3), 393–398. doi:10.1109/THMS.2014.2376519

Basdogan, C., Giraud, F., Levesque, V., and Choi, S. (2020). A Review of Surface Haptics: Enabling Tactile Effects on Touch Surfaces. *IEEE Trans. Haptics* 13 (3), 450–470. doi:10.1109/TOH.2020.2990712

Bau, O., Poupyrev, I., Israr, A., and Harrison, C. (2010). "TeslaTouch: Electrovibration for Touch Surfaces," in UIST '10: Proceedings of the 23nd annual ACM Symposium on User interface software and technology, New York, NY, October 3–6, 2010, 283–292. doi:10.1145/1866029.1866074

Biswas, A., Manivannan, M., and Srinivasan, M. A. (2015). Vibrotactile Sensitivity Threshold: Nonlinear Stochastic Mechanotransduction Model of the Pacinian Corpuscle. *IEEE Trans. Haptics* 8 (1), 102–113. doi:10.1109/TOH.2014.2369422

Burns, D. A., Klatzky, R. L., Peshkin, M. A., and Colgate, J. E. (2021). "Spatial

Perception of Textures Depends on Length-Scale," in IEEE World Haptics Conference (WHC), Canada, July 6–9, 2021, 415–420. doi:10.1109/WHC49131.2021.9517265

Culbertson, H., and Kuchenbecker, K. J. (2017). Importance of Matching Physical Friction, Hardness, and Texture in Creating Realistic Haptic Virtual Surfaces. *IEEE Trans. Haptics* 10 (1), 63–74. doi:10.1109/TOH.2016.2598751

Culbertson, H., Unwin, J., and Kuchenbecker, K. J. (2014). Modeling and Rendering Realistic Textures from Unconstrained Tool-Surface Interactions. *IEEE Trans. Haptics* 7 (3), 381–393. doi:10.1109/TOH.2014.2316797

Culbertson, H. M. (2015). *Data-Driven Haptic Modeling and Rendering of Realistic Virtual Textured Surfaces*. Dissertation. Philadelphia (PA): University of Pennsylvania. Available at: http://repository.upenn.edu/edissertations/1674.

Delhaye, B., Lefèvre, P., and Thonnard, J.-L. (2014). Dynamics of Fingertip Contact during the Onset of Tangential Slip. *J. R. Soc. Interf.* 11 (100), 20140698. doi:10.1098/rsif.2014.0698

Delhaye, B., Barrea, A., Edin, B. B., Lefèvre, P., and Thonnard, J.-L. (2016). Surface Strain Measurements of Fingertip Skin under Shearing. *J. R. Soc. Interf.* 13, 20150874. doi:10.1098/rsif.2015.0874

Fischer-Cripps, A. C. (1999). The Hertzian Contact Surface. *J. Mater. Sci.* 34, 129–137. doi:10.1023/A:1004490230078

Hasegawa, H., Okamoto, S., and Yamada, Y. (2020). Phase Difference between Normal and Shear Forces during Tactile Exploration Represents Textural Features. *IEEE Trans. Haptics* 13, 11–17. doi:10.1109/TOH.2019.2960021

Hertz, H. (1882). *Verhandlungen des Vereins zur Beförderung des Gewerbe Fleisses*. Ch. 6, 61. London: Macmillan, 410. Translated and reprinted in English in "Hertz's Miscellaneous Papers".

ISO 6344 (2013). Coated Abrasives - Grain Size Analysis - Part 3: Determination of Grain Size Distribution of Microgrits P240 to P2500. Available at: https://www.iso.org/standard/56010.html (Accessed November 18, 2021).

Ito, K., Okamoto, S., Elfekey, H., Kajimto, H., and Yamada, Y. (2017). "A Texture Display Using Vibrotactile and Electrostatic Friction Stimuli Surpasses One Based on Either Type of Stimulus," in 2017 IEEE International Conference on Systems, Man, and Cybernetics (SMC), Banff, Canada, October 5–8, 2017, 2343–2348. doi:10.1109/SMC.2017.8122972

Jeon, S., Metzger, J.-C., Seungmoon Choi, S., and Harders, M. (2011). "Extensions to Haptic Augmented Reality: Modulating Friction and Weight," in IEEE World Haptics Conference, Istanbul, Turkey, June 21–24, 2011, 227–232. doi:10.1109/WHC.2011.5945490

Kuchenbecker, K. J., Romano, J., and McMahan, W. (2011). "Haptography: Capturing and Recreating the Rich Feel of Real Surfaces," in *Robotics Research*. Editors C. Pradalier, R. Siegwart, and G. Hirzinger (Berlin-Heidelberg: Springer), 70, 245–260. Springer Tracts in Advanced Robotics. doi:10.1007/978-3-642-19457-3_15

Lee, J., Sinclair, M., Gonzalez-Franco, M., Ofek, E., and Holz, C. (2019). "TORC: A Virtual Reality Controller for In-Hand High-Dexterity Finger Interaction," in Proceedings of the 2019 CHI Conference on Human Factors in Computing Systems, Glasgow, UK, May 4–9, 2019. doi:10.1145/3290605.3300301

Maeda, T., Peiris, R., Masashi, N., Tanaka, Y., and Minamizawa, K. (2016). "HapticAid: Wearable Haptic Augmentation System for Enhanced, Enchanted and Empathised Haptic Experiences," in SA'16: SIGGRAPH ASIA 2016 Emerging Technologies, Macao, China, December 5–8, 2016, 1–2. doi:10.1145/2988240.2988253

Martel, E., and Muldner, K. (2017). Controlling VR Games: Control Schemes and the Player Experience. *Entertain. Comput.* 21, 19–31. doi:10.1016/j.entcom.2017.04.004

Poupyrev, I., and Maruyama, S. (2003). "Tactile Interfaces for Small Touch Screens," in UIST '03: Proceedings of the 16th Annual ACM Symposium on User Interface Software and Technology, Vancouver, Canada, November 2–5, 2003, 217–220. doi:10.1145/964696.964721

Preechayasomboon, P., Israr, A., and Samad, M. (2020). "Chasm: A Screw Based Expressive Compact Haptic Actuator," in CHI '20: Proceedings of the 2020 CHI Conference on Human Factors in Computing Systems, Honolulu, HI, April 25–30, 2020, 1–13. doi:10.1145/3313831.3376512

Strese, M., and Steinbach, E. (2018). "Toward High-Fidelity Haptic Interaction with Virtual Materials: A Robotic Material Scanning, Modelling, and Display System," in IEEE Haptics Symposium, San Francisco, CA, March 25–28, 2018 (IEEE Press), 247–254. doi:10.1109/HAPTICS.2018.8357184

Takasaki, M., Kotani, H., Mizuno, T., and Nara, T. (2005). "Transparent Surface Acoustic Wave Tactile Display," in IEEE/RSJ International Conference on Intelligent Robots and Systems, Edmonton, Canada, August 2–6, 2005, 3354–3359. doi:10.1109/IROS.2005.1545129

Ujitoko, Y., Sakurai, S., and Hirota, K. (2020). "Vibrator Transparency: Re-using Vibrotactile Signal Assets for Different Black Box Vibrators without Redesigning," in IEEE Haptics Symposium (HAPTICS), Crystal City, VA, March 28–31, 2020, 882–889. doi:10.1109/HAPTICS45997.2020.ras.HAP20.80.00957e94

16

A Soft Robotic Wearable Wrist Device for Kinesthetic Haptic Feedback

Erik H. Skorina, Ming Luo and Cagdas D. Onal*

Soft Robotics Lab, Worcester Polytechnic Institute, Worcester, MA, United States

*Correspondence:
Cagdas D. Onal
cdonal@wpi.edu

Advances in soft robotics provide a unique approach for delivering haptic feedback to a user by a soft wearable device. Such devices can apply forces directly on the human joints, while still maintaining the safety and flexibility necessary for use in close proximity to the human body. To take advantage of these properties, we present a new haptic wrist device using pressure-driven soft actuators called reverse pneumatic artificial muscles (rPAMs) mounted on four sides of the wrist. These actuators are originally pre-strained and release compressive stress under pressure, applying a safe torque around the wrist joints while being compact and portable, representing the first soft haptic device capable of real-time feedback. To demonstrate the functional utility of this device, we created a virtual path-following task, wherein the user employs the motion of their wrist to control their embodied agent. We used the haptic wrist device to assist the user in following the path and study their performance with and without haptic feedback in multiple scenarios. Our results quantify the effect of wearable soft robotic haptic feedback on user performance. Specifically, we observed that our haptic feedback system improved the performance of users following complicated paths in a statistically significant manner, but did not show improvement for simple linear paths. Based on our findings, we anticipate broader applications of wearable soft robotic haptic devices toward intuitive user interactions with robots, computers, and other users.

Keywords: soft robotics, wearable devices, haptics, pneumatics, human-robot interaction

1. INTRODUCTION

As computers become increasingly prevalent, the ability of humans and computers to communicate becomes more important. While much can be conveyed visually, humans have access to other senses that can be used to communicate information and provide feedback to a human user.

Haptic feedback devices have been used to convey subtle informational cues to users. These come in two basic categories: tactile and kinesthetic. Tactile haptic feedback uses purely sensory cues, such as vibrations, to inform the user of events or provide the illusion of forces, as in Amemiya and Gomi (2014). This has been used for a range of activities, such as gait training (Dowling et al., 2010) and vision aid (Johnson and Higgins, 2006).

Kinesthetic haptic feedback, which this paper focuses on, utilizes real forces in order provide feedback to the user. The simplest example of this is the force-feedback-enabled joystick. Chciuk et al. (2017) used a force-feedback joystick to teleoperate a robotic arm, and showed that the physical feedback provided a significant improvement to the performance of the user. Another example of a force-feedback joystick was developed by Riecke et al. (2016) for teleoporating robots in space. This system was developed to use the rapid and intuitive flow of information from the force feedback joystick to the operator to compensate for the communication lag in long-distance robot teleoperation. These joystick systems can provide strong, high-bandwidth feedback, but require the user to manipulate an external device. Other applications of rigid, kinesthetic feedback include robotic surgery as discussed by Wagner et al. (2002), where haptic feedback reduced errors by a factor of 3. In addition, work has been done by Metzger et al. (2012) using kinesthetic feedback for rehabilitation.

Similar electric motor techniques can be directly applied to the user's joints. Margineanu et al. (2018) created a 5-DoF haptic arm exoskeleton for use in space telerobotics. This system was effective, but was heavy and bulky. MA and Ben-Tzvi (2015) developed an exoskeletal glove which used rigid links protruding above the hand to apply forces to the user's fingertips. This method is bulky, and can easily become a hindrance when not used in a lab setting. Blake and Gurocak (2009) developed a similar glove, but used magnetorheological fluids to convey variable stiffness information to the user. Bouzit et al. (2002) developed similar device, but one that used pneumatic pistons to apply the forces. An example of a haptic wrist actuator was presented by Erwin et al. (2016). This device used piezoelectric actuators to provide relatively compliant (and Magnetic Resonance Imaging compatible) forces, but required a complicated mechanism, making it suited for use in controlled environments. A hybrid technique combining properties of tactile and kinesthetic was used by Schorr et al. (2013). This work uses a motor to physically stretch the skin of the user to simulate force effects, representing a skin-based haptic feedback that nevertheless involves real forces.

These haptic technologies rely on the user manipulating an external device or being constrained by an inflexible joint. However, there is a significant discrepancy in this approach, since human bodies are soft and flexible. Thus, in order to provide a seamless experience for haptic interactions, we posit that it would be appropriate for haptic devices to be soft and flexible to match the mechanical behavior of the human body. Soft feedback can be applied to the user in many ways, including using soft pneumatic actuators. One example of a soft pneumatic actuator is the McKibben muscle (or the pneumatic artificial muscle) as discussed by Chou and Hannaford (1996). This actuator type consists of a rubber tube wrapped in a mesh which causes it to contract when pressurized. McKibben muscles were used by Jadhav et al. (2015) as part of a soft glove for haptic feedback for a piano-playing VR experience. The soft actuators provided safe forces to the user's fingers, while the compliant nature of the glove made it comfortable and adaptable for a wide range of hand sizes. Patterson and Katz (1992) compared several haptic feedback devices used in active-prosthetic grasping. They found that pneumatic feedback was more reliable and easy to interpret than vibro-tactile haptic or visual feedback. Soft techniques can also be used for purely tactile feedback. One example is the work of Koo et al. (2008), where the authors used a series of small electroactive polymer nodules to apply stimulation to the user without additional electromechanical transmissions.

In this paper, we debut a novel wearable soft haptic wrist device capable of applying feedback to the user in the form of real torques around the wrist. We use soft linear actuators we call reverse pneumatic artificial muscles (rPAMs). These actuators consist of tubes of silicone rubber wrapped in thin helical thread such that when pressurized, they extend. This extension makes them more efficient than McKibben Muscles, which contract axially and expand radially when pressured. We investigated the performance of these actuators operating antagonistically in Skorina et al. (2015), with an actuator mounted on either side of a revolute joint analogous to a wrist. We also performed similar experiments using rPAM actuators as part of a bidirectional bending segment in Luo et al. (2017). In both of these works, we used valve PWM (Pulse-Width Modulation) to approximate pressure control, a technique idea for wearable devices, and could perform precise position control at up to 6 Hz.

We created a device that mounts four rPAMs along the user's wrist, as shown in **Figure 1**. Under pressure, these actuators provide safe haptic torques on the wrist. To test the usability of this device, we created a simple path-following scenario that users underwent. In this scenario, users controlled a virtual agent using the angle of their wrist, with the goal of following a path as precisely as possible, with the haptic wrist device providing kinesthetic feedback. This device can be used as part of a soft haptic robotic arm teleoperation system, conveying forces to the user and also improving their performance via virtual fixturing, such as discussed by Rosenberg (1993).

A different type of soft actuator used in soft robotics the PneuNet. Presented by Ilievski et al. (2011), this actuator type consists of a series of connected chambers within a soft manifold. When pressurized, the chambers expand, causing the PneuNet to deform in a desired direction, usually out-of-plane bending. This bending can follow a similar path to the curling of fingers, and has been used in a soft pneumatic glove by Polygerinos et al. (2015). This system was intended for hand rehabilitation and only had a response time of around 2 s, not fast enough for real-time haptic feedback.

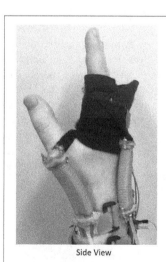

Side View   Top View

FIGURE 1 | Views of the Haptic Wrist device worn by a user.

An example of a soft wrist device was discussed by Sasaki et al. (2005). This system uses pneumatic actuators similar to our rPAMs, but with an inextensible constraint layer that causes them to bend when pressurized. This work focused on EMG-enabled rehabilitation and only performed simple motions, with no precise control or angle feedback. In addition, the nature of the bending actuators used to apply forces meant that this system could only apply forces in a single plane, limiting its usability for haptic feedback. Similarly, a soft wrist device was created by Al-Fahaam et al. (2016) using both extensile and contractile McKibben muscles to actuate the user's wrist. Mounted on a glove [further analyzed in Al-Fahaam et al. (2018)], these actuators can apply high forces, although the authors did not investigate the control of the wrist.

Instead, the wrist device presented in this paper is both faster than other soft kinesthetic devices and safer, lower profile, and more flexible than existing rigid kinesthetic devices. We use precise pulse width modulation control of the soft actuators, which allows the device to provide real-time haptic feedback on the user's wrist.

Section 2 of this paper is devoted to discussing the fabrication of the haptic wrist device, including the actuators and the integrated sensors, as well as its physical capabilities. Section 3 focus on the setup and control required for the path-following trials we used for system verification. Section 4 shows the experimental results of the path-following trials, including both specific trajectories made by users and a aggregated analysis of Root Mean Square Errors (RMS Error). Finally, section 5 is the conclusion as well as a discussion of a possible use for this haptic wrist device as part of a larger system.

2. FABRICATION

The wearable soft haptic wrist device described in this paper uses reverse pneumatic artificial muscles (rPAMs) to apply compliant forces to the wearers wrist. These rPAM actuators consist of a tube of silicone wrapped in a helix of thread. When pressurized, the thread provides a physical constraint that prevents the actuator from expanding into a sphere. Instead, the actuator simply extends, imparting compliant forces as discussed by Skorina et al. (2015) and Luo et al. (2015).

The compliant nature of these linear actuators makes applying compressive forces a difficult proposition. When doing so, the actuators have a tendency to buckle. To compensate for this, we have previously mounted these actuators antagonistically around a 3-D printed joint in a prestrained condition. Thus, when pressurized, the actuators relieve the pre-strain without buckling, allowing them to apply their antagonistic forces.

The rPAMs used in this paper were fabricated using a multi-step process. First, the hollow core of the actuator was created out of silicone rubber (DragonSkin 10) in a 3D printed mold. Next, nylon thread is wrapped in a uniform helical pattern around the actuator. The mold includes grooves around the outside, making it easy for the thread to be wrapped uniformly. To hold the thread

in place, we applied a thin layer of uncured DragonSkin 10 over the outside.

To provide a seal for each end of the actuator, we used a technique we developed by Tao et al. (2015). This consists of a pair of acrylic plates sandwiching a flange at each end of the actuator, with the actuator fitting through the inner plate. These two plates were bolted together over the flange to form a tight seal. On one side of each actuator, a vent screw (a machine screw with a hole drilled through) was slotted though the outer plate, allowing pressure to be applied to the actuator chamber.

Securing these actuators onto the forearm and hand was a challenge, especially considering the desired pre-strain in the rPAM actuators. We had to provide solid mounts for the actuators that would both resist actuator forces and stay put as the user moved their arm. After investigating several options, including nitrile gloves, velcro straps, and an elbow support, we settled on using different attachment methods at the hand and the wrist. To attach at the hand, we used a Flarico Hand Wrap, which is slotted over the thumb and than wrapped above the thumb and around the hand. The acrylic end-plates of the actuators were attached to the lowest layer of this wrap, so that they would be situated around all sides of the user's wrist when the device is worn. The material of the wrap is stretchy enough to adapt to different hand sizes. The donning process can be seen in **Figure 2**.

To mount the actuators on the forearm, we used a Bluecell Velcro strap secured below the user's wrist. Without tightening this Velcro strap to an uncomfortable level, this mount was still subject to sliding, but the bumps below the radius and ulna ensure that the actuators stay attached at a usable position. Again, the acrylic end plates of the actuators were glued to the strap, which allowed for a simple, effective mount.

In order for the system to measure the state of the user's wrist, we need to accurately measure the angle of the wrist in real time. To do this, we mounted a pair of inertial measurement units (IMUs) on the wrist device, one on the forearm and one on the back of the hand. We chose the BNO0055 9-axis absolute IMU for its small size, ease of use, and high reliability. This IMU performs all sensor fusion on-board, and only outputs its orientation which we use to calculate the angle of the wrist, as discussed later.

We mounted the IMU on the forearm by bolting it to an acrylic plate, and attaching the plate to Velcro strap. In order to ensure that this IMU remained stationary during motion, we added a second Velcro strap farther down the forearm, which was attached to the other side of the IMU attachment plate. The hand IMU was initially attached to the hand wrap using the same acrylic plate with the forearm IMU. However, initial user tests indicated that the fixed position of the IMU on the hand wrap was vulnerable to differences in user's hand size. To remedy this, we replaced the direct connection between the IMU plate and the hand wrap with a velcro connection. Thus, the IMU could be placed at a variety of points on the wrap to ensure its location coincided with the back of the user's hand. The IMU was placed on a lower level of the wrap, as shown in **Figure 2**, so the upper level could be used to hold the IMU in place. The entire device that is mounted on the user's wrist (excluding the circuitry and valves) has a mass of around 130 g.

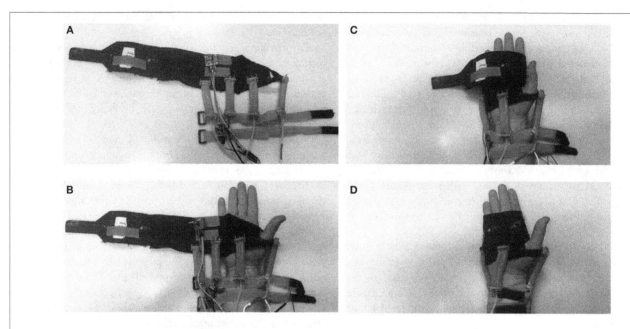

FIGURE 2 | **(A)** The full Haptic Wrist Device, unattached to a user. **(B)** Step one in donning the device, put loop over the thumb. **(C)** Next step in donning the device, begin wrapping. **(D)** Fully wrapped, tighten the forearm straps.

2.1. Physical Capabilities

We created a test setup to verify the forces that the rPAMs can impart on the wrist and ensure that the torques are within a safe range. We 3-D printed a replica of a human hand and forearm. This model included a hinge joint at the wrist, which allowed it to pivot forwards and backwards. This joint also included a potentiometer for reliable and direct angle measurement. We applied known torques around the wrist joint, and adjusted the pressure in the corresponding actuator to return the joint to a neutral angle. This allowed us to determine the torque output of rPAM actuators on a user's wrist. The experimental setup can be seen in **Figure 3**.

We found that the maximum torque the actuators can apply while the hand is maintained at a straight pose is 0.14 Nm at 8 psi input pressure. If the actuators are given a higher pressure, they will start buckling, and the force applied to the wrist will not increase. This is significantly lower than the maximum wrist torque humans can sustain according to Morse et al. (2006) ensuring that our haptic device will be safe to operate regardless of any malfunctions. Thus, this was the pressure we used for all experiments.

3. PATH FOLLOWING TEST

In order to test the usability of the haptic feedback provided by our device, we created a simple scenario where the user would use their wrist to control an agent operating in a simple virtual environment. We initially considered having the user control an agent in a maze or other obstacle-filled environment. However, we decided that the obstacles would add an element of problem-solving to any tests that were performed, adding noise

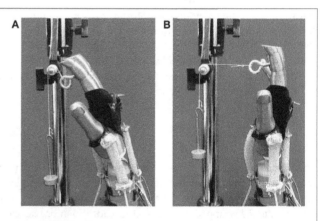

FIGURE 3 | The Haptic Wrist force experimental. **(A)** torque applied, no pressure applied **(B)** torque applied, pressure applied to return the hand to the zero angle. Note, the pressurized actuator is against the palm, and is inflated and extended.

to any direct analysis of the effect of the haptic feedback on user performance.

Instead, we chose to test the benefits of the haptic device on a simple path following task. This would allow the user to only focus on performing the intricate task as steadily as possible without having to worry about internal path planning. In addition, the nature of following an infinitely thin curve means that there is no performance ceiling, that there will always be room for the user to improve. Thus, there will always be room for a haptic device to assist the user.

The environment consists of a path and an agent. We tested the usability of the system on both a straight line and a sinusoidal curve, both traveling left-to-right. The agent that the

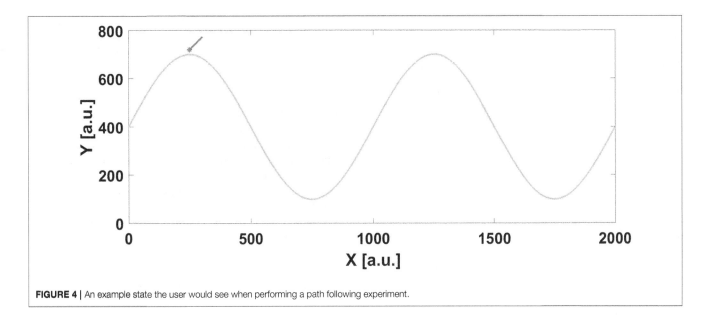

FIGURE 4 | An example state the user would see when performing a path following experiment.

user controls within this environment is represented by a "*" icon. It has a forward velocity, represented by a line branching out from the agent position indicating the direction of travel. The length of this line was adjusted in conjunction with the velocity of the agent, to give some additional visual indication of velocity. A scene from the test environment is shown in **Figure 4**. The goal of the user was to follow the path as closely as possible while traveling all the way to the right side of the screen. We also instituted a time limit in the event that the user was traveling too slowly, to ensure that experiments were completed in a timely fashion.

3.1. Virtual Agent Control

At each simulation time step, the system calculates the motion angle and linear velocity of the agent from user input and iterate agent position on the screen. The user controls the agent using the angle of their wrist. In order to do this, it is first necessary to extract the wrist angle from the readings from the two IMUs. The control code running on the desktop computer receives global orientations of the IMUs in the form of quaternions. From there, we converted them to rotation matrices and used the following equation to find the rotation matrix of the wrist:

$$R_D = R_2 R_1^T, \tag{1}$$

where $R_D \in \Re^{3 \times 3}$ is the rotation matrix between the two IMUs, $R_2 \in \Re^{3 \times 3}$ is the global rotation matrix to the wrist IMU, and $R_1 \in \Re^{3 \times 3}$ is the global rotation matrix to the hand IMU. We convert this back to $D_r \in \Re^{3 \times 1}$, the raw local Euler angle state vector of the wrist. Because of the inconsistencies between human morphologies and the way the wrist device is wrapped around the hand, di⊠erent users, or even the same user during di⊠erent trials, would have di⊠erent rest angles for their hand. Thus, we implemented a calibration routine every time the user puts on the device. This routine calculated the average D_r over 50 iterations of the user holding their hand loose and steady, this was used to

calculate an o⊠set value used during the subsequent experiments as follows:

$$D = D_r - D_o, \tag{2}$$

where $D \in \Re^{3 \times 1}$ is the adjusted angle of the wrist, D_r is the measured raw state discussed previously, and $D_o \in \Re^{3 \times 3}$ is the o⊠set calculated during calibration. From this adjusted value of the state of the wrist, the algorithm calculates the angle of the next state using the following equation:

$$A_i = A_{i-1} - con(D(2)k_a, -1, 1), \tag{3}$$

where A_i is the angle of the current state, A_{i-1} is the angle at the previous state, k_a is a sensitivity constant, $con(.)$ is a constraint function, and $D \in \Re^{3 \times 1}$ is the Euler angle state vector of the wrist in "yaw-pitch-roll" order. Thus, as this equation uses $D(2)$, the angular velocity of the agent is controlled directly by the pitch of the user's wrist, that is the motion along the flexion/extension axis. The angular change per control loop is constrained between −1 and 1, while the angle itself is unconstrained. The control frequency is around 15 Hz, which means that the maximum rotational velocity is around 2.5 revolutions per second. For all experiments performed, $k_a = 1$.

The human wrist has three degrees-of-freedom (DoF), and we use one of them to control the angular velocity of the agent. Thus, we decided to study the use of an additional DoF in the wrist to control the linear velocity of the agent. The user could speed up and slow down the agent, depending on how well they were following the line. This would allow an additional metric of velocity to be examined in order to gauge user performance. The velocity of the agent was controlled by:

$$V_i = con(V_{i-1} + con(D(1)k_v, -0.3, 0.3), 15, 2), \tag{4}$$

where V_i is the linear velocity at the current state, V_{i-1} is the linear velocity at the previous state, and k_v is a sensitivity constant. As this equation uses $D(1)$, the linear acceleration is controlled directly by the yaw of the wrist, that is, the lateral motion in the radial/ulnar direction. We also observed that users could more easily move their hands in the ulnar direction (toward the little finger) than in the radial direction (toward the thumb). Thus, we used a different value for k_v depending on which direction the user was turning their wrist, as follows:

$$k_a = \begin{cases} 15, & \text{if } D(1) < -0.01 \\ 7, & \text{if } D(1) > 0.08 \\ 0 & \text{otherwise.} \end{cases} \quad (5)$$

This equation also creates a deadzone, where it would theoretically be easier for the user to steer the agent without accidentally changing its velocity. However, initial experiments indicated that this method of controlling the agent velocity was still difficult for most users. Some users found that the mental coupling between the two axes of rotation in the wrist made it difficult to control one without changing the other. Thus, we looked into different ways of controlling the linear velocity of the agent using the user's body. We settled on controlling the linear velocity of the agent directly using the angle of their forearm. This would decouple the two DoF, while using our already existing hardware. The velocity control equation for this method is written as:

$$V_i = con(E_2(1)k_{v2}, 20, 3), \quad (6)$$

where $E_2 \in \Re^{3\times1}$ is the global Euler angle of IMU2 (the IMU mounted on the forearm), and k_{v2} is a sensitivity constant. Thus, if the user held their hand and forearm with the little finger downwards, they could directly control the velocity of the agent by moving their forearm up and down. For all of these experiments, we used $k_{v2} = 30$. The velocity was constrained between 20 and 3. This comes out to a maximum velocity of one sixth of the horizontal length of the environment per second, and the minimum velocity being one fortieth of the horizontal length of the environment per second. Thus, the user would reach their maximum velocity when the arm was held at around 40° above horizontal

3.2. Feedback Control

In order for the system to guide the user to the desired path, we created an algorithm to determine the pressure in each rPAM. To do this, we calculated how far the agent was from the nearest point on the path. For faster computation, this distance was only calculated for the 400 nearest points on the horizontal axis. The distance to each of these points was calculated, and the shortest distance was determined. Once that point was determined, we calculated the angle needed for the agent to reach that point, as well as the angle of the path at that point. The desired angle for the agent was then calculated as a weighted average between these two angles:

$$A_d = \alpha a_1 + (1 - \alpha)a_2, \quad (7)$$

where A_d is the desired angle, a_1 is the angle for the agent to reach the nearest point on the path, and a_2 angle of the path at

that point, and $\alpha \in [0, 1]$ is the weight. α becomes smaller as the minimum distance to the nearest point on the path becomes smaller, and is calculated using the following equation:

$$\alpha = \min(\frac{m}{200}, 1) \quad (8)$$

where m is the minimum distance to the desired path. Thus, if $m > 200, \alpha = 1$ and the desired angle is equal to the angle between the agent and the nearest point on the path. As the virtual agent approaches the path, the desired angle becomes more and more aligned with the direction of the path. Entirely following the desired angle, an agent would asymptotically approach the desired path.

Using the desired angle, we calculate the angle error A_e using the following equation:

$$A_e = \begin{cases} A_d - A_i, & \text{if } |A_d - A_i| > dz \\ 0 & \text{otherwise.} \end{cases} \quad (9)$$

where dz is the deadzone. Thus, when the user is pointing their wrist within a certain threshold of the desired angle, it will be considered to be perfectly accurate. From here, the control command to the valves is calculated as:

$$u_1 = con(50 + k_{au}A_e, 0, 100) \quad (10)$$

where u_1 is the angle control input, k_{au} is the sensitivity constant, and A_e is the angle error. We used $k_{au} = 30$ for all experiments. This equation generates a control input between 0 and 100 with 0 resulting in full actuation in one direction and 100 resulting in full actuation in the opposite direction.

We also wanted to investigate the ability of the haptic feedback to help the user regulate their velocity. When the user is following the desired path with a high level of accuracy, we would want them to speed up to reach the end of the path faster. On the other hand, if the user has a large error, we would want them to slow down to better focus on returning to the path. To this end, we implemented the following feedback control law for velocity:

$$V_d = \max(18 - |A_e|k_{vu}, 3), \quad (11)$$

where V_d is the desired velocity, and k_{vu} is the sensitivity constant. For all experiments performed, $k_{vd} = 12$. Through this equation, the desired velocity ranges between 18 and 3, and is linearly related to the angle error. When the user is pointing in the desired direction, the desired velocity will be high, telling the user to speed up to return to the path or speed along it toward the goal. However, when the user is not pointing in the correct direction, the desired velocity will be low, telling the user to slow down. We calculated the velocity error in a similar manner to equation 9, with a corresponding deadzone of 3, and calculated the command to the controller by

$$u_2 = con(50 + k_{vu}V_e, 0, 100), \quad (12)$$

where u_2 is the velocity control input, V_e is the error between the desired velocity and the actual velocity, and k_{vu} is a sensitivity constant.

This feedback on the lateral motion of the hand was still used when the velocity was being controlled by the angle of the forearm. As the hand was directed to be held sideways, the changes in the angle of the arm would be in the same plane as the lateral motion of the hand. Thus, the lateral haptic cues on the hand would still indicate to the user the correct direction to move their arm, even if the forces were not directly affecting the joint used for control.

3.2.1. Valve Control

An Arduino Mega control board receives commands from MATLAB and directly controls 30 Hz pulse-width-modulation (PWM) signals of the four digital valves connected to the rPAM actuators. Several different control schemes were evaluated, including our previous method of both valves operating antagonistically, as in Luo et al. (2017). The final control scheme we settled on is as follows:

For $u_i > 50$:

$$c_1 = 0,$$
$$c_2 = 2(u - 50 + c_O) \times 255/100,$$
(13)

for $u_i < 50$:

$$c_1 = 2(50 - u + c_O) \times 255/100,$$
$$c_2 = 0,$$
(14)

and if $u_i = 50$, then:

$$c_1 = 0,$$
$$c_2 = 0,$$
(15)

where c_1 and c_2 are 8-bit duty cycles sent directly to the two valves and c_O is a command offset. c_O is included because at low duty cycles ($c < 30$) the commands will be too fast to register, and the valve will not actuate. Thus, c_O was set to 15 for all experiments. This saturation behavior also occurs where $c > 70$, but precision is not necessary when the error is high. These equations were used for pairs of actuators on each actuated wrist axis.

4. EXPERIMENTAL RESULTS

We performed a range of path-following experiments with users[1]. In order to collect data under a wide range of circumstances, we studied all combinations of the type of path, the type of feedback used , and the variability of velocity, for a total of ten experiments (velocity feedback was not used when the velocity of the agent was fixed). When a fixed velocity was used, we set it at 50 a.u. per second, or about one twenty-fourth of the horizontal length of the environment. The two paths used were a straight horizontal line and a sine wave with amplitude 300 a.u. and a period of 1,000 a.u. The sine wave trajectory is shown in **Figure 4**, with two periods taking up the entire length of

the environment. Pressure for the haptic feedback was provided though the building and regulated down to 8 psi. Initial positions were on the desired position at $x = 250$ but with an initial angle $\frac{\pi}{2}$, forcing the users to immediately correct their trajectory to match the path. This was particularly relevant on the horizontal line following experiments, where if the initial angle was along the direction of the path, the user wouldn't have to do anything in order to follow it successfully. An example experiment, with haptic feedback and fixed velocity following a sine path, can be seen "Video 1" of the Supplementary Materials.

We first helped the users don the wrist device. We tightened the wrist device, ensuring it was tight enough to keep the actuator mounts from shifting while receiving verbal confirmation that it was not uncomfortably tight.We gave the users instructions about the testing scenarios and about how to control the virtual agent, then asked new users to practice control of the agent without feedback. After this, users were given 10 experiments in random order, with a brief pause in between each where the properties of the next experiment were listed, allowing the users to prepare themselves. Before each set of experiments (or practice runs), the users were asked to hold their wrist at a comfortable neutral pose. This was used as the zero angle by the simulation, compensating for differences in orientation of the IMUs when mounted on each user.

We performed this set of 10 different experiments with nine different volunteers (mostly males ages 21–28) from our research group, with some users performing the random set multiple times. We did an initial run of 18 experiments. In this first set of experiments, we used the lateral motion of the wrist to control the velocity when velocity was variable (see Equation 4) and a deadzone $dz = 4.5^o$ (0.078 rad). We measured the root-mean-square (RMS) error for the user for each of these trials, as well as their average horizontal velocity. The RMS errors (RMSE) were calculated using the distance to the nearest point calculated during the control, while the average velocities were calculated using the final x-coordinate and the final time recorded for a given trial. The means and standard deviations for the RMS errors for each experiential type are shown in **Table 1**.

The first observation we can make from this data is that the addition of feedback provides a noticeable improvement for the sine wave experiments, with and without a variable velocity. In particular, there is around a 30% improvement in the RMSE of the fixed-velocity sine wave following, as well as a smaller improvement during variable velocity experiments. Performing a T-Test, we can see that this improvement is statistically significant for the fixed-velocity trial ($p < 0.05$).

A histogram comparison of the fixed-velocity trials can be seen in **Figure 5**. The data without haptic feedback was fairly uniform, with some users struggling to control the agent. Haptic feedback helped users follow the path more accurately, though the wrist device was not effective enough to help users reduce their RMS error to below 10°.

One example of a trajectory pair, comparing a single user's performance with and without feedback in a sine-following fixed-velocity scenario, can be seen in **Figure 6**, where we show both the full trajectories and the error. We can see that the feedback pulls the user away from their initial divergent trajectory much

TABLE 1 | The errors for all the path following experiments performed with deadzone $dz = 9^o$ (0.156 rad).

	Linear Path		Sine Path	
	Const. Velocity	Var. Velocity	Const. Velocity	Var. Velocity
No Feedback	17.3 ± 14.0	43.5 ± 39.5	**40.1 ± 18.2**	88.2 ± 59.0
Angle Feedback	15.2 ± 8.5	24.4 ± 16.1	**31.4 ± 14.9**	76.6 ± 52.4
Angle & Velocity Feedback	–	32.9 ± 25.3	–	101.5 ± 58.6

Parameters investigated were the quantity of haptic feedback (no feedback, feedback on the agent angle, and combined feedback on both the agent angle and velocity), the velocity of the agent (fixed vs. controllable), and the path type (straight vs. sinusoidal). When variable velocity was used, it was controlled using the Radial/Ulnar deviation of the wrist. Errors are presented in the form Mean ± Standard Deviation and in arbitrary units [a.u.]. The sine path/constant velocity data is bolded to highlight the statistically significant improvements brought on by the haptic angle feedback.

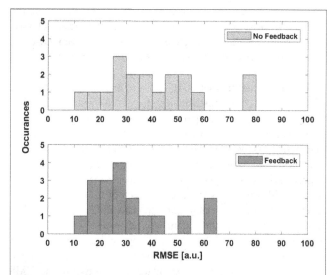

FIGURE 5 | A histogram of user RMS Error for users following a sinusoidal path with and without haptic feedback. The agent velocity was fixed and the deadzone $dz = 4.5^o$ (0.078 rad).

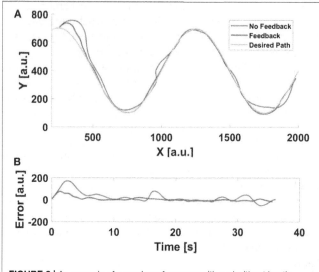

FIGURE 6 | An example of a user's performance with and without haptic feedback when following a sine wave path with a deadzone $dz = 4.5^o$ (0.078 rad). **(A)** the trajectory **(B)** error.

faster. The changing nature of the sine path fosters error on the user, error that the haptic device is able to help correct. In addition to providing correcting forces, some users also reported that the perceived vibration (resulting from the PWM pressure control of the valves) kept them focused on the task when the agent was starting to diverge.

In contrast, an example comparison of a single user's performance following a straight path can be seen in **Figure 7**. This figure shows both the error (which, as the desired path is straight, represents the trajectory), but also the error with respect to the desired angle (see Equation 7). In this case, we can see that the feedback does not help. The feedback seems to drive the user into over-correcting. In addition, because the linear trajectory is easier to follow, much more of the motion occurs within the deadzone. Thus, feedback plays a much smaller role in affecting

performance, which is supported by the aggregate data for the straight line following experiment.

We saw that the haptic feedback provided a slight improvement for the variable-velocity sine following experiments, but the variance in the data was too large to show any statistical significance. This applied to other experiments as well, and was not affected by the haptic velocity control. Users reported that using both DoF on the wrist was difficult, such as increasing the velocity without turning, and vice-versa. This is despite initial calibration experiments that showed that the two degrees of freedom were not coupled. Within the cognitive burden of the path following task, users found it hard to perform pure motions that are decoupled in the 2 DoF we measure through our soft haptic wrist device.

To circumvent this problem, we investigated an alternate method of controlling the linear velocity of the agent. As discussed previously, we performed experiments using the angle of the forearm to directly control velocity (see Equation 6). In addition, we also shrunk to $dz = 3^o$ (0.052 rad), with the goal of improving feedback-performance on the straight line trials. We performed 11 additional experiments under these conditions, with all other aspects of the experimental processes remaining the same. The results of these experiments can be seen in **Table 2**.

From this table, we can see that the changes did improve the effectiveness of the haptic feedback, but not in a statistically significant manner. For the fixed velocity horizontal line following, the decrease in the size of the deadzone did not seem to improve the effects of the haptic feedback. Even when the rPAM in the haptic glove are applying a very small amount of force, the vibration resulting from the PWM pressure control may be causing the users to overcorrect. An example plot of the angle error can be seen in **Figure 8**. While the addition of haptic feedback speeds up the user's ability to approach the desired path,

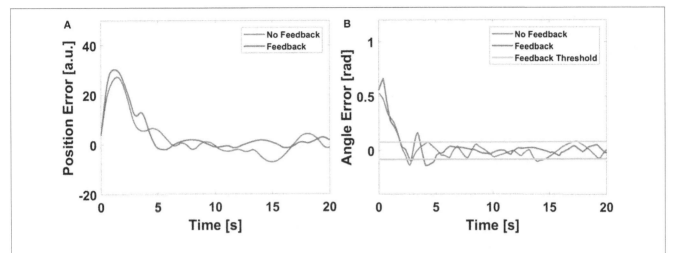

FIGURE 7 | An example of a user's performance with and without haptic feedback when following a linear path with a deadzone $dz = 4.5^o$ (0.078 rad). **(A)** the error with respect to the desired position for each path **(B)** The error with respect to desired angle chosen by the haptic algorithm (as calculated by Equation 7).

TABLE 2 | The errors for all the path following experiments performed with deadzone $dz = 3^o$ (0.052 rad).

	Linear Path		Sine Path	
	Const. Velocity	Var. Velocity	Const. Velocity	Var. Velocity
No Feedback	18.6 ± 13.7	24.5 ± 13.2	**36.2 ± 13.3**	100.4 ± 121.0
Angle Feedback	12.5 ± 4.0	18.4 ± 12.1	**26.1 ± 12.4**	50.2 ± 20.2
Angle & Velocity Feedback	–	16.7 ± 6.2	–	47.1 ± 13.5

Parameters investigated were the quantity of haptic feedback (no feedback, feedback on the agent angle, and combined feedback on both the agent angle and velocity), the velocity of the agent (fixed vs. controllable), and the path type (straight vs. sinusoidal). When variable velocity was used, it was controlled using the angle of the forearm. Errors are presented in the form Mean ± Standard Deviation and are in arbitrary units [a.u.]. The sine path/constant velocity data is bolded to highlight the statistically significant improvements brought on by the haptic angle feedback.

it seems to increase the oscillations once the user is near the target trajectory. The haptic feedback seems to cause the user to overcorrect, zig-zagging around the deadzone.

We also found that the alternate method of controlling velocity was ineffective at increasing velocity-control performance. Users reported that the cognitive burden of controlling both degrees of freedom with their wrist was replaced with the burden of focusing on two entirely separate muscle groups simultaneously: wrist and elbow. In addition, users would often forget about the importance of arm position during fixed-velocity trials, resulting in a high initial velocity and then greater errors during a variable-velocity trial that followed.

However, this new round of data continues to show the improvements the haptic device can bring to fixed-velocity, sine-wave trajectories at $p < 0.05$. Combined with the initial data set, we can conclude that over all experiments the haptic feedback provided an improvement of around 30% with a $p <$

0.01. Our haptic wrist device is useful for providing larger-level feedback, for users following variable dynamic trajectories, while it struggles to provide effective feedback for more precise tasks.

5. CONCLUSION

Haptics can provide new avenues for human users to communicate with computers and robots. In particular, soft wearable haptics can conform to the user's body and apply feedback forces and torques while still remaining flexible to user motion and easily adapting to variations in user body dimensions. We created a soft haptic wrist device constructed using reverse pneumatic artificial muscles (rPAMs). This device is capable of sensing the wrist state and applying 2 degrees-of-freedom haptic cues with torques no higher than 0.15 Nm.

We created a scenario where the user moved their wrist and arm to control an agent following a path in a virtual environment. The user was capable of controlling the angular acceleration of the agent via the position of their wrist along the sagittal plane. The forward velocity of the agent was either fixed, controlled by the transverse motion of the wrist, or controlled directly by the angle of the forearm. The haptic wrist feedback device provided gentle torques, directing the user toward the desired path while not overpowering them.

We performed a number of experiments under various conditions, and found that the haptic feedback device was a significant benefit in helping the user follow non-linear paths with a fixed velocity, making it the first soft robotic device capable of performing real-time kinesthetic feedback. In addition, the device as a whole is safer, lighter, more form-fitting, and adaptable to different users than an equivalent rigid device would be.

However, when following linear paths, the haptic feedback was not precise enough to provide any significant performance improvements, often causing users to overcorrect. Under variable velocity conditions, haptic feedback provided small but

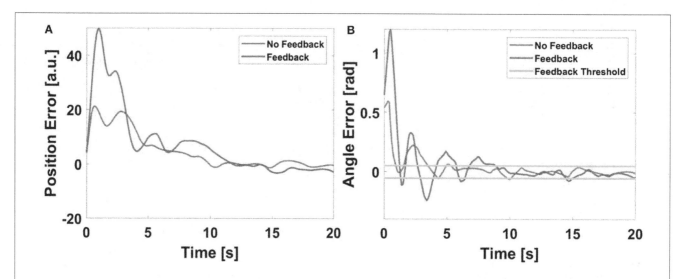

FIGURE 8 | An example of a user's performance with and without haptic feedback when following a linear path with a deadzone $dz = 3^O$ (0.052 rad). **(A)** the error with respect to the desired position for each path **(B)** The error with respect to desired angle chosen by the haptic algorithm (as calculated by Equation 7).

statistically insignificant performance improvements. Velocity was difficult to control under both control schemes test. Velocity represented another property for users to think about, diverting their attention from steering, a particular concern for the forearm velocity control where users had to use different parts of their body to control the agent. This was less of a factor when using the different bending directions of the wrist, but for that scheme users struggled un-coupling the two wrist axes. An increase and decrease in velocity would often cause users to veer off the path. Skilled users were able to effectively utilize these multiple degrees-of-freedom simultaneously, but less skilled ones were not. This, combined with difficulty of path-following at higher speeds, resulted in a much higher variance in the data and eliminated any statistical significance.

One of the main weaknesses of the proposed device is minimum force that the actuators can apply. The nature of the PWM pressure control allows for fast response times, but valves have trouble operating consistently at very low or very high duty cycles. This meant that the actuators struggle to provide useful kinesthetic feedback at low errors (as demonstrated by the only marginal improvements under horizontal line-following conditions). This could be mitigated through a more complex pressure-application scheme, such as through pistons, though any system with the same response time and more precision as our will likely be significantly bulkier and more expensive.

One interesting aspect of our experiments was the discrepancy between the versatility of the wearable haptic device and the user's ability to control the virtual agent. The haptic device was able to measure the local wrist angle regardless of the global orientation, which would theoretically allow the user to control the agent regardless of the orientation of their hand. However, we observed that users struggled to control the agent effectively except in certain preferred orientations, where the motion of the wrist matched the motion of the agent by an intuitive mapping.

This leads to some of the ongoing aspects of this project. We would like to use the haptic wrist device as part of a more complicated wearable haptic system. We plan on integrating this device into a haptic system used to teleoperate a robotic arm for 3-D manipulation tasks. In future work, the device introduced in this paper will be used to simulate gravity and contact forces on the user's wrist, as well as provide haptic cues to improve teleoperation performance. In order to fully apply haptic forces to a user's arm, techniques would have to be developed to apply forces to the user's elbow and shoulder, something the actuators in this paper could not extend and contract enough to effectively accommodate. In addition, this work could be used as part of a self-contained wearable device. It would function as a low-profile force-feedback joystick, allowing a worker to control machinery while in the field. This would require a personal pressure source. Though pumps outputting the pressures used this work are available that can be incorporated into a wearable device, the noise they generate is a problem that would have to be overcome.

AUTHOR CONTRIBUTIONS

CO came up with the idea for the rPAM actuators and their use for haptic feedback. ML developed the techniques for the actuator fabrication, and created the valve control circuitry. ES developed the haptic control algorithms, fabricated the device, oversaw user experiments, and analyzed the data. ES, ML, and CO wrote the paper.

ACKNOWLEDGMENTS

We would like to thank all the volunteers who participated in our path-following trials. We would also like to Raagini Rameshwar for assistance in editing the paper.

REFERENCES

Al-Fahaam, H., Davis, S., and Nefti-Meziani, S. (2016). "Wrist rehabilitation exoskeleton robot based on pneumatic soft actuators," in *Students on Applied Engineering (ICSAE), International Conference* (Lucerne).

Al-Fahaam, H., Davis, S., and Nefti-Meziani, S. (2018). The design and mathematical modelling of novel extensor bending pneumatic artificial muscles (ebpams) for soft exoskeletons. *Rob. Auton. Syst.* 99, 63–74. doi: 10.1016/j.robot.2017.10.010

Amemiya, T., and Gomi, H. (2014). *Distinct Pseudo-Attraction Force Sensation by a Thumb-Sized Vibrator that Oscillates Asymmetrically*. Berlin; Heidelberg: Springer Berlin Heidelberg, 88–95.

Blake, J., and Gurocak, H. B. (2009). Haptic glove with mr brakes for virtual reality. *IEEE ASME Trans. Mechatron.* 14, 606–615. doi: 10.1109/TMECH.2008.2010934

Bouzit, M., Burdea, G., Popescu, G., and Boian, R. (2002). The rutgers master ii-new design force-feedback glove. *IEEE ASME Trans. Mechatron.* 7, 256–263. doi: 10.1109/TMECH.2002.1011262

Chciuk, M., Milecki, A., and Bachman, P. (2017). *Comparison of a Traditional Control and a Force Feedback Control of the Robot Arm During Teleoperation*. Cham: Springer International Publishing, 277–289.

Chou, C.-P., and Hannaford, B. (1996). Measurement and modeling of mckibben pneumatic artificial muscles. *IEEE Trans. Rob. Autom.* 12, 90–102. doi: 10.1109/70.481753

Dowling, V. A., Fisher, D. S., and Andriacchi, T. P. (2010). Gait modification via verbal instruction and an active feedback system to reduce peak knee adduction moment. *J. Biomech. Eng.* 132, 071007. doi: 10.1115/1.4001584

Erwin, A., O'Malley, M. K., Ress, D., and Sergi, F. (2016). Kinesthetic feedback during 2dof wrist movements via a novel mr-compatible robot. *IEEE Trans. Neural Syst. Rehabil. Eng.* 25, 10127–10134. doi: 10.1109/TNSRE.2016.2634585

Ilievski, F., Mazzeo, A. D., Shepherd, R. F., Chen, X., and Whitesides, G. M. (2011). Soft robotics for chemists. *Angew. Chemie Int. Ed.* 50, 1890–1895. doi: 10.1002/anie.201006464

Jadhav, S., Kannanda, V., Kang, B., Tolly, M., and Schulze, J. P. (2015). "Soft robotic glove for kinesthetic haptic feedback in virtual reality environments," in *Engineering Reality of Virtual Reality 2017* (Los Angeles, CA), 19–24 .

Johnson, L. A., and Higgins, C. M. (2006). "A navigation aid for the blind using tactile-visual sensory substitution,". in *2006 International Conference of the IEEE Engineering in Medicine and Biology Society* (New York, NY), 6289–6292.

Koo, I. M., Jung, K., Koo, J. C., Nam, J. D., Lee, Y. K., and Choi, H. R. (2008). Development of soft-actuator-based wearable tactile display. *IEEE Trans. Rob.* 24, 549–558. doi: 10.1109/TRO.2008.921561

Luo, M., Skorina, E., Tao, W., Chen, F., and Onal, C. D. (2015). "Optimized design of a rigid kinematic module for antagonistic soft actuation," in *Technologies for Practical Robot Applications (TePRA), 2015 IEEE International Conference* (Woburn, MA), 1–6 .

Luo, M., Skorina, E. H., Tao, W., Chen, F., Ozel, S., Sun, Y., et al. (2017). Toward modular soft robotics: proprioceptive curvature sensing and sliding-mode control of soft bidirectional bending modules. *Soft Rob.* 4, 117–125. doi: 10.1089/soro.2016.0041

MA, Z., and Ben-Tzvi, P. (2015). Rml glovean exoskeleton glove mechanism with haptics feedback. *IEEE Trans. Mechatron.* 20, 641–652. doi: 10.1109/TMECH.2014.2305842

Margineanu, D., Lovasz, E.-C., Gruescu, C. M., Ciupe, V., and Tatar, S. (2018). *5 DoF Haptic Exoskeleton for Space Telerobotics–Shoulder Module*. Cham: Springer International Publishing, 111–120.

Metzger, J. C., Lambercy, O., and Gassert, R. (2012). "High-fidelity rendering of virtual objects with the rehapticknob-novel avenues in robot-assisted rehabilitation of hand function," in *2012 IEEE Haptics Symposium (HAPTICS)* (Vancouver, BC), 51–56.

Morse, J. L., Jung, M.-C., Bashford, G. R., and Hallbeck, M. S. (2006). Maximal dynamic grip force and wrist torque: The effects of gender, exertion direction, angular velocity, and wrist angle. *Appl. Ergon.* 37, 737–742. doi: 10.1016/j.apergo.2005.11.008

Patterson, P. E., and Katz, J. (1992). Design and evaluation of a sensory feedback system that provides grasping pressure in a myoelectric hand. *J. Rehabil. Res. Dev.* 1, 1–8. doi: 10.1682/JRRD.1992.01.0001

Polygerinos, P., Wang, Z., Galloway, K. C., Wood, R. J., and Walsh, C. J. (2015). Soft robotic glove for combined assistance and at-home rehabilitation. *Rob. Auton. Syst.* 73, 135–143. doi: 10.1016/j.robot.2014.08.014

Riecke, C., Artigas, J., Balachandran, R., Bayer, R., Beyer, A., Brunner, B., et al. (2016). "Kontur-2 mission: The dlr force feedback joystick for space telemanipulation from the iss," in *The Proceedings of The International Symposium on Artificial Intelligence, Robotics and Automation in Space (i-SAIRAS 2016)* (Beijing).

Rosenberg, L. B. (1993). "Virtual fixtures: Perceptual tools for telerobotic manipulation," in *Proceedings of IEEE Virtual Reality Annual International Symposium* (Seattle), 76–82.

Sasaki, D., Noritsugu, T., and Takaiwa, M. (2005). "Development of active support splint driven by pneumatic soft actuator (assist)," in *Proceedings of the 2005 IEEE International Conference on Robotics and Automation (ICRA)* (Barcelona).

Schorr, S. B., Quek, Z. F., Romano, R. Y., Nisky, I., Provancher, W. R., and Okamura, A. M. (2013). "Sensory substitution via cutaneous skin stretch feedback," in *2013 IEEE International Conference on Robotics and Automation* (Karlsruhe), 2341–2346.

Skorina, E. H., Luo, M., Ozel, S., Chen, F., Tao, W., and Onal, C. D. (2015). "Feedforward augmented sliding mode motion control of antagonistic soft pneumatic actuators," in *Robotics and Automation (ICRA), 2015 IEEE International Conference* (Seattle), 2544–2549.

Tao, W., Skorina, E. H., Chen, F., McInnis, J., Luo, M., and Onal, C. D. (2015). "Bioinspired design and fabrication principles of reliable fluidic soft actuation modules," in *Robotics and Biomimetics (ROBIO), 2015 IEEE International Conference on*, (IEEE) 2169–2174.

Wagner, C. R., Stylopoulos, N., and Howe, R. D. (2002). "The role of force feedback in surgery: analysis of blunt dissection," in *Proceedings 10th Symposium on Haptic Interfaces for Virtual Environment and Teleoperator Systems. HAPTICS 2002* (Washington, DC), 68–74.

Permissions

All chapters in this book were first published by Springer; hereby published with permission under the Creative Commons Attribution License or equivalent. Every chapter published in this book has been scrutinized by our experts. Their significance has been extensively debated. The topics covered herein carry significant findings which will fuel the growth of the discipline. They may even be implemented as practical applications or may be referred to as a beginning point for another development.

The contributors of this book come from diverse backgrounds, making this book a truly international effort. This book will bring forth new frontiers with its revolutionizing research information and detailed analysis of the nascent developments around the world.

We would like to thank all the contributing authors for lending their expertise to make the book truly unique. They have played a crucial role in the development of this book. Without their invaluable contributions this book wouldn't have been possible. They have made vital efforts to compile up to date information on the varied aspects of this subject to make this book a valuable addition to the collection of many professionals and students.

This book was conceptualized with the vision of imparting up-to-date information and advanced data in this field. To ensure the same, a matchless editorial board was set up. Every individual on the board went through rigorous rounds of assessment to prove their worth. After which they invested a large part of their time researching and compiling the most relevant data for our readers.

The editorial board has been involved in producing this book since its inception. They have spent rigorous hours researching and exploring the diverse topics which have resulted in the successful publishing of this book. They have passed on their knowledge of decades through this book. To expedite this challenging task, the publisher supported the team at every step. A small team of assistant editors was also appointed to further simplify the editing procedure and attain best results for the readers.

Apart from the editorial board, the designing team has also invested a significant amount of their time in understanding the subject and creating the most relevant covers. They scrutinized every image to scout for the most suitable representation of the subject and create an appropriate cover for the book.

The publishing team has been an ardent support to the editorial, designing and production team. Their endless efforts to recruit the best for this project, has resulted in the accomplishment of this book. They are a veteran in the field of academics and their pool of knowledge is as vast as their experience in printing. Their expertise and guidance has proved useful at every step. Their uncompromising quality standards have made this book an exceptional effort. Their encouragement from time to time has been an inspiration for everyone.

The publisher and the editorial board hope that this book will prove to be a valuable piece of knowledge for researchers, students, practitioners and scholars across the globe.

List of Contributors

Juan S. Martinez and Hong Z. Tan
Haptic Interface Research Laboratory, College of Engineering, School of Electrical and Computer Engineering, Purdue University, West Lafayette, IN, United States

Roger W. Cholewiak
Cutaneous Communication Laboratory, Princeton University, Princeton, NJ, United States

Pornthep Preechayasomboon
Rombolabs, Mechanical Engineering, University of Washington, Seattle, WA, United States

Eric Rombokas
Rombolabs, Mechanical Engineering, University of Washington, Seattle, WA, United States
Electrical Engineering, University of Washington, Seattle, WA, United States

Daniele Leonardis, Massimiliano Gabardi, Michele Barsotti and Antonio Frisoli
Percro Laboratory, Institute of Mechanical Intelligence, Scuola Superiore Sant'Anna, Pisa, Italy

Janis Rosskamp, Hermann Meißenhelter, Rene Weller, Marc O. Rüdel, Johannes Ganser and Gabriel Zachmann
Computer Graphics and Virtual Reality, Faculty 03: Mathematics/Computer Science, University of Bremen, Bremen, Germany

Luis Figueredo, Abdeldjallil Naceri and Sami Haddadin
Munich Institute of Robotics and Machine Intelligence (MIRMI), Technical University of Munich (TUM), Munich, Germany

Ulrich Walter
Chair of Astronautics, TUM School of Engineering and Design, Technical University of Munich (TUM), Munich, Germany

Jean Elsner and Gerhard Reinerth
Munich Institute of Robotics and Machine Intelligence (MIRMI), Technical University of Munich (TUM), Munich, Germany
Chair of Astronautics, TUM School of Engineering and Design, Technical University of Munich (TUM), Munich, Germany

Aliyah K. Shell, Andres E. Pena, James J. Abbas and Ranu Jung
Adaptive Neural Systems Laboratory, Department of Biomedical Engineering and the Institute for Integrative and Innovative Research, University of Arkansas, Fayetteville, AR, United States

Carolin Stellmacher and Michael Bonfert
Faculty of Mathematics and Computer Science, University of Bremen, Bremen, Germany

Ernst Kruijff
Institute of Visual Computing, Bonn-Rhein-Sieg University of Applied Sciences, Sankt Augustin, Germany

Johannes Schöning
School of Computer Science , University of St. Gallen, St. Gallen, Switzerland

Neal Y. Lii, Aaron Pereira, Georg Stillfried, Hadi Beik-Mohammadi, Thomas Baker, Annika Maier, Benedikt Pleintinger, Philipp Reisich and Alin Albu-Schäffer
Institute of Robotics and Mechatronics, German Aerospace Center (DLR), Wessling, Germany

Julian Dietl
Faculty of Mechanical Engineering, Munich University of Applied Science, Munich, Germany

Annika Schmidt
Institute of Robotics and Mechatronics, German Aerospace Center (DLR), Wessling, Germany
Faculty of Informatics, Technical University of Munich, Munich, Germany

Zhaopeng Chen
Department of Informatics, Faculty of Mathematics, Informatics and Natural Science, University of Hamburg, Hamburg, Germany

Amal Elawad
Department of Electrical Engineering, Chalmers University of Technology, Göteborg, Sweden

Lauren Mentzer and Austin Pineault
Department of Computer Science and Electrical Engineering, Stanford University, Stanford, CA, United States

Sigurd Bjarne Rørvik, Marius Auflem, Henrikke Dybvik and Martin Steinert
TrollLABS, Department of Mechanical and Industrial Engineering, Faculty of Engineering, Norwegian University of Science and Technology (NTNU), Trondheim, Norway

Thomas Hulin, Michael Panzirsch, Harsimran Singh, Andre Coelho, Ribin Balachandran, Bernhard M. Weber, Nicolai Bechtel, Cornelia Riecke, Bernhard Brunner, Julian Klodmann, Anja Hellings, Katharina Hagmann, Gabriel Quere, Adrian S. Bauer, Marek Sierotowicz, Roberto Lampariello, Jörn Vogel, Alexander Dietrich, Daniel Leidner, Christian Ott and Gerd Hirzinger
Institute of Robotics and Mechatronics, German Aerospace Center (DLR), Wessling, Germany

François Jourdes, Brice Valentin and Jérémie Allard
InSimo SAS, Strasbourg, France

Christian Duriez
DEFROST Team, UMR 9189 CRIStAL, CNRS, Centrale Lille, Inria, University of Lille, Lille, France

Barbara Seeliger
IHU-Strasbourg, Institute of Image-Guided Surgery, Strasbourg, France
Department of General, Digestive and Endocrine Surgery, University Hospitals of Strasbourg, Strasbourg, France
ICube, UMR 7357 CNRS, University of Strasbourg, Strasbourg, France
IRCAD, Research Institute Against Digestive Cancer, Strasbourg, France

Victor Rodrigo Mercado, Ferran Argelaguet and Anatole Lécuyer
Inria Rennes—Bretagne Atlantique, Rennes, France

Gery Casiez
Univ. Lille, Inria, CNRS, Centrale Lille, UMR 9189 CRIStAL, Lille, France

Mihai Dragusanu, Alberto Villani and Monica Malvezzi
Department of Information Engineering and Mathematics, University of Siena, Siena, Italy

Domenico Prattichizzo
Department of Information Engineering and Mathematics, University of Siena, Siena, Italy
Department of Advanced Robotics, Istituto Italiano di Tecnologia, Genova, Italy

Claudio Pacchierotti
Department of Advanced Robotics, Istituto Italiano di Tecnologia, Genova, Italy

Stefano Scheggi
Surgical Robotics Laboratory, Department of Biomechanical Engineering, MIRA – Institute for Biomedical Technology and Technical Medicine, University of Twente, Enschede, Netherlands

Sarthak Misra
Surgical Robotics Laboratory, Department of Biomechanical Engineering, MIRA – Institute for Biomedical Technology and Technical Medicine, University of Twente, Enschede, Netherlands
Department of Biomedical Engineering, University of Groningen and University Medical Center Groningen, Groningen, Netherlands

Jianyao Zhang and Hiroyuki Kajimoto
Department of Informatics, The University of Electro-Communications, Chofu, Japan

Erik H. Skorina, Ming Luo and Cagdas D. Onal
Soft Robotics Lab, Worcester Polytechnic Institute, Worcester, MA, United States

Index

Printed in the USA
CPSIA information can be obtained
at www.ICGtesting.com
JSHW060754270923
49096JS00029B/54